Fundamentals of Organizational Behavior

John W. Slocum, Jr.
Southern Methodist University

Don Hellriegel
Texas A & M University

THOMSON
SOUTH-WESTERN

Australia · Brazil · Canada · Mexico · Singapore · Spain · United Kingdom · United States

Fundamentals of Organizational Behavior
John W. Slocum, Jr. and Don Hellriegel

VP/Editorial Director:
Jack W. Calhoun

Senior Publisher:
Melissa S. Acuña

Senior Acquisitions Editor:
Joe Sabatino

Senior Developmental Editor:
Emma F. Guttler

Senior Marketing Manager:
Kimberly Kanakes

Production Project Manager:
Margaret M. Bril

Manager of Technology, Editorial:
Vicky True

Technology Project Editor:
Kristen Meere

Web Coordinator:
Karen Schaffer

Senior Manufacturing Coordinator:
Doug Wilke

Production House:
Lachina Publishing Services

Printer:
C&C Offset Printing Co. Ltd.

Art Director:
Tippy McIntosh

Internal Designer:
Grannan Graphic Design, Ltd.

Cover Designer:
Grannan Graphic Design, Ltd.

Cover Images:
© Getty Images

Photography Manager:
Deanna Ettinger

Printed in China
1 2 3 4 5 09 08 07 06

International Student Edition:
ISBN 0-324-42256-3

Library of Congress Control Number:
2005910798

For more information about our products, contact us at:
Thomson Learning Academic Resource Center
1-800-423-0563

Thomson Higher Education
5191 Natorp Boulevard
Mason, OH 45040
USA

Christopher, Bradley, and Jonathan (JWS)
To Jill, Kim, and Lori (DH)

Brief Contents

Part 1: Learning about Organizational Behavior 1

Chapter 1 Organizational Behavior and Foundation Competencies 2

Part 2: The Organization 35

Chapter 2 Managerial and Ethical Decision Making 36
Chapter 3 Designing Organizations 64
Chapter 4 Cultivating Organizational Culture 96
Chapter 5 Guiding Organizational Change 126

Part 3: Leadership and Team Behaviors 159

Chapter 6 Leading Effectively: Foundations 160
Chapter 7 Leading Effectively: Contemporary Developments 186
Chapter 8 Developing and Leading Teams 208
Chapter 9 Managing Conflict and Negotiating Effectively 246
Chapter 10 Fostering Organizational Communication 276

Part 4: Individuals in Organizations 309

Chapter 11 Understanding Individual Differences 310
Chapter 12 Perceptions and Attributions 338
Chapter 13 Learning and Reinforcement 364
Chapter 14 Fundamentals of Motivation 390
Chapter 15 Motivation through Goal Setting and Reward Systems 422
Chapter 16 Managing Stress and Aggressive Behavior 446

References R-1
Index I-1

Contents

PART 1: Learning about Organizational Behavior 1

Chapter 1 **Organizational Behavior and Foundation Competencies 2**

Preview Case: *Jack Gherty of Land O'Lakes* 3
Self Competency 5
Foundation Abilities 5
Career Development 6
Self Competency: *Shelly Lazarus of Ogilvy & Mather* 7
Communication Competency 7
Foundation Abilities 8
Communication Competency: *Lee Korens on Communicating* 9
Diversity Competency 9
Foundation Abilities 9
Categories of Diversity 10
Changing Workforce 12
Gender 13
Race and Ethnicity 13
Age 14
Diversity Competency: *Ted Childs of IBM* 14
Ethics Competency 15
Foundation Abilities 15
Ethical Dilemmas 16
Ethics Competency: *Raytheon Company* 17
Across Cultures Competency 18
Foundation Abilities 19
Work-Related Cultural Values 19
Across Cultures Competency: *Charles Zhang on China's Culture* 22
Teams Competency 23
Foundation Abilities 23
Teams and Individualism 23
Teams Competency: *West Suburban Hospital's Teams* 24
Change Competency 25
Foundation Abilities 25
Technological Forces 26
Change Competency: *Alaska Indoor Sports Distributing Ltd.* 26
Learning Framework for Individual, Team, and Organizational Effectiveness 27
The Organization Itself 27
Leadership and Team Behaviors 28
Individuals in Organizations 29
Foundation Competencies 29
Chapter Summary 29
Key Terms and Concepts 31
Discussion Questions 31
Experiential Exercise and Case 32
Experiential Exercise: Diversity Competency—Attitudes Toward Diversity 32
Case: Communication Competency—James Halpin of CompUSA 33

PART 2: The Organization 35

Chapter 2 **Managerial and Ethical Decision Making 36**

Preview Case: *JC Penney's Golden Rules of Conduct* 37

Making Ethical Decisions 38
Ethical Intensity 39
Decision-Making Principles and Decision Rules 42
Concern for Affected Individuals 45
Benefits and Costs 45
Determination of Rights 46
Ethics Competency: *Norm Brodsky's Drug Testing Dilemma* 47
Managerial Decision-Making Models 48
Rational Model 48
Change Competency: *St. Vincent's Rational Initiatives* 50
Bounded Rationality Model 51
Communication Competency: *Julie Rodriguez of Epic Divers and Marine* 54
Political Model 55
Stimulating Organizational Creativity 56
Lateral Thinking Method 57
Self Competency: *Donna Kacmar of Architect Works, Inc.* 59
Devil's Advocate Method 59
Chapter Summary 60
Key Terms and Concepts 60
Discussion Questions 61
Experiential Exercise and Case 61
Experiential Exercise: Ethics Competency—Living Ethics 61
Case: Change Competency—Is Opportunity Knocking? 62

Chapter 3 **Designing Organizations 64**
Preview Case: *Kellogg Company* 65
Key Factors in Organization Design 67
Environmental Factors 68
Strategic Factors 69
Change Competency: *7-Eleven* 71
Technological Factors 73
Mechanistic and Organic Organizations 74
Hierarchy of Authority 76
Division of Labor 76
Rules and Procedures 77
Impersonality 77
Chain of Command 78
Span of Control 78
Across Cultures Competency: *Latin American versus U.S. Management Practices* 79
Traditional Organization Designs 80
Organizational Design Options 80
Functional Design 81
Place Design 82
Product Design 83
Multidivisional Design (M-Form) 84
Contemporary Organization Designs 85
Multinational Design 85
Communication Competency: *Electrolux* 86
Network Design 87
Communication Competency: *DreamWorks SKG* 89
Chapter Summary 91
Key Terms and Concepts 91
Discussion Questions 92
Experiential Exercise and Case 92
Experiential Exercise: Communication Competency—Is Your Organization Designed for High Performance? 92
Case: Change Competency—Salomon 93

Chapter 4

Cultivating Organizational Culture 96
Preview Case: *Google 97*
Dynamics of Organizational Culture 98
Forming a Culture 101
Across Cultures Competency: *Grupo Carso 102*
Sustaining a Culture 103
Changing a Culture 106
Change Competency: *Harley-Davidson 107*
Types of Organizational Culture 108
Bureaucratic Culture 109
Clan Culture 110
Entrepreneurial Culture 110
Market Culture 111
Culture-Performance Relationships 111
Ethical Behavior and Organizational Culture 112
Impact of Culture 113
Whistle-Blowing 113
Communication Competency: *What Would You Do? 114*
Fostering Cultural Diversity 115
Challenges 115
Self Competency: *Linda Glick at Levi Strauss 116*
Effective Diversity Programs 116
Socialization of New Employees 117
Organizational Socialization Process 118
Dilemmas in Socialization 119
Chapter Summary 120
Key Terms and Concepts 121
Discussion Questions 121
Experiential Exercise and Case 122
Experiential Exercise: Ethics Competency—Assessing a Culture's Ethical Behaviors 122
Case: Teams Competency—Southwest Airlines' Culture 122

Chapter 5

Guiding Organizational Change 126
Preview Case: *Hewlett-Packard 127*
Challenges of Change 128
Pressures for Change 129
Across Cultures Competency: *Western Union 131*
Types of Change Approaches 132
Organizational Use 134
Organizational Diagnosis 136
Resistance to Change 138
Individual Resistance 138
Self Competency: *Are You Ready to Change? 141*
Organizational Resistance 142
Overcoming Resistance 144
Teams Competency: *Shell's Change Process 146*
Promoting Change 147
Interpersonal Methods 147
Team Methods 147
Organizational Methods 150
Communication Competency: *Just in Time at Toyota 151*
Ethical Issues in Organizational Change 152
Chapter Summary 153
Key Terms and Concepts 154
Discussion Questions 154

Experiential Exercise and Case 154
Experiential Exercise: Self Competency—Measuring Support for Change 154
Case: Ethics Competency—Kindred Todd and the Ethics of OD 156

PART 3: Leadership and Team Behaviors 159

Chapter 6 **Leading Effectively: Foundations 160**
Preview Case: *Amy Brinkley of Bank of America* 161
Power and Political Behavior 163
Leaders' Use of Power 163
Use of Political Behavior 165
Self Competency: *Arlivia Gamble of State Farm* 167
Traditional Leadership Models 168
Traits Model of Leadership 168
Ethics Competency: *Norman Augustine of Lockheed Martin* 169
Behavioral Model of Leadership 170
Situational Leadership® Model 173
Leadership Styles 173
Situational Contingency 175
Choosing a Leadership Style 175
Implications for Leaders 175
Communication Competency: *Michelle Miller of Walgreens* 176
Vroom–Jago Leadership Model 177
Leadership Styles 177
Situational Variables 178
Solution Matrix 178
Change Competency: *Your Leadership as Director of Research* 180
Implications for Leaders 181
Chapter Summary 181
Key Terms and Concepts 182
Discussion Questions 182
Experiential Exercise and Case 183
Experiential Exercise: Self Competency—Personal Power Inventory 183
Case: Change Competency—Ashley Automotive—Changing Times 184

Chapter 7 **Leading Effectively: Contemporary Developments 186**
Preview Case: *Ed Breen of Tyco International* 187
Transactional Leadership 188
Key Components 188
Self Competency: *Guangchang Guo of Shanghai Fortune High Technology Group* 189
Implications for Leaders 190
Charismatic Leadership 190
Key Components 190
Communication Competency: *Richard Branson of the Virgin Group* 192
Implications for Leaders 193
Authentic Leadership 194
Key Components 194
Ethics Competency: *Robert Johnson of BET* 196
Implications for Leaders 197
Transformational Leadership 197
Key Components 197
Change Competency: *Mike McGavick of Safeco* 200
Implications for Leaders 201
Similarities and Differences in Models 201
Chapter Summary 202
Key Terms and Concepts 203

Discussion Questions 203
***Experiential Exercise and Case* 203**
Experiential Exercise: Communication Competency—Managing for the Future 203
Case: Change Competency—Meg Whitman of eBay 204

Chapter 8 **Developing and Leading Teams 208**
Preview Case: *Mayo Clinic and Teams 209*
Characteristics of Groups 210
Classifications of Groups 210
Informal Groups 210
Effective Groups 211
Communication Competency: *Mayo Clinic's Surgical Suite Design Team 211*
Types of Work-Related Teams 212
Functional Team 212
Problem-Solving Team 213
Cross-Functional Team 214
Self-Managed Team 215
Teams Competency: *Bayer's High Speed Line Team 217*
Virtual Team 218
Global Team 219
Across Cultures Competency: *Unilever Latin America's Global Virtual Team 220*
Stages of Team Development 221
Forming Stage 221
Storming Stage 222
Norming Stage 223
Performing Stage 223
Adjourning Stage 224
Potential Team Dysfunctions 224
Key Influences on Team Effectiveness 226
Context 226
Goals 227
Team Size 228
Team Member Roles and Diversity 229
Norms 231
Cohesiveness 233
Leadership 234
Self Competency: *Linda Dillman's Team Leadership 234*
Stimulating Team Creativity 235
Nominal Group Technique 235
Traditional Brainstorming 237
Change Competency: *Creative Process at Play 238*
Electronic Brainstorming 238
Chapter Summary 239
Key Terms and Concepts 240
Discussion Questions 240
***Experiential Exercise and Case* 241**
Experiential Exercise: Team Competency—Team Assessment Inventory 241
Case: Team Competency—Artisan Industries' Team 242

Chapter 9 **Managing Conflict and Negotiating Effectively 246**
Preview Case: *KLA-Tencor 247*
Levels of Conflict 249
Intrapersonal Conflict 249
Interpersonal Conflict 250
Intragroup Conflict 251
Intergroup Conflict 252

Diversity Competency: *Georgia Power's Affinity Groups* 253
Interpersonal Conflict-Handling Styles 254
Avoiding Style 255
Forcing Style 255
Accommodating Style 256
Collaborating Style 256
Compromising Style 257
Effectiveness of Styles 258
Communication Competency: *ATM Express* 258
Negotiation in Conflict Management 259
Stages of Negotiation 259
Distributive Negotiations Strategy 261
Integrative Negotiations Strategy 262
Teams Competency: *Cinergy's Residential Collections Negotiations* 263
Four Influences on Negotiation Strategies 264
Negotiating across Cultures 266
Differences in Negotiators 267
Cross-Cultural Emotional Intelligence 268
Negotiation Process 269
Across Cultures Competency: *Chinese Negotiating Style* 270
Chapter Summary 271
Key Terms and Concepts 272
Discussion Questions 272
Experiential Exercises **272**
Experiential Exercise: Self Competency—Conflict-Handling Styles 272
Experiential Exercise: Managing Self—Intervening in Employee Disputes 275

Chapter 10 **Fostering Organizational Communication 276**
Preview Case: *David Radcliffe of Hogg Robinson* 277
Elements of Interpersonal Communication 278
Sender and Receiver 278
Transmitters and Receptors 279
Messages and Channels 279
Meaning and Feedback 280
Interpersonal Barriers 282
Cultural Barriers 284
Across Cultures Competency: *Caterpillar's Piazza* 285
Fostering Ethical Interpersonal Communications 286
Communication Openness 288
Constructive Feedback 289
Appropriate Self-Disclosure 291
Active Listening 292
Communication Competency: *FPA's Culture of Conversation* 292
Nonverbal Communication 293
Types of Nonverbal Cues 293
Cultural Differences 295
Status Differences 297
Organizational Use 298
Interpersonal Communication Networks 298
Individual Network 298
Informal Group Network 300
Formal Employee Network 301
Communication Competency: *Sensis Employee Communication Strategy* 301
Organizational Use 302
Chapter Summary 302
Key Terms and Concepts 304
Discussion Questions 304

Experiential Exercise and Case *304*
Experiential Exercise: Self Competency—Interpersonal Communication Practices *304*
Case: Across Cultures Competency—Juan Perillo and Jean Moore *307*

PART 4: Individuals in Organizations 309

Chapter 11 **Understanding Individual Differences 310**
Preview Case: *Ann Fudge, CEO of Young & Rubicam, Inc.* *311*
Personality Determinants 312
Heredity 313
Environment 313
Self Competency: *David Neeleman of JetBlue* *315*
Personality and Behavior 316
Big Five Personality Factors 316
Self-Esteem 318
Locus of Control 318
Introversion and Extraversion 319
Emotional Intelligence 320
Organizational Uses 321
Teams Competency: *Thrive Networks* *321*
The Person and the Situation 322
Work Attitudes and Behavior 322
Components of Attitudes 323
Key Work-Related Attitudes: Hope, Job Satisfaction, and Organizational Commitment 323
Communication Competency: *The Container Store* *327*
Emotions and Performance 329
A Model of Emotions 330
Change Competency: *Kenneth Chenault of American Express* *331*
Chapter Summary 332
Key Terms and Concepts 333
Discussion Questions 333
Experiential Exercises ***334***
Experiential Exercise: Self Competency—Assessing the Big Five *334*
Experiential Exercise: Self Competency—Emotional IQ *336*

Chapter 12 **Perceptions and Attributions 338**
Preview Case: *Chet Cadieux, CEO of QuikTrip* *339*
The Perceptual Process 340
Across Cultures Competency: *Selling Frito-Lay Chips in China* *341*
Perceptual Selection 342
External Factors 342
Communication Competency: *Just My Type* *343*
Internal Factors 344
Person Perception 346
The Perceived 346
The Perceiver 346
The Situation 347
Impression Management 347
Perceptual Errors 348
Accuracy of Judgment 348
Perceptual Defense 349
Stereotyping 349
Diversity Competency: *Home Depot* *350*
Halo Effect 350
Projection 351

The Role of Culture 351
Self Competency: *Doing Business in Arab Countries 352*
Attributions: Why People Behave as They Do 353
The Attribution Process 354
Internal versus External Causes of Behavior 355
Attributions of Success and Failure 356
Chapter Summary 358
Key Terms and Concepts 359
Discussion Questions 359
Experiential Exercise and Case 359
Experiential Exercise: Diversity Competency—Measuring Perceptions of Women as Managers 359
Case: Ethics Competency—The Foundation for New Era Philanthropy 362

Chapter 13 **Learning and Reinforcement 364**
Preview Case: *Mini Maids 365*
Learning through Rewards and Punishments 366
Classical Conditioning 366
Operant Conditioning 367
Contingencies of Reinforcement 368
Positive Reinforcement 370
Communication Competency: *Gary Logan at Kodak 371*
Organizational Rewards 372
Negative Reinforcement 372
Omission 373
Punishment 374
Change Competency: *Discipline without Punishment 377*
Guidelines for Using Contingencies of Reinforcement 377
Schedules of Reinforcement 378
Continuous and Intermittent Reinforcement 378
Fixed Interval Schedule 378
Variable Interval Schedule 379
Fixed Ratio Schedule 379
Across Cultures Competency: *Northern Shipbuilding of China 380*
Variable Ratio Schedule 380
Social Learning Theory 380
Symbolizing 381
Forethought 382
Vicarious Learning 382
Self-Control 382
Teams Competency: *Rowe Furniture's Focused Factory 383*
Self-Efficacy 383
Organizational Guidelines 384
Chapter Summary 385
Key Terms and Concepts 386
Discussion Questions 386
Experiential Exercise and Cases 386
Experiential Exercise: Self Competency—What Is Your Self-Efficacy? 386
Case: Ethics Competency—Medical Incentives 387
Case: Change Competency—Westinghouse 387

Chapter 14 **Fundamentals of Motivation 390**
Preview Case: *Starbucks 391*
The Basic Motivational Process 392
Core Phases 393
Motivational Challenges 394
Motivating Employees through Satisfying Human Needs 395

Needs Hierarchy Model 395
Achievement Motivation Model 397
Self Competency: *John Schnatter of Papa John's Pizza 400*
Motivating Employees through Job Design 401
Motivator–Hygiene Model 401
Job Characteristics Model 402
Teams Competency: *SEI Investments 405*
Cultural Influences 405
Motivating Employees through Performance Expectations 406
Expectancy Model 406
Across Cultures Competency: *McProgrammers 411*
Motivating Employees through Equity 411
Equity Model: Balancing Inputs and Outcomes 412
Ethics Competency: *Employee Theft 414*
Procedural Justice: Making Decisions Fairly 414
Chapter Summary 416
Key Terms and Concepts 417
Discussion Questions 417
Experiential Exercise and Case 418
Experiential Exercise: Self Competency—What Do You Want from Your Job? 418
Case: Teams Competency—SAS Institute 419

Chapter 15 **Motivation through Goal Setting and Reward Systems 422**
Preview Case: *UPS 423*
Model of Goal Setting and Performance 424
Importance of Goal Setting 424
Challenge 425
Teams Competency: *NASCAR Racing 427*
Moderators 427
Mediators 429
Performance 430
Ethics Competency: *The Gap 430*
Rewards 431
Satisfaction 431
Effects of Goal Setting 432
Impact on Performance 432
Communication Competency: *The Ritz-Carlton Hotel 433*
Limitations to Goal Setting 433
Organizational Guidelines 434
Reward Systems for High Performance 434
Gain-Sharing Programs 435
Profit-Sharing Programs 437
Skill-Based Pay 438
Flexible Benefit Plans 438
Organizational Guidelines 439
Across Cultures Competency: *Reward Practices in Different Cultures 441*
Chapter Summary 441
Key Terms and Concepts 442
Discussion Questions 442
Experiential Exercise and Case 443
Experiential Exercise: Self Competency—Goal Setting 443
Case: Change Competency—Improving Safety 444

Chapter 16 **Managing Stress and Aggressive Behavior 446**
Preview Case: *Erica Benson 447*
Concept of Stress 448

Fight-or-Flight Response 448
The Stress Experience 449
Role of Personality in Stress 450
The Type A Personality 450
The Hardy Personality 452
Primary Sources of Stress 453
Organizational Sources 453
Teams Competency: *Bruce Goode of Works Corporation 454*
Life Stressors 456
Impacts of Stress 458
Impacts on Health 458
Impacts on Performance 459
Impacts on Job Burnout 460
Self Competency: *John Houghom's Burnout Experience 461*
Managing Stress 462
Individual Practices 462
Organizational Practices 463
Change Competency: *Dofasco's Wellness Program 465*
Workplace Aggression 465
Workplace Bullying 466
Sexual Harassment 469
Diversity Competency: *OfficeWorks' Sexual Harassment Policy 469*
Workplace Violence 471
Aggression toward the Organization 474
Chapter Summary 474
Key Terms and Concepts 475
Discussion Questions 475
Experiential Exercise and Case 476
Experiential Exercise: Self Competency—Determining Your Stress Level 476
Case: Change Competency—Stress Management at Metropolitan Hospital 477

References R-1

Index I-1

Preface

For more than four decades, we have been writing, editing, and revising this book. Looking back at the first edition of this book, we notice that there are a lot of similar chapter titles. However, the text in those chapters is substantially revised or changed. For example, in the first edition, we have chapters on learning, leadership, teams, and organizational design. However, in the 1970s, concepts of self-efficacy, transformational and/or authentic leadership, virtual and affinity teams, and networked designed organizations were not even being written about or discussed. Today, many of these and other topics that form the bases for effectively managing people are widely acknowledged. Thus, while the chapter titles look familiar to those of you who used the previous editions, this new international edition of our book is not simply old wine in new bottles—it is a major revision. We tell ourselves that major revisions are not needed, but then undertake them anyway.

If the international edition is a major revision; what's new? First, all opening preview cases are new. Second, the competency features are virtually all new. Third, we have added a new feature *The Competent Leader* that illustrates how leaders use the concepts discussed in the text to manage their organizations more effectively. Fourth, at the end of each chapter, we have added at least one new experiential exercise and/or case.

What stayed the same? First, as in all previous editions, we pursued the goal of presenting fundamental concepts in the field of organizational behavior. These are presented by using contemporary examples, issues, and management practices. Second, to engage students as active participants in the learning process and to assist them in developing their managerial competencies, there are numerous questionnaires that students can take. The objectives of these questionnaires are to help readers assess their behaviors accurately and help them develop the competencies they will need to become successful employees, managers, and leaders. A third goal is to present timely real-life examples to encourage, stimulate, and support learning.

The effective management and leadership of organizations require thoughtful application of competencies related to the behavior of people at work. Few, if any, of the dramatic challenges facing organizations can be handled effectively without a solid understanding of human behavior—both of oneself and others. Highly motivated and committed employees and leaders are critical for organizational success and effectiveness. Organizations fail or succeed, decline or prosper because of people—what people do or do not do every day on the job. Effective organizational behavior is the bedrock on which effectiveness rests. Long-term competitive advantage comes from the rich portfolio of individual and team-based competencies learned by an organization's employees, managers, and leaders.

OUR ROAD MAP TO YOUR LEARNING JOURNEY

Our road map to your learning journey starts in Chapter 1. In this chapter, we detail the seven foundation competencies that all employees, managers, and leaders need to master in order for them to become effective. Through our combined teaching, research, and consulting, we have found that mastering these seven competencies will lead to high performance. Being smart and quick on your feet might land you a spot on the TV show *Jeopardy*, being a social schmoozer may get you invited to the right parties, and being a workaholic might get you a few words of praise from your peers,

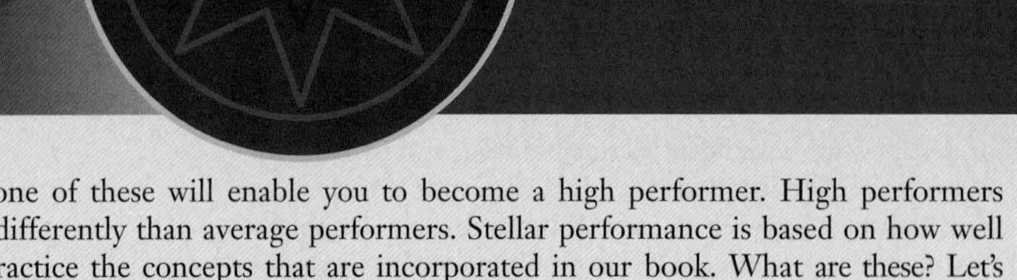

but none of these will enable you to become a high performer. High performers work differently than average performers. Stellar performance is based on how well you practice the concepts that are incorporated in our book. What are these? Let's briefly identify and describe them for you.

Start
Self
Change
Communication
Individual, Team and Organizational Effectiveness
Teams
Diversity
Across Cultures
Ethics

- ***Self Competency*** involves your ability to assess your own strengths and weaknesses, set and pursue professional goals, balance work and personal life, and engage in learning new behaviors.

- ***Communication Competency*** involves your ability to use all ways of sending, understanding, and receiving ideas, thoughts, and feelings. Most of us possess a deep-seated desire to have others understand and respect us for who we really are. Accurately transferring and exchanging information and emotions are critical for this process to occur.
- ***Diversity Competency*** involves your ability to value the unique individual and group characteristics found in organizations. Increasing workforce diversity brings together people with different identities, and managers need to sort out how diverse people understand and relate to one another. You need to embrace the different characteristics as potential sources of organizational strength and appreciate the uniqueness of each individual.
- ***Ethics Competency*** involves your ability to incorporate values and principles that distinguish right and wrong in decision making and taking action on those values. By encouraging employees to discuss their own ethical beliefs, these discussions can lead to a deeper appreciation of other employees' talents.
- ***Across Cultures Competency*** refers to your ability to recognize and embrace the similarities and differences among nations and cultures. Globalization has increased the diversity of the modern workplace. Cultural differences bring out a paradox: On one hand, cultural diversity brings innovation and creativity, but on the other hand, it can sow seeds for conflict and lack of commitment to team and organization goals. Differences in cultures are a fact of life in today's organizations. These cultural differences also create a challenge for managers who must get people to work together productively without harmful conflict.
- ***Teams Competency*** involves your ability to develop, support, facilitate, and lead teams to achieve the organization's goals. Teamwork in organizations is elusive to many managers because they fail to demonstrate the behaviors that will enable members of the organization to develop into a cohesive well-run unit.
- ***Change Competency*** involves your ability to recognize and implement needed changes in people, tasks, structures, or cultures. Most people and organizations resist change. Therefore, you will need to demonstrate the benefits of change to others and overcome some of the barriers to change that others will present to you.

We provide you with a rich portfolio of action learning opportunities to develop your seven competencies. These opportunities include self-assessment instruments, experiential exercises, case studies, and discussion questions. Self-assessment instruments, such as the one at the end of Chapter 1, provide benchmarks against which you can gauge your competencies independently and compare your levels with those of other students and practicing managers.

NEW AND DISTINGUISHING FEATURES

Chapter-Opening Preview Cases

Each chapter opens with a Preview Case that focuses on a person, team, or organization. Our purpose is to engage the learner with the themes of the chapter. We have picked organizations that most students are familiar with, such as Google, Starbucks, UPS, Tyco, Mayo Clinic, and Bank of America. Typically, the Preview Cases illustrate effective or ineffective applications of one or more of the seven foundation competencies. Within the chapter, there are numerous references to how the Preview Case illustrates particular concepts or management practices. All 16 of the Preview Cases are **NEW** to this edition.

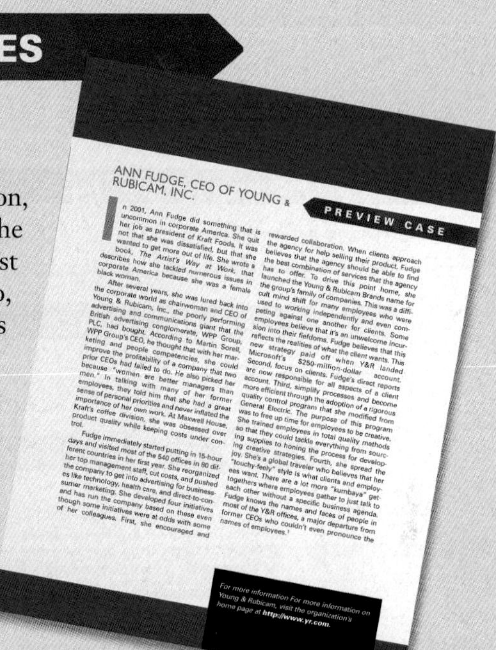
ANN FUDGE, CEO OF YOUNG & RUBICAM, INC.

PREVIEW CASE

For more information on Young & Rubicam, visit the organization's home page at http://www.yr.com.

The Competent Leader Feature

NEW to this international edition is the Competent Leader feature. This feature provides brief insights from practicing managers on how they apply a concept to managing people in their organizations. Leaders' suggestions and comments appear in the margin next to the text materials to which they directly relate. Some of the featured competent leaders include Meg Whitman, CEO of eBay; Gary Ridge, CEO of WD-40; Carol Bartz, CEO of Autodesk; Humberto Gutierrez-Olvera, director of e-commerce for CompUSA; and Colleen Barrett, COO of Southwest Airlines.

utes that I think are important in a leadership position.[6]

THE COMPETENT LEADER

Be true to yourself. That is the foundation of a good life well lived.... Choose organizations and bosses where you feel comfortable being yourself.

Edna Morris, President, Women's Foodservice Forum

Career Development

A **career** *is a sequence of work-related positions occupied by a person during a lifetime.*[7] It embraces attitudes and behaviors that are part of ongoing work-related tasks and experiences. The popular view of a career usually is restricted to the idea of moving up the ladder in an organization. At times, this opportunity is no longer available to many people because of downsizing, mergers, and the increasing tendency of management to place the responsibility on employees to develop their own competencies. A person may remain at the same level, acquiring and developing new competencies, and have a successful career without ever being promoted. A person also can build a career by moving among various jobs in different fields, such as accounting, management information systems, and marketing, or among organizations such as Land O'Lakes, Dell, and Nike. Thus a career encompasses not only traditional work experiences but also the opportunity

In-Chapter Competency Features

We have at least four features in every chapter that relate to one of the seven competencies. The features aid teaching, learning, and reinforcing of chapter content. They lend a real-world flavor to the text materials. We have chosen these 66 competency features to provide additional examples and applications to help you develop your competencies. Ninety-five percent of these are **NEW** to this edition. Those that we have retained have been updated and revised. In many instances, students are challenged to analyze and evaluate the competency being presented. Let's briefly highlight some of the organizations that are illustrated for you in these competency features:

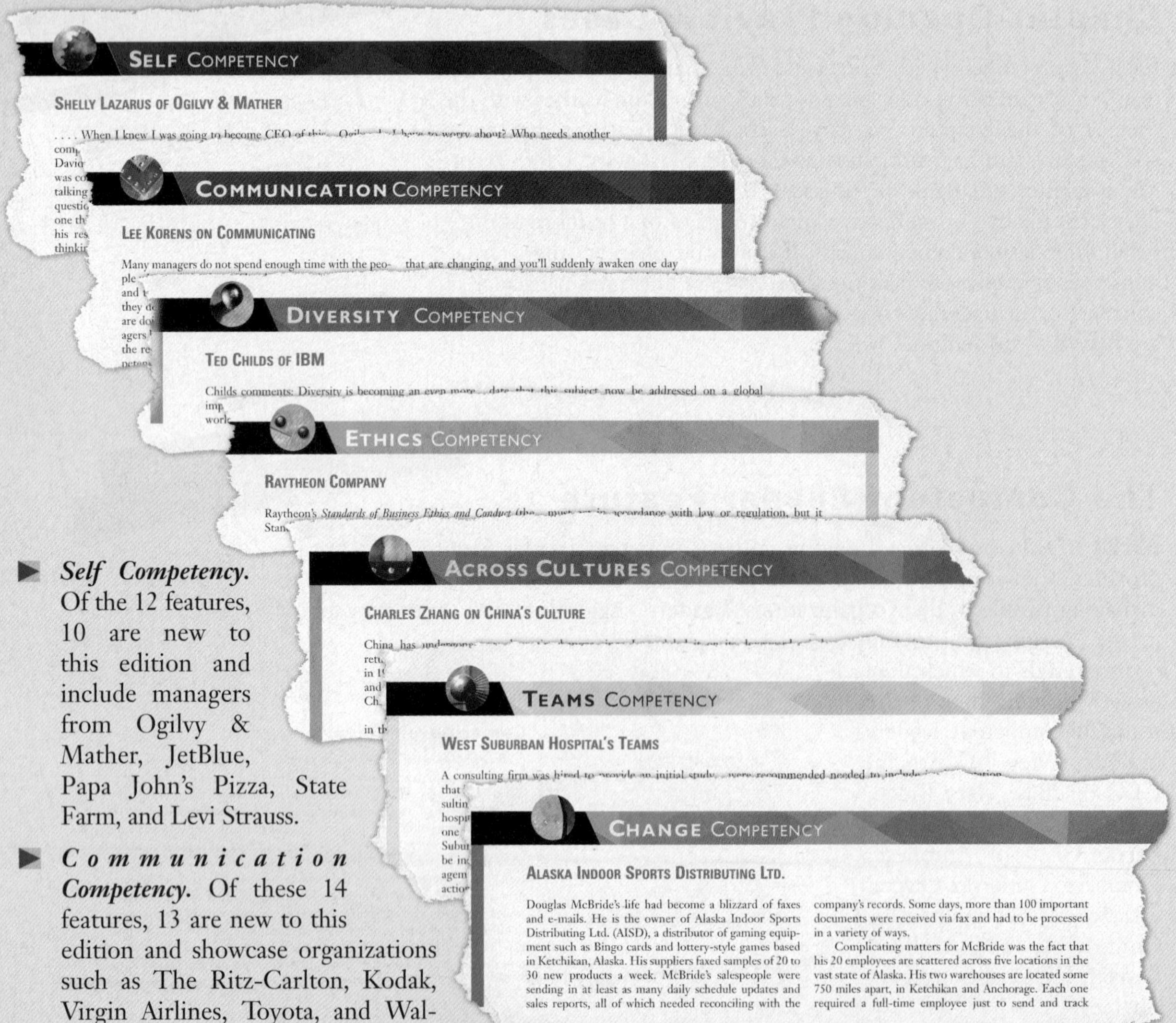

SELF COMPETENCY

SHELLY LAZARUS OF OGILVY & MATHER

COMMUNICATION COMPETENCY

LEE KORENS ON COMMUNICATING

Many managers do not spend enough time with the peo- that are changing, and you'll suddenly awaken one day

DIVERSITY COMPETENCY

TED CHILDS OF IBM

ETHICS COMPETENCY

RAYTHEON COMPANY

ACROSS CULTURES COMPETENCY

CHARLES ZHANG ON CHINA'S CULTURE

TEAMS COMPETENCY

WEST SUBURBAN HOSPITAL'S TEAMS

CHANGE COMPETENCY

ALASKA INDOOR SPORTS DISTRIBUTING LTD.

Douglas McBride's life had become a blizzard of faxes and e-mails. He is the owner of Alaska Indoor Sports Distributing Ltd. (AISD), a distributor of gaming equipment such as Bingo cards and lottery-style games based in Ketchikan, Alaska. His suppliers faxed samples of 20 to 30 new products a week. McBride's salespeople were sending in at least as many daily schedule updates and sales reports, all of which needed reconciling with the company's records. Some days, more than 100 important documents were received via fax and had to be processed in a variety of ways.

Complicating matters for McBride was the fact that his 20 employees are scattered across five locations in the vast state of Alaska. His two warehouses are located some 750 miles apart, in Ketchikan and Anchorage. Each one required a full-time employee just to send and track

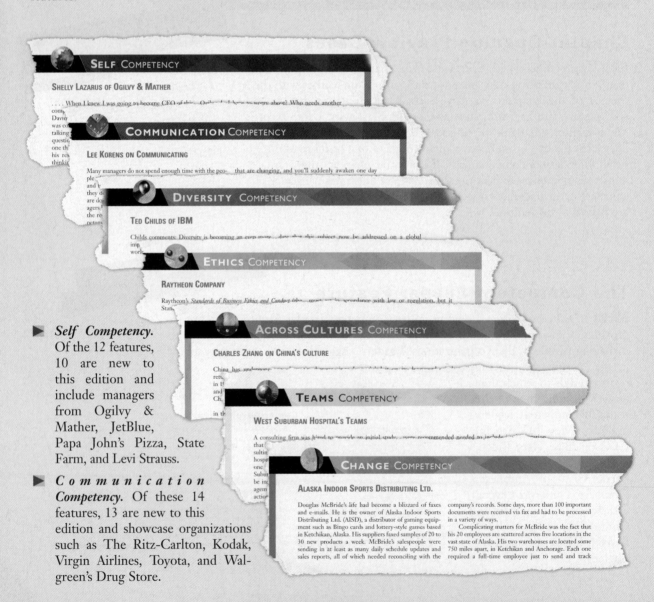

- ***Self Competency.*** Of the 12 features, 10 are new to this edition and include managers from Ogilvy & Mather, JetBlue, Papa John's Pizza, State Farm, and Levi Strauss.
- ***Communication Competency.*** Of these 14 features, 13 are new to this edition and showcase organizations such as The Ritz-Carlton, Kodak, Virgin Airlines, Toyota, and Walgreen's Drug Store.

- **_Diversity Competency._** All of the four diversity competency features are new to this edition and include insights learned from IBM, Home Depot, Georgia Power, and a sexual harassment policy.
- **_Ethics Competency._** Of the six ethics competency features, all are new to this edition and include managers from Raytheon, The Gap, BET, and State Farm.
- **_Across Cultures Competency._** All of these 11 features are new to this edition. We have included examples about employees and managers from global organizations such as Frito-Lay, Unilever, Caterpillar, Western Union, and Grupo Carso.
- **_Teams Competency._** Of the 10 features, nine are new to this edition. Students will be exposed to teams working at Rowe Furniture, DreamWorks SKG, Bayer, and NASCAR, among others.
- **_Change Competency._** Of the nine features, eight are new to this edition. How managers at Safeco, St. Vincent's Hospital, 7-Eleven, and Harley-Davidson achieved change is highlighted in these features.

Key Terms and Concepts

Key terms and concepts appear in boldface in the text, making it easy for students to check their understanding. The definition of each term and concept is in italics to enhance clarity and student learning.

Discussion Questions

Every chapter includes discussion questions. They require students to apply, analyze, discover, and think about important chapter concepts and related competencies. These questions also require students to build their communication competencies because they ask for thoughtful, focused responses. The majority of the more than 150 questions are **NEW** to this edition.

Experiential Exercises and Cases

Each chapter contains at least one experiential exercise and/or case. These end-of-chapter features provide additional means for students to actively engage in their learning process and to further develop their competencies. Some of the experiential exercises include Managing for the Future, Interpersonal Communication Styles, Personal Power Inventory, and Team Assessment Inventory. Among the organizations featured in the cases are Southwest Airlines, CompUSA, SAS Institute, and eBay. Each of these experiential exercises and cases has been used by instructors and has proven to stimulate students to become active learners in their own development process.

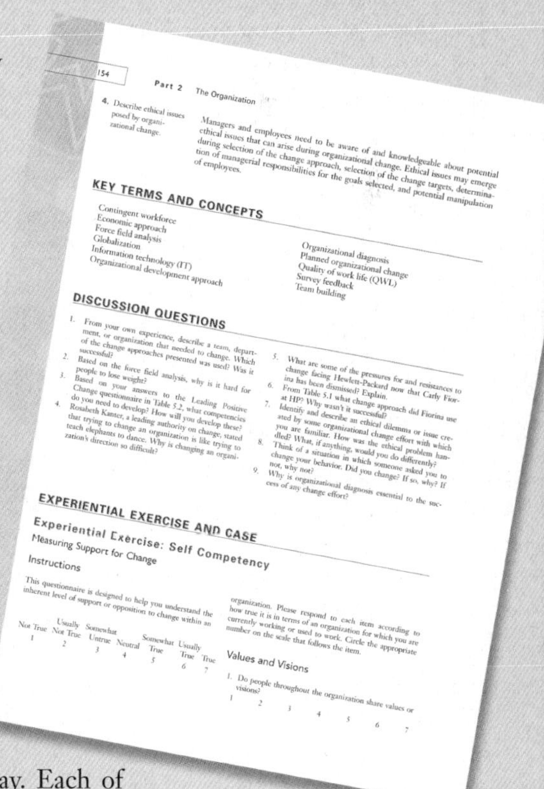

154 Part 2 The Organization

4. Describe ethical issues posed by organizational change.

Managers and employees need to be aware of and knowledgeable about potential ethical issues that can arise during organizational change. Ethical issues may emerge during selection of the change approach, selection of the change targets, determination of managerial responsibilities for the goals selected, and potential manipulation of employees.

KEY TERMS AND CONCEPTS

Contingent workforce
Economic approach
Force field analysis
Globalization
Information technology (IT)
Organizational development approach
Organizational diagnosis
Planned organizational change
Quality of work life (QWL)
Survey feedback
Team building

DISCUSSION QUESTIONS

1. From your own experience, describe a team, department, or organization that needed to change. Which of the change approaches presented was used? Was it successful?
2. Based on the force field analysis, why is it hard for people to lose weight?
3. Based on your answers to the Leading Positive Change questionnaire in Table 5.2, what competencies do you need to develop? How will you develop these?
4. Rosabeth Kanter, a leading authority on change, stated that trying to change an organization is like trying to teach elephants to dance. Why is changing an organization's direction so difficult?
5. What are some of the pressures for and resistances to change facing Hewlett-Packard now that Carly Fiorina has been dismissed? Explain.
6. From Table 5.1 what change approach did Fiorina use at HP? Why wasn't it successful?
7. Identify and describe an ethical dilemma or issue created by some organizational change effort with which you are familiar. How was the ethical problem handled? What, if anything, would you do differently?
8. Think of a situation in which someone asked you to change your behavior. Did you change? If so, why? If not, why not?
9. Why is organizational diagnosis essential to the success of any change effort?

EXPERIENTIAL EXERCISE AND CASE

Experiential Exercise: Self Competency

Measuring Support for Change

Instructions

This questionnaire is designed to help you understand the inherent level of support or opposition to change within an organization. Please respond to each item according to how true it is in terms of an organization for which you are currently working or used to work. Circle the appropriate number on the scale that follows the item.

Not True	Usually Not True	Somewhat Untrue	Neutral	Somewhat True	Usually True	True
1	2	3	4	5	6	7

Values and Visions

1. Do people throughout the organization share values or visions?
1 2 3 4 5 6 7

Chapter Summaries

Every chapter ends with a summary that distills the chapter's main points. These summaries are organized around the chapter's *Learning Objectives*. Students can readily assess their mastery of the material presented for each of these objectives.

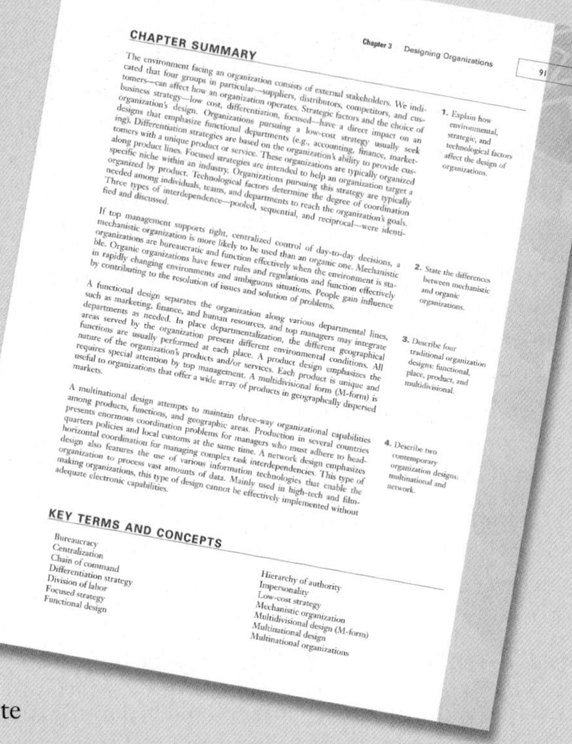

CHAPTER SUMMARY — Chapter 3 Designing Organizations 91

1. Explain how environmental, strategic, and technological factors affect the design of organizations.
2. State the differences between mechanistic and organic organizations.
3. Describe four traditional organization designs: functional, place, product, and multidivisional.
4. Describe two contemporary organization designs: multinational and network.

KEY TERMS AND CONCEPTS

Bureaucracy
Centralization
Chain of command
Differentiation strategy
Division of labor
Focused strategy
Functional design
Hierarchy of authority
Impersonality
Low-cost strategy
Mechanistic organization
Multidivisional design (M-form)
Multinational design
Multinational organizations

Self-Assessment Instruments

Throughout the book, we present over thirty self-assessment instruments that typically focus on one or more of the foundation competencies in the chapter. They are aimed at helping students gain self-insights, readily learn concepts, identify their own strengths and weaknesses, and effectively lead others. These instruments were chosen because they have proven to enhance student learning and development and stimulate classroom discussion.

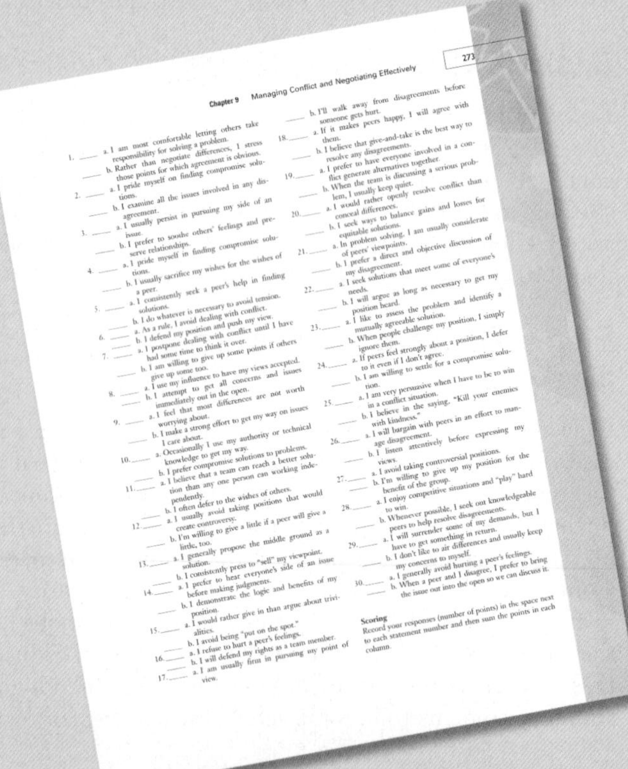

Chapter 9 Managing Conflict and Negotiating Effectively 273

Scoring

Record your responses (number of points) in the space next to each statement number and then sum the points in each column.

LEARNING FRAMEWORK

The framework for learning about organizational behavior and developing your competencies is fully presented in Chapter 1 titled *Learning Framework for Individual, Team, and Organizational Effectiveness.* Our framework moves the reader from the individual level, to the team level, to the organizational level.

In Part 2, we address more macro and system-wide aspects of organizational behavior. Chapter 2 focuses on managerial and ethical decision making and on the ethical dilemmas that confront many managers. The rationale that managers use to make decisions is explored through vivid examples at St. Vincent's Hospital, Epic Divers and Marine, and other organizations. Chapter 3 focuses on how the strategy of an organization impacts its choice of design. It also illustrates the basic building blocks of an organization—division of labor, rules and procedures, chain of command, span of control, responsibility, authority—and how managers use these to create effective organizations. A **NEW** section on network design explores issues surrounding the real-time management of off-site employees and suppliers. DreamWorks SKG, Electrolux, and 7-Eleven are among the organizations used to illustrate various types of designs. Chapter 4 covers the elusive concept of organizational culture. We focus on why understanding culture is important and the manager's role in forming, maintaining, and changing his or her organization's culture. We also explore different types of cultures and how these impact employee behaviors at Google, Harley-Davidson, and other organizations. A **NEW** section on ethical behaviors and effective cultural diversity programs has been added to this edition. The final chapter, Chapter 5, presents contemporary views of organizational change. Due to the various demands on organizations, change is the order of the day. How organizations such as Toyota, Hewlett-Packard, 3M, Shell, and others respond to change provides powerful illustrations of the necessity and complexity of the change process.

The third part of the book moves the reader from individual aspects of organizational behavior to the interpersonal processes that often impact the effectiveness of organizations. We present leadership in a two-chapter sequence, covering the foundations in Chapter 6 and contemporary leadership concepts in Chapter 7. Chapter 6 is a historical perspective on leadership with coverage on power and political behavior, leader traits and behaviors, situational leadership, and the decision-making model of leadership. We have added a **NEW** section on power and political behavior because we believe that leadership is a complex influence process. Chapter 7 focuses on transactional, charismatic, authentic, and transformational leader behaviors. **NEW** material on authentic leadership has been added to this chapter to present a more comprehensive picture of leader behaviors. Chapter 8 presents material on how teams operate in organizations. Using diverse examples from the Mayo Clinic to Bayer, we illustrate the differences between groups and teams, the benefits and costs of teams, and the steps for implementing effective teams in organizations. We have added **NEW** material on virtual teams in global organizations because of their importance in many organizations. Chapter 9 focuses on the many types of conflict found in organizations. It explores both the positive and negative aspects of conflict and how organizations are using effective conflict resolution tactics to improve their effectiveness. **NEW** material on affinity groups and negotiating with the Chinese have been

added. The last chapter in this part is Chapter 10. Chapter 10 addresses a portfolio of concepts, issues, and processes for enhancing interpersonal communication—verbally, nonverbally, and through networks—between two or more individuals within organizations. Special emphasis is given to fostering ethical interpersonal communications.

Part 4 of the book focuses on key aspects of the individual by discussing workforce diversity and cultural values, the psychological nature of people, elements of personality, how emotions affect employee behaviors, how people form attitudes, perceptual and attribution processes, and how people learn. The six chapters in Part 4 are full of real-world examples of how today's leaders and organizations are using these concepts to manage others. For example, in Chapter 11 we use examples from The Container Store to illustrate how store managers can use various tactics to increase employee job satisfaction and commitment, and American Express to demonstrate how Kenneth Chenault, its CEO, funneled the emotions of people after 9/11 to increase their effectiveness and commitment. We have added a **NEW** section on why managers need to understand the role of emotions and how emotions of employees change over time to influence the effectiveness of a team, department, or company. In Chapter 12, we illustrate how perceptions and attributions vary by culture and the manager's role in shaping these individual processes. In addition, we have added materials on diversity programs in use at Home Depot. Chapter 13 describes how managers can use various reinforcement systems to enhance an individual's learning on the job. As new challenges are thrust on managers, they need to be able to tailor their organization's reward system to enhance employee effectiveness. Chapters 14 and 15 focus on specific motivational strategies that managers at Starbucks, Papa John's Pizza, The Ritz-Carlton Hotels, and The Gap use to affect individual performance in organizations. The last chapter of Part 4, Chapter 16, closes with the topics of workplace stress, sexual harassment, and a **NEW** section on aggressive workplace behaviors. It illustrates how organizations are paying more attention to the needs of employees and trying to achieve a work–life balance.

SUPPLEMENTS

Instructor Resources

Instructor's Manual (Available at http://aise.swlearning.com)

Written by Professor Susan Leshnower of Midland College, the *Instructor's Manual* contains comprehensive resource materials for lectures, including enrichment modules for enhancing and extending relevant chapter concepts. It uses jazz bands as a metaphor to explore many of the facets of organizational behavior. It also presents suggested answers to all end-of-chapter discussion questions. It includes notes on using the end-of-chapter *Experiential Exercise and Case* features.

Test Bank

(Available at http://aise.swlearning.com)

Written by Professor Molly Pepper of Gonzaga University, the Test Bank contains almost 4,000 questions from which to choose. A selection of new and revised true/false, multiple-choice, short essay, and critical thinking essay questions is provided for each chapter. Questions are categorized by difficulty level, by learning objective, and according to Bloom's taxonomy. Cross-references to materials in the textbook and pages where answers can be found are also included. Explanations are provided for why statements are false in the true/false sections of the test bank.

ACKNOWLEDGMENTS

Don and John express their sincere and grateful appreciation to the following individuals who provided thoughtful reviews and useful suggestions for improving this edition of their book. Their insights were critical in making a number of important revisions.

Jason Colquitt, *University of Florida*
Cecily Cooper, *University of Miami*
Humberto Gutierrez-Olvera, *CompUSA*
Sue Hammond, *Thin Book Publishing*
David Lei, *Southern Methodist University*
Karl O. Magnusen, *Florida International University*
Padmakumar Nair, *University of Texas, Dallas*
Tom Nevant, *Deep South Insurance Company*
Stephen D. Schuster, *California State University, Northridge*
J. Daniel Sherman, *University of Alabama, Huntsville*
Sydne W. Tustison, *Columbia College*
Don VandeWalle, *Southern Methodist University*

For their assistance with editions past, they would like to thank the following people:

Carole K. Barnett, *University of New Hampshire*
Steve Brown, *University of Houston*
D. Anthony Butterfield, *University of Massachusetts Amherst*
Ken Butterfield, *Washington State University*
William Cron, *Texas Christian University*
Eric B. Dent, *University of North Carolina, Pembroke*
David Elloy, *Gonzaga University*
Larry Garner, *Tarleton State University*
William Joyce, *Dartmouth College*
Dong I. Jung, *San Diego State University*
Andrew (A.J.) Lutz II, *Park University & Avila College*
Kevin Mossholder, *Louisiana State University–Baton Rouge*
Theodore H. Rosen, *George Washington University*
Stephen P. Schappe, *Penn State University at Harrisburg*
Ralph Sorrentino, *Deloitte Consulting*
Michael Trulson, *Amberton University*
Roger Volkema, *American University*
Edward Ward, *St. Cloud State University*

For their valuable professional guidance and collegial support, they sincerely thank the following individuals who served on the team responsible for this edition:

- Joe Sabatino, who was our editor and worked with us in the various stages of this revision
- Emma Guttler, our developmental editor, who worked with us on all facets of this edition and also provided a key interface with the authors of the various supplements
- Lorretta Palagi, our copyeditor
- Marge Bril, our production project manager
- Tippy McIntosh, our art director
- Tina Potter at Southern Methodist University for her superb support with management preparation and keeping John in line once again
- Argie Butler at Texas A&M University for her superb creativity in designing and building the PowerPoint slides for this edition, as well as her support for manuscript preparation

Don Hellriegel expresses his appreciation to his colleagues at Texas A&M University who collectively create a work environment that nurtures his continued learning and professional development. In particular, the learning environment fostered by Jerry Strawser, dean, and by Angelo DeNisi, former head of the Management Department and now dean at Tulane's Freeman School of Business, is gratefully acknowledged.

John Slocum acknowledges his colleagues at SMU—Mel Fugate, Peter Heslin, Tom Perkowski, Bob Rasberry, and Don VandeWalle—for their constructive inputs and reviews. Also, special thanks are extended to Al Niemi, dean of the Cox School, for his support, and to all of the executive MBA students who listened to countless stories and wrote some cases for this book. John also thanks his golfing group at Stonebriar Country Club (Cecil Ewell, Jack Kennedy, Ken Haigler, and Barry Sullivan) for delaying tee-times so that he could finish this project.

Finally, we celebrate this new international edition, some 30 years after the publication of our first U.S. edition in 1976. We thank the many hundreds of reviewers, adopters, students, and others who have supported the development of these 11 editions during the past three decades. Moreover, Don and John thank each other for being great friends since 1962. We met each other in an industrial relations course during our graduate days at Kent State University in 1962 and are still close friends. It's been a lifetime of experiences for both of us. During that time, Don raised three daughters who now are raising 11 children and is still married to Lois, his first love. John raised three sons who are now raising seven children and is still married to Gail. There is a sign in John's den that reads "Missing: Husband-golfer and dog. Reward for the dog."

John W. Slocum, Jr., *Southern Methodist University*

Don Hellriegel, *Texas A&M University*

Author Page

John W. Slocum, Jr.

John W. Slocum, Jr. is the O. Paul Corley Professor of Organizational Behavior at the Edwin L. Cox School of Business, Southern Methodist University, Dallas, Texas. He has also taught on the faculties of the University of Washington, Penn State University, the Ohio State University, the International University of Japan, and Dartmouth's Amos Tuck School. He holds a B. B. A. from Westminster College, an M. B. A. from Kent State University and a Ph.D. in organizational behavior from the University of Washington.

Professor Slocum has held a number of positions in professional societies, including President of the Eastern Academy of Management in 1973–1974, the 39th President of the Academy of Management in 1983–1984, and Editor of the *Academy of Management Journal* from 1979–1981. He is a Fellow of the Academy of Management, Decision Science Institute, and the Pan-Pacific Institute. He has been awarded the Alumni Citation for Professional Accomplishment by Westminster College, and the Nicolas Salgo, Rotunda, and Executive MBA Outstanding Teaching Awards at SMU. Currently he serves as Co-Editor of the *Journal of World Business* and the *Journal of Leadership and Organizational Behavior*, Associate Editor for *Organizational Dynamics*, and is a member of the editorial review board of the *Leadership Quarterly*. He has authored or co-authored more than 127 journal articles.

Professor Slocum has served as a consultant to such organizations as Aramark, OxyChem, Southwest Real Estate Corporation, Celanese, Pier 1, NASA, Pfizer Corporation, Bayer Corporation, Brakke Consulting, and Key Span Energy. He is a regular speaker in senior executive development programs sponsored by Lockheed Martin Corporation, the Governor of Texas, Oklahoma State University, University of Oklahoma, and Wuhan University, among others. He is currently on the Board of Directors of Kisco Senior Living, The Winston School of Dallas, GoToLearn (a non-profit corporation), Applied Management Sciences Institute of Houston, Texas and the School of Business Management at the Bandung Institute of Technology in Indonesia.

Don Hellriegel

Don Hellriegel is Professor of Management within the Mays Business School at Texas A&M University. He received his B.S. and M.B.A. from Kent State University and his Ph.D. from the University of Washington. Dr. Hellriegel has been a member of the faculty at Texas A&M since 1975 and has served on the faculties of the Pennsylvania State University and the University of Colorado.

His research interests include corporate entrepreneurship, effect of organizational environments, managerial cognitive styles, and organizational innovation and strategic management processes. His research has been published in a number of leading journals.

Professor Hellriegel served as Vice President and Program Chair of the Academy of Management (1986), President Elect (1987), President (1988), and Past President (1989). In September 1999, he was elected to a three-year term as Dean of the Fellows Group of the Academy of Management. He served a term as Editor of the *Academy of Management Review* and served as a member of the Board of Governors of the Academy of Management (1979–1981 and 1982–1989). Dr. Hellriegel has performed many other leadership roles, among which include President, Eastern Academy of Management; Division Chair, Organization and Management Theory Division; President, Brazos County United Way; Co-Consulting Editor, *West Series in Management*; Head (1976–1980 and 1989–1994), Department of Management (TAMU); Interim Dean, Executive Associate Dean (1995-2000), Mays School of Business (TAMU); and Interim Executive Vice Chancellor (TAMUS).

He has consulted with a variety of groups and organizations, including—among others—3DI, Sun Ship Building, Penn Mutual Life Insurance, Texas A&M University System, Ministry of Industry and Commerce (Nation of Kuwait), Ministry of Agriculture (Nation of Dominican Republic), American Assembly of Collegiate Schools of Business, and Texas Innovation Group.

Fundamentals of Organizational Behavior

PART 1

Learning about Organizational Behavior

CHAPTER 1 Organizational Behavior and Foundation Competencies

CHAPTER 1

Organizational Behavior and Foundation Competencies

LEARNING OBJECTIVES

When you have finished studying this chapter, you should be able to:

1. Describe the self competency and its contribution to effectiveness.
2. Describe the communication competency and its contribution to effectiveness.
3. Describe the diversity competency and its contribution to effectiveness.
4. Describe the ethics competency and its contribution to effectiveness.
5. Describe the across cultures competency and its contribution to effectiveness.
6. Describe the teams competency and its contribution to effectiveness.
7. Describe the change competency and its contribution to effectiveness.
8. Explain the framework for learning about organizational behavior to enhance individual, team, and organizational effectiveness.

Preview Case: Jack Gherty of Land O'Lakes
SELF COMPETENCY
Foundation Abilities
Career Development
Self Competency—Shelly Lazarus of Ogilvy & Mather
COMMUNICATION COMPETENCY
Foundation Abilities
Communication Competency—Lee Korens on Communicating
DIVERSITY COMPETENCY
Foundation Abilities
Categories of Diversity
Changing Workforce
Gender
Race and Ethnicity
Age
Diversity Competency—Ted Childs of IBM
ETHICS COMPETENCY
Foundation Abilities
Ethical Dilemmas
Ethics Competency—Raytheon Company
ACROSS CULTURES COMPETENCY
Foundation Abilities
Work-Related Cultural Values
Across Cultures Competency—Charles Zhang on China's Culture
TEAMS COMPETENCY
Foundation Abilities
Teams and Individualism
Teams Competency—West Suburban Hospital's Teams
CHANGE COMPETENCY
Foundation Abilities
Technological Forces
Change Competency—Alaska Indoor Sports Distributing Ltd.
LEARNING FRAMEWORK FOR INDIVIDUAL, TEAM, AND ORGANIZATIONAL EFFECTIVENESS
Individuals in Organizations
Leadership and Team Behaviors
The Organization Itself
Foundation Competencies
CHAPTER SUMMARY
KEY TERMS AND CONCEPTS
DISCUSSION QUESTIONS
EXPERIENTIAL EXERCISE AND CASE

JACK GHERTY OF LAND O'LAKES

PREVIEW CASE

Jack Gherty is the recent past president and CEO of Land O'Lakes. He currently serves as chairman of the board of the National Council of Farmers Cooperatives. Headquartered in Arden Mills, Minnesota, Land O'Lakes is a national farmer-owned food and agricultural cooperative with over $6 billion in sales in all 50 states and more than 50 countries. We share excerpts from an interview of Gherty in this Preview Case.

How I convey accountability and performance to my managers and employees is as honestly and candidly as I can. As we have become a bigger organization, our ultimate success or failure has come to depend on how we perform as a business, how we operate as a team, whether we have the right culture, whether we have the right compensation systems, and whether we make the right business decisions. Within our Vision of "being one of the best food and agricultural companies in the world," we ask ourselves, "Are we our employees' first choice for work?" Creating a culture becomes pretty important, because we need to be an organization that is growing. People want to join an organization where they feel they have an opportunity for advancement in the future.

The leader of any organization is the strongest determinant of the culture of the organization. To the extent the leader walks the talk in living whatever those cultural attributes are every day, the stronger the culture will be. But it will not evolve over a day or a week or a month or a year. It will evolve over a period of time, but it is pretty powerful when you get there. The most effective leader is one who creates the right culture and builds the best team. My definition of building the best team is to build a group of people who find that, when you leave, you won't be missed at all. You won't be missed at all because you have built a team that's brighter and stronger.

People would probably define me as a situational leader. There are some pluses and minuses to that. The value of a situational leader is the flexibility or adaptability to adopt different management styles. As a situational leader, I once got some feedback that people were sometimes intimidated and confused. To address this feedback, I took that information to a meeting of managers and spent an hour and a half discussing my management style to help them understand me. Part of the reason for doing that was to say to them, "If you do that same kind of thing with your direct reports, we'll probably be a stronger organization."

The world is changing so quickly. Back at the beginning of my career, you could develop strategies and the plans to implement them over a period of time. You would be successful if you were effective in implementing those original plans. Today, I don't think that works. Today, there is such a sense of accelerating change that you have to not only develop strategies and implement them, you also have to be nimble enough to change your strategies 45 degrees three months into them and be able to implement them on the fly. A real challenge to the best business organizations is not to complain about the fact that this or that is changing, but to accept that it is just the environment they are operating in. You must have a set of competencies to be able to do that.

Several years ago, I used a slogan at our annual meeting that was "Whatever you did to get you there is never enough to keep you there." The whole theory is that if you are performing just to tread water, it is not good enough. You have to keep increasing your performance and adding increased value for customers.[1]

For more information on Land O'Lakes, visit the organization's home page at ***http://www.landolakes.com.***

Jack Gherty recognizes the critical roles of employees, leadership, managing change, and serving customers in the success of Land O'Lakes. The principles and practices of the leadership at Land O'Lakes, not just that of Jack Gherty, represent the latest thinking in organizational behavior. Gherty uses a portfolio of competencies to develop and sustain a winning organizational culture. Also, he suggests that effective leaders need to develop and support employees' organizational competencies throughout the organization.[2]

A **competency** *is an interrelated set of abilities, behaviors, attitudes, and knowledge needed by an individual to be effective in professional and managerial positions.* A number of competencies can be identified as important to the effectiveness of most organizations.[3] From among them, we focus on seven core competencies that significantly affect the behavior and effectiveness of individuals, teams, and organizations. These particular competencies are increasingly important to the effectiveness of most professionals, not just those in managerial and leadership roles, as in the case of Jack Gherty. One of the themes of this book is to define, describe, and illustrate how the seven core competencies can be used in organizations. We weave these ideas into the discussion of organizational behavior and effectiveness throughout.

The first theme of this book is to help you further develop these competencies, which are identified and illustrated in Figure 1.1. The double-headed arrows in Figure 1.1 indicate that these competencies are interrelated and that drawing rigid bound-

FIGURE 1.1 Foundation Competencies for Effectiveness

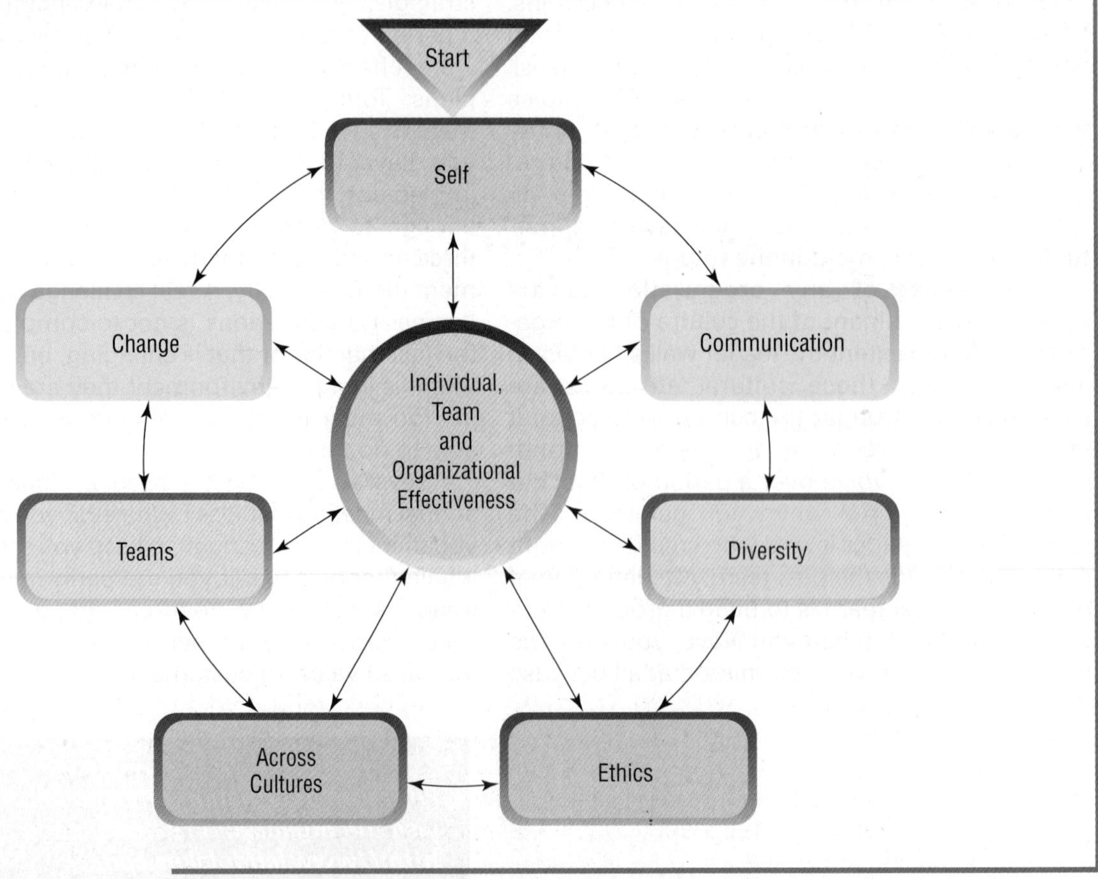

aries between them isn't feasible. We discuss them in considerable depth in specific chapters. For example, most of Chapter 10, *Fostering Organizational Communication*, focuses on developing the communication competency. In addition, in other chapters, we discuss capabilities that build on the foundation competencies and address specific issues. For example, in Chapters 6 and 7, we discuss their importance and that of other capabilities in relation to being an effective leader.

A second theme of this book is to emphasize that there are no easy or complete answers as to why people and organizations function effectively or fail to do so. Thus, we assist you in learning how to look at and understand the behavior of people in organizations. This will guide you in addressing organizational and behavioral issues and developing ways to resolve them. **Organizational behavior** *is the study of individuals and groups within an organizational context, and the study of internal processes and practices as they influence the effectiveness of individuals, teams, and organizations.*[4]

A third theme of this book focuses on the importance of organizational behavior to you and your own effectiveness. You are or probably will be an employee of an organization—and in all likelihood of several organizations—during your career. You may eventually become a team leader, a manager, or an executive. Studying organizational behavior will help you attain the competencies needed to be an effective employee, team leader, manager, and/or executive. The competencies that you acquire will help you diagnose, understand, explain, and act on what is happening around you in your job.

SELF COMPETENCY

LEARNING OBJECTIVE

1. Describe the self competency and its contribution to effectiveness.

The **self competency** *involves the overall ability to assess your own strengths and weaknesses, set and pursue professional and personal goals, balance work and personal life, and engage in new learning—including new or modified skills, behaviors, and attitudes.*

Foundation Abilities

The self competency includes the foundation abilities to be effective in doing the following:

- Understanding your own and others' personality and attitudes (see especially Chapter 11, *Understanding Individual Differences*).
- Perceiving, appraising, and interpreting accurately yourself, others, and the immediate environment (see especially Chapter 12, *Perceptions and Attributions*).
- Understanding and acting on your own and others' work-related motivations and emotions (see especially Chapter 14, *Fundamentals of Motivation*).
- Assessing and establishing your own developmental, personal (life-related), and work-related goals (see especially Chapter 15, *Motivation through Goal Setting and Rewards Systems*).
- Taking responsibility for managing yourself and your career over time and through stressful circumstances (see especially Chapter 16, *Managing Stress and Aggressive Behavior*).

In our view, the self competency is the most basic of the seven competencies. Its achievement creates the underlying personal attributes needed for successfully developing the other six competencies. For example, you can't develop the communication competency if you are unable to perceive, appraise, and interpret your own individual differences and attitudes. This self competency was a cornerstone, for example, of the leadership of Jack Gherty at Land O'Lakes. The self competency includes the concept of **emotional intelligence**—*the capacity for recognizing one's own and others' emotions,* *including self-awareness, self-motivation, being empathetic, and having social skills.*[5] Gherty suggests a keen sense of emotional intelligence in this comment:

> *I got ahead, I think as I reflect back on it, by helping other people win. It just made me feel good. But that, I think, contributed a lot to the things that went on behind the scenes that got me into this position. So, as I think about all of those things, it isn't just one person, but there were things that molded who I am and maybe encouraged some of the attributes that I think are important in a leadership position.*[6]

THE COMPETENT LEADER

Be true to yourself. That is the foundation of a good life well lived.... Choose organizations and bosses where you feel comfortable being yourself.

Edna Morris, President, Women's Foodservice Forum

Career Development

A **career** *is a sequence of work-related positions occupied by a person during a lifetime.*[7] It embraces attitudes and behaviors that are part of ongoing work-related tasks and experiences. The popular view of a career usually is restricted to the idea of moving up the ladder in an organization. At times, this opportunity is no longer available to many people because of downsizing, mergers, and the increasing tendency of management to place the responsibility on employees to develop their own competencies. A person may remain at the same level, acquiring and developing new competencies, and have a successful career without ever being promoted. A person also can build a career by moving among various jobs in different fields, such as accounting, management information systems, and marketing, or among organizations such as Land O'Lakes, Dell, and Nike. Thus a career encompasses not only traditional work experiences but also the opportunity for career alternatives, individual choices, and individual experiences. Let's briefly consider five aspects of a career:

- The nature of a career in itself doesn't imply success or failure or fast or slow advancement. Career success or failure is best determined by the individual, rather than by others.
- No absolute standards exist for evaluating a career. Career success or failure is related to a person's self-concept, goals, and competencies. Individuals should evaluate their own career goals and progress in terms of what is personally meaningful and satisfying.
- An individual should examine a career both subjectively and objectively. Subjective elements of a career include values, attitudes, personality, and motivations, which may change over time. Objective elements of a career include job choices, positions held, and specific competencies developed.
- **Career development** *involves making decisions about an occupation and engaging in activities to attain career goals.* The central idea in the career development process is time. The shape and direction of a person's career over time are influenced by many factors (e.g., the economy, availability of jobs, skill acquisition, personal characteristics, family status, and job history).
- Cultural factors play a role in careers. Cultural norms in countries such as Japan, the Philippines, and Mexico also influence the direction of a person's career. By U.S. standards, women are discriminated against as managers in these cultures. In India and South Korea, social status and educational background largely determine an individual's career paths.

Ralph Waldo Emerson's classic essay "Self-Reliance" offers good advice for a person's career: "Trust thyself." To be successful, people need to commit themselves to a lifetime of learning, including the development of a career plan. A **career plan** *is the individual's choice of occupation, organization, and career path.*

Shelly Lazarus is the chairman and CEO of Ogilvy & Mather Worldwide, a major advertising agency with over 400 offices in 100 countries and headquarters in

New York City. In the following feature, the self competency of Lazarus is suggested in her comments related to employee development.[8]

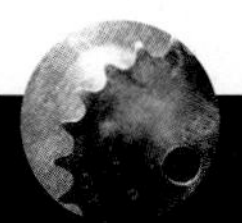

SELF COMPETENCY

SHELLY LAZARUS OF OGILVY & MATHER

. . . . When I knew I was going to become CEO of this company, I spent three days with its legendary founder, David Ogilvy, at his château in France. It was March, it was cold and rainy, and we spent the entire time indoors talking about the business. At one point, I asked him a question point-blank: "David, if you were going to say one thing to me, what would it be?" He didn't hesitate in his response. "No matter how much time you spend thinking about, worrying about, focusing on, questioning the value of, and evaluating people, it won't be enough," he said. "People are the only thing that matters, and the only thing you should think about, because when that part is right, everything else works."

I spend part of every single day hearing David speak that advice, and as a result, I devote a huge amount of time to asking myself: Am I doing enough? Who at Ogilvy do I have to worry about? Who needs another challenge? Who seems a little stale? Who needs a new view on life or a new country to run? David's advice drives not only how I think about and mentor people but also how I form business strategy and make critical decisions.

Let's say, for example, that there was enormous advertising talent in a city where Ogilvy didn't have an office, and the talent refused to leave that city and come to New York, or wherever, to work for us. To me, that's a reason to open a new office. A lot of businesspeople would think primarily about the cost or about whether there were clients in that new city. But ultimately those issues pale in comparison to the need to get, and keep, great talent—great people—at the company.

For more information on Ogilvy & Mather Worldwide, visit the organization's home page at ***http://www.ogilvy.com.***

COMMUNICATION COMPETENCY

LEARNING OBJECTIVE

2. Describe the communication competency and its contribution to effectiveness.

The **communication competency** *involves the overall ability to use all the modes of transmitting, understanding, and receiving ideas, thoughts, and feelings—verbal, listening, nonverbal, written, electronic, and the like—for accurately transferring and exchanging information and emotions.*[9] This competency may be thought of as the *circulatory system* that nourishes the other competencies. Just as arteries and veins provide for the movement of blood in a person, communication allows the exchange of information, thoughts, ideas, and feelings.

Shelly Lazarus, the focus of our previous self competency feature, demonstrates her effective communication competency in this remark:

> *. . . When I have a meeting that's really tense, and when everyone in the office thinks the world is falling apart, I disarm the situation. I'll ask, "Just to be clear, is anyone going to die as a result of our action or inaction? Will Ogilvy go out of business? Will anyone lose a child? Because if that's true, let me know, and I'll get significantly more agitated."*

It just makes everyone laugh, and when we're done laughing, I tell them, "Now let's really focus and get this problem sorted out." [10]

Foundation Abilities

The communication competency includes the foundation abilities to be effective in doing the following:

- Conveying information, ideas, and emotions to others in such a way that they are received as intended. This ability is strongly influenced by the **describing skill**—*identifying concrete, specific examples of behavior and its effects.* This skill also includes recognizing that too often individuals don't realize that they are not being clear and accurate in what they say, resulting from a tendency to jump quickly to generalizations and judgments (see especially Chapter 10, *Fostering Organizational Communication*).
- Providing constructive feedback to others (see especially Chapter 10).
- Engaging in **active listening**—*the process of integrating information and emotions in a search for shared meaning and understanding.* Active listening requires the use of the **questioning skill**—*the ability to ask for information and opinions in a way that gets relevant, honest, and appropriate responses.* This skill helps to bring relevant information and emotions into the dialogue and reduce misunderstandings, regardless of whether the parties agree (see especially Chapters 9, *Managing Conflict and Negotiating Effectively*, and 10).
- Using and interpreting **nonverbal communication**—*facial expressions, body movements, and physical contact are often used to send messages.* The **empathizing skill** *refers to detecting and understanding another person's values, motives, and emotions.* It is especially important in nonverbal communication and active listening. The empathizing skill helps to reduce tension and increase trust and sharing (see especially Chapter 12, *Perceptions and Attributions*, and Chapter 10).
- Engaging in **verbal communication** effectively—*presenting ideas, information, and emotions to others, either one-to-one or in groups.* Recall Jack Gherty's effective verbal communication in the Preview Case when he met with his managers for an hour and a half to discuss his management style. This meeting was in response to the feedback Gherty received that some people were intimidated and confused by his situational leadership. We provide the opportunity for you to apply this skill in the Experiential Exercise and Case section at the end of many chapters.
- Engaging in **written communication** effectively—*the ability to transfer data, information, ideas, and emotions by means of reports, letters, memos, notes, e-mail messages, and the like.*
- Using a variety of computer-based (electronic) resources, such as e-mail and the Internet. The **Internet** *is a worldwide collection of interconnected computer networks.* Through an array of computer-based information technologies, the Internet directly links organizations and their employees to customers, suppliers, information sources, the public, and millions of individuals worldwide. We help you develop this skill throughout the book by presenting numerous Internet addresses and encouraging you to learn more about the organizations, issues, and people discussed.

Lee Korens' distinguished career includes major leadership positions at Merrill Lynch, Pacific Stock Exchange, and at the Security Traders Association. In the following feature, he reflects on the vital role of the communication competency for managers.[11]

COMMUNICATION COMPETENCY

LEE KORENS ON COMMUNICATING

Many managers do not spend enough time with the people who work for them. They hire them, interview them, and then maybe have a weekly meeting with them. But they don't really get involved with the tasks their people are doing. I've found that people like to think their managers have a real interest in how they are proceeding and the results they are getting. If there is one overall competency I think is important, it is to communicate with the people that work for you. Talk to them, listen to them, even if they have complaints, because lots of time the complaints will make a good deal of sense and you will want to make changes.

If you don't have a lot of communication with the people working for you, you won't be aware of things that are changing, and you'll suddenly awaken one day and find that you've lost a couple of good and dedicated employees. If you take a survey of exit interviews in most large firms, you'll find that most people are leaving because they say "No one around here gives a damn about what I do." I think that the number one key to good management is to spend a lot of time talking with the people who are working for you. Your responsibility as a manager is to plan and lead.

Anybody that works in any endeavor likes to feel that what they are doing is important, and managers should show it in some way. Verbal praise is one way to do that, but there are other ways as well.

DIVERSITY COMPETENCY

LEARNING OBJECTIVE

3. Describe the diversity competency and its contribution to effectiveness.

The **diversity competency** *involves the overall ability to value unique individual and group characteristics, embrace such characteristics as potential sources of organizational strength, and appreciate the uniqueness of each individual.*[12] This competency also involves the ability to help people work effectively together even though their interests and backgrounds may be quite different.

Foundation Abilities

The diversity competency includes the foundation abilities to be effective in doing the following:

- Fostering an environment of inclusion with people who possess characteristics different from your own (see especially Chapter 11, *Understanding Individual Differences*, and Chapter 12, *Perceptions and Attributions*).
- Learning from those with different characteristics, experiences, perspectives, and backgrounds. Diversity of thought and behavior is vital to stimulating creativity and innovation (see especially Chapter 2, *Managerial and Ethical Decision Making*, and Chapter 5, *Guiding Organizational Change*).

- Embracing and developing personal tendencies—such as *intellectual openness* and attitudes that demonstrate respect for people of other cultures and races—that support diversity in the workplace and elsewhere (see especially Chapter 11).
- Communicating and personally practicing a commitment to work with individuals and team members because of their talents and contributions, regardless of their personal attributes (see especially Chapter 8, *Developing and Leading Teams*).
- Providing leadership—*walk the talk*—in confronting obvious bias, promoting inclusion, and seeking win–win or compromise solutions to power struggles and conflicts that appear to be based on diversity issues (see especially Chapter 7, *Leading Effectively: Contemporary Developments*, and Chapter 9, *Managing Conflict and Negotiating Effectively*).
- Applying governmental laws and regulations as well as organizational policies and regulations concerning diversity as they relate to a person's position.

The case for the diversity competency within the United States is well stated by Elizabeth Pathy Salett, president of the National Multicultural Institute. She comments:

> *Multiculturalism is an acknowledgment that the United States is a diverse nation and does not assume that any cultural tradition is ideal or perfect. It looks to the equitable participation of all individuals in society. It assumes that our nation can be both unified and diverse, that we can be proud of our heritage and of our individual group identities while at the same time working together on common goals. It is a reciprocal process based on democratic principles and a shared value system.*[13]

Categories of Diversity

As suggested in Figure 1.2, diversity includes many categories and characteristics. Even a single aspect of diversity, such as physical abilities and qualities, contains various characteristics that may affect individual or team behaviors. One challenge for managers is to determine whether those effects (1) deny opportunity and are wasteful and counterproductive, (2) simply reflect a tolerance of differences, or (3) lead to embracing diversity as a value-added organizational resource. A second challenge is to assist in developing individual, team, and organizational competencies—including learning new knowledge, attitudes, skills, and methods of intervention—to value and embrace diversity as a source of creativity and strength.

Figure 1.2 identifies the more common categories of diversity dealt with in organizations. They are subdivided into *primary categories*—genetic characteristics that affect a person's self-image and socialization—and *secondary categories*—learned characteristics that a person acquires and modifies throughout life. As suggested by the arrows, these categories aren't independent. For example, a woman (gender) with children (parental status) is likely to be directly affected by an organization with *family-friendly* or *family-unfriendly* policies and attitudes. An example of a family-unfriendly attitude would be "Your job must always come first if you are to get ahead in this organization."

The following are brief explanations of the primary categories of diversity. Individuals have relatively little influence over these characteristics:

- *Age:* the number of years a person has been alive and the generation into which the individual was born in the United States (e.g., depression era, baby boomers, generation X born between 1965 and 1977, or generation Y born between 1978 and 1998).
- *Race:* the biological groupings within humankind, representing superficial physical differences, such as eye form and skin color. Race accounts for less than 1 percent of the difference in a person's genetic heredity.

FIGURE 1.2 Selected Categories of Diversity

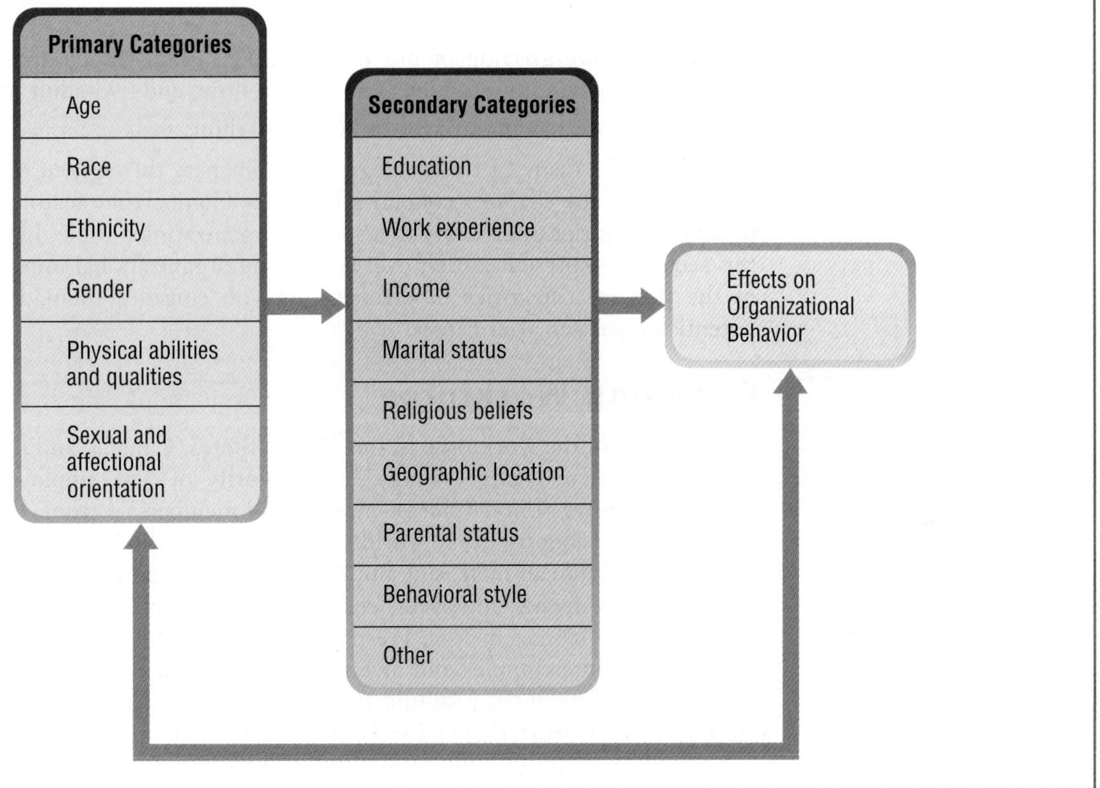

Source: Adapted from Bradford, S. Fourteen dimensions of diversity: Understanding and appreciating differences in the workplace. In J. W. Pfeiffer (ed.), 1996 *Annual: Volume 2, Consulting.* San Diego: Pfeiffer and Associates, 1996, 9–17.

- *Ethnicity:* identification with a cultural group that has shared traditions and heritage, including national origin, language, religion, food, and customs. Some people identify strongly with these cultural roots; others do not.
- *Gender:* biological sex as determined by XX (female) or XY (male) chromosomes.
- *Physical abilities and qualities*: a variety of characteristics, including body type, physical size, facial features, specific abilities or disabilities, and visible and invisible physical and mental talents or limitations.
- *Sexual orientation:* feelings of sexual attraction toward members of the same or opposite gender, such as heterosexual, homosexual, or bisexual.

The following are brief explanations of the secondary categories of diversity. Individuals have relatively more influence over them during their lifetimes by making choices:

- *Education:* the individual's formal and informal learning and training.
- *Work experience:* the employment and volunteer positions the person has held and the variety of organizations for which the person has worked.
- *Income*: the economic conditions in which the person grew up and his current economic status.
- *Marital status:* the person's situation as never married, married, widowed, or divorced.
- *Religious beliefs:* fundamental teachings received about deities and values acquired from formal or informal religious practices.

- *Geographic location:* the location(s) in which the person was raised or spent a significant part of her life, including types of communities and urban areas versus rural areas.
- *Parental status:* having or not having children and the circumstances in which the children are raised, such as single parenting and two-adult parenting.
- *Personal style:* tendency of the individual to think, feel, or act in a particular way.

We discuss many of these categories of diversity throughout the book. In addition, many of the chapters contain a Diversity Competency feature that relates one or more categories of diversity to a specific organizational topic. In the remainder of this section, we present a brief overview of the organizational implications for some of the primary categories of diversity. As you consider them, think about their potential impact on your career.

Changing Workforce

The makeup of the workforce in the United States, Canada, and many other countries continues to change rapidly. The majority of new employees will soon be women, members of non-Caucasian races, and members of ethnically diverse groups (virtually every country in the world is represented in the U.S. population and workforce). In addition, an increasing number of global organizations, such as Coca-Cola and IBM, have many employees, customers, and suppliers in locations throughout the world. Workforces in Asia, Western Europe, Latin America, and North America are growing more complex and diverse. Managers and employees need to recognize and embrace differences resulting from this diversity, particularly in terms of what employees want from their jobs. Three of the many challenges of a diverse workforce include language differences, formation of natural ethnic groupings, and attitudinal and cultural differences.[14]

Language Differences. Unless employees can understand each other, communication is difficult or even impossible. Employees can't train each other or work together if they can't communicate. Translators may be used for hiring, but—for the day-to-day communication that fosters a friendly, informal, and productive work setting—language barriers pose real and often serious problems. Such problems may lead to misunderstandings regarding performance goals, work methods, safety measures, and other essential working conditions.

Formation of Natural Ethnic Groupings. The formation of natural ethnic groupings within an organization is a tendency that needs to be constructively managed. Employees, especially if they don't speak English, may seek out others of the same ethnic group for assistance. At the Marriott's Quorum Hotel in Addison, Texas, a large percentage of its housekeeping staff is from Vietnam. With English as a second language, these employees often seek out other Vietnamese rather than a supervisor for help. They don't want to embarrass themselves because of their inability to speak English fluently. Although natural ethnic groupings may create a strong sense of togetherness, they may not promote working with others who don't share the same language and cultural heritage. At J.C. Penney's corporate headquarters in Plano, Texas, once a month the cafeteria staff prepares meals, hangs flags, and displays other items from countries in which the company does business. This type of observance is one way for employees to get some feeling for living and working in different cultures.

Attitudes and Cultural Differences. Most people have developed attitudes and beliefs about others by the time they seek a job. However, some attitudes and beliefs create frustration, anger, and bitterness in those at whom they're aimed. Managers and others who want to foster employee tolerance recognize that major changes are required. In some organizations, women and minorities are bypassed when important, formal decisions are made. Informally, these people often are left out when others go to lunch or a sporting event. These informal get-togethers often give older employees a chance to counsel younger employees about coping with problems—an advantage not shared by those left out.

Gender

Women now represent nearly half (47 percent) of the workforce in the United States. They earn 57 percent of all bachelor's degrees in the United States, 58 percent of all master's degrees, and 45 percent of all doctorates. Women account for about 16 percent of officer positions and 8 percent of CEO positions at large corporations.[15] One reason for the limited, but improving, number of executive women is the glass ceiling.

The **glass ceiling** *is a barrier so subtle that it is transparent, yet so strong that it prevents women and minorities from moving up in management.* There appear to be three primary causes of the glass ceiling. First, many executives and managers aren't held accountable for results in the areas of equal employment opportunity and affirmative action. Second, women and minorities aren't encouraged to apply for or even made aware of job openings at higher levels. At times, these openings are discussed at golf outings, card games, and other activities to which women and minority employees are not invited. Third, these groups lack training and development opportunities that would allow them to improve their competencies and chances for promotion.

Let's consider one of the programs at Aetna—a global provider of health, retirement, and financial services products—that is intended to help shatter the glass ceiling. The Aetna Emerging Leaders Program is designed to groom the next generation of leaders by guiding participants through a rigorous multiyear development plan. One of the goals is to build wide-ranging diversity into Aetna's talent base. Candidates must have five to seven years of work experience either within Aetna or outside the company. The program guides participants through a series of 12- to 24-month assignments in different areas of the business. According to Orlene Weyland, program director, this program is different because it's highly individualized, and it reaches people early in their careers. Each candidate receives coaching, education, mentoring, and career path guidance. At Aetna, women now hold 56 percent of management positions and people of color hold 9 percent of management positions.[16]

Many women with children hold full-time jobs and still bear primary responsibility for family care. An estimated 75 percent of working women are in their childbearing years. DuPont, Eli Lilly, and Marriott International are among the firms that have family-friendly policies and strategies. Such firms often offer child care, flextime (ability to arrive and leave work at varied hours), job sharing (two individuals, often women, who want to work part time and share a job), telecommuting (opportunity for certain groups of employees to work at home some or most of the time), and other types of flexibility in accommodating employees with urgent family needs.[17]

Race and Ethnicity

The U.S. workforce is approximately 150 million people. Each year, one-third of the newcomers to the U.S. workforce are minority group members. The U.S. workforce has approximately 16 million African Americans, 15 million of Hispanic origin, and 10 million of Asian and other minority origin. By 2012, white non-Hispanics are expected to make up about 66 percent of the labor force, down from a 2005 estimate of 73 percent.[18] In addition to the glass ceiling, minority group members also face **racism,** *the notion that a person's genetic group is superior to all others.* As suggested in Figure 1.3, racism takes three interrelated basic forms: (1) *individual racism*—the extent to which a person holds attitudes, values, and feelings and/or engages in behaviors that promote the person's own racial group as superior; (2) *cultural*

FIGURE 1.3 Interrelated Forms of Racism

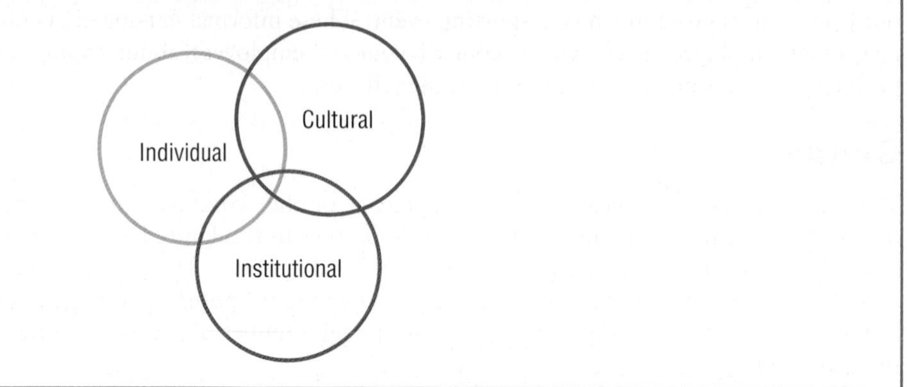

racism—the arrogant elevation of the cultural features and achievements of one race as superior while actively ignoring or denigrating those of other races; and (3) *institutional racism*—organizational and/or social rules, regulations, laws, policies, and customs that serve to maintain the dominant status of and control by one racial group. Each form of racism may operate openly or secretly and intentionally or unintentionally.

Age

The U.S. and Canadian workforces are aging along with the baby boomers. The U.S. growth rate of the 55-and-older group is projected to be 4 percent annually through 2012, nearly four times the rate of growth of the overall labor force.[19] The increase in the number of middle-aged employees has collided with the efforts of many companies, such as Kodak, Sanyo Electric, and British Petroleum, to reduce layers of middle management in order to remain competitive. Over time, the competencies that many of these employees have gained are valuable only to the firms for which they work. Displaced, older employees who lose their jobs often have great difficulty matching previous levels of responsibility and salaries, even when they are able to find new jobs. Moreover, older workers often are less likely than younger workers to relocate or train for new occupations.

IBM has been the recipient of many diversity awards. It is the world's top provider of computer hardware and has a major service arm. With 255,000 employees, IBM has operations throughout the world with headquarters in Armonk, New York.[20] Ted Childs, Jr., is the vice president of global diversity at IBM. The following Diversity Competency presents several of his perspectives on diversity at IBM, including the view that diversity initiatives and results are not only the right thing to do, but a business imperative.[21]

Diversity Competency

Ted Childs of IBM

Childs comments: Diversity is becoming an even more important topic for businesses and employees around the world. For IBM, the issues surrounding diversity mandate that this subject now be addressed on a global scale—from the workplace to the marketplace.

That is why IBM has created an innovative global strategic framework for this new era of diversity, which will help IBM address the emerging issues taking shape in the 160 countries where we do business. . . . Our long-standing commitment to workforce diversity—equal opportunity, affirmative action, cultural awareness, and work/life balance—has evolved into a legacy of leading social change and setting trends before they became fashionable, politically correct, or, more importantly, mandated by law.

IBM orchestrated one of the most dramatic changes to workforce diversity when eight diversity executive task forces were established and the subject became a marketplace issue about talent and getting the best people for the job. These task forces include Asian, Black, Hispanic, Native American, Gay/Lesbian, People with Disabilities, Men, and Women. The task forces are chaired and staffed by executives from that particular constituency.

Each task force was asked to look at IBM through the lens of their group and answer these questions: What is required for your group to feel welcomed and valued here? What can IBM, in partnership with your group, do to maximize your productivity? And, what decisions can IBM make to influence the buying decisions of your group?

The mission of each task force is to increase IBM's success in the marketplace by focusing on the various constituencies as customers. In addition, task force leaders help ensure that our diversity training is fresh, remains well received, and is a priority for our company.

Diversity and the concept of workforce inclusion are key factors in helping define how we do business in today's marketplace and help us compete for the best talent and enhance our ability to create new revenue streams, retain employees, win clients, and maintain our marketplace leadership.

For more information on IBM, visit the organization's home page at ***http://www.IBM.com.***

ETHICS COMPETENCY

LEARNING OBJECTIVE

4. Describe the ethics competency and its contribution to effectiveness.

The **ethics competency** *involves the overall ability to incorporate values and principles that distinguish right from wrong in making decisions and choosing behaviors.* **Ethics** *are the values and principles that distinguish right from wrong.*[22]

Foundation Abilities

The managing ethics competency includes the foundation abilities to be effective in doing the following:

- Identifying and describing the principles of ethical decision making and behavior (see especially Chapter 2, *Managerial and Ethical Decision Making*).
- Assessing the importance of ethical issues in considering alternative courses of action. The decision to shop at Sears versus Target is not related to any ethical issue of consequence for most individuals.
- Applying governmental laws and regulations, as well as the employer's rules of conduct, in making decisions and taking action within a person's level of responsibilities and authority. In general, the greater a person's level of responsibilities and authority, the more the person is likely to face increasingly complex and ambiguous ethical issues and dilemmas. For example, an associate at a Target store is less likely than a store manager to have to make decisions of importance that involve ethical demands (see especially Chapter 6, *Leading Effectively: Foundations*).
- Demonstrating dignity and respect for others in working relationships, such as taking action against discriminatory practices as individually feasible and in terms of a person's position. The manager at a Sears store is more able to stop

an employee from showing disrespect to members of a minority group than is a checkout associate in the store (see especially Chapter 7, *Leading Effectively: Contemporary Developments*).

- Being honest and open in communication, limited only by legal, privacy, and competitive considerations (i.e., do what you say and say what you do). (See especially Chapter 9, *Managing Conflict and Negotiating Effectively*, and Chapter 10, *Fostering Organizational Communication.*)

THE COMPETENT LEADER

Ethics matter. Our capital market systems depend on ethical behavior. You, as future business leaders, have a responsibility to set the tone in your organizations.
Eddie Munson, National Director of University Relations, KPMG

Ethical Dilemmas

The ethical issues facing managers and other employees have grown in significance in recent years, fueled by public concern about how business is conducted. We develop this point through Ethics Competency features throughout the book. Ethical behavior sometimes is difficult to define, especially in a global economy with its varied beliefs and practices. Although ethical behavior in business clearly has a legal component, it involves more than that, and absolutes in one country aren't always applicable in another country.

Managers and employees alike face situations in which there are no clear right or wrong answers. The burden is on individuals to make ethical decisions. An **ethical dilemma** *occurs when an individual or team must make a decision that involves multiple values.* An ethical dilemma doesn't simply involve choosing right over wrong because there may be several competing values. Some ethical dilemmas arise from competitive and time pressures, among other factors.[23] Consider these three real-life examples of ethical dilemmas:

- A customer asked for a product from us today. After telling him our price, he said he couldn't afford it. I know he could get it cheaper from a competitor. Should I tell him about the competitor—or let him go without getting what he needs? What should I do?
- A fellow employee told me that he plans to quit the company in two months and start a new job that has been guaranteed to him. Meanwhile, my boss told me that she wasn't going to give me a new opportunity in our company because she was going to give it to my fellow employee now. What should I do?
- My boss told me that one of my employees is among several to be laid off soon and that I'm not to tell my employee yet or he might tell the whole organization, which would soon be in an uproar. Meanwhile, I heard from my employee that he plans to buy braces for his daughter and new carpet for his house. What should I do?[24]

Top-management leadership, policies and rules, and the prevailing organizational culture can do much to reduce, guide, and help the individual confront and resolve ethical dilemmas.[25] Table 1.1 provides a brief questionnaire that asks you to assess an organization (or manager) that you have worked for with respect to its commitment to various ethical behaviors, practices, and policies.

TABLE 1.1 Ethical Practices Questionnaire

Instructions. Think of an organization for which you have worked or currently work. Respond to the 10 statements that follow the scale in terms of the degree to which you think the organization reflects the behavior, policy, and/or practice in each statement. Use the following 10-point scale, which ranges from 10 (highly descriptive of the organization) to 1 (not at all descriptive). The middle point in the scale, 5, indicates that you are neutral or undecided.

NOT AT ALL DESCRIPTIVE				NEUTRAL					HIGHLY DESCRIPTIVE
1	2	3	4	5	6	7	8	9	10

Record your number next to each statement.

____ 1. I did not fear retaliation from higher management for reporting misconduct by others.

____ 2. Management was trusted to do the right thing by me and other employees.

____ 3. When making important decisions, managers and other employees considered the ethical implications of the alternatives being considered.

____ 4. There were well-established policies and practices by higher management for dealing honestly with customers.

____ 5. The core abilities in the managing ethics competency were seen as important and applied consistently by higher management.

____ 6. I and my coworkers never felt pressured to engage in practices that we found to be questionable or unethical.

____ 7. My organization had a practice of doing what was right, not just what brought quick profits or other benefits.

____ 8. The organization's ethics policies and expected behaviors were effectively communicated to all employees.

____ 9. There were clearly communicated consequences for deviations from or violations of ethics policies and expected behaviors—which were backed up by action in the case of such violations.

____ 10. High levels of individual performance that were achieved by violating or distorting the organization's ethics policies and expected behaviors were not tolerated.

Results and Interpretation. Sum the point values for items 1 through 10. Totals of 80 to 100 provide indicators of a highly ethical organization. Totals of 61 to 79 suggest needed improvements. Totals of 40 to 60 may suggest confusing and inconsistent ethical signals and practices. Scores of 10 to 40 suggest a highly unethical organization that requires a major transformation.

The Raytheon Company, headquartered in Waltham, Massachusetts, has 78,000 employees. The company is a major defense manufacturer and also makes a variety of related communications and electronics products for the private sector. William Swanson, chairman and CEO of Raytheon, comments: "In today's business world, ethics, integrity and honesty are the new mantra of every successful venture; unfortunately not everybody 'gets it' . . ."[26] Raytheon has an extensive ethics and corporate governance program. One component is Raytheon's *Standard of Business Ethics and Conduct.* It is one of Raytheon's resources for guiding Raytheon employees, suppliers, partners, and teammates in making right and proper choices. The following Ethics Competency feature provides a brief glimpse at Raytheon's code and guidelines for employee behavior and decision making.[27]

ETHICS COMPETENCY

RAYTHEON COMPANY

Raytheon's *Standards of Business Ethics and Conduct* (the Standards) addresses not only those areas in which we must act in accordance with law or regulation, but it establishes the responsibilities, policies, and guiding principles that will assist us in doing the right thing on Raytheon's behalf. *The Standards* is not meant to detail all of the rules, regulations, and policies to which employees are expected to adhere. These are available from your supervisor, Human Resources, the Office of Business Ethics and Compliance, the Legal Department, or on the Raytheon intranet home page (http://www.ray.com). *The Standards* provides guidance of a more general nature—guidance that will help us to make decisions in those gray areas where law, regulation, or policy may not be available, or where such guidance is merely a foundation for those decisions.

When you are confronted with an ethical dilemma, it is your responsibility to take action. This **ACTION** decision-making model can help you assess whether or not a particular action is "the right thing to do." Keep in mind that not taking **ACTION** is itself an action that can have serious consequences.

Act Responsibly: Has someone taken responsibility? Do you have all the information you need? Has the information been clarified?

Consider our Ethical Principles: Does the action foster Respect and Trust? Does it reflect Integrity? Promote Teamwork? Does it demonstrate Quality, Innovation, and Citizenship?

Trust your Judgment: Is the action fair? Does it feel comfortable? Is it the "right" thing to do? Could it be shared publicly?

Identify Impact on Stakeholders: Does the action positively impact the Employee? Team? Supplier? Customer? Company? Shareholders? Public?

Obey the Rules: Does the action comply with: The law? Company policy? Regulatory agency requirements? Customer requirements?

Notify Appropriate Persons: Has communication been open and honest? Have potential problems been disclosed?

For more information on Raytheon, visit the organization's home page at ***http://www.raytheon.com.***

Despite the best intentions and formal programs at large firms such as Raytheon, ethical issues and problems do occur. For example, a jury awarded $500,000 to a woman who said Raytheon failed to investigate her sexual harassment complaint against her manager because he was the nephew of the former chief executive officer of Raytheon. Raytheon has filed motions seeking a new trial or a dismissal.[28]

LEARNING OBJECTIVE

5. Describe the across cultures competency and its contribution to effectiveness.

ACROSS CULTURES COMPETENCY

The **across cultures competency** *involves the overall ability to recognize and embrace similarities and differences among nations and cultures and then approach key organizational and strategic issues with an open and curious mind.* **Culture** *is the dominant pattern of living, thinking, and believing that is developed and transmitted by people, consciously or unconsciously, to subsequent generations.*[29] For a *culture* to exist, it must

- be shared by the vast majority of the members of a major group or entire society;
- be passed on from generation to generation; and
- shape behavior, decisions, and perceptions of the world.[30]

A key feature of a culture is its **cultural values**—*those consciously and subconsciously deeply held beliefs that specify general preferences and behaviors, and define what is right and wrong.* Cultural values are reflected in a society's morals, customs, and established practices.

Foundation Abilities

The across cultures competency includes the foundation abilities to be effective in doing the following:

- Understanding, appreciating, and using the characteristics that make a particular culture unique and are likely to influence a person's behaviors.
- Identifying and understanding how work-related values, such as individualism and collectivism, influence the choices of individuals and groups in making decisions.
- Understanding and motivating employees with different values and attitudes. These may range from the more individualistic, Western style of work, to paternalistic, non-Western attitudes, to the extreme "the state-will-take-care-of-me" collectivist mind-set.
- Communicating in the language of the country with which the individual has working relationships. This ability is crucial for employees who have ongoing communications with people whose native language is different from their own.
- Taking assignments in a foreign country or effectively working with those from foreign countries. This ability applies even if the assignment is short term or the person has international responsibilities from the home office.
- Addressing managerial and other issues through a **global mind-set**—*viewing the environment from a worldwide perspective, always looking for unexpected trends that may create threats or opportunities for a unit or an entire organization.* Some call this the ability to *think globally, act locally.*

Work-Related Cultural Values

There are a number of classifications of cultural values. We briefly introduce you to one that is particularly helpful in understanding individual and societal differences in five work-related values.[31] As suggested in Figure 1.4, these values in combination influence the behaviors and decisions of employees in many organizations.

Individualism–Collectivism. Individualism and collectivism are two of the fundamental work-related values that must be thoroughly understood to be effective in today's world. **Individualism** *is the tendency of people to look after themselves and their immediate families.* The culture emphasizes individual initiative, decision making, and achievement. The individual is emotionally detached from organizations and institutions. Everybody is believed to have the right to privacy and personal freedom of expression. Countries characterized by an emphasis on individualism include the United States, Canada, New Zealand, the United Kingdom, and Australia.

In contrast, **collectivism** *is the tendency of people to emphasize their belonging to groups and to look after each other in exchange for loyalty.* The social framework tends to be tight, and in-groups (relatives, communities, and organizations) focus on their common welfare and distinguish themselves from out-groups. Collectivism usually involves emotional dependence of the individual on groups, organizations, and institutions. The sense of belonging and "we" versus "I" in relationships is fundamental. Individuals' private lives are open to the groups and organizations to which they belong. Group goals are generally thought to be more important than the individual's personal goals. When conflict arises between individual goals and in-group goals, the general expectation is that in-group goals and decision making should prevail. Countries characterized by an emphasis on collectivism include Japan, China, Venezuela, and Indonesia.

Harmony is another feature of cultures that emphasize collectivism. People in the same group sense that they have a common fate. Individuals in China, Japan, Taiwan, and South Korea care about whether their behavior would be considered shameful by the other members of their groups. They also avoid pointing out other

FIGURE 1.4 Influence of Culturally Based Work-Related Values

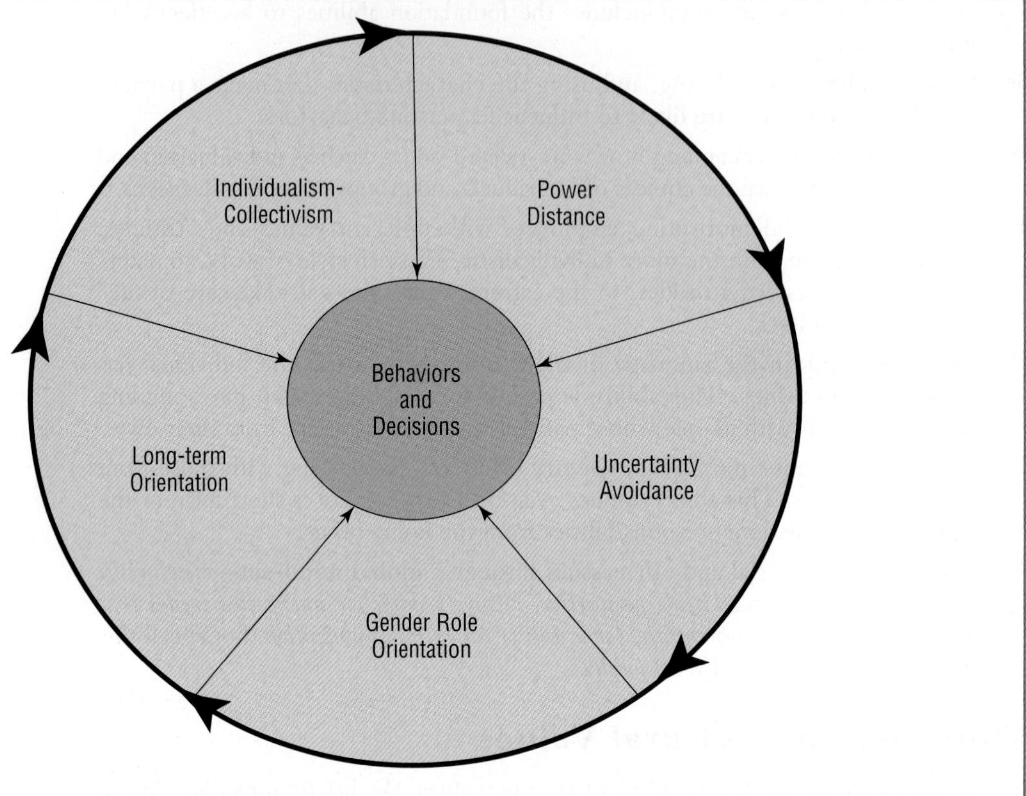

people's mistakes in public so that the others won't lose face. Face-saving is important in these cultures because it allows people to maintain their dignity and status.

In contrast, the people in countries that emphasize individualism, such as Canada, the United States, and the United Kingdom, do not often form such tight-knit groups. Individuals in these countries generally do not believe that they share a common fate with others. They view themselves as independent, unique, and special. They are less likely to conform to the expectations of others. When group goals conflict with personal goals, individuals commonly pursue their own goals. In addition, seeking personal identity is highly valued in individualistic cultures. Confrontation with others within an in-group is acceptable. Personal achievement, pleasure, and competition are all highly valued.

Power Distance. **Power distance** *is the extent to which people in a society accept status and power inequalities as a normal and functional aspect of life.* Countries that are "high in power distance" are those whose citizens generally accept status and power inequalities; those "low in power distance" are those whose citizens generally do *not.* Countries that are high in power distance include Argentina, India, Malaysia, Mexico, the Philippines, and the Commonwealth of Puerto Rico. At the opposite extreme, countries that are low in power distance include Finland, Israel, Norway, and Sweden (the United States is moderately low).

People who are raised in a high power distance culture behave submissively to managers and avoid disagreements with them. High power distance employees are more likely to take orders without question and follow the instructions of their managers. In high power distance societies, subordinates consider bypassing their managers to be an act of insubordination. In low power distance countries, employees are expected to bypass a manager if necessary in order to get their work done. When negotiating in high power distance countries, companies find it necessary to send representatives with titles equivalent to or higher than those of their bargaining partners. Titles, status, and formality are of less importance in low power distance countries.

Uncertainty Avoidance. Uncertainty avoidance *is the extent to which people rely on social norms, procedures, and organizations (including government) to avoid ambiguity, unpredictability, and risk.* With "high" uncertainty avoidance, individuals seek orderliness, consistency, structure, formalized procedures, and laws to cover situations in their daily lives. Societies that are high in uncertainty avoidance, such as Japan, Sweden, and Germany, have a strong tendency toward orderliness and consistency, structured lifestyles, clear specification of social expectations, and many rules and laws. In contrast, in countries such as the United States and Canada and in Hong Kong, there is strong tolerance of ambiguity and uncertainty. More secure and long-term employment is common in "high" uncertainty avoidance countries. In contrast, job mobility and layoffs are more commonly accepted in "low" uncertainty avoidance countries.[32]

Gender Role Orientation. Gender role orientation *refers to the extent to which a society reinforces, or does not reinforce, traditional notions of masculinity versus femininity.* A society is called *masculine* when emotional gender roles are clearly distinct. Men are supposed to be assertive, tough, and focused on material success. Women are supposed to be more modest, tender, and concerned with the quality of life. In masculine-dominated cultures, gender roles are clearly distinct. Japan, Austria, Italy, Mexico, and Ireland are a few of the countries ranked as high in masculinity. Dominant values are material success and progress, money and things. A society is called *feminine* when gender roles overlap: Both men and women are supposed to be modest, tender, and concerned with the quality of life. In feminine-dominated societies, roles are often merged or overlap for sexes. A few of the countries ranked high on femininity are Denmark, Costa Rica, Finland, and Portugal. Dominant values include caring for others, emphasizing the importance of people and relationships, accepting that both men and women can be gentle, stressing the quality of work life, and resolving conflict by compromise and negotiation.[33]

Long-Term Orientation. Long-term orientation *refers to the degree to which the society embraces, or does not embrace, the fostering of virtues oriented toward future rewards.* A long-term orientation ranking indicates that the society prescribes to the values of sustained commitments, perseverance, and thrift. This is thought to support a strong work ethic where long-term rewards are expected as a result of today's hard work. A few of the countries with a long-term orientation are China, Japan, India, and the Netherlands. These countries include characteristics such as adaptation of traditions to the modern context, respect for tradition and obligation within limits, thrift (saving resources), perseverance toward slow results, willing to subordinate oneself for a purpose, and concern with virtue.

A short-term orientation stands for fostering respect for tradition, preservation of "face," concern with status and social obligations, and the belief that efforts should produce quick results. A few of the societies with a short-term orientation include Canada, Czech Republic, Pakistan, Spain, and the United States.[34] From a business perspective, several of the features of a strong short-term orientation include:

- Main work values are freedom, individual rights, achievement, and thinking for oneself.
- Focus is on the bottom line with an emphasis on the importance of this year's profits.
- Managers and workers view themselves as highly distinct groups.
- Personal loyalties vary with business needs (versus investment in lifelong personal networks).

Avoiding Stereotypes. The five cross-culture value dimensions presented here and in later chapters are a useful beginning point for explaining, understanding, and relating to individuals or groups with cultural values different than your own. However, we caution that there are often wide variations of behavior and values by various individuals and groups within a given society.

You need to be wary of stereotyping individuals or groups in a society in simple terms and thus glossing over nuances and complexities in a particular culture.[35] Further, the specific issues and situations—such as work, family, friends, and recreation—can play a significant role in understanding the impact of different cultural values on behaviors. For example, when Japanese businesspeople make contracts, they seek to have them be ambiguous. The dominant value underlying this approach is collectivism (cultural value). In this context, collectivism is revealed as a belief that those entering into an agreement are joined together and share something in common; thus they should rely on and trust one another. Collectivism is more important than high uncertainty avoidance (a cultural value of the Japanese) in this context, but uncertainty avoidance is not completely absent. Some of the uncertainty surrounding the contract is dealt with in the process by carefully choosing and getting to know business partners and by using third parties. An additional consideration is that many Japanese like flexible contracts, because they have a greater recognition of the limits of contracts and the difficulties of foreseeing all contingencies (context of cultural history of business practices). Even though Americans are typically more tolerant of uncertainty (low uncertainty avoidance), they value pragmatism and don't like to take unnecessary risks (context of market economy). If a deal falls through, they rely on the legal system for a resolution (context of cultural history of institutions).

Dr. Charles Chao Yang Zhang is the founder, chairman, and CEO of SOHU.com, Inc. This firm developed the first Chinese-language search engine in the world and is a leading Internet portal in China. In the following Across Cultures Competency feature, we report on a few of Zhang's perspectives on the Chinese culture.[36]

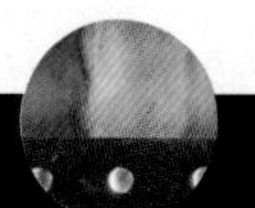

Across Cultures Competency

Charles Zhang on China's Culture

China has undergone very dramatic changes since I returned there in 1995. The differences between China in 1995 and China today are as stark and distinct as night and day. The Internet is helping the whole society in China to become more intelligent and empowered.

Many people have asked me whether China's growth in the past twenty-five years is merely a bubble. In my opinion, it definitely is not. The changes that have taken place are fundamental ones. The government has become more decentralized. What has taken place in China is not just an economic miracle. While the whole society has become better off, almost all people in China continue to think that they are not good enough and therefore need to engage in lifelong learning so that China can reclaim its rightful place in the world. This attitude is cause for hope that China won't again fall into the complacency trap that once plagued the country for many centuries and led it on its downward spiral, culminating in its defeat in the First Opium War.

This Chinese emphasis on education and learning is part of Confucian culture. Confucianism also stresses diligence, hard work, bringing glory to one's family, and self-sacrifice. In considering a person's lifelong achievements, Chinese culture places more emphasis on the individual's responsibilities to family, community, and country than on one's own living comforts. A person's achievements are judged by one's parents, officials, and society. This desire to meet or exceed the expectations of these parties serves as a huge driver/motivator for one to advance and succeed. So, the Chinese are probably the most driven people in the world! In addition, self-sacrifice is imbued in children by their parents from a very early age because Chinese parents are perhaps the world's most selfless and devoted parents.

Another ancient Chinese philosophy, Taoism, emphasizes a holistic approach to problem solving. It has led to the belief that a non-confrontational approach to resolving conflicts may be superior and the need to balance the "yin" and "yang." So people generally believe that there are alternative ways of thinking and that different schools of thought can produce excellence. Thus, Western values and practices are not the only way.

For more information on SOHU.com, visit the organization's home page at ***http://www.sohu.com/about/English/.***

TEAMS COMPETENCY

LEARNING OBJECTIVE

6. Describe the teams competency and its contribution to effectiveness.

The **teams competency** *involves the overall ability to develop, support, facilitate, and lead groups to achieve organizational goals.*[37] The components of this competency are developed in several chapters, especially Chapter 8, *Developing and Leading Teams*, and Chapter 9, *Managing Conflict and Negotiating Effectively*. In addition, the other competencies reviewed in this chapter contribute to the variety of abilities needed to be effective as a team member or leader (as suggested previously in Figure 1.1).

Foundation Abilities

The teams competency includes the foundation abilities to be effective in doing the following:

- Determining the circumstances in which a team approach is appropriate and, if using a team is appropriate, the type of team to use.
- Engaging in and/or leading the process of setting clear performance goals for the team.
- Participating in and/or providing the leadership in defining responsibilities and tasks for the team as a whole, as well as its individual members.
- Demonstrating a sense of mutual and personal accountability for the achievement of team goals, not just an individual's own goals. That is, the individual doesn't approach problems and issues with a mind-set of "That's not my responsibility or concern."
- Applying decision-making methods and technologies that are appropriate to the goals, issues, and tasks confronting the team.
- Resolving personal and task-related conflicts among team members before they become too disruptive.
- Assessing a person's own performance and that of the team in relation to goals, including the ability to take corrective action as needed.

Teams and Individualism

In some countries, people strongly believe in the importance and centrality of the individual. In the United States, the United Kingdom, and Canada, educational, governmental, and business institutions frequently state that they exist to serve individual goals. Two cultural values that strongly affect decisions about whether to use teams and groups in organizations are individualism and collectivism.

The cultural belief in individualism creates uneasiness over the use of teams or groups in organizations. Employees in individualistic cultures are expected to act on the basis of their personal goals and self-interest. In collectivistic countries, such as China and South Korea, the use of teams by organizations is a natural extension of their nations' cultural values. Uneasiness revolves around the relative influence of individuals in teams. Thus we might characterize the basic difference as "fitting into the team" versus "standing out from the team." Even in societies that value individualism, the use of teams is substantial in such firms as Ford, General Electric, and Home Depot.

The potential for teams and individuals to have incompatible goals clearly exists, but these goals need not always conflict; in fact, they are often are compatible. The potential for conflict and commonality is suggested by the following observations:

- Teams do exist, and employees need to take them into account.
- Teams mobilize powerful forces that create important effects for individuals.
- Teams may create both good and bad results.
- Teams can be managed to increase the benefits from them.

The circumstances under which teams should be used versus sole reliance on the individual—that is, a single employee or manager taking primary control and personal accountability for performing a task, resolving an issue, or solving a problem—should be assessed continually.

West Suburban Health Care operates West Suburban Hospital, a not-for-profit, nonsectarian health care provider in a very competitive market on the west side of Chicago and in the western suburbs. The payer mix is challenging, with a high percentage of self-pay and Medicaid patients. After the hospital joined the organization, it became apparent that it was losing $1 million a month. As reported in the following Teams Competency feature, teams were formed to help improve operating income—and were successful at doing so.[38]

Teams Competency

West Suburban Hospital's Teams

A consulting firm was hired to provide an initial study that identified areas of cost containment. The initial consulting review determined areas of focus. Unlike many hospitals in which major cost savings can be achieved in one department, the opportunities for savings at West Suburban touched many departments. Savings tended to be incremental. With this approach in mind, top management and the consultant set out to develop specific action plans, using teams to devise solutions. Teams were structured to include a subject matter specialist from the consultant, a management leader from the discipline being reviewed, a senior hospital leader, and other members as appropriate, for a total of 5 to 10 people per team.

Team members used data collection and analysis, brainstorming, and analysis of policies and procedures to identify opportunities for improvement. Projects that were recommended needed to include implementation plans and timetables to ensure accountability. Teams reported monthly to an oversight panel chaired by the CEO. Bar charts were the typical means of summarizing progress.

The single largest opportunity for improvement that was identified was the hospital's revenue cycle. Team members from the consulting firm as well as hospital billing and accounts receivable (AR) personnel worked on a broad spectrum of issues. Areas for improvement ran the gamut, such as scheduling, insurance verification, billing, registration, financial counseling, and point of service collection. Other teams were more general, focusing on such areas as productivity, supplies, policies for admission and continued stays, and utilization.

Financial progress was relatively quick, but seemed painstaking at the same time. The hospital improved its bottom line by approximately $17 million in annual reductions over a two-year period. In retrospect, top management contends the team approach was an important ingredient in the turnaround. The involvement of hospital employees at different levels to work with partners from the consulting firm was highly effective. It helped ensure that plans were implementable rather than "blue-sky" ideas.

For more information on West Suburban Health Care, visit the organization's home page at ***http://www.westsub.com.***

CHANGE COMPETENCY

LEARNING OBJECTIVE

7. Describe the change competency and its contribution to effectiveness.

The **change competency** *involves the overall ability to recognize and implement needed adaptations or entirely new transformations in the people, tasks, strategies, structures, or technologies in a person's area of responsibility.* Jack Gherty, the focus of our Preview Case, comments on the role of the change competency: "Today, there is such a sense of accelerating change that you have to not only develop strategies and implement them, you also have to be nimble enough to change your strategies 45 degrees three months into them and be able to implement them on the fly."[39]

Foundation Abilities

The change competency includes the foundation abilities to be effective in doing the following:

- Applying the six previously discussed competencies in the diagnosis, development, and implementation of needed changes.
- Providing leadership in the process of planned change (see especially Chapter 6, *Leading Effectively: Foundations*, and Chapter 7, *Leading Effectively: Contemporary Developments*). As described in those chapters, leadership styles and approaches may need to vary under conditions of crisis and the need for major changes. Consider the case of Jack Welch, GE's retired CEO. At one time, he was nicknamed "Neutron Jack" because of his autocratic approach and style of leadership. He was faced with the need to make transformational and difficult decisions, including the elimination of tens of thousands of employees, entire levels of management, and several divisions. After completing this overhaul, Welch shifted his leadership approach and made it known that there was no place for autocrats at GE. Not many leaders can change their behaviors as dramatically as Welch did. In many instances, the directive autocrat needs to be replaced by a more democratic or supportive leader when a crisis has passed.[40]
- Diagnosing pressure for and resistance to change in specific situations. These pressures may be internal—such as the organizational culture—or external—such as new technologies or competitors (see especially Chapter 4, *Cultivating Organizational Culture*, and Chapter 5, *Guiding Organizational Change*).
- Applying the systems model of change and other processes to introduce and achieve organizational change. Individuals with this ability are able to identify key issues and diagnose them by examining the basic factors of *who, what, why, when, where*, and *how*. We provide insights for developing this ability in a number of the chapters.

- Seeking, gaining, sharing, and applying new knowledge in the pursuit of constant improvement, creativity, and entirely new approaches or goals. These behaviors require **risk taking**, or *the willingness to take reasonable chances by recognizing and capitalizing on opportunities while also recognizing their potential negative outcomes and monitoring progress toward goals.*

Technological Forces

Technological forces, especially computer-based information technologies and the Internet, continue to revolutionize how customers are served; employees communicate and network with one another and external stakeholders, such as customers, suppliers, competitors, and governmental agencies; tasks are performed; organizations are structured; human resources are led and managed; and so on.

Technological change may have positive effects, including products and services of higher quality and lower costs. But it also may have negative effects, including erosion of personal privacy, work-related stress, and health problems (e.g., eyestrain, carpal tunnel syndrome, and exposure to toxic substances).

New technologies are increasing the need for constant learning, adaptation, and innovation by individuals, teams, and entire organizations. The revolution in technologies is a driving force in creating the need to actively manage change. Throughout this book, we discuss topics that are related to the introduction and use of technology and how technology affects the behaviors of employees.

The rapid rise in use of the Internet in the United States is the most obvious expression of an economy and a culture that focus on technology. The Internet seems to bring the entire world to a person's desktop, laptop, or personal digital assistant instantaneously and to satisfy quickly any query or curiosity. The ever-expanding online World Wide Web is but the most recent indication of a trend over the past few decades that has brought businesses, customers, and others continually closer in real time. Technologies ranging from PCs to television to ATMs to desktop photo processing to cell phones have shaped our expectations about acceptable time frames for communicating and seeing results.

The following Change Competency feature reveals how Alaska Indoor Sports Distributing Ltd. took advantage of Groove, one of the new generation of software collaboration tools that take advantage of the Internet.[41] Groove Networks, Inc., is headquartered in Beverly, Massachusetts. It provides collaborative software that enables users to directly access files stored on their colleagues' computers and communicate in real time, allowing for file sharing, instant messaging, chatting, calendaring, and collaborative product design.

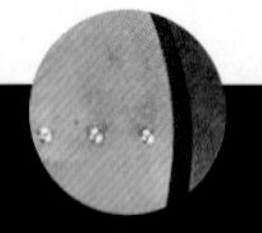

CHANGE COMPETENCY

ALASKA INDOOR SPORTS DISTRIBUTING LTD.

Douglas McBride's life had become a blizzard of faxes and e-mails. He is the owner of Alaska Indoor Sports Distributing Ltd. (AISD), a distributor of gaming equipment such as Bingo cards and lottery-style games based in Ketchikan, Alaska. His suppliers faxed samples of 20 to 30 new products a week. McBride's salespeople were sending in at least as many daily schedule updates and sales reports, all of which needed reconciling with the company's records. Some days, more than 100 important documents were received via fax and had to be processed in a variety of ways.

Complicating matters for McBride was the fact that his 20 employees are scattered across five locations in the vast state of Alaska. His two warehouses are located some 750 miles apart, in Ketchikan and Anchorage. Each one required a full-time employee just to send and track faxes. Face-to-face meetings were nearly impossible, and even getting a colleague on the phone was a hassle.

McBride's business was growing, but the communications problems were taking a toll. Faxes and e-mails were getting lost, and new orders were no longer being processed efficiently. McBride stumbled onto Groove, one of a new breed of relatively inexpensive, easy-to-install collaboration tools. Groove provided a virtual "workspace." It enabled McBride to (1) post documents, spreadsheets, and images; (2) solicit employees' comments; and (3) make notes and changes. The software tracked the various changes automatically. Suddenly, a mundane task like the daily sales report, which meant gathering faxes from four field sales staffers and three phone salespeople and pulling together the seven reports into one, could be done with a simple spreadsheet housed in Groove. It provided McBride with an instant message notification every time the numbers were updated.

Groove, as a new technology, has made all the difference for AISD. When suppliers send new product updates, for example, they're automatically placed into a workspace in Groove, and notices go out to the salespeople. The same goes for inventory updates.

Communications costs are down by more than 70% (faxes between Anchorage and Ketchikan run 14 cents a minute). McBride thinks Groove software's virtual work environment saves his employees between two and eight hours per week in coordination time, allowing them to be more productive, and ultimately makes the company more profitable. From a qualitative standpoint, McBride says Groove gives his "decentralized business a feeling of centrality, or connectedness, that it would otherwise lack."

LEARNING FRAMEWORK FOR INDIVIDUAL, TEAM, AND ORGANIZATIONAL EFFECTIVENESS

LEARNING OBJECTIVE

8. Explain the framework for learning about organizational behavior to enhance individual, team, and organizational effectiveness.

The long-term effectiveness of an organization is determined by its ability to anticipate, manage, and respond to changes in its environment. Shareholders, unions, employees, financial institutions, and government agencies, among others, exert numerous and ever-changing pressures, demands, and expectations on the organization. The foundation competencies are indicated to link environmental forces and the actions of managers and employees. Throughout this book, therefore, we discuss the relationships among these various competencies and organizational behavior in general.

The framework for learning about organizational behavior and improving the effectiveness of employees, teams, and organizations consists of four basic components: (1) the organization itself, (2) leadership and team behaviors, (3) individuals in organizations, and (4) the foundation competencies that underlie and integrate the first three components. Figure 1.5 shows the relationships among these components, as well as the principal elements of each. These relationships are much too dynamic—in terms of variety and change—to define them as laws or rules. As we discuss each component, the dynamics and complexities of organizational behavior will become clear.

The Organization Itself

In Part 2, Chapters 2 through 5, we consider the factors, both internal and external, that influence individual, team, and organizational effectiveness. Decision making in organizations isn't particularly orderly or totally within the control of the

FIGURE 1.5 Learning Framework for Enhanced Individual, Team, and Organizational Effectiveness

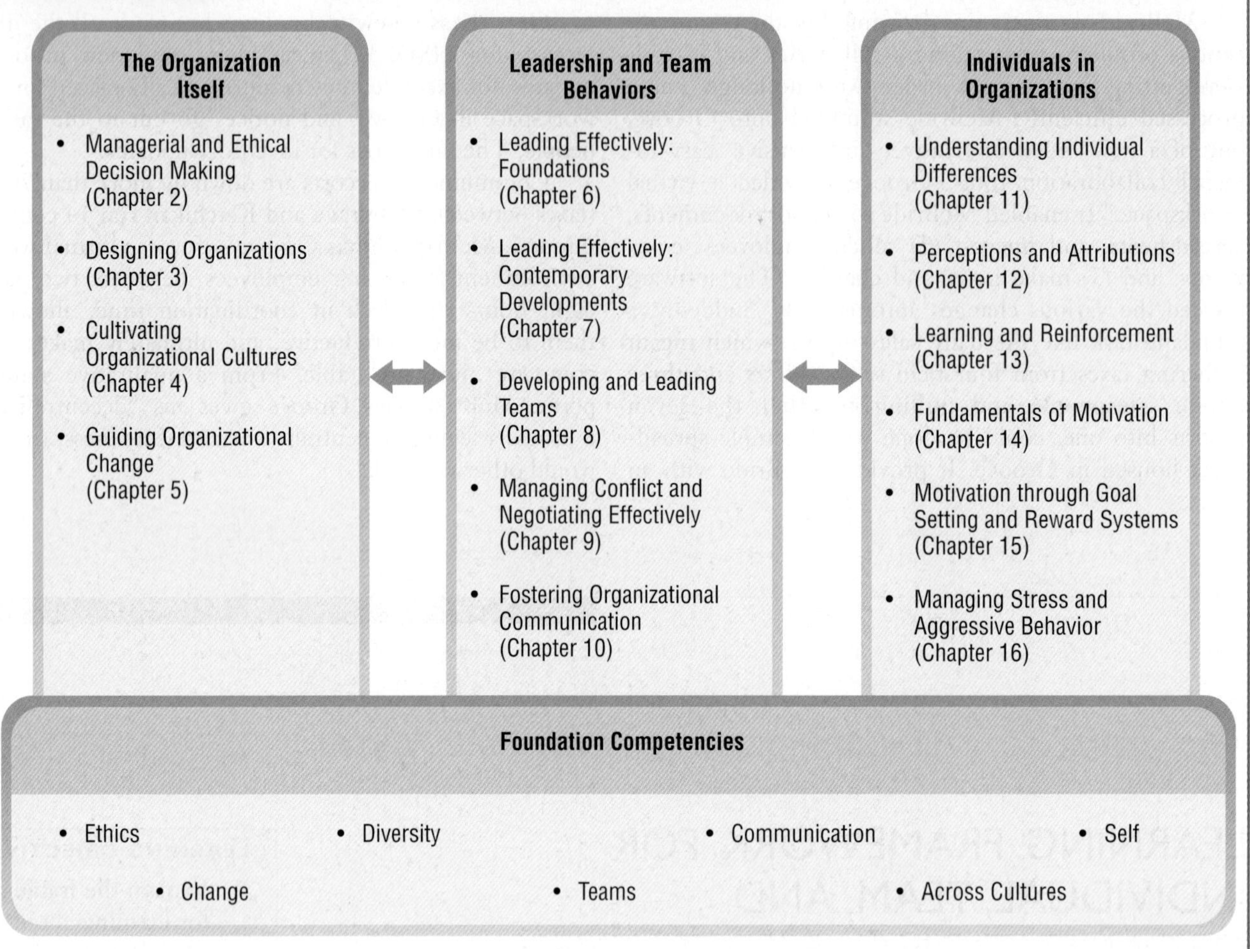

decision makers. We identify and explore the phases of decision making and core ethical concepts and ethical dilemmas encountered.

The Organization Itself
• Managerial and Ethical Decision Making (Chapter 2)
• Designing Organizations (Chapter 3)
• Cultivating Organizational Cultures (Chapter 4)
• Guiding Organizational Change (Chapter 5)
Leadership and Team Behaviors
• Leading Effectively: Foundations (Chapter 6)
• Leading Effectively: Contemporary Developments (Chapter 7)
• Developing and Leading Teams (Chapter 8)
• Managing Conflict and Negotiating Effectively (Chapter 9)
• Fostering Organizational Communication (Chapter 10)
Individuals in Organizations
• Understanding Individual Differences (Chapter 11)
• Perceptions and Attributions (Chapter 12)
• Learning and Reinforcement (Chapter 13)
• Fundamentals of Motivation (Chapter 14)
• Motivation through Goal Setting and Reward Systems (Chapter 15)
• Managing Stress and Aggressive Behavior (Chapter 16)
Foundation Competencies
• Ethics
• Diversity
• Communication
• Self
• Change
• Teams
• Across Cultures

To work effectively, all employees must clearly understand their jobs and the organization's design. We identify factors that influence organization design and present some typical designs that facilitate organizational effectiveness.

Individuals enter organizations to work, earn money, and pursue career goals. We discuss how employees learn what is expected of them. Basically, they do so by exposure to the organization's culture. It is the set of shared assumptions and understandings about how things really work—that is, policies, practices, and norms—that are important to supporting, or perhaps diminishing, individual, team, or organizational effectiveness.

The management of change involves adapting an organization to the demands of the environment and modifying the actual behaviors of employees. We explore the dynamics of organizational change and present several basic strategies for achieving change to improve organizational effectiveness.

Leadership and Team Behaviors

Being inherently social, people generally don't choose to live or work alone. Most of their time is spent interacting with others: People are born into a family group, worship in groups, work in teams, and play in groups. Much of a person's identity is based on the ways in which other individuals and groups perceive and treat that person. For these reasons—and because many managers and employees spend considerable amounts of time interacting with other people—competencies in communication, interpersonal, and team dynamics are vital to everyone in an organization.

Effective organizations have leaders who can integrate customer, employee, and organizational goals. The ability of organizations to achieve their goals depends on the degree to which leadership abilities and styles enable managers and team leaders to control, influence, and act effectively. In Part 3, Chapters 6 through 10, we examine how leaders influence others and how individuals can develop leadership competencies. Effective leadership involves management of conflict, which may arise over any number of issues. How employees communicate with superiors, peers, subordinates, and others can help make them effective team members or lead to low morale, lack of commitment, and reduced organizational effectiveness. For that reason and because most managers and professionals spend considerable amounts of time dealing with others, we stress interpersonal communication in this part.

Individuals in Organizations

People make assumptions about those with whom they work or spend time in leisure activities. To some extent, these assumptions influence a person's behavior toward others. Effective employees understand what affects their own behaviors before attempting to influence the behaviors of others. In Part 4, Chapters 11 through 16, we focus on the behavior and effectiveness of individuals, especially in organizations.

Individual behavior is the foundation of organizational effectiveness. Understanding individual behavior, therefore, is crucial for enhancing organizational effectiveness. Each person is a physiological system composed of various subsystems—digestive, nervous, circulatory, and reproductive—and a psychological system composed of various subsystems—attitudes, perceptions, learning capabilities, personality, needs, feelings, and values. In Part 4, we concentrate on the individual's psychological system. Both internal and external factors shape a person's behavior on the job. Internal factors include learning ability, motivation, perception, attitudes, personality, and values. Among the external factors that affect a person's behavior are the organization's reward system, organizational politics, group behavior, managerial leadership styles, and the organization's design. We examine these factors in Parts 3 and 4.

Foundation Competencies

Our fourth component, foundation competencies, has been the focus of this chapter. The seven competencies serve as an underlying foundation to the other three components and means of integrating them throughout the book.

CHAPTER SUMMARY

1. Describe the self competency and its contribution to effectiveness.

The self competency involves the overall ability to assess a person's own strengths and weaknesses; set and pursue professional and personal goals; balance work and personal life; and engage in new learning—including new or modified skills, behaviors, and attitudes. This competency underlies the other six foundation competencies. Mastering it requires a lifelong process of learning and career management.

2. Describe the communication competency and its contribution to effectiveness

The communication competency involves the overall ability to transmit, receive, and understand data, information, thoughts, and emotions—nonverbal, verbal, written, listening, electronic, and the like. Core abilities included in this competency are describing, active listening, questioning, nonverbal communication, empathizing, verbal communication, and written communication. This competency is like the body's circulatory system, nourishing and carrying the other competencies.

3. Describe the diversity competency and its contribution to effectiveneness.

The diversity competency involves the overall ability to value unique individual and group characteristics, embrace such characteristics as potential sources of organizational strength, and respect the uniqueness of each individual. The core abilities in this competency are related to a framework of six primary categories of diversity: age, race, ethnicity, gender, physical abilities and qualities, and sexual orientation. Eight secondary categories of diversity include education, work background, and religious beliefs. Several types of diversity—changing workforce and customers, gender, race, and ethnicity, and age—affect most employees, managers, teams, departments, and organizations. These types of diversity are important because they often reflect differences in perspectives, lifestyles, attitudes, values, and behaviors. How managers and employees embrace and respond to diversity greatly influences an organization's effectiveness.

4. Describe the ethics competency and its contribution to effectiveness.

The ethics competency involves the overall ability to incorporate values and principles that distinguish right from wrong into decision making and behaviors. Ethics are the values and principles that distinguish right from wrong. Managers and employees often experience ethical dilemmas—situations in which the individual or team must make a decision that involves multiple values.

5. Describe the across cultures competency and its contribution to effectiveness.

The across cultures competency involves the overall ability to recognize and embrace similarities and differences among nations and cultures—even within the same organization—and then to approach key organizational and strategic issues with an open and inquisitive mind. Individualism, collectivism, uncertainty avoidance, power distance, gender role orientation, and long-term orientation are five of the fundamental work-related values that need to be understood in order to develop this competency. These and other values affect people's perceptions, communication, decisions, and behaviors.

6. Describe the teams competency and its contribution to effectiveness.

The teams competency involves the overall ability to develop, support, facilitate, and lead groups to achieve organizational goals. Important also is recognition of the potential for individual and team differences and commonalities in goals.

7. Describe the change competency and its contribution to effectiveness.

The change competency involves the overall ability to recognize and implement needed adaptations or entirely new transformations in the people, tasks, strategies, structures, or technologies in a person's area of responsibility. Technological forces are one of the primary sources of change. The Internet is one of the primary enablers of increasing organizational effectiveness.

8. Explain the framework for learning about organizational behavior to enhance individual, team, and organizational effectiveness.

Organizational behavior involves the dynamic interplay among individuals in organizations, leadership and team behaviors, the organization itself, and the foundation competencies. The seven foundation competencies introduced in this chapter are developed through the dynamic interplay among the parts of this framework, which are addressed throughout this book.

KEY TERMS AND CONCEPTS

Across cultures competency
Active listening
Career
Career development
Career plan
Change competency
Collectivism
Communication competency
Competency
Cultural values
Culture
Describing skill
Diversity competency
Emotional intelligence
Empathizing skill
Ethical dilemma
Ethics
Ethics competency
Gender role orientation
Glass ceiling
Global mind-set
Individualism
Internet
Long-term orientation
Nonverbal communication
Organizational behavior
Power distance
Questioning skill
Racism
Risk taking
Self competency
Teams competency
Uncertainty avoidance
Verbal communication
Written communication

DISCUSSION QUESTIONS

1. Think of a team on which you are currently or have been a member. How would you evaluate its members—in general—with respect to the core abilities of the teams competency? Which members stand out, as either especially strong or especially weak, in terms of these abilities? Briefly describe their characteristics.
2. How would you describe your society's work-related cultural values? What impact have they had on your education?
3. For the most challenging job you now have or have had in the past, list the technologies you are using or have used to help you do the job. How would your performance of the tasks involved change if any two of the technologies were no longer available?
4. Identify two strengths and two weaknesses in your own competencies. What specific steps might you take over the next two years to reduce the weaknesses?
5. Identify three categories of diversity that represent significant issues in a team or an organization of which you are currently a member. How is this team or organization—and its members—addressing these issues?
6. The most successful teams and organizations are those that recognize the challenge and opportunity of embracing a diverse workforce. What obstacles stand in the way of doing so in a team or an organization of which you are or have been a member? Select a team or organization different from the one you chose to respond to Question 5.
7. What competencies are illustrated in the Preview Case about Jack Gherty?
8. Identify two ethical dilemmas that you have faced during the past year. How did you resolve them?
9. What is your dominant personal value orientation—individualism or collectivism? What is the basis for your answer?

EXPERIENTIAL EXERCISE AND CASE

Experiential Exercise: Diversity Competency

Attitudes Toward Diversity

Respond to the following statements. Use a scale of 5 to 1 to indicate how strongly you agree with the statements.

SA = Strongly Agree (5)
A = Agree (4)
N = Neutral (3)
D = Disagree (2)
SD = Strongly Disagree (1)

	SA	A	N	D	SD
1. I make a conscious effort to not think stereotypically.	5	4	3	2	1
2. I listen with interest to the ideas of people who don't think like I do.	5	4	3	2	1
3. I respect other people's opinions, even though I may disagree.	5	4	3	2	1
4. If I were at a social event with people who differed ethnically from me, I would make every effort to talk to them.	5	4	3	2	1
5. I have a number of friends who are not my age, race, or gender, or of the same economic status and education.	5	4	3	2	1
6. I recognize the influence that my upbringing has had on my values and beliefs and that my way isn't the only way.	5	4	3	2	1
7. I like to hear both sides of an issue before making a decision.	5	4	3	2	1
8. I don't care how the job gets done, as long as it is done ethically and I see results.	5	4	3	2	1
9. I don't get uptight when I don't understand everything going on around me.	5	4	3	2	1
10. I adapt well to change and new situations.	5	4	3	2	1
11. I enjoy traveling, seeing new places, eating different foods, and experiencing different cultures.	5	4	3	2	1
12. I enjoy people-watching and trying to understand the dynamics of human interactions.	5	4	3	2	1
13. I have learned from my mistakes.	5	4	3	2	1
14. When I am in unfamiliar surroundings, I watch and listen before acting.	5	4	3	2	1
15. When I get lost, I don't try to figure it out for myself but ask for directions.	5	4	3	2	1
16. When I don't understand what someone is telling me, I ask questions.	5	4	3	2	1
17. I really try not to offend or hurt others.	5	4	3	2	1
18. People are generally good, and I accept them as they are.	5	4	3	2	1
19. I watch for people's reactions whenever I'm speaking to them.	5	4	3	2	1
20. I try not to assume anything.	5	4	3	2	1

Scoring

Total your answers. If your score is 80 or above, you probably value diversity and can adapt easily to a multicultural work environment. Continue to look for areas of improvement. If you scored below 50, you probably need to work on understanding the need to value diversity.[42]

Case: Communication Competency

James Halpin of CompUSA

CompUSA is the largest retailer and seller of personal computer-related products and services in the United States. The company's mission is to market goods and services of high value to help customers manage information to improve their personal and organizational lives. CompUSA currently operates more than 200 computer superstores in major metropolitan markets throughout the United States, serving retail, corporate, governmental, and educational customers, and has more than 20,000 employees. James Halpin joined CompUSA in 1993 as president and chief operating officer (COO) and became CEO later that year. The following excerpts are from a recent in-depth interview of Halpin. They focus on communication within the company, including some aspects of the values and ethics expected of its employees.

We are a very verbal company. We don't write many letters. If you go through my files, the only thing you'll see is things like letters of congratulations I send to employees when I get letters from customers saying somebody did a great job. These are the only letters you'll see, because everything else we do quickly in oral form. If you have an idea, you just walk into somebody's office and say, "OK, what do you think about this?" So we do a lot of brainstorming instead of letter writing. A lot of companies are very much into writing things. We once had a guy from another company who was going to give a presentation using a hundred slides. One of our employees cautioned him: "But Jim, our CEO, has the patience of a gnat. So pick out two." "I can't do it in two," he said. "Then cancel the presentation," my staff member told him, "because after slide five, Jim is going to get antsy." The point of the story is that we try to do things quickly and mostly orally.

We have E-mail, but typically we just walk into each other's offices. Verbal is so much better. We've also got video conferencing, which is great, but you can't get the same intensity of emotion through a TV set as you can eyeball-to-eyeball. I also have coffee and donuts on Friday mornings with our team members in the office and out in the stores. For a while employees were intimidated, but then they would just start talking about everything and anything. They feel like they know us because they see us all the time on video. Every quarter we bring everyone in the home offices together to talk about the results—good, bad, and ugly. We broadcast results to the stores, and anybody can call in with questions and get answers. I've learned a lot of things about our company I would never have known otherwise. For example, I didn't realize we paid everyone once a month. I assumed I got paid once a month because I was an executive. But then I found out we were paying hourly employees once a month too. Now, how would I ever have known that unless they told me? So you find out things like that and you take care of them.

Companies get unions because management stops listening. For instance, an employee asks for a microwave for the break room, and management says, "Yeah, sure," but does nothing about it. Then, all of a sudden the union guy says, "Microwave? I'll get you a microwave." Next thing you know, he gets a microwave for the staff, and you've got a union. So the important thing is we have to continue to listen to our people and communicate down the organization as far as we can. Companies get in trouble through politics because it involves lying. You would get fired at CompUSA for lying. It is well known that if you lie, it's your last day. Just tell the truth. That's why employees don't have to worry about somebody going over their head. For instance, once a merchant was having an argument with the COO and said: "Well, I want to talk to Jim about it. Do you mind?" The COO asked him: "Can you tell the truth?" The merchant said he could, and so he came to see me. As long as you tell the truth, it makes everything so simple.

There is no middle ground. You are either honest or you're not. You can be stupid and get away with it. Because stupid is stupid. But if you lie, it's because you mean to lie. We talk very straight. We don't believe in lying. If something's great, we say so. If it's bad, that's exactly what we call it.[43]

For more information on CompUSA, visit the firm's Web site at ***www.compusa.com.***

Questions

1. What are the similarities and differences in the communication process and practices of higher level management in an organization that you have worked for compared to CompUSA?
2. What do you like best about Halpin's approach to communication? Why? What do you like least? Why?
3. See the core components of the managing communication competency. Which of these components can you identify in Halpin's comments?
4. How are potential ethical dilemmas handled at CompUSA? Do you agree with Halpin's view? Why?

PART 2

The Organization

CHAPTER 2	Managerial and Ethical Decision Making
CHAPTER 3	Designing Organizations
CHAPTER 4	Cultivating Organizational Culture
CHAPTER 5	Guiding Organizational Change

CHAPTER 2

Managerial and Ethical Decision Making

LEARNING OBJECTIVES

When you have finished studying this chapter, you should be able to:

1. Explain the core concepts and principles for making ethical decisions.
2. Describe the attributes of three models of managerial decision making.
3. Explain two methods for stimulating organizational creativity.

Preview Case: JC Penney's Golden Rules of Conduct

MAKING ETHICAL DECISIONS

Ethical Intensity

Decision-Making Principles and Decision Rules

Concern for Affected Individuals

Benefits and Costs

Determination of Rights

Ethics Competency—Norm Brodsky's Drug Testing Dilemma

MANAGERIAL DECISION-MAKING MODELS

Rational Model

Change Competency—St. Vincent's Rational Initiatives

Bounded Rationality Model

Communication Competency—Julie Rodriguez of Epic Divers and Marine

Political Model

STIMULATING ORGANIZATIONAL CREATIVITY

Lateral Thinking Method

Self Competency—Donna Kacmar of Architect Works, Inc.

Devil's Advocate Method

CHAPTER SUMMARY

KEY TERMS AND CONCEPTS

DISCUSSION QUESTIONS

EXPERIENTIAL EXERCISE AND CASE

JC PENNEY'S GOLDEN RULES OF CONDUCT

PREVIEW CASE

JC Penney is one of the largest department store, catalog, and e-commerce retailers in the United States. It has approximately 151,000 employees and annual sales of more than $18 billion. Gary Davis is the executive vice president and chief human resources and administration officer of JC Penney. In this Preview Case, we share excerpts of his remarks on ethical decision making and behavior and how JC Penney strives to practice what it calls its "golden rules" of business conduct.

Highly ethical leaders build values and ethics awareness. They regularly communicate and discuss the organization's shared values, operating principles, and ethical standards. Not in a special meeting . . . but as part of their everyday business style. . . . As business leaders, we are responsible for the assets of the company we serve, and one of those precious assets is the *legacy* of its reputation. James Cash Penney, the founder, understood that capitalism is built on trust. Trust that you will do the right thing. Trust in the quality of the products or services you sell. Trust that if the customer isn't satisfied, the company will make it right.

Many of us have chosen to work for JC Penney because of its strong culture, high ethical standards, and reputation. Companies that are successful decade after decade, such as JC Penney, have one thing in common. They have core values that are supported from the top. They understand that if they serve the customer well, the other stakeholders (such as associates and stockholders) are served as well. JC Penney's core values are *Honor, Confidence, Service,* and *Cooperation.* These four values have been a part of our culture and define the way we work with each other and with our business partners.

Trust must be a part of a culture within an organization—just as integrity must be inside the individual person. An officer in a company today has ultimate *responsibility* but not necessarily ultimate *control* over every decision that is made. That's why trust in your associates is so very important. Here's a quote that sums up this thought: "The power of the wolf is in the pack. The power of the pack is in the wolf." Individually strong—unbeatable as a team.

Today, our Business Ethics Committee is made of individuals from our Senior Management Executive Team. As Chief HR and Administration Officer, I have the responsibility and honor to chair this committee. One of the functions of the Business Ethics Committee is to periodically update and republish the JC Penney Statement of Business Ethics, so that it meets the requirements of changing laws and our business environment.

The document is important to our company because it defines for us our ethical obligations in conducting the company's business. The three key principles in our statement are:

- *Compliance with law:* No associate should take any action on behalf of the company which he or she knows, or reasonably should know, violates any applicable law or regulation.
- *Conflicts of interest:* Each associate of the company shall avoid any activity, interest, or relationship with non-company persons or entities that would create, or might appear to others to create, a conflict with the interests of the company.
- *Preservation of company assets:* Assets of the company may not be diverted to the personal use of any associate. Procedures established for purchase, sale, or other utilization of assets must be followed.

JC Penney requires all management and designated non-management associates to read

For more information on JC Penney, visit the organization's home page at ***http://www.jcpenney.net***

and electronically sign a Certificate of Compliance. But, as you know, Enron too had a Business Ethics Statement. We also know, it is not enough to merely require compliance with a statement. It is the actions and responsibility of individuals to understand and model their everyday behavior after that code of ethics. In business today . . . it is no longer acceptable to say. . .

"I didn't know . . . "
"I wasn't aware . . . "
"They didn't tell me."

Sure you can't know everything that is going on . . . but you *can* ensure that you have the best person in every job: people whom you trust to do the right thing or to tell you when something is *wrong.*[1]

Ethical concepts and issues are increasingly recognized as key components in all types of decision making in leading organizations, such as JC Penney and Johnson & Johnson. The remarks by Gary Davis in the Preview Case provide a glimpse into the efforts by the leadership of JC Penney to instill and shape the ethical obligations of its employees at all levels. The critical obligation of the top leaders to model the firm's stated core values and ethical principles in their decisions and behavior was emphasized by Davis.

We have presented issues related to making managerial, team, and individual decisions in a number of previous chapters. In this chapter, we expand on them. First, we discuss core concepts and principles that are fundamental to ethical decision making and behavior. Next, we review the features of three models of managerial decision making. Then, we conclude with a presentation of two approaches for stimulating creativity in decision making.

LEARNING OBJECTIVE

1. Explain the core concepts and principles for making ethical decisions.

MAKING ETHICAL DECISIONS

Decisions and behaviors in organizations have an underlying foundation of ethical concepts, principles, and rules.[2] Because of the importance of ethics in management, we recognize it throughout this book in the Ethics Competency features, as well as in relation to a number of topics, such as leadership and organizational change. As you will recall from Chapter 1, the *ethics competency* involves the overall ability to incorporate values and principles that distinguish right from wrong in making decisions and choosing behaviors. We noted also that **ethics** are the values and principles that distinguish right from wrong. In the broader sense, ethics refers to the study of moral values, principles, and rules, including the determination of standards of conduct and obligations for individuals and organizations. Ethical issues in organizations are common and complex. In fact, ethical issues influence the decisions that employees make daily. Some ethical issues involve factors that blur the distinction between "right" and "wrong." As a result, employees may experience ethical dilemmas.

THE COMPETENT LEADER

No longer can leaders prosper at the expense of the common good while they hide behind the barriers of language, geography, or cover-up tactics. In this interconnected world, only ethical leaders and companies will survive.

Michael L. Hackworth, Chairman, Former President, and CEO, Cirrus Logic, Inc.

The Ethics Resource Center, headquartered in Washington, D.C., conducts ethical surveys of workers in the United States on an interim basis. In their most recent survey, there were some encouraging findings.[3] The central findings include the first overall drop in observed misconduct as seen by employees in a decade: from 31 to 22 percent. Employee reporting of misconduct increased to 65 percent, continuing an upward trend from 48 percent. In addition, perceptions that top management "keeps promises and commitments" went from 77 to 82 percent over a three-year period. The percentage of employees saying that they feel pressure to compromise ethics standards of their organizations also declined from 13 to 10 percent over a three-year period. The report shows that lying to employees, customers, vendors, and the public is down to 19 percent from 26 percent. Similarly, withholding needed information has dropped to 18 percent from 25 percent, and discrimination on the basis of race, color, gender, and age is down to 13 percent from 17 percent. Of course, these findings are still problematic, but the trend is in the right direction.

In some situations, there are no simple rules for making ethical decisions. Our goal here is to help further develop your competency in applying ethical concepts to decision making. Your assessment of alternatives will be improved by examining five key components that comprise the foundation of ethical decision making: ethical intensity, decision-making principles and decision rules, concern for affected individuals, benefits and costs, and determination of rights. As suggested in Figure 2.1, these components are interrelated and need to be considered as a whole in order to make ethical decisions.

FIGURE 2.1 Components of the Foundation for Making Ethical Decisions

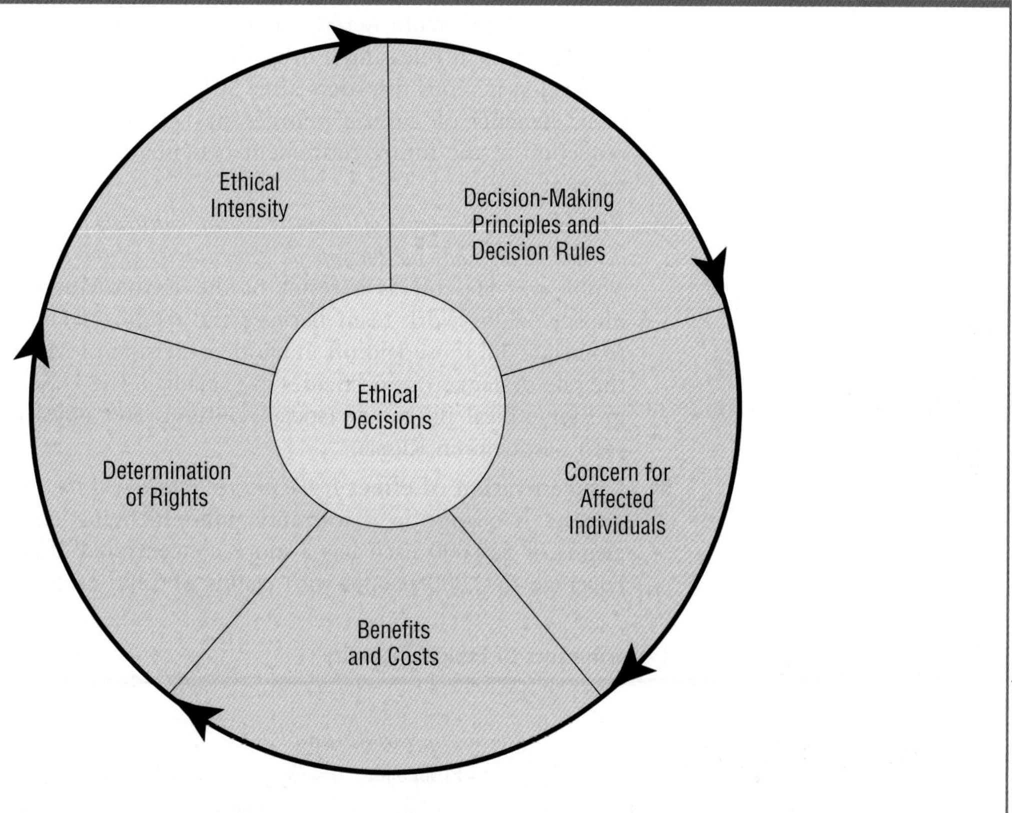

Ethical Intensity

Ethical intensity *is the degree of moral importance given to an issue.*[4] It is determined by the combined impact of six factors, which are shown in Figure 2.2 and described as follows:

- **Magnitude of consequences** *is the harm or benefits accruing to individuals affected by a decision or behavior.* An action that causes 1,000 people to suffer a particular injury has greater consequences than an action that causes 10 people to suffer the same injury. A decision that causes the death of a human being is of greater consequence than one that causes a sprained ankle.

- **Probability of effect** *is the likelihood that a decision will be implemented and that it will lead to the harm or benefit predicted.* The production of an automobile that would be dangerous to occupants during normal driving has greater probability of harm than the production of a NASCAR race car that endangers the driver when curves are taken at high speed. The sale of a gun to a known armed robber has a greater probability of harm than the sale of a gun to a law-abiding hunter.
- **Social consensus** *is the amount of public agreement that a proposed decision is bad or good.* Actively discriminating against minority job candidates is worse than not actively seeking out minority job candidates. Bribing a customs official in Canada evokes greater public condemnation than bribing a customs official in a country such as the Philippines where such behavior is generally accepted as a way of doing business. Managers and employees will have difficulty deciding what is and isn't ethical if they aren't guided by a reasonable amount of public agreement.
- **Temporal immediacy** *is the length of time that elapses from making a decision to experiencing the consequences of that decision.* A shorter length of time implies greater immediacy. Releasing a drug that will cause 1 percent of the people who take it to have acute nervous reactions within 1 month has greater temporal immediacy than releasing a drug that will cause 1 percent of those who take it to develop nervous disorders after 30 years of use. The reduction in the retirement benefits of current retirees has greater temporal immediacy than the reduction in the future retirement benefits of employees who are currently 22 years of age.
- **Proximity** *is the sense of closeness (social, cultural, psychological, or physical) that the decision maker has for victims or beneficiaries of the decision.* When Don Ritter at Mobil was laid off as a result of the Exxon/Mobil merger, it had a greater impact on his work team because the members knew and liked Ritter better than they did those laid off in another division of Mobil. For North Americans, the sale of dangerous pesticides in Canadian, the U.S., and Mexican markets has greater ethical proximity (social, cultural, and physical) than does the sale of such pesticides in Russia.
- **Concentration of effect** *is the inverse function of the number of people affected by a decision.* A change in a warranty policy denying coverage to 20 people with claims of $20,000 each has a more concentrated effect than a change denying coverage to 2,000 people with claims of $200 each. Cheating an individual or

FIGURE 2.2 Determinants of Ethical Intensity

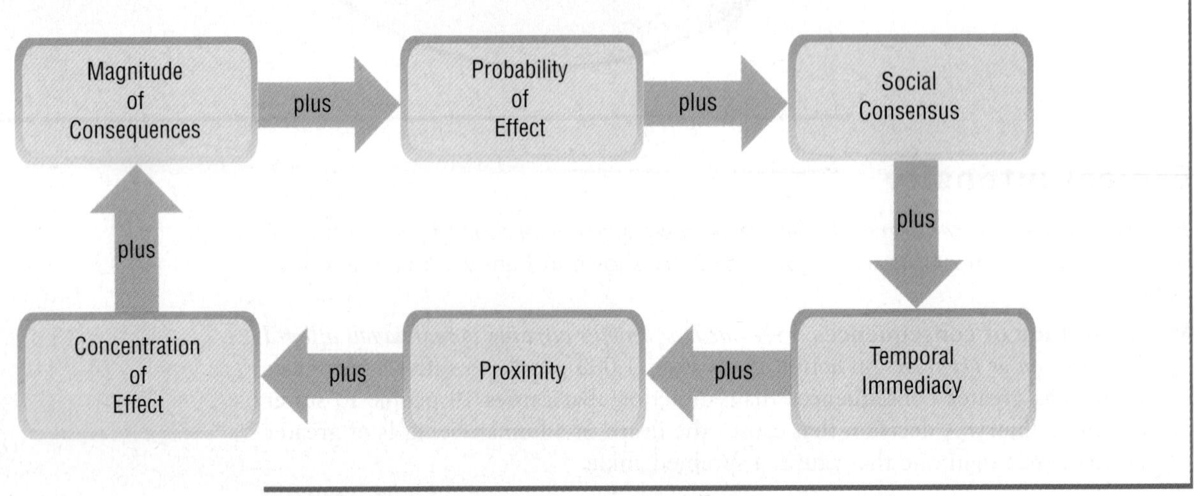

small group of individuals out of $5,000 has a more concentrated effect than cheating an organization, such as the IRS, out of the same sum.

Organizational Use. The six factors of ethical intensity potentially are influenced by the characteristics of the decision issue itself. Ethical intensity rises with increases in one or more of its factors and declines with reductions in one or more of these factors, assuming that all other conditions remain constant. However, different individuals may rate the ethical intensity of the same decision differently because they place different values on the principles and rules of ethics in decision making. Table 2.1 provides a questionnaire for you use in rating the ethical intensity of 10 different behaviors.

TABLE 2.1 Ethical Intensity of Selected Behaviors

Instructions

Evaluate each of the 10 behaviors shown in this questionnaire in terms of its ethical intensity. The overall scale of ethical intensity varies from –5, which indicates highly unethical behavior, to +5, which indicates a highly acceptable and ethical behavior. Write down the number on each scale at or near the point that reflects your assessment. What factors were most important in arriving at your rating of the ethical intensity for each behavior?

Behaviors	Ethical Intensity		
	Unethical/ Negative	Neutral	Ethical/ Positive
1. Covering up mistakes by coworkers.	–5	0	+5
2. Giving a favor to a client out of friendship.	–5	0	+5
3. Giving a favor to a client for a bribe.	–5	0	+5
4. Discriminating against an employee on the basis of race.	–5	0	+5
5. Presenting misleading information to a customer.	–5	0	+5
6. Presenting only positive features of your organization's products to a customer.	–5	0	+5
7. Manipulating performance data and indicators to give the appearance of reaching your goals.	–5	0	+5
8. Rewarding people differently based on differences in performance.	–5	0	+5
9. Bending the rules to help the organization.	–5	0	+5
10. Using an office PC for personal use.	–5	0	+5

Decision-Making Principles and Decision Rules

There are no universally accepted principles and rules for resolving all ethical issues in complex decision-making situations. In addition, individuals and groups differ over what influences both ethical and unethical behaviors and decisions. Numerous principles and rules have been suggested to provide an *ethical justification* for a person's decisions and behaviors.[5] They range from those that justify self-serving decisions to those that require careful consideration of others' rights and costs. In presenting all of these principles, it is recognized that the individual cannot use a principle to justify an act or decision if it is clearly illegal.

Self-Serving Principles. The following three ethical principles are used to justify self-serving decisions and behaviors:

- **Hedonist principle:** *You do whatever is in your own self-interest.*
- **Might-equals-right principle:** *You do whatever you are powerful enough to impose on others without respect to socially acceptable behaviors.*
- **Organization interests principle:** *You act on the basis of what is good for the organization.*

Some of the statements and thoughts that might reflect self-serving principles include the following: (1) "This act really won't hurt anybody"; (2) "I don't feel comfortable doing this, but if this is what it takes to get ahead (via money/work/promotion/prestige), I should probably do it"; (3) "Everybody else does it, so why shouldn't I"; (4) "Because _____ is my boss and told me to do this, I have no choice but to comply"; and (5) "Since this is such a small matter to most people and it will help our organization, who will notice?"[6]

Balancing Interests Principles. The following three ethical principles are used to justify decisions intended to balance the interests of multiple individuals or groups:[7]

- **Means–end principle:** *You act on the basis of whether some overall good justifies a moral transgression.*
- **Utilitarian principle:** *You act on the basis of whether the harm from the decision is outweighed by the good in it—that is, the greatest good for the greatest number.*
- **Professional standards principle:** *You act on the basis of whether the decision can be explained before a group of your peers.*

These principles provide the ethical foundation for many decisions in organizations. They create the basis for helping to resolve ethical dilemmas. For example, organizations—American Airlines, Hewlett-Packard, General Motors—are able to justify employee layoffs for the good of the organization but recognize certain responsibilities for providing career counseling and severance packages for the employees affected.

As a result of the Internet, new surveillance technologies, privacy issues, and governmental legislation and agencies related to homeland security and terrorism in the United States and many other countries have become major concerns in the attempt to balance the interests of individuals, organizations, and the public at large.[8] The growing perception is that employees and consumers have lost too much of their privacy to employers, marketers, and governmental agencies. Although a variety of U.S. laws have been enacted that attempt to protect the privacy of individuals in their roles as citizens, the notion of legal rights to employee privacy in the workplace is quite limited.[9]

Privacy issues in the workplace have become ethical dilemmas in terms of (1) distribution and use of employee data from computer-based human resource information systems; (2) increasing use of paper-and-pencil honesty tests, resulting from polygraph testing being declared illegal in most situations; (3) procedures and bases for substance abuse and AIDS testing; and (4) genetic testing. The ethical dilemmas in each of these areas revolve around balancing the rights of the individual, the needs and rights of the employer, and the interests of the community at large.[10]

Most employers want to ensure a reasonable degree of employee privacy even when they are not legally obligated to do so. This perspective is based on the balancing interests ethical principles. There is wide consensus that employers must protect against actions of employees who download pornography or copyrighted music, send harassing e-mail, reveal company secrets, disclose personal information, sell drugs, or even slack off on their job because of the time they spend surfing the Internet. New technologies make it possible for employers to monitor many aspects of their employees' jobs; especially on telephones, computer terminals, through electronic and voice mail, and when employees are using the Internet. Such monitoring of employees by employers is virtually unregulated by government. Therefore, unless company policy specifically states otherwise (and even this is not assured), the employer may listen, watch, and read almost all workplace communications by employees.[11]

Concern for Others Principles. The following three ethical principles focus on the need to consider decisions and behaviors from the perspective of those affected and the public as a whole:

- **Disclosure principle:** *You act on the basis of how the general public would likely respond to the disclosure of the rationale and facts related to the decision.*
- **Distributive justice principle:** *You act on the basis of treating an individual or group equitably rather than on arbitrarily defined characteristics (e.g., gender, race, age).*
- **Golden rule principle:** *You act on the basis of placing yourself in the position of someone affected by the decision and try to determine how that person would feel.*

These three ethical principles are often *imposed* on certain categories of decisions and behaviors through laws, regulations, and court rulings. In effect, governments impose ethical principles and rules that organizations are expected to comply with in certain situations. For example, U.S. civil rights laws forbid organizations from considering personal characteristics, such as race, gender, religion, or national origin, in decisions to recruit, hire, promote, or fire employees. These laws are based on the ethical principle of distributive justice, which requires the same treatment of individuals regardless of age, race, gender, and the like. For example, employees who are similar in relevant respects should be treated similarly and employees who differ in relevant respects should be treated differently in proportion to the differences between them. On this basis, the U.S. Equal Pay Act of 1963 asserts that paying women and men different wages is illegal when their jobs in the same organization require equal skills, effort, responsibility, and working conditions. This act applies to organizations with 15 or more employees. There are limited exceptions for pay differentials when an employer can show that:

- the difference is due to a seniority or merit system; or
- the difference is due to an employee's education, training, and experience.[12]

Table 2.2 lets you assess a significant course of action that you're considering in relation to the nine ethical principles just described.

Organizational Use. As noted previously, no single factor influences the degree to which decisions and behaviors are likely to be ethical or unethical. However, the following actions can help integrate ethical decision making into the day-to-day life of an organization:[13]

- Top managers must demonstrate their commitment to ethical behaviors and decisions made by other managers and employees. Recall the remark of Gary

TABLE 2.2 Ethical Assessment of an Incident

Incident

After delivering some materials to her supervisor, Mary returns to her office to find one of her coworkers, Bob, downloading a word-processing program from her computer. The company has only a site license for the use of this program. Bob explains that his home computer has no word-processing software and that his son Jeff, a high school senior, needs it to write a lengthy report on World War II. He further says that Jeff's final grade in history is on the line; if the grade isn't high enough, the boy's total grade-point average may make college acceptance impossible. Bob asks Mary to let him finish downloading the program.

Questions

1. What should Mary do? Why?
2. How would you evaluate the ethics of your decision with respect to the degree to which it is based on each of the following ethical principles?

Ethical Principle	High Degree 5	4	Uncertain/ Undecided 3	2	Low Degree (None) 1
To what degree is your decision based on this ethical principle:					
1. Hedonist	5	4	3	2	1
2. Might-equals-right	5	4	3	2	1
3. Organization interests	5	4	3	2	1
4. Means–end	5	4	3	2	1
5. Utilitarian	5	4	3	2	1
6. Professional standards	5	4	3	2	1
7. Disclosure	5	4	3	2	1
8. Distributive justice	5	4	3	2	1
9. Golden rule	5	4	3	2	1

Source: Incident adapted from Duran, G. J., Gomar, E. E., Stiles, M., Vele, C. A., and Vogt, J. F. Living ethics: Meeting challenges in decision making. In *The 1997 Annual: Volume 1, Training.* Copyright 1997 by Pfeiffer, San Francisco: Jossey-Bass, 1997, 127–135.

Davis, an executive at JC Penney, from the Preview Case. "Highly ethical leaders build values and ethics awareness. They regularly communicate and discuss the organization's shared values, operating principles and ethical standards. Not in a special meeting . . . but as part of their everyday business style."

- A clear code of ethics should be promulgated and followed. Recall from the Preview Case that the JC Penney Statement of Business Ethics, which represents its code of ethics, "defines for us our ethical obligations in conducting the company's business," according to Davis.
- A whistle-blowing and/or ethical concerns procedure should be established and followed.

- Managers and employees alike should be involved in the identification of ethical problems to arrive at a shared understanding of them and to help solve them.
- The performance appraisal process should include consideration of ethical issues.
- The organizational priorities and efforts related to ethical issues should be widely publicized. Recall the remark of Davis in the Preview Case: "It is the actions and responsibility of each individual to understand and model their everyday behavior after that code of ethics. It is no longer acceptable to say . . . 'I didn't know,' 'I wasn't aware,' 'They didn't tell me.'"

Concern for Affected Individuals

The highest form of ethical decision making involves a careful determination of who will receive benefits or incur costs as the consequence of a decision. For major decisions, this assessment may include a variety of stakeholders—shareholders, customers, lenders, suppliers, employees, and governmental agencies, among others. The more specific an individual or group can be about who may benefit and who may incur costs from a particular decision, the more likely it is that ethical implications will be fully considered. As discussed in the Preview Case, Gary Davis reflects a concern for stakeholders in describing his and JC Penney's approach to making decisions. He comments: "Companies that are successful decade after decade, such as JC Penney, have one thing in common. They have core values that are supported from the top. They understand that if they serve the customer well, the other stakeholders (such as associates and stockholders) are served as well."

The ethical interpretation of the effects of decisions on specific individuals or groups can change over time. For example, **employment at will** *is an employment relationship in which either party can terminate the employment relationship-at-will with no liability if there was not an express contract for a definite term governing the employment relationship.* Although employment at will allows an employee to quit for no reason, it is also used when an employer wants to fire an employee at any time for any reason or no reason. At-will employment is a creation of U.S. law.

All 50 states recognize retaliatory discharge as an exception to the at-will rule. Under the retaliatory discharge exception, an employer may not fire an employee if it would violate the state's public policy or a state or federal statute, such as if an employee reported illegal behavior by the organization to a government agency. Most states also recognize an implied contract as an exception to at-will employment. Implied employment contracts are most often found when an employer's personnel policies or handbooks indicate that an employee will not be fired except for good cause or when they specify a procedural process for firing. If the employer fires the employee in violation of an implied employment contract, the employer may be found liable for breach of contract.[14]

The employment-at-will doctrine increasingly has been challenged successfully in alleged wrongful termination cases in the courts. These challenges are based on the distributive justice principle and the golden rule principle. Before 1980, companies in the United States were free to fire most nonunion employees "at will." Employees were fired for any reason without explanation and rarely went to court to challenge a termination. The vast majority who did had their suits dismissed. However, the courts have recently ruled in favor of exceptions to the employment-at-will doctrine, especially if questionable termination procedures were followed.[15]

Benefits and Costs

An assessment of the benefits and costs of a decision requires a determination of the interests and values of those affected. For example, a global values survey asked respondents to reply to the following: "Please look at the list of 15 values carefully and check the five values that are most important to you in your daily life." The most frequent choice was truth, followed by compassion, responsibility, freedom, and reverence for life. The five values chosen least—starting with the very least—were respect for elders, devotion, honor, social harmony, and humility.[16]

Care must be taken to guard against assuming that others attach the same importance to these values that you do or that people in different cultures hold the same values. Conflicting values can lead to different interpretations of ethical responsibilities. For example, Greenpeace and other environmental groups have "preservation of nature" as one of their top values. In the survey just cited, it was ranked as eighth in importance and selected as most important by only 2 percent of the respondents. Active members of Greenpeace contend that most managers are irresponsible and unethical in not showing more concern about air and water pollution, land use, protection of endangered species, and the like.[17]

Organizational Use. The utilitarian principle is a common approach to the weighing of benefits and costs in organizations. Utilitarianism emphasizes the provision of the greatest good for the greatest number in judging the ethics of a decision. A manager who is guided by utilitarianism considers the potential effect of alternative actions on employees who will be affected and then selects the alternative benefiting the greatest number of employees. The manager accepts the fact that this alternative may harm others. However, so long as potentially positive results outweigh potentially negative results, the manager considers the decision to be both good and ethical.

According to some critics, utilitarianism has been misused by U.S. organizations. They suggest that there is too much short-run maximizing of personal advantage and too much discounting of the long-run costs of disregarding ethics. Those costs include rapidly widening gaps in income between rich and poor, creation of a permanent underclass with its hopelessness, and harm done to the environment. These critics believe that too many people and institutions are acquiring wealth for the purposes of personal consumption and power and that the end of acquiring wealth justifies any means of doing so. As a result, these critics suggest that trust of leaders and institutions, both public and private, has declined.[18]

Determination of Rights

The notion of rights also is complex and continually changing. One dimension of rights focuses on who is entitled to benefits or participation in decisions to change the mix of benefits and costs. Union–management negotiations frequently involve conflicts and dilemmas over management's rights to hire, promote, fire, reassign union employees, and to outsource work. Slavery, racism, gender and age discrimination, and invasion of privacy often have been challenged by appeals to values based on concepts of fundamental rights.

Organizational Use. Issues of responsibilities and rights in the workplace are numerous and vary greatly. A few examples include unfair and reverse discrimination, sexual harassment, employee rights to continued employment, employer rights to terminate employment "at will," employee and corporate free speech, due process, and the right to test for substance abuse and acquired immune deficiency syndrome (AIDS). Some experts believe that workplace rights and the establishment of trust with employees are the most crucial internal issues facing organizations today.[19]

The following Ethics Competency feature reports on the ethical dilemma experienced by Norm Brodsky in contemplating the implementation of a drug testing policy.[20] Brodsky is a veteran entrepreneur whose six small businesses include a three-time *INC.* magazine top 500 company. Brodsky shares his advice on running small businesses with his coauthor Bo Burlingham in a regular *INC.* magazine column. This competency feature is based on his experience as CEO and founder of Citistorage, an archival storage and retrieval service that he started in 1990. It is located in Brooklyn, New York, and now has more than 400 employees.

Ethics Competency

Norm Brodsky's Drug Testing Dilemma

Often, I've found you do something in business for one reason and only later discover that your decision has had ramifications you never imagined. With luck, they'll be good ones. That's been my experience with drug testing, which I began doing somewhat reluctantly about six years ago.

I knew we had a drug problem in our warehouse at the time. We'd heard rumors about marijuana being bought and sold on our premises. We'd also seen a marked increase in petty theft and minor accidents, which I suspected was related to drug use. People were running forklift trucks into walls and dropping skids of boxes onto the floor as they were being moved from one spot to another. Items would disappear from the shipments of goods that we kept in the warehouse for customers of our trucking business. I couldn't blame all of the problems on drug use, but I felt certain that it was a contributing factor.

Still, I hesitated to start drug testing. Part of my reluctance, I suppose, was a subconscious fear of feeling hypocritical. Like other members of my generation, I'd tried marijuana in my youth, and I'd be lying if I said I didn't inhale. When the testing issue arose, I had reservations about punishing people for doing something I'd also done at their age. In addition, I knew that drug testing could result in our having to let some employees go—maybe even some good, long-term employees. I eventually decided that we had to go forward anyway, mainly because of the accidents. No one had been seriously injured, but I knew our luck would run out sooner or later.

So, after consulting with some experts we had brought in to help us, we announced our new policy. Henceforth, we would test all job applicants for use of illegal drugs and hire only those whose results came back negative. As for our current employees, we wanted to give people using drugs a chance to clean themselves up. Marijuana, we explained, would show up in urine samples for at least a month after use. Other drugs passed through the body's system more quickly. Accordingly, we would wait 45 to 60 days before beginning testing. Thereafter, we would test everyone in the company, including me, my wife, my daughter, the other executives—everyone.

The tests would be random and would not be announced in advance. People who tested positive for drugs other than marijuana would be terminated immediately. Those who tested positive for marijuana use only would be given a second chance. After another 45-day waiting period, we'd do a second round of tests. Employees who failed both tests would be let go.

Despite the warning, we were in for a shock. In the first few days of testing, half of the samples from current employees came back positive. You can imagine how we felt about the prospect of replacing 50 percent of our 130-person workforce, which now totals over 400 employees. We decided to slow down the testing, so that we'd have time to find the new people we'd need. I had hopes for the employees who flunked the first test. Before the second round began, I asked several people if they were ready. Everybody said, "Oh, yeah, I'm clean." In the end, though, only one of them passed the second test. Although we offered the others drug treatment and a chance to reapply for a job, we got no takers. Overall, we wound up losing about 25 percent of our workforce—fewer than we'd feared, but a significant number nonetheless.

Yet, the drug testing did work. The accident rate declined, as did the incidence of petty theft. Even more gratifying was the response of the employees who remained: They thanked us. They said they felt safer. Only then did I begin to appreciate the real importance of having a drug-free company. It wasn't just about reducing our liability, or even keeping someone from getting hurt, as much as we wanted to do both. It was also about creating a better working environment for the other employees, the ones on whom we depend most heavily, the people we absolutely must figure out how to keep.

*For more information about Citistorage, visit the organization's home page at **http://www.citistorage.com**.*

LEARNING OBJECTIVE

2. Describe the attributes of three models of managerial decision making.

MANAGERIAL DECISION-MAKING MODELS

In previous chapters we have presented a variety of concepts and models that are important to understanding individual, team, and managerial decision making. In this section, we describe the main features of three managerial decision-making models: rational, bounded rationality, and political. In doing so, we introduce you to the different ways in which managerial decision making is viewed. Each model is useful for gaining insights into the complex array of managerial decision-making situations in an organization.

Rational Model

The **rational model** *involves a process for choosing among alternatives to maximize benefits to an organization.* It includes comprehensive problem definition, thorough data collection and analysis, and a careful assessment of alternatives. The criteria for evaluating alternatives are well-known and agreed on. The generation and exchange of information among individuals presumably are unbiased and accurate. Individual preferences and organizational choices are a function of the best alternative for the entire organization.[21] Thus, the rational model of decision making is based on the explicit assumptions that

1. all available information concerning alternatives has been obtained,
2. these alternatives can be ranked according to explicit criteria, and
3. the alternative selected will provide the maximum gain possible for the organization (or decision makers).

An implicit assumption is that ethical dilemmas do not exist in the decision-making process. The means–end and utilitarian principles often dominate the consideration of ethical issues.

Xerox's Six-Stage Process. Xerox developed the companywide six-stage rational process for guiding decision making that is presented in Table 2.3. Column 1 shows the six stages, column 2 identifies the key question to be answered in each stage, and column 3 indicates what's needed to proceed to the next stage. Managers and employees receive extensive training in the use of various decision-making tools to help them work through these stages.[22]

In terms of the individual, the rational model puts a premium on logical thinking.[23] Pam Lopker is the cofounder, chairman, and president of QAD, Inc., which is headquartered in Carpinteria, California. It is a leading provider of enterprise

TABLE 2.3 Xerox's Rational Decision-Making Process

Stage	Core Question	To Go to the Next Step, Develop:
1. Identify and select problem	What do we want to change?	Identification of the gap; "desired state" described in observable terms
2. Analyze problem	What's preventing us from reaching the "desired state"?	Key cause(s) documented and ranked
3. Generate potential solutions	How could we make the change?	Solution list
4. Select and plan the solution	What's the best way to do it?	Plan for making and monitoring the change; measurement criteria to evaluate solution effectiveness
5. Implement the solution	Are we following the plan?	Solution in place
6. Evalute the solution	How well did it work?	Verification that the problem is solved, or agreement to address continuing problems

Source: Adapted from Xerox consensus matrix. Available at http://www.xbrg.com (accessed June 2005).

resource planning (ETP) and supply chain software to firms in various industries.[24] She effectively comments on both the merits and limits of attempting to use the rational model, such as Xerox's six-stage process, in these words:

> I make bad decisions all the time. But I've been successful because I've developed a process for identifying and changing those decisions quickly. I approach every decision with an eye to the long-term outcome. That's a hard method to adopt in a fast-paced business environment. . . . I want the people in my organization to learn the lessons that come with making decisions: that everything is a compromise, that nothing is ever completely logical, but that you can deal with things through a logical decision-making process.[25]

Clearly, a feature of the rational model is that it helps keep people from jumping to premature conclusions about the nature of the problem and course of action to take. It encourages more deliberation, including the search for critical pieces of information. However, it provides no guarantee of successful decision making as Xerox experienced in the development of some failed technology and marketing strategies.[26]

Organizational Use. One obvious limitation of the rational model is that its full use can take a considerable amount of time. The resources required to use the rational model may exceed the benefit from it. This approach requires considerable data and information, which may be hard to obtain. Moreover, if the situation keeps changing, the decisions selected from a drawn-out process may quickly become obsolete. Another limitation is that managers may have to act when goals are vague or conflicting. Even when the rational process is used, decision makers may simply change the stated goals, criteria, or weights if a favored alternative doesn't come out on top. In brief, we suggest using the rational model to the extent feasible but don't expect it to be the sole or even primary guide in making many managerial decisions.[27]

The following Change Competency feature reports on the rational decision making at St. Vincent's Hospital, located in Birmingham, Alabama, to eliminate medical errors and improve efficiency.[28] This hospital, which is part of the Ascension Health Corporation, is a not-for-profit hospital.[29]

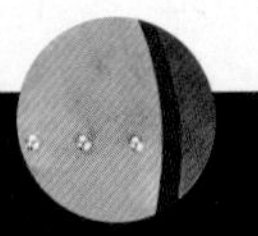

CHANGE COMPETENCY

ST. VINCENT'S RATIONAL INITIATIVES

At St. Vincent's, medical data are literally in the air. X-rays, CAT scans, and lab results can be retrieved immediately off of the hospital's wireless network, saving doctors time. St. Vincent's Wi-Fi network has been turned to an even more important purpose: eliminating medical errors. "Our goal is zero preventable errors," stated Timothy Stettheimer, the hospital's chief information officer.

That's a hard goal to achieve. One study showed one in five hospital medications is given in error. Medical mistakes, including those that occur during surgery and at other stages of patient care, may kill 98,000 people a year. Significantly reducing them could save more lives than curing diabetes.

Consistent with the rational model, St. Vincent has adopted state-of-the-art technologies to prevent mistakes. Robot arms often perform surgery with precision. Machines measure out doses of medicine. Surgical tools are affixed with bar codes so that they can be tracked—ensuring that they are properly maintained and never left inside patients. Nurses use scanners to check bar codes on patients' armbands so that drugs are given as doctors prescribed. For a system to work, physicians must embrace it. "If it's not going to make life easier," Chief Information Officer Stettheimer says, "I don't want to put it out there." That's where Wi-Fi helps. "It's indispensable," says Mark Maldia, an internist at St. Vincent's. At another hospital, he might spend an hour running from floor to floor to get an X-ray. Now he can download it in a few minutes. Lab results come across as soon as they're ready, not hours later. And with his tablet PC, Maldia can show patients images of their broken bones or tumors. He can even compare new images to old ones. Maldia was one of the first doctors at St. Vincent's to begin prescribing drugs by computer. His verdict? "It is a huge time-saver."

The pharmacy information system includes electronic order entry and advanced clinical screening that checks for drug/drug, drug/allergy, and therapeutic class duplications. St. Vincent also deployed automated dispensing cabinets, featuring locked, sealed pockets that prevent clinician access to nonprescribed medications based on order information received from the pharmacy system.

At St. Vincent's, the medical staff can also check every patient test, order, and procedure via an electronic results viewer, accessible from wireless tablets. Approximately 1,500 personal computers (PCs) are deployed throughout patient rooms and nursing stations across the six-building hospital campus. In patient rooms, medical devices such as blood pressure monitors are connected to each bedside PC, so vital sign information doesn't have to be reentered. Through dual-monitor computers at each nursing station, providers can review digital radiographic images alongside current clinical data, such as medication orders, patient allergies, laboratory results, and other clinical observations.

For more information on St. Vincent's Hospital, visit the organization's home page at ***http://www.stv.org.***

Bounded Rationality Model

The **bounded rationality model** *describes the limitations of rationality and emphasizes the decision-making processes often used by individuals or teams.* This model helps explain why different individuals or teams may make different decisions when they have exactly the same information. This model also recognizes the reality that complete information—concerning available alternatives or the outcome of some course of action—may be impossible for an individual or team to obtain, regardless of the amount of time and resources applied to the task. As portrayed in Figure 2.3, the bounded rationality model reflects the individual's or team's tendencies to

1. select less than the best goal or alternative solution (that is, to *satisfice*),
2. undertake a limited search for alternative solutions, and
3. cope with inadequate information and control of external and internal environmental forces influencing the outcomes of decisions.[30]

FIGURE 2.3 Bounded Rationality Model

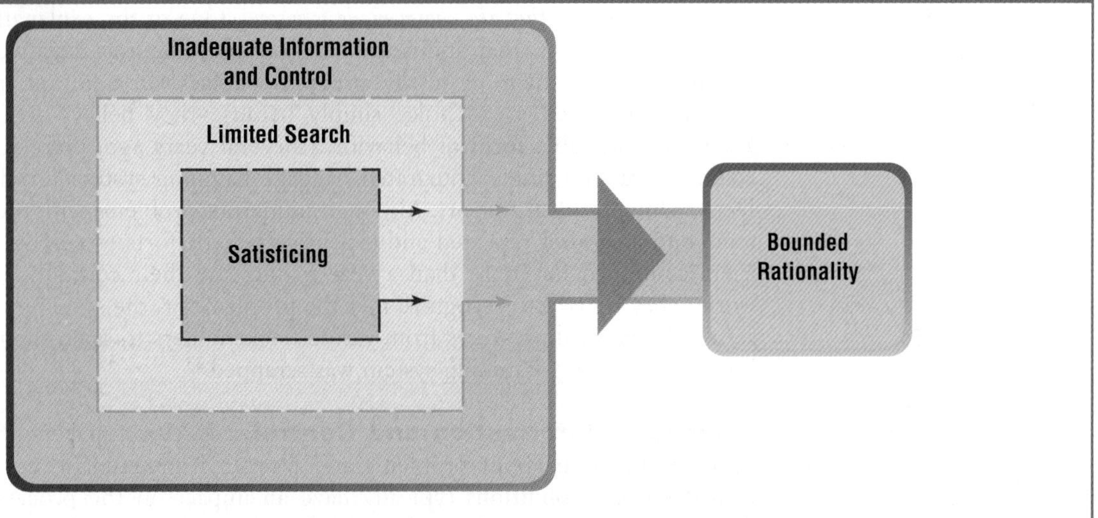

Satisficing. Satisficing *is the tendency to select an acceptable, rather than an optimal, goal or decision.* In this case, *acceptable* might mean easier to identify and achieve, less controversial, or otherwise safer than the best alternative. For example, profit goals are often stated as a percentage, such as a 10 percent rate of return on investment or a 5 percent increase in profits over the previous year. These goals may not be the optimal attainable. They may, in fact, reflect little more than top management's view of reasonable goals that are challenging but not impossible to achieve. Herbert Simon, who introduced the bounded rationality model, comments:[31]

> Satisficing doesn't necessarily mean that managers have to be satisfied with what alternative pops up first in their minds or in their computers and let it go at that. The level of satisficing can be raised—by personal determination, setting higher individual or organizational standards, and by the use of an increasing

THE COMPETENT LEADER

Be humble about your importance, about how many answers you know and how much you don't know (which is always more than you think), humble about the need to engage with and learn from people around you, humble about customers, humble about learning.
Scott Cook, Founder and Chairman, Intuit

range of sophisticated management science and computer-based decision-making and problem-solving techniques.

As time goes on, you obtain more information about what's feasible and what you can aim at. Not only do you get more information, but in many, if not most, companies there are procedures for setting targets, including procedures for trying to raise individuals' aspiration levels [goals]. This is a major responsibility of top management.

Limited Search. Individuals and teams often make a limited search for possible goals or solutions to a problem, considering alternatives only until they find one that seems adequate. For example, in choosing the "best" job, you won't be able to evaluate every available job in your particular field. You might hit retirement age before obtaining all the information needed for a decision! Even the rational decision-making model recognizes that identifying and assessing alternatives cost time, energy, and money. In the bounded rationality model, an individual or team stops searching for alternatives as soon as an acceptable goal or solution is discovered.

One form of limited search is **escalating commitment**—*a process of continuing or increasing the allocation of resources to a course of action even though a substantial amount of feedback indicates that the choice made is wrong.* One of the explanations for escalating commitment is that individuals feel responsible for negative consequences, which motivates them to justify previous choices. In addition, individuals may become committed to a choice simply because they believe that consistency in action is a desirable form of behavior.[32] Several years ago, there was an escalating commitment to a single, integrated baggage-handling system for all airlines at the Denver International Airport. Although numerous problems with the integrated system continued after repeated and expensive failed efforts to resolve them, the managers continued for more than a year to increase their commitment to making it work. They refused to recognize that the problem was the system itself. Finally, as a result of increased pressures from various stakeholders to open the new airport, the integrated baggage-handling system was scrapped.[33]

Inadequate Information and Control. Decision makers often have inadequate information about problems and face environmental forces that they can't control. These conditions typically have an impact on the process and results of their decisions in unanticipated ways. Two of the common decision-making biases that are partially triggered by inadequate information and lack of control are risk propensity and problem framing.

Risk propensity *is the tendency of an individual or team to make or avoid decisions in which the anticipated outcomes are unknown.*[34] A risk-averse individual or team focuses on potentially negative outcomes. The probability of loss is overestimated relative to the probability of gain. Therefore, the decision maker requires a high probability of gain to tolerate exposure to failure. Conversely, a risk-seeking decision maker or team focuses on potentially positive outcomes. Probability of gain is overestimated relative to the probability of loss. Thus, risk seekers may be willing to tolerate exposure to failure with a low probability of gain. Some decisions can be understood in terms of a desire to avoid the unpleasant consequences of a decision that turns out poorly. A choice can be personally threatening because a poor result can undermine the decision maker's sense of professional competence, create problems for the organization, and even get the decision maker demoted or fired. Most individuals have a low propensity for risk. They purchase many types of insurance to avoid the risk of large but improbable losses. They invest in savings accounts, CDs, and money market funds to avoid the risk of extreme fluctuations in stocks and bonds. Generally, they prefer decisions that produce satisfactory results more than risky decisions that have the same or higher expected outcomes.[35]

Problem framing *is the tendency to interpret issues and options in either positive or negative terms.* Individuals or teams in favorable circumstances tend to be risk averse because they think that they have more to lose. In contrast, individuals or teams in unfavorable situations tend to think that they have little to lose and therefore may be risk seeking. Focusing on potential losses increases the importance of risk. In contrast, focusing on potential gains lessens the importance of risk. Thus, a positively framed situation fosters risk taking by drawing managerial attention to opportunities rather than the possibility of failure. An example of positive versus negative framing is that of the certainty of winning $6,000 or the 80 percent probability of winning $10,000. Most people prefer the certain gain to the uncertain chance of larger gain. Which would you choose? Although risk aversion commonly is assumed to hold for most decisions, many exceptions have been documented. People prefer to take risks when making a choice between a certain loss and a risky loss.[36]

Organizational Use. Decision rules are a part of the bounded rationality model. They provide quick and easy ways for managers to reach a decision without a detailed analysis and search. They are written down and easily applied. The **dictionary rule** *involves ranking items the same way a dictionary does: one criterion (analogous to one letter) at a time.* The dictionary rule gives great importance to the first criterion. It is valid in decision making only if this first criterion is known to be of overriding importance.[37]

Consider what can happen when management too hastily uses the dictionary rule. The director and his staff at the Ohio Department of Claims experienced a growing backlog of social benefit appeals. They implemented a change in handling procedures. Their brief analysis led to a pooling idea that grouped similar claims for mass handling. However, the analysis failed to focus on the reason for the growing number of claims. After the backlog grew to the point that claims took a year to process, the director discovered a loophole in the legislation that had inadvertently eased eligibility requirements. The director made the legislature aware of the oversight and the loophole was closed. In the meantime, the agency was subjected to constant criticism and legal action for its slow, error-prone claims management. As the incident suggests, managers often want to find out quickly what is wrong and fix it immediately. The all too common result is poor problem definition and a choice of criteria that proves to be misleading. Symptoms are analyzed while more important concerns may be ignored.[38]

Recall one of the comments by Herbert Simon in the previous quote: "The level of satisficing can be raised—by personal determination, setting higher individual or organizational standards, and by the use of an increasing range of sophisticated management science and computer-based decision-making and problem-solving techniques." Knowledge management is an emerging focus for doing so.

Knowledge management *is the art of adding or creating value by systematically capitalizing on the know-how, experience, and judgment found both within and outside an organization.* Knowledge management is a means of raising the level of satisficing. Knowledge is different from data and information. *Data* represent observations or facts having no context and are not immediately or directly useful. *Information* results from placing data within some meaningful context, often in the form of a message. *Knowledge* is that which a person comes to believe and value on the basis of the systematic organized accumulation of information through experience, communication, and inference. Knowledge can be viewed both as a *thing* to be stored and manipulated and as *process* of applying expertise.[39]

Knowledge can be either tacit or explicit. **Tacit knowledge** *is developed from direct experience and usually is shared through conversation and storytelling.* The campus food director at the University of Washington telling a new manager how to handle abusive students or a sales manager at the Four Seasons Hotel telling a catering person about the habits of a particular client are examples of conveying tacit knowledge.

In contrast, **explicit knowledge** *is more precise and formally expressed*, such as a computer database and software program that creates information and analyses on customer purchasing habits or a training manual describing how to close a sale.

The following Communication Competency feature reports on Julie Rodriguez and her use of knowledge management to raise the level of satisficing in her role as president and CEO of the Epic Divers and Marine.[40] She has accomplished this through her excellent communication competency. Epic Divers and Marine, heaquartered in a suburb of New Orleans, Louisiana, provides (1) underwater commercial diving services and (2) offshore and coastal diving support capabilities, along with production and construction support.[41]

COMMUNICATION COMPETENCY

JULIE RODRIGUEZ OF EPIC DIVERS AND MARINE

Julie Rodriguez isn't a diver. She has never even suited up. Despite that, she has built Epic Divers and Marine from the small outfit she took over from her father in 1991 into a $24 million operation. At first, Rodriguez knew nothing about repairing offshore pipelines and platforms, Epic's bread and butter. Working in her father's office, she took requests for new jobs and would call Epic's divers just to find out if the company was qualified to do the work. She learned fast by listening to the company's accountants and picking up enough to take over the books herself.

Once in charge, Rodriguez listened to her employees, using her divers as consultants to learn about where to expand and which new customers to pursue. Her listening skills proved vital in 1994 when an Epic diver was struck and killed by a loose underwater pipeline. The fatality stunned her. Rodriguez recalls: "I felt rotten. I kept asking myself if it was worth it." She also knew the accident would make it difficult to land new contracts.

Determined to recover, Rodriguez set out to reform Epic's culture around safety. She started by discussing each job with the divers in order to anticipate what tools and procedures they needed to stay safe. The result was an extensive new safety program that's still in place today, emphasizing constant communication so that employees can continually learn from one another. When an incident does happen on a job, Rodriguez uses the error to teach other divers. Rodriguez states: "It's important to share your mistakes with everybody. They go in our manual and become training tools." Today, Epic has the top safety rating with all of its clients, including such industry giants as ChevronTexaco and ExxonMobil.

Rodriguez recently commented:

> In the forefront of all our goals are EPIC's safety statistics. This always seems to be a goal that is harder to achieve, because we will never be satisfied with status quo. Our DIVE 5™ behavior-based safety and quality program teaches us to continuously look for better and safer ways. Will we ever get there? Probably not. Will we ever stop trying? NEVER! Having said that, at a recent bi-weekly safety meeting a question was asked of those in attendance; divers, superintendents, captains, deckhands, engineers, shop personnel and managers: "What has been the most advantageous vehicle used in EPIC's safety program"? The unanimous response was—"the bi-weekly safety meeting"; they all agree that everything else is important; however, the platform they are given at the bi-weekly safety meetings proves to be the best line of communication, support, and education. The bi-weekly safety meetings give the employees the freedom to address safety concerns in front of the decision makers: VP Diving Operations, VP Marine Operations, Chief Operating Officer, and myself. At the same time, it gives the decision makers the opportunity to understand the issues in the field while working with those on the front line to achieve success.

For more information on Epic Divers and Marine, visit the organization's home page at ***http://www.epiccompnies.com.***

Political Model

The **political model** *describes decision making by individuals, groups, or units when the parties perceive that they have separate and different interests, goals, and values.* Preferences based on self-interest goals may not change as new information is learned. Problem definition, data search and collection, information exchange, and evaluation criteria are methods used to bias the outcome in favor of the individual, group, or unit.[42]

The distribution of power in an organization and the effectiveness of the tactics used by managers and employees determine the impact of the decisions. The political model doesn't explicitly recognize ethical dilemmas. However, it often draws on two of the self-serving ethical principles discussed previously: (1) the hedonistic principle—do whatever you find to be in your own self-interest; and (2) the might-equals-right principle—you are strong enough to take advantage without respect to ordinary social conventions.

The political model is prevalent in organizations throughout the world. For example, French culture values relatively high power distance. That is, relationships between superiors and subordinates are unequal, with different levels of status and privilege. The political model in French organizations, such as Altedia, Société Allen SA, and Group Ares, is based on various underlying assumptions and expected behaviors, three of which follow:

- Power, once attained, should not be shared except with the inside group of senior managers. Some are born to lead and others to follow; it is difficult for people to change. Secretaries are there to follow orders. Middle managers need to consult with their bosses as well as many others in the organization before making a decision.
- If individuals have been recognized as having top-management competencies, it does not matter if they are put in a job where they have no experience. They should be able to learn how to do their jobs with experience because of their competencies.
- It is harmful to reveal information unnecessarily because then the decision-making process cannot be controlled. When, where, and how to communicate information is a delicate question that often only the upper echelons can decide.[43]

Organizational Use. The political model is seen in organizations through the use of various **influence methods**—*the means by which individuals or groups attempt to exert power or influence others' behaviors.* The influence methods presented at the top of Table 2.4—rational persuasion, inspirational appeal, and consultation—often are the most effective in many workplace situations. The least effective methods seem to be coalition, legitimating, and pressure. However, to assume that certain methods will always work or that others will always fail is a mistake. Differences in effectiveness occur when attempts to influence are downward rather than upward in the organizational hierarchy. Differences in effectiveness appear when various methods are used in combination rather than independently. This process is complex. To understand fully the effectiveness of various influence strategies, you need to know the power sources available, the direction of attempts to influence (i.e., upward, downward, or laterally), the goals being sought, and the cultural values of the organization.

Having the *capacity* (power) to influence the behaviors of others and effectively using it aren't the same thing. Managers who believe that they can always effectively influence the behaviors of others by acquiring enough power simply to order other people around generally are ineffective. The ineffective use of power has many negative implications, both for the individual and the organization. For example, the consequences of an overreliance on the pressure method are often negative. Managers who are aggressive and persistent with others—characterized by a refusal to

TABLE 2.4 Influence Strategies

INFLUENCE STRATEGY	DEFINITION
Rational persuasion	Use logical arguments and factual evidence.
Inspirational appeal	Appeal to values, ideals, or aspirations to arouse enthusiasm.
Consultation	Seek participation in planning a strategy, activity, or change.
Ingratiation	Attempt to create a favorable mood before making request.
Exchange	Offer an exchange of favors, share of benefits, or promise to reciprocate at later time.
Personal appeal	Appeal to feelings of loyalty or friendship.
Coalition	Seek aid or support of others for some initiative or activity.
Legitimating	Seek to establish legitimacy of a request by claiming authority or by verifying consistency with policies, practices, or traditions.
Pressure	Use demands, threats, or persistent reminders.

Source: Adapted from Yukl, G., Guinan, P. J., and Sottolano, D. Influence tactics used for different objectives with subordinates, peers, and superiors. *Group & Organization Management*, 1995, 20, 275; Buchanan, D., and Badham, R. *Power, Politics and Organizational Change*. London: Sage, 1999, 64.

take *no* for an answer, reliance on repeated reminders, frequent use of face-to-face confrontations, and the like—usually suffer negative consequences. Compared to other managers, the managers who rely heavily on the pressure method typically (1) receive the lowest performance evaluations, (2) earn less money, and (3) experience the highest levels of job tension and stress.[44]

STIMULATING ORGANIZATIONAL CREATIVITY

LEARNING OBJECTIVE

3. Explain two methods for stimulating organizational creativity.

Organizational creativity *is the generation of unique and useful ideas by an individual or team in an organization.* Innovation builds on unique and useful ideas.[45] Creativity helps employees uncover problems, identify opportunities, and make novel choices in solving problems. In Chapter 8, we will present two approaches for stimulating creativity in organizations—namely, the nominal group technique and brainstorming. In addition, we will discuss various ways of reducing roadblocks to creativity and innovation. As suggested in Figure 2.4, three broad categories are perceptual, cultural, and emotional blocks:[46]

1. *Perceptual blocks* include such factors as the failure to use all the senses in observing, failure to investigate the obvious, difficulty in seeing remote relationships, and failure to distinguish between cause and effect.
2. *Cultural blocks* include a desire to conform to established norms, overemphasis on competition or conflict avoidance and smoothing, the drive to be practical and narrowly economical above all else, and a belief that indulging in fantasy or other forms of open-ended exploration is a waste of time.
3. *Emotional blocks* include the fear of making a mistake, fear and distrust of others, grabbing the first idea that comes along, and the like. For many organizations, fostering creativity and innovation is essential to their ability to offer high-quality products and services. Two methods, in particular, may be used to foster creativity with any individual or team: the lateral thinking and devil's advocate methods, as discussed next.

FIGURE 2.4 Potential Roadblocks to Creativity and Innovation

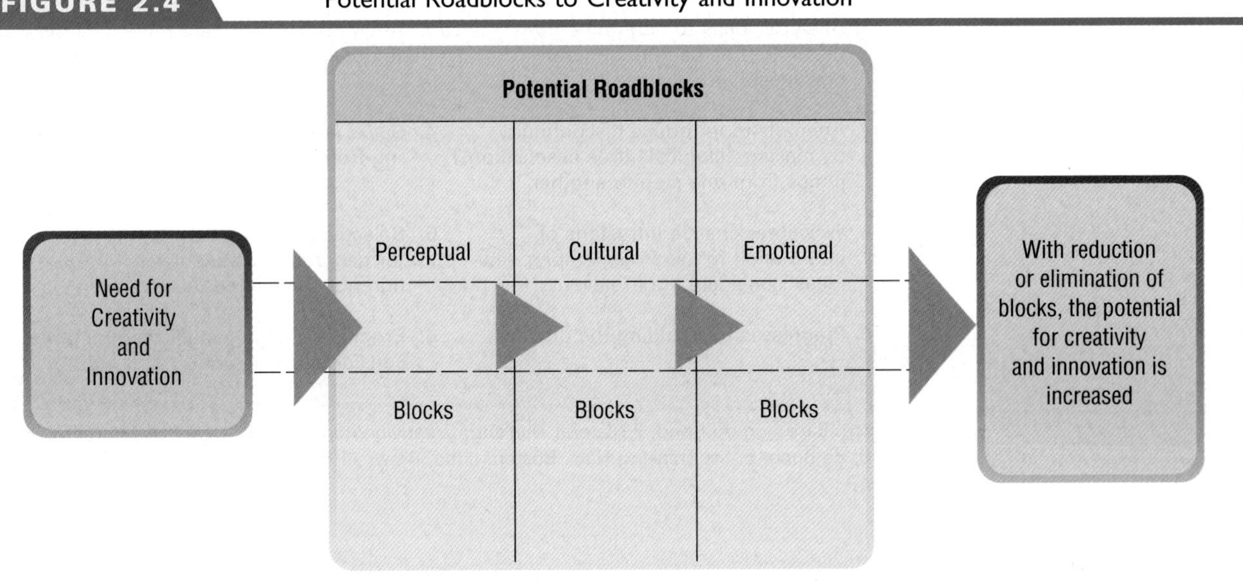

Lateral Thinking Method

The **lateral thinking method** *is a deliberate process and set of techniques for generating new ideas by changing an individual's or team's way of perceiving and interpreting information.* We can best explain this method by contrasting it with the **vertical thinking method,** *which is a logical step-by-step process of developing ideas by proceeding continuously from one bit of information to the next.* Table 2.5 presents the primary differences between lateral thinking and vertical thinking. Edward deBono, the British physician and psychologist who developed the lateral thinking method, stated that the two processes are complementary, and not at odds with each other.

Lateral thinking fosters the generation of unique ideas and approaches. Vertical thinking is useful for assessing them. Lateral thinking enhances the effectiveness of vertical thinking by offering it more from which to select. Vertical thinking improves the impact of lateral thinking by making good use of the ideas generated. You probably use vertical thinking most of the time, but when you need to use lateral thinking, vertical thinking capabilities won't suffice.[47]

The lateral thinking method includes several techniques for (1) developing an awareness of current ideas and practices, (2) stimulating alternative ways of looking at a problem, and (3) aiding in the development of new ideas. Here, we consider only three of the techniques for fostering the development of new ideas: reversal, analogy, and cross-fertilization.

TABLE 2.5 Characteristics of Lateral Versus Vertical Thinking

LATERAL THINKING	VERTICAL THINKING
1. Tries to find new ways for looking at things; is concerned with change and movement.	1. Tries to find absolutes for judging relationships; is concerned with stability.
2. Avoids looking for what is "right" or "wrong." Tries to find what is different.	2. Seeks a "yes" or "no" justification for each step. Tries to find what is "right."

3. Analyzes ideas to determine how they might be used to generate new ideas.	3. Analyzes ideas to determine why they do not work and need to be rejected.
4. Attempts to introduce discontinuity by making "illogical" (free association) jumps from one step to another.	4. Seeks continuity by logically proceeding from one step to another.
5. Welcomes chance intrusions of information to use in generating new ideas; considers the irrelevant.	5. Selectively chooses what to consider for generating ideas; rejects information not considered to be relevant.
6. Progresses by avoiding the obvious.	6. Progresses using established patterns; considers the obvious.

Source: Based on de Bono, E. *Lateral Thinking: Creativity Step by Step.* New York: Harper & Row, 1970; de Bono, E. Six Thinking Hats. Boston: Little, Brown, 1985.

Reversal Technique. The **reversal technique** *involves examining a problem by turning it completely around, inside out, or upside down.* Engineers at Conoco asked, "What's good about toxic waste?" By so doing, they discovered a substance in refinery waste that they now are turning into both a synthetic lubricant and—they hope—a promising new market. Ronald Barbaro, president of Prudential Insurance, considered the idea, "You die before you die," and came up with "living benefit" life insurance. It pays death benefits to people suffering from terminal illnesses before they die. Prudential has sold more than a million such policies.[48]

Analogy Technique. The **analogy technique** *involves developing a statement about similarities among objects, persons, and situations.* Some examples of analogies are "This organization operates like a beehive" or "This organization operates like a fine Swiss watch." The technique involves translating the problem into an analogy, refining and developing the analogy, and then retranslating the problem to judge the suitability of the analogy. If an analogy is too similar to the problem, little will be gained. Concrete and specific analogies should be selected over more abstract ones. Analogies should describe a specific, well-known issue or process in the organization. For an organization that is ignoring increased environmental change, an analogy might be "We are like a flock of ostriches with our heads buried in the sand."

Cross-Fertilization Technique. The **cross-fertilization technique** *involves asking experts from other fields to view the problem and suggest methods for solving it from their own areas of expertise.* For the technique to be effective, these outsiders should be from fields entirely removed from the problem. An attempt can then be made to apply new methods to the problem. Each year, Hallmark Cards brings to its Kansas City headquarters 50 or more speakers who might provide fresh ideas to the firm's more than 700 artists, designers, writers, editors, and photographers. Hallmark staffers often go from Hallmark's midtown headquarters to a downtown loft, where teams of writers and artists get away from phones to exchange ideas. They also may spend days in retreat at a farm in nearby Kearney, Missouri, taking part in fun exercises, such as building birdhouses.[49]

The following Self Competency feature illustrates the importance of lateral thinking. It presents the perspectives of Donna Kacmar, the principal and founder of Architect Works, Inc., headquartered in Houston, Texas.[50] This firm develops well-designed solutions for residential and small-scale commercial projects.[51]

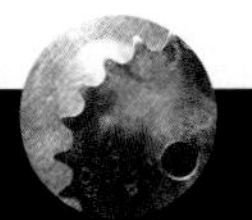

SELF COMPETENCY

DONNA KACMAR OF ARCHITECT WORKS, INC.

My creativity lies in trying to explore new possibilities for what might be considered a dumb or mundane problem. We all think we know how to make an office building or a townhouse or some run-of-the-mill thing like that. Well, do we? Let's question the assumptions that we have and see if there are some new things we can try. I always take risks on projects. But I don't take risks with wacky forms.

I always thought of myself as a problem solver. I also teach architecture at the University of Houston, and I once had a student tell me my buildings were boring. And, yes, they are pretty straightforward. But they're complex in that they allow systems to be expressed. There's a world of limits I operate in and that I am appreciative of. For example, the project that I'm working on right now is a Montessori high school, and part of what they do is have the students help maintain the building. They don't clean it. They maintain it. What does that mean—and what could that mean—for architecture? It's the idea of taking the routine and making it into something more. How do you understand the rituals that take place and then relate them to architecture?

What I'm able to do is help people see things a different way. I think I'm able to see things a little bit more openly—to find relationships between things that aren't as readily apparent and then make something of those relationships. My version of creativity is more like a quest for understanding.

For more information on Architect Works, Inc., visit the organization's home page at ***http://www.architectworks.com.***

Devil's Advocate Method

In the **devil's advocate method,** *a person or team—the devil's advocate—develops a systematic critique of a recommended course of action.* This critique points out weaknesses in the assumptions underlying the proposal, internal inconsistencies in it, and problems that could lead to failure if it were followed. The devil's advocate acts like a good trial lawyer by presenting arguments against the majority position as convincingly as possible. Figure 2.5 illustrates the basic decision-making process when this method is utilized. Individuals assigned to the devil's advocate role should be rotated to avoid any one person or team being identified as a critic on all issues. However, playing this role, even for a short time, may be advantageous for a person and the organization.

Steve Huse, chairperson and CEO of Huse Food Group, indicates that the devil's advocate role is an opportunity for employees to demonstrate their presentation and debating skills. How well someone understands and researches issues is apparent when that person presents a critique. The organization avoids costly mistakes by hearing viewpoints that identify potential pitfalls. In addition, the use of the devil's advocate approach can increase the probability of creative solutions to the problems and reduce the likelihood of groupthink.[52] We will find that groupthink in decision making is caused by excessive consensus and similarity of views in teams—a sure way to kill organizational creativity (see Chapter 8).

FIGURE 2.5 Decision Making with a Devil's Advocate

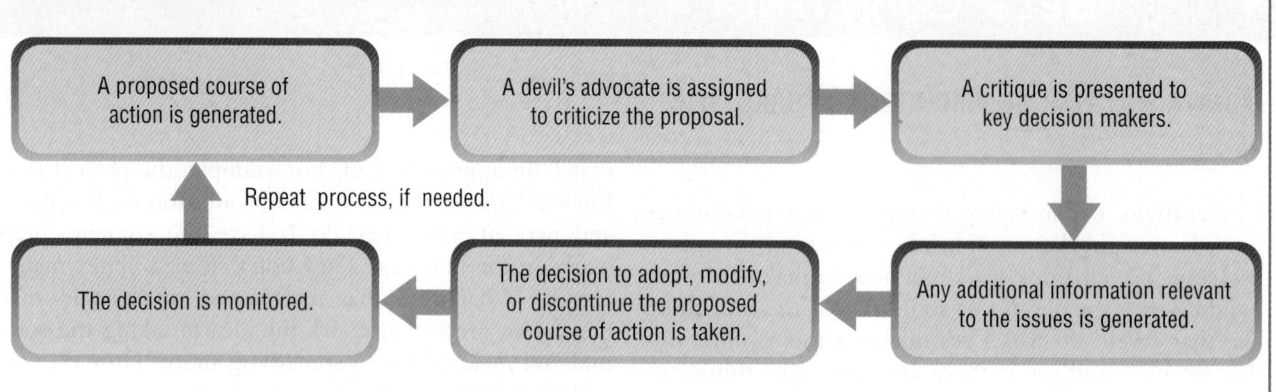

Source: Adapted from Cosier, R. A., and Schrivenk, C. R. Agreement and thinking alike: Ingredients for poor decisions. *Academy of Management,* February 1997, 71.

The devil's advocate method is effective in helping bring to the surface and challenge assumptions on which a proposed course of action is based—an essential element in fostering creativity. This method shouldn't be overused, and it is best applied to important and complex issues where the parties understand the role of the devil's advocate. For instance, those who are not used to this mode of exploring ideas may feel attacked and not do their best thinking.

CHAPTER SUMMARY

1. Explain the core concepts and principles for making ethical decisions.

Individuals often experience ethical dilemmas when making decisions. We addressed five important issues, which can be stated as questions, in ethical decision making: What is the ethical intensity? What are the principles and rules? Who is affected? What are the benefits and costs? Who has rights?

2. Describe the attributes of three models of managerial decision making.

The rational, bounded rationality, and political models are commonly used to explain managerial decision making. Each model explains some aspects of managerial decision-making situations and processes. All three models are needed to grasp the complexity and entire range of decision making.

3. Explain two methods for stimulating organizational creativity.

Creativity is needed in changing, complex, and uncertain environments. This situation often results in ambiguity and disagreement over both the goals to be achieved and the best course of action to pursue. Organizational creativity and innovation are crucial to the discovery and implementation of unique and useful ideas. Two approaches for stimulating organizational creativity are the lateral thinking method and the devil's advocate method.

KEY TERMS AND CONCEPTS

Analogy technique
Bounded rationality model
Concentration of effect
Cross-fertilization technique
Devil's advocate method
Dictionary rule

Disclosure principle
Distributive justice principle
Employment at will
Escalating commitment
Ethical intensity
Ethics
Explicit knowledge
Golden rule principle
Hedonist principle
Influence methods
Knowledge management
Lateral thinking method
Magnitude of consequences
Means–end principle
Might-equals-right principle
Organization interests principle
Organizational creativity
Political model
Probability of effect
Problem framing
Professional standards principle
Proximity
Rational model
Reversal technique
Risk propensity
Satisficing
Social consensus
Tacit knowledge
Temporal immediacy
Utilitarian principle
Vertical thinking method

DISCUSSION QUESTIONS

1. Think of an organization or group in which you are an active member. Describe a choice that seemed to be based on the political model. Why do you think the choice followed the political model?
2. Describe a specific problem that you have experienced that was probably affected by the problem framing bias.
3. Based on Table 2.5, what characteristics of the lateral thinking method are illustrated in the Self Competency feature on Donna Kacmar of Architect Works, Inc.?
4. Evaluate the ethical intensity of the grading system and practices used by an instructor in a course that you have completed. Your evaluation should include an assessment of each of the six components of ethical intensity.
5. What balancing interests principles and concern for others principles are illustrated in the Preview Case on JC Penney's golden rules of conduct? You should relate specific rules to specific principles.
6. What specific decisions and comments by Julie Rodriguez of Epic Divers and Marine illustrate specific features of the bounded rationality model as presented in the Communication Competency feature?
7. What are the differences between the organization interests principle and the utilitarian principle?
8. What are the differences between the professional standards principle and the distributive justice principle?
9. What ethical principles were illustrated in the Ethics Competency feature on Norm Brodsky's drug testing dilemma?
10. Arrange the ethical principles presented in Table 2.2 in rank order from your most preferred to least preferred. What does this ranking tell you about how you are likely to interpret situations involving ethical dilemmas?

EXPERIENTIAL EXERCISE AND CASE

Experiential Exercise: Ethics Competency

Living Ethics[53]

Susan Johnson's Situation

Susan Johnson is a first-line manager. One of her employees, Meg O'Brien, has been in her department for 8 months. Despite Johnson's repeated efforts at training and coaching, O'Brien is performing below an acceptable level, but the supervisors of three other departments gave her "average" ratings. Johnson talked to these supervisors and discovered that they did so in order to avoid hassles resulting from the employee's likely reaction; they explained that O'Brien files grievances and Equal Employment Opportunity (EEO) complaints regularly. Johnson's supervisor, Barbara Lopez, has told Johnson to give O'Brien an excellent rating and a glowing recommendation for a vacant position in another division.

1. What ethical conflict(s) does Johnson face?
2. In addition to Johnson, O'Brien, and Lopez, who might be affected by Johnson's decision?

3. What actions are open to Johnson?
4. Which of these actions best meets ethical considerations while resolving the situation as positively as possible for the people involved/affected? What ethical principles serve as the basis for your actions?
5. How would you evaluate the ethical intensity of this situation?

Frank Epps's Situation

Frank Epps is a manager reviewing applications for an open position in his department. One of the company's standard procedures for the hiring process is a background check. Epps's friend, Michael Kee, is one of the applicants and is well qualified for the position. Kee recently told Frank that 12 years ago he embezzled $4,000 from his employer. The employer pressed charges, and Kee was ultimately sentenced to 1 year of probation. According to organizational policy, this incident would disqualify Kee as a candidate for the position. Kee has convinced Epps that the embezzlement was a one-time error in judgment that will never happen again. He has asked Epps not to do the formal background check.

1. What ethical conflict(s) does Epps face?
2. In addition to Epps and Kee, who might be affected by Epps's decision?
3. What actions are open to Epps?
4. Which of these actions best meets ethical considerations while resolving the situation as positively as possible for the people involved/affected? On what ethical principles did you base your response?
5. What level of ethical intensity would you assign to this situation?

Case: Change Competency

Is Opportunity Knocking?[54]

I was excited just to meet the football legend in person. I never expected that a résumé sent to his corporate offices would produce a response, but it had. Now, I was responding to his telephone call and meeting him at his estate behind the high fence, which was a local landmark. The football stadium was named after him, as well as the expressway and the west wing of the hospital. And he wanted to talk to me, personally, about a job in his new restaurant. Me, a recent graduate of HRM at Tech!

The massive gates were ajar so I drove up the lengthy drive to the mansion on the hill. I couldn't help but notice that the lawn desperately needed attention and that the hedges needed trimming. The flower beds had more weeds than flowers. The fountain out front had stopped working a long time ago, judging from the debris rotting inside. But there was Hugh Aimsworth, on the great veranda, waiting for me. He greeted me with a firm handshake and said, "Glad you could make it." He gracefully led the way inside and told me to have a seat anywhere, pointing to a large dark room dominated by a stone fireplace. Every sofa and chair was cluttered with books, magazines, or newspapers. In one corner was a TV tray containing leftovers from earlier meals. Mr. Aimsworth came in and handed me a cup of coffee, "Way to start the day," he said. It was noon, and I was surprised by the remark. Then he surveyed the room and added, "Better we go sit a spell in another room."

I followed him into a large foyer and in passing the spiral staircase he yelled upstairs, "Bertha Mae, we have company, can you come down, darling?" "I'm not dressed," was the shrill response from somewhere on the second floor along with the loud sound of a slammed door. Into the kitchen area we walked. Dirty dishes were piled everywhere! Both sinks were full of greasy water that smelled like a marina. Then I saw the cat on the counter, licking from a cat food can. Explained the fishy smell!

We passed through the kitchen to the den, complete with a big-screen TV and an array of football trophies. Mr. Aimsworth threw the papers off the easy chairs and motioned for me to sit.

We spoke about his admittedly favorite subject, football; then he said, "Let's head out to the lake and look at the Victorian Manor—been in the family for years, great view. It would make a fine restaurant with a smart young whippersnapper like you running it." Had I been offered the job? I wondered! With that he handed me some worn plans of the Victorian Manor dating back to 1890. "You might need these," he added.

The day was brilliant and I was enjoying the 10-mile drive out of the city. At the next turn the concrete ended and gravel began. "Almost there now," said Mr. Aimsworth as he turned up a dirt road and sang loudly along with the CD playing from the Lincoln Town Car's dash, "I did it my way," trying to keep pace with Sinatra. I couldn't help thinking that Sinatra would cringe at the sound.

Five minutes later the Manor came into sight. What a beauty! It sat atop a hill, like out of a movie, but the closer we got the more apparent became its disrepair. First, I noticed that it badly needed paint, a new roof, and a full-time carpenter. A new veranda was a must. I made mental notes as we carefully stepped over missing floorboards. The wallpaper was peeling off and light fixtures were nonexistent. "Great hardwood floors under this paint some idiot covered it with," remarked Mr. Aimsworth. "Did I tell you this house is listed on the National Historic Register?" My mind focused on how the house needed new windows and how electric wire was running up the wall, askew, as if a giant spider had attempted to spin a web. But the biggest disappointment was the kitchen, or lack of one. Mr. Aimsworth continued, "Granddaddy used to have the cookhouse going full blast all the time. Tore it down though. Put in this little kitchen in the '40s when we rented the place for a spell."

We made our way through some French doors onto a wide veranda that had the most spectacular view I had ever seen. I fell through a piece of banister while leaning a little too far for a better view. "Yep, own all the way down to the water; ever seen anything so splendid?" he asked "No, Mr. Aimsworth, I certainly haven't," I honestly replied.

Mr. Aimsworth slowly walked down to the water, and I followed. He was obviously deep in thought. At the water's edge he turned to me and said, "Well, what do you think, eh? I think this would make a fine French or maybe Italian restaurant. Think of the grand parties we could have here. Make me a list of things you would do if I were to make you the manager here. What do you think it would take to get it going?"

On the trip back to his home he offered, "Bring me some ideas on paper about how you would go about making my final dream come true. Bring along any questions you have. If I like your ideas, you have the job as manager." We agreed that our next meeting would be at noon, 2 weeks later. Mr. Aimsworth dropped me off at my car with "same time, same place."

Questions

You have just been offered an opportunity for your first job in quite an unorthodox manner by an eccentric gentleman. You are excited about the possibilities of the Victorian Manor becoming a popular dining destination. But, you realize that it would take a great deal of your time, hard work, and his money to make his dream of a restaurant a reality. You also realize that in 2 weeks you must come up with

1. a list of questions for Mr. Aimsworth (what will they be?);
2. a concept of how you would make the Victorian Manor into a restaurant (what do you have to do to form a concept?);
3. a rough idea of the amount of time and money that would be required to open and operate the restaurant (how will you go about putting together even a rough estimate?); and
4. further information about Mr. Aimsworth's background and his financial situation (how will you accomplish this?).

CHAPTER 3

Designing Organizations

LEARNING OBJECTIVES

When you have finished studying this chapter, you should be able to:

1. Explain how environmental, strategic, and technological factors affect the design of organizations.
2. State the differences between mechanistic and organic organizations.
3. Describe four traditional organization designs: functional, place, product, and multidivisional.
4. Describe two contemporary organization designs: multinational and network.

Preview Case: Kellogg Company
KEY FACTORS IN ORGANIZATION DESIGN
Environmental Factors
Strategic Factors
Change Competency—7-Eleven
Technological Factors
MECHANISTIC AND ORGANIC ORGANIZATIONS
Hierarchy of Authority
Division of Labor
Rules and Procedures
Impersonality
Chain of Command
Span of Control
Across Cultures Competency—Latin American versus U.S. Management Practices
TRADITIONAL ORGANIZATION DESIGNS
Organizational Design Options
Functional Design
Place Design
Product Design
Multidivisional Design (M-Form)
CONTEMPORARY ORGANIZATION DESIGNS
Multinational Design
Communication Competency—Electrolux
Network Design
Communication Competency—DreamWorks SKG
CHAPTER SUMMARY
KEY TERMS AND CONCEPTS
DISCUSSION QUESTIONS
EXPERIENTIAL EXERCISE AND CASE

KELLOGG COMPANY

PREVIEW CASE

Perhaps one of the best-known companies in the United States, the Kellogg Company has begun to shift its focus away from being the country's largest producer of the ready-to-eat cereals and other breakfast food items that have traditionally been synonymous with the company. Although the company remains highly profitable, Kellogg faces numerous strategic challenges.

Recently, company sales passed the $9 billion mark. Even with such highly recognized brands as Kellogg's Corn Flakes, Frosted Flakes, Special K, Raisin Bran, Rice Krispies, and Nutri-Grain cereal bars, the company has faced increasingly tough competition from other packaged foods producers such as General Mills, PepsiCo's Quaker Oats line of cereals, Kraft Foods, and Ralcorp Holdings. As a result, in the past decade, Kellogg has watched its earnings growth slow down, while its market share in cereals dropped from 37 percent to 31 percent.

Many of the challenges facing Kellogg, however, resulted from changing breakfast trends. Traditionally, Kellogg would introduce a new line of cereal or breakfast food item with an expensive marketing promotion that would emphasize the newness of the product. Unlike its competitors, Kellogg generally prefers not to compete on the basis of price. Although consumers sometimes enthusiastically greet Kellogg's new cereal products (e.g., Raisin Bran Crunch), they often care more about the price of the product, rather than who made it.

In 1999 Kellogg purchased Worthington Foods, a leading natural foods company that develops soy-based products and other vegetarian foods. Veggie burgers and soy-based hot dogs and corn dogs are sold by them. Worthington's best-known brand is Morningstar Farms, which holds more than 50 percent of the market for vegetarian and nonmeat alternative food products in U.S. supermarkets. With the acquisition of Worthington, Kellogg is now able to participate in the fast-growing organic and natural foods segment, which has grown at 20 to 25 percent in recent years.

In 2000, Kellogg purchased Keebler Foods. Keebler is one of the largest snack food companies in the United States, making such well-known products as Cheez-It crackers, Club crackers, and a broad line of cookies (e.g., Chips Deluxe, Fudge Shoppe). The company is also highly recognized through its famous television advertisements that feature its Keebler Elves making and delivering fresh cookies. Kellogg's acquisition of Keebler has transformed the combined entity into a $9 billion breakfast and snack food company. With Keebler's product lines, Kellogg will now derive only 40 percent of its sales from breakfast cereals, as opposed to 75 percent from just a few years ago. More important, Keebler brings to Kellogg not only the potential for much higher earnings growth but also a new set of product development and distribution skills that can help the company grow.

Kellogg has begun new efforts to accelerate its time-to-market of new products from its laboratories. During much of the 1990s, Kellogg's new product launches were comparatively scarce, with the exception of Nutri-Grain bars and Raisin Bran Crunch. Today, about 100 scientists work in a modern research and development (R&D) center in Battle Creek, Michigan, to create new types of food recipes. This laboratory also includes a 9,000-square-foot test kitchen and a scaled-down factory. Kellogg has introduced more than 100 new products this year, compared with just 68 a few years ago. Kellogg's scientists are working on new ways to enhance the freshness of ingredients inside the cereal box, especially fruits and other natural products. The benefits of Kellogg's products development efforts are spilling over to

For more information on Kellogg, visit the organization's home page at ***http://www.kellogg.com.***

Keebler's products as well. For example, Cheez-It Twisters are made with a new technology that twists the dough into a light and airy snack. Keebler did not possess the technology before its merger with Kellogg; Kellogg originally developed the technology to enhance its Fruit Loops cereal. To promote the value of its brands, Kellogg has also commenced a series of marketing programs to enhance the public's awareness of its most famous brands. For example, Kellogg is now working with a leading fashion designer to develop a line of women's apparel based on the Special K consumer. Also, Kellogg has begun looking for new ways to license its Tony the Tiger and other Kellogg characters for use in a new line of toys.[1]

The basis for any successful organization is for people to work together and understand how their actions interrelate with the actions of others to support the organization's strategy. Yet talented people in even the best-managed organizations are sometimes left groping to understand how their own activities contribute to their organization's success. An organization's design is crucial in clarifying the roles of the managers and employees who hold the organization together. **Organization design** *is the process of selecting a structure for the tasks, responsibilities, and authority relationships within an organization.*[2] The connections among various divisions or departments in an organization can be represented in the form of an organization chart. An **organization chart** *is a representation of an organization's internal structure, indicating how various tasks or functions are interrelated.* How is Kellogg organized to compete in the global food industry? Figure 3.1 shows an abridged Kellogg organization chart. Each box represents a specific job, and the lines connecting them reflect the formal lines of communication between individuals performing those jobs.

Organization design decisions often involve the diagnosis of multiple factors, including an organization's culture, power and political behaviors, and job design. Organization design represents the outcomes of a decision-making process that includes environmental factors, strategic choices, and technological factors. Specifically, organization design should:

1. promote the flow of information and speed decision making in meeting the demands of customers, suppliers, and regulatory agencies;
2. clearly define the authority and responsibility for jobs, teams, departments, and divisions; and
3. create the desired balance of integration (coordination) among jobs, teams, departments, and divisions, with built-in procedures for fast response to changes in the environment.

We frequently refer to departments and divisions as we discuss organization design. The term *department* typically is used to identify a specialized function within an organization, such as human resource, production, accounting, and purchasing. In contrast, the term *division* typically is used to identify a broader, often autonomous part of an organization that performs many, if not all, of the functions of the parent organization with respect to a product or large geographic area. At Kellogg, Keebler is responsible for all of the functions involved in developing, producing, and marketing in the snack food business. The president of Keebler reports to the president of Kellogg, North America, as shown in Figure 3.1. Similarly, Morningstar is responsible for developing products to compete in the organic and natural foods segment.

In this chapter, we first note how environmental factors, strategic choices, and technological factors can influence the design of an organization.[3] Then, we introduce and compare mechanistic and organic organizations and show how each type reflects a basic design decision. Strategic choice by top managers also influences the structure of the organization. Next, we describe the functional, place, product, and multidivisional bases of design and the requirements for their integration. Finally, we describe two emerging approaches to organization design: multinational and net-

FIGURE 3.1 Kellogg Company

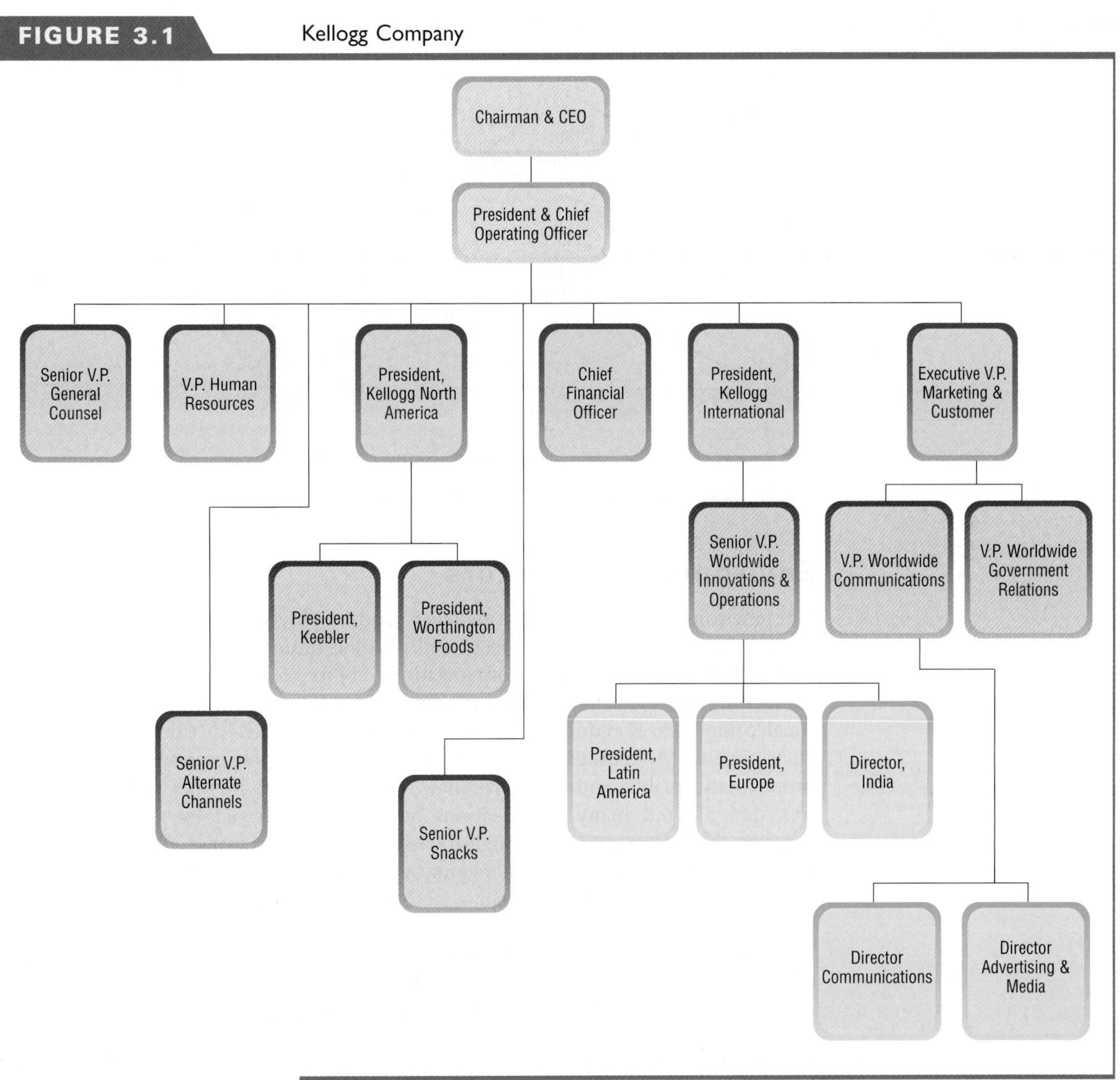

Source: www.hoovers.com, January, 2005.

work organizations. These designs are intended to overcome the limitations of the others in the face of complex, diverse, and changing environments, technologies, and business strategies.

KEY FACTORS IN ORGANIZATION DESIGN

LEARNING OBJECTIVE

1. Explain how environmental, strategic, and technological factors affect the design of organizations.

Every organization design decision (e.g., greater decentralization and empowerment of employees) solves one set of problems but creates others. By definition, the choice of organization design entails a set of trade-offs because every organization design has some drawbacks. The key is to select one that minimizes the drawbacks. Figure 3.2 identifies several variables for each of the three primary factors—environmental, strategic, and technological—that impact organization design decisions. Other factors (e.g., suppliers, customers, and new competitors) can also affect the design of an organization, but we have chosen these three as most important.

FIGURE 3.2 Key Factors in Organization Design

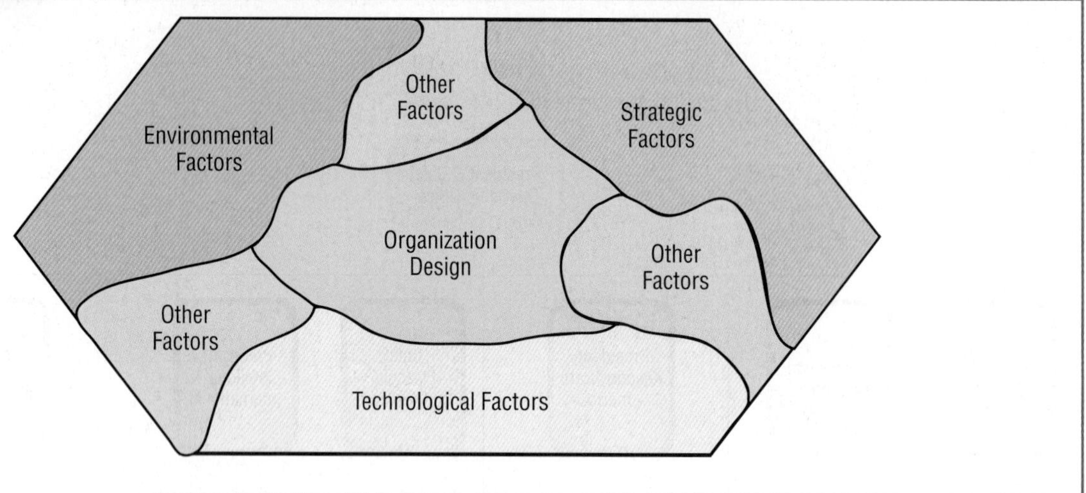

Environmental Factors

The environmental factors that managers and employees need to be aware of are (1) the characteristics of the present and possible future environments and (2) how those characteristics affect the organization's ability to function effectively. Hypercompetition in some industries, including consumer electronics, airlines, and personal computers, is requiring managers to adopt new ways of thinking about their environments. As markets become global and competition escalates, the quest for productivity, quality, and speed has spawned a remarkable number of new organization designs. Yet, many organizations have been frustrated by their inability to redesign themselves quickly enough to stay ahead of their rivals.

Perhaps the best way to understand the impact of the environment on organization design is to look at the various factors that comprise the environment. Every organization exists in an environment and, although specific environmental factors vary from industry to industry, a few broad ones exert an impact on the strategies of most organizations. We chose the four that we believe to be most important.[4] As shown in Figure 3.3, they are suppliers, distributors, competitors, and customers.

Suppliers. To obtain required materials, an organization must develop and manage relationships with its suppliers. Keebler's goal is to secure high-quality materials at reasonable prices. To accomplish this goal, it has established long-term contracts with many suppliers in which it agrees to purchase from them certain quantities of flour, sugar, and cheese. Similarly, McDonald's has a long-term contract with J. R. Simplot to supply it with potatoes. To supply McDonald's, Simplot has contracts with more than 1,000 potato growers throughout the world. Such long-term contracts ensure product uniformity, cost stability, and delivery reliability. Customers are drawn to familiar brands and expect reasonable cost and product consistency.

Distributors. An organization must establish channels of distribution that give it access to customers. Distributors are the various organizations that help other organizations deliver and sell its products. Kellogg does not typically distribute its products directly to the customer; instead, it delivers its products to grocery chain warehouses, which then fill store orders. In other businesses, store managers can develop personalized relationships with customers and devise ways to offer them good quality in both sales and service. Bill Heinecke bought the franchise rights for Pizza Hut in Thailand in 1980 for $5,000. At that time, pizza wasn't sold in Thailand, and cheese wasn't a popular part of a person's diet. Through aggressive adver-

FIGURE 3.3 Forces in an Organization's Environment

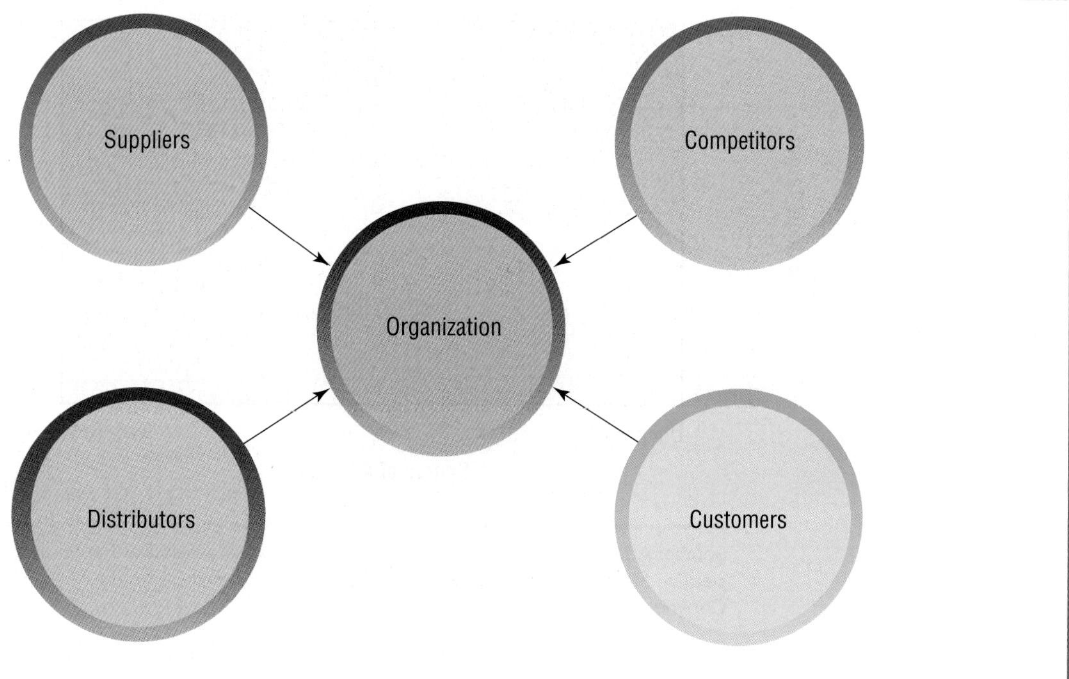

tising, he introduced Pizza Hut's fast-food restaurants in Thailand. Today, he has more than 114 restaurants, which have made him a multimillionaire.

Competitors. Competitors can also influence the design of an organization because they drive the organization to become more productive. As mentioned in the Preview Case, Kellogg faces stiff competition in all of its markets. For example, Ralcorp Holdings makes private-label cereal for Wal-Mart and Target and competes basically on price. General Mills competes on price and value. To compete at low cost requires organization designs that are simple and easy to manage. Cost savings must be gained at every step of the process, including labor, raw materials, acquisition of land, logistics, and human resources.

Customers. Relationships with customers are vital. Customers can easily evaluate the costs of various products and easily switch buying habits with minimal inconvenience. Kellogg tries to manage customer relationships in several ways. On a global level, the company engages in massive countrywide advertising campaigns to create product awareness in customers. As shown in Figure 3.1, Kellogg has created an international organization that focuses its attention on three areas: Latin America, Europe, and India. Managers in each of these three regions of the world are permitted to fine-tune their marketing campaigns and manufacturing and logistical operations to meet the competition in their particular region of the world.

Strategic Factors

Many strategic factors affect organization design decisions. We focus on one of the most popular frameworks of competitive strategies, which was developed by Michael Porter of Harvard University. According to Porter, organizations need to distinguish and position themselves differently from their competitors in order to build and sustain a competitive advantage.[5] Organizations have attempted to build competitive advantages in various ways, but three underlying strategies appear to be essential in doing so: low-cost, differentiation, and focused strategies, which are illustrated in Figure 3.4.

FIGURE 3.4 Strategies Model

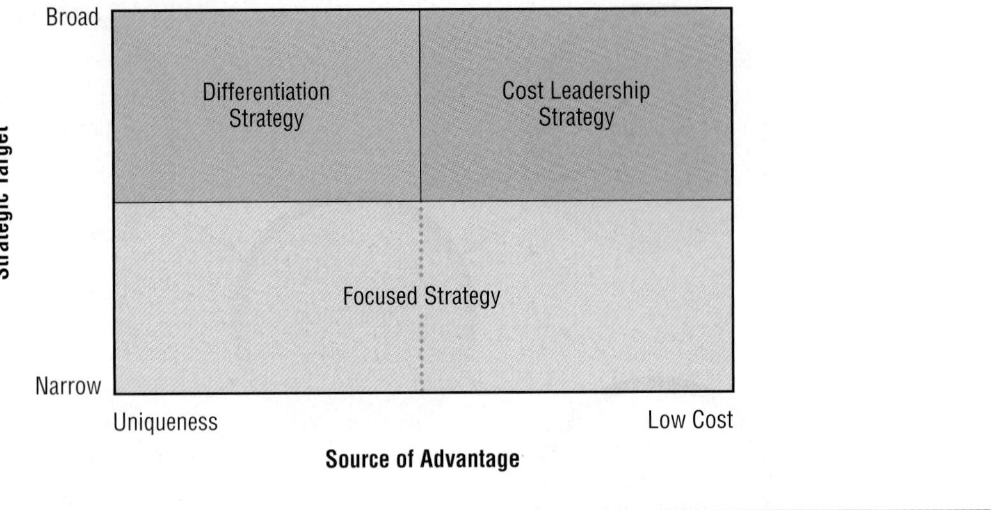

Source: Adapted with permission of The Free Press, a division of Simon and Schuster, from *Competitive Strategy: Techniques for Analyzing Industries and Competitors* (p. 39) by Michael E. Porter. Copyright © 1980 by The Free Press.

> **THE COMPETENT LEADER**
>
> We are now a very large company with a lot of capability to make strategic investments. We failed in Japan, but we're ready to do whatever it takes to be competitive in China. Our relationship with Each-Net in Shanghai now accounts for 70 percent of the total value of goods purchased by Chinese consumers.
>
> Meg Whitman, CEO, eBay

Low-Cost Strategy. A **low-cost strategy** *is based on an organization's ability to provide a product or service at a lower cost than its rivals.* An organization that chooses a low-cost strategy seeks to gain a significant cost advantage over other competitors and pass the savings on to consumers in order to gain market share. Such a strategy aims at selling a standardized product that appeals to an "average" customer in a broad market. The organization must attain significant economies of scale in key business activities (e.g., purchasing and logistics). Because the environment is stable, few product modifications are needed to satisfy customers. The organization's design is functional, with accountability and responsibility clearly assigned to various departments.

Organizations that have successfully used a low-cost strategy include Dollar General, BIC in ballpoint pens, and Wal-Mart in discount stores. The risks involved in following this strategy are (1) getting "locked in" to a technology and organization design that is expensive to change, (2) the ability of competitors to copy the strategy (e.g., Target copying Wal-Mart), or, most important, (3) management not paying attention to shifts in the environment (e.g., customer demand for different types of products and/or services and losing market share, as happened at Kmart).

The low-cost strategy is based on locating and taking advantage of opportunities for an organization to seek cost-based advantages in all of its activities. Dollar General consistently sells quality products to the low end of the market. Its stores are located in small towns and low-income urban areas. Dollar General got its name by offering a broad line of products that cost only one dollar. It carefully selects merchandise that customers can redeem with food stamps. To keep costs low, Dollar General does not take credit cards. The company uses sophisticated information technology at all of its stores to speed up the checkout process and to manage inventory. Recently it doubled the amount of space in the company's distribution centers, thereby reducing the number of runs their retail drivers need to make.

Differentiation Strategy. A **differentiation strategy** *is based on providing customers with something unique that makes the organization's product or service distinctive from its competition.* This is the strategy chosen by Kellogg. An organization that uses a differentiation strategy typically uses a product organization design whereby each product has its own manufacturing, marketing, and R&D departments. The key managerial assumption behind this strategy is that customers are willing to pay a higher price for a product that is distinctive in some way. Superior value is achieved through higher quality, technical superiority, or some special appeal. Toyota's strategy with Lexus is based on exceptional manufacturing quality, the use of genuine wood paneling, advanced sound systems, high engine performance, and comparatively high fuel economy (for luxury cars).

Other organizations that have successfully used a differentiation strategy include Procter & Gamble, American Express in credit cards, Nordstrom in department stores, and Krups in coffeemakers and espresso makers. The biggest disadvantage that these organizations face is maintaining a price premium as the product becomes more familiar to customers. Price is especially an issue when a product or service becomes mature. Organizations may also overdo product differentiation, which places a burden on their R&D departments, as well as a drain on their financial and human resources.

A firm that has succeeded in implementing the differentiation strategy is 7-Eleven. It didn't arrive at this strategy without problems. In the mid-1980s, it expanded rapidly into various businesses, including dairies, gasoline refining, and office rental space. It even constructed a 42-floor office tower in Dallas and leased office space to organizations in the Dallas area. Unfortunately, the recession of 1989–1990, the rise of numerous nontraditional competitors (e.g., Shell, Exxon/Mobil, and ChevronTexaco) in the convenience store industry, and the collapse of the Dallas real estate market brought the firm into bankruptcy. Ito-Yokado purchased the company in 1990 and immediately sold off all businesses not directly related to the convenience stores and adopted a low-cost business strategy. 7-Eleven has more than 5,700 stores in North America and more than 27,000 worldwide generating income of more than $12.1 billion in 2005. The following Change Competency feature illustrates some of the ways in which 7-Eleven uses time and quick responses to pursue a differentiation strategy.[6]

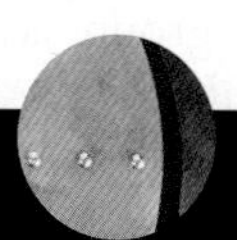

CHANGE COMPETENCY

7-ELEVEN

7-Eleven uses sophisticated computer systems to manage its operations. 7-Eleven uses advanced tracking technology that enables it to compete on the basis of fast inventory restocking. Each 7-Eleven store is equipped with a personal computer network that records every purchase made. These data are fed directly from the cash register into the store's computer. The information generated by each store enables the store manager to make such decisions about which items to add or drop, when to reorder, and what the proper inventory level for different items should be. This system permits fast reordering of products directly from suppliers such as Coca-Cola, PepsiCo, and Frito-Lay. It also enables the manufacturers to improve their forecasts of product demand.

To enhance its quick response strategy, 7-Eleven consolidated a number of its delivery operations for regional markets into combined distribution centers. For example, the distribution system in Lewisville, Texas, serves North Texas 7-Elevens. Dairies, commissaries, bakeries, and snack and drink suppliers ship their goods to this centralized site rather than to each store. 7-Eleven then delivers everything a store needs in one shipment each day. This system enables the company to offer a variety of fresh food, such as deli-style sandwiches and fresh fruit, two major growth product lines for 7-Eleven, and minimize distribution costs. For deli-style sandwiches that are made off-site, the turnaround time for freshness can be as little as 18 hours.

7-Eleven uses one advertising agency for its promotion and marketing. This exclusive contract eases the coordination, design, and implementation of nationwide advertising campaigns. Its ads reflect fair-value price, convenient, portable fresh food, and quality name brands.

7-Eleven locates its stores in high-traffic areas, such as strip shopping centers or busy street corners in large cities. The rental cost per square foot is considerably cheaper in these locations than in shopping malls. These locations also permit shoppers to drive or walk directly to the stores. And because these stores are smaller than the typical grocery store, shoppers have less difficulty locating merchandise and need to spend less time in the store (the typical shopper buys less than five items at a time). Most 7-Eleven stores are open 24 hours a day, spreading the cost of operating the stores over 24 hours. Finally, employees are paid slightly above the minimum wage. The turnover rate is 120 percent per year. Employees receive some training in how to use the systems that manage the stores, but this training period is short.

By the time the 2008 Olympic games are held in Beijing, China, 7-Eleven will have more than 500 stores in that city. To keep products affordable in Beijing, where the annual per capita income is less than US $1,100, 7-Eleven plans to use radio-frequency identification and electronic product codes that can accommodate large volumes of small purchases and improve order fulfillment operations. These technologies will allow each store to improve sales of in-demand products, discontinue stale or dated items, and maintain strict inventory control.

For more information on 7-Eleven, visit the organization's home page at ***http://www.7-eleven.com.***

Focused Strategy. A **focused strategy** *is designed to help an organization target a specific niche in an industry*, unlike both the low-cost and the differentiation strategies, which are designed to target industrywide markets. An organization that chooses a focused strategy may utilize any of a variety of organization designs, ranging from functional to product to network, to satisfy its customers' preferences. The choice of organization design reflects the niche of a particular buyer group, a regional market, or customers that have special tastes, preferences, or requirements. The basic idea is to specialize in ways that other organizations can't effectively match.

Organizations that have successfully used a focused strategy include Karsten Manufacturing, Southwest and JetBlue Airlines, and Chaparral Steel. Karsten Manufacturing has implemented its focused strategy by designing and producing a line of golf clubs under the Ping label. It was able to carve out a defensible niche in the hotly contested golf equipment business. Karsten uses ultrasophisticated manufacturing equipment and composite materials to make golf clubs almost on a customized basis. Southwest Airlines is among the most profitable airlines in the industry. It achieved its success by focusing on short-haul routes, flying into airports located close to or within cities, not serving meals, not transferring baggage, and offering no reserved seating.

The greatest disadvantage that an organization faces in using a focused strategy is the risk that its underlying market niche may gradually shift toward a broader market. Distinctive customer tastes may "blur" over time, thus reducing the defensibility of the niche. For example, when Calloway Golf introduced its own line of golf equipment, it targeted the same customers that Karsten had targeted. In an attempt to differentiate Ping from Calloway, Karsten introduced a broader line of clubs that would appeal to the wider golfing public, thus losing its distinctive niche in the marketplace. Another risk faced by firms pursuing a focused strategy is that of expanding its product offerings (e.g., Calloway Golf) or distribution channels (e.g., Krispy Kreme) too quickly. Krispy Kreme diluted its premium image by selling its doughnuts in gas stations, large supermarket chains, and even in Target stores. As a result, customers felt less desire to pay the high price of a Krispy Kreme doughnut after it had lost its special appeal.

Technological Factors

Technology *is a process by which an organization changes inputs into outputs.* Although there are literally hundreds of technologies, we focus on how technology in general influences the design of an organization. The coordination of teams and departments, the delegation of authority and responsibility, and the need for formal integrating mechanisms are all influenced by the degree to which units must communicate with each other to accomplish their goals. The way in which a firm communicates and shares information directly impacts how well it can design products customers want. In turn, this knowledge of customer needs is fed directly into the organization's information system, which ties together all functional activities that are needed to provide the product.

Task Interdependence. **Task interdependence** *refers to the extent to which work performed by one person or department affects what other members do.*[7] Three types of task interdependence have been identified—pooled, sequential, and reciprocal—and are shown in Figure 3.5.

FIGURE 3.5 Types of Task Interdependence in Organization Design

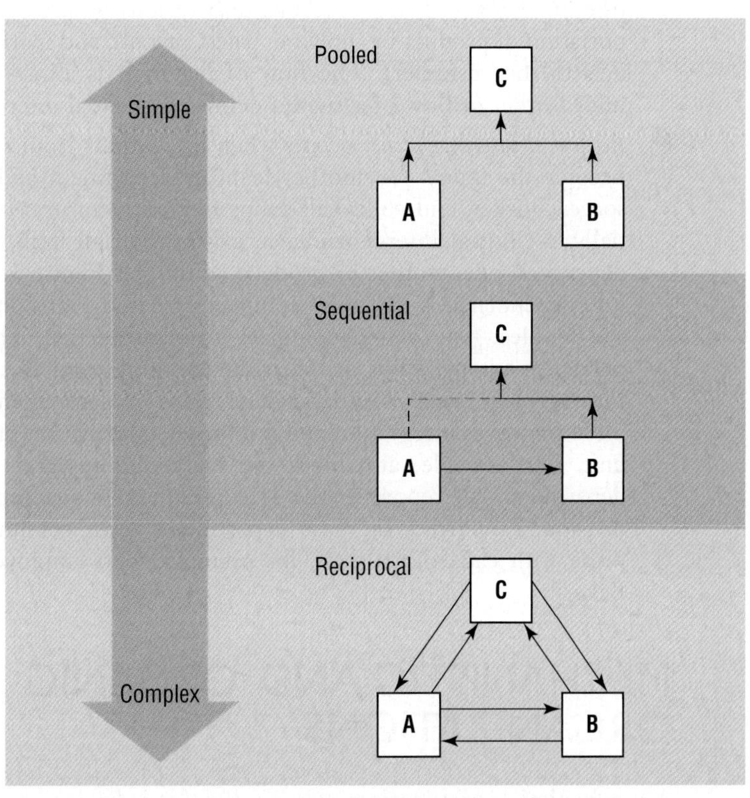

- *Pooled interdependence* occurs when departments or teams are relatively autonomous and make an identifiable contribution to the organization. For example, the many sales and services offices of Farmers Insurance don't engage in day-to-day decision making, coordination, and communication with each other. The local Farmers agents operate their offices without much interaction with other agents. Managers in regional offices coordinate, set policies, and solve problems for agents in their territories. The performance of each agent and regional office is readily identifiable. Pooled interdependence exists when the performance of one person has no direct impact on that of another. Golf and tennis teams rely on pooled interdependence. The scores of the players on each team are added at the end of the match to arrive at the team's total, even though the players on each team may not see or talk with their teammates during play.

  At Brinker International, each global division (such as Chili's, Romano's Macaroni Grill, Maggiano's Little Italy, Rockfish Seafood Grill, and Corner Bakery) is a profit center and responsible for its own casual-dining restaurants, R&D, human resources, and marketing. When a company, such as Brinker, uses a pooled technological interdependence, responsibility for coordinating products is in the hands of product managers. Product managers coordinate the activities of different functions to deliver what the customer wants.
- *Sequential interdependence* occurs when one team or department must complete certain tasks before one or more other teams or departments can perform their tasks. Football teams use sequential interdependence. When the offense is on the field, the defense is resting, waiting to return to the field. British Petroleum uses sequential interdependence to deliver gasoline and other products to a variety of consumers. This process starts with exploration (the search for crude oil and natural gas), production (drilling of wells for retrieval of gas and oil), supply (transport of the raw material via ship and/or pipeline to refineries), refining (the breakdown of hydrocarbons into various by-products), distribution (transportation of product by pipeline, truck, or rail), and marketing (the sale of products to the customer). The flow of materials is always the same. A predetermined order or flow of activities defines sequential interdependence.
- *Reciprocal interdependence* occurs when the outputs from one team or department become the inputs for another team or department and vice versa. Basketball, soccer, hockey, and volleyball teams rely on reciprocal interdependence. Essentially, reciprocal interdependence exists when all units within an organization depend on one another to produce an output. Figure 3.5 shows that reciprocal interdependence is the most complex type and that pooled interdependence is the simplest type of technological interdependence. The greater the interdependence among teams or departments, the greater the need for coordination. Placing reciprocally interdependent teams or departments under one executive often improves integration and minimizes information processing costs within a unit. For example, at Chili's, the marketing research, advertising, and sales departments all report to the vice president of marketing for that restaurant division. Employees in these departments must communicate and coordinate more with each other than, for example, with employees working at Corner Bakery.

LEARNING OBJECTIVE

2. State the differences between mechanistic and organic organizations.

MECHANISTIC AND ORGANIC ORGANIZATIONS

A **mechanistic organization** *is designed so that individuals and functions will behave in predictable ways.* A reliance on formal rules and regulations, centralization of decision making, narrowly defined job responsibilities, and a rigid hierarchy of authority characterize this organization.[8] The emphasis is on following procedures and rules. If you've ever worked at McDonald's, you probably know how highly standardized each step of the most basic operations must be. For example, boxes of fries are stored two inches from the wall and one inch apart. The operations are the same, whether in Tokyo or Dallas.

In contrast, an **organic organization** *is characterized by low to moderate use of formal rules and regulations, decentralized and shared decision making, broadly defined job responsibilities, and a flexible authority structure with fewer levels in the hierarchy.* The degree of job specialization is low; instead, a broad knowledge of many different jobs is required. Self-control is expected and there is an emphasis on reciprocal technological interdependence among employees. Recently, more organizations have started to move toward an organic management approach to promote managerial efficiency and to improve employee satisfaction. Many employees heavily involved in R&D at Adobe Systems, Electronic Arts, and Hewlett-Packard, among others, are likely to enjoy decision-making autonomy.

Top management typically makes decisions that determine the extent to which an organization will operate mechanistically or organically. At Brinker International, the five groups of causal-dining restaurants operate throughout the world with relative autonomy (pooled interdependence). At YUM Brands, until top management decided to merge some of these operations (e.g., KFC, Pizza Hut, Taco Bell) into one at major self-service gas stations in the United States, each brand operated independently. The move to have several restaurants operating out of one location created the need for more coordination of operations between these brands.

A mechanistic organization is essentially a bureaucracy. Max Weber, a German sociologist and economist in the early 1900s, defined a bureaucracy as an organization having the following characteristics:

- The organization operates according to a body of rules or laws that are intended to tightly control the behavior of employees.
- All employees must carefully follow extensive impersonal rules and procedures in making decisions.
- Each employee's job involves a specified area of expertise, with strictly defined obligations, authority, and powers to compel obedience.
- The organization follows the principle of hierarchy; that is, each lower position is under the tight control and direction of a higher one.
- Candidates for jobs are selected on the basis of "technical" qualifications. They are appointed, not elected.
- The organization has a career ladder. Promotion is by seniority or achievement and depends on the judgment of superiors. [9]

A **bureaucracy** *is a system of rules and regulations designed to enhance an organization's efficiency*. The word *bureaucracy* often brings to mind rigidity, incompetence, red tape, inefficiency, and ridiculous rules. In principle, though, the basic characteristics of a mechanistic system may make a bureaucratic organization design feasible or even desirable in some situations. Any discussion of a mechanistic organization must distinguish between the way it should ideally function and the way some large-scale organizations actually operate.

The degrees to which organizations emphasize a mechanistic or an organic system can vary substantially, as suggested in Figure 3.6. Radio Shack and Target have relatively mechanistic organizations in terms of the selected dimensions. They are represented by organization B. Electronic Arts, Deloitte Consulting, and SAS, a software design/integration firm in North Carolina, place more emphasis on the dimensions that represent an organic system. They are represented by organization A. The organic system emphasizes employee competence, rather than the employee's formal position in the hierarchy, as a basis for rewards, including promotion. This type of organization has a flexible hierarchy and empowers employees to make decisions.

FIGURE 3.6 Organic and Mechanistic Design Features

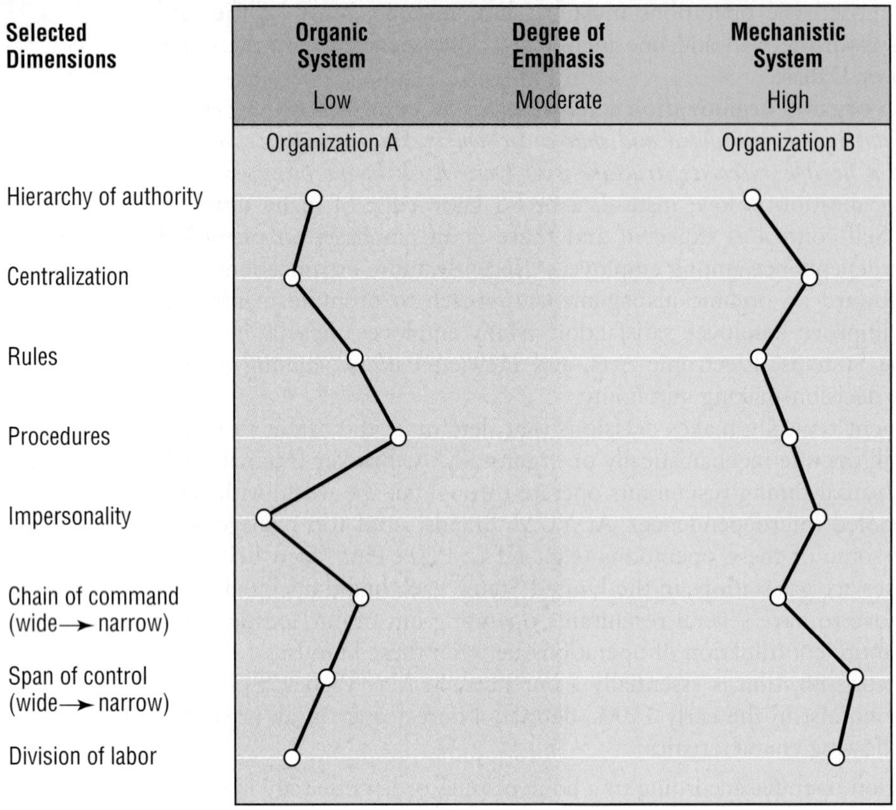

Selected Dimensions	Organic System	Degree of Emphasis	Mechanistic System
	Low	Moderate	High
	Organization A		Organization B
Hierarchy of authority			
Centralization			
Rules			
Procedures			
Impersonality			
Chain of command (wide→narrow)			
Span of control (wide→narrow)			
Division of labor			

Hierarchy of Authority

Hierarchy of authority *indicates who reports to whom.* For example, the Kellogg organization chart (see Figure 3.1) shows that the chief financial officer reports to the president and chief operating officer. In a mechanistic system, higher level departments set or approve goals and detailed budgets for lower level departments and issue directives to them. A mechanistic organization has as many levels in its hierarchy as necessary to achieve tight control. An organic organization has few levels in its hierarchy, which makes coordination and communication easier and fosters innovation.

The hierarchy of authority is closely related to centralization. **Centralization** *means that all major, and oftentimes many minor, decisions are made only at the top levels of the organization.* Centralization is common in mechanistic organizations, whereas decentralization and shared decision making between and across levels are common in organic organizations. At Jiffy Lube, Wendy's, and Pier 1 Imports, top executives make nearly all decisions affecting store operations, including hours of operation, dress codes for employees, starting salaries, advertising, location, and the like. Rules and regulations are sent from headquarters to each store, and detailed reports (e.g., sales and employee attendance) from the stores are sent up the hierarchy.

Division of Labor

Division of labor *refers to the various ways of dividing up tasks and labor to achieve goals.* A mechanistic organization typically has a high division of labor. In theory, the fewer tasks a person performs, the better he may be expected to perform them.

However, a continued increase in the division of labor may eventually become counterproductive. Employees who perform only very routine and simple jobs that require few skills may become bored and frustrated. The results may be low quality and productivity, high turnover, and high absenteeism. This situation developed in numerous U.S. industries (e.g., automobile, consumer electronics, and steel). Excessive division of labor was compounded by rigid union work rules, which eventually compromised these companies' ability to respond to new technologies and customer needs. In addition, the managerial costs (volume of reports, more managers, and more controls to administer) of integrating highly specialized functions usually are high. Many companies in the fast-food industry, including McDonald's, Wendy's, and Burger King, report that employee turnover exceeds 150 percent a year. To cope with such high turnover, most processes are automated and can be quickly learned.

In contrast, the organic organization tends to reduce the costs of high turnover by delegating decision making to lower levels. Delegation encourages employees and teams to take responsibility for achieving their tasks and linking them to those of others in the organization. The organic organization takes advantage of the benefits from the division of labor, but it is sensitive to the negative results of carrying the division of labor too far.

Rules and Procedures

Rules *are formal statements specifying acceptable and unacceptable behaviors and decisions by employees.* One of the paradoxes of rules that attempt to reduce individual autonomy is that someone must still decide which rules apply to specific situations. Rules are an integral part of both mechanistic and organic organizations. In a mechanistic organization, the tendency is to create detailed, uniform rules to cover tasks and decisions whenever possible. United Parcel Service (UPS) has rules that cover all aspects of delivering a package to a customer, including which arm to carry the clipboard under (right arm) for the person to sign and which arm to carry the package with (left arm). In a mechanistic organization, the tendency is to accept the need for extensive rules and to formulate new rules in response to new situations. In an organic system, the tendency is to create rules only when necessary (e.g., safety rules to protect life and property).

Procedures *are preset sequences of steps that managers and employees must follow in performing tasks and dealing with problems.* Procedures often comprise rules that are to be used in a particular sequence. For example, to obtain reimbursement for travel expenses in most organizations, employees must follow specific reporting procedures, including submission of receipts. Procedures have many of the same positive and negative features that characterize rules, and they often proliferate in a mechanistic organization. Managers in organic systems usually know that rules and procedures can make the organization too rigid and thus dampen employee motivation, stymie innovation, and inhibit creativity. Employee input is likely to be sought on changes in current rules and procedures or on proposed rules and procedures when they are absolutely necessary. Employees at all levels are expected to question, evaluate, and make suggestions about such proposals, with an emphasis on collaboration and communication. In a mechanistic system, rules and procedures tend to be developed at the top and issued via memoranda. Such memos may convey the expectation of strict compliance and the adverse consequences of not complying.

Impersonality

Impersonality *is the extent to which organizations treat their employees, customers, and others according to objective, detached, and rigid characteristics.* Managers in a highly mechanistic organization are likely to emphasize matter-of-fact indicators (college degrees, certificates earned, test scores, training programs completed, length of service, and the like) when making hiring, salary, and promotion decisions. Although managers may consider these factors in an organic organization, the emphasis is likely to be on the actual achievements and professional judgments of individuals rather than on rigid quantitative indicators.

Deloitte Consulting is a leading business consulting company that operates as an organic organization. A college graduate applying for a job at Deloitte Consulting goes through an extensive interview process. It may involve several managers, many (if not all) of the employees with whom the applicant would work, and even a casual and informal "interview" by a team of employees. The person responsible for filling the open position solicits opinions and reactions from these employees before making a decision. In most instances, the manager calls a meeting of the employees and other managers who participated in the interview process to discuss a candidate.

Chain of Command

Early writers on organization design stressed two basic ideas about who reports to whom and who has what authority and responsibility.[10] First, the **chain of command** *refers to the hierarchical arrangement of authority and responsibility.* They flow in a clear, unbroken vertical line from the highest executive to the lowest employee. Clarity of direction is the basis for the chain. Second, the **unity of command** *holds that no subordinate should receive direction from more than one superior.* Although some organizations don't rigidly follow unity of command in their designs, overlapping lines of authority and responsibility can make managing a more difficult task than it should be. Without unity of command, who may direct whom to do what becomes cloudy and confusing. Kellogg's president of Latin America has the authority to make decisions about advertising and marketing. Presidents in Latin America and Europe and the director of India report to the president of Kellogg International. Issues surrounding chain of command and unity of control must be addressed in all organization designs.

Span of Control

Span of control *reflects the number of employees reporting directly to one manager.* When the span of control is broad, relatively few levels exist between the top and bottom of the organization, as in many R&D labs. At Kellogg, the president and chief operating officer has a span of control of eight (see Figure 3.1). Conversely, in a military unit, the span of control is narrow because officers and noncommissioned officers need tight control over subordinates in order to get them to respond quickly and precisely. Although there is no "correct" number of subordinates that a manager can supervise effectively, the competencies of both the manager and employees, the similarity of tasks being supervised, and the extent of rules and operating standards all influence a manager's span of control.

In tomorrow's global environment many firms will find that, in order to stay competitive, they must change how they manage. Management blunders by AT&T, Eastman Kodak, and Ford Motor Company have occurred because of their inability to adapt to the speed and turbulence of a changing environment. In some cases, even after massive high-tech investments, management is only beginning to make the organizational changes needed to transform their organizations.

When managers arrive in Latin America from the United States, they instantly notice that they have crossed more than an international border. The forces that drive business success in the United States are different from those in Latin America because of the differences in values, traditions, and expectations; that is, cultural differences. As we have pointed out in various sections of this book, culture colors the way managers view their world. Using the organization design concepts we have presented, the following Across Cultures Competency highlights some of the organizational design differences between a traditional Latin American and U.S. organization.[11]

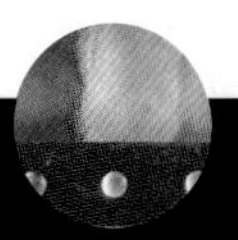

ACROSS CULTURES COMPETENCY

LATIN AMERICAN VERSUS U.S. MANAGEMENT PRACTICES

In Chapter 1, we presented a framework for thinking about how a country's culture affects employee behavior. In this Across Cultures Competency, we examine how three cultural dimensions impact the design of organizations. Recall that *power inequality* refers to the degree to which less-powerful individuals in a society accept that power should be distributed unequally. In Latin America, employees accept power inequality, whereas in the United States, employees believe in meritocracy. Therefore, American employees expect to be consulted about how to perform their jobs, participative management practices are widely accepted, and flat (organic) rather than tall (mechanistic) hierarchies are common.

Uncertainty avoidance describes the degree to which unclear situations create discomfort for individuals. American managers are more likely to be open to new ideas. Efforts to try new methods are often stifled in Latin America because employees set high priority on career stability and are protected by rigid rules and seniority. There is a greater emphasis on retaining their present position than being promoted to a higher position. American managers often view procedures and policies as guidelines, whereas Latin American managers would view those same procedures as absolute and sacrosanct.

Finally, the *individual-collective* dimension refers to the degree to which a culture promotes the role of the individual over the role of the group. As members of the most individualistic culture, American managers tend not to be very loyal to their employers or coworkers and involve fewer people in making decisions than their Latin American counterparts. The tendency to make quick decisions and respond to changing situations has been important for American managers' drive for creativity. In Latin America, social relationships are very important. The need for harmony, the ability to get along with coworkers, and hiring employees based on their connections is important in Latin America. In Latin America, the employer–employee model is based on mutual moral obligations.

Table 3.1 summarizes how these different cultural dimensions can impact management practices in the Americas. We caution you that the risk of overgeneralizing is great when you try to compress a large body of knowledge into one table. Nevertheless, the table gives you trends that you should be aware of if you manage employees who come from a different culture than yours.

TABLE 3.1 Latin American Versus U.S. Management Practices

Management Practice	Latin America	United States
Purpose of hierarchy	To define authority	To define problems and key relationships
Organization chart	Reflects power relationships of key family members	Reflects flow of information
Position in hierarchy	Shows unequal abilities	Shows unequal roles
Responsibility	Employees expect close paternalistic supervisors	Employees look after themselves

Planning process	Short term; impulsive; unstructured deductive	Long term; formal; deliberate; inductive
Decision making	Centralized or top down	Delegated to the lowest level; participative
Hiring criteria	Family or personal ties	Proven performance

Source: Adapted from Becker, T. H. *Doing Business in the New Latin America.* Westport, CT: Praeger, 2004, 135–136.

LEARNING OBJECTIVE

3. Describe four traditional organization designs: functional, place, product, and multidivisional.

TRADITIONAL ORGANIZATION DESIGNS

Now that we have examined the various factors that affect managers' choices of an organization design, let's consider some of the design choices available. As we discuss them, we refer to the factors that influence a particular choice of design.

Organizational Design Options

Figure 3.7 illustrates six commonly used approaches to organization design. These approaches, and the conditions under which they are most likely to be effective, are contrasted in terms of the key factors in organization design. Environmental forces comprise a continuum on the vertical axis, ranging from few to many. Technological interdependence comprises a continuum on the horizontal axis, ranging from pooled to reciprocal. At one end of the continuum is a cluster of choices that reflect uniformity in customers, technologies, and geographic markets, represented by firms such as Avis Rent-a-Car, Allstate Insurance Company, and Motel 6. At the other end of the continuum are organization design choices that reflect diversity in customers, technologies, and geographic markets, represented by firms such as Procter & Gamble, DuPont, and General Electric.

FIGURE 3.7 Organization Design Options

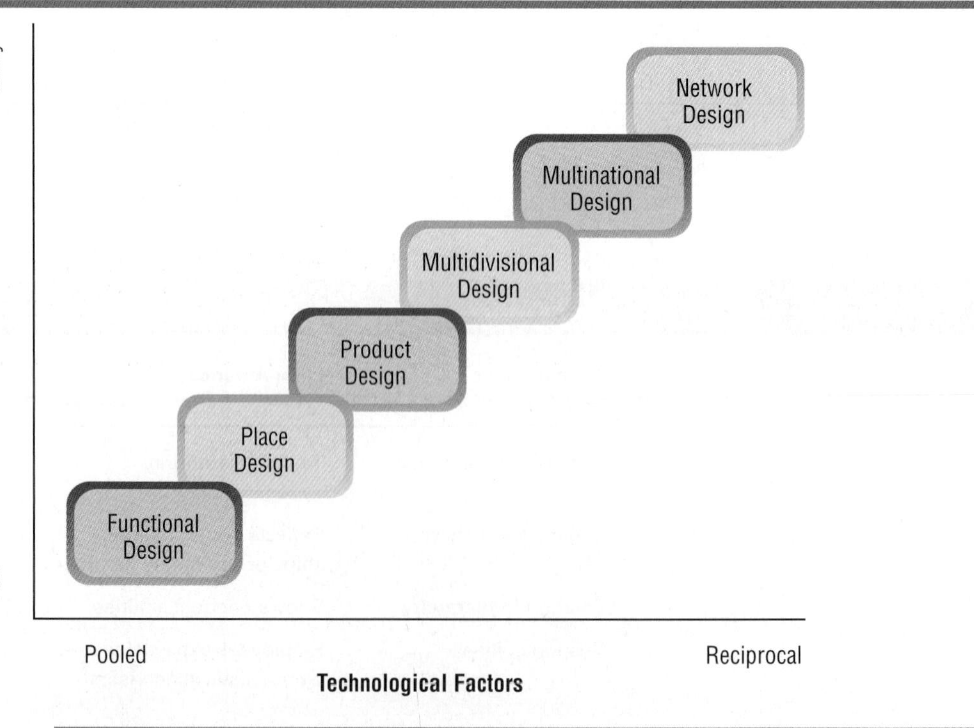

The comparative framework broadly portrays how the design of an organization may differ and change as a result of various patterns of environmental and technological factors. The simplest environment (lower left) implies that some version of the functional organization design is likely to be appropriate. The most complex environment (upper right) implies that a network organization design is likely to be appropriate. In general, designs become more complex as an organization moves from a functional design to a network design. Moreover, the designs require more coordination among people and activities as they become increasingly complex.

Functional Design

Functional design *involves the creation of positions, teams, and departments on the basis of specialized activities.* Functional grouping of employees is the most widely used and accepted form of departmentalization. Although the functions vary widely, depending on the organization (e.g., Christ United Methodist Church does not have a production department, nor does Wells Fargo Bank), grouping tasks and employees by function can be both efficient and economical.

Key Features. Departments of a typical manufacturing firm with a single product line often are grouped by function: engineering, human resource, manufacturing, shipping, purchasing, sales, and finance. Tasks also are usually divided functionally by the process used: receiving, stamping, plating, assembly, painting, and inspection (sequential interdependence). Figure 3.8 shows how Carmike Cinemas, Inc., uses this organization design. Carmike has more than 2,000 movie theaters located in midsized communities in 35 states.[12] A common theme of functional design is the desirability of standardizing repetitive tasks and automating them whenever possible. This approach helps reduce errors and lowers costs. Management then concentrates on exceptions to eliminate gaps or overlaps.

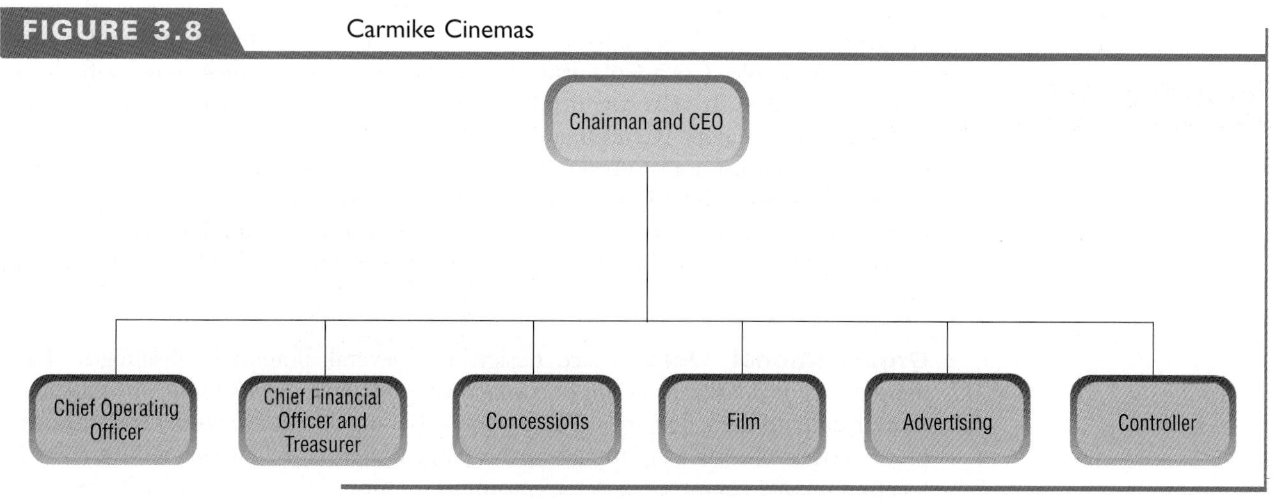

Source: www.hoovers.com, January, 2005.

Organizational Uses. A functional design has both advantages and disadvantages. On the positive side, it permits clear identification and assignment of responsibilities, and employees easily understand it. People doing similar tasks and facing similar problems work together in a functional design. This increases the opportunities for communication and mutual support. A disadvantage is that a functional design fosters a limited point of view that focuses on a narrow set of tasks. Employees tend to lose sight of the organization as a whole. Coordination across functional departments often becomes difficult as the organization increases the number of

THE COMPETENT LEADER

Knowing when to use each design may be a greater source of competitive advantage than knowing how to flawlessly execute them.
Andrew Kohlberg, President, Kisco Senior Living

geographic areas served and the range of goods or services provided. With the exception of marketing, most employees in a functionally designed organization have no direct contact with customers and often lose touch with the need to meet or exceed customer expectations.

A functional design may be effective when an organization has a narrow product line, competes in a uniform environment, pursues a low-cost or focused business strategy, and doesn't have to respond to the pressures of serving different types of customers. The addition of staff departments, such as legal or quality assurance, to a functional design may enable an organization to deal effectively with changes in the organization's environment. As shown earlier in Figure 3.7, functional design is the most elementary type of organization design and often represents a base from which other types of designs evolve.

Place Design

Place design *involves establishing an organization's primary units geographically while retaining significant aspects of functional design.* All functional groups for one geographic area are in one location. State Farm Insurance Company uses a place design. The regions are managed by regional vice presidents who are accountable for the operations and profitability of agents in their areas. Many companies that are marketing intensive and need to respond to local market conditions or customer needs typically use place designs.

Key Features. Many of the functions required to serve a geographic territory are placed under one manager, rather than assigning different functions to different managers or consolidating many of the functions in a central office. Many international firms use place design to address cultural and legal differences in various countries and the lack of uniformity among customers in different geographic markets. For example, Coca-Cola Enterprise, Inc., bottles and distributes soft drinks around the world. It sells soft drinks in 46 states, Canada, and Europe. It is organized into four regions (Central and North America, Eastern North America, Western North America, and Europe). North America accounts for about 75 percent of Coca-Cola sales, while Europe accounts for the rest. The place design enables Coca-Cola to sell products that fit customers' tastes. For example, Coca-Cola sells Appletise, Buxton, and Five-Alive, among 15 other types of drinks, in Europe, but not in the United States.[13]

Organizational Uses. Place design has several potential advantages. Each department or division is in direct contact with customers in its locale and can adapt more readily to their demands. Fast response is a major asset for organizations using place designs. Another advantage of the place design is that it can reduce costs by locating unique resources closer to customers. Coca-Cola learned that it was much cheaper to build bottling plants in Belgium than to bottle Coke in England and then ship it across the English Channel. For Celanese Chemical Corporation, opening a new plant in Singapore to serve the growing demand for its products in the Far East saved it millions of dollars in shipping costs (from the United States).[14] For marketing, locating near customers might mean lower costs and/or better service. Salespeople can spend more time selling and less time traveling. Being closer to the customer may help them pinpoint the marketing tactic most likely to succeed in that particular region.

Organizing by place clearly increases control and coordination problems because of duplication of functions. If regions have their own marketing, human resources, manufacturing, and distribution policies, management may have difficulty achieving coordination. It can be especially difficult and costly to coordinate departments that are thousands of miles apart and whose managers have limited contact with each other. Further, regional and district managers may want to control their own internal activities to satisfy local customers. Employees may begin to emphasize their own geographically based unit's goals and needs more than those of the organization as a whole. To help ensure uniformity and coordination, organizations such as the IRS, Sheraton Hotels, and the U.S. Postal Service make extensive use of rules that apply in all locations.

Product Design

Product design *involves the establishment of self-contained units, each capable of developing, producing, marketing, and distributing its own goods or services.* The Preview Case related how Kellogg used this type of design to manage its product lines (Keebler, Worthington Foods, Kellogg's). Figure 3.9 shows the product organizational structure of United Technologies, an organization that provides high-tech products to the aerospace, building systems, and automotive industries throughout the world.

FIGURE 3.9 United Technologies

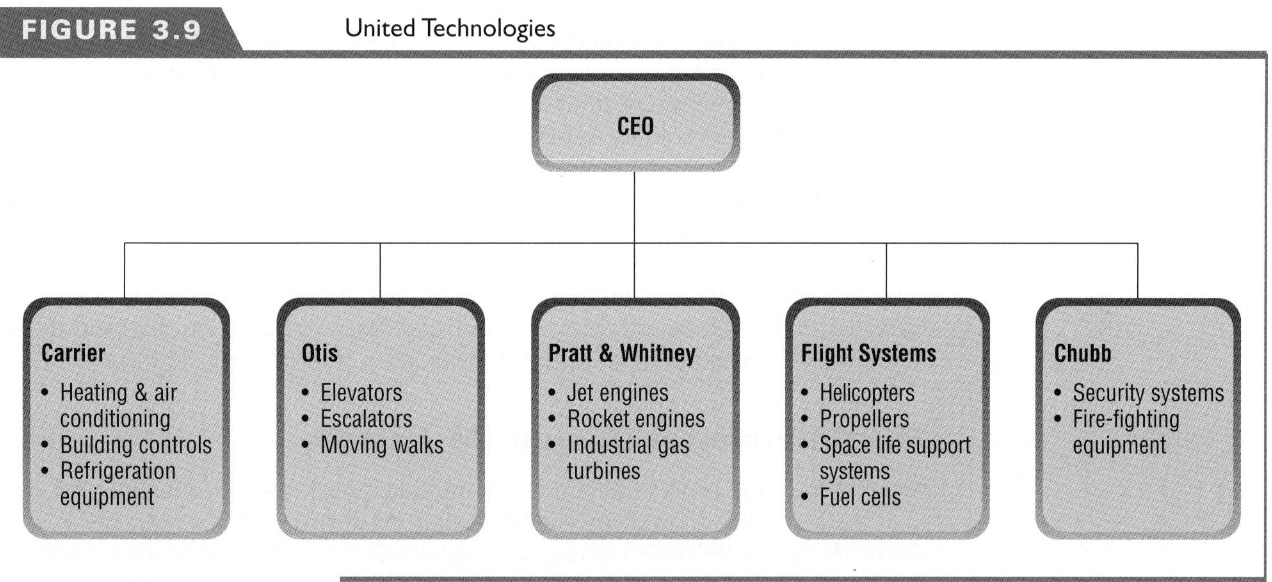

Source: www.hoovers.com, January, 2005.

Key Features. Elisha Graves Otis, who invented the elevator in 1853, provided the foundation for what today is United Technologies.[15] Throughout its existence, various companies having widely different product lines, as illustrated in Figure 3.9, have been added and deleted. Today, United Technologies is a $30 billion company organized around five distinct product lines. Note that, although these five product lines are all involved in technology, there is little overlap among them in terms of customers, distribution channels, and technology. That is, customers such as Boeing buy Pratt & Whitney jet engines but do no business with Chubb. Each product line faces a different set of competitors and has crafted its business strategy to compete in its particular business environment. Pratt & Whitney has developed a *focused business strategy* to compete in its market. For its Flight Systems product line, customers for its Sikorsky helicopters include the major oil companies, which use helicopters to shuttle crews to and from offshore oil platforms; hospitals, which use them to move accident victims and the critically ill to their facilities; and the armed forces of the United States, which use them for troop movement. Managers handling this product line have little need to communicate with those manufacturing elevators as part of the Otis product line.

Organizational Uses. Most organizations that produce multiple goods or services, such as GE, United Technologies, and Boeing, utilize a product design. Such a design reduces the information overload that managers face in a purely functional organization design. Under that type of design, the vice president of marketing at United Technologies would have to be able to market a wide variety of products, understand the competitive forces in many industries, and focus on crafting a business strategy to compete in each industry. When the diversity of goods or services and types of customers reaches a certain point, the creation of multiple marketing vice presidents (one vice president for each product line) to handle the complexity of the business can be the most effective approach. Each division is then evaluated on its own performance. At United Technologies, Carrier contributed 29 percent of the total revenues generated, Otis 25 percent, Pratt and Whitney 24 percent, Flight System 18 percent, and Chubb 4 percent.

Organizations with a product design usually begin with a functional design and then add some place design features as they begin to serve new geographic markets. Eventually, serving multiple customers creates management problems that can't be effectively dealt with by a functional or place design alone. The addition of new product lines, diverse customers, and technological advances also increases the complexity and uncertainty of the organization's business environment.[16] Recently United Technologies sold its Automotive Division and acquired the Chubb group, a London-based security group. Chubb then acquired Kidde PLC, a manufacturer of fire-fighting equipment in the United Kingdom. When changing to a product design, however, companies usually don't completely discard functional or place designs. Instead, the product design may incorporate features of functional and place designs into the organization of each product division. For example, Otis Elevator has functional departments of advertising, finance, manufacturing, and distribution at each of its international plant locations in Russia, Japan, and Korea.

Multidivisional Design (M-Form)

A variation of the product design is the multidivisional design, sometimes referred to as the M-form.[17] In **multidivisional design (M-form),** *tasks are organized by division on the basis of the product or geographic markets in which the goods or services are sold.* Divisional managers are primarily responsible for day-to-day operating decisions within their units. Freed from these day-to-day operating responsibilities, top-level corporate managers can concentrate on strategic issues, such as allocating resources to the various divisions, assessing new businesses to acquire and divisions to sell off, and communicating with shareholders and others. These top-level managers often are supported by elaborate accounting and control systems and specialized staff. Top-level corporate management may also delegate to product divisions the authority to develop their own strategic plans.

Key Features. A multidivisional design eases problems of coordination by focusing expertise and knowledge on specific goods or services. A department or division thoroughly familiar with a product line and its set of customers can best handle that line. Such a design clearly meets the needs of a company such as Kellogg, which provides diverse products to diverse customers in geographic locations throughout the world.

One disadvantage of the multidivisional design is that a firm must have a large number of managerial personnel to oversee all the product lines. Another disadvantage is the higher cost that results from the duplication of various functions by the divisions. Again refer to Kellogg's organization chart in Figure 3.1.

Organizational Uses. Adoption of a multidivisional design often reduces the environmental complexity facing any one team, department, or division. Employees in a product-based unit can focus on one product line, rather than be overextended across multiple product lines. As with a functional design, an organization with a multidivisional design can deal with complex environments by adding horizontal mechanisms, such as linking roles, task forces, integrating roles, and cross-functional teams.

CONTEMPORARY ORGANIZATION DESIGNS

LEARNING OBJECTIVE

4. Describe two contemporary organization designs: multinational and network.

For organizations to function effectively, their designs must not be static; designs have to change to reflect new environmental challenges, threats, and opportunities. The best design for an organization depends on the nature of the environment, the strategy chosen by top managers, and the degree of technological interdependence needed by various parts of the organization. During the past decade, several new forms of organization design have been introduced and used by organizations. In particular, two types of organization design—multinational and network—have emerged in response to certain deficiencies in traditional organization designs and to rapid changes in the environment.[18]

Multinational Design

A **multinational design** *attempts to maintain coordination among products, functions, and geographic areas.*[19] Meeting the need for this extensive three-way cooperation is especially difficult because operating divisions are separated by distance and time. A further complication is that managers often are separated by culture and language. A "perfect" balance, if such were possible, requires a complex design. Hence, most multinational designs focus on the relative emphases that should be given to place and product design options.

Large multibusiness firms, such as Unilever, Nestle, and British Petroleum, operate in various countries, each of which has its own set of customers, governmental officials, and the like. On the one hand, local managers face pressures to be "local insiders"; that is, to design organizations that follow rules and regulations accepted as legitimate by locals. On the other hand, managers face pressures to be "company insiders"; that is, to design organizations that minimize coordination problems with company units in other countries, manage a diverse set of customers, and adhere to rules and regulations viewed as appropriate by the company. The problem of operating companies in many countries presents enormous challenges for managers.

Key Features. **Multinational organizations** *produce and sell products and/or services in two or more countries.* A company can be global without necessarily being multinational. Boeing, for example, produces planes in the United States only, but it works with a worldwide network of suppliers and subcontractors and sells planes all over the world. Companies can become multinational by setting up their own subsidiaries in other countries, by establishing joint ventures in other countries with local partners, or by acquiring companies in other countries. IBM, for example, has built up its worldwide network of subsidiaries by setting up wholly owned companies in a large number of countries. To become fully established in the U.S. auto market, Toyota entered into a joint venture with General Motors in California and then set up a wholly owned subsidiary three years later in the United States. It now produces cars and trucks at several U.S. locations.

Organizational Uses. The forces generating global integration in many industries include (1) the growing presence and importance of global competitors and customers, (2) the global rise in market demand for products, (3) new information technologies, and (4) efficient factories that can manufacture goods for customers throughout the world.[20] Worldwide product divisions in firms dealing with such forces are likely to dominate decisions, overpowering the interests of geographically based divisions. Pressures from national governments and local markets also may be strong, often requiring multinational corporations to market full product lines in all the principal countries they serve. Marketing opportunities, however, may not be open to companies unless they negotiate terms with host governments. Therefore, a worldwide product-line division may not be as effective at opening new markets as a geographically organized division because, under the latter type of organization, local managers can respond more effectively to local governments' concerns. A division operating under a place design often can establish relations with host governments, invest in distribution channels, develop brand recognition, and build competencies that no single product-line division could afford. Thus, valid reasons still exist for country or regional (Europe, North America, Latin America, Central Asia, the Pacific Rim, and the Middle East) organization.

The following Communication Competency feature illustrates how Electrolux uses a multinational design that emphasizes global operations. It also reveals some of the tensions inherent in multinational design when top management tries to balance place, function, and product-line considerations. Since the 1970s, Electrolux has acquired more than 40 different companies throughout Europe and has become the world's largest producer of household appliances.[21]

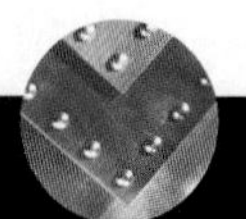

COMMUNICATION COMPETENCY

ELECTROLUX

Until the 1970s, the appliance industry in Europe had been segmented by national markets: Differences in customer tastes and income levels, distribution channels, high transportation costs, and governmental regulations and tariffs all played a part in ensuring that local markets were served by local producers. By the late 1970s, several European countries had formed the Common Market and the appliance industry started to go multinational. In response, Electrolux decided to redesign itself to become a multinational corporation, which required several significant changes.

First, the company needed to centralize its planning process so that products could be produced and introduced in several countries simultaneously. Local plants needed to be coordinated and share resources to achieve a common goal. Second, integration of management philosophy was needed. For example, when Electrolux acquired Zanussi, an Italian appliance maker, it needed to change Zanussi's hierarchical top-down mechanistic system to be more consistent with Electrolux's team-based, organic system. At Electrolux, managers were known by their first names throughout the organization, whereas at Zanussi, managers were addressed by their titles. Third, inefficiencies were rampant. Because of tailor-made specifications for different markets (e.g., Spain, Italy, and France), product development centers in Europe weren't being used efficiently. At one point, these centers were producing hundreds of different motors for vacuum cleaners and refrigerators, even though market research had revealed that the firm needed fewer than 10. Plant utilization was quite low, employment levels were high, and output per employee was unacceptably low. Similarly, Zanussi had too many staff people in relation to its production workers, and staff reductions were needed.

To gain some efficiency from being a multinational corporation, Electrolux tried to match staffing requirements with sales and limited the number of motors it was going to market worldwide. Standardizing motors allowed Electrolux to develop a global product strategy, letting it change certain features for local market tastes but retaining a product's essential features. For example, when Electrolux introduced its new "Jet-System" washing machine that allowed people to use less detergent and reduced water consumption by one-third, it was able to introduce that product throughout Europe. Because nearly 70 percent of the company's production costs are in raw materials and components from external suppliers, Electrolux began to negotiate rates with a few suppliers for all product lines, thus achieving considerable standardization and lowering costs by 17 percent. It also required all suppliers to make a commitment to quality and to use just-in-time (JIT) delivery systems for inventory. Currently, Electrolux organizes its businesses around product lines. These product lines (e.g., vacuum cleaners) have common distribution channels, technologies, customers, competitors, and geographic markets. Managers are responsible for all functions, including manufacturing, advertising, and sales, for their product lines.

For more information on Electrolux, visit the organization's home page at ***http://www.electrolux.com.***

Network Design

A **network design** *subcontracts some or many of its operations to other firms and coordinates them to accomplish specific goals.*[22] Sometimes it is also called a *virtual organization;* managers need to coordinate and link up people (from many organizations) to perform activities in many locations. Contacts and working relationships in the network are facilitated by electronic means, as well as through face-to-face meetings. The use of computer-based technologies permits managers to coordinate suppliers, designers, manufacturers, distributors, and others on an instantaneous, real-time basis. Often, managers in a network design will work as closely with their suppliers and customers as they do with their own employees.

Key Features. All organizations seek to combine the stability and efficiency of their existing designs with a capability for fast response to competitors. However, relying on functional, product, or geographical designs to attain such a balance is very difficult. To meet the dual needs of high efficiency and fast response, many organizations are becoming much more focused and specialized in what they will do in-house. As a result, some activities that used to be performed within the organization are now being given to other firms. Recently, a number of organizations have started to rely on a network design.

Organizations that have used this type of design have seven key features:

- *Distinctive competence.* The organization maintains superiority through innovation and adaptation by combining resources in novel ways. Often these resources come from different parts of the organization or other organizations.
- *Responsibility.* People who must collaborate to perform their tasks share responsibility. The organization's design includes extensive use of cross-functional, special-purpose, and self-managed teams.
- *Goal setting.* Common goals linked to satisfying the needs of one or more important external groups (e.g., customers or clients, suppliers, shareholders, lenders, and governments) are formulated. Performance is less internally driven and more dependent on satisfying customer needs or speeding up product development.

- *Communication.* The primary focus is on lateral rather than vertical communication. The information necessary to make decisions is widely shared and distributed, and open communication is the norm.
- *Information technology.* Many information technologies (including groupware) assist employees in networking internally (with others in the organization who may even be separated geographically by great distances) or externally (with customers, suppliers, regulatory agencies, and others). Typical information technologies and related groupware include e-mail, special PC software decision aids, voice mail, mobile phones, fax, telecommuting, teleconferencing, local-area and wide-area computer networks, and the like.
- *Organization system.* The design has a bias toward an organic system with as few organizational levels as possible. A network design supports individual initiative and collaboration among individuals in teams.
- *Balanced view.* Individuals, teams, departments, and divisions do not view themselves as isolated islands having only their unique goals and ways of doing things. They view themselves in relation to others with common goals and rewards. Forms of cooperation and trust evolve over time, based on a history of past performance. The basic assumption of trust is that each person, team, or department depends on resources controlled by others and that mutual gains are obtained by pooling resources and finding win–win solutions for all.[23]

By connecting people regardless of their location, the network design enhances fast communications so that people can act together. Numerous organizations in the fashion, toy, publishing, software design, and motion picture industries have used this design. Organizing on a network basis allows the organization to compete on the basis of speed and ability to quickly transfer knowledge.

The production of movies has for a long time illustrated many characteristics of a network design. Filmmakers, directors, producers, actors, agents, makeup artists, costume designers, special-effects artists, technicians, and lawyers come together from many different organizations and agencies to produce a film. Although they are all independent, the producer and director need to closely orchestrate and communicate with each of these to produce a film according to very exact specifications. After the production is complete and the film is released, these various people disband and then regroup (often with different people) to produce another film with a different set of actors, producers, directors, and so forth. Thus, the movie industry is actually composed of many different specialized organizations, each of which is critically dependent on the people, knowledge, and skills of other organizations to create a product that is often beyond the scope, capabilities, and means of any one firm.

Organizational Uses. The network design offers many advantages for an organization.[24] First, the organization brings together the special knowledge and skills of others to create value rather than hiring employees to perform this task. The network design enables managers to focus on one set of activities and rely on others to contribute. For example, Medical City of Dallas uses doctors from many specialty practices, such as radiology, oncology, and plastic surgery, to serve its patients. Second, the network design has the advantage of bringing together people with different insights into teams that work exclusively on a given project. Thus, network designs enhance the search for new ideas and creative solutions. Yet, it is important for employees working on such a project to have strong self-management, teamwork, communication, and planning and administration competencies. When a given project is completed, these teams will be disassembled. Third, organizations choosing a network design can work with a wide variety of different suppliers, customers, and other organizations. This gives managers a high degree of flexibility to respond to different circumstances.

With many people working from different locations and often linked by electronic means, some problems can surface. First, other organizations can sometimes fail to live up to the deadlines that were established. Because network designs work in real time, a delay in one part of the process has ripple effects throughout the system. How many times have you waited for a doctor in an office for an opinion? In instances in which time is critical, delays can be very costly because the entire system must wait until a decision is made. Thus, dependence on other organizations can create an operational risk. Often, additional resources or coordination is needed, thus increasing the cost to the consumer. Second, since the network design does not provide managers with knowledge to complete the process on their own, they must constantly monitor the quality of work provided by those in other organizations. Since knowledge resides in people's minds, the network organization is only as competitive as the quality and resources assigned to the project by another organization. Assigning employees with weak communication and planning and administration competencies, for example, can lead to failure. Third, employees in the outsourced organization may not commit to the same values and sense of time urgency to which employees in the networked organization are committed. Therefore, it is crucial that all people working in a network organization understand the critical nature of the project. Last, since the network design requires managers working with many organizations, the lines of authority, responsibility, and accountability are not always clear. Therefore, projects are delayed and cost overruns do occur.

The following Communication Competency feature illustrates how DreamWorks SKG uses a network design to make movies. Some of the benefits and pitfalls of the network design are illustrated in this example.[25]

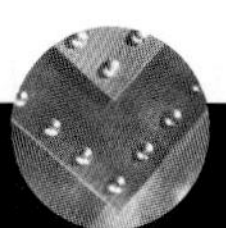

COMMUNICATION COMPETENCY

DREAMWORKS SKG

Created in 1994 by Steven Spielberg, Jeffrey Katzenberg, and David Geffen, this multibillion-dollar company produced such mega box office hits as *Madagascar*, *Shark Tale*, *Shrek 2*, and *A Beautiful Mind*. DreamWorks also produces television shows, as well as music albums for a number of pop artists. With DreamWorks, the three men divide their responsibilities. Spielberg oversees the production of live-action movies, Katzenberg leads the animation division, and Geffen produces the soundtracks and other music activities. Headquartered out of offices at Universal Pictures in Hollywood, California, they have relied on a network organization design to produce movies as shown in Figure 3.10.

DreamWorks relies heavily on many other organizations to provide the critical resources, people, and skills needed to produce a film. As suggested in Figure 14.10, makeup artists, costume designers, actors, and agents are not full-time employees of DreamWorks. These people are hired at the time they are needed. Likewise, DreamWorks works with other specialized organizations to develop many of the newest technologies used to create computer-generated, animated films. A central management task for Spielberg, Katzenberg, and Geffen is communicating with people from different backgrounds, expertise, and competencies to produce a blockbuster film.

As DreamWorks has grown during the past decade, so have the ties it has established to other firms. For example, DreamWorks signed a deal with computer giant Hewlett-Packard (HP) to develop cutting-edge technologies for new forms of animation. HP provides all of the computing resources for DreamWorks' next-generation digital studio at its Glendale, California, location. This facility helps DreamWorks create the latest computer-designed animation more quickly and more cost effectively than previous technology. Hewlett-Packard is a key provider of computer hardware and other technologies that will allow DreamWorks, which cannot develop the technology as effectively or in as timely a manner on its own, to produce even more realistic animation. DreamWorks' TV has signed a contract with NBC. Under this arrangement, NBC pays DreamWorks a fee to cover production costs and gets first look at any new series created by DreamWorks. NBC then finances and owns a majority stake in the projects it chooses to develop. DreamWorks has

FIGURE 3.10 DreamWorks Network Organization

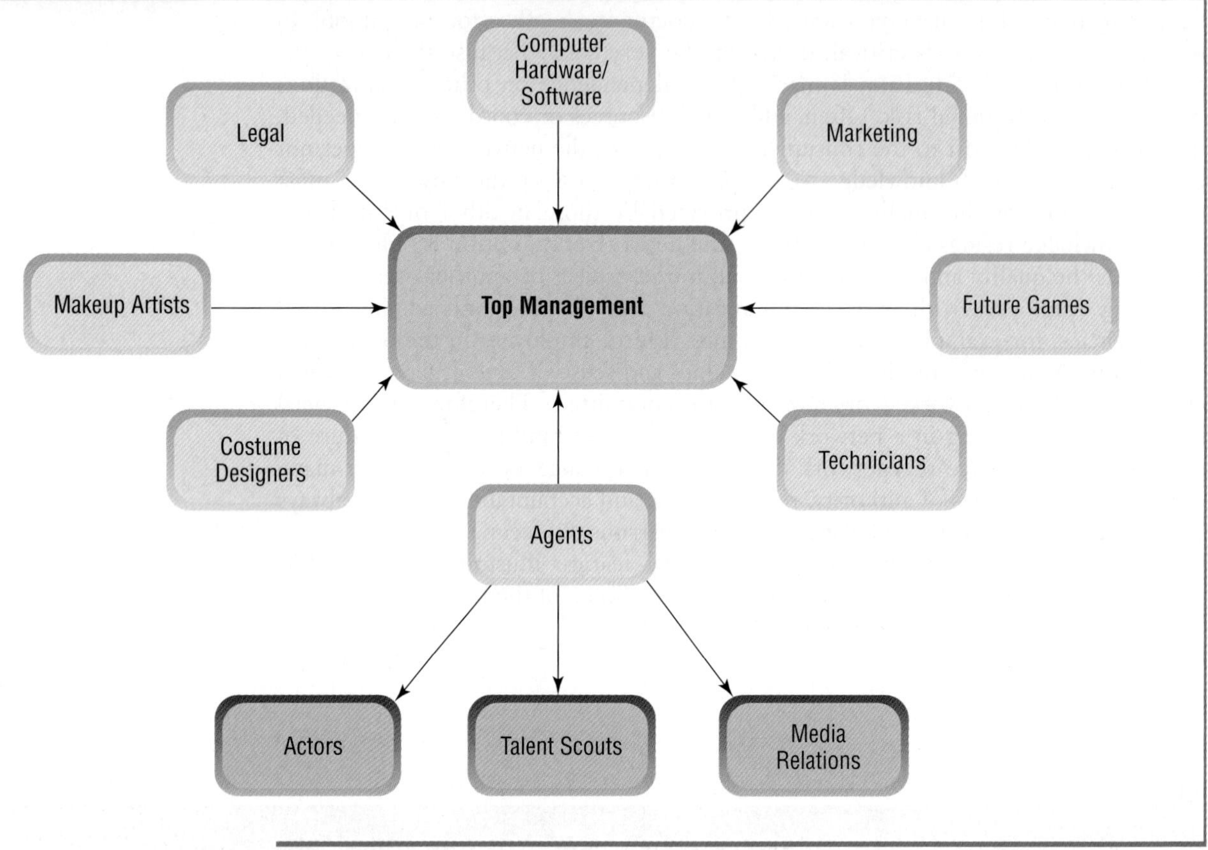

Source: www.hoovers.com, January, 2005.

also entered into an agreement with a Japanese media firm, Kadokawa Holdings, that gives this firm exclusive rights to distribute DreamWorks films, videos, DVDs, and other products in Japan.

Many of DreamWorks' popular movies have become the basis for the newest video game ideas. Yet, DreamWorks does not currently seek to invest in this industry alone, especially after having encountered some product failures in the late 1990s. DreamWorks realizes it does not have the skills or the resources to invest or compete in the video game industry. Yet, DreamWorks recognizes that the video game market is a new channel that could help spark interest in both current and future DreamWorks films. DreamWorks signed a deal with Activision to publish games based on three DreamWorks films: *Sharkslayer*, *Madagascar*, and *Over the Hedge*. In this relationship, Activision helps DreamWorks develop a video game franchise for interactive entertainment, but DreamWorks does not actually develop the games.

For more information on DreamWorks, visit the organization's home page at ***http://www.dreamworks.com.***

The dominant themes of current design strategies are (1) how the factors in the environment affect how the organization must compete for scarce resources, (2) the importance of choosing a strategy to gain a competitive edge in the industry, and (3) how technological interdependence can influence the type of design chosen. Unfortunately, there is no "one best way" to design an organization. Managers must consider multiple factors and design their organization accordingly.

CHAPTER SUMMARY

The environment facing an organization consists of external stakeholders. We indicated that four groups in particular—suppliers, distributors, competitors, and customers—can affect how an organization operates. Strategic factors and the choice of business strategy—low cost, differentiation, focused—have a direct impact on an organization's design. Organizations pursuing a low-cost strategy usually seek designs that emphasize functional departments (e.g., accounting, finance, marketing). Differentiation strategies are based on the organization's ability to provide customers with a unique product or service. These organizations are typically organized along product lines. Focused strategies are intended to help an organization target a specific niche within an industry. Organizations pursuing this strategy are typically organized by product. Technological factors determine the degree of coordination needed among individuals, teams, and departments to reach the organization's goals. Three types of interdependence—pooled, sequential, and reciprocal—were identified and discussed.

1. Explain how environmental, strategic, and technological factors affect the design of organizations.

If top management supports tight, centralized control of day-to-day decisions, a mechanistic organization is more likely to be used than an organic one. Mechanistic organizations are bureaucratic and function effectively when the environment is stable. Organic organizations have fewer rules and regulations and function effectively in rapidly changing environments and ambiguous situations. People gain influence by contributing to the resolution of issues and solution of problems.

2. State the differences between mechanistic and organic organizations.

A functional design separates the organization along various departmental lines, such as marketing, finance, and human resources, and top managers may integrate departments as needed. In place departmentalization, the different geographical areas served by the organization present different environmental conditions. All functions are usually performed at each place. A product design emphasizes the nature of the organization's products and/or services. Each product is unique and requires special attention by top management. A multidivisional form (M-form) is useful to organizations that offer a wide array of products in geographcally dispersed markets.

3. Describe four traditional organization designs: functional, place, product, and multidivisional.

A multinational design attempts to maintain three-way organizational capabilities among products, functions, and geographic areas. Production in several countries presents enormous coordination problems for managers who must adhere to headquarters policies and local customs at the same time. A network design emphasizes horizontal coordination for managing complex task interdependencies. This type of design also features the use of various information technologies that enable the organization to process vast amounts of data. Mainly used in high-tech and film-making organizations, this type of design cannot be effectively implemented without adequate electronic capabilities.

4. Describe two contemporary organization designs: multinational and network.

KEY TERMS AND CONCEPTS

Bureaucracy
Centralization
Chain of command
Differentiation strategy
Division of labor
Focused strategy
Functional design
Hierarchy of authority
Impersonality
Low-cost strategy
Mechanistic organization
Multidivisional design (M-form)
Multinational design
Multinational organizations

Network design
Organic organization
Organization chart
Organization design
Place design
Procedures
Product design
Rules
Span of control
Task interdependence
Technology
Unity of command

DISCUSSION QUESTIONS

1. Global managers must be capable of balancing the often-contradictory pulls of being locally responsive and globally efficient. If Kinko's were going to open stores in Latin America, what are some of the issues that their managers would need to address?
2. ARAMARK Corporation, a global provider of managed services, is organized by product line, including campus dining, business dining, uniform rentals, corrections (feeding prisoners), and sports and recreation (managing concessions at various sports arenas). What are some likely organization design problems that Joe Neubauer, ARAMARK'S CEO, faces?
3. The following are some reasons for organizational ineffectiveness:
   - Lack of goal clarity—strategic goals are not clear or linked to particular aspects of the organization's design.
   - Lack of internal alignment—the design of the organization is internally inconsistent.
   - Ineffective links to customers—the design does not effectively integrate the demands of customers.
   - Lack of external fit—the design does not fit the needs of the environment.

   Identify and describe briefly one organization (Kmart, Krispy Kreme, etc.) whose ineffectiveness you believe reflects these reasons.
4. What are the three most important managerial competencies that Kellogg's leaders need to develop to maintain and increase its global market share in the snack industry?
5. What is the business strategy of Kellogg's? Explain.
6. What practices typically found in a functional organization design have to be changed when top management chooses a network design?
7. What impact does the choice of strategy by 7-Eleven's top managers have on how this organization is designed?
8. How does technological interdependence affect the organization design of DreamWorks?
9. What do you see as the major strengths of Electrolux's organization design? Its major weaknesses?

EXPERIENTIAL EXERCISE AND CASE

Experiential Exercise: Communication Competency

Is Your Organization Designed for High Performance?[26]

Instructions:
Listed are statements describing an effective organization design. Indicate the extent to which you agree or disagree with each statement as a description of an organization you currently work for or have worked for in the past. Write the appropriate number next to the statement.

1. Strongly disagree
2. Disagree
3. Somewhat disagree
4. Uncertain
5. Somewhat agree
6. Agree
7. Strongly agree

___ 1. Employees who try to change things are usually recognized and supported.

___ 2. The organization makes it easy to get the skills needed to progress.

___ 3. Employees almost always know how their work turns out, whether it is good or bad.

___ 4. Employees have flexibility over the pace of their work.

___ 5. Managers facilitate discussion at meetings to encourage participation by subordinates.

___ 6. Few policies, rules, and regulations restrict innovation in this organization.

___ 7. Boundaries between teams, departments, and divisions rarely interfere with solving joint problems.

___ 8. There are few hierarchical levels in this organization.

___ 9. Everyone knows how their work will affect the work of the next person or team and the quality of the final product or service.

___ 10. The organization is well informed about technological developments relevant to its processes, goods, or services.
___ 11. The organization is constantly trying to determine what the customer wants and how to meet customer needs better.
___ 12. The organization can adapt to most changes because its policies, organization design, and employees are flexible.
___ 13. Different parts of the organization work together; when conflict arises, it often leads to constructive outcomes.
___ 14. Everyone can state the values of the organization and how they are used to make decisions.
___ 15. A great deal of information is shared openly, as appropriate.

Scoring and Interpretation

Sum the points given to statements 1–15. A score of 75–105 suggests an effective organization design. A score of 70–89 suggests a mediocre design that probably varies greatly in terms of how specific aspects of the organization work for or against the design's effectiveness. A score of 50–69 suggests a great deal of ambiguity about the organization and how it operates. A score of 15–49 suggests that the design is contributing to serious problems.

Questions

1. What specific design features in your organization led you to rate it as you did?
2. What two or three managerial competencies were most important in that organization?
3. Is the organization a success? Explain.

Case: Change Competency

Salomon

Salomon is a French manufacturer of outdoor sports equipment. Its revenues for 1998 exceeded FF5 billion ($US 840 million). The firm is global, with balanced sales in Asia, North America, and Europe. It is the world leader in winter sports gear, with a market share of 24 percent. In volume, Salomon is number one in downhill ski bindings (43 percent market share) and in cross-country skiing equipment (59 percent market share), and number two in downhill skis (21 percent market share) and downhill boots (23 percent market share). Salomon also serves the golf (Taylor Made), cycling (Mavic), and hiking boots markets. Each of its product lines has achieved a large market share through radical product technological innovation. For Salomon, technology is a means for achieving market share. It does not conduct basic research; rather it builds on its knowledge of advanced materials to develop new products. Its mastery of mechanical skills is essential for production of its ski bindings and cycles; its mastery of composite materials is essential for its production of skis and golf equipment for which gluing and decoration are essential.

Salomon's roots go back to 1947 when the Salomon family opened a workshop to manufacture saws and ski edges in Annecy, in the Haute Savoie region of France. In 1967, Salomon created a revolutionary technology by designing and selling the first ski bindings having a cable. In 1979, it entered the ski boot market by providing a rear-entry boot. By having a limited number of products, Salomon was able to become one of the world's principal manufacturers of ski boots in less than 3 years. In 1980, a Salomon team working in Scandinavia with a large customer developed a new boot and binding system for cross-country skiing. In 1984, Salomon purchased Taylor Made, a manufacturer of golf equipment, primarily in order to compensate for the seasonality of its winter sports lines. In 1994, with the purchase of Mavic, Salomon entered the cycling market (touring and mountain bikes). As had been the case with the purchase of Taylor Made, Mavic had a strong reputation for technological sophistication and innovation. During its history, Salomon has gone through several organization designs. To facilitate diversification into other products, it has moved from a functional structure to a divisional structure, as shown in Figure 3.11. The structure consists of the CEO, various staff functions, three functional directorates, three operational departments (i.e., ski bindings, boots, and golf), and a unit to manage the Salomon brand name. The industrial directorates have three missions: support technological innovation and advance the firm's industrial skills; create, develop, and produce products; and take responsibility for prices, total investment, and the cost structure. The project directorates have seven missions: facilitate relationships between the industrial directorates and the market directorates, formulate and implement product strategies, lead the projects, launch new products, guarantee the overall profitability of the product line, manage long-term planning, and support the creation of "cult products," or those that change the industry structure through its innovative technology. The market directorates have four missions: manage the leaders of subsidiaries, maintain margins and ensure profitability of the subsidiaries, develop sales and distribution channels, and forecast future growth in sales.

As shown in Salomon's organizational chart, the project directorates have been placed in a central position. These directorates play a fundamental interface role between the market directorates and industrial directorates, which often have different goals. They rely heavily on marketing development specialists in the industrial departments, on marketing distribution specialists in the market directorates, and on the brand management group (which has the responsibility for testing prototype products). This role requires the project directorates to gather large amounts of information during product development. All project leaders are located in headquarters to encourage face-to-face communication. They are also in constant communication with the financial controller to ensure compliance with a project's financial goals. The firm's innovation and development activities, which are crucial to the firm's success, encourage people to take on projects. Thus the project directorates play an essential role in the formulation and implementation of ideas, following the general direction set by the firm's top-management team.[27]

Questions

1. How would you characterize the environment in which Salomon operates?
2. What business strategy have Salomon's top managers chosen?
3. What are two potential strengths and limitations of Salomon's organization design?
4. What managerial competencies would you need in order to succeed at Salomon?

FIGURE 3.11 Salomon Organization Chart

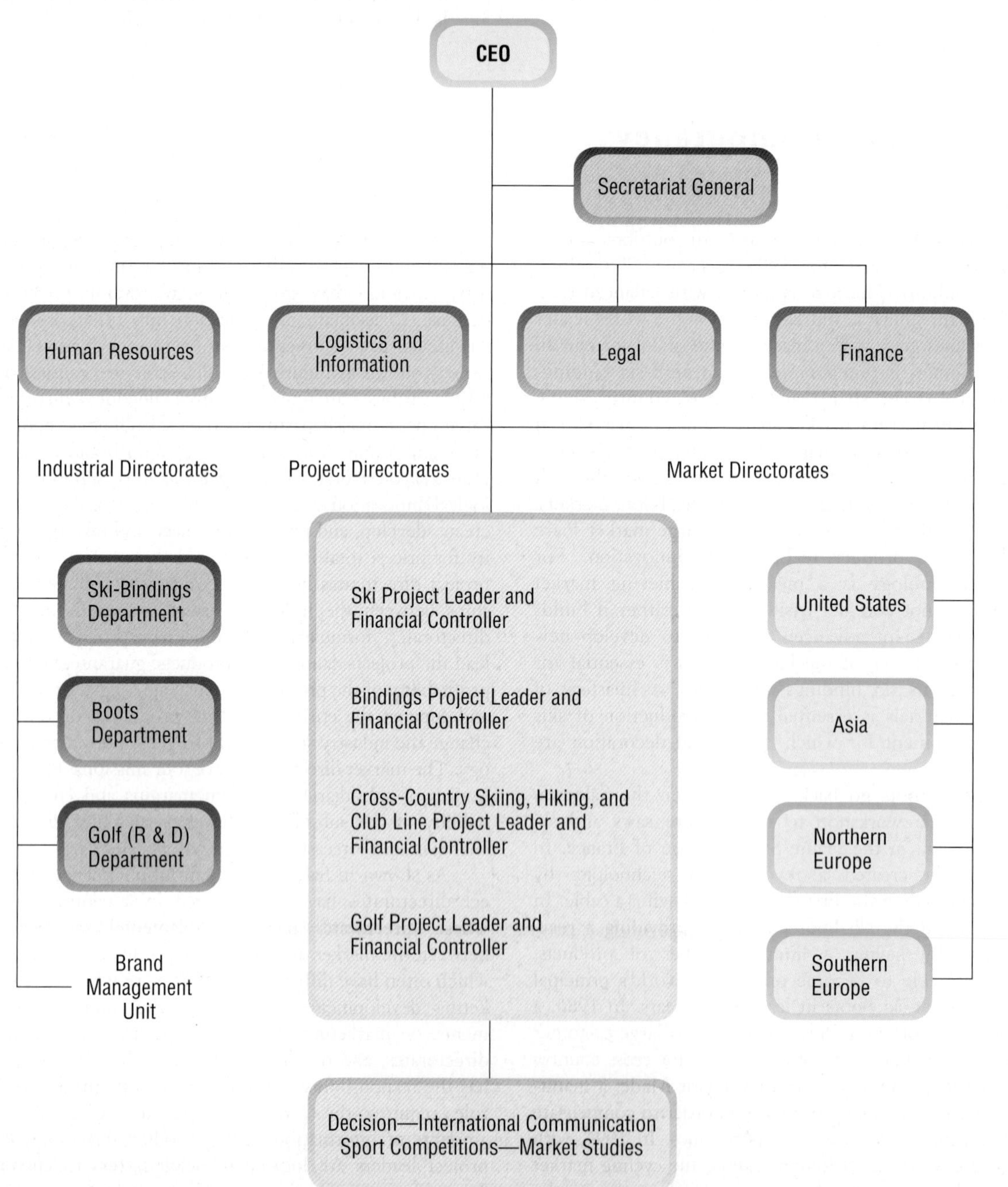

CHAPTER 4

Cultivating Organizational Culture

LEARNING OBJECTIVES

When you have finished studying this chapter, you should be able to:

1. Explain how an organizational culture is formed, sustained, and changed.
2. Describe four types of organizational culture.
3. Discuss how organizational culture can influence ethical behaviors of managers and employees.
4. Explain why fostering cultural diversity is important.
5. Describe the process of organizational socialization and its effect on culture.

Preview Case: Google

DYNAMICS OF ORGANIZATIONAL CULTURE

Forming a Culture

Across Cultures Competency—Grupo Carso

Sustaining a Culture

Changing a Culture

Change Competency—Harley-Davidson

TYPES OF ORGANIZATIONAL CULTURE

Bureaucratic Culture

Clan Culture

Entrepreneurial Culture

Market Culture

Culture-Performance Relationships

ETHICAL BEHAVIOR AND ORGANIZATIONAL CULTURE

Impact of Culture

Whistle-Blowing

Communication Competency—What Would You Do?

FOSTERING CULTURAL DIVERSITY

Challenges

Self Competency—Linda Glick at Levi Strauss

Effective Diversity Programs

SOCIALIZATION OF NEW EMPLOYEES

Organizational Socialization Process

Dilemmas in Socialization

CHAPTER SUMMARY

KEY TERMS AND CONCEPTS

DISCUSSION QUESTIONS

EXPERIENTIAL EXERCISE AND CASE

GOOGLE

PREVIEW CASE

When Omid Kordestani showed up as head of Google in 1999, the founders, Sergey Brin and Larry Page, were working out of a small cramped office. Their business plan was a series of notes scribbled on a whiteboard. Nearly all of the 12 employees had Ph.D.s in engineering or computer science, but nobody had a clue how the sophisticated search engine technology they were working on was supposed to make money. Google is now the world's biggest search engine, answering more than 48 percent of all Internet questions. Its sales exceed $1 billion. How did this happen?

What distinguished Google from most other start-ups is not a vision of what Google would become, but a clear statement of what it should not be. Brin and Page insisted that it would not resemble every other company. It would never be lazy or arrogant or take its users for granted. They created the five lessons of "wisdom" that would be the foundation of Google's culture:

1. Don't sell your soul to the highest bidder. They took the high road to advertising. They refused to allow pop-ups and banners. Brin hated using search sites like Yahoo and waiting for colored ads to cross the screen. All ads on Google had to be tagged to specific search terms that are typed in by users. Google's search ads are among the most effective ways to reach customers.
2. Create a culture of risk taking. Conventional logic held that the ability to do searches should be accompanied by a big, fancy product. But Google stripped its search engine to just a logo in Romper Room colors and a search bar floating on an empty page—no weather, news, or horoscopes. Such an approach attracted free spirits like Brin and Page. All engineers are encouraged to spend 20 percent of their time working on personal projects. Google News was the brainchild of a researcher's self-directed project. The point is to get people thinking creatively and independently. Inside Google, employees ride around in Segway scooters or take time to feed their pets.
3. It's all about the product. Out of the 1,900 employees, roughly 30 percent are engineers and just a few are in marketing. Brin and Page believe that if they build something really good, money will follow. Their two passions are making search results more relevant and delivering them in less than a second.
4. Don't get greedy. Google has sacrificed short-term gain for long-term viability. It advises that customers stop advertising through its site if click-through rates are too low. One small auto accessory business advertising on Google was shocked when it received a letter from Google advising the company to stop wasting its money.
5. Keep your employees motivated and satisfied. Google has a resident chef, masseuses, and doctor on staff. Employees are entitled to parental leaves that include free home food delivery during the first two weeks. Google prides itself on its egalitarian culture. Top executives join employees daily in the company's cafeteria. The executives update employees and respond to their questions each week. Annual employee turnover is in single digits in an industry where turnover rates are much greater. More than 90 percent of people who get offers to join Google accept them.[1]

For more information on Google, visit the organization's home page at ***http://www.google.com.***

The competencies and values of employees and managers play a large role in determining the effectiveness and success of an organization. As illustrated by the Preview Case, certain styles, character, and ways of doing things are powerful guidelines for behavior. Fully understanding the soul of an organization requires plunging below the charts, financial numbers, machines, and buildings into the world of organizational culture.[2]

In this chapter, we examine the concept of organizational culture and how such cultures are formed, sustained, and changed. We also explore some possible relationships between organizational culture and performance; the relationship between organizational culture and ethical behavior; the challenge of managing a culturally diverse workforce; and, finally, how organizations socialize individuals into their particular cultures. We begin with a brief overview of what organizational culture is and how organizational cultures are formed, sustained, and changed.

LEARNING OBJECTIVE

1. Explain how an organizational culture is formed, sustained, and changed.

DYNAMICS OF ORGANIZATIONAL CULTURE

Organizational culture *reflects the values, beliefs, and attitudes of its members.*[3] Organizational cultures evolve slowly over time. Unlike mission and vision statements, they are not usually written down, but are the soul of an organization. A culture is a collection of unspoken rules and traditions that operate 24 hours a day. Culture plays a large part in determining the quality of organizational life. Managers have sought to replicate the strong cultures of successful companies like Southwest Airlines, Mary Kay Cosmetics, and YUM Brands (A&W All-American Food Restaurants, KFC, Pizza Hut, Taco Bell, Long John Silver's) while others have tried to engineer commitment to their own culture in hope of increasing loyalty, productivity, and/or profitability. Culture is rooted in the countless details of an organization's life and influences much of what happens to employees within an organization. The culture of an organization influences who gets promoted, how careers are either made or derailed, and how resources are allocated. Each of these decisions conveys some unique aspect of an organization's culture. While managers are aware of their organization's culture(s), they are often unsure about how to influence it. If cultures are powerful influencers of behavior, they must be created and managed. More specifically, organizational culture includes:

- routine ways of communicating, such as organizational rituals and ceremonies and the language commonly used;
- the norms shared by individuals and teams throughout the organization, such as no reserved parking spaces;
- the dominant values held by the organization, such as product quality or price leadership;
- the philosophy that guides management's policies and decision making, including determining which groups are included or consulted on decisions;
- the rules of the game for getting along in the organization, or the "ropes" that a newcomer must learn in order to become an accepted member; and
- the feeling or climate conveyed in an organization by the physical layout and the way in which managers and employees interact with customers, suppliers, and other outsiders.[4]

None of these components individually represents the culture of the organization. Taken together, however, they reflect and give meaning to the concept of organizational culture. Using these six attributes, how would you describe the culture of Google? These descriptions should give you some insight into why Google has been rated by *Fortune* magazine as one of the 100 best companies to work for.

As indicated in Figure 4.1, organizational culture exists on several levels, which differ in terms of visibility and resistance to change. Just like peeling an onion, the least visible, or deepest, level of organizational culture is that of *shared assumptions and philosophy*, which represent basic beliefs about reality, human nature, and the way things should be done. For example, one key assumption at Google is that employees should focus on technical features of the product and not marketing. Managers and employees alike are committed to a philosophy of trust and the importance of listening to others' thoughts and ideas.

FIGURE 4.1 Layers of Organizational Culture

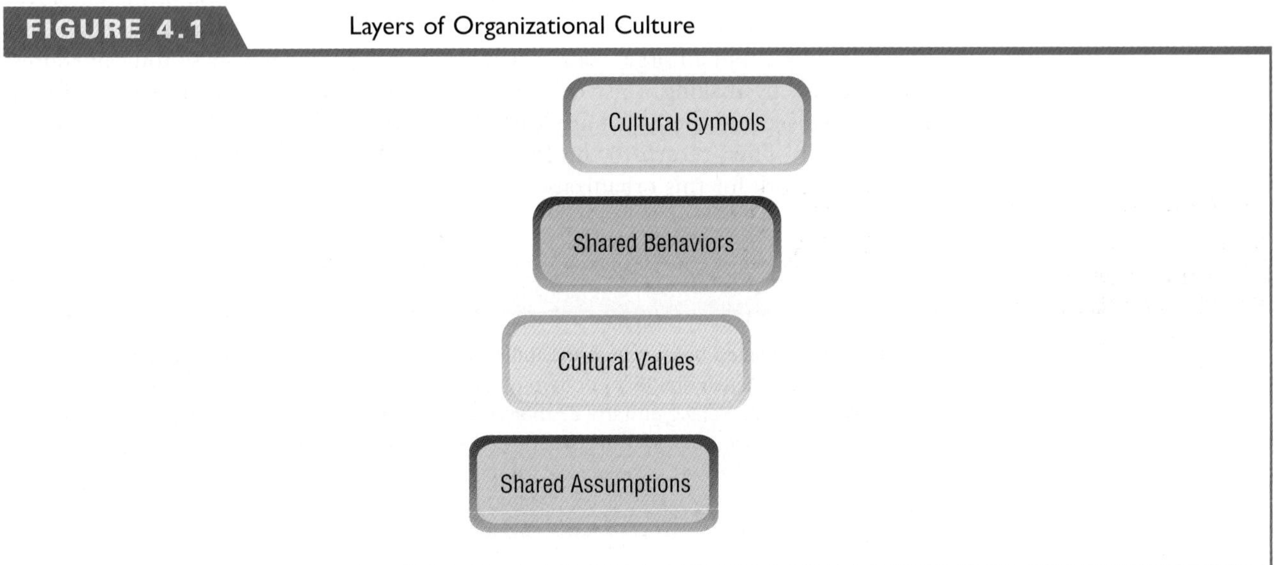

The next level is that of **cultural values,** *which represent collective beliefs, assumptions, and feelings about what things are good, normal, rational, and valuable.*[5] Cultural values can be quite different from organization to organization. In some cultures, employees may care deeply about money, but in others they may care more about technological innovation or employee well-being. These values tend to persist over time, even when organizational membership changes.

The next level is that of **shared behaviors,** *including norms, which are more visible and somewhat easier to change than values.* The five lessons of wisdom at Google are examples of the shared behaviors that are rewarded at Google.

The most superficial level of organizational culture consists of symbols. **Cultural symbols** *are words (jargon or slang), gestures, and pictures or other physical objects that carry a particular meaning within a culture.*[6] Someone entering a New York City Police Department precinct station encounters symbols of authority and spartan surroundings, including physical barriers between officers and civilians; the attire of the duty officer; emblems of authority, such as the American flag, seals, certificates, photos of various city leaders, and signs prohibiting certain behaviors; and hard straight chairs, vending machines, and instructions. In contrast, someone entering the lobby of a Ritz-Carlton hotel encounters warmth, including comfortable chairs and soft couches, decorative pictures, plants and flowers, and reading materials. Bill Arnold, president of Centennial Medical Center in Nashville, Tennessee, symbolized his commitment to an open door communication policy by ripping his door from its hinges and suspending it from the ceiling where everyone could see it.

The cultural symbols of McDonald's also convey a standard meaning. McDonald's restaurants are typically located in rectangular buildings with large windows to let the sun in and with neatly kept surroundings. Parking lots are large and paved; there is rarely any visible litter. A drive-in window indicates that speedy service is available. The most prominent symbol is the golden arch sign that towers over the building, where zoning laws permit. Inside, bright colors and plants create a homey atmosphere. Glistening stainless steel appliances behind the counter provide an up-to-date, efficient, and sanitary appearance. Above all, everything is *clean.* Cleanliness is achieved by endless sweeping and mopping of floors, rapid removal of garbage, instant collecting of dirty trays and cleaning of spills, washing of windows to remove smudges and fingerprints, cleaning of unoccupied tables, and constant wiping of the counter. Both the interior and exterior convey cultural symbols of predictability, efficiency, speed, courtesy, friendliness, and cleanliness.

Organizational culture is important for employees and managers alike. Achieving a good match between the values of the organization and those of the employee first requires that a potential employee figure out what an organization values and second that she find an organization that shares her personal values. You can address the first task by making a list of the 8 values that are most characteristic of your ideal workplace and the 8 that are least characteristic of it from the 54 values shown in Table 4.1. Then return to the Preview Case: What are Google's values? Would you like to work for this organization?

TABLE 4.1 What Do You Value at Work?

The 54 items listed below cover the full range of values you'd likely encounter at an organization. Please divide it into two groups—the 27 that would be most characteristic of your ideal workplace and the 27 that would be the least characteristic. Keep halving the group until you have a rank ordering, then fill in your top and bottom eight choices. Please be sure that you choose four values from the **YOU ARE** list and four values from the **YOUR COMPANY OFFERS** list. Test your fit at a firm by seeing whether the company's values match your top and bottom eight.

Top Eight Choices

Bottom Eight Choices

The Choice Menu

YOU ARE: 1. Flexible 2. Adaptable 3. Innovative 4. Able to seize opportunities 5. Willing to experiment 6. Risk-taking 7. Careful 8. Autonomy-seeking 9. Comfortable with rules 10. Analytical 11. Attentive to detail 12. Precise 13. Team-oriented 14. Ready to share information 15. People-oriented 16. Easygoing 17. Calm 18. Supportive 19. Aggressive 20. Decisive 21. Action-oriented 22. Eager to take initiative 23. Reflective 24. Achievement-oriented 25. Demanding 26. Comfortable with individual responsibility 27. Comfortable with conflict 28. Competitive 29. Highly organized 30. Results-oriented 31. Interested in making friends at work 32. Collaborative 33. Eager to fit in with colleagues 34. Enthusiastic about the job

YOUR COMPANY OFFERS: 35. Stability 36. Predictability 37. High expectations of performance 38. Opportunities for professional growth 39. High pay for good performance 40. Job security 41. Praise for good performance 42. A clear guiding philosophy 43. A low level of conflict 44. An emphasis on quality 45. A good reputation 46. Respect for the individual's rights 47. Tolerance 48. Informality 49. Fairness 50. A unitary culture throughout the organization 51. A sense of social responsibility 52. Long hours 53. Relative freedom from rules 54. The opportunity to be distinctive, or different from others

Source: Adapted from Siegel, M. The perils of culture conflict. *Fortune,* November 9, 1998, 259; Chatman, J. A. and Jehn, K. A. Assessing the relationship between industry characteristics and organizational culture: How different can they be? *Academy of Management Journal,* 1994, 37, 522–553.

Forming a Culture

An organizational culture forms in response to two major challenges that confront every organization: (1) external adaptation and survival and (2) internal integration.[7]

External adaptation and survival *refer to how the organization will find a niche in and cope with its constantly changing external environment.* External adaptation and survival involve addressing the following issues:

- *Mission and strategy:* Identifying the primary purpose of the organization and selecting strategies to pursue this mission.
- *Goals:* Setting specific targets to achieve.
- *Means:* Determining how to pursue the goals, including selecting an organizational structure and reward system.
- *Measurement:* Establishing criteria to determine how well individuals, teams, and departments are accomplishing their goals.

Internal integration *refers to the establishment and maintenance of effective working relationships among the members of an organization.* Internal integration involves addressing the following issues:

- *Language and concepts:* Identifying methods of communication and developing a shared meaning of key values.
- *Group and team boundaries:* Establishing criteria for membership in groups and teams.
- *Power and status:* Determining rules for acquiring, maintaining, and losing power and status.
- *Rewards and punishments:* Developing systems for encouraging desirable behaviors and discouraging undesirable behaviors.[8]

An organizational culture emerges when members share knowledge and assumptions as they discover or develop ways of coping with issues of external adaptation and internal integration. Figure 4.2 shows a common pattern in the emergence of organizational cultures. In relatively new organizations, such as Dell Computers, eBay, and Google, the founder or a few key individuals may largely influence the organization's culture. Later in the life of the organization, its culture will reflect a complex mixture of the assumptions, values, and ideas of the founder or other early top managers and the subsequent experiences of managers and employees.

FIGURE 4.2 How Cultures Emerge

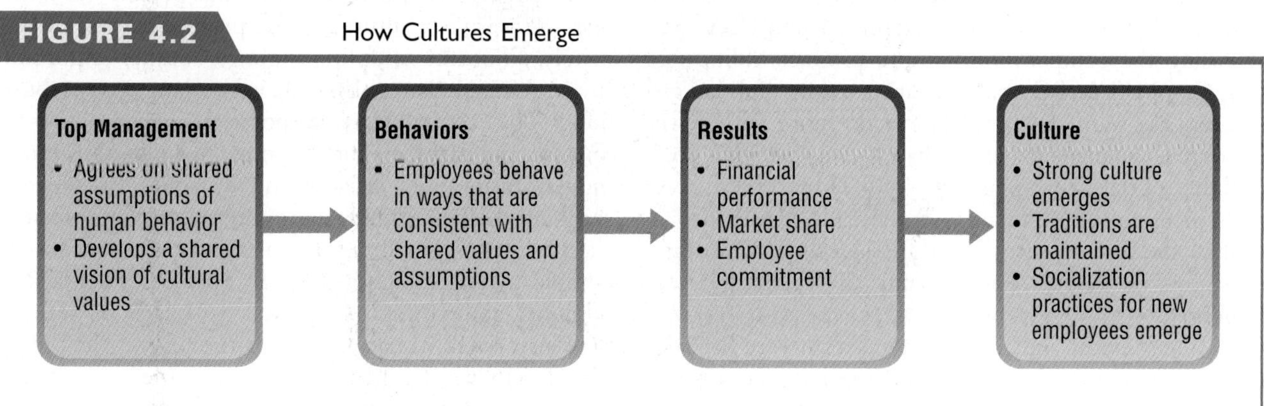

The national culture, customs, and societal norms of a country also shape the culture of the organizations operating within it. The dominant values of a national culture may be reflected in the constraints imposed on the organization by others. For example, a country's form of government may have a dramatic impact on how an organization does business. In addition, the members of the organization have been raised in a particular society and thus bring the dominant values of the society into the firm. For example, in the United States individuals learn values such as freedom of speech and respect for individual privacy from the nation's cultural values. Thus, the presence or absence of these and other values within the larger society has implications for organizational behavior. Finally, increased global operations have forced awareness that differences in national cultures may have a significant impact on the organization's effectiveness. Multinational corporations have discovered that organizational structures and cultures that might be effective in one part of the world may be a struggle in some cases and ineffective in others. The following Across Cultures Competency feature illustrates the impact of both U.S. and Mexican culture on the acquisition of CompUSA by Grupo Carso, one of the largest conglomerates in Latin America.

CompUSA was started in 1975 by Errol Jacobsen, who had a vision of putting a PC in every home in America. It grew from one store to more than 230 CompUSA Computer Superstores and sales of more than $4.5 billion dollars. In an effort to capture market share, it bought archrival Computer City from Radio Shack. Unfortunately, while the sales of PCs have grown steadily, their prices have dropped steadily. With the oversupply of PCs, constantly changing technology, and marketing extravaganzas such as sponsoring the Citrus Bowl, CompUSA profits dropped. Dell and Gateway also emerged as two key players in the marketplace. With their nontraditional retailing model of selling through the Internet, Dell and Gateway were gaining market share at the expense of CompUSA. Finally, in 2000, after its stock lost more than 90 percent of its value, Grupo Carso made an unsolicited bid and acquired the company.[9]

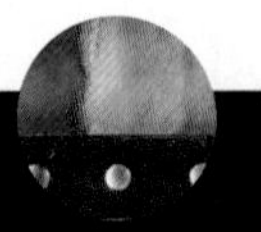

Across Cultures Competency

Grupo Carso

Carlos Slim Helú and his family own the controlling interests in Grupo Carso and wasted no time reducing CompUSA's costs by reorganizing CompUSA and focusing the company on its core products. Slim sold off CompUSA's PC manufacturing plant and its call center. He wanted CompUSA to do more with fewer resources in order to immediately improve the profitability of the firm. A lawsuit was filed by vendors over a "noncommittal" agreement. Eventually, it was thrown out in the Texas courts, but differences between doing business in Latin America and the United States emerged.

The Mexican judicial system makes it very hard for people or organizations to sue each other over contract disputes. In cases where a lawsuit is brought into the court, the process is so lengthy and bureaucratic most people do not use the courts. Slim believed that the American system allowed individuals to make easy money by taking organizations into court as a tactic to gain economic advantage.

Slim appointed a senior manager from Mexico to take charge of CompUSA. While this person was bilingual, he wasn't bicultural. Some problems arose immediately. First, the issue of language became important. In the United States, English is the language of business. The company's incorporation papers were in Spanish and many executives spoke Spanish, thus creating confusion and frustrations in some cases when speaking to their American counterparts. The Mexican executives thought that the American managers should be able to understand and speak Spanish. This lack of bilingual ability was interpreted as a lack of respect. Similarly, when Mexicans answer the phone, they identify themselves by title and name. Titles and names appear on business cards. Managers have certain privileges (e.g., reserved parking, the ability to take long lunches) by right. In the United States, managers need to earn such privileges.

Second, in Mexico, "just now" means nothing more urgent than some time in the future. Elaborate stories are told about why certain tasks were not done on time. Employees have business schedules, but these are adapted due to traffic and personal considerations. Getting to work on time is not critical and most employees stay until 6:30 or 7:00 P.M. In the United States, employees' schedules tend to be less flexible, with most employees arriving at 8:00 A.M. and leaving at 5:00 P.M. For U.S. employees who had direct contact with their Mexican counterparts, this caused frustration.

Third, in Mexico, lunch takes place around 2:00 P.M. and there is a social significance attached to it. It typically is the heartiest meal of the day, in contrast to the U.S. norm of dinner. Mexican managers find drinking socially acceptable at lunch, a practice that many U.S. managers refrain from. It also means that Mexican managers expect their U.S. counterparts to be available for discussions around the noon hour. Last, there are differences in communication. Communication follows the hierarchy of the organization. In Mexico, subordinates believe that their managers are there to provide direction and approve decisions. Managers are available for appointment. At CompUSA, American managers engage in more open and direct communications, often bypassing the chain of command to get things done. Also, there is no formal dress code in the American offices, whereas in Mexico there is an unspoken formal business protocol that includes a dress code for managers.

For more information on Grupo Carso, visit the organization's home page at ***http://www.gcarso.com.mx.***

One perspective is that societal-level cultural differences created the conflicts within CompUSA. Some of the new organization's employees argued that different management philosophies and values were the root of the problem. Most likely, both explanations have some merit. Ultimately, CompUSA will develop its own unique culture—one that blends elements of both the U.S. and Mexican ways of doing business. The sooner that happens, the easier it will be for everyone in the organization to work together productively.

Sustaining a Culture

The ways in which an organization functions and is managed may have both intended and unintended consequences for maintaining and changing organizational culture. Figure 4.3 illustrates a basic approach for maintaining an organization's culture: (1) the organization hires individuals who seem to fit its culture and (2) the organization maintains its culture by removing employees who consistently or markedly stray from accepted behaviors and activities.

Specific methods of maintaining organizational culture, however, are a great deal more complicated than just hiring the right people and firing those who don't work out. The most powerful indicators of the organization's culture are (1) what managers and teams pay attention to, measure, and control; (2) the ways in which managers (particularly top managers) react to critical incidents and organizational crises; (3) managerial and team role modeling, teaching, and coaching; (4) criteria for allocating rewards and status; (5) criteria for recruitment, selection, promotion, and removal from the organization; and (6) organizational rites, ceremonies, and stories.[10]

What Managers and Teams Pay Attention To. One of the more powerful methods of maintaining organizational culture involves the processes and behaviors that managers, individual employees, and teams pay attention to—that is, the events that get noticed and commented on. Dealing with events systematically sends strong signals to employees about what is important and expected of them. For example,

FIGURE 4.3 Methods of Maintaining Organizational Culture

Tom Salonek, president of Go-e-biz.com, an e-business consulting firm, holds a 15-minute meeting every morning at 7:25 A.M. sharp with his salespeople, who use cell phones to call in from the road. They share their challenges and results from the previous day. Salonek closely monitors sales contacts they have made, giving them an extra $20 a day for making their daily contact goal quotas.

Reactions to Incidents and Crises. When an organization faces a crisis, such as the September 11, 2001, terrorism attacks or loss of a major customer, the handling of that crisis by managers and employees reveals a great deal about its culture. The manner in which the crisis is dealt with can either reinforce the existing culture or bring out new values and norms that change the culture in some way. For example, an organization facing a dramatic reduction in demand for its product might react by laying off or firing employees. Or it might reduce employee hours or rates of pay with no workforce reduction. The alternative chosen indicates the value placed on human resources and can reinforce and maintain the current culture or indicate a major change in the culture. Such a situation occurred at Lincoln Electric after the firm formalized a guaranteed continuous employment policy in 1958. Every worker with more than three years of service with the company has been guaranteed at least 30 hours per week, 49 weeks per year. The company responded to declining demand for its arc-welding products and electrical motors during the recession of the 1980s by cutting back all employee hours from 40 to 30. Many employees were reassigned and the total workforce was reduced slightly through normal retirement and restricted hiring. Year-end incentive bonuses were still paid.[11]

Role Modeling, Teaching, and Coaching. Aspects of an organization's culture are communicated to employees by the way managers treat them. At the Ritz-Carlton and Resorts, all new trainees are shown films that emphasize customer service. Managers also demonstrate good customer or client service practices in their interactions with customers. For example, the story is told of the beach attendant who was busy stacking chairs for an evening event when he was approached by a guest who asked to leave two chairs out because he wanted to return to the beach that evening with his girlfriend and propose. Although the beach attendant was going off duty, he didn't just have two chairs on the beach; he put on a tuxedo and brought flowers, champagne, and candles. He met the couple when they arrived at the beach later that evening. He escorted them to the chairs, presented the flowers, lit the candles, and served the champagne to them. The repeated emphasis on good customer relations in both training and day-to-day behavior helps create and maintain a customer-oriented culture throughout the Ritz-Carlton Hotel chain.

Allocation of Rewards and Status. Employees also learn about an organization's culture through its reward system. The rewards and punishments attached to various behaviors convey to employees the priorities and values of both individual managers and the organization. At TDIndustries, a mechanical/electrical/plumbing company, employees are eligible for a 401(k) plan after just 90 days and can earn up to $7,000 for referring a new hire to the company. All employees are cross-trained to perform a variety of tasks to reduce production bottlenecks and status differences among the plumbing, electrical, mechanical, and other trades. At Sara Lee, the baked goods company, programs encourage managers at different levels to own stock in the company. The rationale is that managers should have a stake in the financial health of the firm, based on its overall performance.

Similarly, in many organizations the status system maintains certain aspects of its culture. The distribution of perks (a corner office on an upper floor, executive dining room, carpeting, a private secretary, or a private parking space) demonstrates which roles and behaviors are most valued by an organization. At Chase Manhattan Bank in New York City, Jim Donaldson was promoted to vice president for global trusts. His new office was well furnished with most of the symbols of relatively high status. Before he was allowed to move into his new office, his boss ordered the maintenance department to cut a 12-inch strip from the entire perimeter of the carpet. At Chase Manhattan, wall-to-wall carpeting is a status symbol given only to senior vice presidents and above.

An organization may use rewards and status symbols ineffectively and inconsistently. If so, it misses a great opportunity to influence its culture. An organization's reward practices and its culture are strongly linked in the minds of its members. In fact, some authorities believe that the most effective method of influencing organizational culture may be through the reward system. Within NASA, the crash of the space shuttle *Columbia* has been attributed to a change in the reward system from one that rewarded space safety and technical brilliance to a reward system that focused on efficiency and reuse of the space shuttle. NASA's motto of "faster, better, and cheaper" put an emphasis on meeting schedules and avoiding cost overruns. This motto became a symbol of how rewards were allocated.[12]

Recruitment, Selection, Promotion, and Removal. As Figure 4.3 suggests, one of the fundamental ways in which organizations maintain a culture is through the recruitment process. In addition, the criteria used to determine who is assigned to specific jobs or positions, who gets raises and promotions and why, who is removed from the organization by firing or early retirement, and so on, reinforce and demonstrate basic aspects of an organization's culture. These criteria become known throughout the organization and can maintain or change an existing culture.

Rites and Ceremonies. **Organizational rites and ceremonies** *are planned activities or rituals that have important cultural meaning to employees.* Certain managerial or employee activities can become rituals that are interpreted as part of the organizational culture. Rites and ceremonies that sustain organizational culture include rites of passage, degradation, enhancement, and integration. Table 4.2 contains examples of each of these four types of rites and identifies some of their desirable consequences.[13]

A ceremony used at Mary Kay Cosmetics Company provides a good example of rites of enhancement. During elaborate awards ceremonies, gold and diamond pins, fur stoles, and pink Cadillacs are presented to salespeople who achieve their sales

TABLE 4.2 Organizational Rites and Ceremonies

TYPE	EXAMPLE	POSSIBLE CONSEQUENCES
Rites of passage	Basic training, U.S. Army	Facilitate transition into new roles; minimize differences in way roles are carried out
Rites of degradation	Firing a manager	Reduce power and identity; reaffirm proper behavior
Rites of enhancement	Mary Kay Cosmetics Company ceremonies	Enhance power and identity; emphasize value of proper behavior
Rites of integration	Office party	Encourage common feelings that bind members together

Source: Adapted from Trice, H. M., and Beyer, J. M. *The Cultures of Work Organizations.* Englewood Cliffs, N.J.: Prentice-Hall, 1993, 111

quotas. Music tends to arouse and express emotions, and all the participants know the Mary Kay song, "I've Got That Mary Kay Enthusiasm." It was written by a member of the organization to the tune of the hymn "I've Got That Old Time Religion." This song is a direct expression of the Mary Kay culture and is fervently sung during the awards ceremonies. The ceremonies are reminiscent of a Miss America pageant, with all the participants dressed in glamorous evening clothes. The setting is typically an auditorium with a stage in front of a large, cheering audience. The ceremonies clearly are intended to increase the identity and status of high-performing employees and emphasize the company's rewards for excellence.[14]

Organization Stories. Many of the underlying beliefs and values of an organization's culture are expressed as stories that become part of its folklore. These stories transmit the existing culture from old to new employees and emphasize important aspects of that culture—and some may persist for a long time. The story of how Mary Kay started her cosmetics business in 1963 after taking her entire life's savings of $5,000 to launch her company has been told and retold to all beauty consultants. She quickly realized that if she recognized employees for their achievement, she could motivate people. Mary Kay also believed that all people should have an equal chance of success. Managers retell the story of how Shirly Hutton was making only $11,000 in 1979 and retired in 1996. During those 17 years, she sold enough cosmetics to be retired on a $650,000 income for the next 15 years. How? By maintaining a positive outlook on life, treating customers as friends, calling them just to see how they were doing, sending out birthday cards to customers, and setting goals and working toward that goal each day. These are the core values that Mary Kay Ash spoke about in 1963 when she founded the company.[15]

Changing a Culture

The same basic methods used to maintain an organization's culture may be used to modify it. That is, culture might be modified by changing (1) what managers and teams pay attention to, (2) how crises are handled, (3) criteria for recruiting new members, (4) criteria for promotion within the organization, (5) criteria for allocating rewards, and (6) organizational rites and ceremonies.[16]

Changing organizational culture can be tricky because accurately assessing organizational culture in itself is difficult. Most large, complex organizations actually have more than one culture. The Gainesville (Florida) Police Department, for example, has distinctly different cultures based on the shifts to which officers are assigned and their rank. *When multiple cultures are presented they are referred to as* **subcultures.** Often, if an organization has subcultures they will reflect the following three types: an operating culture (line employees), an engineering culture (technical and professional people), and an executive culture (top management). Each culture stems from very different views typically held by these groups of individuals.[17] Faced with a variety of subcultures, management may have difficulty (1) accurately assessing them and (2) effecting needed changes especially when these subcultures are based in units in different locations.

> **THE COMPETENT LEADER**
>
> Culture change does not occur in a vacuum. All employees must embrace the change. Senior managers need to celebrate behaviors that reinforce and reward the new culture's values.
>
> **David Novak, CEO YUM! Brands**

Despite the presence of subcultures, the change in organizational cultures is feasible. In the case of failing organizations or significant shifts in an organization's external environment, changing the culture is essential. Successfully changing organizational culture requires

- understanding the old culture first because a new culture can't be developed unless managers and employees understand where they're starting from;
- providing support for employees and teams who have ideas for a better culture and are willing to act on those ideas;
- finding the most effective subculture in the organization and using it as an example from which employees can learn;
- not attacking culture head-on but finding ways to help employees and teams do their jobs more effectively;
- treating the vision of a new culture as a guiding principle for change, not as a miracle cure;
- recognizing that significant organizationwide cultural change takes 5 to 10 years; and
- living the new culture because actions speak louder than words.

The transformation of Harley-Davidson is one example of how a company changed its culture, as discussed in the following Change Competency feature. To change a company's culture, reward systems, leader behaviors, and organizational structures must be created to support the change.[18]

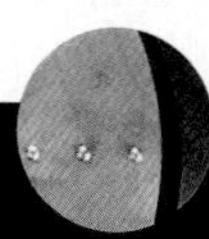

CHANGE COMPETENCY

HARLEY-DAVIDSON

When Richard Teerlink took over as president of Harley-Davidson in 1987, the differences in quality between Harley-Davidson and its competitors were striking. For example, only 5 percent of Honda's motorcycles failed to pass inspection; more than 50 percent of Harleys failed the same test. Honda's value added per employee was three times that of Harley's. Harley's relations with its dealers were poor because they were forced to provide customers with free service because of factory defects. So what did Teerlink do? He set out to change the culture of Harley-Davidson, which he accomplished before retiring in 1999.

First, he emphasized that Harley was a manufacturer of motorcycles, but was in the "experience business."

He said that the real product is not a machine, but a lifestyle, an attitude, a way of being, a perspective on life that has its beginnings before Bill Harley and Arthur Davidson built the first motorized bicycle in 1901. It is the strength and courage that comes from feelings of individuality. Therefore, riding a Harley is the stuff adventure and legends are made of.

Second, he began emphasizing organizational and individual learning at all levels through a Leadership Institute. The institute was designed to introduce new workers to Harley's goals and culture while providing current workers with a better understanding of the organization's design and effects of competition on Harley's performance. Managers prepared a series of nontechnical explanations of how cash flow and flexible production affect financial success. Line workers were taught how products, sales, and productivity affect profitability. Substantial changes in employee job descriptions, responsibilities, and production processes were undertaken in an effort to increase job enrichment and worker empowerment. These efforts were implemented through cross-training and expansion of job responsibilities. Teerlink eliminated the positions of vice presidents of marketing and operations because these jobs didn't add value to the product. Teams of employees, such as a "create-demand team" that is in charge of producing products and a "product-support team," now make these decisions. Employees formed quality circles that became a source of bottom-up ideas for improving quality. Employees created a peer review system to evaluate each other's performance instead of relying solely on first-line supervisors' evaluations. These evaluations help determine employees' pay.

Third, to recapture the Harley mystique, Teerlink revitalized the Harley Hogs, a customer group formed to get people more actively involved in motorcycling. To attract women riders, the Ladies of Harley group was formed to increase ridership and interest among young women motorcyclists. Teerlink and his staff regularly attended road rallies and helped clubs sponsor various charitable events. Harley also issued a credit card to thousands of riders and encouraged them to use the card for the purchase of a motorcycle, service, and accessories. The sale of merchandise, including T-shirts, clothing, jewelry, small-leather goods, and numerous other products, permits customers to identify with the company. As Teerlink noted, "There are very few products that are so exciting that people will tattoo your logo on their body."

Since Teerlink's retirement, CEO Jeff Bleustein has worked hard to sustain Harley's culture. With recent sales exceeding $5 billion and more than 8,800 employees, it appears that his leadership has been able to sustain the culture Teerlink created.

For more information on Harley-Davidson, visit the organization's home page at ***http://www.harley-davidson.com.***

We cover planned organizational change extensively in Chapter 5. Many of the specific techniques and methods for changing organizational behaviors presented in that chapter also may be used to change organizational culture. Indeed, any comprehensive program of organizational change, in some sense, is an attempt to change the culture of the organization.

We can't overemphasize how difficult deliberately changing organizational cultures may be. In fact, the incompatibility of organizational cultures and their resistance to change has been one of the most significant barriers to successful corporate mergers, as illustrated by the Grupo Carso case. For a merger to be effective, at least one (and sometimes both) of the merging organizations may need to change its culture.

LEARNING OBJECTIVE

2. Describe four types of organizational culture.

TYPES OF ORGANIZATIONAL CULTURE

Cultural elements and their relationships create a pattern that is distinct to an organization (e.g., the culture of Google versus that of Grupo Carso). However, organizational cultures do have some common characteristics.[19] One proposed framework is presented in Figure 4.4. The vertical axis reflects the relative control orientation of an organization, ranging from stable to flexible. The horizontal axis reflects the relative focus of attention of an organization, ranging from internal functioning to external functioning. The extreme corners of the four quadrants represent four pure types of organizational culture: bureaucratic, clan, entrepreneurial, and market. In a culturally homogeneous organization such as Mary Kay, one of these basic types of culture will dominate. At the Dallas Police Department, Bank of America, Microsoft, and other organizations with subcultures, multiple cultures are likely not only to exist, but may compete for superiority.

FIGURE 4.4 Framework of Types of Cultures

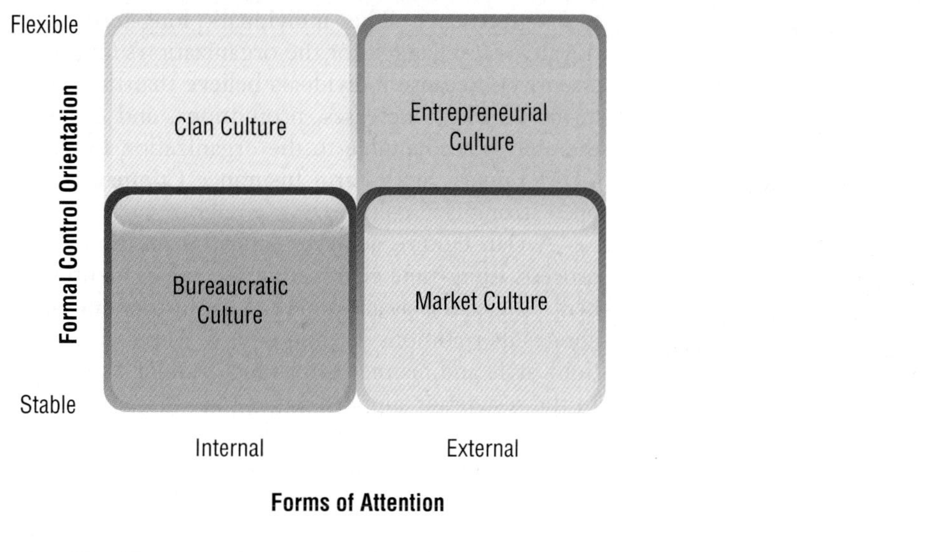

Source: Adapted from Hooijberg, R., and Petrock, F. On cultural change: Using the competing values framework to help leaders execute a transformational strategy. *Human Resource Management*, 1993, 32, 29–50; Quinn, R. E., *Beyond Rational Management: Mastering the Paradoxes and Competing Demands of High Performances.* San Francisco: Jossey-Bass, 1988.

As is true of organization designs, different organizational cultures may be appropriate under different conditions, with no one type of culture being ideal for every situation. However, some employees may prefer one culture to others. As you read about each type of culture, consider which best fits your preferences. Employees who work in an organization with a culture that fits their own view of an ideal culture tend to be committed to the organization and optimistic about its future. Also, a culture should reflect the organization's goals.

Bureaucratic Culture

An organization that practices formality, rules, standard operating procedures, and hierarchical coordination has a **bureaucratic culture.** Recall from Chapter 3 that the goals of a bureaucracy are predictability, efficiency, and stability. Its members highly value standardized goods and customer service. Behavioral norms support formality over informality. Managers view their roles as being good coordinators, organizers, and enforcers of written rules and standards. Tasks, responsibilities, and authority for all employees are clearly defined. The organization's many rules and processes are spelled out in thick manuals, and employees believe that their duty is to "go by the book" and follow legalistic procedures.

Most local, state, and federal governments have bureaucratic cultures, which can impede their effectiveness. The federal personnel manual, which spells out the rules for hiring and firing, runs to thousands of pages. Hundreds of pages are needed just to explain how to fill out some of the forms. The approval process for ordering a computer can take months, during which time the equipment ordered could be a generation old by the time it is installed.

Clan Culture

Tradition, loyalty, personal commitment, extensive socialization, teamwork, self-management, and social influence are attributes of a **clan culture.**[20] Its members recognize an obligation beyond the simple exchange of labor for a salary. They understand that contributions to the organization (e.g., hours worked per week) may exceed any contractual agreements. The individual's long-term commitment to the organization (loyalty) is exchanged for the organization's long-term commitment to the individual (security). Because individuals believe that the organization will treat them fairly in terms of salary increases, promotions, and other forms of recognition, they hold themselves accountable to the organization for their actions. Organizations such as YUM Brands, State Farm Insurance Company, and Southwest Airlines have developed strong clan cultures.

A clan culture achieves unity by means of a long and thorough socialization process. Long-time clan members serve as mentors and role models for newer members. The clan is aware of its unique history and often documents its origins and celebrates its traditions in various rites. Members have a shared image of the organization's style and manner of conduct. Public statements and events reinforce its values. In the restaurant support center (i.e., the headquarters) of YUM Brands (e.g., KFC, Pizza Hut, Taco Bell), there hangs a plaque with the "Founding Truth" and "How we work together principles" proudly displayed for all to see. Statements on these plaques communicate the culture of YUM, such as "Great operations and marketing drive sales," "No finger pointing," and "The restaurant manager is # 1, not senior management."[21]

In a clan culture, members share feelings of pride in membership. They have a strong sense of identification and recognize their common fate in the organization. The up-through-the-ranks career pattern results in an extensive network of colleagues whose paths have crossed and who have shared similar experiences. Shared goals, perceptions, and behavioral tendencies foster communication, coordination, and integration. A clan culture generates feelings of personal ownership of a business, a product, or an idea. In addition, peer pressure to adhere to important norms is strong. The richness of the culture creates an environment in which few areas are left totally free from normative pressures. Depending on the types of its norms, the culture may or may not generate risk-taking behavior or innovation. Success is assumed to depend substantially on sensitivity to customers and concern for people. Teamwork, participation, and consensus decision making are believed to lead to this success.

Entrepreneurial Culture

High levels of risk taking and creativity characterize an **entrepreneurial culture.** There is a commitment to experimentation, innovation, and being on the leading edge. This culture doesn't just quickly react to changes in the environment—it creates change. Many of today's hi-tech companies, such as Apple, DreamWorks SKG, and Get Digital, have developed entrepreneurial cultures. Effectiveness means providing new and unique products and rapid growth. Individual initiative, flexibility, and freedom foster growth and are encouraged and well rewarded. In late 2000 and throughout much of 2001, many of the dot-com companies failed because their leaders lacked the management competencies to build the companies and manage external relationships with financial backers.

Entrepreneurial cultures usually are associated with small to midsized companies that are still run by a founder. Innovation and entrepreneurship are values held by the founder(s). Jeff Bezos started Amazon.com in his two-bedroom home in Seattle. Later, he and his friends converted his garage to an office and ran extension cords from every outlet to power three computers. To save money, Bezos went to Home Depot and bought wooden doors. Using angle brackets and 2 × 4s, he converted the doors into desks that cost $60 each. Today, the firm's desks are still made the same way. Initially, money is tight for most start-ups, and the entrepreneur's ability to raise seed money often is crucial to its survival.

Market Culture

The achievement of measurable and demanding goals, especially those that are financial and market based (e.g., sales growth, profitability, and market share) characterize a **market culture.** PepsiCo, Bank of America, and AIG, among others, have many of the characteristics found in market cultures. Hard-driving competitiveness and a profit orientation prevail throughout the organization. CEO Christos Cotsakos describes the market culture of E*Trade this way: "At E*Trade we're an attacker. We're predatory. We believe in the God-given right to market share."

In a market culture, the relationship between individual and organization is contractual. That is, the obligations of each party are agreed on in advance. In this sense, the control orientation is formal and quite stable. The individual is responsible for some level of performance, and the organization promises a specified level of rewards in return. Increased levels of performance are exchanged for increased rewards, as outlined in an agreed-on schedule. Neither party recognizes the right of the other to demand more than was originally specified. The organization doesn't promise (or imply) security, and the individual doesn't promise (or imply) loyalty. The contract, renewed annually if each party adequately performs its obligations, is utilitarian because each party uses the other to further its own goals. Rather than promoting a feeling of membership in a social system, the market culture values independence and individuality and encourages members to pursue their own financial goals.

A market culture doesn't exert much social pressure on an organization's members, but when it does, members are expected to conform. At Enron, employees (in theory) were permitted to book their business travel themselves with any agency. However, Sharon Lay, Ken Lay's sister, owned a Houston travel agency that received $6.8 million in commissions from Enron for travel. Employees who didn't book their travel through her agency did so only once. Memos from Ken Lay's office reminded them that they should use her travel agency.

In market cultures, superiors' interactions with subordinates largely consist of negotiating performance–reward agreements and/or evaluating requests for resource allocations. Managers aren't formally judged on their effectiveness as role models or mentors. The absence of a long-term commitment by both parties results in a weak socialization process. Social relations among coworkers aren't emphasized, and few economic incentives are tied directly to cooperating with peers. Managers are expected to cooperate with managers in other departments only to the extent necessary to achieve their performance goals. As a result, they may not develop an extensive network of colleagues within the organization. The market culture often is tied to monthly, quarterly, and annual performance goals based on profits. At PepsiCo, managers are driven to make their numbers (sales quotas). The emphasis is on fixing problems quickly and moving up the organization's hierarchy.

Culture-Performance Relationships

Organizational culture has the potential to enhance organizational performance, individual satisfaction, the sense of certainty about how problems are to be handled, and so on. However, if an organizational culture gets out of step with the changing expectations of internal and/or external stakeholders, the organization's effectiveness can decline. Organizational culture and performance clearly are related, although the evidence regarding the exact nature of this relationship is mixed. Studies show that the relationship between many cultural attributes (featured in the popular press as being important for performance) and high performance hasn't been consistent over time. Based on what we know about culture–performance relationships, a contingency approach seems to be a good one for managers and organizations to take. Further investigations of this issue are unlikely to discover one "best" organizational culture (either in terms of strength or type).

We do know the following about the relationships between culture and performance:

- Organizational culture can have a significant impact on a firm's long-term economic performance.
- Organizational culture will probably be an even more important factor in determining the success or failure of firms during the next decade.
- Organizational cultures that inhibit strong long-term financial performance are not rare; they develop easily, even in firms that are filled with reasonable and intelligent people.
- Although tough to change, organizational cultures can be made more performance enhancing if managers understand what sustains a culture.[22]

We can summarize the effects of organizational culture on employee behavior and performance with four key ideas. First, knowing the culture of an organization allows employees to understand both the firm's history and current methods of operation. This knowledge provides guidance about expected future behaviors. Second, organizational culture can foster commitment to corporate philosophy and values. This commitment generates shared feelings of working toward common goals. Third, organizational culture, through its norms, serves as a control mechanism to channel behaviors toward desired behaviors and away from undesired behaviors. Finally, certain types of organizational cultures may be related directly to greater effectiveness and productivity than others.

The need to determine which attributes of an organization's culture should be preserved and which should be modified is constant. In the United States during the 1980s, many organizations began changing their cultures to be more responsive to customers' expectations of product quality and service. During the late 1990s, many organizations began to reassess how well their cultures fit the expectations of the workforce. Since World War II, the U.S. workforce has changed demographically, becoming more diverse. More and more employees have begun to feel that organizational cultures established decades ago are out of step with contemporary values. We address the challenge of adjusting established organizational cultures to meet the expectations of a demographically diverse workforce in the remainder of this chapter.

LEARNING OBJECTIVE

3. Discuss how organizational culture can influence ethical behaviors of managers and employees.

ETHICAL BEHAVIOR AND ORGANIZATIONAL CULTURE

Ethical problems in organizations continue to concern managers and employees greatly. The Enron bankruptcy and scandal is the most prominent recent example of a failure to promote ethical behavior among an organization's managers, employees, and contractors. One organization, Deloitte Touche Tohmatsu, a professional-service firm, has created a web-based ethics course for all employees in the 150 countries in which it operates. It has the kind of 1-800 hotline mandated by the Sarbanes-Oxley Act of 2002 for the anonymous reporting of wrongdoings. It has also customized its ethics program on a country-by-country basis since in some cultures a 1-800 hotline would not be culturally acceptable.[23]

Impact of Culture

Managers and researchers are beginning to explore the potential impact that organizational culture can have on ethical behavior. Organizational culture involves a complex interplay of formal and informal systems that may support either ethical or unethical behavior. Formal systems include leadership, structure, policies, reward systems, orientation and training programs, and decision-making processes. Informal systems include norms, heroes, rituals, language, myths, sagas, and stories.

Organizational culture appears to affect ethical behavior in several ways.[24] For example, a culture emphasizing ethical norms provides support for ethical behavior. In addition, top management plays a key role in fostering ethical behavior by exhibiting the correct behavior. If lower level managers observe top-level managers sexually harassing others, falsifying expense reports, diverting shipments to preferred customers, misrepresenting the organization's financial position, and other forms of unethical behavior, they assume that these behaviors are acceptable and will be rewarded in the future. Thus, the presence or absence of ethical behavior in managerial actions both influences and reflects the culture. The organizational culture may promote taking responsibility for the consequences of actions, thereby increasing the probability that individuals will behave ethically. Alternatively, the culture may diffuse responsibility for the consequences of unethical behavior, thereby making such behavior more likely. In short, ethical business practices stem from ethical organizational cultures.

An employee might use various strategies in attempting to change unethical behavior, including

- secretly or publicly reporting unethical actions to a higher level within the organization;
- secretly or publicly reporting unethical actions to someone outside the organization;
- secretly or publicly threatening an offender or a responsible manager with reporting unethical actions; or
- quietly or publicly refusing to implement an unethical order or policy.

Whistle-Blowing

Whistle-blowing *is the disclosure by current or former employees of illegal, immoral, or illegitimate organizational practices to people or organizations that may be able to change the practice.* The whistle-blower lacks the power to change the undesirable practice directly and so appeals to others either inside or outside the organization.

Time magazine selected three whistle-blowers as their persons of the year in 2002: Cynthia Cooper of WorldCom, Coleen Rowley of the FBI, and Sherron Watkins of Enron. In Cooper's case, this meant reporting falsified accounting records to the Audit Committee at WorldCom; the Audit Committee fired the CFO, who was then prosecuted and found guilty of using illegal accounting procedures. Rowley sent a memo to the director of the FBI alleging mismanagement at the highest levels in regards to the investigation of terrorists on 9/11. The collapse of Enron started when Sherron Watkins sat down at her computer on August 14, 2001, and began typing a questioning and now famous memo to her boss, Kenneth Lay. "I am incredibly nervous that we will implode in a wave of accounting scandals," she wrote. Watkins's seven-page memo has become the smoking gun in an unfolding investigation of alleged financial misdealing at Enron and Arthur

Andersen. Watkins and Cooper both found themselves confronting fraudulent behavior that was illegal and could be related to individuals. Rowley's complaints had to do with the mismanagement of information and ineffective leadership that existed in the FBI. All three acted when the evidence became overwhelming that a significant wrongdoing had occurred. All three feared retaliation.

What do you consider a whistle-blowing offense? The following Communication Competency asks you to decide what a wrongdoing is, and asks you if you would blow the whistle on a person whom you observed engaging in this practice. We also ask you to indicate whether the types of retaliation listed would happen to you if you reported such a wrongdoing to top management and/or the organization's ethics officer. For the purpose of this illustration, you may assume that the average cost of the wrongdoing is $35,000 and that you had observed this wrongdoing frequently. We realize that oftentimes a dollar amount is difficult to place on a wrongdoing (e.g., a safety violation, sexual harassment, mismanagement). On page 445, you can compare your answers to those people who have actually blown the whistle at work.[25]

COMMUNICATION COMPETENCY

WHAT WOULD YOU DO?

We realize that the eight types of wrongdoing presented will be significantly affected by the cost of the wrongdoing. The cost, quality of evidence, and frequency of activity of the wrongdoing are all related to whether you would actually blow the whistle or just threaten to do so. The type of retaliation also varies by the type of wrongdoing and the cost. We want you to indicate the type of retaliation most likely suffered by the whistle-blower.

Type of Wrongdoing	*Would You Report to Management?*
Stealing	YES NO
Waste	YES NO
Mismanagement	YES NO
Safety problems	YES NO
Sexual harassment	YES NO
Unfair discrimination	YES NO
Legal violation	YES NO
Financial reporting	YES NO

Type of Retaliation	*Would This Happen to You?*
Coworkers not associating with person	YES NO
Pressure from coworkers to stop complaint	YES NO
Withholding of information needed to perform job	YES NO
Poor performance appraisal	YES NO
Verbal harassment or intimidation	YES NO
Tighter scrutiny of daily work by management	YES NO
Reassignment to a different job	YES NO
Reassignment to a different job with less desirable duties	YES NO
Denial of a promotion	YES NO

The following actions can help create an organizational culture that encourages ethical behavior:

- Be realistic in setting values and goals regarding employment relationships. Do not promise what the organization cannot deliver.

- Encourage input from throughout the organization regarding appropriate values and practices for implementing the culture. Choose values that represent the views of both employees and managers.
- Develop a *strong* culture that encourages and rewards diversity and principled dissent, such as grievance or complaint mechanisms or other internal review procedures.
- Provide training programs for managers and teams on adopting and implementing the organization's values. These programs should stress the underlying ethical and legal principles and cover the practical aspects of carrying out procedural guidelines.

An effective organizational culture should encourage ethical behavior and discourage unethical behavior. Admittedly, ethical behavior may "cost" the organization and individuals. A global firm that refuses to pay a bribe to secure business in a particular country may lose sales. An individual may lose financially by not accepting a kickback. Similarly, an organization or individual might seem to gain from unethical actions. An organization may flout U.S. law by quietly paying bribes to officials in order to gain entry to a new market. A purchasing agent for a large corporation might take kickbacks for purchasing all needed office supplies from a particular supplier. However, such gains are often short term.

In the long run, an organization can't successfully operate if its prevailing culture and values aren't similar to those of society. That is as true as the observation that, in the long run, an organization cannot survive unless it provides high-quality goods and services that society wants and needs. An organizational culture that promotes ethical behavior is not only compatible with prevailing cultural values in the United States, but it also makes good business sense.

FOSTERING CULTURAL DIVERSITY

LEARNING OBJECTIVE

4. Explain why fostering cultural diversity is important.

In Chapter 1, we emphasized that organizations are becoming increasingly diverse in terms of gender, race, ethnicity, and nationality. More than half of the U.S. workforce consists of women, minorities, and recent immigrants. The growing diversity of employees in many organizations can bring substantial benefits, such as more successful marketing strategies for different types of customers, improved decision making, and greater creativity and innovation. The U.S. Department of Labor forecasts that 60 percent of all new employees entering the U.S. workforce during the period from 2000 to 2010 will be women or people of color. Whether motivated by economic necessity or choice, organizations will be competing in this marketplace for talent. At DuPont, a group of African-American workers recently opened promising new markets for the firm by focusing on black farmers. A multicultural team gained the company about $45 million in new business by changing the way DuPont designs and markets decorating materials (e.g., countertops) in order to appeal more to overseas customers.

Challenges

Along with its benefits, cultural diversity brings costs and concerns, including communication difficulties, intraorganizational conflict, and turnover. Effectively fostering cultural diversity promises to continue to be a significant challenge for organizations for a long time. To succeed, organizations have to work hard at resolving these issues. In the following Self Competency feature, Linda Glick, chief information officer for Levi Strauss and Company, describes both the benefits and the challenges stemming from a multicultural workforce.[26]

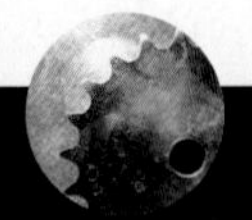

SELF COMPETENCY

LINDA GLICK AT LEVI STRAUSS

Linda Glick started her career at Levi Strauss as a programmer. Soon managers at Strauss recognized her as a person with excellent communication and team competencies, as well as someone who worked very well across cultures. Her ability to speak two foreign languages was a major plus for a company that views its products as having global appeal. Her initial assignment in the international group proved especially valuable because it was a small group where titles and other symbols of Levi's culture were not important. Levi's team members yelled and screamed at each other over business issues, but still went out together for beer later. This assignment gave Glick an opportunity to understand Levi's entire business operations across all product lines. During that early assignment, she learned that effective leaders at Strauss were those who listened, understood others' concerns, and used creative thinking to solve problems—and let others make decisions.

Later, as a manager working overseas, she also faced unique challenges. When she went to Japan, she lacked the ability to speak Japanese. In her first meeting with a supplier of zippers, she encountered gender prejudice. The Japanese managers thought that she was a translator and treated her as such. She was expected to sit quietly, not ask questions, stand up when men left the room, serve tea, and the like. The meeting was conducted entirely in Japanese. When she asked questions in English, the Japanese replied in Japanese. Although Japanese suppliers saw her as a wonderful person, they had a difficult time accepting her as a line manager with responsibility. However, because she understood Levi Strauss's business thoroughly and took a high-energy approach to business (e.g., serious negotiations, on-time meetings, and organized meeting agendas), she eventually was accepted.

Her experience in Mexico required different behaviors. Meetings were chaotic, leaders lost control of conversations, and meetings that were scheduled to start at 9:00 A.M. usually didn't begin until much later. She had a hard time understanding the macho attitudes that were shown toward women. It wasn't her personality to be aggressive, to fight to be heard, but she found that if she didn't speak up, she would be ignored and undervalued.

Glick's philosophy is: "Change is painful and hard. We all gravitate toward the comfortable, familiar and cozy. We don't know if we have the stamina and resilience to take on change and see it through successfully." To be an effective manager in a multicultural corporation such as Levi Strauss, the person needs to stay focused, have a belief in her own abilities, and a belief that others can make good decisions.

*For more information on Levi Strauss, visit the organization's home page at **http://www.levistrauss.com**.*

Effective Diversity Programs

There are no easy answers to the challenges of fostering a culturally diverse workforce. However, research has revealed some common characteristics that are present in organizations having effective diversity management programs. These characteristics have been distilled into the following helpful guidelines:

- Managers and employees must understand that a diverse workforce will embody different perspectives and approaches to work and must truly value variety of opinion and insight.
- Managers must recognize both the learning opportunities and the challenges that the expression of different perspectives presents for the organization.

- The organizational culture must create an expectation of high standards of performance and ethics from everyone.
- The organizational culture must stimulate personal development.
- The organizational culture must encourage openness.
- The organizational culture must make workers feel valued.
- The organization must have a clearly stated and widely understood mission.

Table 4.3 contains a questionnaire that you can use to examine your awareness of diversity issues. Take a moment to complete it now. What did you learn about yourself?

TABLE 4.3 Diversity Questionnaire

Directions

Indicate your views by placing a T (true) or F (false) next to each of these nine statements.

1. I know about the rules and customs of several different cultures. _____
2. I know that I hold stereotypes about other groups. _____
3. I feel comfortable with people of different backgrounds from my own. _____
4. I associate with people who are different from me. _____
5. I find working on a multicultural team satisfying. _____
6. I find change stimulating and exciting. _____
7. I enjoy learning about other cultures. _____
8. When dealing with someone whose English is limited, I show patience and understanding. _____
9. I find that spending time building relationships with others is useful because more gets done. _____

Interpretation

The more true responses you have, the more adaptable and open you are to diversity. If you have five or more true responses, you probably are someone who finds value in cross-cultural experiences.

If you have less than five true responses, you may be resistant to interacting with people who are different from you. If that is the case, you may find that your interactions with others are sometimes blocked.

Source: Adapted from Gardenswartz, L., and Rowe, A. What's your diversity quotient? *Managing Diversity Newsletter,* Jamestown, New York (undated).

SOCIALIZATION OF NEW EMPLOYEES

LEARNING OBJECTIVE

5. Describe the process of organizational socialization and its effect on culture.

Socialization *is the process by which older members of a society transmit to younger members the social skills and knowledge needed to function effectively in that society.* Similarly, **organizational socialization** *is the systematic process by which an organization brings new employees into its culture.*[27] In other words, it involves the transmission of organizational culture from managers and senior employees to new employees, providing the social knowledge and skills needed to perform organizational roles and tasks successfully.

Organizational socialization provides the means by which new employees learn which "ropes" to pay attention to and which to ignore. It includes learning work group, departmental, and organizational values, rules, procedures, and norms; developing social and working relationships; and developing the skills needed to perform a job. Interestingly, the stages that an employee goes through during organizational socialization resemble, in many respects, the five stages of group development discussed in Chapter 8.

Organizational Socialization Process

Figure 4.5 presents an example of an organizational socialization process. It doesn't represent the socialization process of every organization. However, many firms with strong cultures—such as Disney, TDIndustries, and Interstate Battery—frequently follow at least some of these steps in socializing new employees:

FIGURE 4.5 Steps in Socialization

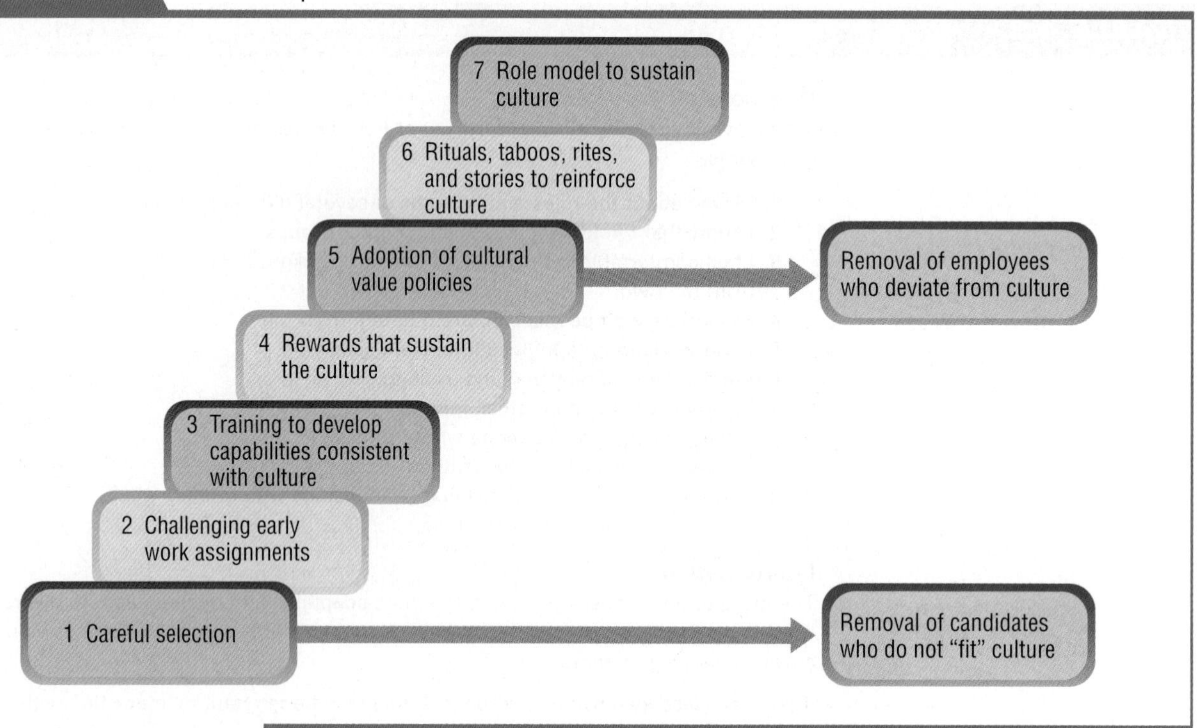

Step One. Entry-level candidates are selected carefully. Trained recruiters use standardized procedures and seek specific capabilities that are related to the success of the business.

> **THE COMPETENT LEADER**
>
> We had a corporate culture here before I knew what it meant. One of my goals is to maintain it. Our culture is what differentiates us from other airlines. Our people give us a competitive advantage and it cannot be copied.
>
> **Colleen Barrett, President and Chief Operating Officer, Southwest Airlines**

Step Two. Humility-inducing experiences in the first months on the job cause employees to question their prior behaviors, beliefs, and values. At the U.S. Naval Academy, this indoctrination includes saluting all upperclassmen, standing at attention while being spoken to by upperclassmen, and memorizing trivial facts about the academy (e.g., its date of founding, number and names of buildings, the score of last year's football game against West Point). Self-questioning promotes openness to acceptance of the organization's norms and values.

Step Three. Tough on-the-job training leads to mastery of one of the core disciplines of the business. Promotion is then tied to a proven track record. At KFC, for example, many restaurant managers have been greeters, busing staff, waiters, chefs, and so forth.

Step Four. Careful attention is given to measuring results and rewarding performance. Reward systems are true indicators of the values that underlie an organization's culture. At KFC, David Novak, its CEO, passes out floppy rubber chickens (all of which are numbered and have a personal note on them) as a reward and to recognize employees for their outstanding contribution(s) to KFC.

Step Five. Adherence to the organization's values is emphasized. Identification with common values allows employees to justify personal sacrifices caused by their membership in the organization.

Step Six. Reinforcing folklore provides legends and interpretations of important events in the organization's history that validate its culture and goals. Folklore reinforces a code of conduct for "how we do things around here."

Step Seven. Consistent role models and consistent traits are associated with those recognized as being on the fast track to promotion and success.[28]

Disney World has an effective socialization process that uses some of these seven steps to help ensure that tens of thousands of visitors a day will have fun.[29] Disney annually hires more than 2,000 people and employs more than 27,500 at Disney World. Those who cannot afford housing are housed in a separate Disney gated complex. Disney carefully screens all potential members (Step One). After recruits complete their applications, they are screened for criminal records. Those who have a record are dropped from consideration.

All workers at Disney World must strictly follow Disney rules (e.g., no mustaches, visible tattoos, dangling body piercing items, and no hair color outside of the "normal" colors) and norms (such as always taking the extra step to make sure guests have a good experience) and behave in a certain way. To learn these rules, norms, and behaviors, new cast members (recruits) receive formal training at Disney University in groups of 45 and follow a rigid program. During the Tradition I program, which lasts a day and a half, new cast members learn the Disney language and the four Disney values: safety, courtesy, show or entertainment, and efficiency. They also receive training in how to answer guests' questions no matter how simple or difficult the question (Step Five). About 40 percent of new cast members complete Tradition I training. Many simply quit when they understand what their jobs and the rules will entail.

Once the cast members have completed the Tradition I phase, they move on to further socialization in the attraction areas (Adventureland, Fantasyland, and so on) that they will join. This session, which can last as long as a day and a half, covers rules for each area. Last but not least is on-the-job training by experienced cast members who actually work in an attraction. This part of the socialization process can take up to two and a half weeks to complete, during which the new cast members wear a costume, learn to sing a song (where appropriate), and begin to relate effectively with other cast members and guests (Step Three).

Dilemmas in Socialization

All organizations and groups socialize new members in some way, but the steps can vary greatly in terms of how explicit, comprehensive, and lengthy they are. Generally, rapid socialization is advantageous. For the individual, it quickly reduces the uncertainty and anxiety surrounding a new job. For the organization, it helps the new employee become productive quickly. Organizations with strong cultures may be particularly skillful at socializing individuals. If the culture is effective, socialization will contribute to organizational success. However, if the culture needs changing, strong socialization reduces the prospects for making needed changes.

Socialization creates some additional dilemmas. For example, GE, Xerox, Disney, and other organizations use executive development programs to socialize new hires. How strong should the socialization be? Does the organization want its hires to think alike, at least in terms of a certain level of logic and intelligent analysis? To have the same business values and sense of professionalism? In some sense, the answer to these questions has to be *yes*. Yet oversocialization runs the risk of creating rigid, narrow-minded corporate men and women. The goal of most organizations' socialization processes is to develop independent thinkers committed to what they believe to be right, while at the same time helping them become collaborative team players who have good interpersonal skills. This goal poses a challenge for socialization, which, to be effective, must balance these two demands.

The socialization process may affect employee and organizational success in a variety of ways.[30] Table 4.4 lists some possible socialization outcomes. These outcomes aren't determined solely by an organization's socialization process. For example, job satisfaction is a function of many things, including the nature of the task, the individual's personality and needs, the nature of supervision, opportunities to succeed and be rewarded, and the like (see Chapter 11). Note that successful socialization may contribute to job satisfaction, whereas unsuccessful socialization may contribute to job dissatisfaction.

TABLE 4.4 Possible Outcomes of Socialization Process

SUCCESSFUL SOCIALIZATION IS REFLECTED IN	UNSUCCESSFUL SOCIALIZATION IS REFLECTED IN
• Job satisfaction	• Job dissatisfaction
• Role clarity	• Role ambiguity and conflict
• High work motivation	• Low work motivation
• Understanding of culture, perceived control	• Misunderstanding, tension, perceived lack of control
• High job involvement	• Low job involvement
• Commitment to organization	• Lack of commitment to organization
• Tenure	• Absenteeism, turnover
• High performance	• Low performance
• Internalized values	• Rejection of values

CHAPTER SUMMARY

1. Explain how an organizational culture is formed, sustained, and changed.

Organizational culture is the pattern of beliefs and expectations shared by members of an organization. It includes a common philosophy, norms, and values. In other words, it expresses the "rules of the game" for getting along and getting things done and ways of interacting with outsiders, such as suppliers and customers. Some aspects of organizational culture are cultural symbols, heroes, rites, and ceremonies. Organizational culture develops as a response to the challenges of external adaptation and survival and of internal integration. The formation of an organization's culture also is influenced by the culture of the larger society within which the organization must function.

The primary methods for both sustaining and changing organizational culture include (1) identifying what managers and teams pay attention to, measure, and control; (2) recognizing the ways in which managers and employees react to crises; (3) using role modeling, teaching, and coaching; (4) developing and applying fair criteria for allocating rewards; (5) utilizing consistent criteria for recruitment, selection, and promotion within the organization and removal from it; and (6) emphasizing organizational rites, ceremonies, and stories.

2. Describe four types of organizational culture.

Although all organizational cultures are unique, four general types are identified and discussed: bureaucratic, clan, entrepreneurial, and market. They are characterized by differences in the extent of formal controls and focus of attention.

Organizational culture also can have a strong effect on ethical behavior by managers and employees alike. One concept linking culture to ethical behavior is principled organizational dissent. Cultures that encourage dissent and permit whistle-blowing provide guidelines for ethical behaviors.

3. Discuss how organizational culture can influence ethical behaviors of managers and employees.

Fostering cultural diversity is expected to be one of the principal challenges facing the leaders of organizations for years to come. How leaders respond to this challenge will determine the effectiveness of culturally diverse teams, an organization's communication process, and employees' personal development.

4. Explain why fostering cultural diversity is important.

Socialization is the process by which new members are brought into an organization's culture. At firms having a strong culture, socialization steps are well developed and the focus of careful attention. All organizations socialize new members, but depending on how it is done, the outcomes could be either positive or negative in terms of job performance, satisfaction, and commitment to the organization. We presented a seven-step process for socializing new employees.

5. Describe the process of organizational socialization and its effect on culture.

KEY TERMS AND CONCEPTS

Bureaucratic culture
Clan culture
Cultural symbols
Cultural values
Entrepreneurial culture
External adaptation and survival
Internal integration
Market culture
Organizational culture
Organizational rites and ceremonies
Organizational socialization
Shared behaviors
Socialization
Subcultures
Whistle-blowing

DISCUSSION QUESTIONS

1. Use the words in Table 4.1 to describe the culture of Starbucks (visit its website at http://www.starbucks.com), Dell Computer (visit its website at http://www.dell.com), or another organization with which you are familiar. How does its organizational culture affect the type of employee who chooses to work there?
2. What role does Google's reward system play in maintaining its culture?
3. Describe the culture at Google. What behaviors led you to describe its culture in this way?
4. Describe the steps used in socializing new employees at an organization with which you are familiar. How successful is this process?
5. What type of organizational culture would you prefer to work in? Why? Table 4.1 can help you understand your own values.
6. How might an organization use its culture to increase the probability of ethical behavior and decrease the probability of unethical behavior by its managers and employees?
7. Can Teerlink's methods at Harley-Davidson be used in other organizations? Explain.
8. What are the primary methods that Richard Teerlink used to change the culture of Harley-Davidson?
9. Provide two examples of how organizational culture is expressed at your college or university.
10. Describe how that culture affects your behavior.

EXPERIENTIAL EXERCISE AND CASE

Experiential Exercise: Ethics Competency

Assessing a Culture's Ethical Behaviors

Instructions: Think of a job you currently hold or used to have. Indicate how you feel about each behavior. Use the following scale and place one number after each behavior to indicate your response. There are no right or wrong answers.

1. Very acceptable
2. Acceptable
3. Somewhat acceptable
4. Uncertain
5. Somewhat unacceptable
6. Unacceptable
7. Very unacceptable

_____ 1. Taking home a few supplies (e.g., paper clips, pencils, and pens).
_____ 2. Calling in sick when some personal time (e.g., play golf or take in a movie) is needed.
_____ 3. Using a company telephone, fax, or computer for personal business.
_____ 4. Making personal copies on a company copy machine.
_____ 5. Using a company car to make a personal trip.
_____ 6. Eating at a very expensive restaurant on a company business trip.
_____ 7. Charging wine and cocktails as well as food on a company business trip.
_____ 8. Taking a significant other along on a company business trip at the company's expense.
_____ 9. Staying at an expensive hotel on a company business trip.
_____10. On a company business trip, charging a $7 cab ride to your expense account when you actually walked.

Interpretation of Results

More than 200 managers responded to this survey. Compare your responses to theirs.

1. 50 percent thought that taking home a few office supplies was acceptable.
2. 70 percent reported that calling in sick to take personal time was unacceptable.
3. 74.7 percent reported that making personal calls on the telephone, using a fax, or computer was unacceptable.
4. 54.6 percent indicated that making personal copies on a copy machine was acceptable.
5. 70.6 percent thought that using a company car for a personal trip was unacceptable.
6. 59.1 percent reported that eating at a very expensive restaurant was acceptable.
7. 50 percent believed that charging wine and cocktails was acceptable.
8. 85 percent thought that taking a significant other along on a business trip at the company's expense was unacceptable.
9. 55 percent indicated that staying at an expensive hotel on a company business trip was acceptable.
10. 41 percent indicated that charging $7 for a cab ride when they walked was very unacceptable.[31]

Questions

1. Would you expect these results to vary by type of culture (e.g., bureaucratic, clan, entrepreneurial, or market)?
2. Choose several items that you and the managerial respondents are in disagreement over. What steps would you recommend to change these behaviors? How do your recommendations reflect your own values (see Table 4.1).

Case: Teams Competency

Southwest Airlines' Culture[32]

San Antonio lawyer Herb Kelleher founded Southwest Airlines in 1966 with one of his clients, Rollin King, at a bar in San Antonio. King came up with the idea of starting a low-fare airline and Kelleher liked it. They doodled a plan on a cocktail napkin and Kelleher put up $10,000 of his own money to get it started. (His stake is now worth more than $200 million.)

He fought competitors in the courts to get the airline started and likened these fights to being in the French Foreign Legion. Texas International, Braniff, and Continental tried to stop Kelleher, but he was determined to show them that Southwest could become a reality and survive. On June 18, 1971, Kelleher told Lamar Muse, then CEO of Southwest Airlines, to go ahead with scheduled flights no matter what the courts decided. Lamar said: "Gee, Herb, what do I do. Suppose the sheriff shows up and tries to prevent the flights?" "So what!" said Kelleher. "Leave tire tracks on his shirt. We're going, come hell or high water." This same spirit also led to at least one fistfight with personnel of another airline. One time, some Braniff people went up to the roof of the terminal building at Hobby Field in Houston and hung a sign over Southwest's to advertise Braniff's service to Dallas. The Southwest station manager went up there and tried to cut it down with a knife. He ended up getting into a fistfight on the top of the terminal building.

According to Kelleher, people are the airline's most important asset, and they provide legendary service. He states that employees are the airline's first customers and passengers are the second. When it was pointed out to Kelleher that mechanics on the graveyard shift could not participate in company picnics, he held a 2:00 A.M. barbecue and several pilots served as chefs. Southwest wants to offer a unique and fun experience to each customer. He also believed that you want to show your people that you value them and that you are not going to hurt them just to get some more money in the short term. Laying people off breeds a lack of trust, a sense of insecurity, and a lack of loyalty. Although 85 percent of Southwest's pilots are members of unions, they identify more with the airline than with their union. As a result, there have been few strikes since Southwest was formed in 1971.

Southwest can hire and hold the very best people. Why would you work longer hours than others doing the same job? This is interesting because Southwest pilots fly 80 hours per month compared with 50 hours in other airlines. Southwest pilots are paid by the trip rather than by the hour. As a result, pilots are interested in minimizing the aircraft's time at the gate, because while at the gate, they are not being compensated. Flight attendants fly 150 hours per month versus the 80 hours for other airlines. The airline does, however, contribute 15 percent of pretax income to all employees' profit-sharing plans. Flight attendants are also required to make a reasonable effort to tidy up the airplane between flights. Many flight attendants have developed catchy phrases to involve customers in this task.

At Southwest Airlines the human resource function is called the People Department, which is crucial to Southwest's success. According to the department's mission statement, "recognizing that our people are the competitive advantage, we deliver resources and services to prepare our people to be winners, to support the growth and profitability of the company, while preserving the values and special culture of Southwest Airlines." Elizabeth Sartain, executive vice president of the People Department, comments that Southwest can change a person's skill levels through training, but it can't change attitudes, so people are hired for their attitudes, not for their technical skills. In fact, the airline rejects about 100,000 applicants a year, and the turnover rate is less than half (e.g., about 7 percent) that of most other airlines. Because its organizational culture is crucial for developing dedication to excellence, a new hire's first six months at Southwest are a period of indoctrination and mentoring. This time is also used to weed out anyone who doesn't fit the culture.

All new hires attend Southwest's University for People. During classes, all are told that they have a responsibility for self-improvement and training. Once a year, all employees, including senior management, are required to participate in a program designed to reinforce shared values. Except for flight training, which is regulated by the FAA, all training is done on the employee's own time. The university operates at capacity, seven days a week. The fun and spirit of Southwest emerge in graduates very early.

Creativity, humor, and service are significant aspects of the culture. At the corporate offices, employees have been allowed to work in pajamas for a day. There are also rocking chairs located throughout the building for impromptu meetings and ways to find relief in high-stress jobs. Employees are taught that, if they want customers to have fun, they must create a fun-loving environment. That means that employees must be self-confident enough to reach out and share their sense of humor and fun. They must be willing to play and expend the extra energy it takes to create a fun experience for their customers. For example, Southwest's "positively outrageous service" stresses friendliness, caring, warmth, and company spirit. Gate attendants are taught how to play games with customers, such as guess the weight of the gate agent, name three things to do in Tulsa, and who has the most holes in his sock to pass the time if a plane is delayed. Flights attendants are liable to say anything over the telecom. The games are never in poor taste and the winners get a free dinner or a Southwest "fun" hat. Recently, Gary Kelly, Southwest Airlines' CEO, showed up at a Halloween party looking like Gene Simmons, the front man for the rock group Kiss. The legacy of Herb seems to be living on.

Another characteristic of the strong culture is employee commitment and motivation, which leads to cooperative relationships among employee teams. That is, the majority of employees share the same goals and basically agree on how to pursue them. For example, gate agents and flight crews clean planes along with members of the maintenance department. All share the goal of a 15-minute turnaround, or about one-third of the time needed by competitors. Because of these team-oriented values, the company has few of the rigid work rules that characterize most of its competitors. At Southwest everybody pitches in regardless of the task. Southwest uses a team measurement instead of individual performance metrics to reinforce the team concept. A team statistic that it uses is percentage of on-time departures. This measurement is the responsibility of all Southwest people at an airport. People from all departments must work together to improve the percentage of on-time departures. There is no finger pointing. Shared knowledge and goals are critical. Just before he retired, Kelleher wrote to all employees and asked them to save $5 a day by cutting nonfuel costs. Employees responded by cutting costs 5.6 percent, or more than $10 a day. Since being diagnosed with prostate cancer a few years ago, Kelleher has retired from active management at Southwest. For him, cancer was never an issue. It was just something that he had to get through, and he has tried to keep a sense of humor about it. For example, one day he walked into an exam room with a lighted cigarette. The doctors went berserk. Told to put it out, he said: "I don't have anywhere to put it out. If you want smokers to put out cigarettes, you ought to have ashtrays."

In 2001, he reached the age of 70 and decided to retire. His biggest concern was that he wanted a successor who would respect Southwest's culture and who was altruistic. Gary Kelly, who joined Southwest in 1986 as a controller, insists that he will keep the airline's maverick spirit that Herb created in 1971.

Questions

1. Use the words in Table 4.1 to describe the organizational culture of Southwest Airlines.
2. Why haven't other organizations, including other airlines, been able to copy Southwest's culture?
3. What role does socialization play at Southwest Airlines?
4. Access the Southwest Airlines website at http://www.iflyswa.com. What symbols does Southwest use on its website to convey its culture?

ANSWERS TO COMMUNICATION COMPETENCY

What Would You Do?

Types of Wrongdoings	Percentage of People Who Would Report the Wrong-doing to Management
Stealing	25%
Waste	17
Mismanagement	42
Safety problems	23
Sexual harassment	40
Unfair discrimination	27
Legal violations	53
Financial reporting	52

Type of Retaliation	Percentage Who Experienced It
Coworkers not associating with person	12%
Pressure from coworkers to stop complaint	5
Withholding information needed to perform job	10
Poor performance appraisal	15
Verbal harassment or intimidation	12
Tighter scrutiny of daily work by management	14
Reassignment to a different job	8
Reassignment to a different job with less desirable duties	7
Denial of a promotion	7

CHAPTER 5

Guiding Organizational Change

LEARNING OBJECTIVES

When you have finished studying this chapter, you should be able to:

1. Identify pressures for change, two types of change programs, and how to perform an organizational diagnosis.
2. Diagnose reasons for individual and organizational resistance to change and describe methods for overcoming it.
3. Discuss three methods for promoting change.
4. Describe ethical issues posed by organizational change.

Preview Case: Hewlett-Packard
CHALLENGES OF CHANGE
Pressures for Change
Across Cultures Competency—Western Union
Types of Change Approaches
Organizational Use
Organizational Diagnosis
RESISTANCE TO CHANGE
Individual Resistance
Self Competency—Are You Ready to Change?
Organizational Resistance
Overcoming Resistance
Teams Competency—Shell's Change Process
PROMOTING CHANGE
Interpersonal Methods
Team Methods
Organizational Methods
Communication Competency—Just in Time at Toyota
ETHICAL ISSUES IN ORGANIZATIONAL CHANGE
CHAPTER SUMMARY
KEY TERMS AND CONCEPTS
DISCUSSION QUESTIONS
EXPERIENTIAL EXERCISE AND CASE

PREVIEW CASE

HEWLETT-PACKARD

It has been more than five years since Carleton Fiorina burst onto the scene at Silicon Valley. Named as *Fortune* magazine's most powerful woman in 1998, her reputation bloomed. She was one of the few businesspeople identifiable by her first name: Carly. She became an instant celebrity.

In 1998, she announced her plans to reinvent HP, but still wanted to maintain the cultural values that Dave Packard held when he formed the company. Ever since its founding in a Palo Alto garage in 1939, HP has represented entrepreneurialism. Packard created a culture that valued engineering and teamwork and rewarded ideas and innovation. Fiorina recognized that HP needed to build capabilities of speed, agility, and collaboration to survive in this industry. Fiorina saw the industry in which HP competed as being in a state of transformation. The digital age is bringing about democratization of information because it removes the traditional barriers of time, distance, and wealth. HP started working with Jeffrey Katzenberg at DreamWorks to help them create cutting-edge entertainment. She thought that the ability of HP to give audiences a new visual experience in movies, such as *Shark Tale, Shrek 2,* or *Polar Express,* was her vision for HP as it moved into the digital age. She also believed that HP needed to work with Orca and other companies to deliver and distribute digital content to consumers in new, compelling, and mobile ways.

On February 9, 2005, the board of directors dismissed her. Many believe that under her leadership, HP was simply trying to do too much. It lacked the resources and management competencies to compete with the best in each industry. According to some, her problems started with the acquisition of Compaq in 2001 for more than $24 billion. By emphasizing size over technology, the board of directors said that she doomed HP to periods of declining margins and lackluster growth. That is, she created a giant company but did not come up with a strategy to fend off Dell in the low end of computing or match IBM's sophistication. She immediately began to exercise leadership over HP's 80 relatively autonomous divisions, instilling a more centralized structure, which resulted in downsizing the firm and eventually laying off thousands of workers. Robert Knowling, a member of HP's board of directors, said that the "merger hasn't met the board's expectations or management's." Recently the stock price was listed as 13 percent below what it was just prior to the Compaq merger. While recent profits have risen, one HP e-mail sent after her firing read "Ding-dong, the witch is dead."

The history of high-tech companies indicates that companies that dominate their segments of the market—such as Intel, Microsoft, and Dell—are big moneymakers. Unfortunately, HP doesn't dominate anything. In personal computers, HP's market share is small compared to Dell's and its profits are less than 1 percent. And HP is often second best to IBM for global corporate computing. In its PC business, HP has two different distribution channels, each with its own goals. The direct-sales, build-to-order model competes with Dell, which carries no inventory. The other is HP's traditional, high-inventory distribution model for units that it ships through its sales partners. If HP tries to match Dell's direct system, it might not have the efficiency and volume to make money. This approach would also risk angering thousands of HP's traditional sellers (e.g., Costco) whom HP needs to sell its printers and ink. The $24 billion dollar Imaging and Printing Division is the only division making a profit. This division generates more than 75 percent of HP profits. HP's chief competitors in this business, Lexmark and Dell, have also seen their profits steadily increase.

For more information on Hewlett-Packard, visit the organization's home page at ***http://www.HewlettPackard.com.***

HP had operational challenges under Fiorina's leadership. HP has developed customized websites for customers where they can place and manage orders. Unfortunately, these B2B (business-to-business) sites have frequently crashed—erasing accounts, losing orders, and shipping wrong products—causing customers (such as Procter & Gamble) to lose faith in HP's ability to deliver. This requires HP sales representatives to spend most of their time working with customers to fix problems as opposed to selling new products. In putting together a package involving servers, printers, and software for a customer, a sales representative must coordinate the efforts of different divisions. As a product designed organization, each division has its own goals. For example, if one division is concerned with its financial picture and is unwilling to cut its price, the whole deal falls apart. The company appears to lack an effective process to resolve conflicts.

HP intended to push its digital technology in the crowded electronic field. The results of HP's push into this field have met with mixed success. To tap into the music industry, HP began selling Apple's iPods. Some thought that HP was straying too far from its reputation as an innovative company and getting into a business that it knows nothing about. Because HP sold less than 320,000 iPods of the more than 4.6 million sold, these critics have a point. HP has also been aggressively buying small software companies in an attempt to enter this market. HP has also entered into the managed services industries, in which companies outsource their IT departments to another organization. Unfortunately, this market has heavy start-up costs and IBM and EDS already hold a large share of this market.[1]

Understanding and managing organizational change presents complex challenges. Planned change may not work, or it may have consequences far different from those intended. In many instances, organizations must have the capacity to adapt quickly and effectively in order to survive. Often the speed and complexity of change severely test the capabilities of managers and employees to adapt rapidly enough. However, when organizations fail to change, the costs of that failure may be quite high. Hence, managers and employees must understand the nature of the change needed and the likely effects of alternative approaches to bring about that change.

Because organizations exist in changing environments, bureaucratic organizations are increasingly ineffective. Organizations with rigid hierarchies, high degrees of functional specialization, narrow and limited job descriptions, inflexible rules and procedures, and impersonal, autocratic management can't respond adequately to demands for change. As we pointed out in Chapter 3, organizations need designs that are flexible and adaptive. Organizations also need reward systems and cultures that allow greater participation in decisions by employees and managers alike.

In this chapter, we examine the pressures on organizations to change, types of change programs, and why accurate diagnosis of organizational problems is crucial. We explore the difficult issue of resistance to change at both the individual and organizational levels and examine ways to cope with that inevitable resistance. In addition, we identify three methods for making organizational and behavioral changes. Finally, we explore some ethical issues associated with organizational change.

LEARNING OBJECTIVE

1. Identify pressures for change, two types of change programs, and how to perform an organizational diagnosis.

CHALLENGES OF CHANGE

Organizational change can be difficult and takes time. Despite the challenges, many organizations successfully make needed changes, but at the same time, failure also is common. There is considerable evidence that adaptive, flexible organizations have a competitive advantage over rigid, static organizations.[2] As a result, managing change has become a central focus of effective organizations.

Pressures for Change

Most organizations around the world have tried to change themselves—some more than once—during the past decade. Yet for every successful change, there is an equally prominent failure. Wal-Mart's dramatic performance improvement stands in stark contrast to a string of disappointments that have plagued Kmart. The rise of Target and Kohl's to leadership in the retailing industry only emphasizes Kmart's inability to reverse its declining market share in that area.

Organizations that are well positioned to change will prosper, but those that ignore change will flounder. For example, Sun Microsystems has lost tremendous market share to its competitors, HP, IBM, and Dell, because it failed to develop a server to run the next version of Microsoft's Windows and instead tried to develop its own software called Solaris. To regain its market share, Scott McNealey, Sun's CEO, is focusing on what he calls "disruptive innovation." While most of Sun's competitors make plain-vanilla computers and compete on price, he plans to change the rules of the game by developing "throughput computing" chips that can handle dozens of tasks at the same time. While this plan sounds appealing, the new strategy calls for Sun to move in two directions at once: build bare-bones servers, while inventing cutting-edge technologies. As a result, Sun will spend 17 percent of its budget on R&D, compared to 2 percent at Dell.[3]

There is an almost infinite variety of *pressures for change*. In this section, we examine three of the most significant ones: (1) globalization of markets, (2) spread of information technology and computer networks, and (3) changes in the nature of the workforce employed by organizations.

Globalization. Organizations face global competition on an unprecedented scale. **Globalization** *means that the main players in the world's economy are now international or multinational corporations.* Their emergence creates pressures on domestic corporations to internationalize and redesign their operations. Global markets now exist for most products, but to compete effectively in them, firms often must transform their cultures, structures, and operations.

Historically, the primary forces at work in globalization have included:

- the economic recoveries of Germany and Japan after their defeat in World War II;
- the emergence of new "industrial" countries, such as South Korea, India, China, and Spain;
- the dramatic shift from planned economies to market economies that has occurred in Eastern Europe, Russia and other republics of the former Soviet Union, and to a certain extent in the People's Republic of China; and
- the emergence of new "power blocks" of international traders, stemming from the economic unification of Europe and the "yen block" of Japan and its Pacific Rim trading partners.

These and other powerful globalization forces are pushing domestic firms around the world to abandon "business as usual" in order to remain competitive. In some industries, global strategies are replacing country-by-country approaches. Although globalization strategies aren't easy to implement, many organizations have effectively moved outside their domestic markets. Ford, Merck & Company, and IBM have strong, profitable operations in Europe. McDonald's, YUM Brands (KFC, Pizza Hut, Taco Bell), and Mary Kay Cosmetics have highly successful Asian operations. Mary Kay sells more than $500 million worth of cosmetics in China each year. KFC and Pizza Hut serve more customers in China and earn more profits from these operations than anywhere else in the world. Procter & Gamble and Gillette have merged to form a $60 billion consumer products company. Together, they hope to do what each has struggled to do on its own—ramp up sales in the developing markets of China and Eastern Europe, bring global products to market more quickly, increase their leverage over Wal-Mart and Costco, and gain savings with media companies from which they buy advertising.[4]

Information Technology. Coping with international competition requires a flexibility that many organizations often do not possess. Fortunately, the revolution in information technology permits organizations to develop the needed flexibility. **Information technology (IT)** *comprises networks of computers (many of them complex), telecommunications systems, and remote-controlled devices.*[5] As discussed throughout this book, IT is having a profound impact on individual employees, teams, and organizations. For example, experts who have studied its impact on organizations have observed that IT:

- changes almost everything about a company—its structure, its products, its markets, and its processes;
- increases the value of invisible assets, such as knowledge, competencies, and training;
- democratizes a company because employees have more information and can talk to anyone in the company;
- increases the flexibility of work by allowing more people to work at home, on the road, or at hours that suit them; and
- allows companies to unify their global operations and to work a 24-hour day spanning the world.

However, the potential effects of IT aren't uniformly positive. Organizations that rely on sophisticated information technologies are more vulnerable to sabotage, espionage, and vandalism. Moreover, IT can create new social divisions (e.g., the computer literate versus the nonuser and the educated versus the uneducated) even as it brings people together. If the full potential of IT is to be realized, employees must be better educated, better trained, and better motivated than at any time in history. However, wisdom and intuition remain essential for good management, and having more information, faster, cannot replace good judgment and common sense.

Still, despite these cautions, the impact of IT is dramatic. The Internet makes it possible for a design, a fashion, or an idea to be known instantaneously around the world.[6] A New York apparel manufacturer put his spring line on the Internet and had five orders from Beijing in the People's Republic of China within hours. Information technology permits an IBM engineer to ask colleagues in virtually any country for help when confronted with a difficult problem. General Electric operates its own private global phone network, allowing employees to communicate directly with each other from anywhere in the world by using just seven digits.[7] Information technology allows CRSS, a large architectural firm, to exchange drawings with 3M, one of its largest clients, almost instantaneously.

The globalization phenomenon and information technologies are linked in interesting ways. Highly decentralized organizations, with operating units scattered throughout the world, face some significant challenges in terms of coordination and cooperation. However, advanced computer and telecommunication technologies provide mechanisms to link employees in ways only imagined in the past. For example, many multinational corporations rely on the use of virtual teams to accomplish their work. As we discussed in Chapter 3, *virtual teams* are groups of geographically and/or organizationally dispersed coworkers who are assembled via a combination of telecommunications and information technologies to accomplish organizational tasks.[8] Such teams rarely meet or work together face to face. Virtual teams may be set up on a temporary basis and used to accomplish a specific task, or they may be relatively permanent and used to address ongoing strategic planning issues. The membership of virtual teams may be quite fluid, with members changing according to task demands even for those teams with an ongoing assignment.[9]

Changing Nature of the Workforce. In addition to coping with the challenges presented by globalization and rapid changes in information technology, organizations must attract employees from a changing labor market. For this reason among others, we have explored the challenges of managing cultural diversity throughout this book.

As discussed in Chapter 1, the labor market continues to grow more diverse in terms of gender and ethnicity. Thus, equal opportunity pressures on hiring, promotion, and layoff practices will persist for some time to come. Other trends add to the challenge for organizations. For example, the dual-career family has become the norm, rather than the exception, in most industrialized societies. Further, the number of temporary workers continues to grow as a percentage of all workers. The **contingent workforce** *includes part-time employees, freelancers, subcontractors, and independent professionals hired by companies to cope with unexpected or temporary challenges.* By some accounts, about 30 percent of U.S. workers now fall into this category. This percentage is expected to continue to grow as companies find that they can operate efficiently and effectively with a smaller core of permanent employees supplemented by a changing cast of temporary help—and save money by not having to provide employee benefits. The U.S. Bureau of Labor Statistics expects the number of temporary workers to increase by another 11 percent in the next three years.[10] Temporary-employment agencies, such as Manpower and Kelly Services, are among the fastest growing organizations in the United States. The largest of the agencies—Manpower, Inc.—has more employees than General Motors or IBM. Among the challenges facing organizations are those of motivating and rewarding temporary and part-time employees whose morale and loyalties may be quite different from those of permanent employees.

The workforce is increasingly better educated, less unionized, and characterized by changing values and aspirations. Although these changes won't lessen the motivation to work, they continue to affect the rewards that people seek from work and the balance that they seek between work and other aspects of their lives. The **quality of work life (QWL)** *represents the degree to which people are able to satisfy important personal needs through their work.*[11] Achieving a high QWL is an important goal for many working women and men. Typically, employees desire pleasant working conditions, participation in decisions that affect their jobs, and valuable support facilities such as day-care centers for their children. These and other employee expectations put additional pressures on organizations and affect their ability to compete effectively in the labor market.

Of course, changes in globalization, information technology, and the workforce represent opportunities for some organizations. When Charles Fote decided to acquire Western Union in 1995, many people questioned the wisdom of this move. Western Union was just emerging from bankruptcy and was facing fierce competition from the widespread use of ATMs, credit cards, and other forms of electronic payment. But Fote was impressed with the number of immigrants he saw coming into the United Stated and believed that he could turn Western Union around to become the chief money-mover for foreign-born workers. The following Across Cultures Competency highlights how he accomplished that change.[12]

ACROSS CULTURES COMPETENCY

WESTERN UNION

Western Union made more than $3.6 billion in fees on cash transfers across country borders, earning more than $1 billion in profits in 2004. It handled more than 81 million transfers from more than 180 countries. On the strength on the increasing number of migrant workers around the world, it has doubled its revenues along with a 150 percent rise in profit. How did Charles Fote and his management team change Western Union around?

When Western Union was up for sale after its bankruptcy, Fote bought the company because of its brand recognition. Western Union has been in existence since 1851. Fote believed that the key to change was to dramatically expand Western Union's customer base to include immigrants. His goal was to make it possible for cash senders to find agents easily and for recipients to get hassle-free pickup. The more agents he could hire, the more cash that would flow from senders in the United States to their family and friends in other countries.

Instead of building or leasing offices, Western Union began to partner with banks and post offices that had room to spare. It pays these companies a small fee for this space. Certified Western Union agents take a 1 to 3 percent transaction fee. Super-agents, those who hire other agents, manage their own groups of agents. Like Amway, Mary Kay Cosmetics, or Avon, the super-agents take an additional percentage fee. For example, when Western Union entered China, it signed up the national postal service as the agent and immediately added thousands of locations. It followed the same strategy in India and Jamaica. In Jamaica, it had just eight branches in 1990; it now has more than 130 locations generating more than $1 billion a year. Presently, there are more than 170 branches in India, which means it has more locations than McDonald's, Starbucks, and Wal-Mart combined.

By focusing its marketing efforts on countries other than the United States, Western Union creates a demand where it exists, with cash recipients, not the senders. When a competitor, such as MoneyGram owned by American Express, was approved to be sold in Wal-Mart stores, Western Union immediately lowered its price. The company also developed a "loyalty card" to promote more repeat business and an online service that allows customers to send cash from their PCs, charging their credit cards for transactions.

For more information on Western Union, visit the organization's home page at ***http://www.westernunion.com.***

Types of Change Approaches

Distinguishing between change that inevitably happens to all organizations and change that is deliberately planned by members of an organization is important. Our focus is primarily on intentional, goal-oriented organizational change. **Planned organizational change** *represents a deliberate attempt by managers and employees to improve the functioning of teams, departments, divisions, or an entire organization in some important way.*[13]

Two radically different approaches are used to achieve organizational change: economic and organizational development.[14] Each approach is guided by a different set of assumptions about the purpose and means for change. We have highlighted these differences in Table 5.1.

TABLE 5.1 Approaches to Change

MEANS	ECONOMIC	ORGANIZATIONAL DEVELOPMENT
Purpose	Profit	Develop employees' competencies
Leadership	Top-down	Participative
Focus	Structure and strategy	Culture
Motivation	Incentives lead performance	Incentives lag performance

Economic Approach. The **economic approach** *refers to creating change for the purpose of creating shareholder value.* Such change is driven by top management with financial incentives for employees to perform. Change is planned and focused. Leaders who create change using this approach set goals based on expectations of the financial markets. They do not involve their management team or employees in discussing ways to reach financial goals. These change agents focus on decisions that affect the strategy, structure, and systems of their organization. The economic approach is mainly used by turnaround artists, and not people who want to build the organization.

THE COMPETENT LEADER

Guys, everyone is going to give blood in this change process. Let me tell you what blood you're going to give. Anyone who thinks Kinko's is doomed for failure, I'll give you 30 days to decide. I want you to vote with [your] feet. I'll personally ensure that you get another job. But on the 31st day, anyone who is not 100 percent aligned with what I'm saying, I will find you and weed you out.

Gary Kusin, CEO Kinko's

When Al Dunlap became CEO of financially troubled Scott Paper, he immediately laid off 11,000 employees. He based his goals on financial returns. "I have a goal of $176 million this year and there is no time to involve others or develop people," Dunlap stated. He believed that this single goal focused all employees' attention. He didn't involve other managers and made it clear that he was commander-in-chief. He also fired many members of the top-management team and recruited new people who believed in his purpose: to restore shareholder wealth. Dunlap attracted them to the organization by promising financial incentives, mainly stock options, if the company returned to profitability. They were instructed simply to follow his commands. Not long after taking these steps, Dunlap sold off several businesses, retaining the core consumer products businesses. He sold Scott Paper's paper division to Scott's long-time competitor Kimberly-Clark. He moved Scott's headquarters from Philadelphia to a much smaller location near his home in Florida. Within 15 months, Dunlap managed to return Scott to profitability, making himself and many of the company's top managers rich. Virtually all of Dunlap's change efforts focused on changing the company's strategy and structure. Dunlap resigned immediately after collecting his bonus and left Scott Paper struggling without his leadership to compete in the businesses to which he had committed the firm.[15]

Organizational Development Approach. The goal of the **organizational development approach** *is to develop employees' competencies to solve problems by having them identify and become emotionally committed to improving the performance of the firm.* By focusing on the effectiveness and efficiency with which employees carry out their jobs, leaders believe that building partnerships, trust, and employee commitment are critical. If commitment is developed, then extensive use of rules and regulations will be unnecessary. Simply changing structure and systems does not change the way people behave. The organizational development approach requires management to engage people emotionally in examining why the existing structure and systems are not meeting the new challenges facing the organization.

Wegman's grocery store, a $3.6 billion company located in Rochester, New York, uses the organizational development approach to empower employees to make changes. It has created a work environment where their contributions count and there are few rules. Wegman's knows that shoppers who are emotionally connected to a store spend 46 percent more than those who aren't. It is each employee's job to create this emotional bond for the shopper by changing the way Wegman's does business. Wegman's selects people who are passionate about customer service, have a genuine interest in food, and are capable of making decisions on their own. When Kelly Shoeneck completed an analysis on a competitor's shopper loyalty program, she handed it to her boss. Her boss told her that she would have to make the presentation to Robert Wegman, CEO, herself. When Maria Benjamin discovered a way to make "chocolate meatball cookies," she went to Jack DePeters, chief of operations, and persuaded him to let her sell them. Her cookie at Wegman's Pittsford, New York, store is the best seller. To instill the Wegman's approach to change, all management employees go through a store manager training program, where they learn how to greet customers, sweep floors, gut fish, bake bread, walk a customer to their car, and the like. All members of the Wegman family have also been through the same training program.[16]

Sequencing the Approaches. Jeff Immelt, CEO of GE, has used a combination of approaches to change the strategic direction of GE. When Immelt took over from Jack Welch in September 2001, he faced a period of intense uncertainty—from the September 11 attacks through new regulations and a shaky economy. He needed to create an agenda for transforming GE into the 21st century. One of his favorite sayings is that "Too many companies have lost the ability to innovate because they have become 'business traders' rather than 'business creators.'" To become a business creator, he knows that GE must become a more customer-driven, global, and diverse company—one that rewards innovation, embraces technology, and grows products internally in a slow-growth global economy. As a result, many of his top managers have marketing, as opposed to engineering, backgrounds because he believes that marketing will carry GE through economic slumps. He has sold off slow-growth businesses, like insurance, and bought companies like Vivendi Universal's entertainment assets and Amersham PLC, a British diagnostics and biotech firm. He hopes that these businesses will sharpen GE's innovative capabilities in the media and medical industries. He has broken up GE Capital into four separate businesses, making each business more accountable for its own profits. In comparison to Jack Welch, who rotated managers through divisions to develop generalists, Immelt wants to keep managers in place to develop leaders as specialists. These specialists must also be excellent teachers. A leader's two primary roles are to be able to work with people who do not necessarily agree with you and to share what he or she has learned. Whereas Welch grew GE through acquisition, Immelt wants to grow GE through innovation. Immelt's central idea is this: "We have to make our own growth."[17]

Organizational Use

Managers who face major changes need to think through the long-term consequences of using either the economic approach or the organizational development approach. Moreover, finding managers with the managerial competencies needed to sequence change properly is difficult. In many small dot-com start-up organizations, the primary goal of the founder and managers is to prepare their organization for the initial public offering (IPO). Maximizing market value prior to the sale of shares is their sole purpose, so they emphasize shaping the organization's strategy, structure, and systems to build quickly its presence in the marketplace. Transactional leaders with a strong top-down style usually lead such firms. They attract others by offering high-powered incentives, such as stock options and various perks. The lure is getting rich quickly. In contrast to the economic approach, change agents who want to build an institution are driven more by the organizational development approach. The focus of these managers often is to build an organization based on a deeply held set of values and a strong culture, such as Southwest Airlines, the Container Store, and Whole Foods. Such leaders attract others who share their passion about the vision and strategies they are pursuing to make their organizations stand out in their industries and contribute to their communities, while at the same time making a profit.

Success Indicators. All successful change approaches share some common characteristics. For example, effective change programs may involve:

- motivating change by creating a readiness for the change among managers and employees and attempting to overcome resistance to change (which we discuss in detail shortly);

- creating a shared vision of the desired future state of the organization;
- developing political support for the needed changes;
- managing the transition from the current state to the desired future state; and
- sustaining momentum for change so that it will be carried to completion.

The initiatives required to address each of these aspects of a change program are summarized in Figure 5.1.

FIGURE 5.1 Initiatives Contributing to Effective Change Management

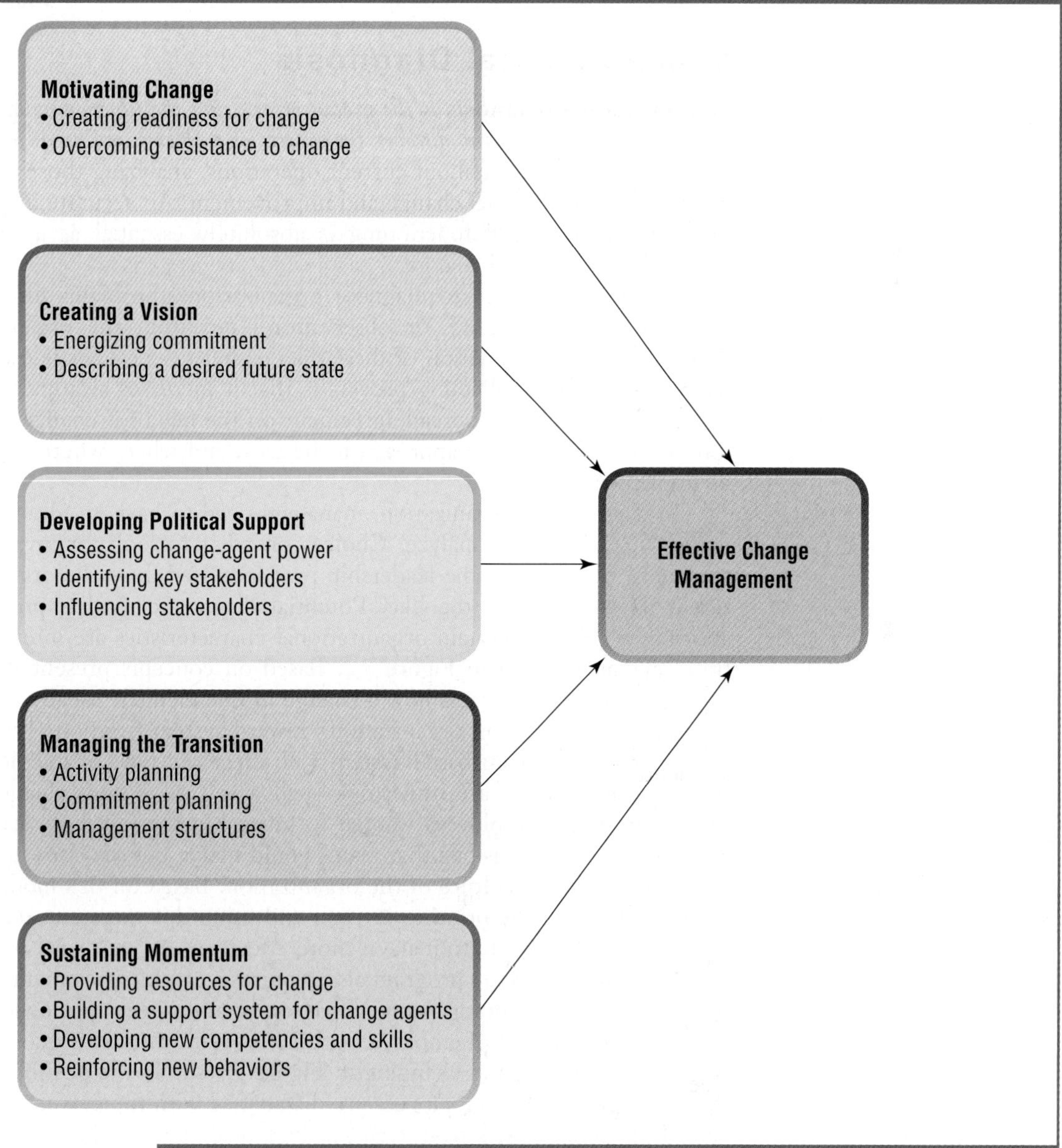

Source: Reprinted with permission from Cummings, J. G., and Worley, C. G. *Organizational Development and Change,* 6th ed. Cincinnati, OH: South-Western, 1997, 154.

Similarly, the conditions necessary for successfully carrying out effective change programs include the following:

- The organization's members must be the key source of energy for change, not some party external to the team or organization.

- Key members of the organization must recognize the need for change and be attracted by the potentially positive outcomes of the change program.
- A willingness to change norms and procedures must exist.

These programs and the conditions necessary for them are similar in certain respects. Change must come from within the organization. People must be aware of the need for change, believe in the potential value of the changes proposed, and be willing to change their behaviors in order to make the team, department, or organization more effective. Absent these beliefs and behaviors, effective organizational change is problematic. Managers must be open to trying different approaches at different times, as Jeff Immelt does at GE.

Organizational Diagnosis

Organizational diagnosis *is the process of assessing the functioning of the organization, department, team, or job to discover the sources of problems and areas for improvement.* It involves collecting data about current operations, analyzing those data, and drawing conclusions for potential change and improvement. An accurate diagnosis of organizational problems and functioning is absolutely essential as a starting point for planned organizational change.

Information needed to diagnose organizational problems may be gathered by questionnaires, interviews, or observation—and from the organization's records. Typically, some combination of these data gathering methods is used. An advantage of the information collecting process is that it increases awareness of the need for change. Even with widespread agreement on the need for change, people may have different ideas about the approach to be used and when, where, and how it should be implemented.

To diagnose an organization, managers need to have an idea about what information to collect and analyze. Choices on what to look for invariably depend on managers' perceptions, the leadership practices used, how the organization is structured, its culture, and the like. Potential diagnostic models provide information about how and why certain organizational characteristics are interrelated. We illustrate one such model in Figure 5.2. Based on concepts presented throughout this book, this model illustrates how a change in one element usually affects others. For example, a change in an organization's reward system from one based on individual performance to a team-based system will affect the type of individuals joining the organization. PacificCare undertook such a reward system change because it reflected the needs employees wanted to satisfy on the job, how leaders made decisions, the type of decisions that teams could make, the structure of the department or division, and the culture of the organization. Based on this model, what changes, such as selling off the printing division and using this money to bolster other products, should HP initiate to make it more effective?

Any planned change program also requires a careful assessment of individual and organizational capacity for change. Two important aspects of individual readiness for change are the degree of employee satisfaction with the status quo and the perceived personal risk involved in changing it. Figure 5.3 shows the possible combinations of these concerns. When employees are dissatisfied with the current situation and perceive little personal risk from change, their readiness for change probably would be high. In contrast, when employees are satisfied with the status quo and perceive high personal risk in change, their readiness for change probably would be low.

With regard to individual readiness for change, another important aspect is employee expectations regarding the change effort because expectations play a crucial role in behavior. If people expect that nothing of significance will change, regardless of the amount of time and effort they might devote to making it happen, this belief can become a self-fulfilling prophecy. And when employee expectations for improvement are unrealistically high, unfulfilled expectations can make matters worse. Ideally, expectations regarding change should be positive yet realistic.

FIGURE 5.2 Diagnostic Model of Change

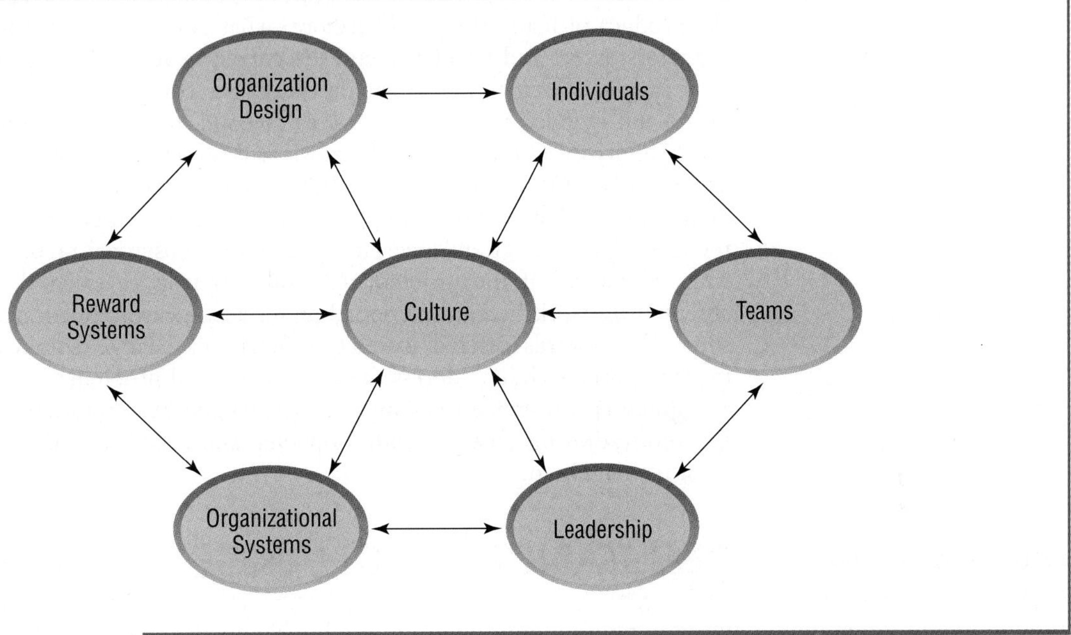

FIGURE 5.3 Employee Readiness for Change

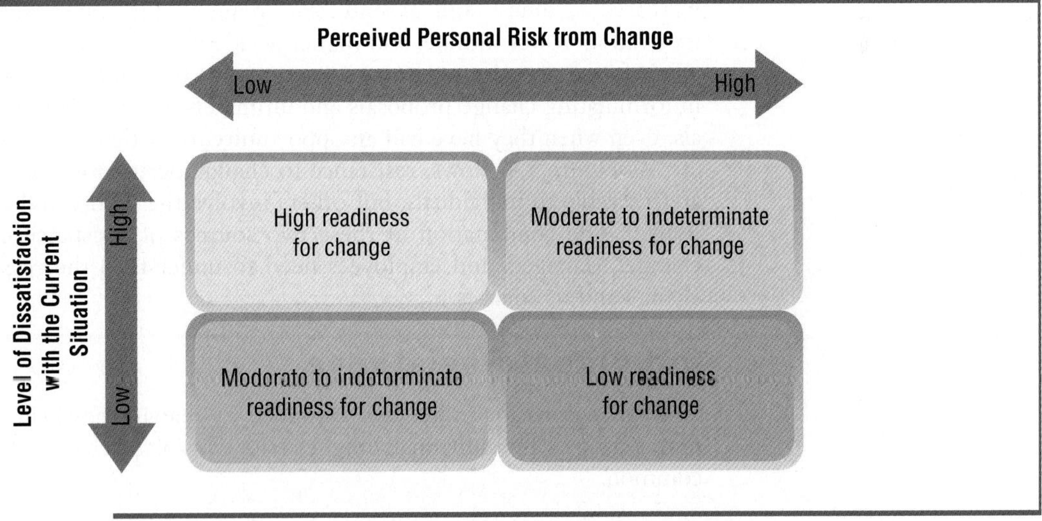

Source: Adapted from Zeira, Y., and Avedisian, J. Organizational planned change: Assessing the chances for success. *Organizational Dynamics*, Spring 1989, 37.

In addition, the organization's capacity for change must be accurately assessed. Approaches that require a massive commitment of personal energy and resources from organizations (such as NASA, IBM, and HP) probably will fail if the organization has few resources and its members don't have the time or opportunity to implement the needed changes. Under such circumstances, the organization may benefit most from starting with a modest effort. Then, as the organization develops the necessary resources and employee commitment, it can increase the depth and breadth of the change.

When managers and employees conduct an organizational diagnosis, they should recognize two additional important factors. First, organizational behavior is the product of many things. Therefore, what is observed or diagnosed—employee behaviors, issues and problems, and the current state of the organization—has multiple causes. Trying to isolate single causes for complex problems can lead to simplistic and ineffective change strategies. Second, much of the information gathered about an organization during a diagnosis will represent symptoms rather than causes of problems. Obviously, change strategies that focus on symptoms won't solve underlying problems. For example, at one Marriott Hotel, an awards program that recognized perfect attendance failed to reduce absenteeism because it didn't deal with the causes of the problem. Careful diagnosis revealed that employees were absent from work because of poor bus service, lack of child care, and family pressures. The awards offered weren't sufficient to change employee behaviors and, more important, didn't address the employees' real problems.

Potential resistance to change represents another important aspect of readiness and motivation for change. Both individual and organizational resistance to change must be diagnosed.

LEARNING OBJECTIVE

2. Diagnose reasons for individual and organizational resistance to change and describe methods for overcoming it.

RESISTANCE TO CHANGE

Change involves moving from the known to the unknown. Because the future is uncertain and may negatively affect people's careers, salary, and competencies, organization members generally do not support change unless compelling reasons convince them to do so. Resistance to change often is baffling because it can take so many forms. Overt resistance may be expressed through strikes, reduced productivity, shoddy work, and even sabotage. Covert resistance may be expressed by increased tardiness and absenteeism, requests for transfers, resignations, loss of motivation, lower morale, and higher accident or error rates. One of the most damaging forms of resistance is passive resistance by employees—a lack of participation in formulating change proposals and ultimately a lack of commitment to the proposals, even when they have had an opportunity to participate in making such decisions.

As Figure 5.4 shows, resistance to change occurs for a variety of reasons. Some are traceable to individuals, but others involve the nature and structure of organizations.[18] The combination of these two sources of resistance can be devastating to change. Managers and employees need to understand the reasons for resistance to change and its sources.

Individual Resistance

The six reasons for individual resistance to change shown in Figure 5.4 aren't the only reasons why individuals might resist workplace change, but they are the most common.

Perceptions. In Chapter 12, we will discuss the notion of perceptual defense—a perceptual error whereby people tend to perceive selectively those things that fit most comfortably with their current view of the world. Once individuals have established an understanding of reality, they may resist changing it. Among other things, people may resist the possible impact of change on their lives by (1) reading or listening only to what they agree with, (2) conveniently forgetting any knowledge that could lead to other viewpoints, and (3) misunderstanding communication that, if correctly understood, wouldn't fit their existing attitudes and values. For example, managers enrolled in management training programs at ARAMARK are exposed to different managerial philosophies and techniques. In the classroom, they may com-

FIGURE 5.4 Sources of Resistance to Change

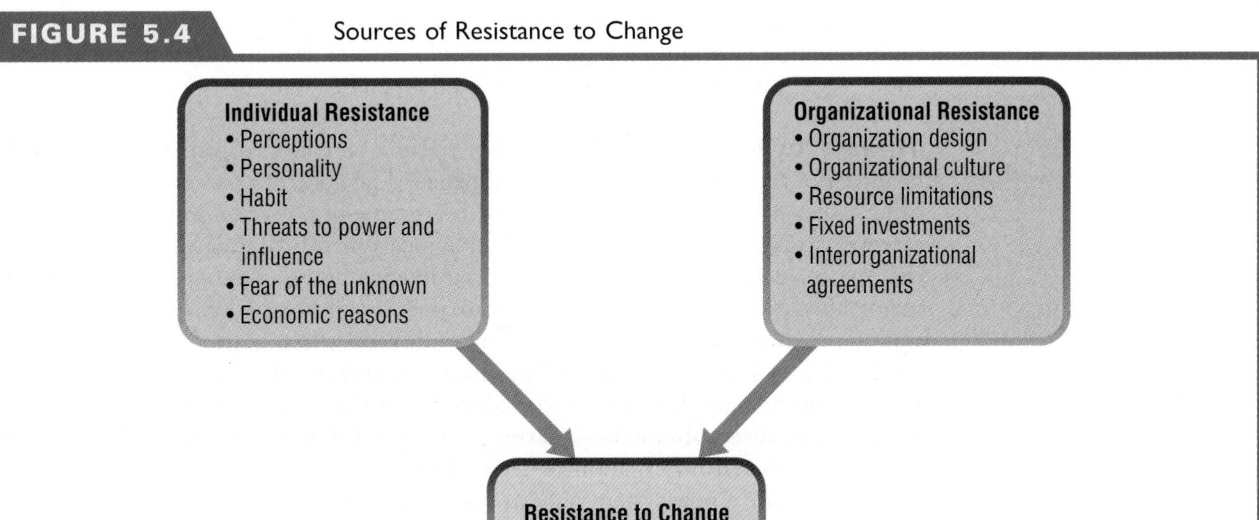

petently discuss and answer questions about these new ideas, yet carefully separate in their minds the approaches that they believe wouldn't work from those that they believe would work or that they already practice.

Personality. Some aspects of an individual's personality may predispose that person to resist change. In Chapter 11, you will find that self-esteem is an important personality characteristic that determines how a person behaves in an organization. People with low self-esteem are more likely to resist change than those with high self-esteem because low self-esteem people are more likely to perceive the negative aspects of change than the positive aspects. Low self-esteem people are not as likely as high self-esteem people to work hard to make change succeed. Another personality characteristic is adjustment. People who are nervous, self-doubting, and moody typically have a difficult time changing their behaviors. They may resist change until those people they depend on endorse it. These employees are highly dependent on their supervisors for performance feedback. They probably won't accept any new techniques or methods for doing their jobs unless their supervisors personally support the changes and indicate how these changes will improve performance and/or otherwise benefit the employees.

Managers must be careful to avoid overemphasizing the role played by personality in resistance to change because they can easily make the fundamental attribution error (see Chapter 12). There is a tendency to "blame" resistance to change in the workplace on individual personalities. Although personality may play a role (as we have just discussed), it seldom is the only important factor in a situation involving change.

Habit. Unless a situation changes dramatically, individuals may continue to respond to stimuli in their usual ways. A habit can be a source of comfort, security, and satisfaction for individuals because it allows them to adjust to the world and cope with it. Whether a habit becomes a primary source of resistance to change depends, to a certain extent, on whether individuals perceive advantages from changing their behaviors. For example, if Texas Instruments suddenly announced that all employees would immediately receive a 10 percent pay raise, few would object even though the pay raise might result in changes in behavior because it would allow employees to pursue a more expensive lifestyle. However, if Texas Instruments announced that all employees could receive a 10 percent pay raise only if they switched from working during the normal workday to working evenings and nights, many might object. Employees would have to change many personal habits about when they slept, ate, talked with family members, and so on.

Threats to Power and Influence. Some people in organizations may view change as a threat to their power or influence. The control of something needed by others, such as information or resources, is a source of power in organizations. Once a power position has been established, individuals or teams often resist changes that they perceive as reducing their ability to influence others. One of Michael Jordan's major hurdles to overcome when he took over as CEO of EDS from Dick Brown was to get divisions to share information with each other. Started by Ross Perot in 1962, EDS had built a culture of rugged individualism. "Fix the problem yourself" was a saying frequently heard in the hallways of EDS. A large statue of an American bald eagle in its corporate headquarters symbolized this culture. Each of its 48 divisions rarely shared information or technology. One division would invest time and money to create a new system only to learn that another division already had such a system in place. EDS's management could not send an e-mail directly to all 132,000 employees because the company used 16 different e-mail systems. Sales results were available only after the finance department closed its books at the end of each quarter. Jordan needed to revamp EDS and did so by consolidating data centers, organizing EDS around four services, and cutting costs.[19]

Fear of the Unknown. Confronting the unknown makes most people anxious. Each major change in a work situation carries with it an element of uncertainty. In July 2002, Ed Breen told his stunned boss at Motorola that he was leaving his job and a good chance to be Motorola's next CEO to take over as CEO of Tyco. His wife told him he was crazy. "I wondered if we'd stay together," he jokes now. CEO Dennis Kozlowski and his CFO Mark Swartz had just been accused of stealing more than $600 million from Tyco and the firm was facing a potential shareholder lawsuit of $4 billion. At 10:00 A.M. on Breen's first day at Tyco, seven major stockholders, representing 15 percent of Tyco's ownership, demanded that he replace the majority of the board of directors that had let the corruption happen under their noses. They stated that a compliant board had created a culture of entitlement, engaged in lucrative financial arrangements with the company, and shared in the lavish perks that Kozlowski had started as CEO. Breen decided to dismiss the entire board on his first day as CEO. He also dismissed 290 of Tyco's 300 highest ranking managers in his first few months as CEO. Breen also hired 110 new auditors and had them report to the board of director's audit committee chairperson. Tyco's ombudsman also reported to that person; employees can call an 800 number and report anything they perceive as a wrongdoing, from sexual harassment to price-fixing. In his first year, more than 1,300 investigations, 25 percent of which resulted in disciplinary action or a change in procedures, were pursued. What have been the results of these massive changes? Tyco's stock price has jumped nearly 300 percent and most people believe that the company has been saved.[20]

Economic Reasons. Money weighs heavily in people's considerations, and they certainly can be expected to resist changes that might lower their incomes. In a very real sense, employees have invested in the status quo in their jobs. That is, they have learned how to perform their work well, how to get good performance evaluations, and how to interact effectively with others. Changes in established work routines or job duties may threaten their economic security. Employees may fear that, after changes are made, they won't be able to perform as well and thus may not be as valuable to the organization, their supervisors, or their coworkers. Since Nestlé brought Perrier in 1992, it has struggled to finds ways to increase the productivity of its French employees. The average Perrier worker produces 600,000 bottles a year compared with 1.1 million bottles per worker at San Pellegrino and Evian, Nestlé's two major competitors. The French employees have resisted change because they will need to take a cut in pay and increase the number of hours worked per week from 35 to 40. Nestlé maintains that when the French employees are not on strike, they earn an average annual salary of $32,000, which is good money for the southern part of France. Nestlé has promised to cut 15 percent of the workforce unless changes are made.[21]

Sometimes the problems and dissatisfaction in a company are so serious that a general readiness for change exists. At Delta, American, USAir, and other airlines, employees knew that major changes were necessary for their organizations to survive. However, the real challenge is for managers to create a sense of readiness to change while things seem to be going well. The following Self Competency feature can help you assess your readiness for change.[22] If your readiness score is low, what competencies do you need to develop to increase your readiness for change?

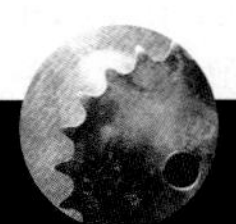

SELF COMPETENCY

ARE YOU READY TO CHANGE?

Read each of the following statements and then use the scale shown to reflect your opinion. Record your answer in the blank at the left of the question's number.

1	2	3	4	5	6	7
Completely disagree			**Neither agree nor disagree**			**Completely agree**

_____1. I believe that an expert who doesn't come up with a definitive answer probably doesn't know too much.

_____2. I think it would be fun to live in a foreign country for a period of time.

_____3. The sooner we all agree on some common values and ideals, the better.

_____4. A good teacher is one who makes you wonder about your way of looking at things.

_____5. I enjoy parties where I know most of the people more than ones where all or most of the people are strangers.

_____6. Supervisors who hand out vague assignments give me a chance to show initiative and originality.

_____7. People who lead even, regular lives—in which few surprises or unexpected events arise—really have a lot to be grateful for.

_____8. Many of our most important decisions are actually based on insufficient information.

_____9. There is really no such thing as a problem that can't be solved.

_____10. People who fit their lives to a schedule probably miss most of the joy of living.

_____11. A good job is one in which what is to be done and how it is to be done are always clear.

_____12. It is more fun to tackle a complicated problem than to solve a simple one.

_____13. In the long run, it is possible to get more done by tackling small, simple problems than large, complicated ones.

_____14. Often the most interesting and stimulating people are those who don't mind being different or original.

_____15. What we are used to is always preferable to what is unfamiliar.

_____16. People who insist on a "yes" or "no" answer just don't know how complicated things really are.

Interpretation

To get your total score, you need to do several things. First, sum your responses to the *odd*-numbered items and write your score here_____. Second, add 64 points to that score to create the first subtotal and record it here_____. Third, sum your responses to the *even*-numbered items and write your score here_____. Then subtract that number from the subtotal for the odd-numbered items to determine your overall score.

Your overall score is ________. Your score should be somewhere between 16 and 112. The lower your overall score, the more willing you may be to deal with the uncertainty and ambiguity that typically go with change. Higher scores suggest a preference for more predictable and structured situations and indicate that you don't respond as well to change. Research data show that the range of scores for a group is usually between 20 and 80, with a mean of 45. How does your score compare to these norms?

Organizational Resistance

To a certain extent, the nature of organizations is to resist change. Organizations often are most efficient at doing routine tasks and tend to perform more poorly, at least initially, at doing something for the first time. Thus, to ensure operational efficiency and effectiveness, some organizations may create strong defenses against change. Moreover, change often opposes vested interests and violates certain territorial rights or decision-making prerogatives that departments, teams, and informal groups have established and accepted over time. Again, Figure 5.4 shows several of the more significant reasons for organizational resistance to change.

Organization Design. Organizations need stability and continuity in order to function effectively. Indeed, the term *organization* implies that the individual, team, and department have a certain structure. Individuals have assigned roles, established procedures for getting the job done, consistent ways of getting needed information, and the like. However, this legitimate need for structure also may lead to resistance to change. Organizations may have narrowly defined jobs, clearly identified lines of authority and responsibility, and limited flows of information from top to bottom. This was a problem facing Michael Jordan at EDS. The use of a rigid design and an emphasis on the authority hierarchy may cause employees to use only certain specific channels of communication and to focus narrowly on their own duties and responsibilities. Typically, the more mechanistic the organization, the more numerous are the levels through which an idea must travel (see Chapter 3). This type of design, then, increases the probability that any new idea will be screened out because it threatens the status quo. More adaptive and flexible organizations are designed to reduce the resistance to change created by rigid organizational structures.

Organizational Culture. Organizational culture plays a key role in change. Cultures are not easy to modify and may become a major source of resistance to needed changes (see Chapter 4). One aspect of an effective organizational culture is whether it has the flexibility to take advantage of opportunities to change. An ineffective organizational culture (in terms of organizational change) is one that rigidly socializes employees into the old culture even in the face of evidence that it no longer works.

One of the key challenges for Bob Nardelli, CEO of Home Depot, was to change the entrepreneurial culture that started the "do it yourself" initiative at Home Depot. During the period of rapid growth, top management at Home Depot encouraged store managers to make decisions on their own. This entrepreneurial culture became a major issue as buyers and store managers continued to place orders and stockpile inventory without coordinating decisions. Store managers did not have e-mail to communicate with each other or with headquarters before Nardelli arrived. In an effort to make efficiency a cultural value at Home Depot, he and his staff consolidated buying offices from nine to one and changed the refund policy to offer the customer store credit rather than cash for returned items without a receipt. To streamline inventory control, stores receive high-tech carts equipped with wireless handheld bar-coded scanners and order entry forms. This change resulted in having 16 fewer employees per store handle in-store inventory. To compete against Lowe's, Lumber 84, and other home improvement retailers, Home Depot has opened special outlets to serve contractors, started soliciting business from companies that buy lumber and construction materials, and offered home repairs and maintenance services to the "do-it-for-me" customer.[23]

Resource Limitations. Some organizations want to maintain the status quo, but others would change if they had the resources to do so. Change requires capital, time, and individuals with a lot of competencies. At any particular time, an organization's managers and employees may have identified changes that could or should be made, but they may have had to defer or abandon some of the desired changes because of resource limitations. When Jay Grinney took over as CEO of the HealthSouth Corporation based in Birmingham, Alabama, he needed to immediately make changes after former CEO Richard Scrushy allegedly inflated earnings. He slashed 250 management jobs, sold unprofitable rehab and diagnostic centers, such as the Doctors Hospital in Coral Gables, and 10 private planes and one helicopter to pay down a $3.3-billion-dollar debt. As a result, HealthSouth has returned to profitability. Grinney wants to move HealthSouth into services that he believes will be increasing in demand, such as skilled nursing and home health care.[24]

Fixed Investments. Resource limitations aren't confined to organizations with insufficient assets. Goodyear Tire and Rubber Company had invested its financial resources to establish more than 5,300 authorized dealers. These dealers mainly sell replacement tires, which account for 70 percent of the company's sales. However, with the proliferation of retail formats—from discounters and convenience stores to warehouse clubs and online shops—the retail loyalty that it earned from its dealers has been lost. Pressured to boost sales, Goodyear had little choice but to sell tires through mass merchandisers (e.g., Discount Tires, Costco, Wal-Mart, Sears). These merchandisers demanded and received bulk discounts. The result was that some of its authorized dealers, who were expected to honor warranties and recalls, were paying more for their tires than what Sears charged at retail. As a result, Goodyear dealers are selling other replacement brand tires about 60 percent of the time. A Goodyear authorized tire dealer for more than 35 years was kicked out of its dealer network because he wasn't buying enough tires. Robert Keegan, Goodyear's CEO, admits that "We lost sight of the fact that it's in our interest that our dealers succeed."[25]

Fixed investments aren't limited to physical assets; they also may be expressed in terms of people. For example, consider employees who no longer are making a significant contribution to an organization but have enough seniority to maintain their jobs. Unless they can be motivated to perform better or retrained for other positions, their salaries and fringe benefits represent, from the organization's perspective, fixed investments that can't easily be changed.

Interorganizational Agreements. Agreements between organizations usually impose obligations on them that can restrain their actions. Labor negotiations and contracts provide some examples. Nike's relationship with colleges and various NFL teams precludes Adidas and other sporting apparel manufacturers from negotiating with them until the current contract expires. Ways of doing things that once were considered the rights of management (the right to hire and fire, assign tasks, promote and demote, and the like) may become subject to negotiation and fixed in a union–management contract. Other types of contracts also may constrain organizations. For example, proponents of change may face delay because of arrangements with competitors, commitments to suppliers and other contractors, and pledges to public officials in return for licenses, permits, financing, or tax abatement. When the Dallas Cowboys football team announced that it had plans to move from its home in Irving, Texas, to a new location in 2009, the city of Arlington, Texas, gave the team $325 million dollars as an inducement to choose Arlington to build their new $650 million, 75,000-seat stadium. The city issued a bond for that amount. This arrangement requires that the Cowboys stay in the city for at least the next 30 years, play all their home games at that stadium, and pay $2 million dollars in rent (with increases depending on inflation) a year for the duration of the contract.[26]

Overcoming Resistance

Realistically, resistance to change will never cease completely. Managers and employees, however, can learn to identify and minimize resistance and thus become more effective change agents. People often have difficulty with clearly understanding situations that involve change. Part of the reason is that even analyzing a change problem may be quite complex when a large number of variables must be considered.

Kurt Lewin, a pioneering social psychologist, developed a way of looking at change that has been highly useful for managers and employees when faced with the challenge of change. Lewin viewed change not as an event but rather as a dynamic balance of forces working in opposite directions. His approach, called **force field analysis,** *suggests that any situation can be considered to be in a state of equilibrium resulting from a balance of forces constantly pushing against each other.* Certain forces in the situation—various types of resistance to change—tend to maintain the status quo. At the same time, various pressures for change are acting opposite to these forces. The combined effect of these two sets of forces is illustrated in Figure 5.5.[27]

FIGURE 5.5 Force Field Analysis

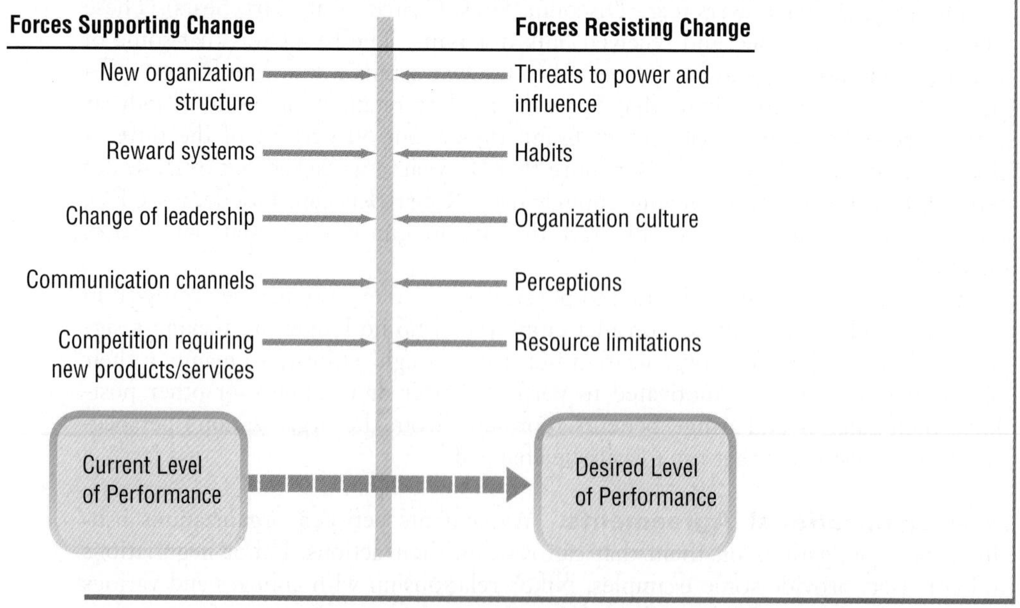

To initiate change, an organization must take one or more of three actions to modify the current equilibrium of forces:

- increasing the strength of pressure for change;
- reducing the strength of the resisting forces or removing them completely from the situation; and/or
- changing the direction of a force—for example, by changing a resistance into a pressure for change.

Using force field analysis to understand the process of change has two primary benefits. First, managers and employees are required to analyze the current situation. By becoming competent at diagnosing the forces pressing for and resisting change, individuals should be able to understand better the relevant aspects of a change situation. Second, force field analysis highlights the factors that can be changed and those that can't be changed. People typically waste time considering actions related to forces over which they have little, if any, control. When individuals and teams focus on the forces over which they do have some control, they increase the likelihood of being able to change the situation.

Of course, careful analysis of a situation doesn't guarantee successful change. For example, people in control have a natural tendency to increase the pressure for change to produce the change they desire. Increasing such pressure may result in short-run changes, but it also may have a high cost: Strong pressure on individuals and teams may create conflicts that disrupt the organization. Often the most effective way to make needed changes is to identify existing resistance to change and focus efforts on removing resistance or reducing it as much as possible.

An important part of Lewin's approach to changing behaviors consists of carefully managing and guiding change through a three-step process:

1. *Unfreezing.* This step usually involves reducing those forces that are maintaining the organization's behavior at its present level. Unfreezing is sometimes accomplished by introducing information to show discrepancies between behaviors desired by employees and behaviors they currently exhibit.
2. *Moving.* This step shifts the organization's behavior to a new level. It involves developing new behaviors, values, and attitudes through changes in organizational structures and processes.
3. *Refreezing.* This step stabilizes the organization's behavior at a new state of equilibrium. It is frequently accomplished through the use of supporting mechanisms that reinforce the new organizational state, such as organizational culture, norms, policies, and structures.

THE COMPETENT LEADER

Changing the attitude and behavior of hundreds of thousands of people is very, very hard to accomplish. You cannot mandate it, or engineer it. What you can do is to create the conditions for transformation by providing incentives, defining marketplace realities and goals. But at some point you must trust.
Lou Gerstner, former CEO of IBM

In addition to completing the three-step process successfully, other important factors play a role in overcoming resistance to change. For example, studies have shown that methods for successfully dealing with resistance to change often include the following components:

1. *Empathy and support.* Understanding how employees are experiencing change is useful. It helps identify those who are troubled by the change and helps management to understand the nature of their concerns. When employees feel that those managing change are open to their concerns, they are more willing to provide information. This openness, in turn, helps establish collaborative problem solving, which may overcome barriers to change.
2. *Communication.* People are more likely to resist change when they are uncertain about its consequences. Effective communication can reduce gossip, rumors, and unfounded fears. Adequate information helps employees prepare for change.

3. *Participation and involvement.* Perhaps the single most effective strategy for overcoming resistance to change is to involve employees directly in planning and implementing change. Involved employees are more committed to implementing the planned changes and more likely to ensure that they work than are employees who have not been involved.

The following Team Competency feature demonstrates the effects of participation and involvement in overcoming resistance to change at Royal Dutch/Shell. The company is the world's tenth largest corporation with operations in more than 135 countries. It operates more than 46,000 gas stations worldwide, has annual sales that exceed $265 billion, and employs more than 119,000 people. Faced with a consolidating industry, Shell tried to restructure itself to stay more competitive. When the effort stalled, Steve Miller, one of Shell's managing directors, stepped in to restart and manage it.[28]

TEAMS COMPETENCY

SHELL'S CHANGE PROCESS

Two years after Shell started a change program several years ago that was designed to restore its competitiveness, Steve Miller concluded that change was happening too slowly. The company had downsized and reorganized, and all senior managers had attended workshops that dealt with the changes needed and the reasons for them. Performance had improved a bit, but morale was low. The company's leaders agreed that Shell had to move aggressively into the Internet Age, but couldn't agree on how to implement the idea and so the change effort stalled.

Miller believed that once the folks at the refineries understood the problems, were empowered, and started to make changes, top-level managers would have to change their behaviors. To get this message across, Miller set aside half this time to work with employees who needed to respond to competitive threats on a daily basis. Week in and week out, he met with Shell employees in 25 countries.

One of the challenges facing Shell was figuring out how better to use its 49,000 gas stations to boost retail sales of all company products. To begin tackling that problem, Miller set up a five-day "retailing boot camp." Cross-functional teams (e.g., a trucker, a gas station manager, and a marketing employee) went to "camp" and then went home to develop a new business plan. Later they returned to camp and received feedback on their plans from other Shell employees. After another cycle of revising their plans and getting more feedback, they went home to put their plans into action. After two more months, they returned to camp for a follow-up session that focused on what had worked, what had failed, and what they had learned. These employees got to design a new Shell and participate in a culture that changed from one where following the rules was rewarded to one where being entrepreneurial was rewarded. These workers taught top-level managers that change could happen.

Miller admits that most of the people in the boot camps found the process to be "scary as hell." Top management had convinced itself that change was essential to Shell's survival, but it didn't believe that lower level employees had the ability to solve "real" problems. Similarly, lower level employees didn't have the polished communication skills to make presentations before top managers and answer strategic questions. Miller soon found out that, as people move up the corporate ladder, they get farther from the real work of Shell and tend to devalue it. Top-level people get caught up in broad strategy issues, such as whether Shell should buy Pennzoil-Quaker State, but what really drives the business is increasing sales at the retail gas station.

For more information on Shell, visit the organization's home page at ***http://www.shell.com.***

PROMOTING CHANGE

LEARNING OBJECTIVE

3. Discuss three methods for promoting change.

The main objective of planned organizational change is to alter the behavior of individuals within the organization. In the final analysis, organizations survive, grow, prosper, decline, or fail because of the things that employees do or fail to do. Behavior, therefore, should be a primary target of planned organizational change. In other words, to be successful, change programs must have an impact on employee roles, responsibilities, and working relationships.

At some fundamental level, all organizational change depends on changes in behavior. Of course, managing effective change also depends on identifying specific aspects of the organization that will be the initial target of change efforts. We use Figure 5.2 from earlier in the chapter as an organizing framework to explore three methods for promoting change.

Interpersonal Methods

Change programs that focus on behavior (the *individuals* variable in Figure 5.2) tend to rely on active involvement and participation by many employees. Successfully changing behaviors can improve individual and team processes in decision making, problem identification, problem solving, communication, working relationships, and the like. One popular approach to focus on people who are having problems fitting in with others or dealing with change is to use survey feedback.

Survey Feedback. In **survey feedback** *information is (1) collected (usually by questionnaire) from members of an organization, department, or team; (2) organized into an understandable and useful form; and (3) fed back to the employees who provided it.*[29] In Chapter 10, we will discuss how 360-degree feedback is used by managers to improve the performance of employees; 360-degree feedback is just one form of survey feedback. It leads to a comprehensive assessment of an employee's performance and usually leads to change methods that increase the likelihood that the person's competencies will be taken into account. This information provides the basis for planning actions to deal with specific issues and problems. The primary objective of all interpersonal methods is to improve the relationships among team members through the discussion of common problems, rather than to introduce a specific change, such as a new computer system. Survey feedback also is frequently used as a diagnostic tool to identify team, department, and organizational problems. Because of its value in organizational diagnosis, survey feedback often is utilized as part of large-scale, long-term change programs in combination with other approaches and techniques.

Take a few minutes to complete the questionnaire found in Table 5.2. This survey feedback instrument is designed to help you discover your competency in leading change. When leading change, most people rely on what they know best and avoid areas where they struggle. What are your best areas? Where might you improve? You might want to identify 20 people who know you well and ask each of these people to take this survey assessing your attitudes and behaviors. When you have obtained their feedback, you will then be able to develop an accurate self-portrait based on this feedback.[30]

Team Methods

As the name suggests, the purpose of team methods is to get a handle on team performance problems. As illustrated in Figure 5.6, team performance is influenced by the competencies of its members, organizational structure, the organization's reward system, organizational culture, and other factors. Team methods are designed to improve relations among team members and their team's performance.[31]

TABLE 5.2 Leading Positive Change

INSTRUCTIONS: Please use the following rating scale to discover your change competency ability. Your answers should reflect your attitudes and behaviors as they are now, not as you would like them to be. Be honest.

RATING SCALE
1. Strongly disagree
2. Disagree
3. Slightly disagree
4. Slightly agree
5. Agree
6. Strongly agree

ASSESSMENT

___ 1. I create positive energy in others when I interact with them.
___ 2. I know how to unlock the positive energy in other people.
___ 3. I express compassion toward people who are facing pain or difficulty.
___ 4. I help promote compassionate responses in others when it is appropriate.
___ 5. I usually emphasize a higher purpose or meaning associated with the work I do.
___ 6. I forgive others for the harm they may have produced or the mistakes they made.
___ 7. I maintain high standards of performance, even though I am quick to forgive.
___ 9. I express gratitude frequently and conspicuously, even for small acts.
___ 10. I keep track of things that go right, not just things that go wrong.
___ 11. I frequently give other people positive feedback.
___ 12. I emphasize building on strengths, not just overcoming weaknesses.
___ 13. I use a lot more positive comments than negative comments.
___ 14. I compare my own (or my group's) performance against the highest standards.
___ 15. When I communicate a vision, I capture people's hearts as well as their heads.
___ 16. I work to close abundance gaps—the difference between good performance and great performance.
___ 17. I exemplify absolute integrity.
___ 18. I know how to get people to commit to my vision of the change.
___ 19. I take advantage of a small-wins strategy in all my change initiatives.
___ 20. I have developed a teachable point of view for subjects I care about.

SCORING KEY

Score	**Quartile**
100 or above	Top quartile
81–99	2nd quartile
60–80	3rd quartile
Below 60	4th quartile

Subscales for Changed Competency Ability	**Items**
Personal capability to lead positive change	2, 3, 5, 6, 7, 9, 10, 12, 13, 16, 17, 20
Ability to mobilize others toward positive change	1, 4, 8, 11
Capacity to create positive deviance in organizations	14, 15, 18, 19

Team Building. In **team building** *team members diagnose how they work together and plan changes to improve their effectiveness.* Many different teams comprise an organization, and much of its success depends on how effectively those teams and the people in them can work together. We will explore how to improve team functioning in Chapter 8 and urge you to read that chapter.

FIGURE 5.6 The Team Performance Curve

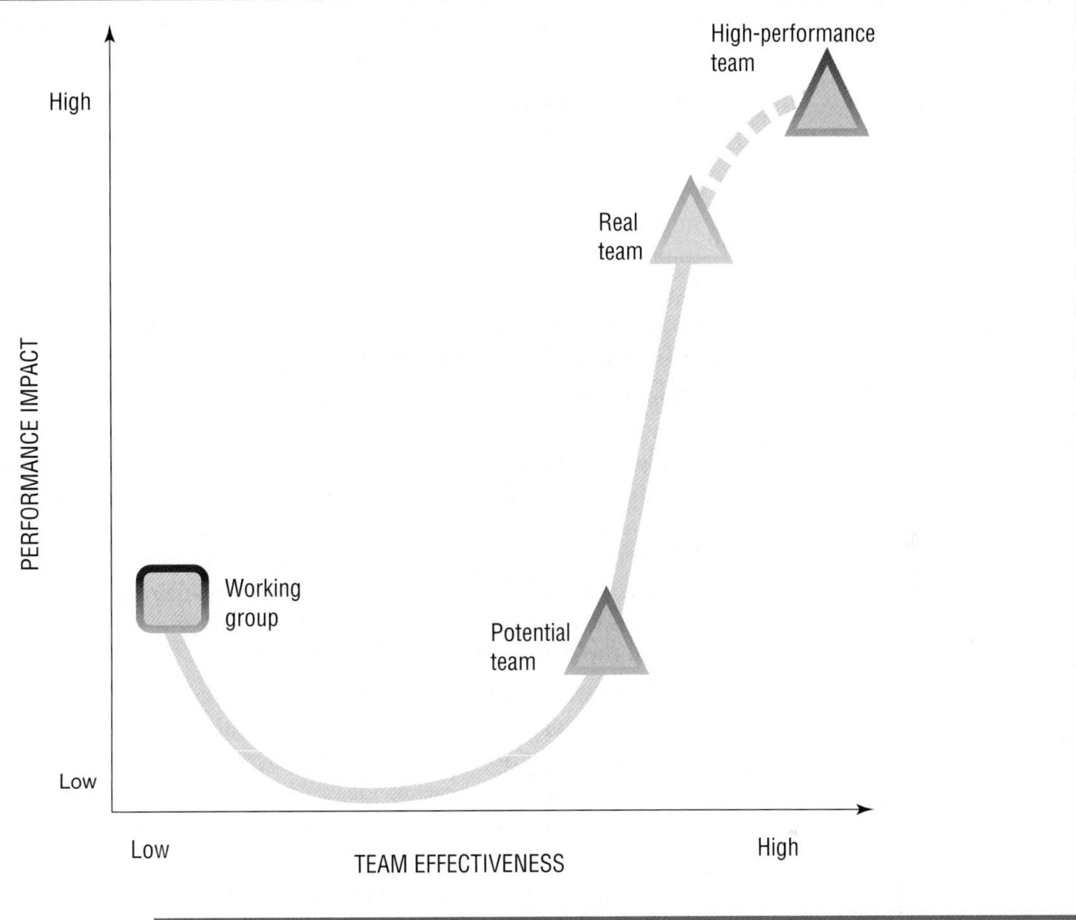

Source: Adapted from Katzenbach, J. R., and Smith, D. K. *The Wisdom of Teams.* Boston: Harvard Business School Press, 1993, 84.

Team building begins when members recognize a problem. An effective team can recognize barriers to its own effectiveness and design and take actions to remove them. During team building, members of the team contribute information concerning their perceptions of issues, problems, and working relationships. Steve Miller at Dutch Royal/Shell used this technique. Usually information is gathered during team meetings or prior to meetings, using interviews or questionnaires. Managers then analyze the information and diagnose work-related problems. Using problem diagnosis as the starting point, team members plan specific actions and assign individuals to implement them. At some later stage, team members evaluate their plans and progress to determine whether their actions solved the problems identified. As team effectiveness grows, the potential impact on organizational performance increases. Another good way to define team building is that it consists of the activities designed to move the team up the performance curve shown in Figure 5.6.

The goal of many team-building methods is to change the culture of the organization. In Chapter 4 we explored changing organizational culture and pointed out just how difficult such changes can be. Among other issues and problems, just assessing accurately the organization's culture before any plans for changes can be developed may be a daunting task. In addition, some aspects of culture (e.g., the deepest core values shared by employees) may be almost impossible to change. Despite these challenges, some organizations have successfully changed their cultures. How did they do it? A detailed examination of successful cultural change suggests that the odds for success can be increased by giving attention to seven main issues:

1. *Capitalize on dramatic opportunities.* The organization needs to take advantage of the moment when obvious problems or challenges that are not being met "open the door" to needed change. When Michael Jordan took over as CEO of EDS, many of EDS problems focused on the internal design of this organization and loss of customers.
2. *Combine caution with optimism.* Managers and employees need to be optimistic with regard to the advantages of cultural change; otherwise they will be unwilling to make the attempt. Yet, because cultural change can have negative impacts, the organization needs to proceed with caution. Expectations for improvement must be positive, yet realistic.
3. *Understand resistance to cultural change.* Resistance to change needs to be diagnosed. Identifying and reducing sources of resistance is valuable in cultural change as well as in other change programs.
4. *Change many elements but maintain some continuity.* "Don't throw the baby out with the bathwater" is a common saying that sums up the importance of recognizing what is of value and retaining it. Southwest Airlines, a firm that we have examined in several places in this book, has grown and prospered since its founding in the early 1970s, yet it managed to retain a core of cultural ideas and beliefs that Herb Kelleher instilled when he founded the organization. Although Kelleher is no longer involved in the day-to-day operations, CEO Gary Kelly and President Colleen Barrett are longtime employees and have been able to sustain the culture that Kelleher created.
5. *Recognize the importance of implementation.* A survey indicated that more than 90 percent of planned changes in strategy and culture were never fully implemented. A large percentage of failed change programs are failures of implementation rather than failures of ideas. Management needs to recognize that having a vision and a plan, although important, are only part of the battle. Planned changes must be carried through.
6. *Modify socialization tactics.* Socialization is the primary way in which people learn about a culture (see Chapter 3). Thus, changing socialization processes can be an effective approach to cultural change.
7. *Find and cultivate innovative leadership.* Cultural change must begin at the top of the organization, and good leadership is crucial. When Joseph Leonard took over as CEO of AirTran in 1999, the airline was almost bankrupt. Today, it is one of the low-cost airlines that is making money. He focused on cutting costs, flying on lucrative short-haul flights, adding routes to smaller markets, and buying fuel-efficient Boeing 737s. For example, it is the only airline that flies directly between New York City and Akron, Ohio. AirTran differentiates itself from its competitors, such as Southwest and JetBlue, that fly point-to-point routes by having Atlanta as its hub. It also doesn't fly long-haul flights from major markets like New York and Los Angeles. Another way in which AirTran differentiates itself from its competitors and maintains its low costs is through cross-training of its employees to perform multiple jobs. When Zakiya Cheris, for example, an employee based in Philadelphia, moves from the counter to conveyor belt to the runway at the airport, she is helping the airline reduce its labor costs.[32]

Organizational Methods

In the past decade, a large number of organizations have radically changed how they operate and satisfy customers' demands. Increased competition has forced many organizations to downsize, become leaner and more efficient, and flexible. Organizations are unlikely to undertake major organizational changes unless there are compelling reasons to do so. Power, habit, culture, and vested interests are organizationwide norms that are difficult to change. Many organizations, such as EDS, Kmart, and Tyco, had to experience a severe threat to their survival before they were motivated to undertake such change.

Organizationwide change programs frequently are aimed at changing an organization's design, reward systems, culture, and organizational systems, as shown earlier in Figure 5.2. Approaches to change that focus on organizational methods involve redefining positions or roles and relationships among positions and redesigning departmental, divisional, and/or organizational structure. Unfortunately, implementing design or structural change has sometimes been used as an excuse for organizations simply to downsize their workforces without identifying and exploring the reasons for inefficiency and poor performance.

A key feature of organizational change methods is the active role of top management in all phases of the change process. Because top managers are responsible for the strategic direction and operation of the organization, they decide when to initiate such changes, what the change should be, how it should be implemented, and who should be responsible for implementing it. In organizations undergoing organizationwide changes, senior managers need to play three roles:

- *Envisioning.* Top management must articulate a clear and credible vision for the change. They must also set new standards of performance.
- *Energizing.* Top management must demonstrate personal excitement for the changes and model behaviors that are expected of others. They must constantly communicate with all employees.
- *Enabling.* Top management must provide the resources necessary for undertaking significant change and use rewards to reinforce new behaviors.[33]

The following Communication Competency illustrates how top management at Toyota played these three roles in making organizationwide changes at Toyota. The problem Toyota was facing was that a customer who wanted a white Tacoma pickup would have to wait weeks for delivery. In Japan and Europe, customers are accustomed to waiting a month or two for their cars and suppliers are typically located near the assembly-line plants. But in North America, customers wanted their cars within two weeks or less or they would go to a dealer that had a vehicle that would satisfy their desires. The goal was to reduce from 70 days to 14 the average time between dealer order and delivery from Toyota North American factories. That change would not only make customers happier, but also cut dealer costs and the need for Toyota to spend money on rebates for slow-selling vehicles.[34]

COMMUNICATION COMPETENCY

JUST IN TIME AT TOYOTA

The dilemma for Toyota was this: How can you be as efficient as the competitors yet give customers the exact vehicle they want? Toyota spent six years revamping its ordering, manufacturing, and distribution processes to make it easier for dealers and customers to make changes before production. It developed its own software that connects dealers to factories and factories to suppliers.

Dealers used to be able to review their allocation of vehicles once a month and request changes that took a week to get approved through Toyota's bureaucracy. Now dealers can log on to a computer daily, see what vehicles are in the pipeline, and make changes to satisfy the customer. The next day the dealer finds out if his order has been accepted. A few days later the car is built to the customer's exact specification.

Toyota builds 10 models in North America, but different engines and option packages make for more than 50,000 combinations. When a request from a dealer comes in, the system figures out the availability of parts nearby, the time to resequence the assembly line, and whether the change would unbalance the line by scheduling, for example, too many models loaded with time-consuming options one right after another.

Toyota then tackled the distribution system. Getting a car from the factory to the dealer takes a lot of time. Toyota wanted to reduce that time. Now Toyota considers the dealers' locations, and makes all vehicles headed for a particular destination at the same time. Instead of shipping a Camry made in Georgetown, Kentucky, to Seattle where it might sit in rail yards for days, Toyota now sends finished vehicles of all models to sorting docks where they can be grouped by destination (e.g., Seattle, Dallas, and Chicago). Arriving by rail, dealers are notified when their shipment has arrived and go to the rail yard to get the customer's car.

This distribution change required changes in certain manufacturing processes. The biggest change involved painting. Half of the time required to build a new car was being spent in the paint shop. When a paint color needed to be changed, every trace of paint had to be cleaned from the tubes used in paint-spraying robots with expensive solvents. Toyota needed to reduce this time, so it installed robots that use individual paint cartridges. The robot grabs a red cartridge for a red car, a green one for a green car, and so on. Cartridges are expensive, but the change made the paint shop more efficient. The Georgetown factory took 2.1 hours out of the 22 person-hours it takes to build a vehicle. It saved $29 per vehicle or $2.5 million a year.

For more information on Toyota, visit this organization's home page at ***http://www.toyota.com.***

LEARNING OBJECTIVE

4. Describe ethical issues posed by organizational change.

ETHICAL ISSUES IN ORGANIZATIONAL CHANGE

Serious ethical issues may arise in any organizational change program, no matter how carefully thought out and well managed it might be. Managers and employees need to be aware of potential ethical issues in four main areas: change approach selection, change target selection, managerial responsibilities, and manipulation.[35]

When choosing the change approach or combination of approaches deemed best for the situation, managers and employees should recognize the ethical issues involved in selecting the criteria to be used. Does the manager or change agent have a vested interest in using a particular technique so that other alternatives might not receive fair consideration? Do individuals involved in the organizational diagnosis have biases that might predetermine the problems identified and thus influence the change approach chosen?

Selection of the change target raises ethical concerns about participation in the change program. What is to be the target of change? Which individuals, teams, or departments of the organization will the change effort focus on? Which members of the organization will participate in diagnosing, planning, and implementing the change and to what degree? Who will make this determination? Issues of power and political behavior raise serious ethical concerns when managers attempt to make inappropriate changes or choices concerning what is to be changed that overstep the boundaries of their legitimate roles. To what extent can managers make choices about changing the behaviors of employees, and where should the line be drawn in this regard?

A major ethical concern in the area of managerial responsibility involves whose goals and values are to guide the change effort. The reason is that organizational change is never value free. The value systems of managers and employees always underlie assumptions about what the organization should be doing. Ethical concerns arise if managers involved in the change process fail to recognize the potential problems associated with incompatible goals and values held by the organization's members. Whose vision guides the change? Whose values influence the adoption of goals and methods chosen to accomplish them?

Finally, the reality of power differences raises the possibility of manipulation in the change process. Making changes in organizations without some employees feeling manipulated in some way is difficult. Often the organization needs to make changes that do, in fact, result in some individuals or groups being worse off after the change than they were before. Ethical issues concern the degree of openness surrounding planned changes. To what extent should the organization disclose all aspects of the change in advance? To what degree do employees have the right to participate in, or at least be aware of, changes that affect them, even indirectly?

These questions are not easily addressed, and we have no simple answers to them. As a starting point, managers and employees need some basis for recognizing the potential ethical concerns involved in organizational change so that fair and informed choices can be made. Organizations must be sensitive to the probability that ethical problems will emerge during planned change programs.

CHAPTER SUMMARY

1. Identify pressures for change, two types of change programs, and how to perform an organizational diagnosis.

A rapidly changing environment places many demands on managers and employees, including the need to plan for and manage organizational change effectively. Pressures for change stem from globalization, the increasingly heavy use of computers and other sophisticated information technology, and the changing nature of the workforce.

The two main types of change approaches are economic and organizational development. The economic approach focuses on changing the organization's structure and decision-making authority relationships, and its goal is to improve the financial well-being of the organization. The organizational development approach focuses on developing employees' competencies and commitment to the organization. An accurate, valid diagnosis of current organizational functioning, activities, and problems is an essential foundation for effective organizational change. The readiness for change, availability of resources for change, and possible resistance to change are among the factors that should be accurately diagnosed.

2. Diagnose reasons for individual and organizational resistance to change and describe methods for overcoming it.

Individuals may resist change because of their perceptions or personalities. In addition, habits, fear of the unknown, economic insecurities, and threats to established power and influential relationships may generate further resistance to change. Organizational resistance to change may be caused by organizational structure and culture, resource limitations, fixed investments not easily altered, and interorganizational agreements. Force field analysis can help managers and employees diagnose and overcome resistance to change. Resistance can also be reduced through open communication and high levels of employee participation in the change process.

3. Discuss three methods for promoting change.

Three methods are available for promoting organizational change: interpersonal, team, and organizational. The interpersonal method focuses on changing employees' behaviors so that they can become more effective performers and usually involves some use of survey feedback. As the name suggests, the team method focuses on ways to improve the performance of entire teams, and team-building activities are its foundation. The organizational method is aimed at changing the organization's structure, reward system, level at which decisions are made, and the like.

4. Describe ethical issues posed by organizational change.

Managers and employees need to be aware of and knowledgeable about potential ethical issues that can arise during organizational change. Ethical issues may emerge during selection of the change approach, selection of the change targets, determination of managerial responsibilities for the goals selected, and potential manipulation of employees.

KEY TERMS AND CONCEPTS

Contingent workforce
Economic approach
Force field analysis
Globalization
Information technology (IT)
Organizational development approach
Organizational diagnosis
Planned organizational change
Quality of work life (QWL)
Survey feedback
Team building

DISCUSSION QUESTIONS

1. From your own experience, describe a team, department, or organization that needed to change. Which of the change approaches presented was used? Was it successful?
2. Based on the force field analysis, why is it hard for people to lose weight?
3. Based on your answers to the Leading Positive Change questionnaire in Table 5.2, what competencies do you need to develop? How will you develop these?
4. Rosabeth Kanter, a leading authority on change, stated that trying to change an organization is like trying to teach elephants to dance. Why is changing an organization's direction so difficult?
5. What are some of the pressures for and resistances to change facing Hewlett-Packard now that Carly Fiorina has been dismissed? Explain.
6. From Table 5.1 what change approach did Fiorina use at HP? Why wasn't it successful?
7. Identify and describe an ethical dilemma or issue created by some organizational change effort with which you are familiar. How was the ethical problem handled? What, if anything, would you do differently?
8. Think of a situation in which someone asked you to change your behavior. Did you change? If so, why? If not, why not?
9. Why is organizational diagnosis essential to the success of any change effort?

EXPERIENTIAL EXERCISE AND CASE

Experiential Exercise: Self Competency

Measuring Support for Change

Instructions

This questionnaire is designed to help you understand the inherent level of support or opposition to change within an organization. Please respond to each item according to how true it is in terms of an organization for which you are currently working or used to work. Circle the appropriate number on the scale that follows the item.

Not True	Usually Not True	Somewhat Untrue	Neutral	Somewhat True	Usually True	True
1	2	3	4	5	6	7

Values and Visions

1. Do people throughout the organization share values or visions?

1 2 3 4 5 6 7

History of Change

2. Does the organization have a good track record in implementing change smoothly?

1 2 3 4 5 6 7

Cooperation and Trust

3. Is there a lot of cooperation and trust throughout the organization (as opposed to animosity)?

1 2 3 4 5 6 7

Culture

4. Does the organization's culture support risk taking (as opposed to being highly bureaucratic and rule bound)?

1 2 3 4 5 6 7

Resilience

5. Are people able to handle change (as opposed to being worn out from recent, unsettling changes)?

1 2 3 4 5 6 7

Punishments and Rewards

6. Does the organization reward people who take part in change efforts (as opposed to subtly punishing those who take time off from other work to get involved)?

1 2 3 4 5 6 7

Respect and Status

7. Will people be able to maintain respect and status when the change is implemented (as opposed to losing these as a result of the change)?

1 2 3 4 5 6 7

Status Quo

8. Will the change be mild (and not cause a major disruption of the status quo)?

1 2 3 4 5 6 7

Interpretation

Scores 1, 2, and 3 are low; 4 and 5 are mid-range; and 6 and 7 are high. However, these are just numbers, and one person's 5 may be another person's 3. The value of the scores lies in understanding the meanings that people attach to them.

Generally, low to mid-range scores should be cause for concern. Lower scores indicate possible areas of resistance to change.

Values and Visions

Low scores may indicate that values may be in conflict and that individuals and groups may not perceive any common ground. This situation is serious and almost guarantees that any major change will be resisted unless people learn how to build a shared set of values. In contrast, low scores may indicate a communication problem. In some organizations, values and visions remain secret, with people not knowing where the organization is headed. Although this communication problem needs to be solved, it may not indicate deeper potential resistance.

History of Change

Low scores indicate a strong likelihood that a change will be resisted forcefully. Those who want the change will need to demonstrate repeatedly that they are serious this time. People are likely to be very skeptical, so persistence will be crucial.

Cooperation and Trust

Low scores should be taken seriously. Building support for any major change without some degree of trust is difficult, if not impossible. The opposite of trust is fear, so a low score indicates not just the absence of trust but the presence of fear.

Culture

Mid-range to low scores indicate that people may have difficulty carrying out changes even though they support the changes. They are saying that the systems and procedures in the organization hinder change. The change agents must be willing to examine these deeper systemic issues.

Resilience

Low scores probably indicate that people are burned out. Even though they may see the need for change, they may have little strength to give to the effort. Two important questions should be asked:

- Is this change really necessary at this time?
- If it is, how can the organizations support people so that the change causes minimal disruption?

Punishments and Rewards

Low scores indicate strong potential resistance. Who in their right minds would support something that they knew would harm them? If the respondents' perceptions are accurate, the change agents must find a way to move forward with the change *and find ways to make it rewarding for others*. If the low scores indicate a misperception, the change agents must let people know why they are misinformed. This message will likely need to be communicated repeatedly (especially if trust also is low).

Respect and Status

Low scores indicate that change agents must find ways to make this a win–win situation.

Status Quo

Low scores indicate that people regard the potential change as very disruptive and stressful. The more involved people are in the change process, the less resistance they are likely to experience. Most often, people resist change when they feel out of control.[36]

Case: Ethics Competency

Kindred Todd and the Ethics of OD

Kindred Todd had just finished her master's degree in organization development and had landed her first consulting position with a small consulting company in Edmonton, Alberta, Canada. The president, Larry Stepchuck, convinced Todd that his organization was growing and that it offered her a great opportunity to learn the consulting business. He had a large number of contacts, an impressive executive career, and several years of consulting experience behind him.

In fact, the firm was growing, adding new clients and projects as fast as Stepchuck could hire consultants. A few weeks after Stepchuck hired Todd, he assigned her to a new client, a small oil and gas company. "I've met with the client for several hours. They are an important and potentially large opportunity for our firm. They are looking to us to help them address some long-range planning issues. From the way they talk, they could also use some continuous quality improvement work as well."

As Todd prepared for her initial meeting with the client, she reviewed financial data from the firm's annual report, examined trends in the client's industry, and thought about the issues that young firms face. Stepchuck indicated that Todd would first meet with the president of the firm to discuss initial issues and next steps.

When Todd walked into the president's office, she was greeted by the firm's entire senior management team. Team members expressed eagerness to get to work on the important issues of how to improve the organization's key business processes. They believed that an expert in continuous quality improvement (CQI), such as Todd, was exactly the kind of help they needed to increase efficiency and to cut costs in the core business. Members began to question Todd directly about technical details of CQI, the likely time frame within which they might expect results, how to map key processes, and how to form quality improvement teams to identify and implement process improvements.

Todd was stunned and overwhelmed. Nothing that Stepchuck had said about the issues facing this company was being discussed, and worse, it was clear that he had sold Todd to the client as an "expert" in CQI. Her immediate response was to suggest that all of their questions were good ones, but that they needed to be answered in the context of the long-range goals and strategies of the firm. Todd proposed that the best way to begin was for team members to provide her with some history about the organization. In doing so, she was able to avert disaster and embarrassment for herself and her company and to appear to be doing all the things necessary to begin a CQI project. The meeting ended with Todd and the management team agreeing to meet again the following week.

The next day, Todd sought out Stepchuck. She reported on the results of the meeting and her surprise at being sold as an expert on CQI to this client. Todd suggested that her competencies didn't fit with the needs of the client and requested that another consultant, with expertise in CQI, be assigned to the project.

Stepchuck responded to her concerns: "I have known these people for over 10 years. They don't know exactly what they need. CQI is an important buzzword. It's the flavor of the month, and if that's what they want, that's what we'll give them." He also told Todd that there were no other consultants available for this project. "Besides," he said, "the president of the client firm had just called to say how much he had enjoyed meeting with you and was looking forward to getting started on the project right away."

Todd felt that Stepchuck's response to her concerns included a strong, inferred ultimatum: If you want to stay with this company, you'd better take this job. "I knew I had to sink or swim with this job and this client," Todd later reported.

As Todd reflected on her options, she pondered the following questions:

- How can I be honest with this client and thus not jeopardize my values of openness and honesty?
- How can I be helpful to this client?
- How much do I know about quality improvement processes?
- How do I satisfy the requirements of my employer?
- What obligations do I have?
- Who's going to know if I do or don't have the credentials to perform this work?
- What if I fail?

After thinking about these issues, Todd summarized her position in terms of three dilemmas: a dilemma of self (who is Kindred Todd?), a dilemma of competence (what can she do?), and a dilemma of confidence (do I like who I work for?). Based on these issues, Todd made the following tactical decisions. She spent 2 days at the library reading about and studying total quality management and continuous improvement. She also contacted several of her friends and former classmates who had experience with quality improvement efforts. Eventually, she contracted with one of them to be her "shadow" consultant—to work with her behind the scenes on formulating and implementing an intervention for the client.

Based on her preparation in the library and the discussions with her shadow consultant, Todd was able to facilitate an appropriate and effective intervention for the client. Shortly after completing her assignment, she resigned from the consulting organization.[37]

Questions

1. Discuss the course of action followed by Kindred Todd in terms of its strengths and weaknesses. What, if anything, would you have done differently if you were Todd?
2. Based on the material in this chapter, describe an effective, and ethical, alternative way to approach helping this organization.

PART 3

Leadership and Team Behaviors

CHAPTER 6 Leading Effectively: Foundations

CHAPTER 7 Leading Effectively: Contemporary Developments

CHAPTER 8 Developing and Leading Teams

CHAPTER 9 Managing Conflict and Negotiating Effectively

CHAPTER 10 Fostering Organizational Communication

CHAPTER 6

Leading Effectively: Foundations

LEARNING OBJECTIVES

When you have finished studying this chapter, you should be able to:

1. Describe the role of power and political behavior in the leadership process.
2. Describe two traditional models of leadership: traits and behavioral.
3. Explain the Situational Leadership® Model.
4. Discuss the Vroom–Jago time-driven leadership model.

Preview Case: Amy Brinkley of Bank of America

POWER AND POLITICAL BEHAVIOR

- Leaders' Use of Power
- Use of Political Behavior
- *Self Competency—Arlivia Gamble of State Farm*

TRADITIONAL LEADERSHIP MODELS

- Traits Model of Leadership
- *Ethics Competency—Norman Augustine of Lockheed Martin*
- Behavioral Model of Leadership

SITUATIONAL LEADERSHIP® MODEL

- Leadership Styles
- Situational Contingency
- Choosing a Leadership Style
- *Communication Competency—Michelle Miller of Walgreens*
- Implications for Leaders

VROOM–JAGO LEADERSHIP MODEL

- Leadership Styles
- Situational Variables
- Solution Matrix
- *Change Competency—Your Leadership as Director of Research*
- Implications for Leaders

CHAPTER SUMMARY

KEY TERMS AND CONCEPTS

DISCUSSION QUESTIONS

EXPERIENTIAL EXERCISE AND CASE

AMY BRINKLEY OF BANK OF AMERICA

PREVIEW CASE

Amy Brinkley is the chief risk officer of Bank of America, the third-largest bank in the United States with over 14,000 employees. She is responsible for risk management activities across the entire company and serves on the Risk and Capital Committee, which oversees the allocation of capital to all business lines of the company. In this Preview Case, we share excerpts of her insights and reflections on leadership.

Let me say first that I do not think of myself as a "woman executive" but rather as an executive who happens to be a woman. What that means is that I want to be helpful wherever I can, but I do not wear my gender like a badge. . . .

Now, leaving gender behind, let's turn to another critical element today's world is calling for in leaders—and that is the importance of achieving and maintaining an enterprise view. This element transcends *who* we are and *where* we are in our organizations—and goes to *how* we see our organizations and the opportunities and challenges they face. To build an enterprise view, we must start with an understanding of our place in the world. And that world has never been more complex and inner-connected. The speed of business has never been faster . . . the opportunity for short-sightedness, myopia, and unintended consequences never greater. It's been said that experience is the hardest kind of teacher: It gives you the test first and the lesson afterward.

But we can build an enterprise view—and avoid the mistakes that come with myopia—only by actively subjecting ourselves to the tests that experience brings with it. In other words, by taking risk. I am fortunate to have had a wide variety of experiences at Bank of America. But it's hardly been a career path I might have mapped out when I was younger. In fact, I know I have probably made a good career move when I hear that people are asking "Why in the world did she do that?" It is the horizontal moves that I have been offered or that I pursued that always have taught me the most. They deepened and broadened my judgment . . . prepared me for larger roles . . . and sharpened my understanding of the working pieces of our enterprise.

The sum of my experiences contributes to the ability to achieve and apply an enterprise view in my current role as chief risk officer. I've had the opportunity to watch and learn from leaders across the enterprise. I've learned that, at the end of the day, it's about much more than one's *technical* ability. It's about the ability to think. It's about having enough perspective to articulate a valid and value-added point of view. It's about the ability to see beyond one's position, ask the tough question, and influence the final results.

The importance of the concept of maintaining an enterprise view . . . that is, maintaining the right perspective . . . goes beyond the organizations where we work and lead . . . to our personal lives as well. I think of this as *balance* and the best advice I ever got on this subject came from the most unlikely source. I have a colleague at the bank—a fellow member of the Management Operating Committee—who has come up through the ranks with me. He has a reputation for being maniacal in his work. The kind of guy you want with you if you are ever in a street fight. One day, he sits me down and, in a serious tone of voice, says he has something he wants me to hear. "You intimidate people," he tells me. "You need to be kinder and gentler." Talk about a wake-up call. Especially coming from this friend and colleague, I realized immediately that I was at risk of damaging my career. What I was missing was balance. Now,

For more information on Bank of America, visit the organization's home page at ***http://bankofamerica.com.***

balance is different for everyone. There is no one formula. I define it as whatever mix it takes to stay fulfilled and energized. What it is not is focusing only on work. Today, I cannot say I have it all figured out . . . or that I don't have my moments of intensity. I do. And, at times, that is what is needed. But that intensity must be balanced by empathy, listening, and inclusion.

Another perspective on leadership is that which we derive from the values we embrace. This is, in short, the sum of *who we are* and *what our organizations are.* And it has never been more important. Stop for a moment and think about all of the cases of corporate irresponsibility. We've witnessed an absence of leaders who asked the tough questions. We've also witnessed a failure of perspectives, of governance and of organizational discipline that might have kept those enterprises on course. In the end—leadership is about *both* practicing the right values and putting in place the right management framework for governing your organization. Leadership is also an individual equation that reflects our personal potential. So I encourage you to find the equation for success that *fits you . . . your* experiences, *your* skills and talents, *your* life, and *your* aspirations.[1]

Amy Brinkley's thoughtful insights on leadership are further discussed in this and the following chapter and are reflective of the foundation competencies developed throughout the book. Leadership embraces the seven foundation competencies developed throughout this book, but it also goes beyond them. A team's or organization's success is greatly influenced by its leadership. Amy Brinkley clearly reflects core leadership qualities.

Leadership *is the process of developing ideas and a vision, living by values that support those ideas and that vision, influencing others to embrace them in their own behaviors, and making hard decisions about human and other resources.* Noel Tichy, who has studied many outstanding business leaders, describes leadership in these words:

> *Leadership is accomplishing something through other people that wouldn't have happened if you weren't there. And in today's world, that's less and less through command and control, and more and more through changing people's mindsets and hence altering the way they behave. Today, leadership is being able to mobilize ideas and values that energize other people.*[2]

A **leader** *is a person who exhibits the key attributes of leadership—ideas, vision, values, influencing others, and making tough decisions.* In this and the next chapter, you will discover that leadership is like a prism—something new and different appears each time you look at it from another angle. Our purpose is to identify and describe for you diverse leadership issues, ideas, and approaches. In doing so, we present various leadership perspectives and suggest some of their strengths, limitations, and applications. These chapters also are intended to give you personal insights into your own leadership abilities and those that need further development. Our assumption is simple: Leadership can be learned but not taught. Learning leadership means that you are actively seeking to make the personal changes required to become a leader.

As indicated in the Preview Case, Amy Brinkley sees herself as a leader and executive first who happens to be a woman. She focuses on *ideas* and *vision* in her comment about the need to take an enterprise view to avoid the mistakes that come with myopia. Brinkley notes the foundation role of *values* in her discussion of leadership being about "both practicing the right values and putting in place the right management framework for governing your organization." One of her several remarks about *influencing others* is that "intensity must be balanced by empathy, listening, and inclusion." Brinkley recognizes the need for leaders to *make tough decisions,* both personally and in their jobs, throughout the Preview Case. Consider this remark by Brinkley: The enterprise view and leadership is "about the ability to see beyond one's position, ask the tough question, and influence the final results."

POWER AND POLITICAL BEHAVIOR

LEARNING OBJECTIVE

1. Describe the role of power and political behavior in the leadership process.

All leaders use power and engage in political behavior to influence others.[3] Some leaders do so effectively and ethically. Others in leadership roles, but who do not qualify as effective leaders, use power and political behavior in ways that are ineffective and counterproductive.

Leaders' Use of Power

There are five important interpersonal sources of power—legitimate power, reward power, coercive power, referent power, and expert power—that leaders and others use in various situations.[4] Leaders use these sources of power to influence followers by appealing to one or more of their needs. Effective leadership depends as much on the acceptance of influence by the follower as on the leader's providing it. Let's review those sources of power in relation to the roles of leader and follower.

Legitimate Power. **Legitimate power** *is an individual's ability to influence others' behaviors because of the person's formal position in the organization.* Subordinates may respond to such influence because they acknowledge the leader's legitimate right to tell them what to do. Nonmanagerial employees also may possess legitimate power. For example, John Ogden, a safety inspector at Lockheed Martin Vought's plant in Camden, Arkansas, has the legitimate power to shut down production if there is a safety violation, even if the plant manager objects and tries to stop the safety inspector.

Legitimate power is an important concept. Typically, a leader is given the right to make decisions within a specific area of responsibility, such as customer service, quality control, marketing, or accounting. This area of responsibility defines the activities for which the leader (and sometimes other employees) can expect to exercise legitimate power to influence behavior. The farther removed that leaders get from their specific areas of responsibility, the weaker their legitimate power becomes. Employees have a zone of indifference with respect to the exercise of power.[5] The **zone of indifference** *is an area within which employees will accept certain directives without questioning the leader's power.* The leader may have considerable legitimate power to influence subordinates' behavior. Outside that zone, however, legitimate power disappears rapidly. For example, a secretary will type letters, answer the phone, open the mail, and do similar tasks for a leader without question. However, if the leader asks the secretary to go out for a drink after work, the secretary may refuse. The leader's request clearly falls outside the secretary's zone of indifference. The leader has no legitimate right to expect the secretary to comply. Consider this example of legitimate power:

> *My boss is Piero Di Matteo at Los Angeles Air Force Base. He believes that if you carry out your assignments on time, there will be no problem. If you get stuck, he's there to guide you.*[6]

Reward Power. **Reward power** *is an individual's ability to influence others' behaviors by providing valued things.* To the extent that subordinates value rewards that the leader can give—praise, promotions, money, time off, and so on—they may comply with requests and directives. A leader who controls the allocation of merit pay raises in a department has reward power over the employees in that department. Accordingly, employees may comply with some attempts by leaders to influence their behaviors because they expect to be rewarded for their compliance. Consider this example of reward power:

> *Bill Weingart at First Data Merchant Services Corporation in Hagerstown, Maryland, realizes the importance of recognizing and rewarding employees when they achieve their goals. Also, he encourages education and self-improvement. He is a mentor to all who*

have the opportunity to work with or for him. I expect never to encounter anyone like him again in my entire working career.[7]

Coercive Power. **Coercive power** *is an individual's ability to influence others' behaviors by punishing them.* For example, subordinates may comply because they expect to be punished for failure to respond favorably to a leader's request. Punishment may take the form of reprimands, undesirable work assignments, closer supervision, tighter enforcement of work rules, suspension without pay, and the like. The organization's ultimate punishment is to fire the employee.

However, that punishment can have undesirable side effects (see Chapter 13). For example, the employee who receives an official reprimand for shoddy work may find ways to avoid punishment, such as by refusing to perform the task, falsifying performance reports, or being absent frequently. Coercive power doesn't necessarily encourage desired behavior, but it may stop or reduce undesirable behaviors. Consider this example of the application of coercive power:

The boss looked at me and shouted, "I don't care what your [expletive] job title is or what they [expletive] told you when you were hired. You'll do what I [expletive] tell you to do, the [expletive] way I tell you to do it, and if you don't like it, there's the [expletive] door." I had my résumé out the very next day.[8]

At times, leaders do need to exercise coercive power, which is based on their legitimate power. Demoting or dismissing subordinates for poor performance, unacceptable behaviors (e.g., sexual harassment, bullying, workplace violence), and the lack of integrity (e.g., lying, deceitful conduct, and the like) may require the use of coercive power.

Referent Power. **Referent power** *is an individual's ability to influence others because she is respected, admired, or liked.* For example, subordinates' identification with a leader often forms the basis for referent power. This identification may include the desire of subordinates to be like the leader. A young manager may copy the leadership style of an older, admired, and more experienced leader. The senior leader, thus, has some referent power to influence the behavior of the younger manager.

Referent power usually is associated with individuals who possess admired personality characteristics, charisma, or a good reputation. It often is associated with political leaders, movie stars, sports figures, or other well-known individuals (hence, their use in advertising to influence consumer behavior). However, leaders and employees also may have considerable referent power because of the strength of their personalities. Meg Whitman, CEO of eBay, uses her referent power to motivate employees to achieve the organization's goals. Consider this example of the use of referent power:

Rudy Gragnani, a manager of the Coca-Cola Company bottler in Richmond, Virginia, displayed true leadership for me. A customer, an expressive New Yorker, and I were loudly discussing a problem when Rudy walked by. Later, he chewed me out for yelling at my customer. But at the next management meeting, he thanked me. Rudy understood that what he saw as an argument was just "New York" style. He apologized to me for misreading the situation and forwarded the thanks from the accounting area for my efforts.[9]

THE COMPETENT LEADER

You will never get people to follow you and you will never be able to lead, if you can't manage your own life and you can't act in a moral and ethical way in all environments. That doesn't mean you have to be perfect. What it means is that personal integrity is a core characteristic that will permit people to follow you.
Michael E. Moroone, President and Chief Operating Officer, Auto Nation

Expert Power. **Expert power** *is an individual's ability to influence others' behaviors because of recognized competencies, talents, or specialized knowledge.* To the extent that leaders can demonstrate their competencies, they will acquire expert power. However, expert power often is relatively narrow in scope. For example, a team member at Overhead Door Company might carefully follow the advice of her team leader about how to program a garage door opener, yet ignore advice from the team leader regarding which of three company health plans she should choose. In this instance, the team member is recognizing expertise in one area while resisting influence in another.

A lack of expert power often causes problems for new managers and employees. Even though a young accountant might possess a great deal of knowledge about accounting theory and procedures, that expertise must be correctly demonstrated and applied over time to be recognized and accepted. Consider this example of the exercise of expert power:

> *I went to work for a manager who was one of the sharpest people I have ever worked for. The applications we worked on were some of the most intelligently constructed, flexible, reusable, modular applications I had ever seen. It was a fantastic environment for me to learn in.*[10]

An effective leader—whether a first-line manager or top-level executive like Amy Brinkley—uses all of these sources of power. For successful leaders and organizations, the emphasis is on reward, referent, and expert power, with less reliance on coercive and legitimate power. This pattern is affected by changing technologies, increasing abilities of employees and teams to make decisions, flattening of organizational hierarchies, and changing work and personal life expectations of employees.

Use of Political Behavior

Political behavior *involves attempts by individuals to influence the behaviors of others and the course of events in the organization in order to protect their self-interests, meet their own needs, and advance their own goals.*[11] Defined in this way, almost all behavior may be regarded as political. Labeling behavior as political, however, usually implies a judgment that certain people are gaining something at the expense of others or the organization as a whole. However, a balanced understanding of political behavior and its consequences is needed. People often are self-centered and biased when labeling actions as political behavior. Employees may justify their own political behavior as defending legitimate rights or interests. Some may say it's "playing politics."

Organizational Politics. **Organizational politics** *involves actions by individuals, teams, or leaders to acquire, develop, and use power and other resources in order to obtain preferred outcomes.*[12] When people share power but differ about what must be done, many decisions and actions quite naturally will be the result of a political process.

Employees are often concerned about office politics.[13] Typically, they also believe that an ideal work setting would be free from political behavior. Negative attitudes about political behavior and organizational politics can hinder organizational effectiveness. Examples of behaviors often seen as political are shown in Table 6.1. People tend to assume that political behavior doesn't yield the best organizational decisions or outcomes—that somehow, by pushing for their own positions, they cause inferior actions or decisions to be produced. Although this result can occur, political behavior isn't always detrimental to an organization. For example, a study involving managers in 30 organizations indicated that they were able to identify beneficial, as well as harmful, effects of political behavior.[14] Beneficial effects included career advancement, recognition and status for individuals looking after their legitimate interests, and achievement of organizational goals—getting the job done—as a result of the normal political process in the organization. Harmful effects included demotions and loss of jobs for "losers" in the political process, a misuse of resources, and creation of an ineffective organizational culture. Organizational politics may arouse anxieties that cause employees to withdraw emotionally from the organization. Their withdrawal makes creating an organization characterized by high performance and high commitment very difficult.

TABLE 6.1 Common Political Tactics

Taking counsel	The individual exercises great caution in seeking or giving advice.
Maneuverability	The individual maintains flexibility and never completely commits to any one position or program.
Communication	The individual never communicates everything. Instead information is withheld and/or at times it's released carefully.
Compromising	The individual accepts compromise only as a short-term tactic, while continuing to press ahead with one's own agenda.
Confidence	Once the individual has made a decision, he must always give the impression of knowing what he is doing, even when he does not.
Always the boss	An atmosphere of social friendship limits the power of the leader; thus the leader always maintains a sense of distance and separation from subordinates.

Source: Adapted from Buchanan, D., and Badham, R. *Power, Politics, and Organizational Change*. London: Sage, 1999.

Political behavior, then, can meet appropriate and legitimate individual and organizational needs, or it can result in negative outcomes. In any event, leaders and employees must understand political behavior because it definitely will occur. Eliminating political behavior isn't possible—it can only be managed.

Drivers of Political Behavior. The probability of political behavior occurring typically increases in proportion to disagreements over goals, different ideas about the organization and its problems, different information about the situation, the need to allocate scarce resources, and so on.[15] If these forces didn't exist, perhaps political behavior wouldn't exist either. However, results are never certain, resources are never infinite, and people must make difficult choices between competing goals and methods to attain them. Thus, political behavior will naturally occur as individuals, teams, and departments attempt to obtain their preferred outcomes. Leaders shouldn't try to prevent the inevitable, but rather should try to ensure that these activities do not have negative consequences for the organization and its employees.

Leaders and employees are more likely to act politically when (1) decision-making procedures and performance measures are uncertain and complex, and (2) competition for scarce resources is strong. Conversely, in less complex situations where decision-making processes are clear and competitive behavior is not rewarded, excessive political behavior is unlikely.

Even though individual differences may contribute to political behavior, such behavior is typically more strongly influenced by aspects of the situation. Leaders make engaging in political behavior easier when they provide few rules or policies. Ambiguous circumstances allow individuals to define situations in ways that satisfy their own needs and desires. Further, when employees want more of a resource (e.g., equipment or office space) than is available, political behavior is likely to occur.

Political behavior is higher when leaders reward it. A reward system may focus solely on individual accomplishment and minimize team contributions. When that's the case, individuals may be tempted to behave politically to ensure that they receive much more of the rewards than other team members. If their actions result in more rewards, employees are even more likely to engage in such political actions in the future. Similarly, individuals who had avoided political behavior may start behaving politically when they observe such behavior being rewarded by leaders. In sum, the organizational reward system can be a significant factor in the occurrence of political behavior.

Relation to Performance Appraisal. The performance appraisal process provides a good example of a situation in which leaders may stimulate political behavior among employees. Performance for employees in many departments—accounting, human resources, quality control, legal, information systems, and so on—isn't easily measured. Thus, the process used by leaders results in the allocation of scarce resources (pay, bonuses, benefits, etc.) based on complex criteria.[16]

Some leaders ignore the existence of politics in the appraisal process or may assume that use of quantitative performance appraisal (e.g., number of units sold, downtime, wastes) will minimize it. However, political behavior is a fact of life in the appraisal process. In particular, because of the ambiguous nature of managerial work, appraisals of managers by higher level leaders are susceptible to political manipulation. What is the risk, ethical or otherwise, of using performance appraisal as a political tool? Among other things, political performance appraisals by leaders can

- undermine organizational goals and performance;
- compromise the link between performance and rewards;
- increase political behavior in other organizational processes and decisions; and
- expose the organization to litigation if employees are terminated.[17]

Leaders should adopt the following guidelines to help cope with the problem:

- Develop goals and standards that are as clear and specific as possible.
- Link specific actions and performance results to rewards.
- Conduct structured, professional reviews, including specific examples of observed performance and explanations for ratings given.
- Offer performance feedback on an ongoing basis, rather than once a year.
- Acknowledge that appraisal politics exists and make this topic a focus of ongoing discussions throughout the organization.[18]

The following Self Competency feature presents the perspectives of G. Arlivia Babbage Gamble on her experiences with organizational politics at State Farm Insurance Companies.[19] She is a division vice president. State Farm Insurance Companies is a major provider of insurance and financial services with headquarters in Bloomington, Illinois, and 760 offices throughout the United States. The firm has 76,000 employees.[20]

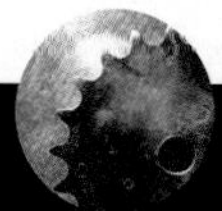

SELF COMPETENCY

ARLIVIA GAMBLE OF STATE FARM

G. Arlivia Babbage Gamble, a division vice president, is used to being the only female or African American in high-level meetings at State Farm Insurance Companies. She says: "I've got reasonable amounts of power, reputation, and results. Sometimes, I feel I have to stand up and scream to get noticed. When you walk into somebody else's game, you're invisible to them if they choose you to be."

Gamble regrets not learning how to play golf, despite her successful rise through the ranks. She states: "I've never felt I was intentionally left out. Golf certainly could be an opportunity I might have used to have something in common." The golf course is where strategic alliances can be formed—relationships with coworkers, supervisors, and executives who can further your cause.

Gamble may not be sports-minded, but she's known for years that office politics is a game that she needs to play. She had a major encounter with organizational politics a couple of years ago when leading a team. The team's objective was to solve a distribution problem that was affecting State Farm's 17,000-agent network. Fixing the problem was tough enough, but what made it worse was a white male colleague who constantly shot down Gamble's ideas, undercutting them to whoever would listen. Plus, he had the ear of one of the company's most senior leaders.

"It was the most difficult thing I had to do, because I am a harmony seeker," says Gamble, who wrestled for over a year with this issue. Her subordinates warned her that this colleague was out to get her. "It became so serious that my credibility was on the line. My job then became to develop one-on-one relationships to build the strength, which took away some of the power that person had. I very deliberately went about building a team that was more collaborative and that he couldn't afford not to support."

During her 19-year career at State Farm, Gamble has worked mostly with men. "I can't remember being in a room when there was more than one female vice president," says Gamble. Gamble thinks a well-connected mentor is important for a rising executive. Mentors are also allies who will speak on your behalf, clarify speculations, and trumpet your efforts. Gamble comments: "You have to make lots of deposits in order to have any returns. You have to realize that not every battle is a war."

She also sees the need to build alliances with subordinates as well as executives. With 80 employees in her division, Gamble schedules each one for a one-hour, get-to-know-you session each year. It is worth the time investment. "I have felt many times that [my staff] protected me from things I wasn't aware of. So, knowing my employees gives me inside intelligence. The people who get the job done are the ones below you. They have to know that you are supportive of them and their concerns."

Known for being direct, Gamble remembers ruffling the feathers of some fellow male executives during a meeting several years ago because of her persistent questioning of the presenter. Confronted later by one meeting participant, she went to her boss to "solicit feedback and coaching." While the incident did no permanent damage to her reputation, Gamble earned points with her boss by being willing to seek counsel from him.

For more information on State Farm Insurance Companies, visit the organization's home page at ***http://www.statefarm.com.***

LEARNING OBJECTIVE

2. Describe two traditional models of leadership: traits and behavioral.

TRADITIONAL LEADERSHIP MODELS

The traits and behavioral models are probably the most basic, oldest, and most popular of the leadership models. The more recent and complex leadership models often draw on parts of these two models.

Traits Model of Leadership

The **traits model of leadership** *is based on characteristics of many leaders—both successful and unsuccessful—and is used to predict leadership effectiveness.* The resulting lists of traits are then compared to those of potential leaders to assess their likelihood of success or failure. There is support for the notion that successful leaders have interests and abilities and, perhaps, even personality traits that are different from those of less effective leaders.

Key Traits. Some evidence suggests that four traits are shared by most (but not all) successful leaders:

- *Intelligence.* Successful leaders tend to have somewhat higher intelligence than their subordinates.
- *Maturity and breadth.* Successful leaders tend to be emotionally mature and have a broad range of interests.

- *Achievement drive.* Successful leaders are results oriented; when they achieve one goal, they seek another. They do not depend primarily on employees for their motivation to achieve goals.
- *Integrity.* Successful leaders, over the long term, usually have integrity. When individuals in leadership positions state one set of values but practice another set, followers quickly see them as untrustworthy. Many surveys show that honesty is the most important characteristic when employees are asked to rank and comment on various traits of successful and unsuccessful leaders. Trust is crucial and translates into the degree of willingness by employees to follow leaders. Confusion over the leader's thinking and values creates negative stress, indecision, and personal politics.[21]

The following Ethics Competency feature reports on the essential need for integrity in leaders.[22] It presents excerpts of remarks by Norman Augustine, recently retired chairman and CEO of Lockheed Martin Corporation, upon receipt of the Stanley C. Pace Leadership in Ethics Award from the not-for-profit Ethics Resource Center headquartered in Washington, D.C.[23] The award was bestowed in 2005 and in recognition of Mr. Augustine's extraordinary commitment to ethics throughout his career. Lockheed Martin is the world's number one defense contractor with the following major business segments: aeronautics, electronic systems, space systems, integrated systems, and solutions and information and technology services. The firm has approximately 130,000 employes.[24]

ETHICS COMPETENCY

NORMAN AUGUSTINE OF LOCKHEED MARTIN

I am afraid that any honest assessment would have to conclude that, overall, these are not "the best of times" when it comes to ethics. In sports, we have illegal drugs, corked bats, and fighting with the fans. In the media, we have faked stories and the use of apparently forged documents. In academia, we have cases of plagiarism . . . one blatant example of which was recently found in, of all places, a book on plagiarism. In government, we have contracting abuses. In entertainment, we have wardrobe malfunctions and scurrilous, so-called "reality" shows. In business, we have Enron, Rite Aid, Sunbeam, WorldCom, Imclone, Tyco, and . . . well, you get the idea. Particularly troublesome is the recent survey of college seniors in which fifty-six percent of the respondents said they believe that the only difference between the executives at Enron and those of other large companies was that those at Enron got caught.

The road to wrongdoing is not a cliff over which one consciously jumps, but rather is a slippery slope along which one slides; a ski jump of morality, if you will. I have often drawn the analogy of ethical collapses to the actions of a boa constrictor as it devours its prey. Many believe that a boa constrictor simply wraps itself around you and crushes you. This is not the case. It wraps itself around you and each time you exhale it tightens up the slack a bit until eventually you can breathe no more.

I very much doubt that the Enron executives came to work one morning and said, "Let's see what sort of illegal scheme we can cook up to rip off the shareholders today." More likely, they began by setting extremely high goals for the firm . . . and for a time exceeded them. In so doing, they built a reputation for themselves and a demanding expectation among their investors. Eventually, the latter could no longer be sustained. Confronting the usual number of decision situations executives encounter every day, and not wanting to face reality, they gradually began to lean more and more towards extreme interpretations of established accounting principles. The next thing they knew, they had fallen off the bottom of the ski jump. Their accounting shortcuts seemed to parallel the adventures of the renowned if injudicious Evel Knievel, who became famous for attempting to leap deep chasms in two bounds!

Does all this suggest that acting ethically is hopelessly complex? Does it mean that even honest businesspersons may fall onto the slippery slope encountered by the leaders of Enron? I believe the answer is "No." I have found that there are four useful tests that one can apply when facing difficult ethical decisions. The first of these is to ask whether you are prepared to publicly disclose what you are doing and why you are doing it. The second is to ask whether you would feel wronged were someone else to do to you what you were considering doing. This, of course, is simply the Golden Rule. The third and by far the most demanding is to ask if you would mind if your mother watched you doing whatever it is that you are contemplating doing. (My own mother lived to be 105, so that tended to keep the pressure on!) The fourth is to ask yourself if you are getting too caught up in a debate over subtleties and passing issues . . . and if so, should you not simply turn the argument around, using the uncertainties to dictate against the aggressive approach? Simply stated, "When in doubt, don't!"

For more information on the Lockheed Martin Corporation, visit the organization's home page at ***http://www.lockheedmartin.com.***

Implications for Leaders. The traits model of leadership is inadequate for successfully predicting leadership effectiveness for at least three reasons.[25] First, in terms of personality traits, there are no consistent patterns between specific traits or sets of traits and leadership effectiveness. More than 100 different traits of successful leaders in various leadership positions have been identified. For example, the traits pattern of successful leaders of salespeople includes optimism, enthusiasm, and dominance. The traits pattern of successful leaders of production workers usually includes being progressive, introverted, and cooperative. These descriptions are simply generalities. Many successful leaders of salespeople and production workers do not have all, or even some, of these characteristics. There also is often disagreement over which traits are the most important for an effective leader.

The second limitation of the traits model is that it often attempts to relate physical traits—such as height, weight, appearance, physique, energy, and health—to effective leadership. Most of these factors are related to situational factors that can have a significant impact on a leader's effectiveness. For example, people in the military or law enforcement must be a particular minimum height and weight in order to perform certain tasks well. Although these traits may help an individual rise to a leadership position in such organizations, neither height nor weight correlates highly with effective leadership. In business and other organizations, height and weight generally play no role in performance and thus are not requirements for a leadership position.

The third limitation of the traits model is that leadership itself is complex. A relationship between specific traits and a person's interest in particular types of jobs could well exist, which a study relating personality and effectiveness might not identify. The traits approach paints a somewhat fatalistic picture, suggesting that some people, by their traits, are more prone to be leaders than others.

Behavioral Model of Leadership

The **behavioral model of leadership** *focuses on what leaders actually do and how they do it.* There are several versions of this model, but the one we present suggests that effective leaders help individuals and teams achieve their goals in two ways. First, they build task-centered relations with employees that focus on the quality and quantity of work accomplished. Second, they are considerate and supportive of employees' attempts to achieve personal goals (e.g., work satisfaction, promotions, and recognition) and work hard at settling disputes, keeping people happy, providing encouragement, and giving positive reinforcement.

The greatest number of studies of leader behavior has come from the Ohio State University leadership studies program, which began in the late 1940s. This research was aimed at identifying leader behaviors that are important for attaining team and organizational goals. These efforts resulted in the identification of two main dimensions of leader behavior: consideration and initiating structure.[26] Our review of the behavioral model is based on that leadership studies program. Table 6.2 provides the opportunity for you to diagnose your own leadership style according to the behavioral style of leadership.

Consideration. **Consideration** *is the extent to which the leader has relationships with subordinates that are characterized by mutual trust, two-way communication, respect for employees' ideas, and empathy for their feelings.* This style emphasizes the satisfaction of employee needs. The leader typically finds time to listen, is willing to make changes, looks out for the personal welfare of employees, and is friendly and approachable. A high degree of consideration indicates psychological closeness between leader and subordinates; a low degree shows greater psychological distance and a more impersonal leader.

When is consideration effective? The most positive efforts of leader consideration on productivity and job satisfaction occur when (1) the task is routine and denies employees little, if any, satisfaction from the work itself; (2) followers are predisposed toward participative leadership; (3) team members must learn something new; (4) employees feel that their involvement in the decision-making process is legitimate and affects their job performance; and (5) employees feel that strong status differences should not exist between them and their leader.

Initiating Structure. **Initiating structure** *is the extent to which a leader defines and prescribes the roles of subordinates in order to set and accomplish goals in their areas of responsibility.* This style emphasizes the direction of team or individual employee activities through planning, communicating, scheduling, assigning tasks, emphasizing deadlines, and giving orders. The leader maintains definite standards of performance and expects subordinates to achieve them. In short, a leader with a high degree of initiating structure concerns herself with accomplishing tasks by setting performance goals, giving directions, and expecting them to be followed.

When is initiating structure effective? The most positive effects of leader initiating structure on productivity and job satisfaction occur when (1) a high degree of pressure for output is imposed by someone other than the leader; (2) the task satisfies employees; (3) employees depend on the leader for information and direction on how to complete the task; (4) employees are psychologically predisposed toward being instructed in what to do and how to do it; and (5) more than 12 employees report to the leader.

Figure 6.1 suggests that the dimensions of consideration and initiating structure are not necessarily mutually exclusive and, in fact, may be related in various ways. A "leader" may be high, low, or moderate on both consideration and initiating structure, as suggested in Figure 6.1. For example, Amy Brinkley and Arlivia Babbage Gamble appear to be at the high end of both dimensions.

Implications for Leaders. Some studies suggest that a leader who emphasizes initiating structure generally improves productivity, at least in the short run. However, leaders who rank high on initiating structure and low on consideration generally have large numbers of grievances, absenteeism, and high employee turnover rates. The view now widely accepted is that effective leaders can have high consideration and initiating structure at the same time. Showing consideration is beneficial insofar as it leads to high levels of team morale and low levels of turnover

TABLE 6.2 Behavioral Leadership Style Questionnaire

The following statements can help you diagnose your leadership style according to the behavioral model of leadership. Read each item carefully. Think about how you usually behave when you are the leader (or if you were in a leader role). Then, using the following, record the letter that most closely describes your style next to the item.

A = Always O = Often ? = Sometimes S = Seldom N = Never

_____ 1. I take time to explain how a job should be carried out.
_____ 2. I explain the part that others are to play in the team.
_____ 3. I make clear the rules and procedures for others to follow in detail.
_____ 4. I organize my own work activities.
_____ 5. I let people know how well they are doing.
_____ 6. I let people know what is expected of them.
_____ 7. I encourage the use of uniform procedures for others to follow in detail.
_____ 8. I make my attitude clear to others.
_____ 9. I assign others to particular tasks.
_____ 10. I make sure that others understand their part in the team.
_____ 11. I schedule the work that I want others to do.
_____ 12. I ask that others follow standard rules and regulations.
_____ 13. I make working on the job more pleasant.
_____ 14. I go out of my way to be helpful.
_____ 15. I respect others' feelings and opinions.
_____ 16. I am thoughtful and considerate of others.
_____ 17. I maintain a friendly atmosphere in the team.
_____ 18. I do little things to make it more pleasant for others to be a member of my team.
_____ 19. I treat others as equals.
_____ 20. I give others advance notice of change and explain how it will affect them.
_____ 21. I look out for others' personal welfare.
_____ 22. I am approachable and friendly toward others.

Scoring
The point values for Always (A), Often (O), Sometimes (?), Seldom (S), and Never (N) are as follows: A=5; O=4; ?=3; S=2; and N=1. Sum the point values for items 1 through 12. Then, sum the point values for items 13 through 22.

Point values for initiating structure:
_____ 1, _____ 2, _____ 3, _____ 4, _____ 5, _____ 6, _____ 7, _____ 8, _____ 9, _____ 10, _____ 11, _____ 12, = Total ☐

Point values for consideration:
_____ 13, _____ 14, _____ 15, _____ 16, _____ 17, _____ 18, _____ 19, _____ 20, _____ 21, _____ 22 = Total ☐

Interpretation
Items 1 through 12 reflect an initiating structure or task leadership style. A score greater than 47 indicates that you describe your leadership style as high on initiating or task structure. You see yourself as planning, directing, organizing, and controlling the work of others. Items 13 through 22 reflect a considerate or relationship style. A score greater than 40 indicates that you see yourself as a considerate leader. A considerate leader is one who is concerned with the comfort, well-being, and personal welfare of her subordinates. In general, individuals rated high on initiating structure and at least moderate on consideration tend to be in charge of more productive teams than those whose leadership styles are low on initiating structure and high on consideration.

Source: Schriesheim, C. Leadership Instrument. Used by permission, University of Miami, Miami, Florida, 2005.

FIGURE 6.1 Behavioral Leadership Grid

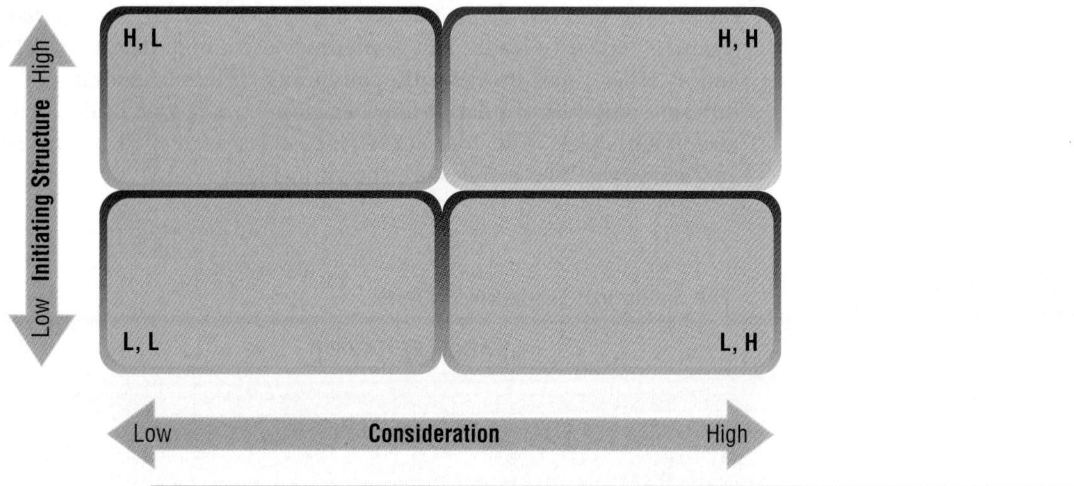

and absenteeism. At the same time, high levels of initiating structures are useful in promoting high levels of efficiency and performance.

Perhaps the main limitation of the behavioral model was the lack of attention it gave to the effects of the situation. It focused on relationships between leaders and employees but gave little consideration to the situation in which the relationships occurred. A better understanding of behavior usually results when both the person and the situation are examined.

Developers of the traits and behavioral models sought to find characteristics that apply to most leadership situations. In contrast, situational (contingency) leadership models identify variables that permit certain leadership characteristics and behaviors to be effective in given situations. In the next two sections, we present two contingency models of leadership: the Situational Leadership® Model, and the Vroom–Jago leadership model.

> **THE COMPETENT LEADER**
>
> Leadership is what it is all about. Without people being motivated and committed to magnificence, you will have an average company. Leadership is about creating the environment that motivates people to reveal their magnificence every day.
> **Garry C. Ridge, President and CEO, WD-40 Company**

SITUATIONAL LEADERSHIP® MODEL

> **LEARNING OBJECTIVE**
> 3. Explain the Situational Leadership® Model.

The **Situational Leadership® Model** *states that the style of leadership should be matched to the level of readiness of the followers.*[27] Like other contingency models of leadership, this one contains three basic components: a set of several possible leadership styles, a description of several alternative situations that leaders might encounter, and recommendations for which leadership styles are most effective in each situation.

Leadership Styles

According to the model, leaders can choose from among four leadership styles. These four leadership styles involve various combinations of task behavior and relationship behavior. Task behavior is similar to initiating structure, and relationship behavior is similar to consideration as described in the behavioral model. More specifically, **task behavior** *includes using one-way communication, spelling out duties, and telling followers what to do and where, when, and how to do it.* An effective leader might use a high degree of task behavior in some situations and only a moderate amount in other situations. **Relationship behavior** *includes using two-way communication, listening, encouraging, and involving followers in decision making, and giving emotional support.* Again, an effective leader may sometimes use a high degree of relationship behavior, and at other times use less. By combining different amounts of task behavior with different amounts of relationship behavior, an effective leader may use four different leadership styles. The four leadership styles are called *telling*, *selling*, *participating*, and *delegating*. These styles are shown in Figure 6.2.[28]

FIGURE 6.2 The Situational Leadership® Model

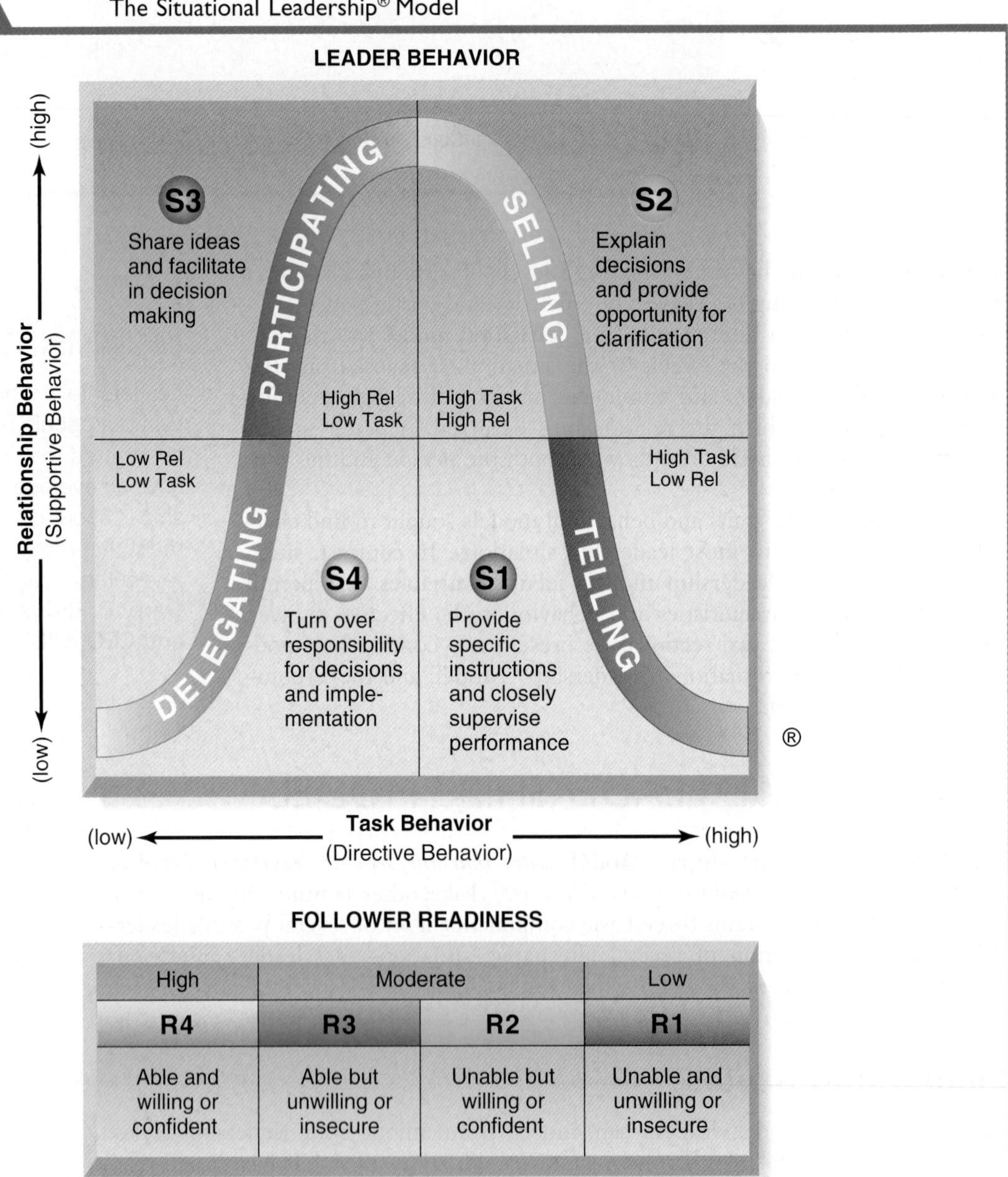

Source: P. Hersey et al. *Management of Organizational Behavior: Leading Human Resources,* 8th ed. (Upper Saddle River, NJ: Prentice Hall, 2001), p. 182. Copyright © 2001, Center for Leadership Studies, Escondido, CA. Used with permission.

Situational Contingency

According to this model, a leader should consider the situation before deciding which leadership style to use. The situational contingency in this model is the degree of follower readiness. **Readiness** *is a follower's ability to set high but attainable task-related goals and a willingness to accept responsibility for reaching them.* Readiness is not a fixed characteristic of followers—it depends on the task. The same group of followers may have a high degree of readiness for some tasks, but a low degree of readiness for others. The readiness level of followers depends on how much training they have received, how committed they are to the organization, their technical expertise, experience with the specific task, and so on.

Choosing a Leadership Style

As Figure 6.2 shows, the appropriate leadership style depends on the level of follower readiness. The curve running through the graph indicates the leadership style that best fits each readiness level of the individual or team. Note that high readiness levels appear on the left and low readiness levels appear on the right.

For a follower who is at the stage of low readiness for a task, a telling style is effective. In using a **telling style,** *the leader provides clear instructions, gives specific directions, and supervises the work closely.* The telling style helps ensure that new employees perform well, which provides a solid foundation for their future success and satisfaction.

As the follower's task-specific readiness increases, the leader needs to continue to provide some guidance behavior because the employee isn't yet ready to assume total responsibility for performing the task. In addition, the leader needs to begin using supportive behaviors in order to build the employee's confidence and maintain enthusiasm. That is, the leader should shift to a selling style. In using a **selling style,** *the leader provides direction, encourages two-way communication, and helps build confidence and motivation on the part of the follower.*

When the follower feels confident about performing the task, the leader no longer needs to be so directive. The leader should maintain open communication but now does so by actively listening and assisting the follower as he or she makes efforts to use what has been learned. In using a **participating style,** *the leader encourages followers to share ideas and facilitates the work by being encouraging and helpful to subordinates.*

Finally, when an employee is at a high level of readiness for the task, effective leadership involves more delegation. In using a **delegating style,** *the leader turns over responsibility for making and implementing decisions to followers.* Delegating is effective in this situation because the follower is both competent and motivated to take full responsibility for his work. Even though the leader may still identify problems, the responsibility for carrying out plans is given to the follower. The follower who is fully ready for a project is permitted to manage the project and decide how, when, and where tasks are to be done.

The Communication Competency feature on page 176 reports on how Michelle Miller adjusted her leadership style in relation to the characteristics of one of her subordinates.[29] Miller is the manager who opened Walgreens' 4,000th store in Redondo Beach, California. Walgreens is a major drugstore and health service chain with 4,600 stores and headquarters in Deerfield, Illinois, a suburb of Chicago.[30]

Implications for Leaders

The Situational Leadership® Model helps leaders recognize that the same leadership style may be effective in some situations but not others. Furthermore, it highlights the importance of considering the followers' situation when choosing a leadership style, as Michelle Miller did. This model has generated quite a bit of interest among

COMMUNICATION COMPETENCY

MICHELLE MILLER OF WALGREENS

Michelle Miller's wall of her back office is papered with work schedules. Miller's store in Redondo Beach, California, employs people with sharply different skills and potentially disruptive differences in personality. A critical part of her job, therefore, is to put people into roles and shifts that will allow them to shine—and to avoid putting clashing personalities together. At the same time, she attempts to find ways for individuals to grow.

There's Jeffrey, for example, a "goth rocker" whose hair is shaved on one side and long enough on the other side to cover his face. Miller almost didn't hire him because he couldn't quite look her in the eye during his interview. But he wanted the hard-to-cover night shift, so she decided to give him a chance. After a couple of months, she noticed that when she gave Jeffrey a vague assignment, such as "Straighten up the merchandise in every aisle," what should have been a two-hour job would take him all night—and wouldn't be done very well. But if she gave him a more specific task, such as "Put up all the risers for Christmas," all the risers would be in line, with the right merchandise on each one, perfectly priced, labeled, and "faced" (turned toward the customer). Give Jeffrey a general task, he would struggle. Give him one that forced him to be accurate and analytical, and he would excel. Miller concluded that this was Jeffrey's strength. So, as a good leader, she told Jeffrey what she had learned about him and praised him for his good work.

Miller knew she could get more out of Jeffrey. So she devised a plan to reassign responsibilities across the entire store to capitalize on his unique strengths. In every Walgreens, there is a responsibility called "resets and revisions." A reset involves stocking an aisle with new merchandise, a task that usually coincides with a predictable change in customer buying patterns (at the end of summer, for example, the stores will replace sun creams and lip balms with allergy medicines). A revision is a less time-consuming but more frequent version of the same thing: Replace these cartons of toothpaste with this new and improved variety. Display this new line of detergent at this end of the row. Each aisle requires some form of revision at least once a week.

In most Walgreens stores, each employee "owns" one aisle, where the person is responsible not only for serving customers but also for "facing" the merchandise, keeping the aisle clean and orderly, tagging items with a Telxon gun, and conducting all resets and revisions. This arrangement is simple and efficient, and it affords each employee a sense of personal responsibility. But Miller decided that since Jeffrey was so good at resets and revisions—and didn't enjoy interacting with customers—this should be his full-time job, in every single aisle.

It was a challenge. One week's worth of revisions requires a binder three inches thick. But Miller reasoned that not only would Jeffrey be excited by the challenge and get better and better with practice, but other employees would be freed from what they considered a chore and have more time to greet and serve customers. The store's performance proved her right. After the reorganization, Miller saw not only increases in sales and profit but also in that most critical performance metric, customer satisfaction. In subsequent months, her store netted perfect scores in Walgreens' mystery shopper program.

For more information on Walgreens, visit the organization's home page at ***http://www.walgreens.com.***

practitioners and researchers.[31] The idea that leaders should be flexible with respect to the leadership style they use is appealing. An inexperienced employee may perform as well as an experienced employee if properly directed and closely supervised. Michelle Miller demonstrated this in her leadership of Jeffrey. An appropriate leadership style should also help followers gain more experience and become more competent. Thus, as a leader helps followers develop to higher levels of readiness, the leader's style also needs to evolve. Therefore, this model requires the leader to be constantly monitoring the readiness level of followers in order to determine the combination of task and relationship behaviors that is most appropriate.

Like other contingency models, this one assumes that managers can accurately assess each situation and change their leadership styles to match different situations. Some people can read situations and adapt their leadership style more effectively than others. For those who can't, what are the costs of training them to be able to do so? Do these costs exceed the potential benefits? Before an organization adopts a management training program to teach managers to use this model of leadership, they need to answer questions such as these.

VROOM–JAGO LEADERSHIP MODEL

LEARNING OBJECTIVE

4. Discuss the Vroom–Jago time-driven leadership model.

Victor Vroom and Arthur Jago developed a model that focuses on the leadership role in decision-making situations.[32] Victor Vroom revised this model to (1) give greater consideration to ranges that may exist in situational variables; (2) clarify the presentation of the five leadership styles in the earlier model; and (3) further emphasize the time-driven dimension to the choice of leadership style in relation to decision-making situations. The **Vroom–Jago time-driven leadership model** *prescribes a leader's choice(s) among five leadership styles based on seven situational factors, recognizing the time requirements and costs associated with each style.*[33]

Leadership Styles

There are five core leadership styles that vary in terms of the levels of empowerment and participation available to the leader's subordinates. These styles are summarized here in increasing levels of empowerment and participation:

- **Decide style**—*the leader makes the decision alone and either announces or sells it to the team.* The leader uses personal expertise and collects information from the team or others who can help solve the problem. The role of employees is clearly one of providing specific information that is requested, rather than generating or evaluating solutions.
- **Consult individually style**—*the leader presents the problem to team members individually, getting their ideas and suggestions and then makes the decision without bringing them together as a group.* This decision may or may not reflect their influence.
- **Consult team style**—*the leader presents the problem to team members in a meeting, gets their suggestions, and then makes the decision.* It may or may not reflect their influence.
- **Facilitate style**—*the leader presents the problem to the team in a meeting, acts as a facilitator, defines the problem to be solved, and sets the boundaries within which the decision must be made.* The objective is to get agreement on a decision. Above all, the leader takes care to ensure that her ideas are not given any greater weight than those of others simply because of her position. The leader's role is much like that of chairperson, coordinating the discussion, keeping it focused on the problem, and being sure that the essential issues are discussed. The leader doesn't try to influence the team to adopt "her" solution. The leader is willing to accept and implement any solution that has the support of the entire team.
- **Delegate style**—*the leader permits the team to make the decision within prescribed limits.* The team undertakes the identification and diagnosis of the problem, developing alternative procedures for solving it and deciding on one or more alternative solutions. The leader doesn't enter into the team's deliberations unless explicitly asked, but plays an important role by providing needed resources and encouragement. This style represents the highest level of subordinate empowerment.

Situational Variables

The Vroom–Jago time-driven leadership model focuses on seven situational factors (contingency variables) that should be assessed by the leader to determine which leadership style to use. Victor Vroom developed a Windows-based computer program called Expert System that enables the leader to record judgments on a five-point scale as to the extent to which a factor is present in a particular situation. Specifically, 5 = high presence, 3 = moderate presence, and 1 = low presence. Following our presentation of the seven situational factors, we demonstrate their use with a simplified "high" or a "low" presence evaluation.

- *Decision significance*—the degree to which the problem is highly important and a quality decision is imperative. In brief, how important is the technical quality of the decision?
- *Importance of commitment*—the degree to which subordinates' personal willingness to support the decision has an impact on the effectiveness of implementation. In brief, how important is subordinate commitment to the decision? Employees are more likely to implement enthusiastically a decision that is consistent with their goals, values, and understanding of the problem.
- *Leader expertise*—the degree to which the leader has relevant information and competencies to understand the problem fully and select the best solution to it. In brief, does the leader believe that he has the ability and information to make a high-quality decision?
- *Likelihood of commitment*—the degree to which subordinates will support the leader's decision if it is made. Followers who have faith and trust in the judgments of their leaders are more likely to commit to a decision, even if the subordinates were not heavily involved in making it. In brief, if the leader were to make the decision, would subordinate(s) likely be committed to it?
- *Team support*—the degree to which subordinates relate to the interests of the organization as a whole or a specific unit in solving the problem. In brief, do subordinates share the goals to be achieved by solving this problem?
- *Team expertise*—the degree to which the subordinates have the relevant information and competencies to understand fully the problem and select the best solution to it. In brief, does the leader think that subordinates have the abilities and information to make a high-quality decision?
- *Team competence*—the degree to which team members have the abilities needed to resolve conflicts over preferred solutions and work together in reaching a high-quality decision. In brief, are team members capable of handling their own decision-making process?

Solution Matrix

The solution matrix shown in Table 6.3 represents the basic features of the Vroom–Jago time-driven leadership model. This matrix begins on the left where you evaluate the significance of the situation—high (H) or low (L). The column headings denote the situational factors that may or may not be present. You progress across the matrix by selecting high (H) or low (L) for each relevant situation factor. After you determine the significance of the decision, you then evaluate the degree (high or low) to which employee commitment is important to implementation of the decision. As you proceed across the matrix, record a value (H or L) for only those situational factors that call for a judgment, until you reach the recommended leadership style.

Decision-Time Penalty. The **decision-time penalty** *is the negative result of decisions not being made when needed.* Leaders often must make decisions when time is

TABLE 6.3 Vroom–Jago Time-Driven Leadership Model

PROBLEM STATEMENT

Note: Dashed line (—) means not a factor.

DECISION SIGNIFICANCE	IMPORTANCE OF COMMITMENT	LEADER EXPERTISE	LIKELIHOOD OF COMMITMENT	TEAM SUPPORT	TEAM EXPERTISE	TEAM COMPETENCE	
H	H	H	H	—	—	—	Decide
			L	H	H	H	Delegate
						L	Consult Team
					L	—	
				L	—	—	
		L	H	H	H	H	Facilitate
						L	Consult Individually
					L	—	
				L	—	—	
			L	H	H	H	Facilitate
						L	Consult Team
					L	—	
				L	—	—	
	L	H	—	—	—	—	Decide
		L	—	H	H	H	Facilitate
						L	Consult Individually
					L	—	
				L	—	—	
L	H	—	H	—	—	—	Decide
			L	—	—	H	Delegate
						L	Facilitate
	L	—	—	—	—	—	Decide

Source: Vroom, V. H. Leadership and decision-making. *Organizational Dynamics,* Spring 2000, 82–94.

of the essence. For example, air traffic control supervisors, emergency rescue squad leaders, and nuclear energy plant managers may have little time to get inputs from others before having to make a decision. The time penalty is low when there are no severe pressures on the leader to make a quick decision.

Negative effects on "human capital" occur because the delegate and consult styles (especially the consult team version) use time and energy, which can be translated into costs even if there are no severe time constraints. Many managers spend almost 70 percent of their time in meetings and that time always has a value, although the precise costs of meetings vary with the reasons for them. For example, while Jonathan Wheeler, vice president of human resources at Centex Homes, is in a meeting, other decisions are being delayed. What's the cost to Centex for these delays? One cost, obviously, is the value of time lost through the use of participative decision making. Benefits gained from employee participation in meetings include being members of a team, strengthening their commitment to the organization's goals, and contributing to the development of their leadership capabilities (mainly as related to the self and communication competencies). Thus, the cost of holding a meeting must be compared to the cost of not holding a meeting.

Although participation can have negative effects on human capital, it can also have positive effects. As we emphasize throughout this book, participative leader behaviors help develop the technical skills and managerial competencies of employees, build teamwork, and foster loyalty and commitment to organizational goals. The Vroom–Jago model considers the trade-offs among four criteria by which a leader's decision-making style can be evaluated: decision quality, employee commitment to implementation, costs, and employee development. The consult and delegate styles are viewed as most supportive of employee development.

This model is applied in the following Change Competency feature.[34] We ask you to assume the role of the director of research and select the leadership style that you would use.

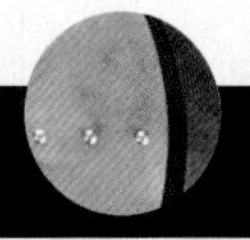

CHANGE COMPETENCY

YOUR LEADERSHIP AS DIRECTOR OF RESEARCH

After receiving your Ph.D. in chemistry, you joined a large pulp and paper firm and gradually worked your way up to the position of director of research. Several years ago, you persuaded top management to allocate the funds necessary to build a brand new research facility and to hire the brightest research scientists that you could persuade to work in the forest products industry. The scientists that you were able to hire are technically excellent but, unfortunately, have a strong preference for working on basic rather than applied research. You have accepted that preference in order to keep this highly cohesive team satisfied. However, the pulp and paper industry, as a whole, has fallen on hard times. You are finding it increasingly difficult to justify the bottom-line contributions made by R&D to top management.

Recently, a new research problem with considerable promise has been suggested by another division. Your group would be ideally qualified to work on the problem. Unfortunately, they are likely to regard it as devoid of scientific interest. The projects on which they are currently working provide them with intellectual satisfaction. It will be necessary to get back to the division soon with a decision concerning what resources, if any, you can devote to their problem. In the past, you have found this team of scientists to speak with one voice. If you can find a solution that satisfied one team member, it would probably go a long way toward satisfying everyone on the team.

As director of research—and armed with the solution matrix shown in Table 6.3—what leadership style should you choose when making a decision about how to lead? Start with *decision significance* on the left-hand side of the matrix. This first column requires that you make a decision about the importance of the issue. After you make that decision, go to the next column, *importance of commitment*. Again, you must make a decision about the importance of having staff members committed. After you make this decision, you face another decision and then another. As you make each decision, follow the columns across the matrix. Eventually, at the far right-hand side of the matrix, you will arrive at the recommended best style of leadership to use, which is based on your previous seven decisions. We used this method and obtained the results shown in the following table. Based on this analysis, we selected the style of leadership that we recommend for this situation. Do you agree?

Problem Statements in Table 6.3	Answers
• Decision significance	High
• Importance of commitment	High
• Leader expertise	High
• Likelihood of commitment	Low
• Team support	Low
• Team expertise	Not applicable in this situation
• Team competence	Not applicable in this situation

We recommend that you use the consult team style in this situation. A different answer to one or more of these situational factors would probably result in a different recommended leadership style.

Implications for Leaders

The Vroom–Jago time-driven leadership model is consistent with work on group and team behaviors, as we will discuss in Chapter 8. If leaders can diagnose situations correctly, choosing the best leadership style for those situations becomes easier. These choices, in turn, enable them to make high-quality, timely decisions. If the situation requires delegation, the leader must learn how to establish the desired goals and limitations and then let employees determine how best to achieve the goals within those limitations. If the situation calls for the leader alone to make the decision, the leader should be aware of potential positive and negative consequences of not asking others for their input.

The model does have some limitations. First, subordinates may have a strong desire to participate in decisions affecting their jobs, regardless of the model's recommendation of a style for the leader to use. If subordinates aren't involved in the decision, they may become frustrated and not be committed to the decision. Second, certain competencies of the leader play a key role in determining the relative effectiveness of the model. For example, in situations involving conflict, only leaders skilled in communication and conflict resolution may be able to use the kind of participative decision-making strategy suggested by the model. A leader who hasn't developed such abilities may obtain better results with a more directive style, even though this leadership style is different from the style that the model proposes. Third, the model is based on the assumption that decisions involve a single process. Often, decisions go through several cycles and are part of a solution to a bigger problem than the one being addressed at the time.

Choosing the most appropriate leadership style can be difficult. A theme of employee empowerment has begun to prevail in many leading business organizations. Evidence shows that this leadership style can result in productive, healthy organizations. Participative management is not appropriate for all situations, as the model in Table 6.3 suggests.

CHAPTER SUMMARY

1. Describe the role of power and political behavior in the leadership process.

Leaders draw on five sources of power to influence the actions of followers: legitimate, reward, coercive, referent, and expert. All leaders engage in political behavior to influence others—sometimes ineffectively. Political behavior and organizational politics focus on efforts to protect or enhance self-interests, goals, and preferred outcomes. The drivers of political behavior were noted with special emphasis on how leaders can foster or minimize political behaviors of subordinates in relation to the performance appraisal process.

2. Describe two traditional models of leadership: traits and behavioral.

Two of the traditional leadership models are the traits and behavioral models. The traits model emphasizes the personal qualities of leaders and attributes success to certain abilities, skills, and personality characteristics. This model fails to explain why certain people succeed and others fail as leaders. The primary reason is that it ignores how traits interact with situational variables. The behavioral model emphasizes leaders' actions instead of their personal traits. We focused on two leader behaviors—initiating structure and consideration—and how they affect employee performance and job satisfaction. The behavioral model tends to ignore the situation in which the leader is operating. This omission is the focal point of the two contingency models of leadership that we reviewed. The contingency approach emphasizes the importance of various situational factors for leaders and their leadership styles.

3. Explain the Situational Leadership® Model.

The Situational Leadership® Model states that leaders should choose a style that matches the readiness of their subordinates to follow. If subordinates are not ready to perform a task, a directive leadership style will probably be more effective than a relationship style. As the readiness level of the subordinates increases, the leader's style should become more participative and less directive.

4. Discuss the Vroom–Jago time-driven leadership model.

The Vroom–Jago model presents a leader with choices among five leadership styles based on seven situational (contingency) factors. Time requirements and other costs associated with each style are recognized in the model. The leadership styles lie on a continuum from decide (leader makes the decision) to delegate (subordinate or team makes the decision). A solution matrix (Table 6.3) is used to diagnose the situation and arrive at the recommended leadership style.

KEY TERMS AND CONCEPTS

Behavioral model of leadership
Coercive power
Consideration
Consult individually style
Consult team style
Decide style
Decision-time penalty
Delegate style
Delegating style
Expert power
Facilitate style
Initiating structure
Leader
Leadership
Legitimate power
Organizational politics
Participating style
Political behavior
Readiness
Referent power
Relationship behavior
Reward power
Selling style
Situational Leadership® Model
Task behavior
Telling style
Traits model of leadership
Vroom–Jago time-driven leadership model
Zone of indifference

DISCUSSION QUESTIONS

1. Describe a manager that you have worked for in terms of the use (or lack of use) of the five sources of power: legitimate, reward, coercive, referent, and expert. How effective was this manager in using each of these sources of power to influence you? Explain.
2. Assume that you have been selected as a team leader for four other classmates. The team's assignment is to develop a 20-page paper on the traits model of leadership and then to present the paper to the class. This project represents 30 percent of the course grade. How might the Vroom–Jago time-driven leadership model be helpful to you as the team leader? What limitations does this model impose on you as team leader?
3. In the Ethics Competency feature, we presented excerpts of Norman Augustine's views of ethics. Based on the Situational Leadership® Model, what style or styles of leadership does he represent? Relate his specific comment(s) to each style identified.
4. Based on the five sources of power presented, which ones are illustrated in the remarks by Amy Brinkley in the Preview Case? Relate her specific comment(s) to each source of power identified.
5. Based on the traits model of leadership, what leadership traits are emphasized by Amy Brinkley in the Preview Case? Relate her specific comment(s) to each trait identified.
6. Think of a manager you have worked for. Did this manager engage in political performance appraisals or do things to minimize politics in the performance appraisal process? Explain with specific examples.
7. Based on the Self Competency feature related to Arlivia Gamble, what examples of consideration and/or initiating structure behaviors can you identify for her? How would you characterize her on the behavioral leadership grid (Figure 6.1)? Justify your interpretation.
8. Think of an organization you have worked for. What drivers of political behavior can you identify?
9. Based on the Communications Competency feature related to Michelle Miller, what behaviors and decisions by her reflected elements of the Situational Leadership® Model?
10. Based on a problem situation in which you were a team member or leader, was the appropriate leadership style used according to an assessment of the situational variables in the Vroom–Jago time-driven leadership model? Use Table 6.3 to guide your assessment.

EXPERIENTIAL EXERCISE AND CASE

Experiential Exercise: Self Competency

Personal Power Inventory[35]

Instructions: Think of a group of which you are a member. For example, it could be a team at work, a committee, or a group working on a project at your school. Use the scale shown to respond to the following statements.

1 = Strongly disagree
2 = Disagree
3 = Slightly disagree
4 = Neither agree nor disagree
5 = Slightly agree
6 = Agree
7 = Strongly agree

_____ 1. I am one of the more vocal members of the group.
_____ 2. People in the group listen to what I have to say.
_____ 3. I often volunteer to lead the group.
_____ 4. I am able to influence group decisions.
_____ 5. I often find myself on "center stage" in group activities or discussions.
_____ 6. Members of the group seek me out for advice.
_____ 7. I take the initiative in the group for my ideas and contributions.
_____ 8. I receive recognition in the group for my ideas and contributions.
_____ 9. I would rather lead the group than be a participant.
_____ 10. My opinion is held in high regard by group members.
_____ 11. I volunteer my thoughts and ideas without hesitation.
_____ 12. My ideas often are implemented.
_____ 13. I ask questions in meetings just to have something to say.
_____ 14. Group members often ask for my opinions and input.
_____ 15. I often play the role of scribe, secretary, or note taker during meetings.
_____ 16. Group members usually consult me about important matters before they make a decision.
_____ 17. I clown around with other group members.
_____ 18. I have noticed that group members often look at me, even when not talking directly to me.
_____ 19. I jump right into whatever conflict the group members are dealing with.
_____ 20. I am very influential in the group.

Scoring and Interpretation

Visibility		Influence	
Item	**Your Score**	**Item**	**Your Score**
1.	_______	2.	_______
3.	_______	4.	_______
5.	_______	6.	_______
7.	_______	8.	_______
9.	_______	10.	_______
11.	_______	12.	_______
13.	_______	14.	_______
15.	_______	16.	_______
17.	_______	18.	_______
19.	_______	20.	_______
Total	_______	Total	_______

Use the scores calculated and mark your position on the power matrix shown in Figure 6.3. The combinations of visibility and influence shown are described as follows.

1. *High power*: Individuals in quadrant I exhibit behaviors that bring high visibility and they are able to influence others. In organizations, these individuals may be considered to be on the "fast track."
2. *Low power*: Individuals in quadrant II are highly visible but have little real influence. This condition could reflect their personal characteristics but also could indicate that formal power resides elsewhere in the organization. Often these people may hold staff, rather than line, positions that give them visibility but that lack "clout" to get things done.

FIGURE 6.3 Power Matrix

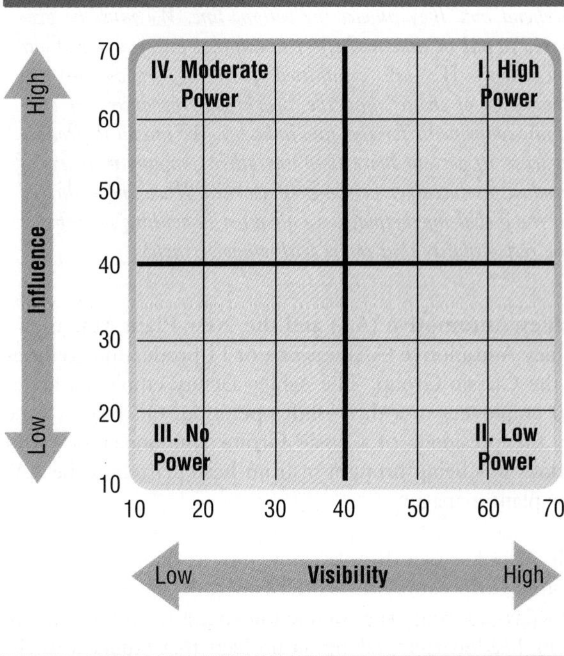

Source: Adapted from Reddy, W. B., and Williams, G. The visibility credibility inventory: Measuring power and influence. In J.W. Pfeiffer (ed.), *The 1988 Annual: Developing Human Resources.* San Diego: University Associates, 1988, 124.

3. *No power.* Individuals in quadrant III, for whatever reason, are neither seen nor heard. Individuals in this category may have difficulty advancing in the organization.
4. *Moderate power.* Individuals in quadrant IV are "behind the scenes" influencers. These individuals often are opinion leaders and "sages" who wield influence but are content to stay out of the limelight.

Case: Change Competency

Ashley Automotive—Changing Times[36]

The sale of U.S. cars and trucks was once again on a roller coaster. Since September 11, 2001, deep discounting, rebates, and low interest rates had increased auto sales. But with escalating production costs and a strong dollar, U.S. manufacturers had fared poorly compared with their foreign rivals. The fierce competition in the automotive industry had spilled over to suppliers. In an effort to compete effectively, supplies had gotten bigger and bigger. Their overall number had declined 75 percent in the last 25 years.

The Classic Group

With eleven production facilities in three Midwestern states, Classic Group, Inc., was a primary source of electronic components for the auto industry. The ambitions of Classic's current president appeared to surpass those of his predecessors. He believed that the company could become a "world-class" supplier of automotive components. He envisioned adding divisions in other parts of the United States and eventually, even overseas. An e-mail sent to all employees stated:

> *Employees must understand the role they play in our organization. They must be literate in financial language and comprehend how they impact the bottom line. We must be prepared to put in time and effort to improve every aspect of our operations. We are committed to being known as the "employer of choice" and the "world-class producer" of electronic components for the auto industry. We intend to produce at least 50 percent more than any other company in terms of product produced per person-hour worked. If we are to succeed in the global marketplace, we all must be willing to embrace the responsibility that comes with empowerment.*

Ashley Automotive (AA) and the New Plant Manager

Ashley Automotive (AA) was one of 11 production facilities in the Classic Group. The Ashley facility employed about 450 employees in a three-shift operation. On Friday, June 13, the president of Classic Group announced that Bill Brooks was being brought in from headquarters to be AA's new plant manager.

Bill Brooks. Bill Brooks grew up working in General Motors Corporation's Delco Divisions. At age 40, he joined the Classic Group as a production specialist in the Toledo, Ohio, headquarters, taking on projects that required working on the "cutting edge." Brooks held a bachelor's degree in industrial engineering and had completed most of the requirements toward an MBA in an evening and weekend program.

Attendance at various management seminars coupled with required reading in the MBA program led him to embrace the idea that "leadership is an observable, learnable set of practices. Given the opportunity for feedback and practice, those with desire and persistence to lead can substantially improve their abilities to do so."[37]

On Tuesday, June 16, Brooks spent the morning walking the Ashley plant and talking with employees. Early that afternoon, he met with the materials managers and the engineering staff. At 4 P.M., he met with all managerial and professional staff. At this meeting, he outlined his philosophy of management:

> *Delivering the finest quality product to customers—on time—and maintaining a safe work environment are the most important goals for this division. Keeping employees motivated is a key concern—participation in decision making is expected. Employees must be encouraged to look for ways to do the job better. Allowing people to make mistakes enables them to learn what not to do in the future. Catching people doing something right motivates them—we will celebrate success.*

Brooks went on to echo the sentiments of the Classic Group's president in reaffirming that the long-term success of the Classic Group and Ashley Automotive hinged on finding ways to produce high-quality products at a substantially reduced cost. Brooks indicated that he expected a minimum of a 10 percent reduction in production costs per part this year.

Discussion of Change

After the meeting, several managers stopped off at the Dew Drop Inn for refreshments as they often did. Over drinks, they reflected on Brooks's comments. In general, they had each enjoyed a good working relationship with the previous plant manager who believed that "the buck stopped with them" with regard to the work of their subordinates. He wanted them to keep their "people in line" and always know what their subordinates were doing.

Al Abrams listened as Tony complained about how they (the first-shift managers) were now expected to spend two hours or more after regular working hours with no additional compensation so they could listen to the new plant manager. Their shift ended at 3:30 P.M., yet they were expected to be at the four o'clock meeting. Al sympathetically countered, "I know how you feel. My good friend Sid, who worked at Farmer's and Merchant's Bank, felt the same way when Bank One bought them. They brought in a bunch of out-of-town managers and the culture of the bank changed—for the worse."

Al Abrams. Al Abrams had a broad background in production and had risen to the position of first-shift materials manager. He had a limited view of employees' capabilities and felt they had to be told to do exactly what needed to be done. He felt that he and he alone was capable of making decisions—his experiences had taught him that the manager's job was to issue directives and that subordinates' jobs were to hear and obey. After all, he was ultimately responsible for the results. Except for a couple of supervisory training programs, his formal education ended when he graduated from high school 20 years ago.

Abrams, a veteran of 11 years of service with AA, had worked hard to get where he was. He had high expectations of others, but often felt they let him down. He expected others to work as hard as he did and often made suggestions as to how to accomplish tasks. Coworkers, subordinates, and others often found him to be too demanding and control oriented.

Some of the management group hung around the Dew Drop Inn and continued to discuss the events of the day and the state of the economy. Most were apprehensive since the global economy was in a recession the likes of which many of them did not understand. Corporate profits had all but disappeared. Retail sales were down and even the Dew Drop Inn appeared to have fewer customers every time they paid a visit.

Most of the discussion centered on the future of AA, and since the group's fate hinged on its future, the opinions were varied. Several expressed that they found the Classic Group president's vision for the future to be threatening. Did he really mean that the Classic Group would be building new plants with newer technologies in low-wage states and developing nations that were known for their low wages? If so, the end might be near for AA. Some expressed fears that if they lost their jobs at AA, they might never find others that were as economically rewarding.

As the group was breaking up, Al got in the last word. He left no doubt that he found the president's new philosophy to be threatening. In conclusion, he retorted,

> *I don't think I'm going to like this Brooks guy. I didn't like what he said or how he said it, and the gall of him to keep us over to hear that crap. My job is to tell people what to do. If he wants cost improvements, he needs to ask us—not them! He never should have gotten that job. Several people here have paid their dues and should have gotten the plant manager job.*

As they departed, others nodded their heads in agreement.

Questions

1. What aspects of discussion of power and political behavior are illustrated in this case?
2. Based on the behavioral model of leadership, how would you describe the leadership styles of Bill Brooks and Al Abrams? Explain.
3. Based on the Vroom–Jago time-driven leadership model, what style of leadership do you think Brooks should use at this time to identify and implement the needed changes? Explain.
4. What potential problems and issues might Brooks face in introducing the needed changes?

CHAPTER 7

Leading Effectively: Contemporary Developments

LEARNING OBJECTIVES

When you have finished studying this chapter, you should be able to:

1. State the characteristics of transactional leadership.
2. Describe the features of charismatic leadership.
3. Discuss the attributes of authentic leadership.
4. Explain the nature of transformational leadership.

Preview Case: Ed Breen of Tyco International

TRANSACTIONAL LEADERSHIP
- Key Components
- *Self Competency—Guangchang Guo of Shanghai Fortune High Technology Group*
- Implications for Leaders

CHARISMATIC LEADERSHIP
- Key Components
- *Communication Competency—Richard Branson of the Virgin Group*
- Implications for Leaders

AUTHENTIC LEADERSHIP
- Key Components
- *Ethics Competency—Richard Johnson of BET*
- Implications for Leaders

TRANSFORMATIONAL LEADERSHIP
- Key Components
- *Change Competency—Mike McGavick of Safeco*
- Implications for Leaders
- Similarities and Differences in Models

CHAPTER SUMMARY

KEY TERMS AND CONCEPTS

DISCUSSION QUESTIONS

EXPERIENTIAL EXERCISE AND CASE

ED BREEN OF TYCO INTERNATIONAL

PREVIEW CASE

Ed Breen became the CEO and chairman of Tyco International Ltd. in July 2002. At that time, there was much speculation in the news that Tyco would file for bankruptcy within days. The firm had more than $11 billion in debt coming due in 2003 with no apparent ability to make the payments. The former CEO, Dennis Kozlowski, and some of the other top executives had been charged with massive accounting fraud and misuse of company assets for personal gain.

Tyco is a global diversified company that provides products and services in five business segments: fire and security, electronics, health care, engineered products and services, and plastics and adhesives. Revenues are now over $40 billion annually and the firm employs approximately 260,000 people worldwide. Since 2002, the stock has recovered from $8 per share to over $36 per share as of 2005.

Ed Breen's leadership, along with the leaders he hired, represents a major ingredient in the remarkable transformation of Tyco. Let's consider a few examples of the strong leadership provided by Breen.

Early on, Breen decided that the entire board of directors needed to be replaced. Breen comments: "To reassure investors, we had to go overboard on corporate governance. Tyco needed a clean sweep to send a message to the market that this is going to be a different company. There's no way I could've backed down. If we didn't replace the board, we wouldn't have been able to proceed." But the process required hard-nosed leadership. In a dramatic five-hour meeting held by speakerphone on September 12, 2002, Breen asked the directors to vote that none of the veterans of the Kozlowski era could stand for reelection at the next annual meeting in early 2003. Breen's position caused an uproar. "Directors were saying, 'This will make it look like we're guilty.' They were worried about liability, " recalls current lead director Jack Krol, a former chairman of DuPont. "They also thought continuity was important. Breen wanted the opposite of continuity." With the vote deadlocked at 5–5, Breen cast the deciding vote to replace the entire board. "It was a tough all-day meeting," says Krol. "But Breen won. He was very determined."

Breen replaced the old, weak board with a strong group of current and former CEOs who bring diverse skills. Breen set up the new board, with the assistance of experts on corporate governance, so that he is the only insider on the board. Breen instituted an internal audit staff, consisting of 110 people. The audit chief reports to the director who heads the board's audit committee, not to Breen. Tyco's ombudsman also reports to this director. Also, employees can call an 800 number to report anything they perceive as wrongdoing, from sexual harassment to price fixing. In the first year of this system, Tyco conducted almost 1,300 investigations—a quarter of which have resulted in disciplinary action or a change in procedures.

Tyco's operating principle had been all about frenzied deal making, not thoughtful leadership and integration. That culture had to change: Breen dismissed 290 of Tyco's 300 highest-ranking managers and staff at corporate headquarters in the first few months. Breen comments: "I didn't know what people knew or what they should have known. So, I decided to start with a clean slate."

Breen's leadership is amplified in a letter to Tyco's stakeholders on the firm's website. We share excerpts of it here:

> *Nothing is more important to a company than its credibility—credibility with investors, customers, government leaders and employees. Since my arrival in July 2002 my*

For more information on Tyco International Ltd., visit the organization's home page at ***http://www.tyco.com.***

biggest challenge has been to begin the process of restoring genuine trust in the leadership of this company. We've already come a long way in rebuilding Tyco's credibility—by demanding of ourselves the highest standards of integrity. For example, we have devoted considerable time and effort to drafting a new employee Guide to Ethical Conduct. That document, approved by the new Board of Directors, sets forth our rules in such areas as harassment, conflicts of interest, compliance with laws, and fraud. All the senior executives, including myself, will be evaluated annually on their adherence to the Guide. In addition, the new Board has enacted Delegation of Authority policies that clearly delineate the lines of authority and accountability to commit or expend funds, and have adopted Board Governance Principles to direct how they will oversee the strategic planning and operations of the company.[1]

Recall our comment from Chapter 6: The topic of leadership is like that of a prism—there is something new and different each time you look at it from a new angle. In this chapter, we present additional lenses for understanding and addressing the range of leadership issues and the pressures on leaders in particular situations. Our focus is on the contemporary perspectives of transactional, charismatic, authentic, and transformational leadership. Clearly, the leadership of Ed Breen had a significant influence in transforming the scandal-ridden state of Tyco International when he assumed the role of CEO in 2002.

Leadership is future oriented. It involves influencing people to move from where they are (here) to some new place (there).[2] In the case of the crisis state of Tyco in 2002, Breen concluded that the core requirement was not one of influencing changes in the board and top personnel at corporate headquarters, but to replace them with new personnel. However, different leaders define or perceive *here* and *there* differently. For some, the journey between here and there is relatively routine, like driving a car on a familiar road. Others see the need to chart a new course through unexplored territory. Such leaders perceive fundamental differences between the way things are and the way things can or should be. They recognize the shortcomings of the present situation and offer a sense of passion and excitement to overcome them. As suggested in the Preview Case, Breen has done this passionately in a variety of ways with special emphasis on restoring integrity and ethics from the top-down at Tyco. He introduced new formal mechanisms to help prevent, detect, and correct lapses in ethical and legal behaviors that apply to all employees, including himself. Breen provided critical leadership in a number of other domains as well.

LEARNING OBJECTIVE

1. State the characteristics of transactional leadership.

TRANSACTIONAL LEADERSHIP

Transactional leadership *involves motivating and directing followers primarily through appealing to their own self-interest.* The transactional leader tends to focus on a carrot (but sometimes a stick) approach, set performance expectations and goals, and provide feedback to followers. The primary power of transactional leaders comes from their formal authority and responsibilities in the organization. They focus on the basic management processes of controlling, organizing, and short-term planning.

Key Components

Three primary components of transactional leadership are usually viewed as prompting followers to achieve their performance goals.

- *Provides contingent rewards.* Transactional leaders identify paths that link the achievement of goals to rewards, clarify expectations, exchange promises and resources for support, arrange mutually satisfactory agreements, negotiate for resources, exchange assistance for effort, and provide commendations for successful performance. These leaders set and clarify detailed goals to obtain short-term and measurable results.

- *Exhibits active management by exception.* Transactional leaders actively monitor the work performed by subordinates, use corrective methods if deviations from expected standards occur, and enforce rules to prevent mistakes.
- *Emphasizes passive management by exception.* Transactional leaders intervene after unacceptable performance or deviations from accepted standards occur. They may wait to take action until mistakes are brought to their attention.[3] Corrective methods and possibly punishment are used as a response to unacceptable performance.

Transactional leadership is best viewed as insufficient, but not bad, in developing maximum leadership potential. One leadership expert makes the following point:

> Without the transactional base, expectations are often unclear, direction is ill-defined, and the goals you are working toward are too ambiguous. . . . Transactions clearly in place form the base for more mature interactions.[4]

The following Self Competency feature reports on the transactional leadership of Guangchang Guo, general manager and chairman of the Shanghai Fortune High Technology Group.[5] His leadership appears to fit the cultural, human resources, market, and political environment of the firm, which is headquartered in Shanghai, China.

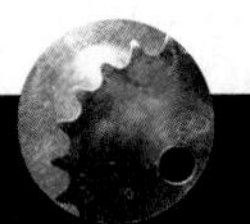

SELF COMPETENCY

GUANGCHANG GUO OF SHANGHAI FORTUNE HIGH TECHNOLOGY GROUP

Guangchang Guo is a pragmatist. He set up a strict performance appraisal system to improve the efficiency of his company. His standards are to create value with minimum cost, to operate with higher efficiency and better quality, and to improve profit. Guo manages his company as a group of interrelated but distinct parts. Guo believes the following:

1. Every division of the company should have its own goal and a detailed plan to achieve it. If necessary, such goal and plan can be adjusted when the environment changes.
2. Every division should have a common vision and have great enthusiasm.
3. Each division should be a distinct organization, so it can operate and be evaluated on its own.

Guo believes that the quantitative performance standards of a division are the key to motivating the division to advance. He says, "You should make a division realize that its effort is related directly to its performance appraisal."

Guo has set a clear vision for the whole company. The target of the Shanghai Fortune High Technology Group is to set standards in every industry in which the firm participates. In recent years, the Shanghai Fortune High Technology Group has invested in many industries such as medicine, finance, steel, and real estate. This is evidence that this firm is acting as a leader and standard setter for modern Chinese enterprises. He thinks that the greatest business opportunity in China is in setting standards of excellence. In a public speech, Guo said, "The mission of our company is to lead in this area, and to create value for our stockholders and for the whole society."

In the area of risk taking, Guo is quite bold. His firm invested more than 500 million yuan RMB (about US $60 million) to set up a joint-venture securities corporation. Since the whole securities industry was in bad shape at the time, many people thought this investment overly risky. However, Guo considered the worst time could be the best time simply because the entry cost was lower. In relating and communicating, Guo does reasonably well. When he meets subordinates, he takes the initiative to say hello. He is concerned about the employees, not only about their jobs but also about their lives.

For more information on the Shanghai Fortune High Technology Group, visit the organization's home page at ***http://www.fosun.com.***

Implications for Leaders

Effective transactional leaders are likely to engage in the following five practices:

- They ask: "What needs to be done?"
- They ask: "What is right for the organization?"
- They develop action plans.
- They take responsibility for decisions.
- They take responsibility for communicating.[6]

A "pure" transactional leader may tend to overemphasize detailed and short-term goals, standard operating procedures, rules, and policies. This emphasis may tend to stifle creativity and the generation of new ideas. They often accept without question the goals, structure, rules, and culture of the existing organization. As a result, the pure form may work only where organizational problems are simple, clear, and well defined. There may be a tendency for transactional leaders to not reward or ignore ideas that do not fit with existing plans and goals.

The "pure" transactional leader attempts to influence others by exchanging good performance for extrinsic rewards such as wages, financial incentives, benefits, and status symbols such as a larger office. The failure to perform is more likely to be followed by punishment. On the other hand, transactional leaders may be quite effective in guiding efficiency initiatives designed to cut costs and improve productivity in the short term.[7] They tend to be highly directive and action oriented, if not dominating. The relationship between transactional leaders and followers tends to be transitory and not based on emotional bonds.

LEARNING OBJECTIVE

2. Describe the features of charismatic leadership.

CHARISMATIC LEADERSHIP

Charismatic leadership *involves motivating and directing followers primarily by developing in them a strong emotional commitment to a vision and set of shared values.* Through their unique personal qualities in the eyes of followers and by showing great passion and devotion to the vision and values, charismatic leaders influence followers by appealing to their heart and emotions at a deep level.

Key Components

The model of charismatic leadership includes the following interrelated components, as shown in Figure 7.1:

FIGURE 7.1 Model of Charismatic Leadership

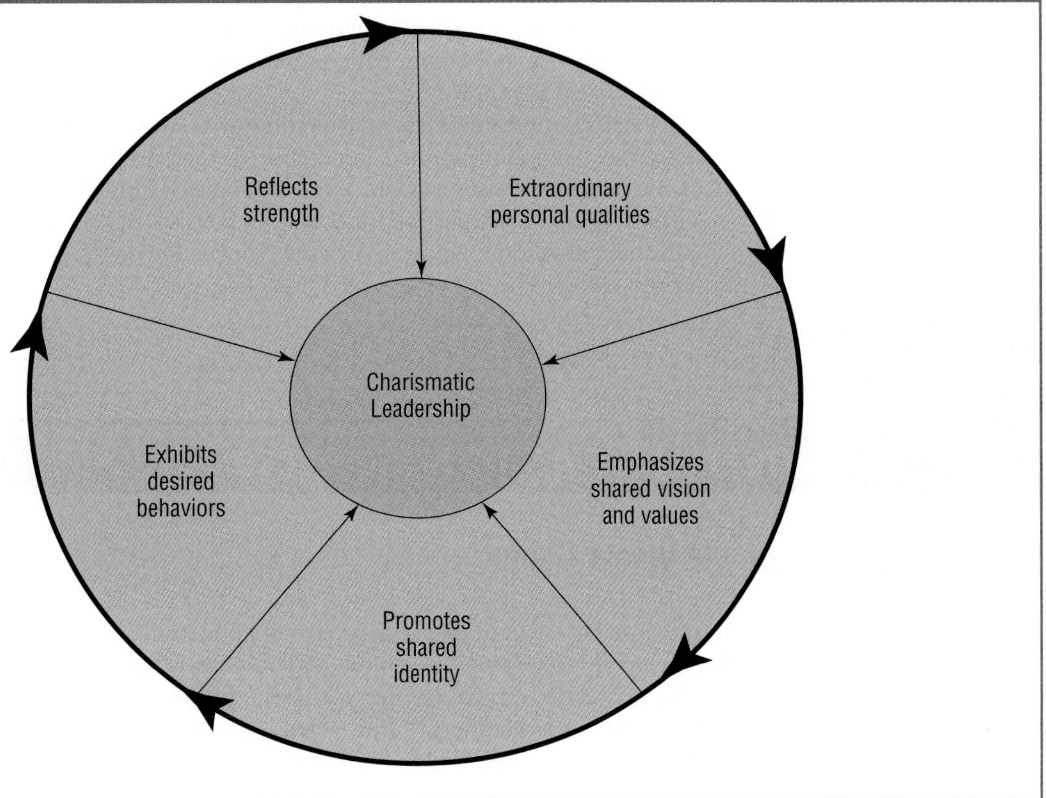

- *Possesses extraordinary personal qualities.* Charismatic leaders possess extraordinary gifts and qualities. Followers are personally and emotionally attracted to these leaders. They communicate extensively and well through the use of metaphors, stories, symbols, slogans, and examples. Their verbal and nonverbal communications capture and stimulate emotional responses in followers.
- *Emphasizes shared vision and values.* Charismatic leaders focus on creating a mental image of a highly desirable future and their values, linking these values to the organization's mission, goals, and expected behaviors. Through this, they challenge the status quo. Remember, vision is all about what could be and should be. It is not about what is likely if the organization proceeds on the present path.
- *Promotes shared identity.* Charismatic leaders focus on creating common bonds among followers and a shared a sense of "who we are" and "what we stand for" as an organization.
- *Exhibits desired behaviors.* Charismatic leaders display personal commitment to the values, identity, and goals that are being promoted, engaging in self-sacrifice to show commitment to those values and goals.
- *Reflects strength.* Charismatic leaders display and create the impression of self-confidence, social and physical courage, determination, optimism, and innovation.[8] They reduce the sense of perceived risk in followers by focusing on success rather than the potential for failure.

Charismatic leaders gain power because their followers identify with them. Followers identify with and are inspired by charismatic leaders in the hope (and with the leader's promises) that they will succeed. Charismatic leaders, such as Richard Branson of the Virgin Group and Oprah Winfrey, have the ability to distill complex ideas into simple messages, communicating with symbols, metaphors, and stories. They relish risk and emotionally put themselves on the line, working on followers' hearts as well as minds.[9]

Charismatic leaders are outstanding in their communication competency. The following Communication Competency feature on Sir Richard Branson, chairman of the Virgin Group, provides a few examples of his charismatic leadership.[10] The Virgin Group, headquartered in London, consists of 160 companies in such diverse industries as Virgin Atlantic Airways, Virgin Records, Virgin Cola, Virgin Active (health clubs), Virgin Books, and Virgin Energy.

COMMUNICATION COMPETENCY

RICHARD BRANSON OF THE VIRGIN GROUP

Many chief executives focus on creating shareholder value and devote their attention primarily to customers. Branson believes that the correct pecking order is employees first, customers next, and then shareholders. His logic is this: If your employees are happy, they will do a better job. If they do a better job, the customers will be happy, and thus business will be good and the shareholders will be rewarded. Branson regularly takes entire flight crews out to dinner and parties when he arrives on a Virgin Atlantic flight. He even stays at the crew's hotel rather than in expensive hotels downtown away from the crew. He gives every Virgin employee a Virgin card, which provides big discounts on the airline as well as at Virgin Megastores and other Virgin businesses.

While vacationing on his private Caribbean island, called Necker, he brought 20 employees from various Virgin companies to the island. These were not senior executives, but the rank and file—a housekeeper, a switchboard operator, a reservations clerk, a pilot. They were invited because of excellent performance—a regular perk for Virgin employees. Branson notes: "The idea is to have fun, but by talking to employees, you learn a lot as well." Reminded that it is the rare chief executive who takes employees along on vacation, Branson laughs and says, "I can assure you, it's no sacrifice." He attends as many orientations for new staff as possible in order to set the tone and send the message: "Get out there and have a good time. Really enjoy yourself, because most of your life is spent working, and you ought to have a great time doing it. It's much nicer paying the bills when everybody is having a good time."

He is frequently on the road to visit Virgin businesses, talking with employees and customers. He is known for his ever-present notebook and pen, which he pulls out whenever he chats with employees and customers. Branson insists that talking and writing things down is a crucial element in his role as chairman. His writings create lists of items for immediate action. He reads mail from employees every morning before he does anything else. This habit, which he started in Virgin's early days, influences company–employee dynamics. Employees don't hesitate to air their grievances directly with him. Branson has proved with his actions that he actively listens. Virgin has more than 35,000 employees around the world, and he gets some 50 e-mail messages or letters each day from nonmanagerial employees. They vary from small ideas to frustrations with middle management to significant proposals. He addresses each concern by answering personally or by initiating some action. Branson states, "Instead of needing a union when they have a problem, they come to me. I will give the employee the benefit of the doubt on most occasions."

To learn more about the Virgin Group Ltd., visit the organization's home page at ***http://www.virgin.com.***

Implications for Leaders

Charismatic leadership is rare in business. That's why a leader such as Richard Branson is seen as so unique, if not novel. Even the corporate web page on "About Virgin" reflects the charisma of Richard Branson. Here is what you will find when you go to the "About Virgin" page. It starts with the statement: "Get the low-down on all things Virgin, from how it all began, who we are, and what we do, to details on how to let us know about your feedback or great ideas." Below this statement, there are icons to click on for categories along with short statements about each category. We share four of those categories to give you a sense of how Branson has attempted to integrate his charisma into the corporate culture:

- *All about Virgin.* Want to find out how Virgin happened, why we do things differently, or what Richard Branson gets up to in his spare time?
- *Getting in touch.* What's on your mind? We always welcome your feedback—especially if it's to tell us how fabulous we are! Whatever your query, we're all ears.
- *Have some fun.* If it's not fun, you're not doing it right! Here's some fun stuff for you to get into.
- *How it all works.* There is a kind of "Virgin-ness" in everything we do, from recruiting great people to keeping our promises, or doing business with a cheeky grin. Find out all about the Virgin spirit.[11]

Martin Luther King also illustrates the rarity and uniqueness of a high degree of charismatic leadership through his impact on followers. The crisis in civil rights, King's extraordinary personal characteristics, his ability to inspire commitment to a radical vision (at the time), followers who were attracted to him and his expressed vision, and a series of successes (breaking down the walls of segregation through nonviolent protest) all came together and resulted in a growing social movement.[12] Recall the vision and values he dramatically expressed in his "I Have a Dream" speech:

> I say to you today, my friends, that in spite of the difficulties and frustrations of the moment, I still have a dream . . . it is a dream deeply rooted in the American dream.
>
> I have a dream that one day this nation will rise up and live out the true meaning of its creed: "We hold these truths to be self-evident: that all men are created equal."
>
> When we let freedom ring, when we let it ring from every village and every hamlet, from every state and every city, we will be able to speed up that day when all of God's children, black men and white men, Jews and Gentiles, Protestants and Catholics, will be able to join hands and sing in the words of the old Negro spiritual, "Free at last! Free at last! Thank God Almighty, we are free at last."[13]

The role of followers is especially critical in the model of charismatic leadership. Followers play a very active role in creating a personal relationship with the leader and empowering the leader. The relationship, such as the one between Richard Branson and his employees, is strongly influenced by the followers' identification with the Virgin organization and what it stands for. In this type of charismatic relationship, the followers are likely to have strong self concepts, find meaning in their work, have a sense of self-determination.[14] Richard Branson supports and fosters that kind of role for Virgin employees. He does not expect or want blind followership. He represents what is referred to as a *socialized charismatic* leader—one who possesses an egalitarian and empowering personality. Charismatic leaders who are unethical and self-centered can be disastrous for the long-term effectiveness of the organization.[15] Some individuals suggest that Dennis Kozlowski, the former CEO of Tyco, was a *personalized charismatic leader*—one who possesses a dominant, Machiavellian, and self-centered personality.

LEARNING OBJECTIVE

3. Discuss the attributes of authentic leadership.

AUTHENTIC LEADERSHIP

Authentic leadership *refers to individuals who (1) know and understand themselves, (2) know what they believe and value, and (3) act upon their values and beliefs through open and honest communications with subordinates and others.*[16] As a result of these attributes, subordinates are more willing to trust and follow the authentic leader. These leaders can be directive or participative. The person's leadership style is not what distinguishes inauthentic leaders from authentic leaders. Authentic leaders build credibility and win the respect of followers by encouraging and respecting diverse viewpoints. They seek to foster collaborative and trusting relationships with followers, customers, shareholders, and other stakeholders.

They convey a genuine desire to serve rather than primarily control others through their leadership. These individuals strive to find ways to empower the people they lead in the pursuit of making a difference. These leaders recognize and value individual differences in goals and competencies. They also have the ability and desire to identify the underlying talents of subordinates and to help build them into workable strengths and competencies.

Key Components

The model of authentic leadership includes the interrelated components discussed next and shown in Figure 7.2.[17]

FIGURE 7.2 Model of Authentic Leadership

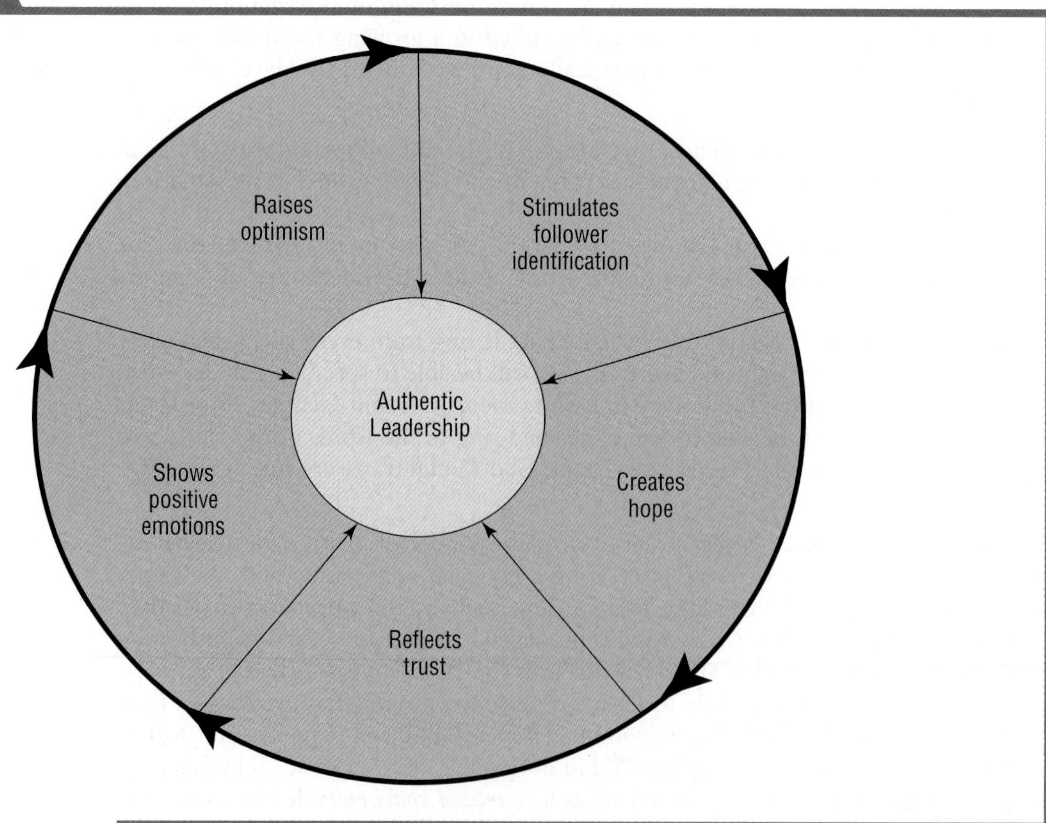

Source: Based on Avolio, B. J., Gardner, W. L., Walumbwa, F. O., Luthans, F., and May, D. R. Unlocking the mask: A look at the process by which authentic leaders impact follower attitudes and behaviors. *Leadership Quarterly*, 2004, 15, 801–823.

Stimulates Follower Identification. Authentic leaders influence followers' attitudes and behaviors, which, in turn, positively affect their self-esteem. These leaders are able to determine the followers' strengths, and develop them. Authentic leaders help followers link their strengths to a common purpose or mission. This is fostered through leading by example and setting high moral standards of honesty and integrity. They are open, positive, and highly ethical. There is an orientation toward doing "what is right and fair" for the leader and followers. Thus, authentic leaders identify with their followers by being up front, openly discussing their own and followers' limitations while constantly nurturing the growth of followers.

Authentic leaders have a clear sense of how their roles as leaders require a responsibility to act ethically and in the best interests of others. Through their high moral values, honesty, and integrity, followers' social identification with the work team, department, or organization is increased. Followers are able to connect and identify with the leaders over time. The followers' self-concept and related self-control become identified with or tied to the purpose or mission of the organization.

Creates Hope. Authentic leaders create positive motivations for followers through fostering goal setting and helping them identify the ways for achieving goals. The role of hope is discussed in Chapter 11. We noted that *hope* involves a person's willpower (determination) and waypower (road map) to achieve goals. Followers accept and become committed to the goals that can be achieved. Also, they believe that successful plans can be developed to achieve these goals. Authentic leaders are able to enhance followers' sense of hopefulness by (1) showing high levels of commitment, sharing, and openness; (2) communicating important information needed for them to reach the goals; and (3) encouraging questioning and open discussions.

Reflects Trust. Based on attributes of authentic leaders reviewed, they are more likely to be trusted by followers and others. They build trust by (1) encouraging open two-way communications, (2) sharing critical information—the bad and the good, and (3) revealing their perceptions and feelings about the people with whom they work—the good and the bad in a constructive way. Followers come to know what the leader values and stands for. In turn, the leader comes to know what the followers value and stand for.

Shows Positive Emotions. The positive emotions of authentic leaders broaden followers' thoughts on how to achieve goals and solve problems, discover novel ways for doing things, and foster creative thinking. They are more likely to stimulate positive feelings among followers and a sense of identification with the purposes being championed.

Raises Optimism. Authentic leaders tend to be optimists and stimulate a sense of optimism among followers. Optimists persevere in the face of obstacles or difficulties, assess personal failures and setbacks as temporary, and exhibit higher levels of work motivation, performance, and job satisfaction. Optimism includes the assumption that individuals can do something to change situations for the better. Pessimism includes the assumption that probably nothing individuals do will make much of a difference. Optimists want to take action, which increases the likelihood that goals will be set, pursued, and achieved. That's how optimism may create a self-fulfilling outcome. Optimists are less stressed by ordinary ups and downs. They tend to see bad situations as temporary and specific—something they can address.

The following Ethics Competency feature provides some of the perspectives of Robert L. Johnson that reflect a number of the components of authentic leadership.[18]

Johnson is the founder, chairman, and CEO of Black Entertainment Television (BET) and majority owner of the NBA's Charlotte Bobcats. BET is a subsidiary of Viacom. It is the leading African-American media and entertainment company in the United States.

ETHICS COMPETENCY

ROBERT JOHNSON OF BET

When you are an African-American, you wake up knowing you are in a society that has vestiges of racism including institutionalized racism throughout. You know you are going to get hit with it, but you don't let it stop you from trying to be the best you can be at what you do. I never give up because I am going to run into racism or I am going to be held back because of lack of access to education, capital, or whatever comes from racism. I have always looked at it as "part of the game." It is like rain. You know you're going to get wet so grab your umbrella and get up and go out to work.

What I have always said to people is that you must have a vision. As a leader, my goal in life is to be able to articulate that vision to people at BET, marshal the resources that they need to execute that vision, and to be there as a source of information or direction if they feel that they need more direction or guidance in pursuing the vision. Our vision at BET was always to become the preeminent African-American entertainment media company in the world. We pursued that vision to the best of our abilities. Because it was clearly understood and clearly articulated, people bought into it, and we were able to successfully grow to be the preeminent brand in African-American life today. I think any leader first has to have a vision, communicate that vision, and then effectively build a consensus among people who are part of achieving that vision.

Every organization has a core culture or core set of values. People are told that when they first come into an organization. We have always had that at BET. We wanted to be the preeminent African-American media company. We wanted to be creative while growing. We wanted to respect the people who worked for us and the people we did business with. We wanted to run a business based on integrity and on mutual respect. That is what we have done, and that is what we continue to do. In most cases, you do not have to remind people. They buy into it if they are able to grow in that culture. If they are not able for some reason, then more than likely these people either leave or they are asked to leave.

We have some very talented people. I have always said that when you hire very talented people, you have to create an environment where they see a future within the organization that is compatible with their lifestyle, their economic interests, their social interests, and everything else that is important to them. If you do that, they are likely to do one of two things. They are going to stay or, if they leave, they will have built a base of people behind them who can step right in and take their place. And that is what we have done successfully at BET.

We have had some very talented people come through BET who have now gone on to do things in television and do things in other businesses very successfully. Those who have done that, for the most part, have left behind a talented group of people to step in and take their place. I am always proud when I can say that "so and so" started at BET and now is the host on that show or is the talent on that show. I love it when people grow, and if they grow into better things, that is OK.

For more information on Black Entertainment Television (BET), visit the organization's home page at ***http://www.bet.com.***

Implications for Leaders

Authentic leaders influence followers' attitudes and behaviors through identification, hope, trust, positive emotions, and optimism. The focus is on the positive attributes and strengths of people and not focusing on their weaknesses. Authentic leadership focuses on understanding enough about yourself to be able to state with confidence things like:

- I know what I'm good at and what I'm not so good at. I will build on my strengths and shore up my weaknesses.
- I will surround myself with people who are good, really good at what I neither have the time for or the ability to do myself. I will build a truly diversified team who can get the job done, who can achieve the focus.
- When I mess up I will fess up. I will forgive myself and move on. I will do the same with other committed team players. I recognize that when I trip up and fall, it's because I am moving, and that without movement there can be no progress.
- I will be myself at all times. I will not wear a mask.

THE COMPETENT LEADER

Without self-discipline, you can't gain the respect of your followers. Most people profess to having good values but lack the discipline to convert those values into consistent actions. Authentic leaders have the self-discipline to show their values through their actions. When they fall short, they admit their mistakes.
Bill George, former CEO of Metronics and author of *Authentic Leadership*

The model mirrors the public outcry for ethical leaders. The leader is, in a sense, a "servant" to followers. The leader is called on to engage employees' hearts and minds in a purpose greater than any of them. Authentic does not mean being "soft." Tough assignments, accountability, and high standards of performance are embedded in this model.

This model also suggests that such leadership will, over the long run, result in superior organizational performance. Although this may prove to be the case, data on this perspective are limited. Moreover, many contextual factors and forces are likely to influence the leadership process. Some of these include organizational power and politics, organizational structure, and organizational culture. Top executives such as Richard Johnson of Black Entertainment Television may be able to shape and influence such contextual factors. However, that may not be as feasible for first- and middle-level managers who strive to be authentic leaders if there is not top-level support and modeling of this kind of leadership.

TRANSFORMATIONAL LEADERSHIP

LEARNING OBJECTIVE

4. Explain the nature of transformational leadership.

Transformational leadership *involves anticipating future trends, inspiring followers to understand and embrace a new vision of possibilities, developing others to be leaders or better leaders, and building the organization or group into a community of challenged and rewarded learners.*[19] Transformational leadership may be found at all levels of the organization: teams, departments, divisions, and the organization as a whole. Visionary, inspiring, daring, and ethical are words that describe transformational leaders. They are assertive risk-takers who seize or create new opportunities. They are also thoughtful thinkers who understand the interactions of technology, culture, stakeholders, and external environmental forces.

As suggested in Figure 7.3 and this discussion, the transformational leadership model clearly is the most comprehensive and challenging to implement. As you will see, there are some similarities between the transformational and authentic leadership models.

Key Components

The key interrelated components of transformational leadership include inspirational motivation, intellectual stimulation, idealized influence, and individualized consideration.[20]

FIGURE 7.3 Model of Transformational Leadership

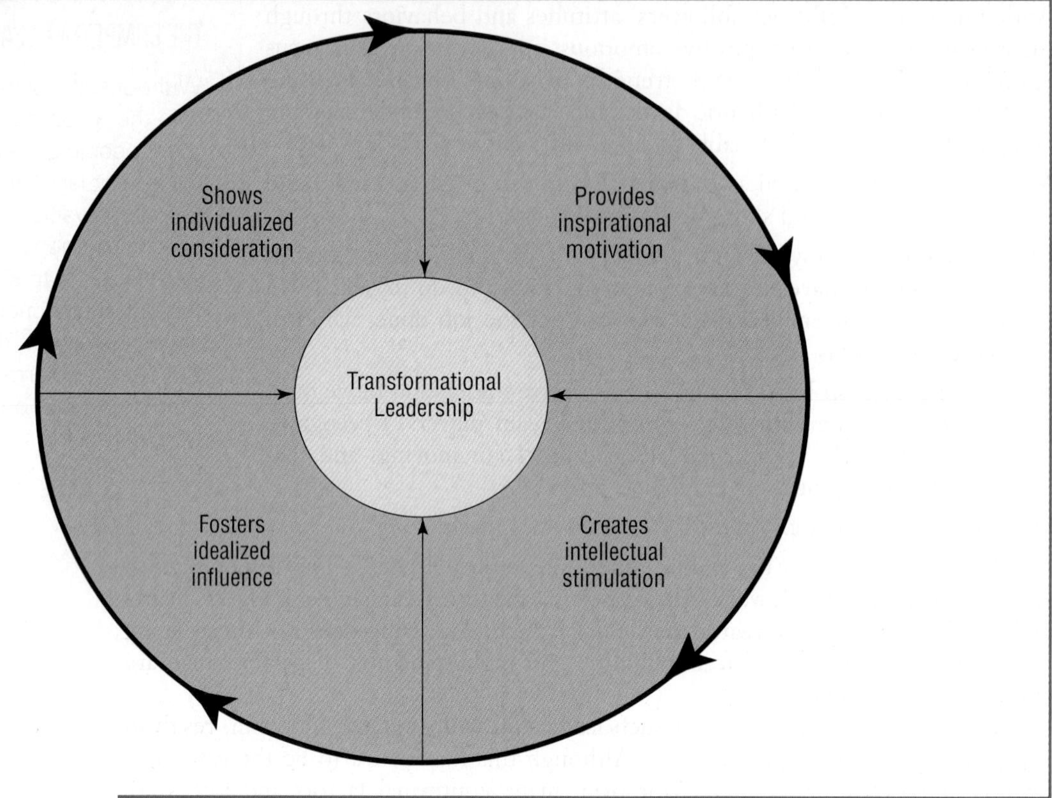

Provides Inspirational Motivation. Transformational leaders guide followers by providing them with a sense of meaning and challenge. For example, Ed Breen of Tyco displays great enthusiasm and optimism, which carries over into the lives of followers and fosters a sense of team spirit. Such leaders get followers involved in, and eventually committed to, a vision of a future that may be significantly different from the present. Transformational leaders inspire others by what they say and do. Ed Breen provided inspirational motivation in a number of ways. His unqualified commitment to and demand for integrity is one such example. Recall his statement to employees and other stakeholders: "Nothing is more important to a company than its credibility—credibility with investors, customers, government leaders and employees." These leaders appeal to followers' sense of pride, self-esteem, and other intrinsic motivators.

A **vision** *is a view of a future desired state.* Martin Luther King's vision was framed in his "I Have a Dream" speech in these words:

> I have a dream that one day this nation will rise up and live out the true meaning of its creed: "We hold these truths to be self-evident: that all men are created equal."

The framing and inspirational promotion of a consistent vision and set of values is the foundation of transformational leadership. One leadership expert sums it up this way:

> Transformational leaders are shapers of values, creators, interpreters of institutional purpose, exemplars, makers of meanings, pathfinders, and molders of organizational culture. They are persistent and consistent. Their vision is so

compelling that they know what they want from every interaction. Their visions don't blind others, but empower them.[21]

Creates Intellectual Stimulation. Transformational leaders encourage followers to "think out of the box" by being innovative and creative. They urge followers to question assumptions, explore new ideas and methods, and approach old situations with new perspectives. In addition, such leaders actively seek new ideas and creative solutions from followers. Followers' ideas aren't criticized just because they may differ from those of the leader. Leaders have a relatively high tolerance for mistakes made by followers, who aren't publicly criticized for those errors. Transformational leaders focus on the "what" in problems rather "whom" to blame for them. Followers feel free to encourage leaders to reevaluate their own perspectives and assumptions.

Transformational leaders are willing to abandon practices that are no longer useful even if they developed them in the first place. Nothing is too good, fixed, political, or bureaucratic that it can't be changed or discontinued. The prevailing view is that it is better to question ourselves than to leave all the questioning about us to our competitors. They view risk taking as necessary and desirable for the long-term development and success of the organization. In brief, they promote creativity, rationality, and thoughtful problem solving from multiple points of view.

Fosters Idealized Influence. Transformational leaders demonstrate the behaviors that followers strive to mirror. Followers typically admire, respect, and trust such leaders. They identify with these leaders as people, as well as with the vision and values that they are advocating. Positive idealized influence allows followers to feel free to question what is being advocated. The goals of followers are often personally meaningful and consistent with their self-concepts. They willingly give extra effort because of the intrinsic rewards obtained from performing well, not just because of the potential for receiving greater monetary and other extrinsic rewards. Immediate short-term goals are viewed as a means to the followers' commitments to a greater vision.

To further earn such idealized influence, transformational leaders often consider the needs and interests of followers over their own needs. They may willingly sacrifice personal gain for the sake of others. Such leaders can be trusted and demonstrate high standards of ethical and moral conduct. Followers come to see such leaders as operating according to a pattern of open communication. Thus, they can be very direct and challenging to some followers (e.g., poor performers) and highly empathetic and supportive of others (e.g., those with a seriously ill family member).

Although transformational leaders minimize the use of power for personal gain, they will use all the sources of power—expert, legitimate, reward, referent, and coercive—at their disposal to move individuals and teams toward a vision and its related goals. As an example of referent power, followers often describe transformational leaders as individuals who have had a major impact on their own personal and professional development.

Shows Individualized Consideration. Transformational leaders provide special attention to each follower's needs for achievement and growth. They may act as coaches, mentors, teachers, facilitators, confidants, and counselors. Followers and colleagues are encouraged to develop to successively higher levels of their potential. Individual differences are embraced and rewarded to enhance creativity and innovation. An open dialogue with followers is encouraged and "management by continuous engagement" is standard practice. Listening skills are sharp and reflect this observation: It's not what you tell them, it's what they hear.

Transformational leaders empower followers to make decisions. At the same time, they monitor followers to determine whether they need additional support or direction and to assess progress. With trust in leaders' intentions, followers think, "This person is trying to help me by noting mistakes, as opposed to pointing a finger at me in some accusatory way."

The following Change Competency shares excerpts of an interview of Mike McGavick, the chairman, president, and CEO of Safeco Insurance Company headquartered in Seattle, Washington.[22] Safeco sells a comprehensive mix of insurance products. He has led the company through an organization-wide restructuring, through a 10 percent layoff of the workforce, and other major changes.

CHANGE COMPETENCY

MIKE MCGAVICK OF SAFECO

Coming in as the first outside CEO in Safeco's history, there was an enormous set of questions about what this was all about and how this might work. The caveat was that each of the things was made somehow a little more acute by my being alone and needing to sort through the talent that was here and recruit some new talent. There was no team to help build a strategy. The initial strategies were of my own invention, but that phase was very short.

I had five basic ideas underlying our turnaround strategy:

- Focus on what makes the organization different from any other in the market.
- Don't be afraid to perform radical surgery.
- Take the pain sooner rather than later.
- Reinforce what is working properly in the organization, and change or add what is missing.
- Communicate, communicate, communicate. But you have no credibility until the actions back up the words.

In a world where corporate leadership has managed to ruin its reputation so profoundly, you spend an awful lot of your time on trust issues. I started from a deficit position as an outsider. I didn't have a deep insurance background. Trust is just the biggest thing you think about. Trust is strained by necessary actions like job losses. You know, we've had two layoffs—one very large one, and one modest. But the size doesn't matter if you're one of the individuals laid off.

It's been a very difficult set of things. In addition, we've sold off very large businesses. We've been through a lot. But I find that we seem to have maintained real credibility as a leadership team. Not always deep affection. But that's a different issue. We get that credibility or respect by continuously doing what we say we'll do. We work very hard to lay out what we're going to do—like adult to adult. If things are changing, we tell people they're changing. If there's a risk of a layoff at some point, or a certain layoff in the future, we say so. Many companies would try to hide that fact. We get a lot of credibility out of delivering what we say we'll do. We think that's more important than morale campaigns. We think the most important forms of trust and energy are built by a combination of doing what you say you'll do and having it turn out to be in the best interest of the organization.

I would argue that the reason Safeco came back so fast is largely the result of the strong culture built over seven decades that people have a great way of working here. They responded very fast and very powerfully by going back to some old ways of doing things. However, we also needed to make some changes in the culture, additions that make our present culture stronger.

We at Safeco tend to know culture by eight attributes. Four of these attributes have been present at Safeco for a long time, and we never want to lose them: integrity, compassion, discipline, and delivering excellent results. Two additional attributes—accountability and wise frugality—I would suggest used to be present at Safeco, and we have brought them back by our actions, by our processes, by all that we do. And then there are two which I would suggest are missing at Safeco—competitive aggression and diversity inclusion—that we're just starting to introduce.

We also have to create a way of working so that people's ideas get discussed openly, so that we have an inclusion of ideas. And after a time of layoffs, it's very challenging because many people just want some safety. Expressing ideas isn't a way to be safe. We've got to learn how to solicit ideas in a respectful way, in a disciplined way, in a way that allows work to keep moving.

But we have to figure out a way to get all the ideas on the table. That's why there's been so much focus on leadership development to try and get out of old habits and learn some new tools for including more ideas and supporting the new culture.

For more information on the Safeco Insurance Company, visit the organization's home page at ***http://www.safeco.com.***

Implications for Leaders

Faced with increasing turbulence in their environments, organizations need transformational leadership more than ever—and at all levels, not just at the top. The need for leaders of vision, confidence, and determination, whether they are leading a small team or an entire organization, is increasing rapidly. Such leaders are needed to motivate others to assert themselves, to join enthusiastically in team efforts, and to have positive feelings about what they're doing. Top managers must come to understand, appreciate, and support as never before employees who are willing to make unpopular decisions, who know when to reject traditional ways of doing something, and who can accept reasonable risks. A "right to fail" must be nurtured and be an integral part of an organization's culture. This leadership is vital to the most difficult, complex, and vague organizational threats, opportunities, and weaknesses.

Transformational leadership fosters synergy. **Synergy** *occurs when people together create new alternatives and solutions that are better than their individual efforts.* The greatest chance for achieving synergy is when people don't see things the same way; that is, differences present opportunities. Relationships don't break down because of differences but because people fail to grasp the value of their differences and how to take advantage of them. Synergy is created by people who have learned to think win–win and who listen in order to understand the other person. One of the messages of Martin Luther King's "I Have a Dream" speech was that of synergy. He challenged people to confront their differences and to learn from them. Stereotyping keeps people from appreciating and building on their differences because they limit listening for understanding.

THE COMPETENT LEADER

One task of a leader is to understand the changing needs of customers and employees. I've seen a lot of leaders tripped up by their inability to be flexible and adaptable. Leaders need to have people follow them. They need to energize people so that they rally behind a vision and take leadership roles themselves in bringing that vision to life.
Cynthia Tragge-Lakra, Global Director, Commercial Leadership and Development, General Electric.

Similarities and Differences in Models

Table 7.1 highlights the relative similarities and differences between the four contemporary leadership models—transactional, charismatic, authentic, and transformational—discussed in this chapter. We do this by presenting our judgment of the relative emphasis of each of the models placed on the seven foundation competencies discussed throughout this book.

A brief overview of our assessments of the four contemporary leadership models, as presented in Table 7.1, suggests that (1) the transactional model is the simplest and places the fewest demands on the leader; (2) the charismatic model places the greatest demands on the leader's appeal to the "heart" of followers; (3) the authentic model places the greatest demands on the leader to be deeply ethical, sensitive to followers, and revealing of one's own strengths and limitations; (4) the transformational model is the most complex and challenging to implement, especially

TABLE 7.1 Similarities and Differences in Four Contemporary Leadership Models

RELATIVE EMPHASIS ON:	CONTEMPORARY LEADERSHIP MODELS			
	TRANSACTIONAL	CHARISMATIC	AUTHENTIC	TRANSFORMATIONAL
Self competency	Low	High	Very high	High
Communication competency	Moderate	Very high	Very high	High
Diversity competency	Low	Low	Very high	High
Ethics competency	Low	Moderate	Very high	High
Across cultures competency	Low	Low	Moderate	Moderate
Teams competency	Low	Moderate	High	Very high
Change competency	Low	High	Moderate	Very high

given the demand to balance the forces for change with the need to be developmental, responsive, and open with followers; and (5) none of the models directly places high emphasis on the across cultures competency.

CHAPTER SUMMARY

1. State the characteristics of transactional leadership.

Transactional leadership involves influencing followers primarily through contingent reward-based exchanges. Leaders attempt to identify clear goals for followers, the specific paths for achieving the goals, and the rewards that will be forthcoming for achieving them. A follower's performance is monitored and corrective actions are taken if there are deviations from the expected path. The emphasis is on exchanging units of work for units of rewards (salary, bonuses, size of office, etc.).

2. Describe the features of charismatic leadership.

Charismatic leadership involves influencing followers primarily through developing their emotional commitment to a vision and set of shared values. The leader relies on referent and reward power in contrast to the transactional leader's reliance on reward, legitimate, and expert power. Charismatic leadership emphasizes extraordinary personal qualities and a shared vision and values, promotes a shared identity, exhibits desired behaviors, and reflects strength.

3. Discuss the attributes of authentic leadership.

Authentic leadership involves influencing followers' attitudes and behaviors through the core interrelated processes of identification, hope, trust, positive emotions, and optimism. These leaders know and understand themselves; they know what they believe and value, and act on their values and beliefs through open and honest communications with subordinates and others. They are highly ethical leaders.

4. Explain the nature of transformational leadership.

Transformational leadership involves influencing followers through a complex and interrelated set of behaviors and abilities. Some of these include anticipating the future, inspiring relevant stakeholders (especially followers) to embrace a new vision or set of ideas, developing followers to be leaders or better leaders, and guiding the organization or group into a community of challenged and rewarded learners. This model extends and incorporates features of authentic leadership. The components of transformational leadership that primarily relate to followers include inspirational motivation, intellectual stimulation, idealized influence, and individualized consideration. Transformational leaders are both challenging and empathetic—and are people of integrity.

KEY TERMS AND CONCEPTS

Authentic leadership
Charismatic leadership
Synergy
Transactional leadership
Transformational leadership
Vision

DISCUSSION QUESTIONS

1. Assume that you have just taken a job at a large manufacturing facility. What insights provided in this chapter can help you be an effective "follower" in this situation?
2. Think of a person that you know who comes closest to exhibiting charismatic leadership. Describe three behaviors of this person that are consistent with being a charismatic leader.
3. What are the three competencies that you need to develop most in order to become a transformational leader?
4. Based on Ed Breen's leadership, as described in the Preview Case, identify those aspects of his behavior that are consistent with one or more features of transformational leadership.
5. In what three ways did a manager you have worked for use transactional leadership?
6. Based on the manager identified in Question 5, in what ways did that person exhibit or fail to exhibit the components of authentic leadership?
7. Based on Guangchang Guo's leadership, as described in the Self Competency feature, what aspects of his behavior illustrate one or more of the components of transactional leadership?
8. Review the Change Competency feature concerning Mike McGavick. Identify three of his statements that reflect transformational leadership.
9. Review the Ethics Competency feature concerning Richard Johnson. Identify three of his statements that reflect authentic leadership.

EXPERIENTIAL EXERCISE AND CASE

Experiential Exercise: Communication Competency

Managing for the Future[23]

Instructions: After reviewing the following list of behaviors and activities, check those items that you believe best describe what "managers of the future" need to do with their time. Don't overthink your responses; your initial reactions most accurately reflect your perceptions.

_____ 1. Managers spend as much as 75 percent of their time being involved with other people.
_____ 2. Managers go around the formal chain of command.
_____ 3. Managers focus on building networks.
_____ 4. Managers discuss anything and everything associated with their organization.
_____ 5. Managers ask a lot of questions.
_____ 6. Managers rarely make big decisions.
_____ 7. Managers focus on developing agendas (goals, objectives, etc.).
_____ 8. Managers joke, kid around, use humor, and talk about nonwork activities.
_____ 9. Managers "waste" time discussing issues that appear to be nonsubstantive.
_____ 10. Managers seldom tell people what to do.
_____ 11. Managers frequently attempt to influence others.
_____ 12. Managers frequently respond to others' initiatives.

_____13. Managers focus on executing their agendas.
_____14. Managers invest significant amounts of time in short and disjointed discussions.
_____15. Managers work long hours (e.g., 60 hours per week).
_____16. Managers rely on conversations with others for information, not on books, magazines, or reports.
_____17. Managers realize that the size of their networks largely determines their degree of success.
_____18. Managers seek out cooperative relationships with people who will have to help implement their agendas.
_____19. Managers seek to maximize teamwork and minimize politics.
_____20. Managers' network members are chosen for their ability to help accomplish the managers' agendas.

Interpretation

Give yourself five points for each item that you checked.

Your total score is _____.

90–100 = You have a strong grasp of the behaviors that characterize an effective manager in the future. Your main tasks for the future include patiently helping your organization and your colleagues learn more about these behaviors, being sure to model and reward these new behaviors and systematically coaching everyone around you to begin implementing appropriate leadership models.

80–89 = You have a moderately good understanding of what it takes to be an effective manager in the future. Your main tasks for the future include strengthening your familiarity with the behaviors, experimenting with the behaviors in low-to-moderate-risk situations, rewarding yourself when you are successful in using the behaviors, establishing goals for yourself that focus on increasing the frequency with which you use the behaviors, and letting others know about your efforts.

70–79 = You are aware of the management behaviors needed for the future but do not find them compelling, or you may work in a setting in which you cannot presently use the behaviors. Your main tasks for the future include continuing to learn about these new management behaviors, finding someone with whom you can talk about them, and identifying settings in which you can try out selected behaviors.

60–69 = You have a below-average understanding of what it takes to be a successful manager in the future. Your main tasks for the future include looking around to see what your organization's top competitors or peer organizations are doing as they prepare to meet the challenges ahead. You also should consider the long-term needs of your organization. How will your employer become steadily more competitive while utilizing fewer resources and responding to growing customer demands for higher levels of product and service quality? Armed with responses to questions such as these, you are then ready to examine the degree to which your current leadership or management style will help you and your employer to be successful in the future.

0–59 = You have little or no awareness of the management practices needed for the future. For a variety of reasons, you also may have little or no interest in altering that situation. Your main tasks for the future include taking time to reflect on where you want your career to lead, your effectiveness in working with other people, how you feel about yourself as a leader/manager, and how other people with whom you work seem to react to your present style of leadership.

Case: Change Competency

Meg Whitman of eBay[24]

Founded in 1995 and headquartered in San Jose, California, eBay is the leading online marketplace for the sale of goods and services by a diverse community of individuals and businesses. eBay has more than 135 million registered users and is the most popular shopping site on the Internet.

eBay's mission is to provide a global trading platform where practically anyone can trade practically anything. It features a variety of international sites, specialty sites, 45,000 categories of merchandise, and services that aim to provide users with the necessary tools for efficient online trading in both auction-style and fixed-price formats. Recent innovations in trading formats, such as *Want In Now* and *Best Offer*, provide new ways for shoppers to find and buy what they want on the website. Europe, Asia, and cross-border trade are major areas of growth for eBay. On any given day, millions of items are listed on eBay in thousands of categories. People from all over the world buy and sell on eBay. Through its Pay Pal service, the company enables any consumer or business with e-mail in 38 countries, and more being added continuously, to send and receive online payments. Pay Pal has over 64 million user accounts, more than many major banks and credit card companies. eBay recently acquired Rent.com, an Internet listing service in the apartment and rental housing industry. eBay continues to make targeted acquisitions that fit with its business model.

Meg Whitman joined eBay as its CEO in 1998. She works in an open cubicle, reflecting eBay's casual setup. Her cubicle with low walls and no view—and surfaces piled with paper—is wedged between two other cubicles. When Whitman needs to talk with technology chief Maynard Webb, she calls out through the partition; when she wants to show him something, she simply walks around the partition to his cubicle. When she sits down to speak as CEO of eBay, however, there is nothing casual about her style. She is all about profit margins, sales growth, and leading the firm's 8,100 employees.

Whitman is many things—a mom, wealthy, a Wall Street darling, and maybe even, as some say, the best CEO in America. One thing she isn't is the stereotype of a new-economy executive. A onetime Procter & Gamble brand manager, Bain consultant, and Hasbro division manager, Whitman is a person with experience and discipline. The casual trappings, the cubicle, and the like only go so far in explaining her leadership style.

This company looks like a dotcom, but its approach is corporate. Whitman's executives handle categories (e.g., toys, cars, and collectibles) like brand managers at P&G handle Bounty or Tide. They dwell on data, following every transaction and customer nuance just as executives do at Wal-Mart. Whitman is one of eBay's greatest strengths. She is considered the reason it's the only startup among all its once promising peers that isn't dead or under the gun. Four years after Whitman came to run this online market, eBay is thriving.

When Whitman arrived at eBay, she promised to transform the company from an online auction house into a much bigger, general-purpose shopping destination—the first place people turn when they want to buy anything. Analysts, who applaud this strategy and are reassured by Whitman's record, see eBay as the one company that really taps into the boundless potential of the Internet. eBay owns no inventory or warehouses, which helps make it highly profitable. It has cleverly used e-mail, message boards, and the natural watchfulness of its virtual community to forge bonds with customers and to police the behavior of its buyers and sellers. Its website enables small sellers to participate in a vast marketplace—and lets eBay collect fees on even the tiniest of transactions. A key element in the firm's growth strategy is to continuously expand the eBay marketplace to new communities around the world.

The superficially casual, fundamentally business-like quality permeates eBay. Employees are cheerful and informal. Their no-nonsense cubicles are littered with sports souvenirs, Godzilla figurines, and Beanie Babies. There are free sodas in the break rooms. But when you talk to eBay people, you don't hear much about fun and games. You hear about plans, systems, numbers, and results.

Whitman has a craving for statistics and, more specifically, for bottom-line results. Asked what it is like reporting to Whitman, one manager says, "I have numbers. I know them. They're very clear. And the expectations are high." Another manager comments: "Several years ago we were a secondary collectibles marketplace. Now we're a trading platform." In plain English, that means eBay is diversifying, offering not just old ceramic plates and baseball cards but a wide array of products from bigger brand-name stores, including new items at set prices. "We want people to think of eBay first when they're in shopping mode, the way they might think of Wal-Mart," says a marketing executive.

In response to a question about eBay being an Internet survivor, Whitman states: "People are really pleased to have a survivor—a thriver. They're enthusiastic that eBay has done well because it bodes well for other companies. eBay will not be the only great company that comes out of the Internet."

Whitman has provided a number of insights and perspectives on her strategic thinking and leadership. "One of the reasons I believe eBay has been so successful is that we have stuck to our business plan from inception. At eBay, we do one thing: We work every day to be the world's most compelling commerce platform on the Internet. Despite the turmoil in the financial markets, we have stayed focused on our goals. Those goals include attracting more customers, expanding the goods traded on the site, spreading eBay to more global markets, and making the user experience more fun, exciting, and easier.

"I think at all good companies, employees are excited by the mission of the company. And at eBay the mission is about creating this global online marketplace where your next-door neighbor's chance of success is equal to a large corporation's. We look for people who are energized by the mission of the company. Once they're here, we want to make sure that they have a chance to understand the company in a really deep way. I said to our head of strategy when he came to work for us: 'Don't do anything for three months. Just absorb, understand, get the counterintuitive nature of the business.' We give people a chance to settle in, and then we make sure that they are well managed, that they are focused on high-impact projects, and that they understand the results that they are going to be accountable for.

"To keep up with our growth, we have reorganized early and often. That keeps people fresh; it brings a new set of eyes to problems. It keeps people excited because they get repotted into new opportunities. That's something we've done since the beginning of the company. We've probably made about 10 to 12 changes in how we have structured the organization. Some were major, some were more evolutionary.

"We come up with a lot of good ideas, but we will not be the fountain of all good ideas. Users that have good ideas about how to make the platform more effective can tap into it through our API [application programming interface]. We now have 10,000 outside developers; 18 months ago it was just 400. We think it's important to open up the platform because it makes eBay better, it makes eBay stronger, as other people develop applications to the platform. And it's not only software. It's also businesses that grow up to support eBay, like AuctionDrop here in the Bay Area. That is another way of supporting and extending the platform in a way that we will probably never get to, at least not in the foreseeable future.

I think we are one of the pioneers of a different kind of business model. And I think the Web has certainly made self-organizing and empowerment of different groups far easier than it was prior to the Internet. But I think we are still at the earliest stages. So we're watching it very carefully. We know it is central to our business. Enabling our customers and our partners to be successful is critical."

Whitman's free-market philosophy goes only so far. Sometimes she has had to play censor of items traded on the site. "We crossed the Rubicon in 1999," she says. That's when she decided to ban firearms, alcohol, and tobacco. She also outlawed murder memorabilia less than a century old. (You can sell Lizzie Borden's ax but not Jeffrey Dahmer's refrigerator on eBay.) Trading one's virginity is not permitted, but selling a simple lunch date is. A lunch with Warren Buffett recently went for $202,000, prompting Buffett to remark to Whitman, "It's always interesting to see what your market value is in real time."

She struggled most over her decision to ban Nazi memorabilia. Several years ago Starbucks chairman Howard Schultz, an eBay director at the time, returned from a trip to Auschwitz and passionately urged Whitman to take Nazi items off the site. The debate inside the company was intense. As some execs and board members clung to eBay's libertarian ethos, Whitman recalls, "I finally said, 'Okay, I know, but I can't stand this.'" She banned all Nazi items except documents, coins, and copies of historical books like *Mein Kampf.* "This decision doesn't yield to analysis," she says. "It's a judgment call. There has to be one person making the decision, and it's the CEO."

Whitman was pursued for the position of chief executive officer of Walt Disney Co. in 2005 to replace Michael Eisner. She withdrew from consideration and decided to stay at eBay. On several occasions, Whitman has indicated that 10 years is the longest any CEO should remain at a company. She arrived at eBay in 1998. Companies need a fresh perspective and an energized leader to tackle corporate challenges, she has said in analyst meetings and media interviews. Whitman has put in place what appears to be the beginning of a succession process by grooming several senior managers who many believe may eventually be in the running to be tapped by the board to replace her at some time. In early 2005, three senior eBay executives—Bill Cobb, Matt Bannick, and Jeff Jordan—swapped their jobs, which involve overseeing the eBay auctions business in North America, the international auctions business, and electronic-payment processing unit PayPal. The rotations were interpreted as Whitman's way to get each executive to learn aspects of another corporate unit and share their expertise with others.

To learn more about eBay, visit the organization's home page at **http://www.ebay.com/aboutebay**.

Questions

1. What aspects of Meg Whitman's leadership style reflect transactional leadership? Explain.
2. What aspects of Meg Whitman's leadership style reflect authentic leadership? Explain.
3. What aspects of Meg Whitman's leadership style reflect transformational leadership? Explain.

CHAPTER 8

Developing and Leading Teams

LEARNING OBJECTIVES

When you have finished studying the chapter, you should be able to:

1. State the basic characteristics of groups, including informal groups.
2. Describe the attributes of six types of work-related teams.
3. Explain the five-stage model of team development.
4. Describe seven key factors that influence team effectiveness.
5. Explain how team creativity can be stimulated through the nominal group technique, traditional brainstorming, and electronic brainstorming.

Preview Case: Mayo Clinic and Teams

CHARACTERISTICS OF GROUPS

- Classifications of Groups
- Informal Groups
- Effective Groups
- *Communication Competency—Mayo Clinic's Surgical Suite Design Team*

TYPES OF WORK-RELATED TEAMS

- Functional Team
- Problem-Solving Team
- Cross-Functional Team
- Self-Managed Team
- *Teams Competency—Bayer's High Speed Line Team*
- Virtual Team
- Global Team
- *Across Cultures Competency—Unilever Latin America's Global Virtual Team*

STAGES OF TEAM DEVELOPMENT

- Forming Stage
- Storming Stage
- Norming Stage
- Performing Stage
- Adjourning Stage
- Potential Team Dysfunctions

KEY INFLUENCES ON TEAM EFFECTIVENESS

- Context
- Goals
- Team Size
- Team Member Roles and Diversity
- Norms
- Cohesiveness
- Leadership
- *Self Competency—Linda Dillman's Team Leadership*

STIMULATING TEAM CREATIVITY

- Nominal Group Technique
- Traditional Brainstorming
- *Change Competency—Creative Process at Play*
- Electronic Brainstorming

CHAPTER SUMMARY

KEY TERMS AND CONCEPTS

DISCUSSION QUESTIONS

EXPERIENTIAL EXERCISE AND CASE

MAYO CLINIC AND TEAMS

PREVIEW CASE

The Mayo Clinic is a charitable, not-for-profit organization ith headquarters in Rochester, Minnesota. Its mission is to provide the best care to every patient every day through integrated clinical practice, education, and research. This world-renowned medical organization thoroughly diagnoses and treats complex medical problems in every specialty. It consists of a network of clinics and hospitals in Minnesota, Florida, Arizona, Iowa, and Wisconsin. Teams are central to all aspects of the Mayo Clinic.

In 1910, William Mayo said: "In order that the sick may have the benefit of advancing knowledge, a union of forces is necessary. . . . It has become necessary to develop medicine as a cooperative science." Dr. Mayo's vision profoundly influences the organization's approach to care to this day. Patients experience the Mayo Clinic as a team of experts who are focused on patients' needs above all else.

Patients experience an integrated, coordinated response to their medical conditions. The Mayo Clinic assembles the expertise and resources needed to solve the patient's problem. If a Mayo doctor can't answer a question and needs to bring someone else onto a team, she freely admits it to the patient. The doctors meet with one another and with the patient—visible evidence that they are collaborating to solve the patient's problem rather than passing it from one doctor to another. One patient expressed a common sentiment when he said, "I have a lot of problems, and I like that I can go to Mayo and be seen by a team of specialists who work together to see the big picture."

Collaboration is particularly important because the institution's reputation has become so well known that patients often come in looking for a miracle. Many have consulted several other doctors and consider the Mayo Clinic the last resort, so the physicians there regularly see patients with complex problems and high expectations. This situation puts the doctors under extra pressure to make the right diagnoses and treatment decisions.

The Mayo Clinic encourages team collaboration through various organizational incentives. All physicians are salaried, so they don't lose income by referring patients to their colleagues. The organization explicitly shuns the star system, downplaying individual accomplishments in favor of organizational achievements.

Mayo also supports teamwork with its use of technology. Staff members partner via a combination of face-to-face and remote collaboration using a sophisticated internal paging, telephone, and videoconferencing system that connects people quickly and easily. Remote teamwork through voice or virtual interaction is just as common as in-person teamwork in the hallway or at bedside. One physician told us, "I never feel I am in a room by myself, even when I am." For example, a Mayo ENT specialist in Scottsdale called together 20 doctors from all three campuses to discuss a difficult case—a patient with skin cancer at risk for metastasis and, owing to the necessary surgery, nerve injury and disfigurement. The team, assembled in a day, met by videoconference for an hour and a half and reached a consensus for a course of treatment. This included specific recommendations on how aggressively to sample the patient's lymph nodes and how best to reconstruct the surgical wound.[1]

For more information on the Mayo Clinic, visit the organization's home page at ***http://www.mayoclinic.org.***

The Preview Case illustrates two important points about outstanding organizations like the Mayo Clinic: (1) Individual performance by committed individuals is crucial, and (2) individuals working together as a team can often achieve more than if they work in isolation. The Mayo Clinic is a team-based organization.

In this chapter, we focus on one of the seven core competencies introduced in Chapter 1. Recall that the *teams competency* involves the overall ability to develop, support, facilitate, and lead groups to achieve organizational goals. Throughout the chapter, we discuss ways to understand and increase the effectiveness of groups and teams. We focus on (1) the characteristics of groups, (2) the types of teams frequently used in organizations, (3) the ways in which team members develop and learn, (4) the principal factors that influence team effectiveness, and (5) two of the many methods that can be used to encourage team creativity.

LEARNING OBJECTIVE

1. State the basic characteristics of groups, including informal groups.

CHARACTERISTICS OF GROUPS

For our purposes, a **group** *is any number of people who share goals, often communicate with one another over a period of time, and are few enough so that each individual may communicate with all the others, person to person.*[2]

Classifications of Groups

Most individuals belong to various types of groups, which can be classified in many ways. For example, a person concerned with obtaining membership in a group or gaining acceptance as a group member might classify groups as open or closed to new members. A person evaluating groups in an organization according to their primary goals might classify them as friendship groups or task groups. A **friendship group** *evolves informally to meet its members' personal security, esteem, and belonging needs.* A **task group** *is created by management to accomplish certain organizational goals.* However, a single group in an organization may serve both friendship and task purposes. The primary focus of this chapter is on types of task groups, commonly known today as teams.

Informal Groups

An **informal group** *is one that develops out of the day-to-day activities, interactions, and sentiments that the members have for each other.* Informal groups typically satisfy their members' security and social needs. At work, informal groups may oppose higher management and organizational goals, reinforce and support such goals, or simply be unrelated to the organizational goals. The organization often has considerable influence on the development of informal groups through the physical layout of work, the leadership practices of managers, and the types of technology used.[3] For example, EDS, a business and technology consulting firm that is headquartered in the Dallas area, found that moving its professionals from one building to another had an impact on who belonged to informal groups. The physical distance between members may make face-to-face communication difficult and cause groups to disband or reform themselves. In contrast, a new manager taking over a department and telling its employees to "shape up or ship out" may cause an informal group to form, with its members uniting against the manager. Some managers believe that close-knit informal groups have undesirable effects on an organization. They view groups as a potential source of anti-establishment power, as a way of holding back information when the group doesn't identify with organizational goals, or as a means of pressuring individuals to slow production.

Informal groups can provide their members with desirable benefits (e.g., security and protection). Some informal groups set production limits for their members, fearing that management might use an outstanding worker as a standard for output and that increased production might lead to some workers being laid off. An informal group can provide positive feedback to other members. The all-too-common belief that higher productivity will work against the interests of workers is kept alive and enforced by some informal groups within organizations.[4]

Informal groups can also exercise undesirable power over individual members. Such power usually falls into two categories. First, a group may be able to manipulate rewards and punishments and thus pressure members to conform to its standards of behavior. Second, a group may restrict the ways by which social needs can be satisfied on the job. Informal groups have been known to ridicule certain members or to give them the silent treatment for not conforming to group standards of "acceptable" behavior. This treatment may threaten the individual's safety, social, and esteem needs. Managers should probably try to minimize the undesirable effects of informal groups rather than try to eliminate them.[5] Informal groups in organizations can't always be classified simply as positive or negative because many exhibit both characteristics from time to time, depending on the circumstances or issues facing the organization.

Effective Groups

To make groups more effective, a manager must know how to recognize effective and ineffective groups. In brief, an effective group has the following basic characteristics. Its members

- know why the group exists and have shared goals;
- support agreed-on guidelines or procedures for making decisions;
- communicate freely among themselves;
- receive help from one another and give help to one another;
- deal with conflict within the group; and
- diagnose individual and group processes and improve their own and the group's functioning.[6]

The degree to which a group lacks one or more of these characteristics determines whether—and to what extent—it is ineffective. These basic characteristics apply both to formal groups (e.g., the teams at the Mayo Clinic discussed in the Preview Case) and to informal groups (e.g., a friendship group to which you may belong). The following Communication Competency feature reports on the effective design team that developed the new surgical suites at the Mayo Clinic's Saint Mary's Hospital in Rochester, Minnesota.[7]

COMMUNICATION COMPETENCY

MAYO CLINIC'S SURGICAL SUITE DESIGN TEAM

The first step in any operating room construction or renovation project is to determine the type and amount of space available. For this project, the Mayo Clinic design team began with some established boundaries because the hospital had an existing shell of space set aside from an earlier expansion. The total available space was 10,000 square feet. The building structure dictated that each operating room would be 500 square feet. Because cardiology operating rooms require an additional 200 square feet of space, the team decided not to include that specialty in the design of the operating room suites. However, all other surgical specialties would be included in the design.

Developing a list of requirements was the next step toward designing an efficient, comfortable space. The design team first met with the chair of surgery, clinical director of surgical services, physicians, and the architect. This leadership group defined the general needs—such as determining that the operating room would be used for all specialties except cardiac surgery—and also listed special services or design features they wanted, such as a nearby clean core and decontamination area accessible to all of the new operating room suites. They also were interested in the potential for natural light.

Because the operating rooms would be utilized for many types of surgeries, equipment storage was a high priority. The Mayo team insisted that every piece of movable equipment and supply, including soiled linens, have a "home." Hallways were not an option for this purpose. Dividing the space into 500-square-foot spaces allowed for nine new surgical suites but did not leave adequate room for the clean core, storage, or other needs. As a result, the team decided to build seven new suites and use the rest of the space for the other items on the list.

Once these general design considerations had been established, the design team met with physicians, anesthesiologists, surgical nurses, core staff, and facilities and operations staff to answer detailed questions and consider additional inputs. Answers to questions helped to highlight opportunities for promoting efficiency and solving travel distance concerns. The responses enabled the designers to visualize the space in action, a necessary element for sensible and efficient design. Visualizing where all of the team members will be located, the path for equipment and supplies moving in and out of the room, and the patient's travel helped the design team create a space that maximized the efficiency and effectiveness of the surgical suites.

For more information on the Mayo Clinic's Saint Mary's Hospital, visit the organization's home page at ***http://www.mayoclinic.org/saintmaryshospital/.***

LEARNING OBJECTIVE

2. Describe the attributes of six types of work-related teams.

TYPES OF WORK-RELATED TEAMS

A **team** *is a small number of employees with complementary competencies (abilities, skills, and knowledge) who are committed to common performance goals and working relationships for which they hold themselves mutually accountable.*[8] The heart of any team is a shared commitment by its members for their joint performance. Team goals could be as basic as responding to all customers' calls within 24 hours or as involved as reducing defects by 20 percent during the next 6 months. The key point is that such goals can't be achieved without the cooperation and communication of team members. When a team is formed, its members must have (or quickly develop) the right mix of competencies to achieve the team's goals. Also, its members need to be able to influence how they will work together to accomplish those goals. The design team at Mayo Clinic's Saint Mary's Hospital had the goal and shared commitment of developing surgical suites that were efficient and effective for different personnel. The team was relatively small and brought together a range of specialties to achieve an optimal design.

Of the many basic types of teams, we consider six of the most common: functional teams, problem-solving teams, cross-functional teams, self-managed teams, virtual teams, and global teams. As suggested in Figure 8.1, all of these types of teams may be found in a single organization. It is quite possible that a single employee may work in all of these teams over a period of time.

Functional Team

A **functional team** *usually includes employees who work together daily on similar tasks and must coordinate their efforts.* Functional teams often exist within functional

FIGURE 8.1 Common Types of Work-Related Teams

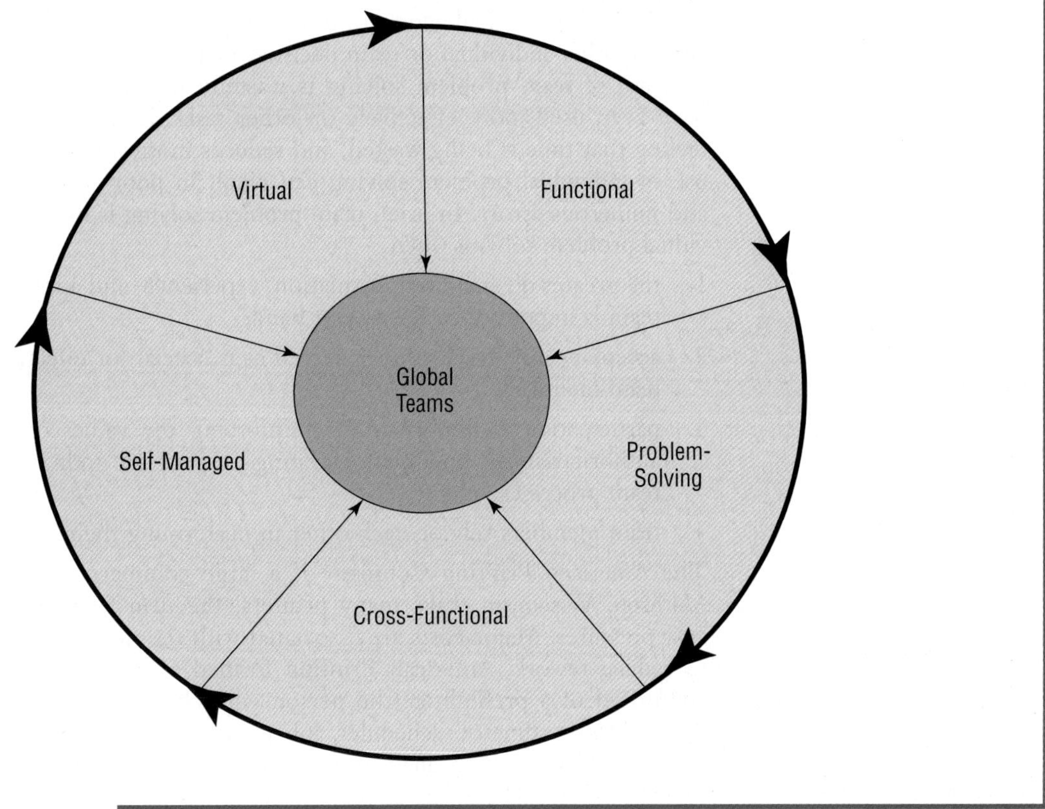

departments: marketing, production, finance, auditing, human resources, and the like. Within a human resource department, one or more functional teams could perform recruiting, compensation, benefits, safety, training and development, affirmative action, industrial relations, and similar functions.

Stoner, Inc., is headquartered in Quarryville, Pennsylvania, and has 48 full- and part-time employees. The firm manufactures more than 500 cleaning, lubrication, and coating products for other businesses. The firm is run on two operational levels: the leadership team and six functional teams. The functional teams include (1) inside sales; (2) manufacturing, warehousing, and purchasing; (3) technology; (4) sales; (5) marketing; and (6) accounting, logistics, and information technology. As a small organization, you can see that several functions have been combined. Stoner's functional teams are connected to the leadership team through representatives, but each has the authority to make a variety of decisions related to their functions.[9]

Problem-Solving Team

A **problem-solving team** *refers to members who focus on a specific issue, develop a potential solution, and are often empowered to take action within defined limits.* These teams frequently address quality or cost problems. Their members may be employees from a specific department who meet at least once or twice a week for an hour or two or members from several units, even including representatives from outside the organization, such as suppliers and customers. Teams may have the authority to implement their own solutions if they don't require major procedural changes that might adversely affect other operations or require substantial new resources. Problem-solving teams do not fundamentally reorganize work or change the role of managers. In effect, managers delegate certain problems and decision-making responsibilities to a team.

The many different types of goals, problems, and tasks confronting an organization require varying degrees of cooperation among individuals and teams. Some require both individual and team problem solving. Organizations can incur excessive costs if either individual or team decision making is used improperly. The unnecessary use of team problem solving is wasteful because the participants' time could have been used more effectively on other tasks; it creates boredom, resulting in a feeling that time is being wasted, and reduces motivation. Conversely, the improper use of individual problem solving can result in poor coordination, little creativity, and numerous errors. In brief, team problem solving is likely to be superior to individual problem solving when

1. the greater diversity of information, experience, and approaches to be found in a team is important to the task at hand;
2. acceptance of the decisions arrived at is crucial for effective implementation by team members;
3. participation is important for reinforcing the values of representation versus authoritarianism and demonstrating respect for individual members through team processes; and
4. team members rely on each other in performing their jobs.

The American Printing Company is a large commercial printing firm located in Madison, Wisconsin. Like many printers, the firm faces intense competition and cost pressures. Major costs are associated with the need to rework jobs. To attempt to reduce rework, American Printing formed a five-person problem-solving team comprised of a preflighter (the person who checks the content of incoming electronic files), estimator, scheduler, job planner, and prepress layout specialist. The team was charged with analyzing jobs for potential problems and taking action to prevent and reduce rework. Shawn Welch, the vice president of operations for American Printing, comments on the results from this team's and related efforts: "We reduced the rework rate from over 3% of sales to below 2%. It is not zero-defect, but it is closer to where we want to be."[10]

Cross-Functional Team

A **cross-functional team** *refers to members from various work areas who identify and solve mutual problems*. Cross-functional teams draw members from several specialties or functions and deal with problems that cut across departmental and functional lines to achieve their goals. Cross-functional teams may operate on an extended basis. Other cross-functional teams may be disbanded after the problems they addressed have been solved and their goals achieved.

Cross-functional teams are often most effective in situations that require innovation, speed, and a focus on responding to customer needs.[11] They may design and introduce quality improvement programs and new technology, meet with customers and suppliers to improve inputs or outputs, and link separate functions (e.g., marketing, finance, manufacturing, and human resource) to increase product or service innovations.

Bell Helicopter Textron is a subsidiary of Textron, Inc., with major production operations in Fort Worth, Texas, and elsewhere. At Bell Helicopter, safety and a safe work environment are not the sole responsibility of the safety department, but of every employee. While many companies make this statement, not all "walk the talk" by backing it up with the resources Bell Helicopter devotes to creating an accident- and injury-free environment.

Two of the most successful tools the company uses to engage employees in safety have been cross-functioning Safety Summits (for both hourly employees and managers) and cross-functional Operations Managers Safety Training programs. Participants in the cross-functional Operations Managers Safety Training program review the company's current culture and look at factors that have caused problems with compliance and safety performance. They study what other best-in-class organizations have done when faced with the same challenges, conduct a cultural analysis and culture gap analysis, and discuss what is needed for change to occur.

The Safety Summits involve cross-functional teams of 20 to 30 Bell employees—evenly split between hourly and managerial. They gather to discuss ways to make Bell a safer place to work. They review current activities, discuss safety challenges, and break up into three teams to consider three questions: What is Bell doing well as a company? What is Bell not doing well as a company? What should Bell be doing? The results of the team activities are submitted to senior management for their review and approval. The summits have proven so popular with employees, and so valuable to the safety effort, that they are conducted four times a year with different groups of employees.[12]

Self-Managed Team

A **self-managed team** *refers to highly interdependent and empowered members who must work together effectively daily to manufacture an entire product (or major identifiable component) or provide an entire service to a set of customers.*[13] A major characteristic of such teams is that they are empowered.

Team Empowerment. **Team empowerment** *refers to the degree to which its members perceive the group as (1) being effective (potency), (2) performing important and valuable tasks (meaningfulness), (3) having independence and discretion (autonomy) in performing the work, and (4) experiencing a sense of importance and significance (impact) in the work performed and goals achieved.*[14] You may relate the key dimensions of empowerment—*potency, meaningfulness, autonomy,* and *impact*—to your own experience when responding to the brief questionnaire in Table 8.1. To obtain your team empowerment score, follow the directions in the table.

TABLE 8.1 Team Empowerment Questionnaire

Instructions: Think of a team that you have been (or are) a member of in a work setting. Respond to each statement below by indicating the degree to which you agree or disagree with it in terms of the team identified. The scale is as follows.

5	4	3	2	1
Strongly Agree	Agree	Undecided/ Neutral	Disagree	Strongly Disagree

Place the appropriate number value next to each item.

Potency Items

_____ 1. The team had confidence in itself.
_____ 2. The team believed that it could be very good at producing high-quality work.
_____ 3. The team expected to be seen by others as high performing.
_____ 4. The team was confident that it could solve its own problems.
_____ 5. The team viewed no job as too tough.

Meaningfulness Items

_____ 6. The team cared about what it did.
_____ 7. The team thought that its work was valuable.
_____ 8. The team viewed its group goals as important.
_____ 9. The team believed that its projects were significant.
_____ 10. The team considered its group tasks to be worthwhile.

Autonomy Items

_____11. The team could select different ways to do its work.

_____12. The team determined how things were done.

_____13. The team had a lot of choice in what it did without being told by management.

_____14. The team had significant influence in setting its goals.

_____15. The team could rotate tasks and assignments among team members.

Impact Items

_____16. The team assessed the extent to which it made progress on projects.

_____17. The team had a positive impact on other employees.

_____18. The team had a positive impact on customers.

_____19. The team accomplished its goals.

_____20. The team made a difference in the organization.

_____**Total**: Add points for items 1 through 20. This total is your perceived team empowerment score. Scores may range from 20 to 100. Scores of 20 through 45 suggest low team empowerment. Scores of 46 through 74 indicate moderate levels of team empowerment. Scores of 75 through 100 reveal a state of significant to very high team empowerment.

Source: Adapted from Kirkman, B. L., and Rosen, B. Beyond self-management: Antecedents and consequences of team empowerment. *Academy of Management Journal*, 1999, 42, 58–74; Kirkman, B. L., and Rosen, B. Powering up teams. *Organizational Dynamics*, Winter 2000, 48–65.

Self-managed teams are often empowered to perform a variety of managerial tasks, such as (1) scheduling work and vacations by members, (2) rotating tasks and assignments among members, (3) ordering materials, (4) deciding on team leadership (which can rotate among team members), (5) setting key team goals, (6) budgeting, (7) hiring replacements for departing team members, and (8) sometimes even evaluating one another's performance.[15] Each member may even learn all tasks that have to be performed by the team.

The impact of self-managed teams on productivity can be enormous. They have raised productivity 30 percent or more and have substantially raised quality in organizations that have used them. They fundamentally change how work is organized and leadership is practiced.[16] The introduction of self-managed teams typically eliminates one or more managerial levels, thereby creating a flatter organization.

Conditions for Use. Empowered self-managed teams aren't necessarily right for every situation or organization. Both costs and benefits accompany such a system. A number of questions need to be addressed in considering the introduction of empowered self-managed teams, including the following:

1. Is the organization fully committed to aligning all management systems with empowered work teams, including selection of leaders, team-based rewards, and open access to information?
2. Are organizational goals and the expected results from the teams clearly specified?
3. Will the teams have access to the resources they need for high performance?
4. Will team members carry out interdependent tasks (i.e., tasks that require a high degree of coordination and communication)?
5. Do employees have the necessary maturity levels to effectively carry out peer evaluations, selection and discipline decisions, conflict management, and other administrative tasks?

6. Are employee competency levels sufficient for handling increased responsibility and, if not, will increased training result in appropriate competency levels?[17]

We discuss additional aspects of the conditions and actions necessary for creating effective teams throughout this chapter and book. The following Teams Competency reports on the High Speed Line Team of the Consumer Care Division manufacturing facility of BayerUS in Myerstown, Pennsylvania.[18] BayerUS has more than 21,000 employees at 50 manufacturing operations in the United States. BayerUS produces approximately 10,000 products in health-care, material science, and crop science divisions. The Myerstown plant produces more than 4 billion Bayer Aspirin tablets a year and several other over-the-counter brands such as Milk of Magnesia, Midol, and Flintstones vitamins.

TEAMS COMPETENCY

BAYER'S HIGH SPEED LINE TEAM

BayerUS uses self-managed teams at its manufacturing facility in Myerstown, Pennsylvania. Peter Grazier, the founder and president of Teambuilding, Inc., visited this facility for a day. We share several of his observations related to one of these self-managed teams—the High Speed Line Team. This team had operated as a self-managed team for three years and was comprised of six operators, one mechanic, and one material handler. The team took finished Bayer Aspirin caplets (produced in another area), put them into plastic bottles, labeled them, boxed them, and then packaged them for shipping. The team also performed other operations such as bottle cleaning, inventory control, capping, shrink wrapping, and such.

When the self-managed team approach was introduced three years earlier, two of the members, Fern and Delores, said that at first they were afraid of their new responsibilities. They were particularly concerned with doing their own quality assurance and accurately recording information that would be audited by the FDA (Food and Drug Administration). They were nervous about making mistakes and being knowledgeable enough to do their new jobs well. They stated: "We had doubts that we could learn it."

Each line controls its own method for work assignments. On the high-speed line, they rotate positions every hour to relieve stress and share work equally. During the rotation, there is a "floater" position that allows some rest from the hands-on operations, but does focus on the paperwork. When they first started as a self-managed team, the members had frequent meetings to set up their process, but today everyone knows the system, so meetings are less frequent. The High Speed Line Team has made simple, but brilliant innovations to reduce changeover time to different bottles. In one application alone, the changeover time was reduced from two hours to ten minutes.

Everyone spoke highly of the self-managed team approach, including such comments as:

- "Before, the supervisor made all the decisions. You didn't know why the decisions were made . . . now we do."
- "We now have more responsibility, more pride in our work. We are solely responsible."
- "I am now more secure as a person . . . this is a wonderful challenge. You never knew where you were going to be from one day to day, now you do."
- "I don't ever want to go back to the old way."

For more information on BayerUS, visit the organization's home page at ***http://www.bayerus.com.***

Virtual Team

Functional, problem-solving, cross-functional, and even self-managed teams increasingly operate as virtual teams. A **virtual team** *refers to members who collaborate through various information technologies on one or more tasks while located at two or more locations.*[19] Unlike teams that operate primarily through person-to-person settings by members of the same organization, virtual teams work primarily across distance (any place), across time (any time), and increasingly across organizational boundaries (members from two or more organizations). Accordingly, some of the potential benefits of virtual teams include the following:

- Members can work from anywhere at any time.
- Members can be recruited for their competencies, not just the physical location where they primarily work and live.
- Members with physical handicaps that limit travel can participate.
- Expenses associated with travel, lodging, and leasing or owning as much physical space may be reduced.

Core Features. The core dimensions of a virtual team are goals, people, and technology links. Goals are important to any team, but especially so to a virtual team. Clear, precise, and mutually agreed-on goals are the glue that holds a virtual team together. The ability to hire and fire by a superior and reliance on rules and regulations are minimized in effective virtual teams.

As in all teams, people are at the core of effective virtual teams, but with some unique twists. Everyone in a virtual team needs to be autonomous and self-reliant while simultaneously working collaboratively with others. This duality requires a certain type of person and a foundation of trust among team members. The most apparent feature of a virtual team is the array of technology-based links used to connect members and enable them to carry out its tasks. Virtual teams are increasingly common because of rapid advances in computer and telecommunications technologies.[20]

A variety of suggestions have been offered for enhancing the *people* dimension of virtual teams.[21] We share five of them here:

- If feasible, bring the members together for an initial face-to-face session, which could last one to three days depending on the scope and complexity of the team's responsibilities and goals. Members need to be given adequate time to get to know one another. This initial session may include team-building activities. Of course, the work-related goals, team member roles, and team responsibilities should be thoroughly discussed in this session. With advances in communication technologies, there are some who hold the view that an initial face-to-face session may not be essential and could be too costly for team members located around the world. This may be more applicable to teams that have a relatively short duration.[22]
- Discuss and establish the ways in which team members are interdependent and need to collaborate to achieve the team goals.
- For long-term or permanent teams, establish a schedule of periodic face-to-face meetings—quarterly, semiannual, or annual, if feasible.
- Agree on what, when, and how information, issues, and problems will be shared as well as on how team members will respond to them.
- Establish clear norms and procedures for surfacing and resolving conflicts.

Technology Links. Three broad categories of technologies are often used in the operation of virtual teams: desktop videoconferencing systems, collaborative software systems, and Internet/intranet systems.[23] Virtual teams can function with only simple e-mail and telephone systems, including voice mail. However, desktop videoconferencing systems (DVCSs) re-create some of the aspects of face-to-face interactions of conventional teams. This technology makes possible more complex communication among team members. The DVCS is a relatively simple system for users to operate. A small camera mounted atop a computer monitor provides the video feed to the system; voice transmissions operate through an earpiece–microphone combination or speakerphone. Connection to other team members is managed through software on the user's computer.

Collaborative software systems (group support systems) comprise the second category of technologies that enable the use of virtual teams. Collaborative software is designed for both independent and interactive use. For example, Lotus Notes, a dominant collaborative software product, is designed specifically for communication and data sharing when team members are working at different times, at the same time, independently, or interactively. It combines scheduling, electronic messaging, and document and data sharing. Although Lotus Notes and other such software may be used to support teamwork in a traditional work environment, they are vital to the operation of empowered virtual teams. Instant messaging (IM) is a virtual Post-it note. It is informal and interactive. IM helps to keep tabs on each other's availability.

Internet and intranet technologies represent the third main enabler of virtual teams. Intranets give organizations the advantage of using Internet technology to disseminate organizational information and enhance interemployee communication while maintaining system security. They allow virtual teams to archive text, visual, audio, and numerical data in a user-friendly format. The Internet and intranets also allow virtual teams to keep other organizational members and important external stakeholders, such as suppliers and customers, up to date on a team's progress.[24]

Global Team

A **global team** *has members from a variety of countries who are, therefore, often separated significantly by time, distance, culture, and native language.*[25] As suggested earlier in Figure 8.1, global teams may operate like any of the other types of teams we have discussed—functional, problem solving, cross-functional, self-managed, and virtual. Global teams typically conduct a substantial portion of their tasks as virtual teams.

Four of the principal reasons for the use of global teams are as follows:[26]

1. The desire to develop goods and services in a variety of countries with a minimum level of customization. In this circumstance, global teams help to define common features of goods and services that will appeal to customers in different countries.
2. In contrast to reason 1 just given, there is a desire to develop goods or services that are tailored to the unique needs and requirements of local markets. The global team members from different countries can provide insight into and input about these unique market needs and requirements for specific attributes of goods and services.
3. Global teams enable organizations to leverage and capitalize on expertise that exists in different countries. This eliminates the need to bring the required expertise to a single country by relocating team members and encountering all of the costs of doing so, including the costs of removing team members from family and friends or relocating entire families.
4. For some organizations, the location of manufacturing facilities, distribution centers, and marketing units in various countries requires the use of global teams. The teams serve as a mechanism for coordinating these dispersed resources. Global teams allow companies to take advantage of lower manufacturing costs in one country, the central location of a distribution center in another, and "on-site" marketing units by bringing together individuals virtually. These global teams usually meet face to face only occasionally.

Global virtual teams face a variety of special challenges relative to most virtual or face-to-face teams because of differences in the members' cultures and native languages as well as significant time zone differences in their normal working hours. For example, virtual teams with members from China, Germany, Japan, France, and the United States are more culturally, socially, and linguistically diverse (even if the work-related communications are undertaken in English) than virtual teams with members from California, Colorado, Florida, Massachusetts, and New York. We discuss in a number of chapters the special challenges associated with across cultural differences.

With respect to time, the normal working hours for global virtual team members may vary by 12 or more hours due to differences in the time zones where members reside. Moreover, the cultural meaning of *time* may vary among team members in different societies, which we discuss in more detail in the following chapter. Cultural orientations about time may affect team members' perceptions of schedules and deadlines. In some cultures, like Germanic and Scandinavian countries, they are seen as absolutes, and in other societies, like Mexico and Italy, they are often seen as guidelines. In recognition of the potential for different views of time among global virtual team members, it is recommended that these perspectives be actively managed through such steps as (1) creating an awareness of the different views members may have with respect to time after the formation of the team; (2) facilitating the development of agreed-on norms and expectations with respect to time and other aspects of the team functioning; and (3) encouraging the use of precise language with respect to time and avoiding the use of time-related language unique to a society, such as "Wait a minute," "I'll be in touch shortly," and "Let's keep in contact as time permits."[27]

The following Across Cultures Competency feature provides an example of the successful use of a global virtual team by Unilever Latin America.[28] The important role of the leader is emphasized, which is typically the case in all types of successful virtual teams.[29] Unilever Latin America manufactures and markets hundreds of consumer packaged goods in the Latin American region of the world, comprising 19 countries. It is a subsidiary of Unilever NV, which is headquartered in Rotterdam, Netherlands.

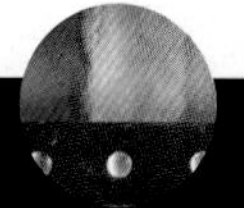

ACROSS CULTURES COMPETENCY

Unilever Latin America's Global Virtual Team

A diverse global virtual team at Unilever Latin America was formed to redesign a deodorant for the Colombian and Venezuelan markets. The packaging for the roll-on, stick, and cream formats was to be manufactured in Brazil; the engineer who was to develop the cream packaging was situated in Argentina. The roll-on formula itself was going to be made in Mexico and Brazil, the stick in Chile, and the cream in Colombia. But because the packaging and formula for the Colombian and Venezuelan markets differed from those the factories were already making for the rest of Latin America, the company needed the existing suppliers and manufacturing engineers, who were spread across five countries, to participate in the redesign of the new product.

A variety of communication technologies were used by the team. In this global virtual team, much of the work of generating solutions happened in conference calls, which were carefully orchestrated by the team leader. "I didn't know the team members very well, didn't know how they thought and worked," the leader, who was based in Argentina, recalls, "so I couldn't always go directly to the point on an issue. Instead, I encouraged a lot of conversation, trying to reach a common view that included all of their points. We discussed different alternatives, always asking everyone, 'What do you think about this?'

"If we had ignored even one country," the leader continues, "we would have run the risk of creating a product that could not be rolled out according to schedule. But by surfacing our differences early, we didn't ignore anyone's needs, and we rolled out the product without problems on time."

This level of attention paid to soliciting and discussing everyone's opinions made for detailed and clear conversations. These conversations proved to be indispensable for the team. Although in the beginning their discussions took a lot of time, results more than made up for that. As the leader of the Unilever team says, "We got to a shared view much more quickly than any of us anticipated." Of course, teleconferencing was not the whole story.

Early in the life of the team, the leader pushed it to adopt a common language. The members of the Unilever team adopted what they called "Portuñol," a hybrid of Spanish and Portuguese. The team prepared a glossary, mostly of technical terms and figures of speech, to make sure there was a common and agreed-on understanding in the use of important terms, concepts, and sayings.

For more information on Unilever Latin America, visit the parent organization's home page at ***http://www.unilever.com.***

STAGES OF TEAM DEVELOPMENT

LEARNING OBJECTIVE

3. Explain the five-stage model of team development.

The formation of effective teams is not automatic. Various conditions for success or failure occur throughout a team's development. To provide a sense of these conditions, we present a basic five-stage developmental sequence that teams may go through: forming, storming, norming, performing, and adjourning.[30] The types of work-related and socially related behaviors that may be observed differ from stage to stage. Figure 8.2 shows the five stages on the horizontal axis and the level of team maturity on the vertical axis. It also indicates that a team can fail and disband during a stage or when moving from one stage to another. Pinpointing the developmental stage of a team at any specific time is difficult. Nevertheless, managers and team members need to understand these developmental stages because each can influence a team's effectiveness. In the following discussion, we describe behaviors that might occur at each stage. Of course, teams and groups do not necessarily develop in the straightforward manner depicted in this model.[31] Team members with high levels of the seven core competencies presented throughout this book are likely to speed up and alter the stages of development presented here.

Forming Stage

Team members often focus on defining or understanding goals and developing procedures for performing their tasks in the forming stage. Team development in this stage involves getting acquainted and understanding leadership and other member roles. In terms of social behaviors, it should also deal with members' feelings and the tendency of most members to depend too much on one or two of the team's members. Otherwise, individual members might (1) keep feelings to themselves until they know the situation, (2) act more secure than they actually feel, (3) experience confusion and uncertainty about what is expected of them, (4) be nice and polite, or at least certainly not hostile, and (5) try to size up the personal benefits relative to the personal costs of being involved with the team or group.

Two researchers investigated the impact of a collaborative software system on the development and performance of two corporate teams.[32] One strength of their study involved investigation of actual corporate teams solving real problems. They were fortunate in having access to an organization whose top managers were as interested in the results of the study as they were. This interest allowed the investigators to study the two teams in detail, using meeting transcripts and individual interviews. One team studied had used a collaborative software system from the

FIGURE 8.2 Stages of Team Development

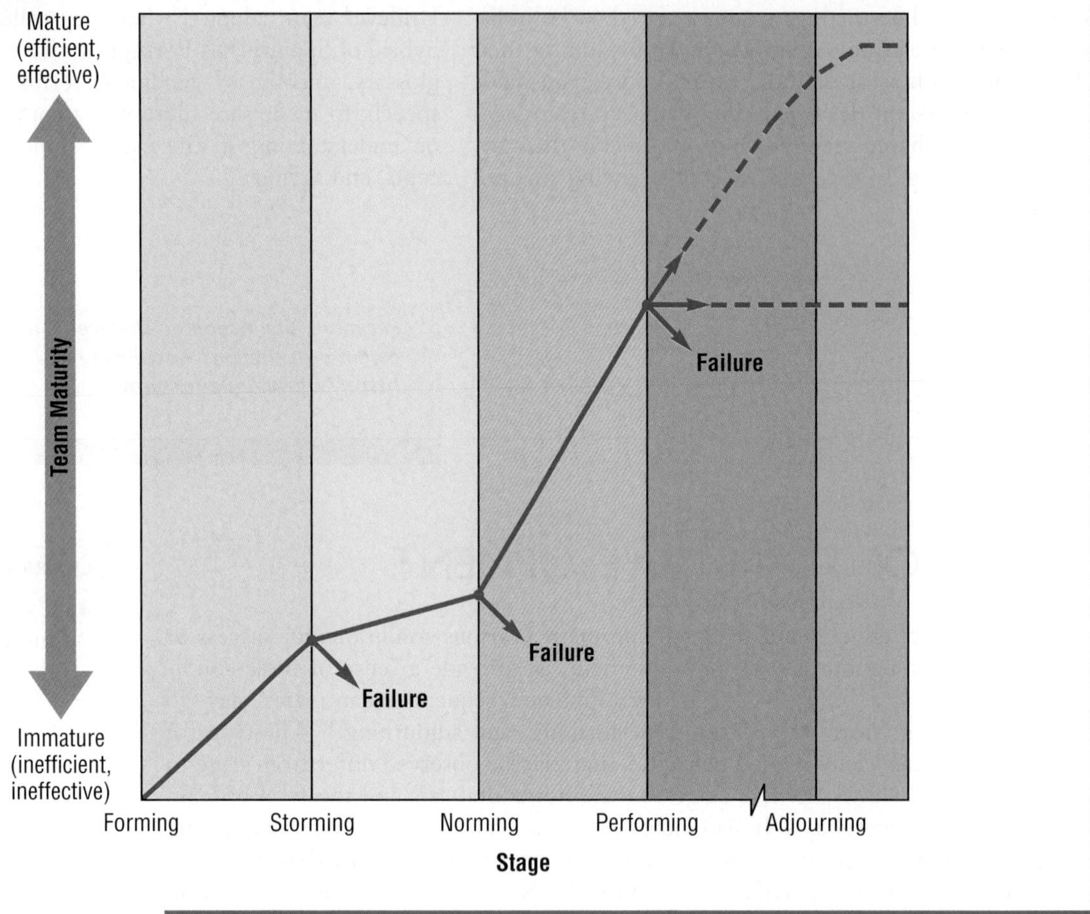

Source: Adapted from Tuckman, B. W., and Jensen, M. A. C. Stages of small-group development revisited. *Groups and Organization Studies*, 1977, 2, 419–442; Kormanski, C. Team interventions: Moving the team forward. In J. W. Pfeiffer (ed.). *The 1996 Annual: Volume 2 Consulting*. San Diego: Pfeiffer and Company, 1996, 19–26.

start, whereas the second team used the system only after the team had met a few times. The investigators' findings indicated that the two teams developed and performed quite differently. The team that started with the collaborative system improved faster than the other team at each stage of development, but most noticeably at the storming stage. The researchers found that a collaborative software system can help a group get started (forming), but only when the group considers that use of the system is important to doing the task at hand.

Storming Stage

The storming stage is characterized by conflicts over work behaviors, relative priorities of goals, who is to be responsible for what, and the task-related guidance and direction of the team leader. Social behaviors are a mixture of expressions of hostility and strong feelings. Competition over the leadership role and conflict over goals may dominate this stage. Some members may withdraw or try to isolate themselves from the emotional tension generated. The key is to manage conflict during this stage, not to suppress it or withdraw from it. The team can't effectively evolve into the third stage if its members go to either extreme. Suppressing conflict will likely create bitterness and resentment, which will last long after team members attempt to express their differences and emotions. Withdrawal may cause the team to fail.

This stage may be shortened or mostly avoided if the members use a team-building process from the beginning. This process involves the development of decision-making, interpersonal, and technical capabilities when they are lacking. Team-building facilitators can help team members work through the inevitable conflicts that will surface during this and the other stages.

Let's consider the findings of a study of six virtual project teams at FOODCO.[33] FOODCO is a food service distributor to schools, fast-food chains, and individually owned and operated restaurants. It also manufactures a limited number of its own products. The virtual project teams were cross-functional and consisted of five members each. Each team addressed a business issue that FOODCO's top executives considered to be "critical" to the company's performance. For example, one team was to develop an integration strategy for acquisitions. Another team was to determine how to transfer best practices from one division of the company to another. The team had three face-to-face periods prior to making their project presentations to seven top executives and five independent assessors. Most of the work of these teams was conducted virtually. Each project was evaluated for content, quality, and anticipated effectiveness.

In the storming stages, most of the FOODCO teams had not identified or agreed on a project leader. More than half of the members of the various teams reported difficulties in working on their projects. Lack of commitment by some team members became evident, and concerns were expressed that they were not doing their fair share. Typical comments included these: (1) "We have not made the project the priority that it deserves"; (2) "Team members' day-to-day tasks are being used as an excuse to avoid doing the project"; and (3) "It has been difficult to get all members to attend each conference call," which is the equivalent of a team meeting.

Norming Stage

Behaviors at the norming stage evolve into a sharing of information, acceptance of different options, and positive attempts to make decisions that may require compromise. During this stage, team members set rules by which the team will operate. For teams that become effective, social behaviors often focus on empathy, concern, and positive expressions of feelings that lead to a sense of cohesion. Cooperation and a sense of shared responsibility develop among members of effective teams.

Returning to FOODCO, by the end of the third face-to-face meeting of the six virtual project teams, most of them had recognized the need for reaching agreement on how they would operate in the future. The teams reconsidered (and reinforced) existing norms or established new norms regarding information collection, document sharing, task responsibilities, acceptable attendance at conference calls, and team commitment. Teams discussed ways in which members could be held more accountable for timely delivery of project assignments and openly confronted problems that might interfere with the completion of their projects. Most teams expressed some regret about their initial passivity, lack of initiative, and delays in collecting information. The comments by members of several teams suggested that they continued to struggle with issues of commitment and trust during the norming stage. It was believed that this adversely impacted their effectiveness in the performing stage.[34]

Performing Stage

Team members show how effectively and efficiently they can achieve results together during the performing stage. The roles of individual members are accepted and understood. The members have learned when they should work independently and when they should help each other. The two dashed lines in Figure 8.2 suggest that teams may differ after the performing stage. Some teams continue to learn and develop from their experiences, becoming more efficient and effective. Other teams—especially those that developed norms not fully supportive of efficiency and effectiveness—may perform only at the level needed for their survival. Excessive self-oriented behaviors, development of norms that inhibit effective and efficient task completion, poor leadership, or other factors may hurt productivity.

In the performing stage of the six FOODCO virtual project teams, the differences among the teams became even more evident. These differences emerged with respect to team commitment, higher executive level sponsor involvement and support, coordination, intra-team trust, and member "loafing." Teams that perceived greater amounts of resource availability at the onset of their projects performed better at the end of the project. Teams with greater mission clarity, more time to examine work process effectiveness, and higher levels of executive sponsor support were more effective.

A profile of the "best" team shows that at each stage of development it was proactive, focused, resourceful, and unafraid to seek support and guidance as needed The best team, as compared to the least effective team, developed a much stronger consensus regarding team mission. The best team reported greater levels of executive sponsor support and more frequent assessments by team members of its own processes than the least effective team. Members of the best team realized they needed to revise their work processes to meet the deadline and perform well. In contrast, members of the least effective team continued to struggle to the end of the project on how they could best accomplish their mission. In the performing stage, the best team, as compared to the least effective team, saw themselves as having a high level of mission clarity, communication, commitment, and trust among team members. There were a variety of other findings related to the stages of development for the six virtual project teams at FOODCO, but are beyond the scope our discussion.[35]

Adjourning Stage

The termination of work behaviors and disengagement from social behaviors occur during the adjourning stage. A problem-solving team or a cross-functional team created to investigate and report on a specific issue within six months has well-defined points of adjournment. After the presentations were made to the top executives and several other assessors by the six virtual project teams at FOODCO, they were disbanded. The reports and presentations represented the "outputs" from their projects. Top management accepted these projects as "inputs" for their consideration and possible implementation by others. Another example of a team with a specific adjournment stage is the surgical suite design team for the Mayo Clinic's Saint Mary's Hospital.

In contrast, BayerUS, as presented in our discussion of self-managed teams, uses teams to perform various tasks on an ongoing basis. Recall that the High Speed Line Team had been operating for three years at the time of its description. Accordingly, some teams go on indefinitely. These teams will "adjourn" only if top management decides to revise the current team system. In terms of relations-oriented behaviors, some degree of adjourning occurs when team members resign or are reassigned. The developmental stages of teams—regardless of the framework used to describe and explain them—are not easy to move through. Failure or reduced effectiveness can occur at any point in the sequence, as indicated in Figure 8.2. Our discussion of FOODCO's virtual project teams suggested some of the factors that influence team effectiveness.

Potential Team Dysfunctions

A number of potential dysfunctions for teams in the performing stage have been identified.[36] To enrich your understanding of the potential sources of team ineffectiveness noted in our discussion of FOODCO's virtual project teams, we present three additional team dysfunctions here—groupthink, free riding, and absence of trust.

Groupthink. Groupthink *is an agreement-at-any-cost mentality that results in ineffective group decision making and poor decisions.* Irving L. Janis, who coined the term *groupthink,* focused his research on high-level governmental policy groups faced with difficult problems in a complex and dynamic environment. Of course, team or group decision making is quite common in all types of organizations. The possibility of groupthink exists in private sector organizations as well as those in the public sector. Several of the characteristics of groupthink include the following:

- An *illusion of invulnerability* is shared by most or all group members, which creates excessive optimism and encourages taking extreme risks. "No one can stop us now" or "The other team (or organization) has a bunch of jerks" are statements made by members suffering from an illusion of invulnerability.
- *Direct pressure* is exerted on any member who expresses strong arguments against any of the team's illusions, stereotypes, or commitments, making clear that such dissent is contrary to what is expected of all loyal members. The leader might say, "What's the matter? Aren't you a member of the team anymore?"
- *Self-censorship* of deviations from the apparent team's consensus reflects the inclination of members to minimize the importance of their doubts and not present counterarguments. A member might think: "If everyone feels that way, my feelings must be wrong."
- A shared *illusion of unanimity* results, in part, from self-censorship and is reinforced by the false assumption that silence implies consent.[37]

Free Riding. The potential for conflicting team and individual interests is suggested by the free-rider concept. A **free rider** *refers to a team member who obtains benefits from membership but does not bear a proportional share of the responsibility for generating the benefit.*[38] Students sometimes experience the free-rider problem when an instructor assigns a group project for which all of the members receive the same (group) grade. Let's assume that there are seven students in the team and that one member makes little or no contribution. This noncontributing member obtains the benefit of the team grade but does not bear a proportional share of the demands in earning the team grade.

> **THE COMPETENT LEADER**
>
> You all remember the term groupthink—the idea that very cohesive groups value harmony above all. This has been the setting for some of the worst decisions ever made.
>
> **Sharon Allen, Chairman of the Board, Deloitte & Touche USA LLP**

When team members fear that one or more other members may free ride, a phenomenon may occur known as the **sucker effect,** *which refers to one or more individuals in the team deciding to withhold effort in the belief that others (the free riders) are planning to withhold effort.* The sucker role is repulsive to many team members for three reasons. First, the free riding of others violates an equity standard: Members don't want others receiving the same levels of rewards for less input or effort. Second, it violates a standard of social responsibility: Everyone should do their fair share. Third, the free riding of others may violate a standard of reciprocity or exchange.[39] A team is doomed to ineffectiveness with both free riders and other members acting on the basis of the sucker effect.

Absence of Trust. The absence of trust among team members can severely hamper its effectiveness.[40] This was found to be somewhat of a problem in the least effective virtual project team at FOODCO. Members of teams with absence of trust tend to:

- Conceal their weaknesses and mistakes from one another.
- Hesitate to ask for help or provide constructive feedback.
- Hesitate to offer help outside their own areas of responsibility.
- Jump to conclusions about the intentions and aptitudes of others without attempting to clarify them.
- Fail to recognize and tap into one another's skills and experiences.[41]

The important role of trust in interpersonal, team, and organizational relationships was addressed in our previous two chapters on leadership. We further address the role of trust and how to increase it in our chapters on conflict (Chapter 9) and organizational communication (Chapter 10).

LEARNING OBJECTIVE

4. Describe seven key factors that influence team effectiveness.

KEY INFLUENCES ON TEAM EFFECTIVENESS

The factors that influence team and group effectiveness are interrelated. Figure 8.3 identifies seven of the main factors. They should be analyzed both separately and in relation to each other. This approach is necessary to gain an understanding of team dynamics and effectiveness—and to develop the competencies needed to be an effective team member and leader.

FIGURE 8.3 Some Influences on Team Effectiveness

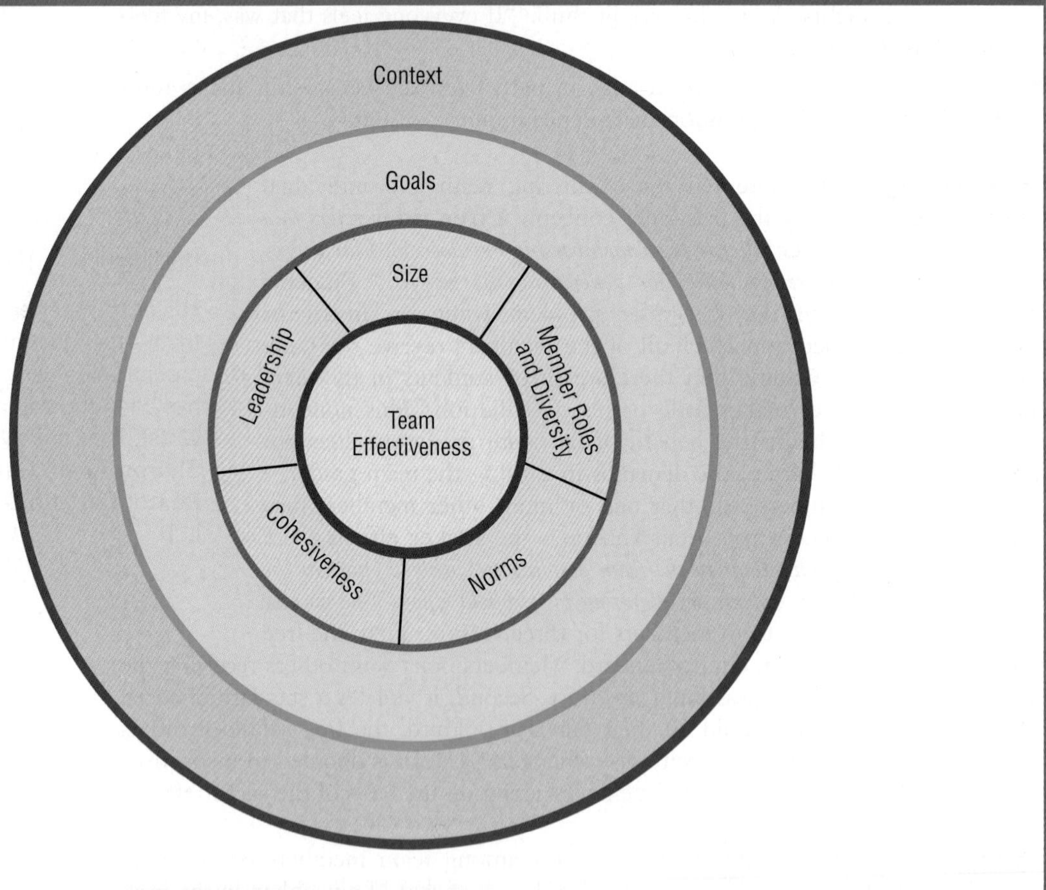

Context

The **context** *refers to the external conditions within which a team works.* Moreover, the context can directly affect each of the six other factors that affect a team. Examples of a team's context include technology, physical working conditions, management practices, and organizational rewards and punishments. Our discussion of virtual teams illustrated the contextual influence of technology. We also noted the contextual influence of the differences in the executive sponsor involvement and support among the virtual project teams at FOODCO.

If the members of a team are more focused on themselves than their peers, perhaps the compensation system should be tailored so that individuals see how their own interests are being served by being strong team contributors. This notion is based on three perspectives:

1. Motivation primarily comes from the individual, not the team.
2. The development of competencies and the application of behaviors are individual undertakings.
3. Fairness in dealing with teams does not mean equal pay for all.

The team system at Mayo Clinic considers these perspectives by not selecting physicians and others who are so individualistic that they want to maximize their own personal income. A physician at the Mayo Clinic states:

> *The Mayo culture attracts individuals who see the practice of medicine best delivered when there is an integration of medical specialties functioning as a team. It is what we do best, and most of us love to do it. What is most inspiring is when a case is successful because of the teamwork of a bunch of docs from different specialties; it has the same feeling as a homerun in baseball.*[42]

Kendall-Futuro Inc. of Newport, Kentucky, has had a great deal of success with teams, and management contends that credit is due to its compensation program. The company uses gain sharing (see Chapter 15), in which team members are financially rewarded for gains in productivity. It no longer bases pay on a salary plus piecework combination but rather on a salary plus team performance combination. Gain sharing has been around for decades, and has been increasingly used to reward team performance. Gain sharing measures performance against a standard, and a bonus is awarded for meeting it. In gain sharing, team members normally aren't penalized for failing to meet the standard. Each team member receives a basic salary and, in addition, a gain-sharing bonus when it has been earned.[43]

Kendall-Futuro's approach is one way to compensate teamwork, but it's not for everyone. There are few hard-and-fast rules for fostering team performance, but there are several general guidelines. For example, companies that use teams most effectively in the United States generally still base a substantial portion of pay on the individual's contributions but with a significant difference. They make teamwork and the ability to work with others a key factor in determining an individual's annual adjustment in pay based on the person's performance review.

Goals

Many aspects of goals are discussed in Chapter 15. Throughout the book, we focus on how goals influence individual, team, and organizational effectiveness. Obviously, individual and organizational goals are likely to influence team goals and behaviors in pursuit of these goals. **Team goals** *are the outcomes desired for the team as a whole, not just goals of the individual members.*

Both compatible and conflicting goals often exist within a team. Moreover, teams typically have both relations-oriented and task-oriented goals. Effective teams spend two-thirds or more of their time on task-oriented issues and roughly one-third or less of their time on relations-oriented issues. The pursuit of only one or the other type of goal over the long run can hurt performance, increase conflicts, and cause a team to disband. The influence of goals on group dynamics and outcomes becomes even more complex when the possible compatibilities and conflicts among member goals, broader team goals, and even broader organizational goals are considered.

One mechanism for dealing with these issues is the use of **superordinate goals,** *which two or more individuals, teams, or groups might pursue but can't be achieved without their cooperation.* These goals do not replace or eliminate individual or team goals and may be either qualitative or quantitative. An example of a qualitative goal is "We need to pull together for the good of the team." An example of a quantitative goal is "We need to work together if we are to reach the team goal of launching a new line within nine months." Superordinate goals are likely to have a more powerful effect on the willingness of individuals or teams to cooperate if they are accompanied by team rewards. Team rewards are given to team members and are determined by the results of their joint efforts. Kendall-Futuro's gain-sharing compensation system is designed to link an individual's goals (higher individual pay and good merit reviews) with team goals (working together to earn bonuses awarded for meeting standards), which represent superordinate goals for each team member.

At times, the way the organization's principles and values are expressed and implemented may serve as superordinate goals. For example, the core principles set forth by Dr. William J. Mayo late in his life continue to serve as superordinate goals at the Mayo Clinic. They include

- continuing pursuit of the ideal of service and not profit,
- continuing primary and sincere concern for the care and welfare of each individual patient, and
- continuing interest by every member of the staff in the professional progress of every other member.[44]

Team Size

The effective size of a team can range from 3 members to a normal upper limit of about 16 members.[45] Collaborative software systems and the Internet are enabling larger teams to work effectively on some tasks. Twelve members probably is the largest size that allows each member to interact easily with every other member face to face. Table 8.2 shows six dimensions of teams in terms of leader behaviors, member behaviors, and team process. The likely effects of team size on each dimension are highlighted. Note that members of teams of 7 or less interact differently than do members of teams or groups of 13 to 16. A 16-member board of directors will operate differently from a 7-member board. Large boards of directors often form committees of 5 to 7 members to consider specific matters in greater depth than can the entire board.

TABLE 8.2 Typical Effects of Size on Teams

	TEAM SIZE		
DIMENSION	2–7 MEMBERS	8–12 MEMBERS	13–16 MEMBERS
1. Demands on leader	Low	Moderate	High
2. Direction by leader	Low	Moderate	Moderate to high
3. Member tolerance of direction by leader	Low to moderate	Moderate	High
4. Member inhibition	Low	Moderate	High
5. Use of rules and procedures	Low	Moderate	Moderate to high
6. Time taken to reach a decision	Low	Moderate	High

As with all influences on teams, the effects identified in Table 8.2 need to be qualified. For example, adequate time and sufficient member commitment to a team's goals and tasks might lead to better results from a team of nine or more members than from a hurried and less committed team of five members. If a team's primary task is to tap the knowledge of the members and arrive at decisions based primarily on expertise rather than judgment, a larger team won't necessarily reflect the effects identified in Table 8.2.

In one recent survey of companies, the typical upper limit on team size was 15 members. Larger teams were associated with the performance of simpler tasks and where there was somewhat less hour-by-hour task interdependence among team members. Recall the eight-person High Speed Line Team at BayerUS manufacturing facility in Myerstown, Pennsylvania. Although the production tasks performed by this team on a daily basis were relatively simple, this self-managed team was quite interdependent on other tasks, such as controlling its own process for making work assignments and developing ways to improve the performance of its production tasks. In contrast, the production teams at a Volvo plant that manufactures truck cabins in the Netherlands consist of 11 to 13 members. The members of these teams are less interdependent throughout the work day in performing their production tasks than the High Speed Line team members. Thus, although the Volvo teams function as self-managed teams, they are effective with more members.[46]

Team Member Roles and Diversity

Similarities and differences among members and their roles influence team behaviors. Obviously, managers can't alter the basic personalities or attributes of team members (see Chapters 11 and 12). Therefore, attempts to influence their roles in a team or group are more useful. These roles may be formally classified as task-oriented, relations-oriented, and self-oriented roles. Each member has the potential for performing each of these roles over time.[47]

Task-Oriented Role. The **task-oriented role** *of a team member involves facilitating and coordinating work-related decision making.* This role may include

- *initiating* new ideas or different ways of considering team problems or goals and suggesting solutions to difficulties, including modification of team procedures;
- *seeking information* to clarify suggestions and obtain key facts;
- *giving information* that is relevant to the team's problem, issue, or task;
- *coordinating* and clarifying relationships among ideas and suggestions, pulling ideas and suggestions together, and coordinating members' activities; and
- *evaluating* the team's effectiveness, including questioning the logic, facts, or practicality of other members' suggestions.

Relations-Oriented Role. The **relations-oriented role** *of a team member involves building team-centered feelings and social interactions.* This role may include

- *encouraging* members through praise and acceptance of their ideas, as well as indicating warmth and solidarity;
- *harmonizing* and mediating intrateam conflicts and tensions;
- *encouraging* participation of others by saying "Let's hear from Susan" or "Why not limit the length of contributions so all can react to the problem?" or "Juan, do you agree?";
- *expressing* standards for the team to achieve or apply in evaluating the quality of team processes, raising questions about team goals, and assessing team progress in light of these goals; and

- *following* by going along passively or constructively and serving as a friendly member.

Self-Oriented Role. The **self-oriented role** *of a team member involves the person's self-centered behaviors that are at the expense of the team or group.* This role may include

- *blocking progress* by being negative, stubborn, and unreasoningly resistant—for example, the person may repeatedly try to bring back an issue that the team had considered carefully and rejected;
- *seeking recognition* by calling attention to oneself, including boasting, reporting on personal achievements, and in various ways avoiding being placed in a presumed inferior position;
- *dominating* by asserting authority, manipulating the team or certain individuals, using flattery or proclaiming superiority to gain attention, and interrupting the contributions of others; and
- *avoiding* involvement by maintaining distance from others and remaining insulated from interaction.

Effective teams often are composed of members who play both task-oriented and relations-oriented roles over time. A particularly adept individual who reveals behaviors valued by the team probably has relatively high *status*—the relative rank of an individual in a team. A team dominated by individuals who exhibit mainly self-oriented behaviors is likely to be ineffective because the individuals don't adequately address team goals and engage in needed collaboration.

Table 8.3 provides a questionnaire for evaluating some of your task-oriented, relations-oriented, and self-oriented behaviors as a team member. The questionnaire asks you to assess your tendency to engage in each role, on a scale of 1 to 5 (or almost never to almost always). Member composition and roles greatly influence team or group behaviors. Either too much or too little of certain member behaviors can adversely affect team performance and member satisfaction.[48]

TABLE 8.3 Assessing Your Role-Oriented Behavior as a Team Member

Instructions: Assess your behavior on each item for the team that you selected by using the following scale.

1	2	3	4	5
Almost Never	Rarely	Sometimes	Often	Almost Always

Place the appropriate number value next to each item.

Task-oriented behaviors: In this team, I . . .

_____ 1. initiate ideas or actions.
_____ 2. facilitate the introduction of facts and information.
_____ 3. summarize and pull together various ideas.
_____ 4. keep the team working on the task.
_____ 5. ask whether the team is near a decision (determine consensus).

Relation-oriented behaviors: In this team, I . . .

_____ 6. support and encourage others.

_____ 7. harmonize (keep the peace).
_____ 8. try to find common ground.
_____ 9. encourage participation.
_____ 10. actively listen.

Self-oriented behaviors: In this team, I . . .

_____ 11. express hostility.
_____ 12. avoid involvement.
_____ 13. dominate the team.
_____ 14. free ride on others.
_____ 15. take personal credit for team results.

_____ Total: Add points for items 1 through 15.

Interpretation: Scores of 20–25 on task-oriented behaviors, 20–25 on relations-oriented behaviors, and 5–10 on self-oriented behaviors probably indicate that you are an effective team member. This conclusion assumes that other team members perceive you as you see yourself.

Team Diversity. The growing diversity of the workforce adds complexity—beyond individuals' personalities and team roles—to understanding team behavior and processes. We have discussed how the composition of the workforce is undergoing continued change in terms of age, gender, race, cultural values, physical well-being, lifestyle preferences, ethnicity, educational background, religious preference, occupational background, and the like. Team effectiveness will be hampered if members hold false stereotypes about each other in terms of such differences.[49]

Although attitudes are changing, diversity all too often still is viewed more negatively than positively. This negative reaction may be due, in large part, to four underlying attitudes involving stereotypical false assumptions:

1. Diversity poses a threat to the organization's effective functioning.
2. Expressed discomfort with the dominant group's values is perceived as oversensitivity by minority groups.
3. Members of all groups want to become and should be more like the dominant group.
4. Equal treatment means the same treatment.

The goal of achieving diversity creates unique challenges in making it work for rather than against the long-term interests of individuals, teams, and organizations.[50] Once a we-versus-them distinction is perceived, people tend to discriminate against others who are different. Moreover, they tend to perceive these others as inferior, adversarial, and competitive.[51]

THE COMPETENT LEADER

The power of any group or team of people is the power of the mix. You may do all right, but you're not going to create any magic as a manager unless you bring together people with diverse perspectives.

Renée Wingo, Chief People Officer, Virgin Mobile USA

Norms

Norms *are the rules and patterns of behavior that are accepted and expected by members of a team.* They help define the behaviors that members believe to be necessary to help them reach their goals. Over time, every team establishes norms and enforces them on its members.[52] Norms often are more rigidly defined and enforced in informal groups—by peer pressure—than in formally organized teams. Such norms may further or inhibit achievement of organizational goals.

Norms versus Organizational Rules. Norms differ from organizational rules. Managers may write and distribute formal organizational rules to employees in the form of manuals and memoranda. At times, employees refuse to accept such rules or simply ignore them. In contrast, norms are informal, often unwritten expectations that are enforced by team members. If a member consistently violates these norms, the other members sanction the individual in some way. Sanctions may range from physical abuse to threats to ostracism to positive inducements (rewards) for compliance. Those who consistently adhere to the team's norms typically receive praise, recognition, and acceptance from the other members.

Team members may be only vaguely aware of some of the norms that are operating, but they should be made aware of these norms for at least two reasons. First, awareness increases the potential for individual and team freedom and maturity. Second, norms can positively or negatively influence the effectiveness of individuals, teams, and organizations. For example, team norms of improving quality are likely to reinforce an organization's formal quality standards.

Relation to Goals. Teams often adopt norms to help them attain their goals. Moreover, some organizational development efforts are aimed at helping members evaluate whether their team's norms are consistent with, neutral with respect to, or conflict with organizational goals. For example, a team may claim that one of its goals is to become more efficient. However, the team members' behaviors might be inconsistent with this stated goal; that is, members take long lunch breaks, let products that are not quite up to quality standards pass to customers, ignore some quality control steps in the production process, and the like.

Even if team members are aware of such norms, they may think of them as being necessary in order to achieve their own goals. Members may claim that producing more than the norm will "burn them out" or reduce product or service quality, resulting in lower long-term effectiveness. If a team's goals include minimizing managerial influence and increasing the opportunity for social interaction, its members could perceive norms restricting employee output as desirable.

Enforcing Norms. Teams don't establish norms for every situation. They generally form and enforce norms with respect to behaviors that they believe to be particularly important. Members are most likely to enforce norms under one or more of the following conditions:

- Norms aid in team survival and provide benefits. For instance, a team might develop a norm not to discuss individual salaries with other members in the organization to avoid calling attention to pay inequities.
- Norms simplify or make predictable the behaviors expected of members. When coworkers go out for lunch together, there can be some awkwardness about how to split the bill at the end of the meal. A group may develop a norm that results in some highly predictable way of behaving—split the bill evenly, take turns picking up the tab, or individually pay for what each ordered.
- Norms help avoid embarrassing interpersonal situations. Norms might develop about not discussing romantic involvements in or out of the office (so that differences in moral values don't become too obvious) or about not getting together socially in members' homes (so that differences in taste or income don't become too obvious).[53]

Norms express the central values and goals of the team and clarify what is distinctive about its identity. Employees of an advertising agency may wear unconventional but stylish clothing. Other professionals may view their doing so as deviant behavior. However, the advertising agency personnel may say, "We think of ourselves, personally and professionally, as trendsetters, and being fashionably dressed conveys that to our clients and the public."

Conforming to Norms. Conformity may result from the pressures to adhere to norms. The two basic types of conformity are compliance and personal acceptance. **Compliance conformity** *occurs when a person's behavior reflects the team's desired behavior because of real or imagined pressure.* In fact, some individuals may conform for a variety of reasons, even though they don't personally agree with the norms. They may think that the appearance of a united front is necessary for success in accomplishing team goals. On a more personal level, someone may comply in order to be liked and accepted by others. Meeting this need may apply especially to members of lower status in relation to those of higher status, such as a subordinate and a superior. Finally, someone may comply because the costs of conformity are much less than the costs of nonconformity, which could threaten the personal relationships in the team.

The second type of conformity is based on positive personal support of the norms. In **personal acceptance conformity,** *the individual's behavior and attitudes are consistent with the team's norms and goals.* This type of conformity is much stronger than compliance conformity because the person truly believes in the goals and norms.[54]

All of the preceding helps explain why some members of highly conforming teams may easily change their behavior (compliance type of conformity), whereas others may oppose changes and find them highly stressful (personal acceptance type of conformity). Without norms and reasonable conformity to them, teams would be chaotic and few tasks could be accomplished. Conversely, excessive and blind conformity may threaten expressions of individualism and a team's ability to change and learn.

Cohesiveness

Cohesiveness *is the strength of the members' desire to remain in a team and their commitment to it.* Cohesiveness is influenced by the degree of compatibility between team goals and individual members' goals. Members who have a strong desire to remain in a team and personally accept its goals form a highly cohesive team.[55]

This relationship between cohesiveness and conformity isn't a simple one. Low cohesiveness usually is associated with low conformity. However, high cohesiveness doesn't exist only in the presence of high conformity. High-performing teams may have high member commitment and a desire to stick together while simultaneously respecting and encouraging individual differences. This situation is more likely to develop when cohesiveness arises from trusting relationships and a common commitment to performance goals.

In confronting problems, members of a cohesive team are likely to encourage and support nonconformity. For example, a **hot group** *usually is small, and its members are turned on by an exciting and challenging goal.* A hot group completely engages its members, capturing their attention to the exclusion of almost everything else. For its members, the characteristics of a hot group are the same: vital, absorbing, full of debate and laughter, and very hard working.[56] Hot groups may arise from the need to deal with major challenges and changes, innovation, complex projects, or crises. For example, the development of the Boeing 777 jetliner spawned several hot groups.

Previously, we discussed groupthink as a potential team dysfunction. When decision-making teams are both conforming and cohesive, groupthink can emerge. Accordingly, highly cohesive teams need to guard against conformity and the poor decision making that is likely to result from it.

Impact on Effectiveness. Team performance and productivity can be affected by cohesiveness. **Productivity** *is the relationship between the inputs consumed (labor hours, raw materials, money, machines, and the like) and the outputs created (quantity and quality of goods and services).* Cohesiveness and productivity can be related, particularly for teams having high performance goals. If the team is successful in reaching those goals, the positive feedback of its successes may heighten member commitment and satisfaction. For example, a winning basketball team is more likely to be cohesive than one with a losing record, everything else being equal. Also, a cohesive basketball team may be more likely to win games. Conversely, low cohesiveness may interfere with a team's ability to win games. The reason is that members aren't as likely to communicate and cooperate to the extent necessary to reach the team's goals. High team cohesiveness actually may be associated with low efficiency if team goals conflict with organizational goals. Team members might think that the boss holds them accountable rather than that they hold themselves accountable to achieve results. Therefore, the relationships among cohesiveness, productivity, and performance can't be anticipated or understood unless the team's goals and norms are also known.

Leadership

Studies of teams emphasize the importance of emergent, or informal, leadership in accomplishing goals. An **informal leader** *is an individual whose influence in a team grows over time and usually reflects a unique ability to help the team reach its goals.*

Multiple Leaders. Team leadership is often thought of in terms of one person. The Mayo Clinic has different leaders over time and for different tasks. Moreover, because a team often has both relations-oriented and task-oriented goals, it may have two or more leaders. These two types of goals may require different skills and leadership styles, creating a total set of demands that one person may have difficulty satisfying. Informal leaders of teams aren't likely to emerge unless the formal leader ignores task-related responsibilities or lacks the necessary skills to carry them out. In contrast, relations-oriented leaders of teams are likely to emerge informally.

Effective Team Leaders. Leaders greatly influence virtually all aspects of team composition and behaviors (e.g., size, members and roles, norms, goals, and context). A leader often assumes a key role in the relations between the team and external groups, such as customers or suppliers, and often influences the selection of new members. Even when the team heavily participates in the selection process, the team leader may screen potential members, thereby limiting the number and range of candidates, as at the Mayo Clinic. Our previous two chapters on leadership provided many insights related to being an effective team leader. The seven key factors that influence team effectiveness discussed in this chapter so far (see Figure 8.3) make the creation and maintenance of effective teams no easy task.

The following Self Competency feature reports on Linda Dillman's team leadership practices. She is the executive vice president and chief information officer of Wal-Mart.[57]

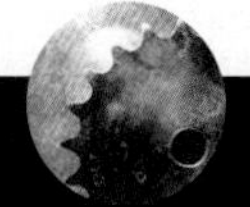

Self Competency

Linda Dillman's Team Leadership

Linda Dillman heads an information technology (IT) staff of more than 2,400 employees at Wal-Mart. She provides the overall strategic and team-based leadership on some 2,500 IT projects, the most significant of which is leading the way for RFID (radio-frequency identification) on the items sold by Wal-Mart. Dillman contends that collaboration is critical for speed, efficiency, and innovation. She notes: "The [application] development isn't successful if the infrastructure team that builds the physical system isn't successful. The infrastructure team isn't successful if the operations team doesn't know how to measure the system. They all are measured in their success based on the final impact to the business."

Dillman objects to being seen as the star behind any of Wal-Mart's IT projects, including the RFID project.

But she's been out in front collaborating with her competitors to make sure that the industry's efforts succeed, has been involved in helping to clear up confusion about RFID's costs and benefits, has worked with suppliers to overcome their initial skepticism, and helped drive the adoption of global standards for RFID. "The fun part about working with Wal-Mart [Information Systems Division] is we're treated as business enablers, not computer nerds," says Dan Phillips, VP of operations, data warehousing, databases, large systems, and communications, who was Dillman's first manager at Wal-Mart. "I've worked at companies where if you were in information systems, you are looked upon as a necessary evil or drain on expenses." Under Dillman's guidance, the division is viewed as just the opposite. "She approaches everything that you bring her as it is today on paper, but also looks at it with a new set of eyes—are there ways to make it better?" says Mark Porter, director of information security. "She's a businessperson first. And that's what I think is the best thing."

Typically, the best project leaders get promoted to managers, and Dillman's goal is to foster within those ranks "executives who manage people who manage projects." Dillman has twice-weekly team-building meetings for her division's senior executives and directors to promote the idea that "a constant sense of accomplishment means multiple people collaborating in the project from start to finish." "Under Linda, there's really been a focus on our people, making sure programs are in place that everyone can build a career," says Sam Moses, strategy manager, merchandising systems.

Dillman's father, Leonard Wayne Dillman, a U.S. Postal Service letter carrier for 35 years, had a big influence on her in this area. "He did things for other people for no reason other than it was the correct thing to do," she says. "It was a great role model in understanding what real success looks like." Dillman is clear that not even one project would happen if it weren't for the team at her back. She states: "There's such an overwhelming feeling when I receive recognition because it's really about the team. There's so little that I do; there's so much the team delivers."

For more information on Wal-Mart, visit the organization's home page at ***http://www.walmart.com.***

STIMULATING TEAM CREATIVITY

LEARNING OBJECTIVE

5. Explain how team creativity can be stimulated through the nominal group technique, traditional brainstorming, and electronic brainstorming.

Before discussing three of the many approaches for fostering team creativity, we note that the broader issues of stimulating organizational creativity are covered in Chapter 2. The stimulation of creativity is in the hands of managers as they think about and establish the work environment. For example, poorly designed motivational and reward systems will likely result in ineffective team approaches. One creativity expert comments: "The thing about creativity is that you can't tell at the outset which ideas will succeed and which will fail. . . . Now, leaders pay a lot of lip service to the notion of rewarding failure. . . . Often, they have a forgive-and-forget policy. Forgiveness is crucial but it's not enough. In order to learn from mistakes, it's even more important to forgive and *remember*."[58]

The three approaches presented in this section—the nominal group technique, traditional brainstorming, and electronic brainstorming—can assist team members with the process of defining problems, generating possible solutions, and evaluating alternative solutions.

Nominal Group Technique

The **nominal group technique** (NGT) *is a structured process designed to guide and stimulate creative team decision making where agreement is lacking or team members have incomplete knowledge about the nature of the problem or alternative solutions.* This technique has a special purpose: to make individual judgments the essential inputs in arriving at a team decision. Team members must pool their judgments in order to determine a satisfactory course of action leading to solution of a problem or resolution of an issue. It may also be used to identify desirable goals and the relative priorities that should be placed among them.

The NGT is most beneficial for (1) identifying the critical variables in a specific situation, (2) identifying key elements of a plan designed to implement a particular solution to some problem, or (3) establishing priorities with regard to the problem to be addressed and goals to be attained. The NGT isn't particularly well suited for routine team meetings that focus primarily on coordination or information exchange. Nor is it usually appropriate for negotiations that take place between incompatible groups (e.g., a union's representatives and a management committee).

The NGT consists of four distinct stages: generating ideas, recording ideas, clarifying ideas, and voting on ideas.[59] Various suggestions have been made for modifying or tailoring these stages to specific situations. Collaborative software technology is now available to aid in doing the tasks called for in these stages. Some research suggests that computer-assisted implementation of the NGT can be more effective than the traditional face-to-face process. In face-to-face sessions, the NGT should normally be used with no more than 12 individuals. When the NGT is implemented through the use of computer-based software, the groups may include up to 50 people. The participants sit at computer terminals in a room or at different locations. Issues are presented and responses are typed. Individual responses and comments are aggregated anonymously and posted on a projection screen or on each participant's PC screen. This approach may be very useful with virtual teams. Effectiveness is defined as generating more and better ideas in less time. Also, the computer-assisted approach enables the participants to remain at their normal locations, thus saving on travel time and costs.[60]

Generating Ideas. The first stage in the process is to have team members generate ideas. Each participant separately writes down ideas in response to a statement of the problem, a question, or some other central focus of the team. A question could be something as simple as "What problems do you think we should consider over the next year?" followed by "Take 5 minutes to write down some of your own ideas on a piece of paper." The generation of ideas or solutions privately by team members avoids the direct pressures of status differences or competition among members to be heard. This procedure, however, retains some of the peer and creative tension in the individual generated by the presence of others. This stage and the subsequent stages provide time for thinking and reflection to avoid premature choices among ideas.

Recording Ideas. The second stage is to record one idea (generated in the first stage) from each group member in turn on a flip chart, white board, or other device displayed for all team members to see. A variation is to have members submit their ideas anonymously on index cards. The process continues until the team members are satisfied that the list reflects all the ideas individually generated. This round-robin approach emphasizes equal participation by team members and avoids losing ideas that individuals consider significant. Listing them for everyone to see depersonalizes the ideas and reduces the potential for unnecessary conflict. Team members often are impressed and pleased with the list of ideas presented, which provides momentum and enthusiasm for continuing the process.

Clarifying Ideas. Team members then discuss in turn each idea on the list during the third stage. The purpose of this discussion is to clarify the meaning of each idea and allow team members to agree or disagree with any item. The intent is to present the logic behind the ideas and minimize misunderstanding, not to win arguments concerning the relative merits of the ideas. Differences of opinion aren't resolved at this stage, but rather by the voting procedure in the fourth stage.

Voting on Ideas. Using the list, which may contain 15 to 30 or more ideas, the team may proceed in one of several ways. Perhaps the most common voting procedure is to have team members individually select a specific number (say, 5) of the ideas that they believe are the most important. Each person writes these 5 ideas on index cards. The team leader then asks the members to rank their items from most to least important. The index cards are collected and the votes tabulated to produce a priority list. An alternative to this single vote is to feed back the results of a first vote, allow time for discussion of the results, and then vote again. Feedback and discussion are likely to result in a final decision that most closely reflects the members' actual preferences.

Regardless of format, the voting procedure determines the outcome of the meeting: a team decision that incorporates the individual judgments of the participants. The procedure is designed to document the collective decision and provide a sense of accomplishment and closure.

Organizational Use. The advantages of the NGT over traditional team discussion include greater emphasis and attention to idea generation, increased attention to each idea, and greater likelihood of balanced participation by each member. Nominal groups may not be superior when people are aware of existing problems and willing to communicate them. The approach may be most effective when certain blockages or problems exist in a team, such as domination by a few team members. The NGT is being used by managers and team leaders in numerous organizations—ranging from Coca-Cola to General Motors to the U.S. Marines.

Traditional Brainstorming

Traditional brainstorming *is a process whereby individuals state as many ideas as possible during a 20- to 60-minute period.* It is usually done with 5 to 12 people. Guidelines for brainstorming include (1) the wilder the ideas the better, (2) don't be critical of any ideas, (3) hitchhike on or combine previously stated ideas, and (4) quantity is wanted. The team setting for traditional brainstorming is supposed to generate many more and better ideas than if the same number of individuals worked alone.[61] Some research indicates that brainstorming may not be nearly as effective as once thought.

To brainstorm effectively is to think of an idea, express it, and get on with thinking of and expressing more new ideas. In face-to-face brainstorming, however, people may be prevented from doing so because someone else is talking. As a result, team members may get bogged down waiting for other people to finish talking. Team members also may be anxious about how others will view them if they express their ideas. This problem may be particularly acute when ideas can be interpreted as critical of current practice or when superiors or others who may affect team members' futures are present. Withholding ideas for these reasons defeats the purpose of brainstorming.[62]

The following Change Competency feature reveals how Play, a consulting firm, uses brainstorming, among other methods, to help its clients foster creativity.[63] This firm helps create ideas that make products better, strategies smarter, brands richer, and cultures stronger. Play's definition of creativity is "Look at more stuff, think about it harder." The firm is headquartered in Richmond, Virginia, and has additional offices in New York, Washington, D.C., and Mexico City. A few of its clients include BMW, Coca Cola, Frito-Lay, Kraft, and Rawlings.

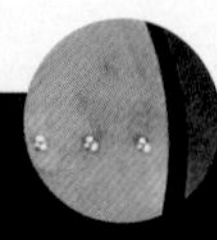

CHANGE COMPETENCY

CREATIVE PROCESS AT PLAY

At Play, the crux of creativity is putting old ideas together in new ways or giving common concepts a twist that makes them uncommon. "You can get better at doing that if you practice," says Andy Stefanovich, Play's cofounder. For example, there's a chalkboard in one hallway that has daily random topics, such as "H_2O," "city," "marathon running," or "teens." People who pass by the board then jot down related words and thoughts, which go into a file and are used in brainstorming sessions on those topics. Stefanovich states: "We get some of our best ideas from 'recreational' thinking. Like the brainstorming you do while getting to work or exercising, when your mind is not completely task-focused."

You can't come up with new ideas if you approach each problem the same way. Play's creativity exercises are built around "forcing connections"—making yourself connect seemingly unrelated ideas. For instance, coaches in brainstorming sessions give clients lists of random quotes from kindergartners and ask them to relate those sayings to their business problem.

One way to lose your fear of looking foolish and to come up with great ideas is to offer the worst possible idea you can think of, and then riff off it. When Play was asked by the Woolmark Company to come up with an event that would promote summer-weight wool clothing, the brainstorming team started with a strange question: What's the worst way to promote wool? How about letting a bunch of sheep loose in New York City? From there, the team refined it. The final iteration was to have wool-clad models walk sheep on leashes on Madison Avenue. The stunt snared more than 8 million media impressions—the number of times individuals observed wool-clad models walking sheep on leashes.

For more information on Play, visit the organization's home page at ***http://www.lookatmorestuff.com.***

Electronic Brainstorming

Electronic brainstorming *involves the use of collaborative software technology to enter and automatically disseminate ideas in real time to all team members, each of whom may be stimulated to generate other ideas.* For example, GroupSystems, headquartered in Broomfield, Colorado, in Denver's metropolitan area is one of the leading providers of electronic brainstorming software. For this approach to work, each team member must have a computer terminal that is connected to all other members' terminals. The software allows individuals to enter their ideas as they think of them. Every time an individual enters an idea, a random set of the team's ideas is presented on each person's screen. The individual can continue to see new random sets of ideas by pressing the appropriate key.[64]

Research on electronic brainstorming is encouraging. It tends to produce more novel ideas than traditional brainstorming. It also removes the main barrier of traditional brainstorming: Members seeing and hearing which ideas are whose. Electronic brainstorming permits anonymity and lets team members contribute more freely to idea generation. They need not fear "sounding like a fool" to other employees and managers when spontaneously generating ideas. These advantages appear to be greater for teams of seven or more people or where there is distrust among team members.[65]

Eastman Chemical used the electronic meeting software by GroupSystems. During one two-hour session, nine people generated 400 ideas to resolve customer problems. There was a need for more ideas and better methods to meet customers' needs. They had not been getting anywhere with traditional methods for resolving customer problems. After categorizing similar items among the 400 ideas generated, the team established common decision criteria to pick the top three ideas. The team used software tools for establishing and agreeing on the criteria. These ideas eventually led to the development of an action plan.

In another session with electronic brainstorming software from GroupSystems, 100 research and development managers and professionals at Eastman Chemical generated 2,200 ideas related to possible strategies to pursue during the next year or two. The team categorized, ranked, and reduced the ideas to eight core strategic opportunities and developed an action to select the top three. Henry Gonzales, the manager of polymer technology at Eastman Chemical comments: "We had more unusual ideas, a richer pool to choose from and we got to the point a lot faster."[66]

CHAPTER SUMMARY

In this chapter, we focused on developing the *teams competency*—the ability to develop, support, facilitate, and lead groups to achieve team and organizational goals. Groups and teams are classified in numerous ways. In organizations, a basic classification is by the group's primary purpose, including informal groups and task groups (now commonly called teams). Informal groups develop out of the day-to-day activities, interactions, and sentiments of the members for the purpose of meeting their security or social needs. Informal groups may support, oppose, or be indifferent to formal organizational goals. Effective groups, formal or informal, have similar basic characteristics.

1. State the basic characteristics of groups, including informal groups.

Functional teams include members from the same functional department, such as marketing, production, or finance. Problem-solving teams include individuals from a particular area of responsibility who address specific problems such as cost overruns or a decline in quality. Cross-functional teams include individuals from a number of specialties and departments who deal with problems that cut across areas. Self-managed teams include employees who must work together daily to manufacture an entire product (or major identifiable component) or provide an entire service to a set of customers. For maximum effectiveness, self-managed teams need to be empowered; that is, have a strong sense of potency, meaningfulness, autonomy, and impact. A variety of organizational, team, and individual factors must be satisfied for introduction of self managed teams. Any type of task group could function somewhat or primarily as a virtual team, which collaborate through various information technologies. Global teams refer to members from a variety of countries and are, therefore, often separated significantly by time, distance, culture, and native language.

2. Describe the attributes of six types of work-related teams.

The five-stage developmental model focuses on forming, storming, norming, performing, and adjourning. The issues and challenges a team faces change with each stage. Teams do not necessarily develop in the straightforward manner presented in this model, especially when the members possess strong team management and related competencies. Several other models are available to aid in understanding the developmental sequence of teams.

3. Explain the five-stage model of team development.

Team dynamics and effectiveness are influenced by the interplay of context, goals, size, member roles, norms, cohesiveness, and leadership. One type of changing

4. Describe seven key factors that influence team effectiveness.

contextual influence on how teams work, interact, and network with other teams is that of information technology, especially the rapid developments in collaborative software systems. Other contextual influences are the nature of the organization's reward system and how it fits the basic value orientations of team members, especially in terms of individualism and collectivism. Team members need to clearly understand and accept team goals as outcomes desired by each member for the team as a whole. Team size can substantially affect the dynamics among the members and the ability to create a sense of mutual accountability. Teams of about 16 or more members typically break into smaller task groups. Member may take on task-oriented, relationship-oriented, or self-oriented roles. Norms differ from rules in important ways and can have a positive or negative impact on performance. The pressures to adhere to norms may result in either compliance conformity or personal acceptance conformity. Another factor having an impact on the effectiveness of teams is cohesiveness, which is related to conformity, groupthink, and productivity. Team leaders may be selected formally or emerge informally.

5. Explain how team creativity can be stimulated through the nominal group technique, traditional brainstorming, and electronic brainstorming.

The nominal group technique (NGT) is a structured process designed to guide and stimulate creativity where agreement is lacking or there is incomplete knowledge about the problem or alternative solutions. It consists of four distinct stages: (1) generating ideas, (2) recording ideas, (3) clarifying ideas, and (4) voting on ideas. It is especially useful when agreement is lacking or team members have incomplete knowledge as to the nature of a problem. Traditional brainstorming involves using a set of guidelines for a face-to-face session in which the individuals state as many ideas as possible during a 20- to 60-minute period. Electronic brainstorming involves the use of collaborative software technology by each team member to enter into a computer and automatically disseminate ideas to all other members.

KEY TERMS AND CONCEPTS

Cohesiveness
Compliance conformity
Context
Cross-functional team
Electronic brainstorming
Free rider
Friendship group
Functional team
Global team
Group
Groupthink
Hot group
Informal group
Informal leader
Nominal group technique
Norms
Personal acceptance conformity
Problem-solving team
Productivity
Relations-oriented role
Self-managed team
Self-oriented role
Sucker effect
Superordinate goals
Task group
Task-oriented role
Team
Team empowerment
Team goals
Traditional brainstorming
Virtual team

DISCUSSION QUESTIONS

1. Assume that you had to complete a class project as a member of a virtual team that could meet face to face only twice. Identify at least four special challenges that your virtual team would face in undertaking the project.
2. Based on your answers to the questions in Table 8.1, what actions are needed to increase the degree of empowerment for this team? Are those actions feasible?

3. For a team or group of which you have been a member, describe its environment (context) in terms of technology, organizational rules, and management's influence. In what ways did the context appear to affect the team's or group's effectiveness?
4. What were the formal and informal goals of the team or group you identified in Question 3? Were the informal goals consistent and supportive of the formal goals? Explain.
5. Think of one informal and one task group of which you are or have been a member during the past two years. In terms of the types of groups and teams presented in this chapter, how would you classify each of them? Did either of them appear to be of more than one type? Explain.
6. For one of the groups you identified in Question 5, how would you evaluate it in terms of the basic characteristics of effective groups?
7. What are the similarities and differences between the nominal group technique (NGT) and electronic brainstorming?
8. Think of a new team or group in which you participated during the past three years. Describe and explain the degree to which the development of this team or group matched the five-stage model of team development discussed in this chapter.
9. If you were employed at the Mayo Clinic, what would you tend to like or dislike about its team-based approach?

EXPERIENTIAL EXERCISE AND CASE

Experiential Exercise: Team Competency

Team Assessment Inventory[67]

Instructions:

Think of a student or work-related team in which you have been a member and that was formed to achieve one or more goals. This team could be associated with a specific course, student organization, or job.

1. Evaluate the *success* of your team on each *item* in this instrument. Use the following scale and assign a value from 1 to 5 to each item. Record the number next to each numbered item. How successful do you think your team was on each of the items?

   1 Not at all successful (well below expectations)
   2 Somewhat successful (though below expectations)
   3 Moderately successful (meets expectations)
   4 Fairly high level of success (exceeds expectations)
   5 Very high level of success (far exceeds expectations)

2. Based on the item assessments and any other related dimensions for each factor, evaluate the *overall success* of your team on each of the seven summary *factors*. Sum the item scores for each factor. Divide the sum (total) by the number of items in that factor.

I. Goals Factor

_____ 1. Team members understood the goals and scope of the team.

_____ 2. Team members were committed to the team goals, and took ownership of them.

Overall Goals Factor:

Add the scores for items 1 through 2 and divide by 2 = ________.

II. Team Performance Management Factor

_____ 3. Individual roles, responsibilities, goals, and performance expectations were specific, challenging, and accepted by team members.

_____ 4. Team goals and performance expectations were specific, challenging, and accepted by team members.

_____ 5. The workload of the team was shared more or less equally among team members.

_____ 6. Everyone on my team did his or her fair share of the work.

_____ 7. No one on my team depended on other team members to do his or her work.

_____ 8. Nearly all the members on my team contributed equally to the work.

Overall Team Performance Management Factor:

Add the scores for items 3 through 8 and divide by 6 = ________.

III. Team Basics Factor

_____ 9. My team had enough members to handle the tasks assigned (i.e., small enough to meet and communicate frequently and easily, and yet not too small for the work required of the team).

_____ 10. The team as a whole possessed the competency levels required to achieve its goals.

_____ 11. The team members possessed the complementary competencies required to achieve the team's goals.

Overall Team Basics Factor:

Add the scores for items 9 through 11 and divide by 3 = ________.

IV. Team Processes Factor

_____ 12. My team was able to solve problems and make decisions.

_____ 13. My team was able to encourage desirable but to discourage undesirable team conflict.

_____ 14. My team members were able to communicate, listen, and give constructive feedback.

_____ 15. Team meetings were conducted effectively.

_____ 16. Members of my team were very willing to share information with other team members about our work.

_____ 17. Members of my team cooperated to get the work done.

_____ 18. Being on my team gave me the opportunity to work on a team and to provide support for other team members.

_____ 19. My team increased my opportunities for positive social interaction.

_____ 20. Members of my team helped each other when necessary.

Overall Team Processes Factor:

Add the scores for items 12 through 20 and divide by 9 = _______.

V. Team Spirit Factor

_____ 21. Members of my team had great confidence that the team could perform effectively.

_____ 22. My team took on the tasks assigned and completed them.

_____ 23. My team had a lot of team enthusiasm.

_____ 24. My team had high morale.

_____ 25. The team developed norms (i.e., expectations concerning team member behavior) that contributed to effective team functioning and performance.

_____ 26. Team members invested energy intensely on behalf of the team.

Overall Team Spirit Factor:

Add the scores for items 21 through 26 and divide by 6 = _______.

VI. Team Outcomes Factor

_____ 27. The team attained measurable results (if objective or quantifiable measures were available).

_____ 28. The product or service delivered by the team met or exceeded the expectations of those receiving it.

_____ 29. My team carried out its work in such a way as to maintain or enhance its ability to work together on future team tasks.

_____ 30. Generally, the team experience served to satisfy, rather than frustrate, the personal needs of team members.

Overall Team Outcomes Factor:

Add the scores for items 27 through 30 and divide by 4 = _______.

VII. Team Learning Factor

_____ 31. We took time to figure out ways to improve team processes.

_____ 32. Team members often spoke up to test assumptions about issues under discussion.

_____ 33. Team members got all the information they needed from others.

_____ 34. Someone always made sure that we stopped to reflect on the team's processes.

_____ 35. The team as a whole asked for feedback from others as it progressed.

_____ 36. The team actively reviewed its own progress and performance.

Overall Team Learning Factor:

Add the scores for items 31 through 36 and divide by 6 = _______.

Interpretation

An overall score of 4 or 5 on a factor suggests considerable success (exceeding expectations and success). An overall score of 3 on a factor suggests a satisfactory level of success and a feeling of just "okay." An overall score of 1 or 2 on a factor suggests that the team processes needed considerable improvement. You might consider all seven factors as a whole to arrive at a final summary assessment. Insights for action steps are likely to be learned through each factor and the specific items that are in it.

Case: Team Competency

Artisan Industries' Team[68]

Part I

In mid October, 29-year-old Bill Meister, president of Artisan Industries, had to meet with his management team to consider increasing prices. A year before, he had taken over the failing $13-million-a-year wooden gift manufacturing company from his father. It had been a hectic year, but he had stopped the company's slide toward bankruptcy. However, much work remained to be done to improve almost every area of the company.

The following team members met in his office at 11:00 A.M. one morning.

1. Bob was the 30-year-old vice president of finance. He had been with the company 3 years, coming from the staff of a major accounting firm. He headed accounting and the office staff in general.
2. Cal was 35 years old and had been with the company 8 years. Although he had a bachelor's degree in accounting, he had held many jobs in the company. Currently, he was installing a small computer system and reported directly to Bob.
3. Edith was Bill Meister's 40-year-old sister and manager of routine sales from the home office. The external sales force that called on firms was made up of independent sales representatives. Only clerical people reported to Edith. She had no college training.
4. Consultant: A 40-year-old woman with bachelors and MBA degrees. She had 10 years experience in consulting.

Bill called the meeting to order in the presence of a management consultant who happened to be visiting to discuss other plans for improvement.

Bill: OK, we've been discussing the need for a price increase for some time now. Bob recommends increasing prices 16 percent right away. I'd like to get all of your thoughts on this. Bob?

Bob: My analysis of profit statements to date indicates that a 16 percent increase is necessary right now if we are to have any profit this year. My best estimate is that we're losing money on every order we take. We haven't raised prices in over a year and have no choice but to do so now.

Cal: I agree. What's the sense in taking orders on which we lose money?

Bob: Exactly. If we raise prices across the board immediately, we can have a profit of about $500,000 at year end.

Cal: It would've been better to have increased prices with our price list last May or June, rather than doing it on each order here in the middle of our sales season, but we really have no choice now.

Bob: There's just no way we can put it off.

Bill (pausing, looking around the room): So, you all recommend a price increase at this time?

Cal and **Bob:** Yes.

Bob: We can't wait to increase prices as new orders are written in the field or through a new price list. Right now, we already have enough of a backlog of orders accepted at the old prices and orders awaiting our acknowledgement to fill the plant until the holiday season ends in six to eight weeks. We must accept orders only at the new prices.

Cal: If we acknowledge all the orders we have now, like that 30-page one Edith has for $321,000, then the price change won't even be felt this year.

Bob: No, we should acknowledge any orders at the old prices. I would hold the orders and send each customer a printed letter telling them of the price increase and asking them to reconfirm their orders with an enclosed mailer if they still want them.

Cal: Orders already acknowledged would keep the plant busy until they responded.

Bill: So, is this the best thing to do?

Bob: We're in business to make money; we'd be crazy not to raise prices!

Bill: Edith, you look unhappy. What do you think?

Edith (shrugging): I don't know.

Bob (visibly impatient): We're losing money on every order.

Edith: I'm just worried about trying to raise prices right in the middle of the season.

Cal: Well, if we wait, we might as well forget it.

Bob: Just what would you suggest we do, Edith?

Edith: I don't know. (Pause.) This order (picking up the 30-page order) took the salesman a month to work up with the customer. There are over 175 items on it, and the items must be redistributed to the customer's nine retail outlets in time for the holidays. I'm worried about it.

Bob: It's worthless to us as it is.

Cal: Look, in our letter, we can mention inflation and that this is our first increase in a long while. Most customers will understand this. We've got to try. It's worth the risk, isn't it, Edith?
(Edith shrugs.)

Bill: What do you suggest, Edith?

Edith: I don't know. We need the increase, but it bothers me.

Bob: Business is made of tough decisions; managers are paid to make 'em.
(All become quiet, look around the room, and finally look at Bill.)

Questions for Part I

1. Explain what happened at this meeting: What was each person's role? What was each person doing and trying to do? Was it a good meeting? Why or why not?
2. What is the decision going to be? Give all the specifics of the decision.
3. What do you think of the decision? Can you think of ways to improve on it?
4. What would you do if you were there?

Part II

Consultant (calmly): I think Edith has raised a good point. *You are* considering making a big move right in the middle of your busy season. It will cause problems. If you can't avoid the increase, then what can you do to avoid or minimize the problems?

Bob (hostile and obviously disgusted): It would be

ridiculous to put off the price increase.

Consultant (calmly): That may be true, but is it being done in the best way? There are always alternatives to consider. I don't think you are doing a good job of problem solving here. (Pause.) Even with the basic idea of an increase, it can be done poorly or done well. There is room for more thought. How can it be done with the least penalty? (All are quiet as the consultant looks around the team, waiting for anyone to add comments. Hearing none, she continues.) For example, by the time you mail them a letter and they think about it and mail it back, two or three weeks may pass. The price increase wouldn't take effect until the season is almost over. How can you get the increase to make money right away? And though you are bound to lose some orders, what can you do to minimize these losses? (She pauses to allow comments).

Edith: Yes, that's what I meant.

Consultant: On this order, for example (picking up the $321,000 order), we could call them right now and explain the situation and possibly be shipping at the higher prices this afternoon.

Bob: (with no hostility and with apparent positive attitude): OK. I will call them as soon as we leave here.

Cal: We have a pile of orders awaiting acknowledgement...

Bob: Right, we can get some help and pick out the bigger orders and start calling them this afternoon.

Consultant: How about involving the sales force? Some could lose their commissions because clients cancel their orders.

Edith: Yes, the salespeople know the customers best. We should call them to contact the customer. They got the order and know the customer's needs. But we will have to convince the salespeople of the necessity for the increase. I can start getting in touch with them by phone right away.

Bob: OK, we can handle the bigger orders personally by phone and use a letter for the small ones.

Consultant: Why not make it so that no action keeps the order? Tell them that we are saving their place in our shipping schedule and will go ahead and ship if they don't contact you in 5 to 7 days. Is it best to put the control in their hands?

Edith: That bothered me. Increasing the price is serious, and we need to handle it carefully if it's to work. I think most people will go ahead and accept the merchandise.

Bob: Edith and I can get together this afternoon on the letter. (All become silent again.)

Bill: OK, can you all get started after lunch? Let's meet in the morning to see how it's going.

Questions for Part II

1. What do you think of the decision now? Is it better than the first one? Why might you call the first decision *suboptimal*?
2. Would the team have made the new decision without the help of the consultant? Why or why not?
3. Initially, the team was not involved in problem solving. Why wasn't it?
4. What does this incident say about empowerment of the management team and the work environment at Artisan? Using the items in Table 8.1, evaluate this team's empowerment.
5. What does this case illustrate about team problem solving? About communication?

CHAPTER 9

Managing Conflict and Negotiating Effectively

LEARNING OBJECTIVES

When you have finished studying this chapter, you should be able to:

1. Describe the four basic levels of conflict in organizations.
2. Explain five interpersonal conflict-handling strategies and the conditions for their use.
3. Discuss the core stages, strategies, and influences in negotiations.
4. State several of the unique aspects and recommendations for negotiating across cultures.

Preview Case: KLA-Tencor

LEVELS OF CONFLICT
- Intrapersonal Conflict
- Interpersonal Conflict
- Intragroup Conflict
- Intergroup Conflict
- *Diversity Competency—Georgia Power's Affinity Groups*

INTERPERSONAL CONFLICT-HANDLING STYLES
- Avoiding Style
- Forcing Style
- Accommodating Style
- Collaborating Style
- Compromising Style
- Effectiveness of Styles
- *Communication Competency—ATM Express*

NEGOTIATION IN CONFLICT MANAGEMENT
- Stages of Negotiation
- Distributive Negotiations Strategy
- Integrative Negotiations Strategy
- *Teams Competency—Cinergy's Residential Collections Negotiations*
- Four Influences on Negotiation Strategies

NEGOTIATING ACROSS CULTURES
- Differences in Negotiators
- Cross-Cultural Emotional Intelligence
- Negotiation Process
- *Across Cultures Competency—Chinese Negotiating Style*

CHAPTER SUMMARY

KEY TERMS AND CONCEPTS

DISCUSSION QUESTIONS

EXPERIENTIAL EXERCISES

KLA-TENCOR

PREVIEW CASE

KLA-Tencor is one of the largest and best-run makers of semiconductor production equipment in the world. The firm is headquartered in San Jose, California, and has approximately 5,200 employees.

At KLA-Tencor, a materials executive in each division oversees a number of buyers who purchase the materials and component parts for machines that the division makes. When negotiating a companywide contract with a supplier, a buyer often must work with the company commodity manager, as well as with buyers from other divisions who deal with the same supplier. There used to be conflict, for example, over the delivery terms for components supplied to two or more divisions under the contract. Today, in such cases, the commodity manager and the division materials executive encourage the division buyer to (1) consider the needs of the other divisions, (2) identify alternatives that might best address the collective needs of the different divisions, and (3) assess the standards to be applied in assessing the trade-offs between alternatives. The aim is to help the buyer see solutions that haven't been considered and to resolve the conflict with the buyer in the other division.

Initially, this approach required more time from senior managers than if they had simply made the decisions themselves. But it has now paid off in fewer disputes that senior managers need to resolve, speedier contract negotiation, and improved contract terms both for the company as a whole and for multiple divisions. For example, the buyers from three KLA-Tencor product divisions locked horns with each other over a global contract with a key supplier. At issue was the trade-off between (1) the supplier's level of liability for materials it needs to purchase in order to fulfill orders and (2) the flexibility granted the KLA-Tencor divisions in modifying the size of the orders and their required lead times.

Each division wanted a different balance between these two factors. The buyers took the conflict to their senior managers, wondering if they should try to negotiate different deals into the contract or pick among them. After being coached by a person to consider how each division's business shaped its preference and with the use of brainstorming, the buyers and commodity manager arrived at a creative solution that worked for everyone. They would request a clause in the contract that allowed them to increase and decrease flexibility in order of volume and lead time, with corresponding changes in supplier liability, as required by changing market conditions.[1]

*For more information on KLA-Tencor, visit the organization's home page at **http://www.kla-tencor.com**.*

The need to manage conflict occurs every day in organizations. **Conflict** *refers to a process in which one party (person or group) perceives that its interests are being opposed or negatively affected by another party.*[2] This definition implies incompatible concerns among the people involved and includes a variety of conflict issues and events. **Conflict management** *consists of diagnostic processes, interpersonal styles, and negotiation strategies that are designed to avoid unnecessary conflict and reduce or resolve excessive conflict.* The ability to understand and correctly diagnose conflict is essential to managing it.

In this chapter, we examine conflict and negotiation from several perspectives. First, we present the basic dimensions of conflict and note different attitudes about it. Second, we identify four levels of conflict found in organizations. Third, we discuss five interpersonal styles in conflict management and the conditions under which each style may be appropriate. Fourth, we address the types of negotiation, and basic negotiation strategies, and highlight the role of third-party mediation in the negotiation process. Fifth, we discuss some of the complications and recommendations for negotiations across cultures.

Our attitude is that conflict may sometimes be desirable and at other times destructive. In Chapter 16, we will review a variety of destructive conflicts that were related to high levels of stress and workplace aggression. Although some types of conflict can be avoided and reduced, other types of conflict have to be properly managed. The balanced approach is sensitive to the consequences of conflict, ranging from negative outcomes (loss of skilled employees, sabotage, low quality of work, stress, and even violence) to positive outcomes (creative alternatives, increased motivation and commitment, high quality of work, and personal satisfaction). Top-level managers at KLA-Tencor effectively guided the buyers from the several divisions to resolve their conflicts over a global contract.

The balanced approach recognizes that conflict occurs in organizations whenever interests collide. Sometimes, employees will think differently, want to act differently, and seek to pursue different goals. When these differences divide individuals, they must be managed constructively.[3] How easily or effectively conflict can be managed depends on various factors, such as how important the issue is to the people involved and whether strong leadership is available to address it. Table 9.1 identifies some of the factors that distinguish types of conflict that are difficult to resolve from types of conflict that are easier to resolve.

TABLE 9.1 Effects of Various Dimensions of Conflict

DIMENSION	DIFFICULT TO RESOLVE	EASY TO RESOLVE
The issue itself	A matter of principle	Simply dividing up something
Size of the stakes	Large	Small
Continuity of interaction	Single transaction	Long-term relationship
Characteristics of participants' "groups"	Disorganized, with weak leadership	Cohesive, with strong leadership
Involvement of third parties	No neutral third party available	Trusted, prestigious, neutral third party available

Source: Adapted from Greenhalgh, L. Managing conflict. In R. J. Lewicki, D. M. Saunders, and J. W. Minton (eds.), *Negotiation*, 3rd ed. Boston: Irwin/McGraw-Hill, 1999, 7.

LEVELS OF CONFLICT

LEARNING OBJECTIVE

1. Describe the four basic levels of conflict in organizations.

Four primary levels of conflict may be present in organizations: intrapersonal (within an individual), interpersonal (between individuals), intragroup (within a group), and intergroup (between groups). Figure 9.1 suggests that these levels are often cumulative and interrelated. For example, an employee struggling with whether to stay on a certain job may show hostility toward coworkers, thus triggering interpersonal conflicts.

FIGURE 9.1 Levels of Conflict in Organizations

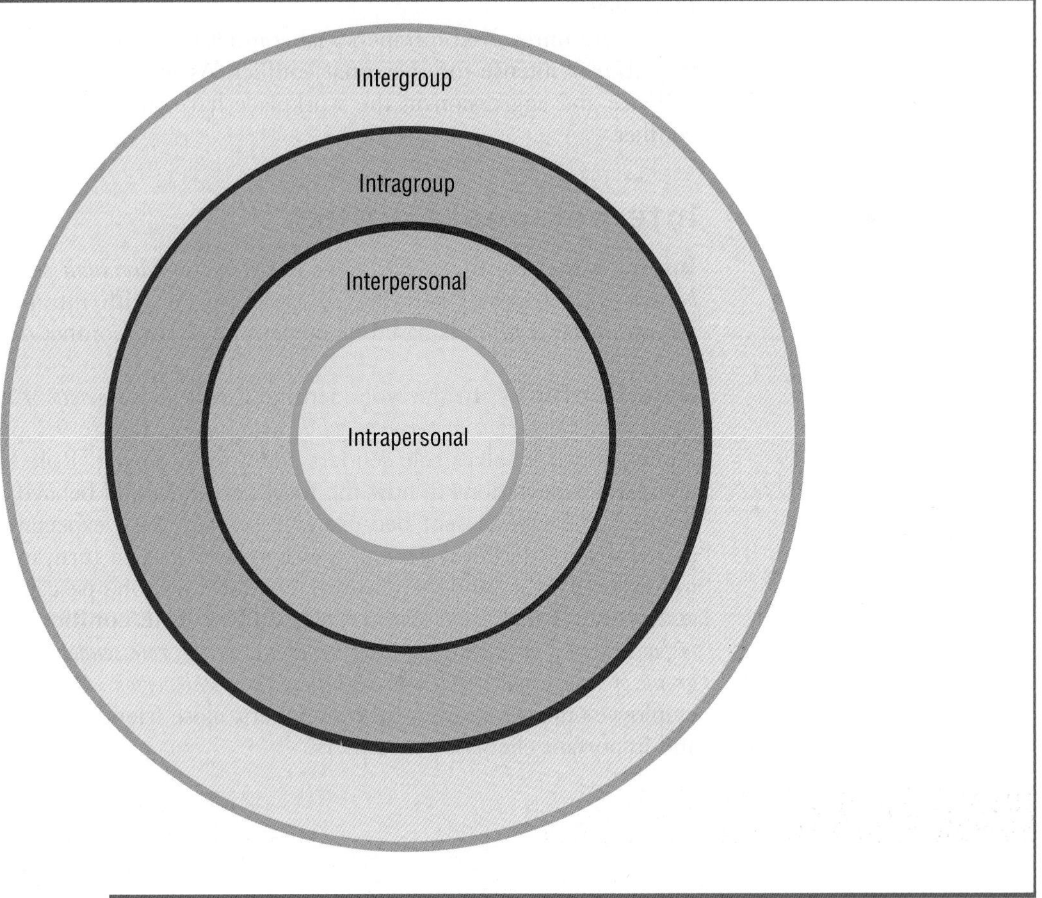

Intrapersonal Conflict

Intrapersonal conflict *occurs within an individual and usually involves some form of goal, cognitive, or affective conflict.* It is triggered when a person's behavior will result in outcomes that are mutually exclusive. Inner tensions and frustrations commonly result. For example, a graduating senior may have to decide between jobs that offer different challenges, pay, security, and locations. Trying to make such a decision may create one (or more) of three basic types of intrapersonal goal conflict:

1. *Approach–approach conflict* means that an individual must choose between two or more alternatives, each of which is expected to have a positive outcome (e.g., a choice between two jobs that appear to be equally attractive).

2. *Avoidance–avoidance conflict* means that an individual must choose between two or more alternatives, each of which is expected to have a negative outcome (e.g., relatively low pay or extensive out-of-town traveling).
3. *Approach–avoidance conflict* means that an individual must decide whether to do something that is expected to have both positive and negative outcomes (e.g., accepting an offer of a good job in a bad location).

Many decisions involve the resolution of intrapersonal goal conflict. The intensity of intrapersonal conflict generally increases under one or more of the following conditions: (1) Several realistic alternative courses of action are available for handling the conflict, (2) the positive and negative consequences of the alternative courses of action are roughly equal, or (3) the source of conflict is important to the individual.

Severe unresolved intrapersonal conflict within employees, customers, or others may trigger intense interpersonal conflict. As we will discuss in Chapter 16, much violence and aggression in the workplace have their source in severe intrapersonal conflict.

Interpersonal Conflict

Interpersonal conflict *occurs when two or more individuals perceive that their attitudes, behaviors, or preferred goals are in opposition.* As with intrapersonal conflict, much interpersonal conflict is based on some type of role conflict or role ambiguity.

Role Conflict. In the work setting, a **role** *is the group of tasks and behaviors that others expect a person to perform while doing a job.* Figure 9.2 presents a role episode model, which involves role senders and a focal person. Role senders are individuals who have expectations of how the focal person should behave. A role episode begins before a message is sent because role senders have expectations, perceptions, and evaluations of the focal person's behaviors. These, in turn, influence the actual role messages that the senders transmit. The focal person's perceptions of these messages and pressures may then lead to role conflict. **Role conflict** *occurs when a focal person responds with behaviors that serve as inputs to the role senders' process.* A **role set** *is the group of role senders that directly affect the focal person.* A role set might include the employee's manager, other team members, close friends, immediate family members, and important clients or customers.

FIGURE 9.2 Role Episode Model

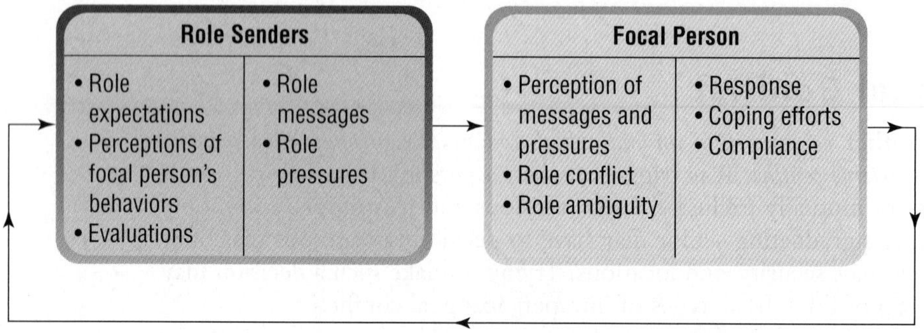

Source: Based on Kahn, R.L., et al. *Organizational Stress: Studies in Role Conflict and Ambiguity.* New York: John Wiley & Sons, 1964, 26.

Four types of role conflict may occur as a result of incompatible messages and pressures from the role set:

- *Intrasender role conflict* may occur when different messages and pressures from a single member of the role set are incompatible.
- *Intersender role conflict* may occur when the messages and pressures from one role sender oppose messages and pressures from one or more other senders.
- *Interrole conflict* may occur when role pressures associated with membership in one group are incompatible with pressures stemming from membership in other groups.
- *Person–role conflict* may occur when role requirements are incompatible with the focal person's own attitudes, values, or views of acceptable behavior. Intrapersonal conflict typically accompanies this type of role conflict.[4]

Role Ambiguity. **Role ambiguity** *is the uncertainty and lack of clarity surrounding expectations about a single role.* Like role conflict, severe role ambiguity causes stress and triggers subsequent coping behaviors. These coping behaviors often include (1) initiating aggressive action (e.g., verbal abuse, theft, and violence) and hostile communication, (2) withdrawing, or (3) approaching the role sender or senders to attempt joint problem solving. Research findings suggest that high levels of role conflict and role ambiguity have numerous dramatic effects, including stress reactions, aggression, hostility, and withdrawal behaviors (turnover and absenteeism).[5] Stress is a common reaction to severe role conflict and role ambiguity (see Chapter 16). However, effective managers and professionals possess the ability to cope with the many ambiguities inherent in their roles.

Intragroup Conflict

Intragroup conflict *refers to disputes among some or all of a group's members, which often affect a group's dynamics and effectiveness.* For example, family-run businesses can be especially prone to intragroup and other types of conflict. Such conflicts typically become more intense when an owner-founder approaches retirement, actually retires, or dies. Only 3 in 10 family-run businesses make it to the second generation, and only 1 in 10 survives into the third generation. The biggest obstacles to succession are the relationships among the family members who own the business and bear responsibility for keeping it alive for another generation. What determines whether a family business soars or nosedives? It depends, in large part, on the respect that family members give each other in the workplace, their willingness to take on roles at work different from those they have at home, and their ability to manage conflict.[6]

Siblings can have the most volatile and complex family relationships—and the issues become magnified in a business. The conflicts are often practical. Can one sibling work for another? Should birth order determine hierarchy? Should siblings give in to the one who whines the most to preserve peace, then work around him or her?

The answers depend on the situation. Underlying these problems, there are often some ongoing factors. Although they share parents and many memories, siblings often must come to grips with having different attitudes and preferences because they grew up at different times in a changing family environment. The fact that parents try to interest their children in the family business but give them little assistance in understanding how to work with each other puts the siblings in a double bind: an obligation with no road map.[7] The insights provided in this chapter and throughout this book provide at least a portion of the needed road map. There are many other types of intragroup conflicts in organizations, as we have discussed in previous chapters, especially in the previous chapter on developing and leading teams.[8]

Intergroup Conflict

Intergroup conflict *refers to opposition, disagreements, and disputes between groups or teams.* At times, intergroup conflict is intense, drawn out, and costly to those involved. Under high levels of competition and conflict, the groups develop attitudes toward each other that are characterized by distrust, rigidity, a focus only on self-interest, failure to listen, and the like.

Intergroup conflict within organizations can occur horizontally across teams, departments, or divisions and vertically between different levels of the organization, such as between top management and first-level employees. In some companies, this type of vertical conflict is clearly seen in union–management disputes through collective bargaining. Horizontal conflicts often occur between manufacturing and marketing or internal auditors and the other business functions.

Let's consider four of the various sources of intergroup conflict:[9]

- *Perceived goal incompatibility.* The perception and perhaps the reality of goal incompatibility is probably the greatest source of intergroup conflict. The potential conflicts between marketing and manufacturing are significant because some of the goals for these two functions may be at odds. A priority marketing goal to achieve sales (for which bonuses and commissions are received) is to satisfy the unique requests of customers. Manufacturing often has the priority goal of long production runs to maximize efficiency. Accordingly, marketing states: "Our customers demand variety." Manufacturing counters: "The product line is already too broad—all we get are short, uneconomical runs."
- *Perceived differentiation.* The greater the number of ways in which groups see themselves as different from each other, the greater the potential for conflicts between them. These differences may actually be sources of strength, such as the specialized expertise and insights that those from different functions and backgrounds contribute to achieve the organization's goals. Unfortunately, these differences too often serve as the base for stimulating distrust and conflicts between the groups or teams.
- *Task interdependency.* **Task interdependency** *refers to the interrelationships required between two or more groups in achieving their goals.* For example, marketing needs manufacturing to produce the required products on a timely and cost-effective basis. Manufacturing needs marketing to generate sales of those products that it is able to produce. In general, as task interdependency increases, the potential for conflict between the groups increases. Of course, there is often task interdependency between organizations. For example, the National Hockey League owners canceled the 2004–2005 season with its players. Both sides knew that without cooperation, there could be no NHL hockey played in the United States or Canada. They were interdependent with each other. Eventually, the strike was settled and league play resumed in October 2005.
- *Perceived limited resources.* The perception of limited resources creates the condition for groups competing and engaging in conflict over the available resources. Organizations have limited money, physical facilities, and human resources to allocate among different groups. The groups may think they need more of the resources than are available to meet the goals for which they will be held accountable.

Diversity-Based Conflict. In previous chapters, we've discussed how serious intergroup conflicts may arise from workforce diversity. The most difficult diversity-based conflicts to resolve in organizations are related to issues of race, gender, ethnicity, and religion. Leading organizations adhere to the letter and spirit of laws and regulations related to nondiscrimination and affirmative action to reduce diversity-based conflicts. In addition, these leading organizations are proactive in other ways to prevent, minimize, surface, and resolve diversity-based conflicts.[10]

One of the ways leading organizations are attempting to be proactive in preventing or resolving diversity-based conflicts is through the acceptance and support of affinity groups—sometimes called employee networks, advocacy groups, support groups, or resource groups.[11] Within organizations, **affinity groups** *are typically voluntary, employee-driven groups that are organized around a particular shared interest, background, or goal.* These groups are usually initiated by employees and typically focus on a shared interest or characteristic, such as race, ethnicity, gender, or sexual orientation. Each group's main goals are to create an open forum for idea exchange, strengthen the links to and within diverse communities, and represent their employee-related interests and goals to higher management. Affinity groups may be composed of African Americans, Asian Americans, Hispanics, older workers, workers with disabilities, gays and lesbians, transgender people, women, or members of religious groups, and other classifications. They frequently serve as advisory groups to higher management. They are open to all employees of the organization. Each group usually has a structure with leaders, periodic meetings, and goals.[12]

The following Diversity Competency feature reports on the use of affinity groups and other initiatives to prevent, reduce, and resolve diversity-related conflicts at Georgia Power.[13] This firm is a subsidiary of Georgia Southern. It provides electricity to 2 million customers in Georgia and has more than 8,700 employees.

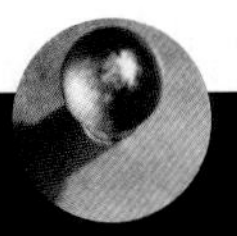

DIVERSITY COMPETENCY

GEORGIA POWER'S AFFINITY GROUPS

Georgia Power encourages employees to form affinity groups they can turn to for support. Any Georgia Power employee can initiate the process to form an affinity group. Employees must develop a business case and submit it to the Affinity Group Review Board, which includes a cross section of people in the company with various beliefs, personalities, life experiences, and work experiences.

A group becomes an officially recognized and company-supported affinity group upon approval by the Affinity Group Review Board. Two of the affinity groups are as follows:

- *African-American Women's Network Group.* This group serves as a support group for African-American women. The group offers leadership development, mentoring, and community involvement.
- *Amigos.* This group assists in the recruiting, retention, and development of Hispanic/Latino employees. Besides mentoring opportunities, the group serves as a bridge between the company and its growing internal and external Latino community. Amigos seeks ways to share information about Hispanic/Latin culture and enhance company representation at community events.

In addition to its various affinity groups, Georgia Power formed five employee committees to improve diversity at the company. The committees developed 33 separate initiatives after evaluating considerable data, conducting focus groups with employees, and visiting other companies to learn about their diversity efforts. The initiatives fell into two broad categories that focused on leadership accountability, supervisory and management training, and communication and awareness. Almost two-thirds of the initiatives called for changes in processes and policies. The process initiatives included

- changes in job selection processes to increase selection committees' diversity and eliminate nepotism, better prepare candidates for job interviews, and provide honest, candid feedback to candidates who were not selected;

- creation of formal employee retention, recruitment, and development programs;
- addition of a career-planning component to the performance management process already used throughout the company; and
- development of a mentoring program for all new employees and supervisors.

For more information on Georgia Power, visit the organization's home page at ***http://www.georgiapower.com.***

LEARNING OBJECTIVE

2. Explain five interpersonal conflict-handling strategies and the conditions for their use.

INTERPERSONAL CONFLICT-HANDLING STYLES

Individuals handle interpersonal conflict in various ways.[14] Figure 9.3 presents a model for understanding and comparing five interpersonal conflict-handling styles. The styles are identified by their locations on two dimensions: *concern for self* and *concern for others.* The desire to satisfy your own concerns depends on the extent to which you are *assertive* or *unassertive* in pursuing personal goals. Your desire to satisfy the concerns of others depends on the extent to which you are *cooperative* or *uncooperative.* The five interpersonal conflict-handling styles thus represent different combinations of assertiveness and cooperativeness. Although you may have a natural tendency toward one or two of the styles, you may use all of them as the situation and people involved change. For example, the style you use in working through a conflict with a good friend may be quite different from the style you use with a stranger after a minor auto accident. The Experiential Exercise and Case section at the end of this chapter contains a questionnaire that you can use to assess your own styles for handling conflict. We suggest that you complete this questionnaire now.

FIGURE 9.3 Interpersonal Conflict-Handling Styles

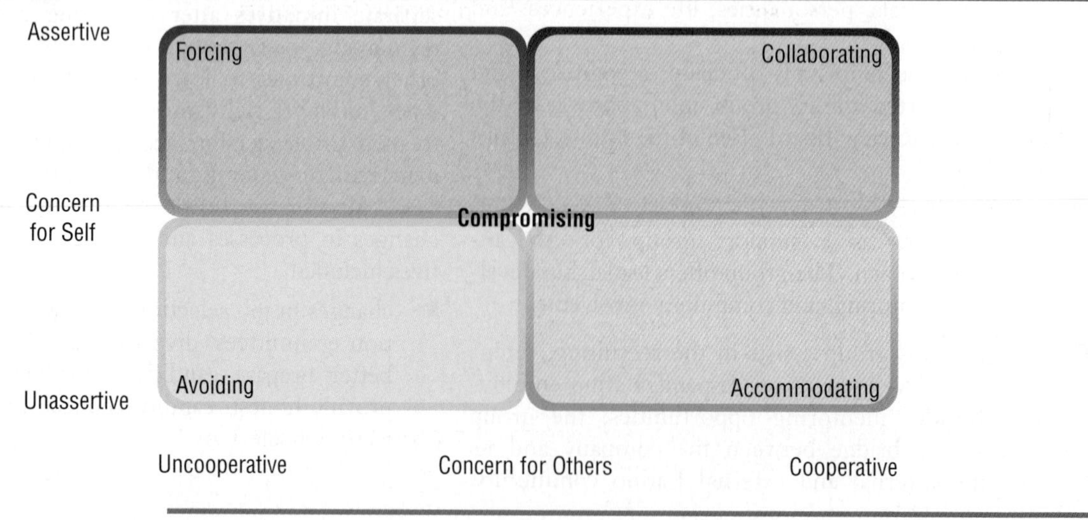

Avoiding Style

The **avoiding style** *refers to unassertive and uncooperative behaviors.* A person uses this style to stay away from conflict, ignore disagreements, or remain neutral. The avoidance approach reflects an aversion to tension and frustration and may involve a decision to let a conflict work itself out. Because ignoring important issues often frustrates others, the consistent use of the avoidance style usually results in unfavorable evaluations by others. The following statements illustrate the avoiding style:

- If there are rules that apply, I cite them. If there aren't, I leave the other person free to make her own decision.
- I usually don't take positions that will create controversy.
- I shy away from topics that are sources of disputes with my friends.
- That's okay. It wasn't important anyway. Let's leave well enough alone.

When unresolved conflict gets in the way of accomplishing goals, the avoiding style will lead to negative results for the organization. This style may be desirable under some situations, as when (1) the issue is minor or only of passing importance and thus not worth the individual's time or energy to confront the conflict; (2) the individual doesn't have enough information to deal effectively with the conflict at that time; (3) the individual's power is so low relative to the other person's that there's little chance of causing change (e.g., disagreement with a new strategy approved by top management); and (4) others can resolve the conflict more effectively.

THE COMPETENT LEADER

We don't have any of the aggressive behavior that some teams show. But conflict can grow under the surface, like a cancer. You can't treat it until you acknowledge that it exists.

Craig Mangean, Director of Human Resources, Field Sales, Sankyo Pharma

Forcing Style

The **forcing style** *refers to assertive and uncooperative behaviors and represents a win–lose approach to interpersonal conflict.* Those who use the forcing approach try to achieve their own goals without concern for others. This style relies on coercive power, which is explained in Chapter 6. It may help a person achieve individual goals, but like avoidance, forcing tends to result in unfavorable evaluations by others. The following statements illustrate the forcing style:

- I like to put it plainly: Like it or not, what I say goes, and maybe when others have had the experience I have, they will remember this and think better of it.
- I convince the other person of the logic and benefits of my position.
- I insist that my position be accepted during a disagreement.
- I usually hold on to my solution to a problem after the controversy starts.

Forcing-prone individuals assume that conflict resolution means that one person must win and the other must lose. When dealing with conflict between subordinates or departments, forcing-style managers may threaten or actually use demotion, dismissal, negative performance evaluations, or other punishments to gain compliance. When conflict occurs between peers, employees using the forcing style might try to get their way by appealing to their manager. This approach represents an attempt to use the manager to force the decision on the opposing individual.

Overreliance on forcing by a manager lessens employees' work motivation because their interests haven't been considered. Relevant information and other possible alternatives usually are ignored. In some situations the forcing style may be necessary, as when (1) emergencies require quick action, (2) unpopular courses of action must be taken for long-term organizational effectiveness and survival (e.g., cost cutting and dismissal of employees for unsatisfactory performance), and (3) the individuals need to take action for self-protection and to stop others from taking advantage of them.

The forcing style becomes escalated when the parties bring lawsuits against one another. Take the case of Hidetomo Morimoto, who was hired by Pacific Software Publishing, headquartered in a suburb of Seattle, Washington. The firm translates English software into Japanese. Because of the poor job market for his programming skills several years ago, he took the job for $1,800 a month to start. Morimoto claims he soon found himself regularly working 60 hours a week, and during crunch times often didn't leave until 1:00 A.M. Yet, he indicates that he never received any overtime pay.

Morimoto complained in an Internet posting that some Japanese employers took advantage of their staff's strong work ethic, but did not mention his employers' name, Pacific Software. He soon found himself out of work. The firm claims it fired him for "a number of improprieties," including the Internet posting. Morimoto is suing his former employer, demanding the overtime pay he says he should have received. Pacific Software Publishing maintains it wasn't wrong because Morimoto spent all of his extra hours in the office on personal matters, not work. The firm is countersuing, alleging defamation. Although these two suits have not been resolved by the court as of this writing, they reflect clear expressions of the forcing approach to conflict management with each party attempting to use the legal process to "force" its preferred outcome on the other party. This case is only one of many recent legal suits by high-tech employees regarding charges of employers denying overtime pay, substituting stock options of little value for cash bonuses, and not paying promised salaries. Lynne Hermle, an attorney for high-tech firms, comments: "Wage-and-hour class-action lawsuits have now invaded high-tech in the Valley."[15]

Accommodating Style

The **accommodating style** *refers to cooperative and unassertive behaviors.* Accommodation may represent an unselfish act, a long-term strategy to encourage cooperation by others, or just complying with the wishes of others. Individuals using the accommodating style are typically evaluated favorably by others, but they may also be perceived as weak and submissive. The following statements illustrate the accommodating style:

- Conflict is best managed through the suspension of my personal goals in order to maintain good relationships with others.
- If it makes other people happy, I'm all for it.
- I like to smooth over disagreements by making them appear less important.
- I ease conflict by suggesting that our differences are trivial and then show goodwill by blending my ideas into those of the other person.

When using the accommodating style, an individual may act as though the conflict will go away in time and appeal for cooperation. The person will try to reduce tensions and stress by providing support. This style shows concern about the emotional aspects of conflict but little interest in working on its substantive issues. The accommodating style simply results in the individual covering up or glossing over personal feelings. It is generally ineffective if used consistently. The accommodating style may be effective in the short run when (1) the individual is in a potentially explosive emotional conflict situation, and smoothing is used to defuse it; (2) maintaining harmony and avoiding disruption are especially important in the short run; and (3) the conflicts are based primarily on the personalities of the individuals and cannot be easily resolved.

Collaborating Style

The **collaborating style** *refers to strong cooperative and assertive behaviors.* It is the win–win approach to interpersonal conflict handling. The person using collaboration desires to maximize joint results. An individual who uses this style tends to (1) see conflict as natural, helpful, and leading to a more creative solution if handled properly; (2) exhibit trust in and candor with others; and (3) recognize that when conflict is resolved to the satisfaction of all, commitment to the solution is likely. An individual who uses the collaborating style is often seen as dynamic and evaluated favorably by others. The following statements illustrate the collaborating style:

- I first try to overcome any distrust that might exist between us. Then I try to get at the feelings that we mutually have about the topics. I stress that nothing we decide is cast in stone and suggest that we find a position for which we can do a trial run.
- I tell the others my ideas, actively seek out their ideas, and search for a mutually beneficial solution.
- I like to suggest new solutions and build on a variety of viewpoints that may have been expressed.
- I try to dig into an issue to find a solution good for all of us.

With this style, conflict is open and evaluated by all concerned. Sharing, examining, and assessing the reasons for the conflict should lead to development of an alternative that effectively resolves it and is acceptable to everyone involved. Collaboration is most practical when (1) a high level of cooperation is needed to justify expending the extra time and energy needed to make working through the conflict worthwhile; (2) sufficient parity in power exists among individuals so that they feel free to interact candidly, regardless of their formal status; (3) the potential exists for mutual benefits, especially over the long run, for resolving the dispute through a win–win process; and (4) sufficient organizational support is given for investing the necessary time and energy in resolving disputes in this manner. The norms, rewards, and punishments of the organization—especially those set by top management—provide the framework for encouraging or discouraging collaboration.

Compromising Style

The **compromising style** *refers to behaviors at an intermediate level of cooperation and assertiveness.* The individual using this style engages in give-and-take concessions. Compromising is commonly used and widely accepted as a means of resolving conflict. The following statements illustrate the compromising style:

- I want to know how and what others feel. When the timing is right, I explain how I feel and try to show them where they are wrong. Of course, it's often necessary to settle on some middle ground.
- After failing to get my way, I usually find it necessary to seek a fair combination of gains and losses for all of us.
- I give in to others if they are willing to meet me halfway.
- As the old saying goes, half a loaf is better than nothing. Let's split the difference.

An individual who compromises with others tends to be evaluated favorably. Various explanations are suggested for the favorable evaluation of the compromising style, including that (1) it is seen primarily as a cooperative "holding back," (2) it reflects a pragmatic way of dealing with conflict, and (3) it helps maintain good relations for the future.

The compromising style shouldn't be used early in the conflict resolution process for several reasons. First, the people involved are likely to compromise on the stated issues rather than on the real issues. The first issues raised in a conflict often aren't the real ones, and premature compromise will prevent full diagnosis or exploration of the real issues. For example, students telling professors that their courses are tough and challenging may simply be trying to negotiate an easier grade.

Second, accepting an initial position is easier than searching for alternatives that are more acceptable to everyone involved. Third, compromise is inappropriate to all or part of the situation when it isn't the best decision available. That is, further discussion may reveal a better way of resolving the conflict.

Compared to the collaborating style, the compromising style doesn't maximize mutual satisfaction. Compromise achieves moderate, but only partial, satisfaction for each person. This style is likely to be appropriate when (1) agreeing enables each person to be better off, or at least not worse off than if no agreement were reached; (2) achieving a total win–win agreement simply isn't possible; and (3) conflicting goals or opposing interests block agreement on one person's proposal.

Effectiveness of Styles

Studies conducted on the use of different interpersonal conflict-handling styles indicate that collaboration tends to be characteristic of (1) more successful rather than less successful individuals and (2) high-performing rather than medium- and low-performing organizations. People tend to perceive collaboration in terms of the constructive use of conflict. The use of collaboration seems to result in positive feelings in others, as well as favorable self-evaluations of performance and abilities. In contrast to collaboration, forcing and avoiding often have negative effects. These styles tend to be associated with a less constructive use of conflict, negative feelings from others, and unfavorable evaluations of performance and abilities. The effects of accommodation and compromise appear to be mixed. The use of accommodation sometimes results in positive feelings from others. But these individuals do not form favorable evaluations of the performance and abilities of those using the accommodating style. The use of the compromising style generally is followed by positive feelings from others.[16]

The following Communication Competency reports on the use of the collaboration and compromise styles of conflict by Marty Ambuehl and Neil Clark, the cofounders of ATM Express.[17] This firm, headquartered in Billings, Montana, is in the business of providing automated teller machine sales and transaction processing services to a national market. ATM Express has revenues of approximately $25 million annually, 30 employees, and more than 10,000 ATM locations throughout the United States.

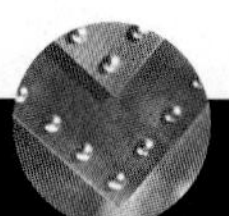

Communication Competency

ATM Express

In the early 1990s, Marty Ambuehl and Neil Clark were college friends who owned a piano-moving company. They formed that first partnership with little more than a handshake and a slap on the back. When they founded ATM in 1999, they decided to establish a more formal structure, partly because they intended to seek outside investing. They hired a lawyer and formed a corporation.

That turned out to be a wise action. The incorporation process encouraged them to face tough issues right at the outset. The incorporation documents they developed clearly defined the specific roles each owner was expected to play and also addressed other issues like how to bring in a third owner or secure additional financing. Ambuehl and Clark faced a tough question when launching ATM Express. Their main investor asked, "What happens if the two of you get to a point where you don't want to be partners anymore?" Ambuehl and Clark answered the question by drafting employment contracts that committed them to the partnership for five years.

Ambuehl and Clark truly enjoy being business partners. They appreciate each other's relaxed and playful attitude toward what they do, and like the way each partner challenges the other to do better, more creative work. Ambuehl comments: "We push each other. We balance each other very well. We don't let things fester. We have close to the same values." Clark adds: "We don't play the petty games others play. Also, we're not easily offended. It's OK to get upset. That's just reality."

Still, they don't agree on everything. In fact, they found themselves in the midst of a fairly significant disagreement. A tempting acquisition target presented itself. Ambuehl saw the purchase as a great expansion opportunity, but Clark was reluctant to take such a big step. Fortunately, they had prepared for just such a scenario years ago. Careful planning at the beginning, it turns out, has been one of the keys to the success of their partnership and their company.

Ambuehl and Clark were not too worried about their disagreement over the acquisition. When they founded their business, they decided that they would make a major move like an acquisition only if they both agreed on it. "If there's no agreement, there's no deal," Clark maintains. "That's the solution." Whether or not they decided to make the purchase, both men are convinced that their partnership—and their company—will survive. "You're fooling yourself if you think there's never going to be a disagreement," Clark says. Ambuehl agrees: "Neil and I don't draw lines in the sand and say, 'This is the way it is, period.' We don't try to back one another into a corner. We know we have to bend."

The partners complement one another's competencies. Clark is the marketing whiz, for instance, while Ambuehl is the operations manager. "We knew going in that we had these strengths," says Ambuehl. "It offers us two viewpoints on everything, and even though we can step into each other's roles, we've always been real careful not to step outside our bounds."

For more information on ATM Express, visit the organization's home page at ***http://www.atmexpress.com.***

NEGOTIATION IN CONFLICT MANAGEMENT

LEARNING OBJECTIVE

3. Discuss the core stages, strategies, and influences in negotiations.

Negotiation *is a process in which two or more interdependent individuals or groups, who perceive that they have both common and conflicting goals, state and discuss proposals and preferences for specific terms of a possible agreement.* Negotiation includes a combination of compromise, collaboration, and possibly some forcing on vital issues. A negotiation situation is one in which

- two or more individuals or groups must make decisions about their combined goals and interests,
- the individuals are committed to peaceful means for resolving their disputes, and
- there is no clear or established method or procedure for making the decisions.[18]

Stages of Negotiation

Negotiations can be viewed as a process with a series of distinct stages. Table 9.2 provides a list of a few of the questions that might be presented in each of the four stages of negotiations, as discussed next:

- The first stage is (1) assessing the situation to ensure that it is appropriate for negotiation and (2) preparing to enter into negotiations, and determining that the other party has some reason to negotiate with you. A critical issue to address in this stage is the **BATNA,** *which refers to the* ***B****est* ***A****lternative* ***T****o a* ***N****egotiated* ***A****greement and means the negotiator's absolute bottom line.* If an agreement isn't better than the BATNA, it actually makes the negotiator worse off. To protect negotiators from escalating to irrational commitments during negotiations, they need to identify and assess the alternatives if an agreement is not reached.

- The second stage is establishing and agreeing on the process by which the negotiations will proceed. Matters that require discussion and prior agreement between the parties include the scope of the issues, who will participate, deadlines, and understandings regarding how the negotiators will approach the problem and each other.
- The third stage is negotiating the substantive agreement. In this stage, the negotiators will make a number of strategic decisions regarding tactics and acceptable outcomes.
- The fourth stage is implementing the agreement. It is important that the agreement reached will be and can be implemented. Experienced negotiators will consider what understandings need to be reached to ensure timely and effective implementation.[19]

TABLE 9.2 Sample Questions in Each Stage of Negotiations

Stage 1: Assessing the Situation

- Are you clear on your interests and priority issues?
- Have you defined the criteria by which you will determine whether or not you will enter into an agreement?
- Have you defined your BATNA (Best Alternative To a Negotiated Agreement)? That is, do you know what you will do if there is no agreement?
- Have you considered the interests and constraints of the other party?

Stage 2: Establishing the Process

- Have you agreed on the scope of the issues?
- Do you understand how agreements will be approved or ratified?
- Are you in agreement on time frames and deadlines?
- Have you discussed what information may be required and how it will be acquired and managed (e.g., confidentiality)?

Stage 3: Negotiating the Agreement

- Are you entering negotiations committed to meet your interests—not your positions?
- Are you identifying and addressing the interests of the other party?
- Are you jointly identifying mutual interests and expanding the "pie"?
- Are you building a relationship that will support the agreement?

Stage 4: Implementing the Agreement

- Are all of the agreements clearly understood and perhaps spelled out in writing?
- Does the agreement spell out the responsibilities of the parties in the implementation of the agreement?
- Is there a provision for assessing the implementation of the agreement and improving it as necessary?

- Are there procedures for jointly resolving disputes under the agreement in a timely manner?

Source: Adapted from Cormick, G. W. *Negotiation Skills for Board Professionals.* Mill Creek, WA: CSE Group, 2005; Dietmeyer, B. *Strategic Negotiation: A Breakthrough Four-Step Process for Effective Business Negotiation.* Chicago: Dearborn Trade, 2004.

Distributive Negotiations Strategy

Distributive negotiations *involve traditional win–lose situations in which one party's gain is the other party's loss.* This strategy often occurs over economic issues, communications are guarded, and expressions of trust are limited. The use of threats, distorted statements, and demands is common. In short, the parties are engaged in intense, emotion-laden conflict. The forcing and compromise conflict-handling styles characterize distributive negotiations.[20]

Some individuals and groups believe in distributive (win–lose) negotiations, and negotiators have to be prepared to counter them. Awareness and understanding probably are the most important means for dealing with win–lose negotiation ploys by the other party. Four of the most common win–lose strategies that you might face as a negotiator are the following:[21]

- *I want it all.* By making an extreme offer and then granting concessions grudgingly, if at all, the other party hopes to wear down your resolve. You will know that you have met such a negotiator when you encounter the following tactics: (1) The other party's first offer is extreme; (2) minor concessions are made grudgingly; (3) you are pressured to make significant concessions; and (4) the other party refuses to reciprocate.
- *Time warp.* Time can be used as a powerful weapon by the win–lose negotiator. When any of the following techniques are used, you should refuse to be forced into an unfavorable position: (1) The offer is valid only for a limited time; (2) you are pressured to accept arbitrary deadlines; (3) the other party stalls or delays the progress of the negotiation; and (4) the other party increases pressure on you to settle quickly.
- *Good cop, bad cop.* Negotiators using this strategy hope to sway you to their side by alternating sympathetic with threatening behavior. You should be on your guard when you are confronted with the following tactics: (1) The other party becomes irrational or abusive; (2) the other party walks out of a negotiation; and (3) irrational behavior is followed by reasonable, sympathetic behavior.
- *Ultimatums.* This strategy is designed to try to force you to submit to the will of the other party. You should be wary when the other party tries any of the following: (1) You are presented with a take-it-or-leave-it offer; (2) the other party overtly tries to force you to accept its demands; (3) the other party is unwilling to make concessions; and (4) you are expected to make all the concessions.

Because of their severe financial problems, a number of the major airlines—such as American, United, and Continental—have engaged in distributive negotiations with their employee unions. For the most part, management wanted larger wage and benefit concessions than the unions representing the employees. For example, Continental Airlines sought $500 million in annual wage and benefit reductions along with the dire warnings of likely bankruptcy and running out of cash. The Airlines Pilot Association membership approved $213 million in cost cuts annually by a vote of 58 percent for and 42 percent against. This vote demonstrates the conflict within the membership. The reluctant "yes" votes are based on the lack of a better option. Jay Panarello, the chairman of the Continental branch of the Airline Pilots Association, comments: "This union fought for our pilots from start to finish. We were willing to help our company, but only on terms acceptable to the pilots." In exchange for the wage cuts, Continental made available 10 million stock options for employees that may be exercised in installments over a three-year period. The purchase price of each share is the price of the stock at the date of the signed agreements in 2005.[22]

In essence, the distributive negotiations involved wage cuts to benefit Continental Airlines in exchange for stock options to benefit employees if the stock increases in price and improved profit sharing. If the stock price declines over the three-year period for exercising the options, they will be of no value to the union members. If Continental's profits do not increase, the improved profit sharing plan will be of no value to the employees.

Integrative Negotiations Strategy

Integrative negotiations *involve joint problem solving to achieve results benefiting both parties.* With this strategy, the parties identify mutual problems, identify and assess alternatives, openly express preferences, and jointly reach a mutually acceptable solution. Rarely perceived as equally acceptable, the solution is simply advantageous to both sides. Although most of the negotiations between Continental and its labor unions were distributive in terms of the wage and benefit concessions, the parties did employ some integrative negotiations as well. For example, management, employees, and the union leadership mutually recognized that Continental's costs were too high to compete with other airlines like Southwest and JetBlue. Those involved in integrative negotiations are strongly motivated to solve problems, exhibit flexibility and trust, and explore new ideas. The collaborative and compromise conflict-handling styles are dominant in this strategy.

A variety of principles and prescriptions are used during integrative (win–win) negotiations. The following four principles provide a foundation for an integrative negotiations strategy:[23]

- *Separate the people from the problem.* The first principle in reaching a mutually agreeable solution is to disentangle the substantive issues of the negotiation from the interpersonal relationship issues between the parties and deal with each set of issues separately. Negotiators should see themselves as working side by side, dealing with the substantive issues or problems instead of attacking each other.
- *Focus on interests, not positions.* People's egos tend to become identified with their negotiating positions. Furthermore, focusing only on stated positions often obscures what the participants really need or want. Rather than focusing only on the positions taken by each negotiator, a much more effective strategy is to focus on the underlying human needs and interests that had caused them to adopt those positions.
- *Invent options for mutual gains.* Designing optimal solutions under pressure in the presence of an adversary tends to narrow people's thinking. Searching for the one right solution inhibits creativity, particularly when the stakes are high. These blinders can be removed by establishing a forum in which various possibilities are generated before decisions are made about which action to take.
- *Insist on using objective criteria.* The parties should discuss the conditions of the negotiation in terms of some fair standard, such as market value, expert opinion, custom, or law. This principle steers the focus away from what the parties are willing or unwilling to do. By using objective criteria, neither party has to give in to the other, and both parties may defer to a fair solution.

Ron Shapiro is coauthor of *The Power of Nice: How to Negotiate So Everyone Wins—Especially You* and CEO of the Shapiro Negotiation Institute. He has negotiated numerous agreements, ranging from real estate acquisitions to corporate mergers, from major financial packages to home loans, from settling symphony orchestra and umpire strikes to completing contracts for professional athletes. Consistent with integrative negotiations, he suggests:

> Don't negotiate as if you'll never again do business with the person across the table. . . . Forget about conquerors and victims. Negotiation is not war. It isn't about getting the other side to wave a flag and surrender. Don't think hurt. Think help. Don't demand. Listen. The best way to get most of what you want is to help the other side get some of what it wants. . . . On the surface, negotiation may seem to be about winning and losing. After all, to the victor belong the spoils. Can it be true that only the hardest, toughest and meanest negotiators will be the most successful?. . . These types of negotiators will undoubtedly achieve success in deals, but most will fall short in the long run. I believe that you can be "nice" and still get what you are after. In fact, you often get better results, achieve more of your goals and build long-term relationships with even greater returns. Win–win simply means the best way to get what you want is to help them get what they want.[24]

The following Teams Competency feature reports on the negotiations by managers of Cinergy Corporation with four unions. The negotiations related to changes wanted by Cinergy in the residential collections process.[25] Cinergy generates, transmits, and distributes electricity to more than 1.5 million customers and natural gas to more than 500,000 customers in Ohio, Indiana, and Kentucky.[26] You will note that the integrative negotiations strategy was the primary strategy used with some use of the distributive negotiations strategy.

TEAMS COMPETENCY

CINERGY'S RESIDENTIAL COLLECTIONS NEGOTIATIONS

Grady Reid, manager of revenue collections for Cinergy, helped lead the negotiations to make changes in the company's residential collections process. Considering the number of parties involved in the issues, reaching an agreement with buy-in from all groups was a major achievement. Moreover, the agreement has led to increased productivity. Reid comments: "We knew we were on a 'burning platform,' and a decision had to be made to make changes. We knew trying to work the changes we wanted, with four unions, would not be easy, as we had tried in the past with no results." Reid notes there was a commitment that "this time would be different" and that the changes were absolutely critical. "We had to make everyone involved understand the importance of working together to make the changes we contemplated," says Reid.

Still, it was not easy. Participants from the four unions and the Cinergy management team all had different ideas about what the collections problems were and how they should be fixed. Reid states: "There were serious discussions concerning outsourcing the work, but most of us wanted to work toward a win–win solution that would keep the work in-house." In fact, there were outsourcing companies that bid on the work even as discussions were ongoing, and these companies were prepared to step in and take on the job if needed.

After nine months of discussion, analysis, and compromise, Reid and the management team agreed to solve the problems by creating a centralized group of people to focus on residential collections/disconnections for nonpayment. The work would be kept in-house, with major changes in the wage structure, the filling of future jobs, and restructuring of field work. Reid comments: "It was a decision that required all five groups (four unions and management) to give and take. None of the groups walked away cheering, but we all agreed it was a workable solution."

The result is that Cinergy has shifted various responsibilities and added a centralized work group focused on collections and nonpayment activity. Reid remarks: "We've added some resources and some hardware/software technology that increase our productivity and allow real-time system updates. As we look at our overall results, we are very happy with where we are and believe we will continue to see improvements as we tweak the plan. When it was all said and done, we had won support from senior management, and the unions had won the support of their membership to make the necessary changes."

*For more information on Cinergy Corporation, visit the organization's home page at **http://www.cinergy.com**.*

Four Influences on Negotiation Strategies

In this section, we highlight four of the common influences on the distributive and integrative negotiation strategies: attitudinal structuring, intraorganizational negotiations, negotiator's dilemma, and mediation.

Attitudinal Structuring. **Attitudinal structuring** *is the process by which the parties seek to establish feelings and relationships.* Throughout any negotiations, the parties reveal certain attitudes (e.g., hostility or friendliness and competitiveness or cooperativeness) that influence their communications. Recall our previous quote from Ron Shapiro that related to the attitudes that he thinks the parties should hold to establish effective negotiations. Reflect on his statement: "I believe that you can be 'nice' and still get what you are after."

William Ury is a well-known scholar on negotiations and heads the Global Negotiation Project, which is part of the Program on Negotiation at the Harvard Law School. We share a few of his remarks related to attitudinal structuring in negotiations:

> Deal with the people and their emotions first. Be soft on the people so that you can be hard on the problem. . . . It's important not to react without thinking, but instead to "go to the balcony," a mental place of calm and perspective where you can step back and remember what your interests are. The truth is that we can't have a whisper of a chance of influencing the other side until we are able to influence ourselves. . . . It's important to put yourself in the other side's shoes, understand their interests and how they feel. Negotiation is an exercise in influence. You're trying to influence another person. You can't influence their mind unless you know where their mind is right now. Try to be inventive. Open up to other options besides your position.[27]

In the previous Teams Competency feature related to Cinergy's residential collections negotiations, Grady Reid, the manager of revenue collections, recognized the importance of attitudinal structuring in this remark: "We had to make everyone involved understand the importance of working together to make the changes we contemplated."

Intraorganizational Negotiations. Groups often negotiate through representatives. For example, representatives of OPEC nations set oil prices for the cartel. However, these representatives first have to obtain agreement from the leaders of their respective nations before they can work out an agreement with each other. **Intraorganizational negotiations** *involve negotiators building consensus for agreement and resolving intragroup conflict before dealing with the other groups' negotiators.*

Several of the comments by Grady Reid reflect the intraorganizational negotiations that took place among members of management, such as, "There were serious discussions [among managers] concerning outsourcing the work, but most of us [managers] wanted to work toward a win–win solution that would keep the work in-house" and "When it was all said and done, we had won support from senior management."

Negotiator's Dilemma. Negotiators increasingly realize the importance of cooperatively creating value by means of integrative negotiations. However, they must also acknowledge the fact that both sides may eventually seek gain through the distributive process. The **negotiator's dilemma** *is a situation in which the tactics of self-gain tend to repel moves to create greater mutual gain.* An optimal solution results when both parties openly discuss the problem, respect each other's substantive and relationship needs, and creatively seek to satisfy each other's interests. However, such behavior doesn't always occur.[28]

Win–win negotiators are vulnerable to the tactics of win–lose negotiators. As a result, negotiators often develop an uneasiness about the use of integrative strategies because they expect the other party to use distributive strategies. This mutual suspicion often causes negotiators to leave joint gains on the table. Moreover, after win–win negotiators have been stung in several encounters with experienced win–lose strategists, they soon "learn" to become win–lose strategists. Finally, if both negotiators use distributive strategies, the probability of achieving great mutual benefits is virtually eliminated. The negotiations will likely result in both parties receiving only minimal benefits.

Graphically, the integrative and distributive negotiation strategies can be placed on vertical and horizontal axes, representing the two negotiating parties. Then, a matrix of possible outcomes emerging from the negotiating process can be developed to illustrate the negotiator's dilemma, as shown in Figure 9.4 for person A and person B.

FIGURE 9.4 Matrix of Negotiated Outcomes

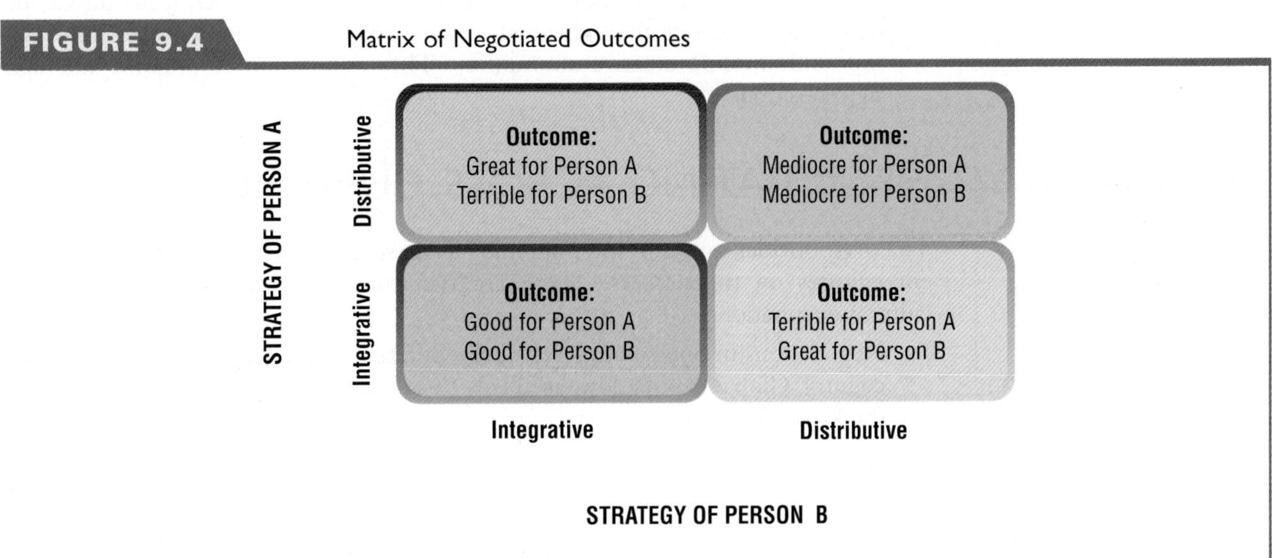

Source: Adapted from Anderson, T. Step into my parlor: A survey of strategies and techniques for effective negotiation. *Business Horizons*, May–June 1992, 75.

Mediation. At times, the parties engaged in negotiations get stuck and are not able to resolve one or more issues. As you would expect, this situation occurs more frequently with the distributive negotiations strategy than with the integrative negotiations strategy. In this situation, the parties may elect to use **mediation**—*a process by which a third party helps two (or more) other parties resolve one or more conflicts.* Most of the actual negotiations occur directly between the involved individuals. But, when the parties appear likely to become locked in win–lose conflict, a mediator, acting as a neutral party, may be able to help them resolve their differences.[29]

Recall the Preview Case on KLA-Tencor. The buyers from three KLA-Tencor divisions locked horns with each other over a contract with a key supplier. After being coached by a mediator to consider how each division's business model shaped its preference—and using this understanding to jointly brainstorm alternatives—the buyers and commodity manager arrived at a creative solution that worked for everyone.

Mediators need special competencies. They must (1) be able to diagnose the conflict, (2) be skilled at breaking deadlocks and facilitating discussions at the right time, (3) show mutual acceptance, and (4) have the ability to provide emotional support and reassurance. In brief, an effective mediator must instill confidence in and acceptance by the parties in conflict.

Key tasks in the mediator's role include the following:

- *Ensure mutual motivation.* Each party should have incentives for resolving the conflict.
- *Achieve a balance of power.* If the power of the individuals isn't equal, establishing trust and maintaining open lines of communication may be difficult.
- *Coordinate confrontation efforts.* One party's positive moves must be coordinated with the other party's readiness to do likewise. A failure to coordinate positive initiatives and readiness to respond can undermine future efforts to work out differences.
- *Promote openness in dialogue.* The mediator can help establish norms of openness, provide reassurance and support, and decrease the risks associated with openness.
- *Maintain an optimum level of tension.* If the threat and tension are too low, the incentive for change or finding a solution is minimal. However, if the threat and tension are too high, the individuals involved may be unable to process information and envision creative alternatives. They may begin to polarize and take rigid positions.[30]

LEARNING OBJECTIVE

4. State several of the unique aspects and recommendations for negotiating across cultures.

NEGOTIATING ACROSS CULTURES

The most obvious aspect of international business negotiations is the effect of different cultures on the process. There are two common perspectives about cross-cultural negotiations:

- Negotiations in one country are totally different from negotiations in any other country. Global negotiations are likely to be completely different from domestic transactions.
- Negotiating globally is essentially the same as negotiating domestically. They're all business transactions.[31]

Both perspectives are inadequate, if not wrong. Cultural differences are critical. However, the core concepts of conflict management and negotiations addressed in previous sections of this chapter are useful and important across cultures as well. In this section, we focus on those aspects of negotiations that are unique in cross-cultural negotiations.

Differences in Negotiators

The numerous issues and complexities relevant to all negotiations are increased—sometimes dramatically—when negotiators are from different cultures.[32] Table 9.3 provides examples of some of these differences from a study of more than 300 negotiators in 12 countries. As previously discussed, two fundamental strategies to negotiation are integrative (win–win) versus distributive (win–lose). Note that 100 percent of the respondents from Japan emphasized win–win in their approach to negotiations. In contrast, only 37 percent of the Spanish negotiators utilized a win–win approach. The table also compares negotiators from these countries in terms of the degree of formality in their negotiations, whether their communication tends to be direct or indirect, and whether they emphasize attaining general agreement or detailed understandings or contracts.

TABLE 9.3 Cultural Effects on Negotiating Style

NEGOTIATING ATTITUDE: WIN–WIN OR WIN–LOSE?

	Japan	China	Argentina	France	India	USA	UK	Mexico	Germany	Nigeria	Brazil	Spain
Win–Win (%):	100	82	81	80	78	71	59	50	55	47	44	37

PERSONAL STYLE: FORMAL OR INFORMAL?

	Nigeria	Spain	China	Mexico	UK	Argentina	Germany	Japan	India	Brazil	France	USA
Formal (%):	53	47	46	42	35	35	27	27	22	22	20	17

COMMUNICATION STYLE: DIRECT OR INDIRECT?

	Japan	France	China	UK	Brazil	India	Germany	USA	Argentina	Spain	Mexico	Nigeria
Indirect (%):	27	20	18	12	11	11	9	5	4	0	0	0

AGREEMENT FORM: GENERAL OR SPECIFIC?

	Japan	Germany	India	France	China	Argentina	Brazil	USA	Nigeria	Mexico	Spain	UK
General (%):	46	45	44	30	27	27	22	22	20	17	16	11

Source: Adapted from Salacuse, J. W. Ten ways that culture affects negotiating style: Some survey results. *Negotiation Journal,* July 1998, 221–240.

The degree of formality refers to a negotiator's style. For example, a negotiator from Germany with a very formal style might insist on addressing individuals by their titles, avoid the use of personal stories and anecdotes, and avoid any mention of private or family life. In contrast, a negotiator from the United States with an informal style might use first names as a form of address, strive to develop a personal relationship with other parties, and dress more casually on purpose. The contrast between direct and indirect communications has to do primarily with how straightforward and to the point communication typically is during the negotiations. Indirect communication consists of heavy use of nonverbal communication (see Chapter 10) and many vague statements. German and U.S. negotiators are typically viewed as very direct in their negotiations. French and Japanese negotiators are viewed as more indirect, relying a great deal on nonverbal cues to help understand the negotiations.

The traditional assumptions and generalizations may not always apply when long-term and insider relationships have been established. This situation applies particularly to negotiations by the Japanese with each other, whom they view as insiders. Almost by definition, Japanese businesspeople consider Westerners to be outsiders. Thus, Westerners often incorrectly assume that the Japanese never use direct or confrontational approaches to conflict resolution and negotiation. In fact, they often are very direct in resolving differences of opinion with other Japanese. They explicitly state the principal differences among group members and state demands, rejections, and counteroffers directly with each other.[33]

Cross-Cultural Emotional Intelligence

Negotiators and others are likely to be more effective if they possess emotional intelligence. We discuss emotional intelligence (EI) in Chapter 11. Let's extend that discussion by noting the relationship of the components of EI with the specific skills and abilities that increase cross-cultural effectiveness for negotiators. These components and relationships include the following:

- *Self-awareness:* acknowledging differences between home and host cultures; realizing the impact of cultural values on performance; recognizing initial difficulties in adjusting to new cultural norms and seeking assistance; being open to new perspectives; managing uncertainties by seeking cultural coaching; resisting the urge to impose one's own values on the host culture; understanding the link between the host culture and cross-cultural conflicts; and being flexible and patient when uncomfortable situations arise during negotiations;
- *Self-motivation:* maintaining optimism in the face of new challenges; effectively handling stress; seeking new ways of achieving goals during negotiation impasses; and consciously balancing the advantages of global negotiations against challenges and stressors in such negotiations;
- *Social empathy:* developing good listening skills; being sensitive to differences; asking questions and seeking to understand before reacting; being willing to change so as to show respect for other negotiators; openly sharing information that provides others with more understanding; and respecting opposing viewpoints; and
- *Social skill:* being outgoing and friendly; building relationships; seeking common ground despite cross-cultural differences; being open-minded and engaging in discussion rather than immediately passing judgment; and communicating informally to build rapport and future cooperation in negotiations.[34]

A mastery of these components of EI provides the foundation for becoming an effective negotiator in cross-cultural work situations. Moreover, EI enables the negotiator to avoid applying simplistic stereotypes to specific negotiators from other cultures, such as the following:

> Americans are impatient, direct, aggressive, creative, friendly, materialistic, and often tactless. Germans are rigid, hardworking, disciplined, domineering, and well-organized. Asians are inscrutable, reserved, status-conscious, patient negotiators who avoid open conflict and emphasize personal relationships. Latinos are romantic, impractical, leisure oriented, disorganized, and obsessed with honor and principle. British negotiators are arrogant, eccentric, reserved, tradition-minded, and fair. Italians are warm, outgoing, emotional, and flirtatious. The list could go on and on.[35]

Consistent with the attributes of EI and the competencies emphasized throughout this book, the better approach is to focus on the qualities and attributes of the specific negotiators with a deeper appreciation and understanding of their cultural context. This will short circuit the natural tendency toward simplistic stereotypes and erroneous attributions.

THE COMPETENT LEADER

I've been very fortunate that for 26 years every job I've ever had has been a global job.... You've got to step back and be able to have respect for every culture and every business type of customer in the world.... What you'll find is if the issue is truly a cultural decision, it's very easy to come to a compromise if you come at it with respect and with integrity.

Steve Ward, Chief Executive Officer, Lenovo Group Ltd.

Negotiation Process

Many features of the negotiation process, such as the key questions in each stage of negotiations, are similar across cultures. We note a few of the features that are unique or require tailoring to across culture negotiations:[36]

- *Dealing with people.* It is essential to take adequate time to get to know the other negotiators as professionals and people. More time is needed than in domestic business negotiations, since cultural, as well as personal, knowledge has to be acquired. Almost every negotiation involves a face-saving situation, and the successful international negotiator avoids making people uncomfortable. To save face, the negotiator needs to avoid arrogance, be careful in the choice of words so as not to offend the other party, and treat the other negotiators with respect. This will help generate trust. When people trust one another, they communicate more openly and are more receptive to each other's proposals and point of view.

- *Time.* Allow plenty of time. In particular, give time to think: Do not respond too quickly to new proposals. The timing of verbal exchange is crucial in negotiations. Some Westerners find gaps or pauses in conversations to be disturbing, while people from other cultures (e.g., Japan, China) prefer to leave a moment of silence between the statements. Patience is an asset in global negotiations, but can be destroyed by time pressure.

- *Managing issues.* Be flexible with the negotiation agenda if the other party does not stick to it. It may be somewhat frustrating when a negotiation agenda has been agreed on and then slowly eroded bit by bit. Such a situation may mean that the other party prefers a global rather than a step-by-step negotiation; he or she may not see negotiation as a linear process in which issues are addressed one after the other and settled before proceeding to the next issue.

- *Communication process.* The basic guideline for effective communication in international negotiations is to be ready for different communication styles. Be cautious in interpreting silence, emotions, threats, and any kind of manipulative communication. Start by assessing as accurately as possible the intercultural obstacles, such as language and problems of communication in general. Businesspeople often underestimate or even completely overlook this point, since they often share a technical or business culture with their negotiators. Beware that what is explicitly said is not necessarily what is implicitly meant. Check, verify. Spend time on checking communication accuracy, especially when the stakes are high.

- *Developing relationships.* The agreement should foster the development of the relationship and be flexible enough to deal with expected and unexpected changes. A major concern is to balance the *relationship* and *deal orientations.* The ultimate goal of negotiation is to establish a mutually trustworthy relationship. This is, of course, true in all negotiations, but especially so in cross-cultural negotiations where so many things can and do go wrong. With trust, the parties are more able to work through the inevitable problems.

The following Across Cultures Competency feature provides a glimpse into the complexities of negotiating in one culture, namely, China.[37]

Across Cultures Competency

Chinese Negotiating Style

A number of cultural elements underpin the Chinese negotiating style in business relationships. We review two of the more important ones here:

1. *Relationships.* Whereas Americans put a premium on networking, information, and institutions, the Chinese place a premium on individuals' social capital within their group of friends, relatives, and close associates. Though the role of *guanxi* (relationships) is fading a bit, it remains an important social force. More often than not, the person with the best *guanxi* wins.

   Here's an example of how *guanxi* works. Upon learning that China Post Savings Bureau planned to modernize its computer network, C. T. Teng, the general manager of Honeywell-Bull's Greater China Region, asked his Beijing sales director to approach the China Post executive responsible for this project. Because the sales director and the China Post executive were old university friends, they had *guanxi.* That connection enabled Teng to invite the China Post executive to a partner's forum at Honeywell-Bull headquarters in Boston. He also invited the CEO of Taiwan's Institute of Information Industry to the event. Over the course of the meeting, Teng proposed a banking system using Honeywell-Bull hardware and Taiwan Institute software to China Post's CEO, and the deal was accepted.

   Good *guanxi* also depends on a strict system of reciprocity. This does not mean immediate, American-style reciprocity: "I make a concession, and I expect one in return at the table that day." In China, favors are almost always remembered and returned, though not right away. This long-term reciprocity is a cornerstone of enduring personal relationships. Ignoring reciprocity in China is not just bad manners; it's immoral. If someone is labeled as one who forgets favors and fails on righteousness and loyalty, it poisons the well for all future business.

2. *Intermediary.* Handling business negotiations and agreements for Americans in China is problematic without an intermediary. In the United States, people tend to trust others until or unless we're given a reason not to. In China, suspicion and distrust characterize meetings with strangers. In business, trust can't be earned because business relationships can't even be formed without it. Instead, trust must be transmitted via *guanxi.* In China, the crucial first step in this phase of negotiation is finding the personal links to the organization or negotiators.

   A talented Chinese intermediary is useful even after the initial meeting takes place. Consider what happens during a typical Sino-Western negotiation session. Rather than just saying no outright, Chinese businesspeople are more likely to change the subject, turn silent, ask another question, or respond by using ambiguous and vaguely positive expressions with subtle negative implications, such as "seems not wrong," "seems fairly all right," and "appears fairly passable."

   Only a native Chinese intermediary can read and explain the moods, intonations, facial expressions, and body language Chinese negotiators exhibit during a formal negotiation session. A vice president of a New York–based software company went to Beijing to negotiate a distribution contract with a Chinese research institute. Having attended meetings arranged by the intermediary—a former senior executive with the institute—the VP was pleased with the progress during the first two days. But on the third day, the two sides became embroiled in a debate over intellectual property rights. Feeling they were losing face, the Chinese ended the meeting. That night, the VP and the China country manager met independently with the intermediary. The following day, the intermediary called the head of the institute and worked his magic. In the end, both sides agreed that the intellectual property rights were to be jointly owned, and the contract was signed.

For more information on China's culture and business practices, visit websites such as ***http://www.index-china/com*** *and* ***http://www.chineseculturesite.com/.***

CHAPTER SUMMARY

Conflict occurs at four different levels within organizations: intrapersonal, interpersonal, intragroup, and intergroup. Intrapersonal conflict occurs within the individual. Interpersonal conflict occurs when someone's wishes or desires are perceived to be in opposition to another's. Intragroup conflict occurs between or among group members. Intergroup conflict occurs between groups or teams.

1. Describe the four basic levels of conflict in organizations.

The five styles for handling interpersonal conflict are avoiding, forcing, accommodating, collaborating, and compromising. An individual may have a natural preference for one or two of these styles. Most individuals are likely to use all of them over time when dealing with various interpersonal conflict situations. As a reminder, an instrument for measuring your own conflict-handling style is presented in the Experiential Exercise and Case section at the end of this chapter.

2. Explain five interpersonal conflict-handling strategies and the conditions for their use.

Negotiation is a component in conflict management. It is a process in which two or more interdependent individuals or groups, who perceive that they have both common and conflicting goals, state and discuss proposals and preferences for specific terms of a possible agreement. The four core stages of negotiation include (1) assessing the situation, (2) establishing the process, (3) negotiating the agreement, and (4) implementing the agreement. Table 9.2 provides examples of questions that need to be addressed in each stage. The two major negotiating strategies are distributive (focus is on win–lose outcomes) and integrative (focus is on win–win outcomes). Four of the influences that affect the selection or implementation of each of these strategies are attitudinal structuring, intraorganizational negotiations, negotiator's dilemma, and mediation when stalemates occur over particular issues.

3. Discuss the core stages, strategies, and influences in negotiations.

Negotiators across cultures may differ with respect to (1) negotiating attitude with a focus on the win–lose (distributive) strategy versus win–win (integrative) strategy, (2) personal style with a formal versus informal approach, (3) communication style with a direct versus indirect approach, and (4) agreement form with a preference for a set of general versus highly specific provisions or understandings. Global negotiators are likely to be more effective if they possess emotional intelligence, which increases their cross-cultural adaptation in the components of self-awareness, self-motivation, social empathy, and social skill. Aspects of the negotiation process that may be unique when negotiating across cultures include dealing with people, allowing enough time, managing issues, handling the communication process, and developing relationships over time.

4. State several of the unique aspects and recommendations for negotiating across cultures.

KEY TERMS AND CONCEPTS

Accommodating style
Affinity group
Attitudinal structuring
Avoiding style
BATNA
Collaborating style
Compromising style
Conflict
Conflict management
Distributive negotiations
Forcing style
Integrative negotiations
Intergroup conflict
Interpersonal conflict
Intragroup conflict
Intraorganizational negotiations
Intrapersonal conflict
Mediation
Negotiation
Negotiator's dilemma
Role
Role ambiguity
Role conflict
Role set
Task interdependency

DISCUSSION QUESTIONS

1. Have you been involved in negotiations when the other party used the distributive negotiations strategy? Describe the situation. What did you do in response to the tactics used with this strategy? How did you feel? What was the outcome?
2. Think of a current or past relationship with someone who had much more power than you. How would you describe that person's relative use of the five interpersonal conflict management styles? How would you evaluate that person's conflict management effectiveness?
3. What levels of conflict are apparent in the KLA-Tencor Preview Case? Explain.
4. What conflict-handling styles were used in the KLA-Tencor Preview Case? Explain.
5. How would you evaluate yourself on the components of emotional intelligence in relation to your ability to be an across cultures negotiator? Use a scale of 100 (perfect) to 0 (nonexistent) to assess yourself on each component. What are the implications of this self-assessment for you?
6. Reread the Communication Competency feature on ATM Express. What levels of conflict are illustrated? Explain. What interpersonal conflict-handling styles are illustrated? Explain.
7. Reread the Diversity Competency feature on Georgia Power's affinity groups. Do you think the actions taken by Georgia Power are likely to be effective over the long run? Explain.
8. Provide examples of (a) intrasender role conflict, (b) intersender role conflict, (c) interrole conflict, and (d) person–role conflict that you have experienced.
9. Give personal examples of (a) approach–approach conflict, (b) avoidance–avoidance conflict, and (c) approach–avoidance conflict.

EXPERIENTIAL EXERCISES

Experiential Exercise: Self Competency

Conflict-Handling Styles[38]

Instructions

Each numbered item contains two statements that describe how people deal with conflict. Distribute 5 points between each pair of statements. The statement that more accurately reflects your likely response should receive the highest number of points. For example, if response (a) strongly describes your behavior, then record

5 a.
0 b.

However, if (a) and (b) are both characteristic, but (b) is slightly more characteristic of your behavior than (a), then record

2 a.
3 b.

1. _____ a. I am most comfortable letting others take responsibility for solving a problem.
   _____ b. Rather than negotiate differences, I stress those points for which agreement is obvious.
2. _____ a. I pride myself on finding compromise solutions.
   _____ b. I examine all the issues involved in any disagreement.
3. _____ a. I usually persist in pursuing my side of an issue.
   _____ b. I prefer to soothe others' feelings and preserve relationships.
4. _____ a. I pride myself in finding compromise solutions.
   _____ b. I usually sacrifice my wishes for the wishes of a peer.
5. _____ a. I consistently seek a peer's help in finding solutions.
   _____ b. I do whatever is necessary to avoid tension.
6. _____ a. As a rule, I avoid dealing with conflict.
   _____ b. I defend my position and push my view.
7. _____ a. I postpone dealing with conflict until I have had some time to think it over.
   _____ b. I am willing to give up some points if others give up some too.
8. _____ a. I use my influence to have my views accepted.
   _____ b. I attempt to get all concerns and issues immediately out in the open.
9. _____ a. I feel that most differences are not worth worrying about.
   _____ b. I make a strong effort to get my way on issues I care about.
10. _____ a. Occasionally I use my authority or technical knowledge to get my way.
    _____ b. I prefer compromise solutions to problems.
11. _____ a. I believe that a team can reach a better solution than any one person can working independently.
    _____ b. I often defer to the wishes of others.
12. _____ a. I usually avoid taking positions that would create controversy.
    _____ b. I'm willing to give a little if a peer will give a little, too.
13. _____ a. I generally propose the middle ground as a solution.
    _____ b. I consistently press to "sell" my viewpoint.
14. _____ a. I prefer to hear everyone's side of an issue before making judgments.
    _____ b. I demonstrate the logic and benefits of my position.
15. _____ a. I would rather give in than argue about trivialities.
    _____ b. I avoid being "put on the spot."
16. _____ a. I refuse to hurt a peer's feelings.
    _____ b. I will defend my rights as a team member.
17. _____ a. I am usually firm in pursuing my point of view.
    _____ b. I'll walk away from disagreements before someone gets hurt.
18. _____ a. If it makes peers happy, I will agree with them.
    _____ b. I believe that give-and-take is the best way to resolve any disagreements.
19. _____ a. I prefer to have everyone involved in a conflict generate alternatives together.
    _____ b. When the team is discussing a serious problem, I usually keep quiet.
20. _____ a. I would rather openly resolve conflict than conceal differences.
    _____ b. I seek ways to balance gains and losses for equitable solutions.
21. _____ a. In problem solving, I am usually considerate of peers' viewpoints.
    _____ b. I prefer a direct and objective discussion of my disagreement.
22. _____ a. I seek solutions that meet some of everyone's needs.
    _____ b. I will argue as long as necessary to get my position heard.
23. _____ a. I like to assess the problem and identify a mutually agreeable solution.
    _____ b. When people challenge my position, I simply ignore them.
24. _____ a. If peers feel strongly about a position, I defer to it even if I don't agree.
    _____ b. I am willing to settle for a compromise solution.
25. _____ a. I am very persuasive when I have to be to win in a conflict situation.
    _____ b. I believe in the saying, "Kill your enemies with kindness."
26. _____ a. I will bargain with peers in an effort to manage disagreement.
    _____ b. I listen attentively before expressing my views.
27. _____ a. I avoid taking controversial positions.
    _____ b. I'm willing to give up my position for the benefit of the group.
28. _____ a. I enjoy competitive situations and "play" hard to win.
    _____ b. Whenever possible, I seek out knowledgeable peers to help resolve disagreements.
29. _____ a. I will surrender some of my demands, but I have to get something in return.
    _____ b. I don't like to air differences and usually keep my concerns to myself.
30. _____ a. I generally avoid hurting a peer's feelings.
    _____ b. When a peer and I disagree, I prefer to bring the issue out into the open so we can discuss it.

Scoring

Record your responses (number of points) in the space next to each statement number and then sum the points in each column.

Column 1	Column 2	Column 3	Column 4	Column 5
3 (a) ____	2 (a) ____	1 (a) ____	1 (b) ____	2 (b) ____
6 (b) ____	4 (a) ____	5 (b) ____	3 (b) ____	5 (a) ____
8 (a) ____	7 (b) ____	6 (a) ____	4 (b) ____	8 (b) ____
9 (b) ____	10 (b) ____	7 (a) ____	11 (b) ____	11 (a) ____
10 (a) ____	12 (b) ____	9 (a) ____	15 (a) ____	14 (a) ____
13 (b) ____	13 (a) ____	12 (a) ____	16 (a) ____	19 (a) ____
14 (b) ____	18 (b) ____	15 (b) ____	18 (a) ____	20 (a) ____
16 (b) ____	20 (b) ____	17 (b) ____	21 (a) ____	21 (b) ____
17 (a) ____	22 (a) ____	19 (b) ____	24 (a) ____	23 (a) ____
22 (b) ____	24 (b) ____	23 (b) ____	25 (b) ____	26 (b) ____
25 (a) ____	26 (a) ____	27 (a) ____	27 (b) ____	28 (b) ____
28 (a) ____	29 (a) ____	29 (b) ____	30 (a) ____	30 (b) ____
Total ____	Total ____	Total ____	Total ____	Total ____

Next carry over the totals from the column totals and then plot your total scores on the following chart to show the profile of your conflict-handling styles. A total score of 36 to 45 for a style may indicate a strong preference and use of that style. A total score of 0 to 18 for a style may indicate little preference and use of that style. A total score of 19 to 35 for a style may indicate a moderate preference and use of that style.

	Total	**0**	**10**	**20**	**30**	**40**	**50**	**60**
Column 1 (Forcing)	____							
Column 2 (Compromising)	____							
Column 3 (Avoiding)	____							
Column 4 (Accommodating)	____							
Column 5 (Collaborating)	____							
		0	**10**	**20**	**30**	**40**	**50**	**60**

Interpretation

When used appropriately, each of these styles can be an effective approach to conflict handling. Any one style or a mixture of the five can be used during the course of a dispute. Are you satisfied with this profile? Why or why not? Is this profile truly representative of your natural and primary conflict-handling styles?

Experiential Exercise: Managing Self

Intervening in Employee Disputes

Imagine yourself in the following two situations in an organization.

Scenario A: Two days before major contract work was to begin at the worksite of an important client, a dispute had erupted between the project director and the controller of a small emission-testing (pollution control) company with regard to hiring temporary workers. The project director argued that the extra workers were necessary for a timely completion of the work and, further, that she had the authority to hire temporary workers as well as do anything else necessary to complete the contract successfully. The controller strongly disagreed, arguing that company policy and regulations allowed the project director to purchase equipment and materials *only*. Adding employees to payroll, in the opinion of the controller, required the approval of both the human resources and finance departments. The dispute was brought to the president of the firm for resolution.

Scenario B: The marketing manager and the production manager of a manufacturing company were in sharp disagreement over some design changes. The production manager was upset about current procedures, which allowed marketing to make changes to product design in order to satisfy customers. Frequently, such changes were made right before production runs were scheduled to start, often resulting in delays that affected the manufacture of other products. Each change typically took 3 days of work to alter the specifications of the components, caused a loss of production line time that had already been reserved for manufacturing other products, and, in general, lowered cost-effectiveness. The production manager wanted to limit design changes to a minimum of 2 weeks before production was scheduled to begin. In other words, the deadline for the final design would be 2 weeks prior to production. The marketing manager was outraged by this suggestion and argued that last-minute design changes were often necessary to meet customer demands and keep the business. They had to cope with their competitor's willingness to make last-minute changes, as well as some disorganization from their customers who often seemed to come up with ideas (some of which were quite good) at the last moment. The marketing manager pointed out that they were having a tough enough time as it was maintaining market share in the global environment and it was crazy to do anything to reduce market share. The conflict had escalated to an extent that coordination and cooperation between marketing and production was suffering and morale was adversely affected. Finally, the president had to step in.[39]

Questions

1. Imagine that you are the president of the firm in these two situations. How would you intervene in the disputes? Would you attempt to facilitate a discussion between the disputants but leave the final solution in their hands? Would you listen carefully to their positions, analyze the situation, and then mandate a solution? Or would you stay aloof from the disputes, emphasizing to the individuals involved that they needed to learn how to handle such conflicts on their own? Select a strategy to resolve these conflicts. Using material from this chapter, explain and defend your decisions.
2. Based on your own experience (at work or school), describe a situation in which you had to decide whether to intervene in a dispute between two individuals. What did you do? Would you now do anything differently, and if so, what?

CHAPTER 10

Fostering Organizational Communication

LEARNING OBJECTIVES

When you have finished studying this chapter, you should be able to:

1. Describe the basic elements of interpersonal communication.
2. Explain the fabric of abilities that foster ethical interpersonal communications.
3. Describe how nonverbal communication affects dialogue.
4. State the role of communication networks in interpersonal communication.

Preview Case: David Radcliffe of Hogg Robinson
ELEMENTS OF INTERPERSONAL COMMUNICATION
- Sender and Receiver
- Transmitters and Receptors
- Messages and Channels
- Meaning and Feedback
- Interpersonal Barriers
- Cultural Barriers
- *Across Cultures Competency—Caterpillar's Piazza*

FOSTERING ETHICAL INTERPERSONAL COMMUNICATIONS
- Communication Openness
- Constructive Feedback
- Appropriate Self-Disclosure
- Active Listening
- *Communication Competency—FPA's Culture of Conversation*

NONVERBAL COMMUNICATION
- Types of Nonverbal Cues
- Cultural Differences
- Status Differences
- Organizational Use

INTERPERSONAL COMMUNICATION NETWORKS
- Individual Network
- Informal Group Network
- Formal Employee Network
- *Communication Competency—Sensis Employee Communication Strategy*
- Organizational Use

CHAPTER SUMMARY
KEY TERMS AND CONCEPTS
DISCUSSION QUESTIONS
EXPERIENTIAL EXERCISE AND CASE

DAVID RADCLIFFE OF HOGG ROBINSON

PREVIEW CASE

David Radcliffe is the chief executive officer of Hogg Robinson Limited, which has 7,500 employees and is headquartered in Hampshire, United Kingdom. This international organization has offices in 20 countries and focuses on corporate travel services as well as sporting events and meetings management. Radcliffe is a recent recipient of the European Excellence in Communication Leadership Award from the International Association of Business Communicators. Radcliffe seeks out ideas in both formal and informal ways. He spends two days every six weeks meeting with employees in their offices around the world. "Rather than going around one of our buildings with 200 people, I am better to get 20 of them for an hour and say, 'Ask me questions,'" he says, explaining that those 20 will then relate their conversations to the 200.

He also meets regularly with different groups of 12 people from throughout the company. They fly in for a few hours to discuss different matters with him and other senior directors. The participants are guaranteed confidentiality. He shares feedback from these visits with employees via an internal newsletter.

When Radcliffe became chief executive and launched this initiative, most of the questions were about local issues and tended to focus on the individual, such as "Why is my manager never talking to me?" "Why am I never given a chance to talk about my career?" or "Why are you being unfair to that person?" Today, communications have improved so that people's concerns are now more about the company and its acquisition plans and growth prospects. "This happened because the local issues have already been dealt with," says Radcliffe, citing yearly staff appraisals, Internet-based feedback programs, and internal publications that cover these areas.

Radcliffe's great sense of humor is a powerful ally in the pursuit of a corporate culture conducive to openness and better communication. Also, he states: "The best way is to treat other people how you like to be treated yourself. . . . If you have to have things in the company that are not nice, the thing to do is to explain why you have them. At least then everyone understands." Employee feedback, through Hogg Robinson's many internal communication programs, is critical. Radcliffe comments: "If employees do not understand what we are trying to do, then my whole desk is a waste of time. This is why spending time on communication becomes very important."

Understanding that "not everyone feels they have to work 24 hours a day," Radcliffe also introduced an internal *E-Mail Free Friday* to help create a more relaxed working environment and promote personal communication. Each Friday, employees are encouraged to focus on traditional forms of internal communication by picking up the telephone or walking to an office to speak to a colleague, rather than use e-mail. It also prevents overeager employees from e-mailing last-minute requests on Friday afternoon, forcing their colleagues to prepare a response over the weekend.[1]

For more information on Hogg Robinson Limited, visit the organization's home page at ***http://www.hoggrobinson.co.uk.***

Recall from Chapter 1 that the *communication competency* involves the overall ability to use all the modes of transmitting, understanding, and receiving ideas, thoughts, and feelings—verbal, listening, nonverbal, written, electronic, and the like—for accurately transferring and exchanging information and emotions. This chapter focuses on enhancing your communication competency with an emphasis on interpersonal communication. **Interpersonal communication** *involves a limited number of participants who (1) are usually in proximity to each other, (2) use many sensory channels, and (3) are able to provide immediate feedback.*[2] First, we discuss the process, types, and patterns of verbal, nonverbal, and other forms of communication used by employees on the job. Second, we present ways to foster ethical interpersonal dialogue in organizations. Third, we examine the nature and importance of nonverbal communication in interpersonal communication. Fourth, we review the role of communication networks in organizations.

In the Preview Case, it is clear that David Radcliffe recognizes the importance of interpersonal communication in Hogg Robinson. For example, recall his emphasis on meeting with small groups of employees, including the practice of meeting regularly with different groups of 12 employees from throughout the company. His introduction of the *E-Mail Free Friday* helped create a more relaxed working environment and promote personal communication.

LEARNING OBJECTIVE

1. Describe the basic elements of interpersonal communication.

ELEMENTS OF INTERPERSONAL COMMUNICATION

For accurate interpersonal communication to take place, the thoughts, facts, beliefs, attitudes, or feelings that the sender intended to send must be the same as those understood and interpreted by the receiver. Recall Radcliffe's comment from the Preview Case: "If employees do not understand what we are trying to do, then my whole desk is a waste of time. This is why spending time on communication becomes very important." Figure 10.1 presents the elements of interpersonal communication involving only two people; the process is not easy, and by considering its components, you can readily see that it becomes increasingly complex as more people participate.

Sender and Receiver

Exchanges between people are an element of interpersonal communication. Labeling one person as the sender and the other as the receiver is arbitrary. These roles shift back and forth, depending on where the individuals are in the process. When the receiver responds to the sender, the original receiver becomes the sender and the initiating sender becomes the receiver.

Consider the comment of a manager at CIBC Oppenheimer about dealing with a stockbroker who made a mistake in a client's statement but failed to notify the client:

> I was facing a tough decision about whether to fire this broker or just reprimand him for knowingly violating our policy. I wrestled with it in my head for almost a week and pretty much made up my mind about what I was going to do. But I gave his former boss a call and talked it through with her. She was really sympathetic and knew that I was struggling. She made me talk out my decision and asked me hard questions along the way. We looked at the problem from several perspectives: mine, my boss's, the broker's and the client's.[3]

This manager's statement suggests that the goals of the sender and receiver substantially influence the communication process. For example, the sender may have certain intentions in communicating, such as adding to or changing the thoughts,

FIGURE 10.1 Elements of Interpersonal Communication

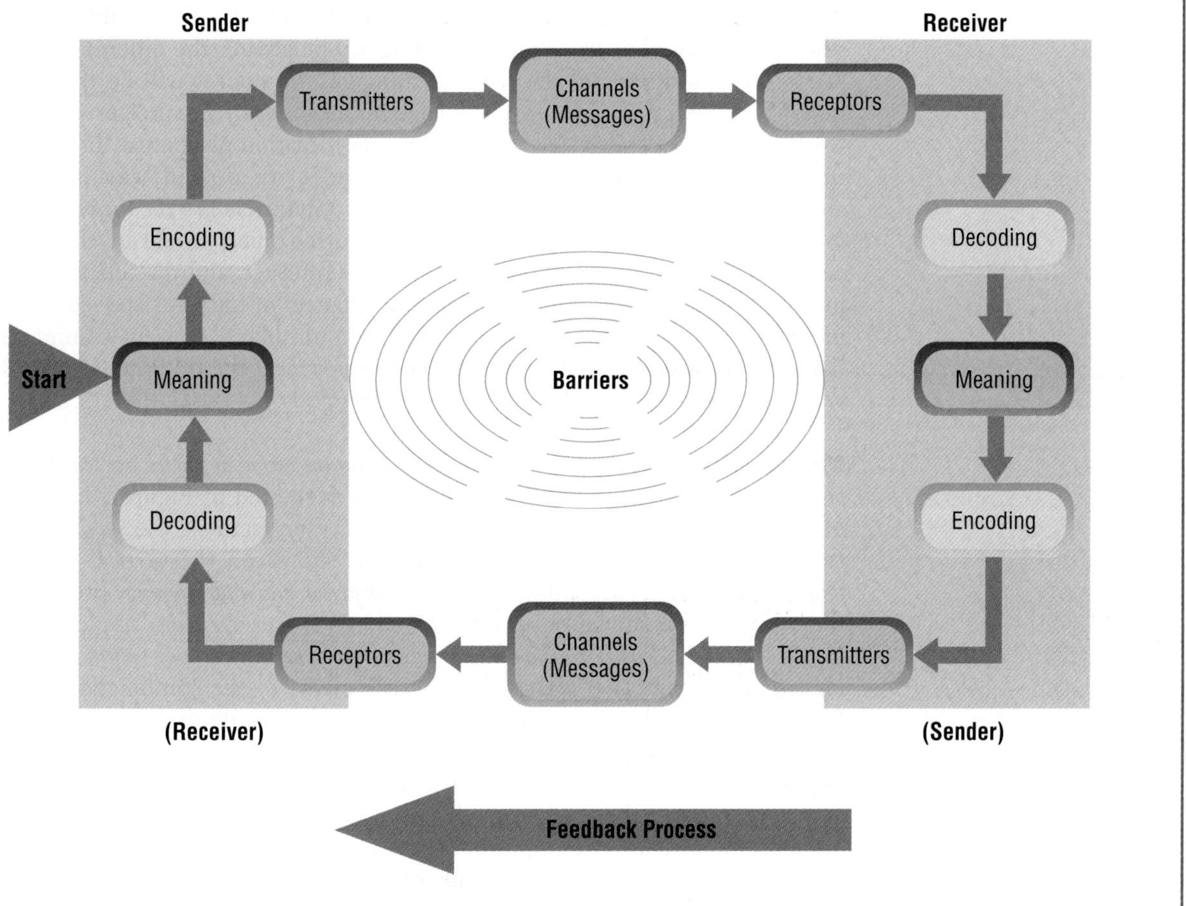

beliefs, attitudes, and/or behaviors of the receiver or changing the sender's relationship with the receiver. These intentions may be presented openly (the manager wanted a new broker) or developed deceptively. If the receiver doesn't agree with them, the probability of distortion and misunderstanding can be quite high (the manager concluded that the broker was immature and too embarrassed to call the client). The fewer the differences in goals, attitudes, and beliefs, the greater the probability that accurate communication will occur.

Transmitters and Receptors

Transmitters *(used by the sender)* and **receptors** *(used by the receiver) are the means available for sending and receiving messages.* They usually involve one or more of the senses: seeing, hearing, touching, smelling, and tasting. Transmission can take place both verbally and nonverbally. Once transmission begins, the communication process moves beyond the direct control of the sender. A message that has been transmitted cannot be brought back. How many times have you thought to yourself: I wish I hadn't said that?

Messages and Channels

Messages *include the transmitted data and the coded (verbal and nonverbal) symbols that give particular meaning to the data.* By using both verbal and nonverbal symbols, the sender tries to ensure that messages are interpreted by the receiver as the sender intended. To understand the difference between an original meaning and a received message, think about an occasion when you tried to convey inner thoughts and feelings of happiness, rage, or fear to another person. Did you find it difficult or impossible to transmit your true "inner meaning"? The greater the difference between the interpreted meaning and the original message, the poorer will be the communication. Words and nonverbal symbols have no meaning by themselves. Their meaning is created by the sender, the receiver, and the situation or context. In our discussion of potential interpersonal and cultural barriers, we explain why messages aren't always interpreted as they were meant to be. **Channels** *are the means by which messages travel from sender to receiver.* Examples of channels would be the "air" during person-to-person conversation, e-mail via the Internet, and the telephone. Radcliffe in the Preview Case indicated the importance of face-to-face communication, including acknowledging things employees do not like. Recall his comment: "If you have to have things in the company that are not nice, the thing to do is explain why you have them. At least then everyone understands."

Media Richness. *The capacity of a communication approach to transmit cues and provide feedback is called* **media richness.**[4] As suggested in Figure 10.2, the richness of each medium is a blend of several factors. One factor is the *speed of personalized feedback* provided through the medium. It is shown on the vertical axis as varying from slow to fast. A second factor is the *variety of cues and language* provided through the medium. It is shown on the horizontal axis as varying from single to multiple. A **cue** *is a stimulus, either consciously or unconsciously perceived, that results in a response by the receiver.* Figure 10.2 relates 10 different media to the combination of these two factors. Because these two factors are continual, a medium may vary somewhat in richness, depending on its use by sender and receiver. For example, e-mail may be associated with slower or quicker feedback than indicated in Figure 10.2. The speed depends on accessibility to e-mail messages and the receiver's tendency to reply immediately or later. Messages that require a long time to digest or that can't overcome biases are low in richness. Radcliffe, in the Preview Case, makes special efforts to employ rich media such as conversations with small groups of employees. Also, recall that he spends two days every six weeks meeting with employees in their offices around the world.

Data are the output of the communication. The various forms of data include words spoken face to face and in telephone calls; words written in e-mail messages, letters, and memos; and words compiled in computer printouts. They become information when they reinforce or change the receivers' understanding of their thoughts, feelings, attitudes, or beliefs. The use of groupware (various information technologies) may help such information exchange but can't always substitute for face-to-face dialogue. The reason is that, as suggested in Figure 10.2, face-to-face dialogue is the richest medium. It provides immediate feedback so that receivers can check the accuracy of their understanding and ask for clarification if they need to. It also allows sender and receiver simultaneously to observe body language, tone of voice, and facial expression. These observations add meaning to the spoken words. Finally, it enables sender and receiver quickly to identify symbols and use language that is natural and personal. Because of these characteristics, solving important and tough problems—especially those involving uncertainty and emotional content—almost always requires face-to-face dialogue.

Meaning and Feedback

The sender's message is transmitted through channels to the receiver's five senses in interpersonal communications. As Figure 10.1 suggests, received messages are changed from their symbolic form (e.g., spoken words) to a form that has meaning. **Meaning** *represents a person's thoughts, feelings, beliefs, and attitudes.*

FIGURE 10.2 Examples of Media Richness

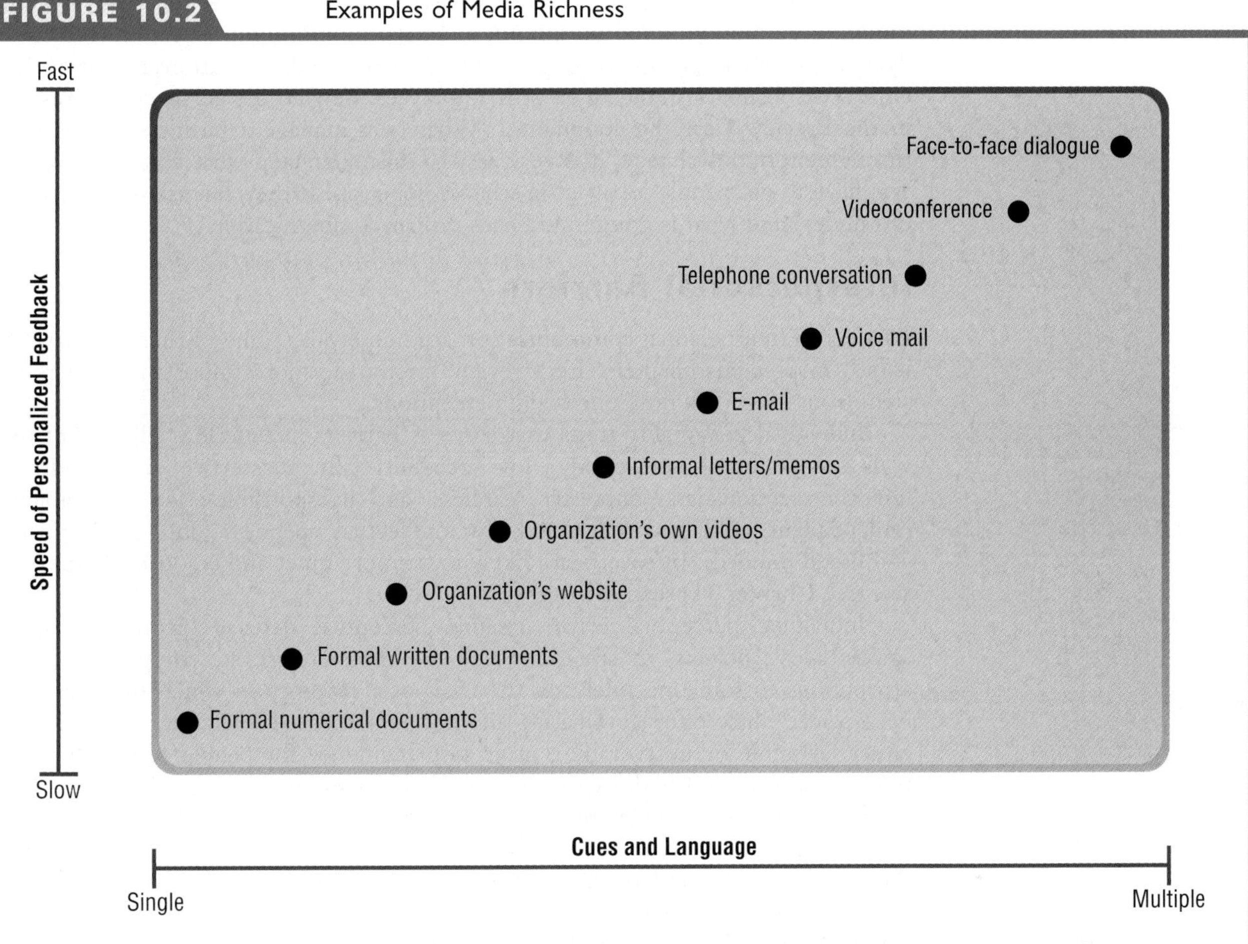

Encoding *gives personal meaning to messages that are to be sent.* Vocabulary and knowledge play an important role in the sender's ability to encode. Unfortunately, some professionals have difficulty communicating with people in general. They often encode meaning in a form that only other professionals in the same field can understand. Lawyers often encode (write) contracts that directly affect consumers but use language that only other lawyers can decode. Consumer groups have pressed to have such contracts written in language that almost everyone can understand. As a result, many banks, credit card firms, and other organizations have simplified the language in their contracts.

Decoding *gives personal, interpreted meaning to messages that are received.* Through a shared language, people can decode many messages so that the meanings received are reasonably close to the meanings transmitted. The accurate decoding of messages is often a major challenge in communicating.[5]

Interpersonal communication accuracy should be evaluated in relation to the ideal state, which occurs when the sender's intended meaning and the receiver's interpretation of it are the same. The transmission of factual data of a nonthreatening nature approximates the ideal state. For example, the sharing of the time, place, and procedures for a high school or college commencement ceremony generally results in easy and accurate interpersonal communication. The communication between a manager and a subordinate during a performance review session is a different, more complex, matter.

Feedback *is the receiver's response to the message.* It lets the sender know whether the message was received as intended. Interpersonal communication becomes a dynamic, two-way process through feedback, rather than just an event. David Radcliffe seeks feedback in meetings with employees. Beyond the perspectives presented in the Preview Case, he comments: "When you manage a business that is going through enormous change, it is very easy to misunderstand what communication is. You have to get people involved in what is going on. If they can ask questions, they can understand what is going on. That's proper communication."[6]

Interpersonal Barriers

Barriers to interpersonal communication are numerous. Some of them we have discussed in previous chapters. Let's review briefly the more important barriers that stem from individual differences and perceptions.

Individual personality traits that serve as barriers include low adjustment (nervous, self-doubting, and moody), low sociability (shy, unassertive, and withdrawn), low conscientiousness (impulsive, careless, and irresponsible), low agreeableness (independent, cold, and rude), and low intellectual openness (dull, unimaginative, and literal minded). Introverts are likely to be more quiet and emotionally inexpressive (see Chapter 11) than extroverts.

Individual perceptual errors include perceptual defense (protecting oneself against ideas, objects, or situations that are threatening), stereotyping (assigning attributions to someone solely on the basis of a category in which the person has been placed), halo effect (evaluating another person based solely on one impression, either favorable or unfavorable), projection (tendency for people to see their own traits in others), and high expectancy effect (prior expectations serving to bias how events, objects, and people are actually perceived). Individuals who make the fundamental attribution error (underestimating the impact of situational or external causes of behavior and overestimating the impact of personal causes of behavior when they seek to understand why people behave the way they do) are less likely to communicate effectively. This error too readily results in communicating blame or credit to individuals for outcomes. A related attribution error is the self-serving bias (communicating personal responsibility for good performance but denying responsibility for poor performance). (See Chapter 12.)

In addition to these underlying interpersonal communication barriers, there also are some direct barriers.

Noise. **Noise** *represents any interference with the intended message in the channel.* A radio playing loud music while someone is trying to talk to someone else is an example of noise. Noise sometimes can be overcome by repeating the message or increasing the intensity (e.g., the volume) of the message.

Semantics. **Semantics** is *the special meaning assigned to words.* Thus, the same words may mean different things to different people. Consider this comment by a manager to a subordinate: "How about the report for production planning? I think that they want it soon!" The manager could have intended one of several meanings in her comment:

Directing: You should get the report to me now. That's an order.

Suggesting: I suggest that we consider getting the report out now.

Requesting: Can you do the report for me now? Let me know if you can't.

Informing: The report is needed soon by production planning.

Questioning: Does production planning want the report soon?

Consider the semantics for five words in American (U.S.) English versus British English vocabularies:

- *Pavement:* American—a hard road surface; British—footpath, sidewalk.
- *Table (verb):* American—to remove from discussion; British—to bring to discussion.
- *Tick off (verb):* American—to anger; British—to rebuke.
- *Canceled check:* American—a check paid by the bank; British—a check that is stopped or voided.
- *Ship:* American—to convey by boat, train, plane, truck, or other means; British—to convey only by boat.[7]

Language Routines. *A person's verbal and nonverbal communication patterns that have become habits are known as* **language routines.** They can be observed by watching how people greet one another. In many instances, language routines are quite useful because they reduce the amount of thinking time needed to produce common messages. They also provide predictability in terms of being able to anticipate what is going to be said and how it is going to be said. The strategy of Wal-Mart and its image is reinforced through language, including its slogan: "Always Low Prices, Always Wal-Mart."

Language routines sometimes cause discomfort, offend, and alienate when they put down or discriminate against others. Many demeaning stereotypes of individuals and groups are perpetuated through language routines. For example, several years ago a manager at Texaco (now ChevronTexaco) made tapes of company conversations available to the public. These tapes contained demeaning comments made by board members and managers about minorities within the company, including blacks, Jews, other minorities, and women. Public outrage led to boycotts of Texaco, which ended up settling a racial discrimination case out of court for $176 million. After the lawsuit was settled, boycotts were called off, criticism trickled off, and Texaco's sales rebounded.[8]

Lying and Distortion. **Lying** *means the sender states what is believed to be false in order to seriously mislead one or more receivers.* The intention to deceive implies a belief that the receiver will accept the lie as a fact. In contrast, honesty means that the sender abides by consistent and rational ethical principles to respect the truth. Everyday social flattery in conversations may not be completely honest, but it is normally considered acceptable and rarely regarded as dishonest (lying). **Distortion** *represents a wide range of messages that a sender may use between the extremes of lying and complete honesty.* Of course, the use of vague, ambiguous, or indirect language doesn't necessarily indicate a sender's intent to mislead. This form of language may be viewed as acceptable political behavior. Silence may also be a form of distortion, if not dishonesty. Not wanting to look incompetent or take on a manager in a departmental meeting, a subordinate may remain quiet instead of expressing an opinion or asking a question.

Personal distortion in interpersonal communications may occur through **impression management**—*the process by which a sender knowingly attempts to influence the perceptions that the receivers form* (see Chapter 12).[9] Three impression management strategies—ingratiation, self-promotion, and face-saving—are commonly used:

- *Ingratiation* involves using flattery, supporting others' opinions, doing favors, laughing excessively at others' jokes, and so on.
- *Self-promotion* involves describing the sender's personal attributes to others in a highly positive and exaggerated way.
- *Face-saving* involves using various tactics, such as (1) apologizing in a way to convince others that the bad outcome isn't a fair indication of what the sender is really like as a person; (2) making excuses to others by admitting that the sender's behavior in some way caused a negative outcome, but strongly suggesting that

the person isn't really as much to blame as it seems (because the outcome wasn't intentional or there were extenuating circumstances); or (3) presenting justifications to others by appearing to accept responsibility for an outcome, but denying that the outcome actually led to problems.

Impression management strategies can range from relatively harmless minor forms of distortion (being courteous to another person even if you don't like the individual) to messages that use extreme ingratiation and self-promotion to obtain a better raise or promotion than others. The personal ethics, self-awareness of the sender, and the political climate of the individual's organization combine to influence the degree to which distortion tactics are used. In brief, the greater the frequency of distortion tactics and the more they approach the lying end of the distortion continuum, the more they will serve as a hurdle to interpersonal communication.

Cultural Barriers

Recall that *culture* refers to the distinctive ways in which different populations, societies, or smaller groups organize their lives or activities. **Intercultural communication** *occurs whenever a message sent by a member of one culture is received and understood by a member of another culture.*[10] The effects of cultural differences on barriers to interpersonal communication can be wide ranging. They depend on the degrees of difference (or similarity) between people in terms of language, religious beliefs, economic beliefs, social values, physical characteristics, use of nonverbal cues, and the like. The greater the differences, the more likely it is that there will be barriers to achieving intercultural communication.

Cultural Context. *The conditions that surround and influence the life of an individual, group, or organization are its* **cultural context.**[11] Differences in cultural context may represent a hurdle to intercultural communication. Nations' cultures vary on a continuum from low context to high context. Figure 10.3 shows the approximate placement of various countries along this continuum.

A **high-context culture** *in interpersonal communication is characterized by (1) the establishment of social trust before engaging in work-related discussions, (2) the high value placed on personal relationships and goodwill, and (3) the importance of the surrounding circumstances during an interaction.* In a high-context culture people rely on paraphrasing, tone of voice, gesture, posture, social status, history, and social setting to interpret spoken words, all of which require time. Factors such as trust, relationships among friends and family members, personal needs and difficulties, weather, and holidays must be taken into consideration. For example, Japanese executives—when meeting foreign executives for the first time—do not immediately "get down to business." They engage in a period of building trust and getting to know each other that foreign executives often are impatient with but must conform to.

In contrast, a **low-context culture** *in interpersonal communication is characterized by (1) directly and immediately addressing the tasks, issues, or problems at hand; (2) the high value placed on personal expertise and performance; and (3) the importance of clear, precise, and speedy interactions.* The use of behavioral modification techniques and other reinforcement approaches discussed in Chapter 14 are based on low-context communication. There we described how a manager can motivate employees with statements focusing on positive or corrective feedback and goal setting. In a heterogeneous country, such as the United States, multiple subcultures have their own unique characteristics. In contrast, the cultural context of a homogeneous country, such as Japan, reflects the more uniform characteristics of its people. We address the important role of nonverbal communication differences across cultures later in the chapter.

Ethnocentrism. **Ethnocentrism** *occurs when individuals believe that only their culture makes sense, has the "right" values, and represents the "right" and logical way to behave.*[12] This may be the greatest barrier to intercultural communication because it

FIGURE 10.3 Examples of Cultures on the Cultural Context Continuum

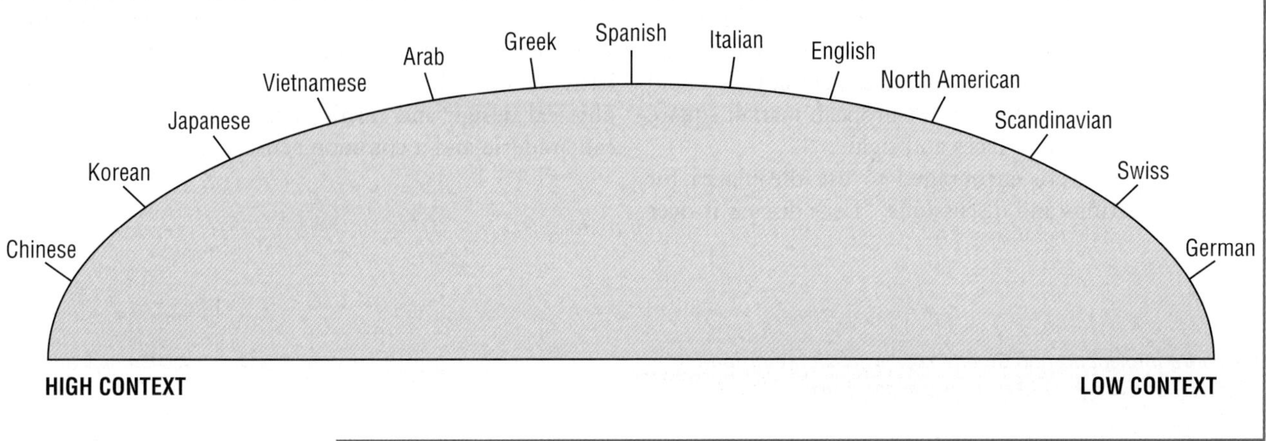

Source: Based on Hall, E. *Understanding Cultural Differences.* Yarmouth, ME.: Intercultural Press, 1989; Munter, M. *Guide to Managerial Communication: Effective Business Writing and Speaking,* 5th ed. Englewood Cliffs, N.J.: Prentice Hall, 1999.

involves judging others from our own cultural point of view. It also involves making false assumptions about the ways others behave based on our own limited experiences. Individuals are not even aware that they are being ethnocentric because "we don't understand that we don't understand." When two highly ethnocentric people from different cultures interact, there is little chance that they will achieve a common understanding. Ethnocentric reactions to strongly differing views are anger, shock, or even amusement. Such people view all others as inferior and may recognize cultural diversity, but only as a source of problems. Their strategy is to minimize the sources and impacts of cultural diversity. Ethnocentric executives and managers ignore or deny that cultural diversity can lead to advantages.

The following Across Cultures Competency feature reports on one initiative by Caterpillar to reduce cultural barriers at its European headquarters in Geneva, Switzerland.[13] The corporate headquarters for Caterpillar, Inc., is in Peoria, Illinois. It is the world's number one maker of earthmoving equipment and a leading supplier of agricultural equipment. The firm has approximately 77,000 employees with production facilities and offices around the globe.[14]

Across Cultures Competency

Caterpillar's Piazza

At Caterpillar's European headquarters in Geneva, Switzerland, employees represent a mixture of nationalities. Although essential for a successful global operation, this diversity complicates communication: Not only are employees dealing with multiple languages and backgrounds, they're also interacting with people from different communication cultures. The challenge was figuring out how to make members of this diverse population begin to think of themselves as a team.

Gottardo Bontagnali, the employee communication manager, kept thinking about the role played by the central market square—"piazza" in Italian—in virtually all European villages. In addition to going to the piazza for necessities of daily life, villagers go there to exchange news, pick up gossip, pass on information, and socialize. It was, and still is in many places, the village's most efficient communication tool.

So Bontagnali decided to create a "piazza" at Caterpillar's Geneva headquarters. Local artists were brought in to paint the walls of the top-floor cafeteria with large village scenes, dotted with bright yellow Cat machines as well as sights from multiple Cat locations. The "villagers" portrayed in the panoramas were actual Cat employees. With a little imagination, employees could actually picture themselves in a European market square surrounded by familiar faces and sights.

Employees were encouraged to use the piazza for informal meetings and discussions. "Let's discuss it over a cup of coffee in the piazza" has become part of Caterpillar's culture in Geneva. Because so many people use the piazza for regular exchanges, it's become an important means of sharing information on an impromptu basis as well. But the most impressive result is how physical design and furnishings helped build workforce camaraderie and a common sense of purpose.

For more information on Caterpillar, Inc., visit the organization's home page at ***http://www.cat.com.***

David Radcliffe, the focus of our Preview Case, also works hard to minimize cultural barriers in his own interpersonal communications. Recently, a division of his firm, Business Travel International (BTI), set up majority-controlled joint ventures in China, Hong Kong, Macau, and Taiwan. BTI Jin Jiang is the only corporate travel management company to have obtained licenses to do business in China's major cities. This is a major advantage in a country whose corporate travel market has experienced double-digit growth in recent years as a result of both direct foreign investment and the expanding domestic economy.

Radcliffe made sure he learned about China's culture as well as its business prospects. He comments: "China's culture is much older than any other, so they've got to have something right. Go and find out what that is, and then blend it with what you want. . . . When you go into a different country, with all the best technology in the world, you still encounter a huge history; and that means that different people have different needs. Never assume you have the right answer."[15]

LEARNING OBJECTIVE

2. Explain the fabric of abilities that foster ethical interpersonal communications.

FOSTERING ETHICAL INTERPERSONAL COMMUNICATIONS

Recall from Chapter 1 that the *ethics competency* involves the overall ability to incorporate values and principles that distinguish right from wrong in making decisions and choosing behaviors. In this section, we discuss the fabric of abilities that foster ethical interpersonal communications. The individual is more likely to incorporate values and principles that distinguish right from wrong in interpersonal communications through effective dialogue. The barriers to effective interpersonal communication—such as noise, confusing semantics, inappropriate language routines, and lying—will be reduced when effective dialogue takes place.

Dialogue *is a process whereby people suspend their defensiveness to enable a free flow of exploration into their own and others' assumptions and beliefs.* Dialogue includes (1) asking questions to learn, (2) seeking shared meanings, (3) integrating multiple perspectives, and (4) uncovering and examining assumptions. As a result, dialogue can build mutual trust, common ground, and the increased likelihood of ethical interpersonal communication.[16] A necessary condition for dialogue is assertive communication. **Assertive communication** *means confidently expressing what you think, feel, and believe while respecting the right of others to hold different views.* Ethical dialogue requires that interacting individuals demonstrate multiple abilities and behaviors. Figure 10.4

illustrates the idea that ethical dialogue is characterized by a specific group of interrelated abilities and behaviors. They include communication openness, constructive feedback, appropriate self-disclosure, active listening, and supportive nonverbal communication.

Through the elements of ethical dialogue and assertive communication, workplace honesty will be more prevalent. Joan Weisman is president and CEO of the Sheridan Press, which is a major division of the Sheridan Group and headquartered in East Hanover, New Hampshire. The Sheridan Press is a print and communication provider to publishers and associations. Weisman comments on the commitment to honesty in interpersonal and other forms of communication, as follows:

> My requirement that all employees be honest in all things is not presented as a lofty ideal that everyone is asked to aspire to. Rather, being honest is viewed at our company as enlightened self-interest that clearly defines how each employee's day-to-day behavior contributes to the success of our business. . . . Our commitment to being honest in all things—not just the easy things—is our lifeline to the soul and character of who we are and why we exist as a company. Being honest, especially when we are tested most severely, simply makes us stronger.[17]

One of the five core values of the Sheridan Press is stated as "We Have Integrity" and includes these components, which mandate ethical interpersonal communications:

- Are honest and up-front in dealing with each other.
- Respect, show courtesy, and treat each other fairly.
- Build trust among each other, and with our customers, suppliers, and communities.
- Obey the law.
- Make principle-based decisions.[18]

FIGURE 10.4 Interrelated Abilities and Behaviors That Foster Dialogue

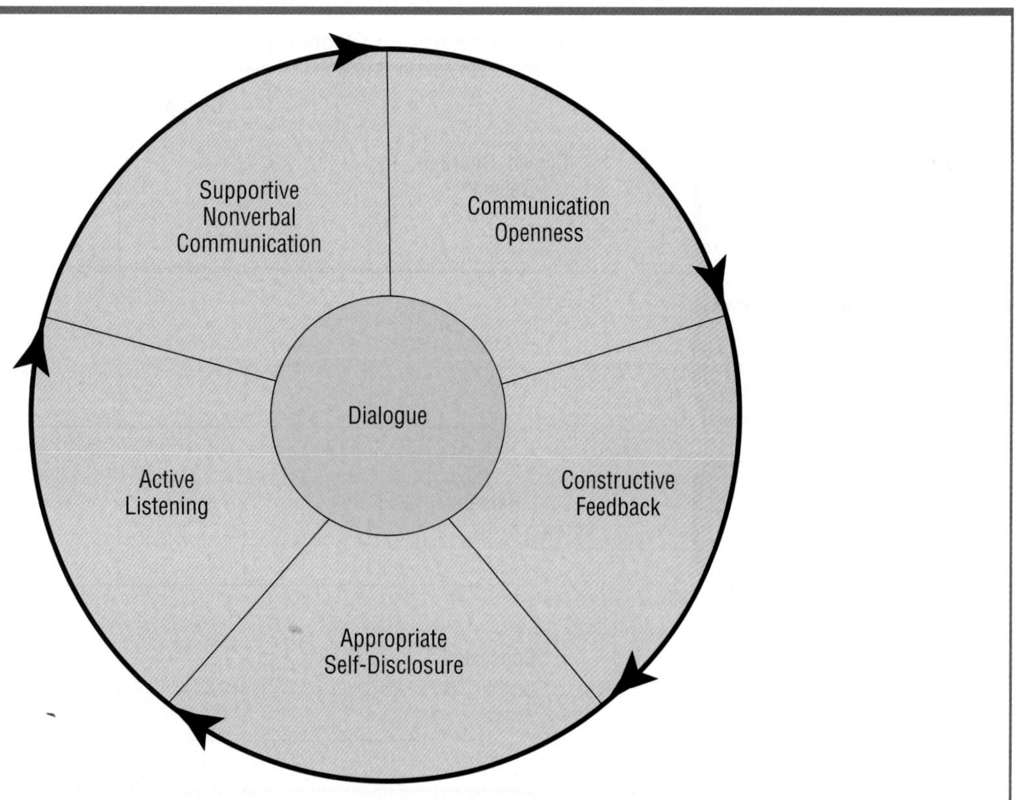

THE COMPETENT LEADER

Employees want the truth. And, they can handle the truth. Too often employers don't give employees enough credit for being able to cope with bad news.

Reggie Hall, Client Relationship Manager, Mellon Financial Corporation

Communication Openness

Communication openness may be viewed as a continuum ranging from closed, guarded, and defensive to open, candid, and nondefensive. Figure 10.5 shows that, at the extreme left-hand side of the continuum, messages are interpreted through low trust, hidden agendas, and concealed goals.

Communication occurs on two levels: direct and meta-communication.[19] **Meta-communication** *brings out the (hidden) assumptions, inferences, and interpretations of the parties that form the basis of open messages.* In closed communication, senders and receivers consciously and purposely hide their real agendas and "messages," and game playing is rampant. Meta-communication focuses on inferences such as (1) what I think you think about what I said, (2) what I think you really mean, (3) what I really mean but hope you don't realize what I mean, (4) what you're saying but what I think you really mean, and (5) what I think you're trying to tell me but aren't directly telling me because . . . (you're afraid of hurting my feelings, you think being totally open could hurt your chances of promotion, and so on).

At the extreme right-hand side of the continuum in Figure 10.5, communication is totally open, candid, and supportive. Messages are interpreted through high trust, shared agendas, and revealed goals. The words and nonverbal cues sent convey an authentic message that the sender chose without a hidden agenda. The purpose of communication is to reveal actual intent, not conceal it. The individuals ethically express what they mean and mean what they convey. Breakdowns in communication at this end of the continuum are due primarily to honest errors (e.g., the different meanings that people assign to words such as *soon* or *immediately*). Communication openness usually is a matter of degree rather than an absolute. The nature of language, linguistics, and different situations (coworker to coworker, subordinate to superior, friend to friend, or spouse to spouse) creates situations that allow for degrees of shading, coloring, emphasis, and deflection in the use of words and nonverbal cues as symbols of meaning.

FIGURE 10.5 Elements in Communication Openness

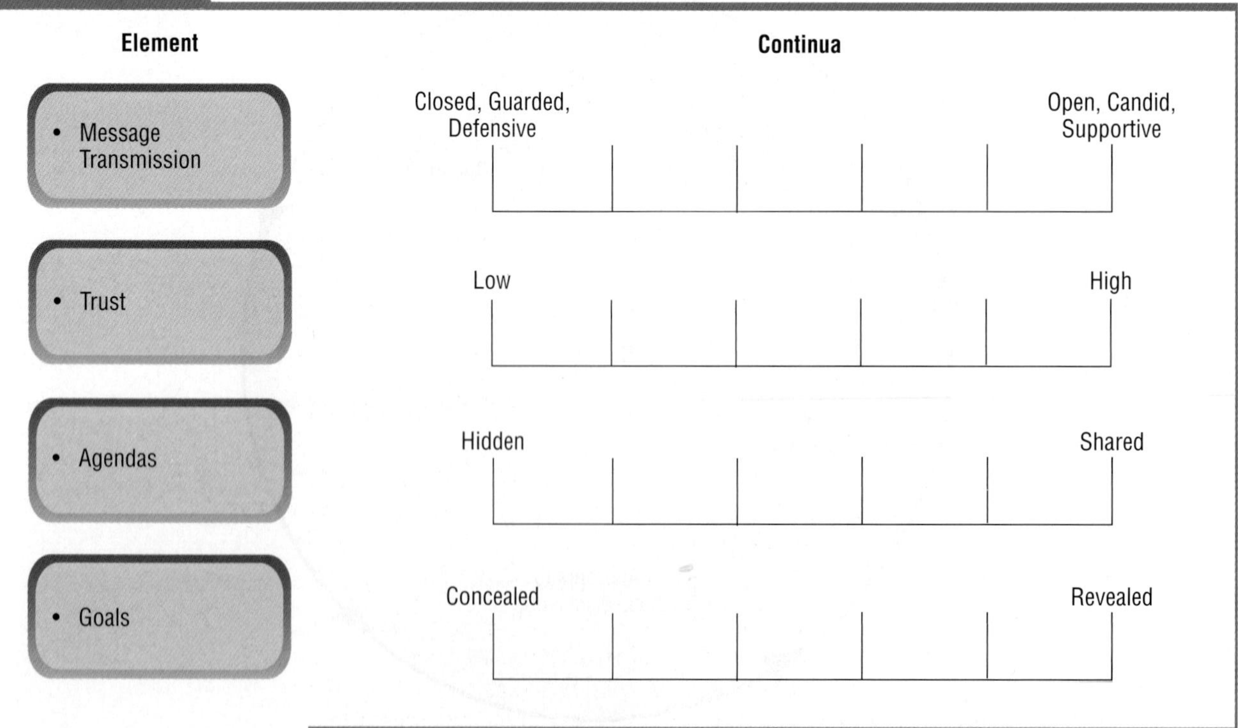

Organizational Use. The degree of openness must be considered in relation to the setting. We note several of these factors here briefly. First, the history of the relationship is perhaps the most significant factor affecting trust and risk taking in communication. Has the other person violated your or others' trust in the past? Has the other person been dishonest and unethical with you or others? Has the other person provided cues (verbal and/or nonverbal) soliciting or reinforcing your attempts to be open and candid? Or has the other person provided cues to the contrary? Has the history of the relationship created a level of such comfort that both you and the other person can focus on direct communication, rather than metacommunication?

Second, if the communication is likely to be partly adversarial or the other person is committed to damaging or weakening your position or gaining at your expense through unethical acts, guarded communication is rational. Conversely, if the communication is likely to be friendly and the other person is trying to please you, strengthen your position, or enhance your esteem, guarded communication may be viewed as irrational.

Third, when you communicate with someone of higher status and power, you are communicating with someone who has some control over your future. That person may be responsible for appraising your performance, judging your promotability, and determining the amount of your merit pay increase. The tendency is to project a favorable image and to encode negative messages with qualifiers. This is understandable and certainly may be rational, especially if past encounters with that person reinforce your use of some distortion. In contrast, the pattern of behaviors by David Radcliffe discussed in the Preview Case encourages and supports communication openness.

Constructive Feedback

In giving feedback, people share their thoughts and feelings about others with them. Feedback may involve personal feelings or reactions to others' ideas or proposals. The emotional impact of feedback varies according to how personally it is focused. When you attempt to achieve dialogue, feedback should be supportive (reinforcing ongoing behavior) or corrective (indicating that a change in behavior is appropriate). The following are principles of constructive and ethical feedback that can foster dialogue:

- Constructive feedback is based on a foundation of trust between sender and receiver. When an organization is characterized by extreme personal competitiveness, the emphasis is on the use of power to punish and control, rigid superior–subordinate relationships, and a lack of trust for constructive and ethical feedback.
- Constructive feedback is specific rather than general. It uses clear and recent examples. Saying "You are a dominating person" isn't as useful as saying "Just now when we were deciding the issue, you did not listen to what others said. I felt I had to accept your argument or face attack from you."
- Constructive feedback is given at a time when the receiver appears to be ready to accept it. When a person is angry, upset, or defensive, that probably isn't the time to bring up other issues.
- Constructive feedback is checked with the receiver to determine whether it seems valid. The sender can ask the receiver to rephrase and restate the feedback to test whether it matches what the sender intended.
- Constructive feedback covers behaviors that the receiver may be capable of doing something about.
- Constructive feedback doesn't include more than the receiver can handle at any particular time. For example, the receiver may become threatened and defensive if the feedback includes everything the receiver does that annoys the sender.[20]

Organizational Use. Individuals, teams, and organizations all depend on relevant feedback to improve the way they develop and perform. One approach to obtaining such feedback is through the collection and tabulation of perceptions from multiple individuals about the behaviors and performance of a single individual. For example, **360-degree feedback** *is a questionnaire-based process that gathers structured feedback from a number of sources about the competencies and behaviors of an individual or team.* For a manager, questionnaires on observed behaviors might be completed by oneself, subordinates, peers, superior, and customers. The results are compiled in a feedback report, with data from each source presented separately. These data and results are provided to the individual who then develops a plan for building strengths and improving personal performance. Normally, this discussion would take place with the person's superior.

The use and application of 360-degree feedback is controversial. Clearly, there needs to be an ethical environment of trust and communication openness before the implementation of a formal 360-degree feedback process. It doesn't work in a highly political or bureaucratic organization. It may not work as well when the feedback is used in a person's performance review process unless specific abilities and behaviors can be linked to specific performance goals. In general, 360-degree feedback appears to work best if it is used for coaching and professional development purposes. A number of other issues and recommendations with respect to the 360-degree feedback process are beyond our scope here.[21]

Table 10.1 provides a questionnaire that can be used by employees to diagnose interpersonal feedback practices within their organization. The scoring system goes from 1 point (strongly disagree) to 5 points (strongly agree) for each statement. Thus, the greater the frequency of "agree" and "strongly agree" responses to the 15 feedback practices, the greater the degree of open and, most likely, ethical interpersonal communications within the organization.

TABLE 10.1 Diagnosis of Feedback Practices

Read each of the following statements and record your perceptions about the feedback practices you experienced in a previous job. Respond on the continuum that ranges from strongly disagree to strongly agree, as follows:

1	2	3	4	5
Strongly Disagree	Disagree	Neutral	Agree	Strongly Agree

CORRECTIVE FEEDBACK

_____ 1. Your manager lets you know when you make a mistake. 1 2 3 4 5

_____ 2. You receive a formal report of poor performance. 1 2 3 4 5

_____ 3. Coworkers tell you that you have done something wrong. 1 2 3 4 5

_____ 4. You are told when you should be doing something else. 1 2 3 4 5

POSITIVE FEEDBACK FROM YOUR MANAGER

_____ 5. You receive thanks after completed jobs. 1 2 3 4 5

_____ 6. Your manager tells you when you are doing a good job. 1 2 3 4 5

_____ 7. You have a regular performance review with your manager. 1 2 3 4 5

_____ 8.	The manager treats you as a mature adult.	1 2 3 4 5
POSITIVE FEEDBACK FROM PEERS		
_____ 9.	Peers congratulate you for how much you accomplish.	1 2 3 4 5
_____10.	Peers compliment you for the quality of your work.	1 2 3 4 5
_____11.	You know more people are using the company's product or service because of your efforts.	1 2 3 4 5
_____12.	Peers like you very much.	1 2 3 4 5
INTERNAL FEEDBACK		
_____13.	You know when you have met your goals.	1 2 3 4 5
_____14.	You can see the results of finding better ways of doing the job.	1 2 3 4 5
_____15.	You know how much you can do without making a mistake.	1 2 3 4 5

The first four items in Table 10.1 concern corrective feedback from superiors and coworkers. Corrective feedback is not necessarily bad for the person who is receiving it. Its effectiveness is largely determined by how the feedback is given. The second section in Table 10.1 concerns the degree to which positive feedback is given by individuals at higher organizational levels (items 5 through 8). Positive feedback reinforces and rewards certain behaviors so that they will be repeated in the future. The third section (items 9 through 12) concerns the degree to which positive feedback is given by your peers. Thus, the first three sections all concern the degree to which positive or negative feedback is received from sources external to the individual. By contrast, the fourth section (items 13 through 15) focuses on internal feedback, or the degree to which individuals observe and assess themselves.

This diagnostic questionnaire clearly shows that several forms of feedback are available to individuals in organizations. A lack of compatibility among these forms of feedback for a number of employees may indicate serious problems in an organization's system of interpersonal communication.

Appropriate Self-Disclosure

Self-disclosure *is any information that individuals communicate (verbally or nonverbally) about themselves to others.* People often unconsciously disclose much about themselves by what they say and how they present themselves to others. The ability to express yourself to others usually is basic to personal growth and development.[22] Nondisclosing individuals may repress their real feelings because to reveal them is threatening. Conversely, total-disclosure individuals, who expose a great deal about themselves to anyone they meet, actually may be unable to communicate with others because they are too self-centered. The presence of appropriate self-disclosure, say, between superior and subordinate or team members and customers, can facilitate dialogue and sharing of work-related problems.

Organizational Use. A person's level in an organization often complicates self-disclosure. An individual is likely to reduce self-disclosure to those having greater formal power because of their ability to punish. Even when a subordinate is able and willing to engage in "appropriate" forms of self-disclosure at work, a perception of the superior's trustworthiness in not using the revealed information to punish, intimidate, or ridicule is likely to influence the amount and form of self-disclosure.

> **THE COMPETENT LEADER**
>
> I don't care how busy you are. It's critical for leaders to have an ear on what's going on by listening. Or, they are going to turn around and there's not going to be anyone standing behind them.
>
> Linda Pittenger, CEO and President, People3, Inc.

Active Listening

Active listening is necessary to encourage appropriate levels of ethical feedback and openness. **Listening** *is a process that integrates physical, emotional, and intellectual inputs in a search for meaning and understanding.* Listening is effective when the receiver understands the sender's message as intended.

As much as 40 percent of an eight-hour workday for many employees is devoted to listening. However, tests of listening comprehension suggest that people often listen at only 25 percent efficiency. Listening skills influence the quality of peer, manager–subordinate, and employee–customer relationships. Employees who dislike a manager may find it extremely difficult to listen attentively to the manager's comments during performance review sessions. The following guidelines are suggested for increasing active listening skills to foster ethical interpersonal communications through dialogue:

- Having a reason or purpose for listening. Good listeners tend to search for value and meaning in what is being said, even if they are not predisposed to be interested in the particular issue or topic. Poor listeners tend to rationalize any or all inattention on the basis of a lack of initial interest.
- Suspending judgment, at least initially. Good listening requires concentrating on the sender's whole message, rather than forming evaluations on the basis of the first few ideas presented.
- Resisting distractions, such as noises, sights, and other people, and focusing on the sender.
- Pausing before responding to the sender.
- Rephrasing in your own words the content and feeling of what the sender seems to be saying, especially when the message is emotional or unclear.
- Seeking out the sender's important themes in terms of the overall content and feeling of the message.
- Using the time differential between the rate of thought (400 or 500 words per minute) and the rate of speech (100 to 150 words per minute) to reflect on content and search for meaning.[23]

Organizational Use. Active listening skills are interrelated. That is, you can't practice one without improving the others. Unfortunately, like the guidelines for improving feedback, the guidelines for improving active listening are much easier to read about than to develop and practice. The more you practice active listening skills, the more likely you will be able to enter into effective dialogue.

The following Communications Competency feature reports on a sample of recent initiatives by the leadership of the Financial Planning Association (FPA) to foster dialogue within its organization.[24] The FPA has approximately 27,000 members in the financial planning community. It is headquartered in Washington, D.C.

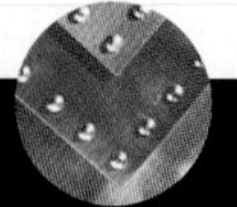

COMMUNICATION COMPETENCY

FPA's Culture of Conversation

Janet McCullen recently served as president of the Financial Planning Association (FPA). She comments:

One aspect of FPA that I am most proud of having helped nurture is a culture of conversation. A culture of conversation focuses on dialogue, not debate. Dialogue is collaborative; multiple sides work towards shared understanding. Debate is oppositional; two sides try to prove each other wrong. In dialogue, one listens to understand, to make meaning, and to find common ground. Dialogue enlarges and possibly changes a participant's view. It reveals assumptions for reevaluation. Dialogue creates an open-minded attitude, openness to being wrong and openness to change. In dialogue, one submits one's best thinking, expecting that the reflections of others will help improve it rather than threaten it.

FPA began its work to create a culture of conversation by introducing several initiatives, such as the following:

- *Circle:* At board of directors meetings and other staff and leadership gatherings, FPA introduced a Circle process. The Circle means much more than just chairs in a circle without a table. Circle means bringing your full, whole self, with intention, openness, and respect. It means prizing discovery and creativity in conversation. Circle means slowing down and listening for what isn't said as well as what is said—it's seeking the questions underneath the questions. Circle means trusting the wisdom of the group.
- *Knowledge Cafés:* At chapter and national meetings, FPA began gathering members to engage with each other on important issues and questions for planners and the profession. Participants share their questions and perspectives and explore others' assumptions. The amazing thing about the Knowledge Cafés is that no matter what question they used to start the dialogue, the conversation always seemed to center on the public's understanding and value of financial planning—a place where the board's conversation is often centered too.
- *Conversation Spaces:* At FPA national meetings, as well as online, space is offered for those who want to join in conversation. This space is provided for planned and spontaneous gatherings, and to help ensure that members are making the connections they want and need with others.
- *Quarterly Chapter Calls:* Each quarter, chapter leaders are invited to participate in conference calls to talk with board and staff leaders about what's happening at FPA. They hear about new initiatives, provide feedback on issues, and learn the reasoning behind what FPA is doing, so that they can share what they learn with chapter members.

For more information on the Financial Planning Association, visit the organization's home page at ***http://www.fpnat.com.***

NONVERBAL COMMUNICATION

LEARNING OBJECTIVE

3. Describe how nonverbal communication affects dialogue.

Nonverbal communication *includes the process of sending "wordless" messages by such means as facial expressions, gestures, postures, tones of voice, grooming, clothing, colors, and use of space.*[25] Nonverbal cues may contain many hidden messages and can influence the process and outcome of face-to-face communication. Even a person who is silent or inactive in the presence of others may be sending a message, which may or may not be the intended message (including boredom, fear, anger, or depression). Nonverbal signals are a rich source of information. One's own nonverbal behavior can be useful in responding to others, making stronger connections with others, and conveying certain impressions about oneself. The proportion of emotional reactions that are expressed through nonverbal signals often exceeds 90 percent.[26]

Types of Nonverbal Cues

A framework for considering types of *personal* nonverbal cues is *PERCEIVE*, an acronym that stands for the following terms: (1) **P**roximity, (2) **E**xpressions, (3) **R**elative orientation, (4) **C**ontact, (5) **E**yes, (6) **I**ndividual gestures, (7) **V**oice, and (8) **E**xistence of adapters. A brief review of each follows[27]:

- *Proximity* is the distance between individuals. Generally, individuals sit, stand, and want to be near those they like. Increased proximity is usually an indication of feelings of liking and interest in the North American environment.
- *Expressions* are observed on the face and can last as little as 1/15 of a second. These very brief expressions occur when people are trying to hide a feeling. Interestingly, when people begin to experience an emotion, their facial muscles are triggered. If they suppress the expression, it's shown for only 1/15 of a second. If they do not suppress it, the expression will appear prominently. The six universal expressions that most cultures recognize are happiness, sadness, anger, fear, surprise, and disgust. Smiling can be real or false, interpreted by differences in the strength and length of the smile, the openness of the eyes, and symmetry of expression.
- *Relative orientation* is the degree to which individuals face one another. Individuals sitting side by side is usually an indication that they are interested in and focused on the other person. As individuals become less interested in another person, they tend to angle their bodies away. A good way to decode orientation is to observe where a person's feet are placed. Often individuals will point their feet in the direction they truly want to go.
- *Contact* refers to physical contact. Generally, the amount and frequency of physical contact demonstrate closeness, familiarity, and degree of liking. A lot of touching usually indicates strong liking for another person.
- *Eyes* primarily show whom or what people are most interested in or like. One can gauge liking and interest by the frequency, duration, and total amount of time spent looking. Few gestures carry more weight than looking someone in the eyes or face in the North American environment. Eye and face contact displays your willingness to listen and your acknowledgment of the other person's worth. Although eye contact does not indicate truthfulness or honesty (as some people believe), it does usually show interest in the other person's idea or point of view. However, prolonged and intense eye contact does not usually occur unless feelings of hostility, defensiveness, or romantic interest are present. Lack of interest may be indicated through contractions of the pupils or wandering eyes.
- *Individual gestures* can convey an image in a person's mind that is sometimes not communicated with spoken language. Some typical gestures are ones in which people indicate what refers to them and what refers to others (e.g., the hands come near the body or motion away), gestures that describe an emotion or experience (e.g., sobbing gesture or frenetic moving of the hands) or gestures that identify where objects are in relation to one another. Gestures can provide information about how things are organized in a person's mind. They can also reveal how people are feeling. People tend to gesture more when they are enthusiastic, excited, and energized. People tend to gesture less when they are demoralized, nervous, or concerned about the impression they are making.
- *Voice* or speech often provides information about the demographics of a speaker (e.g., gender, age, area of origin, social class). Voice can also reveal emotions, which are transmitted through the tone of the voice, accentuation of words, rapidity of speech, and number of speech errors. Typically, speech errors indicate discomfort and anxiety. A person who begins to produce a lot of speech errors may be anxious and ill at ease.
- *Existence of adapters* is the last element of *PERCEIVE*. Adapters are small behaviors that tend to occur when people are stressed or bored with a situation. Examples are playing with rings, twirling a pen, or touching one's hair. As meetings extend, an increasing number of adapter behaviors tend to emerge among the people in the room.

There are, of course, other types of nonverbal cues that are not as specific to the interpersonal communications of individuals. We note two of them here:

- *Time.* Being late or early, keeping others waiting, cultural differences in time perception, and the relationship between time and status.
- *Physical environment.* Building and room design, furniture and other objects, interior decorating, cleanliness, lighting, and noise.

Some organizations are attempting to influence interpersonal communications through the physical environment with use of **feng shui**—*the Chinese art of design and placement of buildings, furniture, and even small objects.*[28] In literal terms, the Chinese phrase "feng shui" means "wind and water" to represent the flow of energy and harmony. It consists of a complex and interrelated set of concepts and principles. A few of the common recommendations for office design based on feng shui include:

1. You should have a full view of the room's entrance door by merely looking up from your desk.
2. You should be able to see outside while sitting at your desk. If the office doesn't have a window, brighten up the lighting and use a picture of the outdoors.
3. Your desk should not be placed at the side of the door. You can place a screen in the space between your desk and the doorway if necessary.
4. You should have a wall at your back while seated. Presumably, it gives you a "commanding" position.[29]

Although the ability of feng shui to impact "harmony and energy" has been questioned, its principles for designing buildings and offices are increasingly used in Western societies.[30]

Nonverbal communication is important to verbal communication in that neither is adequate by itself for effective dialogue. A few of the ways in which verbal and nonverbal cues can be related are as follows:

- Repeating, as when verbal directions to some location are accompanied by pointing.
- Contradicting, as in the case of the person who says "What, me nervous?" while fidgeting and perspiring anxiously before taking a test—a good example of how the nonverbal message might be more believable when verbal and nonverbal signals conflict.
- Substituting nonverbal for verbal cues, as when an employee returns to the office with a stressful expression that says "I've just had a horrible meeting with my manager"—without a word being spoken.
- Complementing the verbal cue through nonverbal "underlining," as when a person pounds the table, places a hand on the shoulder of a coworker, uses a tone of voice indicating the great importance attached to the message, or presents a gift as a way of reinforcing an expression of gratitude or respect.

Nonverbal cues have been linked to a wide variety of concepts and issues. We briefly consider two: (1) cultural differences and (2) status differences, in terms of the relative ranking of individuals and groups.

Cultural Differences

Throughout this book, we have noted the impact of culture on communication. Because of the many differences in nonverbal expression, people from different cultures often misunderstand each other. This is a significant barrier to cross-cultural communication.[31] Earlier in this chapter, we examined how cultural context and ethnocentrism may affect interpersonal communications. Let's now examine three forms of nonverbal cross-cultural communication: chromatics, chronemics, and body language.

Chromatics. **Chromatics** *is communication through the use of color.* Colors of clothing, products, packaging, or gifts send intended or unintended messages when people communicate cross-culturally. For example, in Hong Kong red signifies happiness or good luck. The traditional bridal dress is red, and at Chinese New Year luck money is distributed in *hong bao*, or red envelopes. Men in Hong Kong avoid green because of the Cantonese expression "He's wearing a green hat," which means "His wife is cheating on him." In Chile, a gift of yellow roses conveys the message "I don't like you," whereas in the Czech Republic giving red roses indicates a romantic interest.

Chronemics. **Chronemics** *reflects the use of time in a culture.*[32] Before reading any further, please complete the instrument in Table 10.2 to determine how you use your personal time. A **monochronic time schedule** *means that things are done linearly, or one activity at a time.* Time is seen as something that can be controlled or wasted by people. This time schedule is followed in individualistic cultures, such as those in Northern Europe, Germany, and the United States. Being a few minutes late for a business appointment is an insult, so punctuality is extremely important. Keith Hughes, the former CEO of the Associates First Capital Corporation, used to lock the doors when a meeting was supposed to start and didn't unlock them until the meeting was over.

TABLE 10.2 The Polychronic Attitude Index

Please consider how you feel about the following statements. Circle your choice on the scale provided: strongly agree, agree, neutral, disagree, or strongly disagree.

	STRONGLY DISAGREE	DISAGREE	NEUTRAL	AGREE	STRONGLY AGREE
I do not like to juggle several activities at the same time.	5	4	3	2	1
People should not try to do many things at once.	5	4	3	2	1
When I sit down at my desk, I work on one project at a time.	5	4	3	2	1
I am comfortable doing several things at the same time.	1	2	3	4	5

Add up your points, and divide the total by 4. Then plot your score on the scale.

1.0	1.5	2.0	2.5	3.0	3.5	4.0	4.5	5.0
Monochronic								Polychronic

The lower the score (below 3.0), the more monochronic your organization or department is; the higher the score (above 3.0), the more polychronic it is.

Source: Adapted from Bluedorn, A. C., Kaufman, C. F., and Lane, P. M. How many things do you like to do at once? An introduction to monochronic and polychronic time. *Academy of Management Executive*, 1992, 6(4), 17–26. Used with permission of Bluedorn, A. C., 1999.

A **polychronic time schedule** *means that people tend to do several things at the same time.* Many people may like to drive and conduct business at the same time (cars and cellular phones) or watch the news and a ball game at the same time (picture-in-picture TV). Schedules are less important than personal involvement and the completion of business. In Latin America and the Middle East, time schedules are less important than personal involvement. In Ecuador, businesspeople come to a meeting 15 or 20 minutes late and still consider themselves to be on time.

Body Language. Posture, gestures, eye contact, facial expression, touching, voice pitch and volume, and speaking rate differ from one culture to another.[33] As a simple, but potentially disastrous example, nodding the head up and down in Bulgaria means "no," not "yes." You must avoid using any gestures considered rude or insulting. For instance, in Buddhist cultures, the head is considered sacred, so you must never touch anyone's head. In Muslim cultures, the left hand is considered unclean, so never touch, pass, or receive with the left hand. Pointing with the index finger is rude in cultures ranging from the Sudan to Venezuela to Sri Lanka. The American circular "A-OK" gesture carries a vulgar meaning in Brazil, Paraguay, Singapore, and Russia. Crossing your ankle over your knee is rude in Indonesia, Thailand, and Syria. Pointing your index finger toward yourself insults the other person in Germany, the Netherlands, and Switzerland. Avoid placing an open hand over a closed fist in France, saying "tsk tsk" in Kenya, and whistling in India.

Prepare yourself to recognize gestures that have meaning only in the other culture. Chinese stick out their tongues to show surprise and scratch their ears and cheeks to show happiness. Japanese suck in air, hissing through their teeth to indicate embarrassment or "no." Greeks puff air after they receive a compliment. Hondurans touch a finger to the face below the eye to indicate caution or disbelief.

Finally, resist applying your own culture's nonverbal meanings to other cultures. Vietnamese may look at the ground with their heads down to show respect, not to be "shifty." Russians may exhibit less facial expression and Scandinavians fewer gestures than Americans are accustomed to, but that doesn't mean that they aren't enthusiastic. The British may prefer more distant personal and social space and might consider it rude if you move too close. Closely related is the concept of touch. Anglos usually avoid touching each other very much. In studies of touching behaviors, researchers observed people seated in outdoor cafes in each of four countries and counted the number of touches during an hour of conversation. The results were San Juan, Puerto Rico, 180 touches per hour; Paris, 110 per hour; Gainesville, Florida, 1 per hour; and London, 0 per hour.[34]

Status Differences

The following are only three of the many relationships between nonverbal cues and organizational status:

- Employees of higher status typically have better offices than do employees of lower status. For example, executive offices are typically more spacious, located on the top floors of the building, and have finer carpets and furniture than those of first-line managers. Most senior offices are at the corners, so they have windows on two sides.
- The offices of higher status employees are better "protected" than those of lower status employees. *Protected* refers to how much more difficult it would be for you to, say, arrange to visit the governor of your state than for the governor to arrange to visit you. Top executive areas are typically least accessible and are often sealed off from others by several doors and assistants. Having an office with a door and a secretary who answers the telephone protects even lower level managers and many staff personnel.
- The higher the employee's status, the easier that employee finds it to invade the territory of lower status employees. A superior typically feels free to walk right in on subordinates, whereas subordinates are more careful to ask permission or make an appointment before visiting a superior.[35]

Carried to excess, these and other nonverbal status cues are likely to create barriers to dialogue, especially from the perspective of the employees with lower formal status. However, effective managers often use supportive nonverbal cues when meeting with subordinates, such as (1) lightly touching subordinates on the arm when they arrive and shaking hands, (2) smiling appropriately, (3) nodding to affirm what was said, (4) slightly pulling their chairs closer to subordinates and maintaining an open posture, and (5) engaging in eye contact to further demonstrate listening and interest.

Organizational Use

You need to be cautious in assuming that there are hard and fast rules for quickly interpreting a particular nonverbal cue. In this section, we present three brief incidents to illustrate stereotypical and simple interpretations of nonverbal cues, which are then followed by the facts.

- You're a sales rep presenting your organization's latest planning software to a senior-management prospect. Midway through your presentation, the potential customer leans back in her chair, looks briefly away, and crosses her arms in front of her. You read this body language as unspoken resistance to your price or benefits and immediately shift gears. It turns out that she liked your software but was simply chilled by the cold temperature in the conference room.
- A presenter stands fixed behind a lectern, exhibiting little noticeable body language. The content of his presentation features real-world illustrations, stories, and supporting visual aids. He throws in some self-deprecating humor for good measure. Aside from solid eye contact and periodic head movements, he could be a mannequin. For the audience, this noticeable lack of body energy likely has an effect equivalent to passing out sleeping pills. In fact, the speaker scores high on audience evaluations for authenticity, pragmatic content, and storytelling.
- You're being introduced to the sponsors of an important presentation that you're giving next week. To create a good first impression, you arrive full of energy. You talk fast, and shake hands firmly and quickly. Your gestures are sharp and energetic. You walk away convinced that your hosts were impressed by your enthusiasm and credibility. In fact, to establish a credible first impression, it's often best to talk and move less, with fewer gestures, and to use a slower, lower manner of speaking. People subconsciously associate self-confidence and empathy with a more controlled body style. Your hosts likely thought you were either trying too hard to impress or were wired on too much coffee.[36]

LEARNING OBJECTIVE

4. State the role of communication networks in interpersonal communication.

INTERPERSONAL COMMUNICATION NETWORKS

An **interpersonal communication network** *is the pattern of communication flows, relationships, and understandings developed over time among people, rather than focusing on the individual and whether a specific message is received as intended by the sender.* Networks involve the ongoing flow of verbal, written, and nonverbal messages between two people or between one person and others. Communication networks can influence the likelihood of a match between messages as sent and as actually received and interpreted. The more accurately the message moves through the channel, the more clearly the receiver will understand it.

Individual Network

The elements of interpersonal communication shown earlier in Figure 10.1 are based on a network of only two people. Obviously, communication often takes place among many individuals and larger groups. Claudia Gonzales, a telecommunications manager for Abaco Grupo Financiero in Mexico, normally has ongoing links with many people both inside and outside her organization. Her communication network extends laterally, vertically, and externally. *Vertical networks* typically include her immediate superior and subordinates and the superior's superiors and the subordinates' subordinates. *Lateral networks* include people in the same department at the same level (peers) and people in different departments at the same level. *External networks* include customers, suppliers, regulatory agencies, pressure groups, professional peers, and friends. Thus, a person's communication network can be quite involved.

Size limits the possible communication networks within a team or informal group. In principle, as the size of a team increases arithmetically, the number of possible communication interrelationships increases exponentially. Accordingly, communication networks are much more varied and complex in a 12-person team than in a 5-person team. Although each team member (theoretically) may be able to communicate with all the others, the direction and number of communication channels often are somewhat limited. In committee meetings, for example, varying levels of formality influence who may speak, what may be discussed, and in what order. The relative status or ranking of team members also may differ. Members having higher status probably will dominate communications more than those with lower status. Even when an open network is encouraged, a team member may actually use a limited network arrangement.

A common prescription, especially for college graduates when they join an organization, is to work on developing an individual communication network. At present or in the future, how might you know if you have developed a strong inside individual network? If you are able to answer "yes" to most of the following questions, you are probably on the right track:[37]

1. Do you know people at more than one level of the organization? Do they know your name and what you do?
2. Do you know a number of the people whose work relates to yours in any way beyond your own work unit?
3. Are you involved in any interdepartmental activities (temporary assignments, committees, task forces, special projects, volunteer activities)?
4. Are you plugged into the grapevine? Do you find out quickly what's up?
5. Do you take every opportunity to meet face to face to define and discuss complex problems, shifting priorities, areas of responsibility?
6. Do you know and talk with others about trends that will impact your job in the future and tools to get the job done today?
7. When you become aware of a problem that involves people from various areas, do you take the initiative to indicate your willingness to work on it?
8. Do you drop by to see people—even when you don't need anything—as time permits?

Effective individual networking focuses on serving customers, streamlining internal processes, solving problems, and achieving organizational and unit goals. Networking that focuses on immediate and apparent self-serving interests and goals is often counterproductive and even more so when it serves to hurt or take advantage of others. For individual network effectiveness, the individual needs **political skill**—*the ability to effectively understand others at work, and to use such knowledge to influence others to act in ways that enhance one's long-term personal and/or organizational goals.*[38] Political skill, which is a component of both our communication and self competencies, is characterized this way:

> Politically skilled individuals convey a sense of personal security and calm self-confidence that attracts others and gives them a feeling of comfort. This self-confidence never goes too far so as to be perceived as arrogance but is always properly measured to be a positive attribute. Therefore, although self-confident, those high in political skill are not self-absorbed (although they are self-aware)

because their focus is outward toward others, not inward and self-centered. This allows politically skilled individuals to maintain proper balance and perspective, and also, along with their tendency to be conscientious, to ensure that they keep a healthy gauge on their accountability to both others and themselves.[39]

Informal Group Network

An informal group network involves the communication pattern of multiple individual networks. By *informal* we mean those communication channels and messages that do not strictly follow the formal organization paths, such as when the president meets with or sends all employees an e-mail, or when a manager holds a weekly meeting with employees.

The most common form of informal group network is the **grapevine**—*the unofficial, and at times confidential, person-to-person or person-to-group chain of verbal, or at times e-mail, communication.*[40] The most common messages of the grapevine are *rumors*—unverified information, which may be of uncertain origin, that is usually spread by word of mouth or perhaps e-mail. Four of the major ways that messages move through grapevines in organizations are as follows:[41]

- *Single-strand chain* refers to one person telling a rumor to the next, who then tells the next person, who tells the next, and so on. As such, the rumor is told to one person at a time and passed on to others. Accuracy is lower in this type of chain than in the others because of the many alterations the story is subject to with each retelling.
- *Gossip chain* refers to only one person spreading the message, telling the story to almost everyone the person comes in contact with. This chain is likely to be the most slow moving.
- *Probability chain* refers to one person randomly contacting several others and telling them the message. Those individuals, in turn, randomly contact several others and continue to spread it. This chain is not a definite channel because the message is spread to different people, bypassing others altogether.
- *Cluster chain* refers to one person telling several close contacts who then pass it on to several people they have close contacts with. Regardless, people receive and transmit the message in terms of their personal biases, which results in the general theme being maintained but the details potentially being changed. It is often used to spread rumors and other news in organizations.

Informal group networks, like grapevines, cannot be eliminated by managers. In fact, managers often participate in them. The best approach is to understand grapevines and develop strategies to use in preventing and combating false or inaccurate rumors and gossip both internally and externally to the organization.[42] In an organization with low levels of communication openness, it is to be expected that informal group networks are likely to conflict with the formal employee network established by higher management. As you will recall from Figure 10.5, low communication openness is characterized by (1) closed, guarded, and defensive message transmission; (2) low trust; (3) hidden agendas; and (4) concealed goals. In this situation, it is likely that different informal group networks are likely to conflict with each other as well and be engaged in continuous power struggles. In contrast, with high levels of communication openness and other attributes of ethical interpersonal communication, individual networks, informal group networks, and formal employee networks will more often be mutually supportive and reasonably consistent with one another, thereby reducing barriers, inconsistencies, and confusion in communications within the organization.[43]

Formal Employee Network

By formal employee network, we mean the intended pattern and flows of employee-related communication vertically—between levels—and laterally—between individuals, teams, departments, and divisions. In the Preview Case, we discussed the many initiatives by David Radcliffe of Hogg Robinson to shape, develop, and use its formal employee network. Our discussion of Caterpillar's piazza represented a way in which Gottardo Bontagnali, the employee communication manager at the firm's Geneva headquarters, fostered informal meetings and discussions, built camaraderie, and developed a common sense of purpose. Through sponsoring the development of informal group networks and across culture communications, Bontagnali was attempting to further the effectiveness of the formal employee network.

In the Communication Competency feature on the Financial Planning Association's culture of conversation, we discussed the leadership by Janet McCullen in developing formal and informal group networks to foster dialogue, including the *Circle*, *Knowledge Cafés*, *Conversation Spaces*, and *Quarterly Chapter Calls*. Of course, in most chapters throughout this book, we have provided competency features on how managers can foster or hinder the development of effective formal employee networks. Our discussion of six types of formal teams in Chapter 8—such as self-managed, virtual, and global—are examples of higher management's initiatives to form and influence various lateral and vertical formal employee networks. Also, we discuss the *network design* as one of the contemporary organizational designs in Chapter 3, *Designing Organizations*.

The following Communication Competency feature reports on a major initiative by Sensis to assess and modify its formal employee network.[44] Sensis is a leading Australian advertising and search company. It provides integrated search solutions via print, online, voice, and wireless. Sensis has more than 2,600 employees and revenues in excess of $1 billion annually.[45]

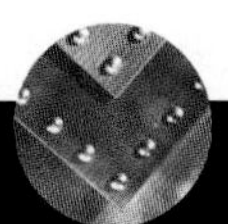

COMMUNICATION COMPETENCY

SENSIS EMPLOYEE COMMUNICATION STRATEGY

Several yeas ago, Sensis launched a program called *Discussion Groups*. The aim was to involve employees in discussions about the next phase of the company's strategy. All of the company's 2,600 employees were invited to attend a three-hour session hosted by a member of the CEO's executive leadership team. Each session involved just 20 employees and one executive—groups small enough to encourage open, meaningful discussion. These discussions unleashed a torrent of feedback on surprised executives, as employees took advantage of the opportunity to vent their frustrations. More than 1,000 specific issues were raised.

The experience had a sobering effect on the executive team. Few had guessed the extent of employee discontent, or the many issues hindering their ability to do their jobs effectively. Poor communication between the leadership team and employees was a key problem. In a move applauded by employees, the CEO decided to delay the launch of several strategic initiatives to fix the operational and communication problems. An internal communication team was formed with a mandate to radically transform the communication environment and engage employees more fully in the business.

A series of leadership-specific communication programs was designed to create a knowledgeable, skilled team of leaders to be advocates for the business and champion change internally. This was a two-pronged attack: building business literacy in all levels of Sensis's leadership and providing them with the skills to communicate that knowledge effectively to their people, through a development and coaching program. As a result of the Discussion Group example, an ongoing program was developed to establish regular two-way communication between leaders and employees. This involved creating regular information sessions delivered by the executive team to employees at each site. The sessions provide employees with an update on business performance against key metrics, plus an opportunity for them to ask questions and make suggestions.

Discussion Groups have become a regular feature on the communication landscape, taking place in the first half of each year. The first series of Discussion Groups addressed very short-term issues. The subsequent sessions have been more positive, with fewer immediate tactical problems raised and more focus on providing constructive input and solutions. In addition to these regular channels, an internal philosophy that focuses on communicating key business information to employees via leaders, together with a more consultative approach around planned operational changes, has emerged. Tools such as newsletters and the intranet have been retained, but they now serve to reinforce key messages, rather than act as the first source of business-critical information.

To monitor engagement levels, Sensis uses an Employee Engagement Index that measures the extent to which employees feel connected to their firm. According to this index, employee engagement at Sensis rose to 81 percent, 8 percent ahead of the Australian norm. The role of internal communication in facilitating regular dialogue between leadership and employees has paid off. Seventy-five percent of people surveyed felt that Sensis did a good to excellent job of keeping its people informed of matters affecting them. This was up from 52 percent in the previous two-year period. Eighty-one percent said they understood the future direction of the company. This was up from 52 percent in the previous two-year period. Overall, Sensis is performing 17 percent better than the Australian norm against all communication factors. The challenge now lies in maintaining the momentum of its employee engagement and formal internal communication programs.

For more information on Sensis, visit the organization's home page at ***http://www.sensis.com.***

Organizational Use

All types of networks are important for day-to-day communication in organizations. First, no single network is likely to prove effective in all situations for a team with a variety of tasks and goals. The apparently efficient, low-cost, and simple method of a superior instructing subordinates is likely to be ineffective if used exclusively. Dissatisfaction may become so great that members will leave the team or lose their motivation to contribute. Second, individuals and teams that face complex problems requiring a lot of coordination may deal with them ineffectively because of inadequate sharing of information, consideration of alternatives, and the like. Management must consider trade-offs or opportunity costs. The use of the fully engaged formal employee network may deal poorly with simple problems and tasks that require little member coordination. For example, members also may become bored and dissatisfied with meetings. They often simply come to feel that their time is being wasted. Another trade-off with the fully engaged formal network is higher labor costs. That is, employees must spend too much time on a problem and its solution in meetings when a simpler network would do well. Hence, management should use the level of networking that is most appropriate to the goals and tasks.

CHAPTER SUMMARY

1. Describe the basic elements of interpersonal communication.

The basic elements in the communication process—senders, receivers, transmitters, receptors, messages, channels, noise, meaning, encoding, decoding, and feedback—are interrelated.

Face-to-face interpersonal communication has the highest degree of information richness. An information-rich medium is especially important for performing complex tasks and resolving social and emotional issues that involve considerable uncertainty and ambiguity. Important issues usually contain significant amounts of uncertainty, ambiguity, and people-related (especially social and emotional) problems.

There are many potential challenges to effective interpersonal communication. We briefly reviewed the underlying interpersonal barriers discussed in previous chapters. Direct barriers include aggressive communication approaches, noise, semantics, demeaning language, and lying and distortion. The barriers stemming from cultural differences are always present. They may be especially high when the interaction takes place between individuals from high-context and low-context cultures.

2. Explain the fabric of abilities that foster ethical interpersonal communications.

Through mastering the interrelated group of abilities and behaviors that constitute dialogue, the likelihood of engaging in ethical interpersonal communications is magnified. Dialogue includes communication openness, constructive feedback, active listening, appropriate self-disclosure, and supportive nonverbal communication. Dialogue requires senders and receivers to play a dynamic role in the communication process. In open communication, senders and receivers are able to discuss, disagree, and search for understanding without resorting to personal attacks or hidden agendas. Feedback received from others provides motivation for individuals to learn and change their behaviors. By being an active listener, the receiver hears the whole message without interpretation or judgment. How much individuals are willing to share with others depends on their ability to disclose information.

3. Describe how nonverbal communication affects dialogue.

Nonverbal cues play a powerful role in supporting or hindering dialogue. We noted many types of personal nonverbal cues through the acronym PERCEIVE, which stands for the following terms: proximity, expressions, relative orientation, contact, eyes, individual gestures, voice, and existence of adapters. Throughout this chapter, we described how cultural barriers can impede communication effectiveness. We examined specifically how certain nonverbal messages—the use of gestures, color, and time—can affect cross-cultural communication. Formal organizational position is often tied to status. Status symbols, such as office size, the floor on which the office is located, number of windows, location of a secretary, and access to senior-level employees, all influence communication patterns. We concluded with some cautionary comments on the need to avoid simplistic stereotypes as to the meaning of nonverbal cues employed by an individual.

4. State the role of communication networks in interpersonal communication.

An individual's communication network extends laterally, vertically, and externally. The development of a strong inside individual network can be determined by being able to respond "yes" to most of the eight questions presented, such as "Do you know a number of the people whose work intersects with yours in any way beyond your own work unit?" For individual networking effectiveness, the individual needs political skill, which is a component of both our communication and self competencies. The informal group network involves the pattern of multiple individual networks. The most common form of informal group network is the grapevine, which may take the pattern of a single-strand chain, gossip chain, probability chain, or cluster chain. The formal employee network focuses on the intended pattern of employee-related communication vertically and laterally. Management needs to be proactive in creating an open and ethically based pattern to ensure that individual and employee group networks are not in conflict with the formal employee network and, for the most part, supportive of it as well.

KEY TERMS AND CONCEPTS

Assertive communication
Channels
Chromatics
Chronemics
Cue
Cultural context
Decoding
Dialogue
Distortion
Encoding
Ethnocentrism
Feedback
Feng shui
Grapevine
High-context culture
Impression management
Intercultural communication
Interpersonal communication
Interpersonal communication network
Language routines
Listening
Low-context culture
Lying
Meaning
Media richness
Messages
Meta-communication
Monochronic time schedule
Noise
Nonverbal communication
Political skill
Polychronic time schedule
Receptors
Self-disclosure
Semantics
360-degree feedback
Transmitters

DISCUSSION QUESTIONS

1. Based on your diagnosis of feedback practices you experienced in a current or previous job through the completion of the instrument in Table 10.1, which practices are least effective? How might they be improved?
2. The Internet and e-mail are making it easier to communicate with people from different cultures. Do you agree or disagree with that statement? Explain.
3. Describe your individual communication network at work or at school. Is it effective? Would you like to make any changes in it? Why or why not?
4. If your job transfers you to a foreign culture, what nonverbal communication practices must you be sensitive to?
5. Describe the common nonverbal cues used by someone you have worked for. Are they usually consistent or inconsistent with that person's verbal expressions? Explain.
6. How would you assess the level of ethical interpersonal communication in an organization at which you are or have been employed? Give concrete examples that serve as a basis of your assessment.
7. How would you evaluate David Radcliffe, as discussed in the Preview Case and elsewhere in the chapter, in terms of the four dimensions of communication openness shown in Figure 10.5? Give examples of his actions and communications to justify your assessment on each dimension.
8. The development of Caterpillar's piazza appears to have had a positive impact on across culture and interpersonal communications at its European headquarters in Geneva. What are three aspects of interpersonal and cultural barriers that the piazza is not likely to impact? Explain.
9. Why is media richness important in interpersonal communication? Do changes need to be made in the pattern and frequency of use of the various media employed by management in the organization for which you currently work or have worked? Explain.
10. Think of a team of which you are a member. How would you assess the members' self-awareness?

EXPERIENTIAL EXERCISE AND CASE

Experiential Exercise: Self Competency

Interpersonal Communication Practices[46]

Instructions:
This survey is designed to assess your interpersonal communication practices. For each item in the survey, indicate which of the alternative reactions best represents how you would handle the situation described. Some alternatives

may be equally characteristic or equally uncharacteristic of your reaction. Although that is a possibility, choose the alternative that is relatively more characteristic of your reaction. For each item, distribute five points between the alternatives in any of the following combinations.

	A	B
1.	5	0
2.	4	1
3.	3	2
4.	2	3
5.	1	4
6.	0	5

Thus, there are six possible combinations for responding to the pair of alternatives presented to you with each survey item. Be sure that the numbers you assign to each pair sum to 5. To the extent possible, please relate each situation in the survey to your own personal experience. In this survey, we alternate the words *he* and *she* and *him* and *her* to balance use of the feminine and masculine genders.

1. If a friend of mine had a personality conflict with a mutual acquaintance of ours with whom it was important for her to get along, I would
   _______A. tell my friend that I felt she was partially responsible for any problems with this other person and try to let her know who the person being affected by her is.
   _______B. not get involved because I wouldn't be able to continue to get along with both of them once I had entered into the conflict.

2. If one of one of my friends and I had a heated argument in the past and I realized that he would be ill at ease around me from that time on, I would
   _______A. avoid making things worse by discussing his behavior and just let the whole thing drop.
   _______B. bring up his behavior and ask him how he felt the argument had affected our relationship.

3. If a friend began to avoid me and act in an aloof and withdrawn manner, I would
   _______A. tell her about her behavior and suggest she tell me what was on her mind.
   _______B. follow her lead and keep our contacts brief and aloof because that seems to be what she wants.

4. If two of my friends and I were talking and one of my friends slipped and brought up a personal problem of mine that involved the other friend, and of which he was not yet aware, I would
   _______A. change the subject and signal my friend to do the same.
   _______B. fill in my uninformed friend on what the other friend was talking about and suggest that we go into it later.

5. If a friend were to tell me that, in her opinion, I was doing things that made me less effective than I might be in social situations, I would
   _______A. ask her to spell out or describe what she has observed and suggest changes that I might make.
   _______B. resent the criticism and let her know why I behave the way I do.

6. If one of my friends aspired to an office in our student organization for which I felt he was unqualified and if he had been tentatively assigned to that position by the president of the student organization, I would
   _______A. not mention my misgivings to either my friend or the president and let them handle it in their own way.
   _______B. tell my friend and the president of my misgivings and then leave the final decision up to them.

7. If I felt that one of my friends was being unfair to me and her other friends, but none of them had mentioned anything about it, I would
   _______A. ask several of those people how they perceived the situation to see if they felt that she was being unfair.
   _______B. not ask the others how they perceived our friend but wait for them to bring it up to me.

8. If I were preoccupied with some personal matters and a friend told me that I had become irritated with him and others and that I was jumping on him for unimportant things, I would
   _______A. tell him I was preoccupied and would probably be on edge for a while and would prefer not to be bothered.
   _______B. listen to his complaints but not try to explain my actions to him.

9. If I had heard some friends discussing an ugly rumor about a friend of mine that I knew could hurt her and she asked me what I knew about it, if anything, I would
   _______A. say that I didn't know anything about it and tell her no one would believe a rumor like that anyway.
   _______B. tell her exactly what I had heard, when I had heard it, and from whom I had heard it.

10. If a friend pointed out the fact that I had a personality conflict with another friend with whom it was important for me to get along, I would
   _______A. consider his comments out of line and tell him I didn't want to discuss the matter any further.
   _______B. talk about it openly with him to find out how my behavior was being affected by this.

11. If my relationship with a friend has been damaged by repeated arguments on an issue of importance to us both, I would

_______A. be cautious in my conversations with her so that the issue wouldn't come up again to worsen our relationship.

_______B. point to the problems that the controversy was causing in our relationship and suggest that we discuss it until we had resolved it.

12. If in a personal discussion with a friend about his problems and behavior, he suddenly suggested we discuss my problems and behavior as well as his own, I would

_______A. try to keep the discussion away from me by suggesting that other, closer friends often talked to me about such matters.

_______B. welcome the opportunity to hear what he felt about me and encourage his comments.

13. If a friend of mine began to tell me about her hostile feelings about another friend who she felt was being unkind to others (and I wholeheartedly agreed), I would

_______A. listen and also express my own feelings to her so she would know where I stood.

_______B. listen but not express my own negative views and opinions because she might repeat what I said to her in confidence.

14. If I thought an ugly rumor were being spread about me and suspected that one of my friends had quite likely heard it, I would

_______A. avoid mentioning the issue and leave it to him to tell me about it if he wanted to.

_______B. risk putting him on the spot by asking him directly what he knew about the whole thing.

15. If I had observed a friend in social situations and thought that she was doing a number of things that hurt her relationships, I would

_______A. risk being seen as a busybody and tell her what I had observed and my reactions to it.

_______B. keep my opinions to myself, rather than be seen as interfering in things that are none of my business.

16. If two friends and I were talking and one of them inadvertently mentioned a personal problem that involved me but of which I knew nothing, I would

_______A. press both of them for information about the problem and their opinions about it.

_______B. leave it up to my friends to tell me or not tell me, letting them change the subject if they wished.

17. If a friend seemed to be preoccupied and began to jump on me for seemingly unimportant things and to become irritated with me and others without real cause, I would

_______A. treat him with kid gloves for a while on the assumption that he was having some temporary personal problems that were none of my business.

_______B. try to talk to him about it and point out to him how his behavior was affecting people.

18. If I had begun to dislike certain habits of a friend to the point that it was interfering with my enjoying her company, I would

_______A. say nothing to her directly but let her know my feelings by ignoring her whenever her annoying habits were obvious.

_______B. get my feelings out in the open and clear the air so that we could continue our friendship comfortably and enjoyably.

19. In discussing social behavior with one of my more sensitive friends, I would

_______A. avoid mentioning his flaws and weaknesses so as not to hurt his feelings.

_______B. focus on his flaws and weaknesses so he could improve his interpersonal skills.

20. If I knew that I might be assigned to an important position in our group and my friends' attitudes toward me had become rather negative, I would

_______A. discuss my shortcomings with my friends so I could see where to improve.

_______B. try to figure out my own shortcomings by myself so I could improve.

Scoring Key

In this survey 10 of the items deal with your receptivity to feedback and 10 are concerned with your willingness to disclose information about yourself. Transfer your scores from each item to this scoring key. Add the scores in each column. Now, transfer these scores to Figure 10.6 by drawing a vertical line through the feedback score and a horizontal line through the self-disclosure line.

Receptivity to Feedback	Willingness to Self-Disclose
2. B _______	1. A _______
3. A _______	4. B _______
5. A _______	6. B _______
7. A _______	9. B _______
8. B _______	11. B _______
10. B _______	13. A _______
12. B _______	15. A _______
14. B _______	17. B _______
16. A _______	18. B _______
20. A _______	19. B _______
Total: _______	Total: _______

As Figure 10.6 suggests, higher scores in receptivity to feedback and willingness to disclose information about

FIGURE 10.6 Personal Openness in Interpersonal Communication

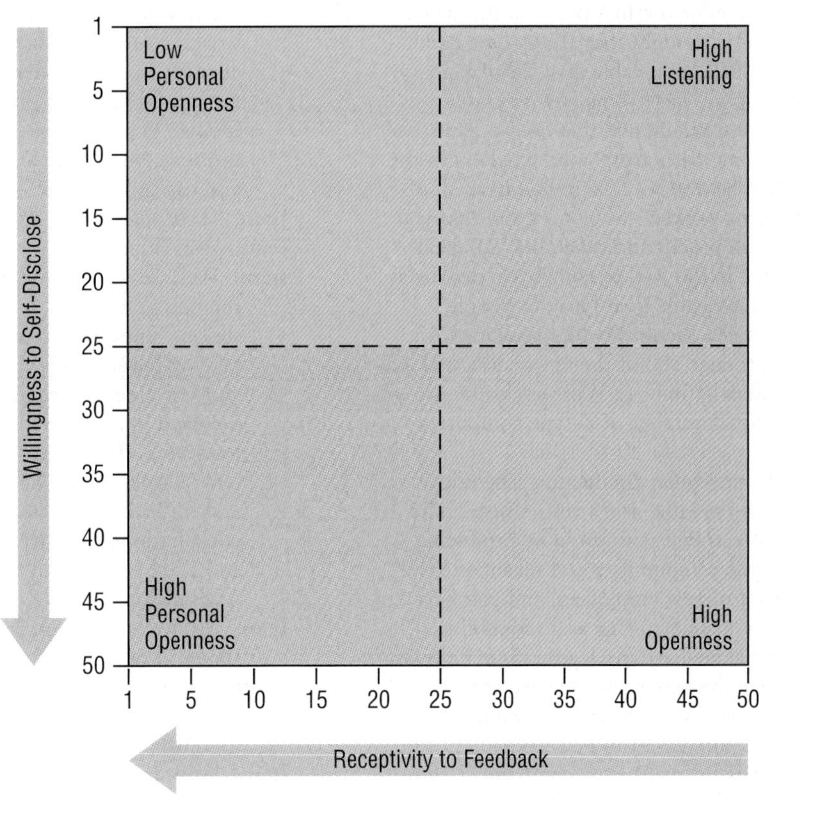

yourself indicate a greater willingness to engage in open interpersonal communication. Of course, you need to be mindful of the situational factors that may influence your natural personal preference to be relatively more open or closed in interpersonal communication.

Questions

1. Based on your profile of scores, what communication abilities do you need to develop further?
2. What are some barriers that you might encounter in developing these abilities?

Case: Across Cultures Competency

Juan Perillo and Jean Moore

Scene I: February 15, San Juan, Puerto Rico

Juan: Welcome back to Puerto Rico, Jean. It is good to have you here in San Juan again. I hope that your trip from Dayton was a smooth one.

Jean: Thank you, Juan. It's nice to be back here, where the sun shines. Fred sends his regards and also asked me to tell you how important it is that we work out a firm production schedule for the next three months. But first, how is your family? All doing well, I hope.

Juan: My wife is doing very well, but my daughter, Marianna, broke her arm and has to have surgery to repair the bone. We are very worried about that because the surgeon says she may have to have several operations. It is very difficult to think about my poor little daughter in the operating room. She was out playing with some other children when it happened. You know how rough children sometimes play with each other. It's really amazing that they don't have more injuries. Why, just last week, my son. . . .

Jean: Of course I'm very sorry to hear about little Marianna, but I'm sure everything will go well with the surgery. Now, shall we start work on the production schedule?

Juan: Oh, yes, of course, we must get started on the

production schedule.

Jean: Fred and I thought that June 1 would be a good cutoff date for the first phase of the schedule. And we also thought that 100 A-type computers would be a reasonable goal for that phase. We know that you have some new assemblers whom you are training, and that you've had some problems getting parts from your suppliers in the past few months. But we're sure you have all of those problems worked out by now and that you are back to full production capability. So, what do you think? Is 100 A-type computers produced by June 1 a reasonable goal for your people?

Juan: (Hesitates a few seconds before replying) You want us to produce 100 of the newly designed A-type computers by June 1? Will we also be producing our usual number of Z-type computers, too?

Jean: Oh, yes. Your regular production schedule would remain the same as it's always been. The only difference is that you would be producing the new A-type computers, too. I mean, after all, you have a lot of new employees, and you have all of the new manufacturing and assembling equipment that we have in Dayton. So, you're as ready to make the new product as we are.

Juan: Yes, that's true. We have the new equipment and we've just hired a lot of new assemblers who will be working on the A-type computer. I guess there's no reason we can't meet the production schedule you and Fred have come up with.

Jean: Great, great. I'll tell Fred you agree with our decision and will meet the goal of 100 A-type computers by June 1. He'll be delighted to know that you can deliver what he was hoping for. And, of course, Juan, that means that you'll be doing just as well as the Dayton plant.

Juan: E-mail me the final decision after you talk to Fred.

Scene II: May 1, San Juan, Puerto Rico

Jean: Hello, Juan. How are things here in Puerto Rico? I'm glad to have the chance to come back and see how things are going.

Juan: Welcome, Jean. It's good to have you here. How was the weather last winter? How is your family?

Jean: The weather was bad—typical of Ohio. The family is fine, just fine. You know, Juan, Fred is really excited about that big order we just got from the Defense Department for 50 A-type computers. They want them by June 10, so we will ship them directly to Washington from San Juan as the computers come off your assembly line. Looks like it's a good thing we set your production goal at 100 A-type computers by June 1, isn't it?

Juan: Um, yes, that was certainly a good idea.

Jean: So, tell me. Have you had any problems with the new model? How are your new assemblers working out? Do you have any suggestions for changes in the manufacturing specs? How is the new quality control program working with this model? We're always looking for ways to improve, you know, and we appreciate any ideas you can give us.

Juan: Well, Jean, there is one thing. . . .

Jean: Yes? What is that?

Juan: Well, Jean, we have had a few problems with the new assemblers. Three of them have had serious illnesses in their families and have had to take off several days at a time to nurse a sick child or elderly parent. And another one was involved in a car accident and was in the hospital for several days. And you remember my daughter's surgery? Well, her arm didn't mend properly and we had to take her to Houston for additional consultations and therapy. But, of course, you and Fred knew about that. I e-mailed you in April about these.

Jean: Yes, we were aware that you had had some personnel problems and that you and your wife had to go to Houston with Marianna. But what does that have to do with the 50 A-type computers for the Defense Department?

Juan: Well, Jean, because of all these problems, we have had a few delays in the production schedule. Nothing serious, but we are a little bit behind our schedule.

Jean: How far behind is "a little bit"? What are you trying to tell me, Juan? Will you have 50 more A-type computers by June 1 to ship to Washington to fill the Defense Department order?

Juan: Well, I certainly hope we will have that number ready to ship. You know how difficult it can be to predict a precise number for manufacturing, Jean. You probably have many of these same problems in the Dayton plant, don't you?[47]

Questions

1. Based on the communication model (see Figure 10.1), what were some hurdles that prevented effective communication between Juan and Jean?
2. What are some cultural differences between the mainland and Puerto Rico that could have hindered communications?
3. What recommendations would you suggest to improve the communications between Juan and Jean?

Individuals in Organizations

CHAPTER 11	Understanding Individual Differences
CHAPTER 12	Perceptions and Attributions
CHAPTER 13	Learning and Reinforcement
CHAPTER 14	Fundamentals of Motivation
CHAPTER 15	Motivation through Goal Setting and Reward Systems
CHAPTER 16	Managing Stress and Aggressive Behavior

CHAPTER 11

Understanding Individual Differences

LEARNING OBJECTIVES

When you have finished studying this chapter, you should be able to:

1. Explain the basic sources of personality determinants.
2. Identify some personality traits that affect behavior.
3. State the role and importance of work attitudes.
4. Describe how emotions affect performance.

Preview Case: Ann Fudge, CEO of Young & Rubicam, Inc.

PERSONALITY DETERMINANTS

Heredity

Environment

Self Competency—David Neeleman of JetBlue

PERSONALITY AND BEHAVIOR

Big Five Personality Factors

Self-Esteem

Locus of Control

Introversion and Extraversion

Emotional Intelligence

Organizational Uses

Teams Competency—Thrive Networks

The Person and the Situation

WORK ATTITUDES AND BEHAVIOR

Components of Attitudes

Key Work-Related Attitudes: Hope, Job Satisfaction, and Organizational Commitment

Communication Competency—The Container Store

EMOTIONS AND PERFORMANCE

A Model of Emotions

Change Competency—Kenneth Chenault of American Express

CHAPTER SUMMARY

KEY TERMS AND CONCEPTS

DISCUSSION QUESTIONS

EXPERIENTIAL EXERCISES

ANN FUDGE, CEO OF YOUNG & RUBICAM, INC.

PREVIEW CASE

In 2001, Ann Fudge did something that is uncommon in corporate America. She quit her job as president of Kraft Foods. It was not that she was dissatisfied, but that she wanted to get more out of life. She wrote a book, *The Artist's Way at Work,* that describes how she tackled numerous issues in corporate America because she was a female black woman.

After several years, she was lured back into the corporate world as chairwoman and CEO of Young & Rubicam, Inc., the poorly performing advertising and communications giant that the British advertising conglomerate, WPP Group, PLC, had bought. According to Martin Sorell, WPP Group's CEO, he thought that with her marketing and people competencies, she could improve the profitability of a company that two prior CEOs had failed to do. He also picked her because "women are better managers than men." In talking with many of her former employees, they told him that she had a great sense of personal priorities and never inflated the importance of her own work. At Maxwell House, Kraft's coffee division, she was obsessed over product quality while keeping costs under control.

Fudge immediately started putting in 15-hour days and visited most of the 540 offices in 80 different countries in her first year. She reorganized her top management staff, cut costs, and pushed the company to get into advertising for businesses like technology, health care, and direct-to-consumer marketing. She developed four initiatives and has run the company based on these even though some initiatives were at odds with some of her colleagues. First, she encouraged and rewarded collaboration. When clients approach the agency for help selling their product, Fudge believes that the agency should be able to find the best combination of services that the agency has to offer. To drive this point home, she launched the Young & Rubicam Brands name for the group's family of companies. This was a difficult mind shift for many employees who were used to working independently and even competing against one another for clients. Some employees believe that it's an unwelcome incursion into their fiefdoms. Fudge believes that this reflects the realities of what the client wants. This new strategy paid off when Y&R landed Microsoft's $250-million-dollar account. Second, focus on clients. Fudge's direct reports are now responsible for all aspects of a client account. Third, simplify processes and become more efficient through the adoption of a rigorous quality control program that she modified from General Electric. The purpose of this program was to free up time for employees to be creative. She trained employees in total quality methods so that they could tackle everything from sourcing supplies to honing the process for developing creative strategies. Fourth, she spread the joy. She's a global traveler who believes that her "touchy-feely" style is what clients and employees want. There are a lot more "kumbaya" get-togethers where employees gather to just talk to each other without a specific business agenda. Fudge knows the names and faces of people in most of the Y&R offices, a major departure from former CEOs who couldn't even pronounce the names of employees.[1]

For more information on Young & Rubicam, visit the organization's home page at ***http://www.yr.com.***

As the Preview Case indicates, people react to how they are treated by others. You might ask yourself whether you would be willing to work for Fudge. Depending on your personality, preferences, and goals, you might answer either *yes* or *no*. As an employee and future manager, you must recognize and appreciate individual differences in order to understand and respond appropriately to the behavior of people in organizations.[2]

In Part 4 of this book, we cover individual processes in organizations. We focus first on the individual to help you develop an understanding of organizational behavior. **Individual differences** *are the personal attributes that vary from one person to another*. Individual differences may be physical, psychological, or emotional. The individual differences that characterize you make you unique. Perhaps you have a dynamic personality and enjoy being the center of attention, whereas others you know avoid crowds and do not have the same energy level as you. Is that good or bad? The answer, of course, is that it depends on the situation. Whenever managers attempt to understand individual differences, they must also analyze the situation in which the behavior occurs. A good starting point in developing this understanding is to appreciate the role of personality in organizations. In this chapter, we discuss individual differences in personality attitudes and emotions. We begin by addressing the concept of personality. Later in the chapter, we explore the role of attitudes and emotions in organizational behavior.

LEARNING OBJECTIVE

1. Explain the basic sources of personality determinants.

PERSONALITY DETERMINANTS

Behavior always involves a complex interaction between the person and the situation. Events in the surrounding environment (including the presence and behavior of others) strongly influence the way people behave at any particular time; yet people always bring something of themselves to the situation. This "something," which represents the unique qualities of the individual, is *personality*.[3] No single definition of personality is accepted universally. However, one key idea is that personality represents personal characteristics that lead to consistent patterns of behavior. People quite naturally seek to understand these behavioral patterns in interactions with others.

Personality *represents the overall profile or combination of stable psychological attributes that capture the unique nature of a person.* Therefore, personality combines a set of physical and mental characteristics that reflect how a person looks, thinks, acts, and feels. This definition contains two important ideas.

First, theories of personality often describe what people have in common and what sets them apart. To understand the personality of an individual, then, is to understand both what that individual has in common with others and what makes that particular individual unique. Thus each employee in an organization is unique and may or may not act differently in a similar situation. This uniqueness makes managing and working with people extremely challenging.

Second, our definition refers to personality as being "stable" and having "continuity in time." Most people intuitively recognize this stability. If your entire personality could change suddenly and dramatically, your family and friends would confront a stranger. Although significant changes normally don't occur suddenly, an individual's personality may change over time. Personality development occurs to a certain extent throughout life, but the greatest changes occur in early childhood.

THE COMPETENT LEADER

Fine shadings of personality, though they may be invisible to some and frustrating to others, are crystal clear to and highly valued by great managers.
Marcus Buckingham, Consultant with One Thing Productions

How is an individual's personality determined? Is personality inherited or genetically determined, or is it formed after years of experience? There are no simple answers because too many variables contribute to the development of each individual's personality. As Figure 11.1 shows, two primary sources shape personality

FIGURE 11.1 Sources of Personality Differences

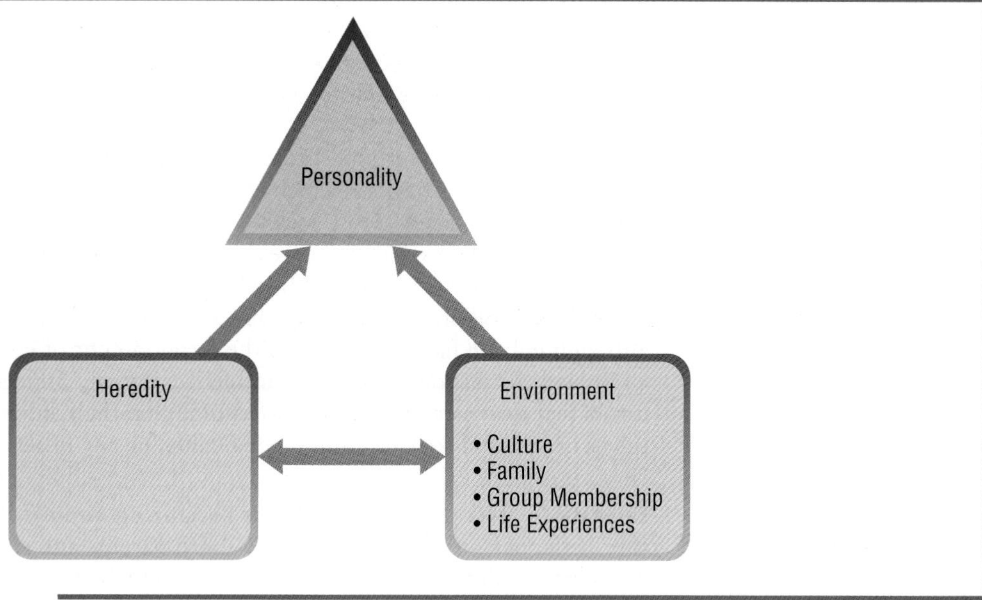

differences: heredity and environment. An examination of these sources helps explain why individuals are different.

Heredity

Deeply ingrained in many people's notions of personality is a belief in its genetic basis. Expressions such as "She is just like her father" or "He gets those irritating qualities from your side of the family, dear" reflect such beliefs. Some people believe that personality is inherited; others believe that a person's experiences determine personality. Our thinking is balanced—both heredity (genes) and environment (experiences) are important, although some personality characteristics may be influenced more by one factor than the other. Some personality traits seem to have a strong genetic component, whereas other traits seem to be largely learned (based on experiences).[4]

Some people argue that heredity sets limits on the range of development of characteristics and that within this range environmental forces determine personality characteristics. However, recent research on the personalities of twins who have been raised apart indicates that genetic determinants may play a larger role than many experts had believed. Some studies of twins suggest that as much as 50 to 55 percent of personality traits may be inherited. Further, inherited personality traits seem to explain about 50 percent of the variance in occupational choice. In other words, you probably inherited some traits that will influence your career choices.

Environment

Many people believe that the environment plays a large role in shaping personality; in fact, the environment plays a more important role than do inherited characteristics. Aspects of the environment that influence personality formation include culture, family, group membership, and life experiences.

Culture. The term *culture* was defined in Chapter 1 and refers to the distinctive ways in which people in different societies organize and live their lives. Anthropologists have clearly demonstrated the important role that culture plays in personality development.[5] Individuals born into a particular society are exposed to family and societal values and to norms of acceptable behavior—the culture of that society. Culture also defines how various roles in that society are to be performed. For example, U.S. culture generally rewards people for being independent and competitive, whereas Japanese culture generally rewards individuals for being cooperative and group oriented.

Culture helps determine broad patterns of behavioral similarity among people, but differences in behavior—which at times can be extreme—usually exist among individuals within a society. Most societies aren't homogeneous (although some are more homogeneous than others). For example, the work ethic (hard work is valued; an unwillingness to work is sinful) usually is associated with Western cultures. But this value doesn't influence everyone within Western cultures to the same degree. Thus, although culture has an impact on the development of employees' personalities, not all individuals respond to cultural influences equally. Indeed, one of the most serious errors that managers can make is to assume that their subordinates are just like themselves in terms of societal values, personality, or any other individual characteristic.

Family. The primary vehicle for socializing an individual into a particular culture is the person's immediate family. Both parents and siblings play important roles in the personality development of most individuals. Members of an extended family—grandparents, aunts, uncles, and cousins—also can influence personality formation. In particular, parents (or a single parent) influence their children's development in three important ways:

- Through their own behaviors, they present situations that bring out certain behaviors in children.
- They serve as role models with which children often strongly identify.
- They selectively reward and punish certain behaviors.[6]

The family's situation also is an important source of personality differences. Situational influences include the family's size, socioeconomic level, race, religion, and geographic location; birth order within the family; parents' educational level; and so on. For example, a person raised in a poor family simply has different experiences and opportunities than does a person raised in a wealthy family. Being an only child is different in some important respects from being raised with several brothers and sisters.

Group Membership. The first group to which most individuals belong is the family. People also participate in various groups during their lives, beginning with their childhood playmates and continuing through teenaged schoolmates, sports teams, and social groups to adult work and social groups. The numerous roles and experiences that people have as members of groups represent another important source of personality differences. Although playmates and school groups early in life may have the strongest influences on personality formation, social and group experiences in later life continue to influence and shape personality. Understanding someone's personality requires understanding the groups to which that person belongs or has belonged in the past.

Life Experiences. Each person's life also is unique in terms of specific events and experiences, which can serve as important determinants of personality. For example, the development of self-esteem (a personality dimension that we discuss shortly) depends on a series of experiences that include the opportunity to achieve goals and meet expectations, evidence of the ability to influence others, and a clear sense of being valued by others. Thus a complex series of events and interactions with other people helps shape the adult's level of self-esteem.

As we weave an understanding of personality and other individual differences into our exploration of a variety of topics in organizational behavior, we hope that you will come to understand the crucial role that personality plays in explaining behavior. People clearly pay a great deal of attention to the attributes of the personalities of the coworkers with whom they interact. The following Self Competency feature shows how JetBlue CEO David Neeleman's personality was shaped by various forces.[7]

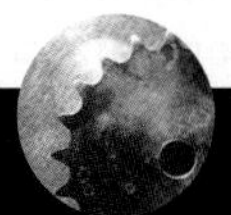

SELF COMPETENCY

DAVID NEELEMAN OF JETBLUE

If you want to understand the culture of a company, it helps to understand the personality of the CEO. Neeleman spent the first five years in Brazil where his father was a journalist. His family moved from Brazil, but he visited every summer. Brazil is a country that is divided between the haves and haves-not. He grew up in the rich part of the country and enjoyed a big house, a membership in country clubs, etc. During his junior year at Utah, he decided to return to Brazil to go on a mission for his church and ended up living in the slums or "favelas" of Brazil. The slums are where the desperately poor people live like caged animals behind barbed wire fences.

He was struck by a few things living in the slums. First, most wealthy people have a sense of entitlement. They thought that they were better than the people in the slums. This bothered him tremendously. Second, most of the poor people were happier than the rich people and they generously shared what little they had. As a college student living away from home, he was only allowed to write letters home once a week and call home twice a year—he should have been miserable. But he wasn't because of the enormous pleasures and satisfaction he gained from working with these people.

These experiences had a tremendous impact on the formation of his personality and his drive to manage JetBlue differently. When he travels on a business trip, he flies coach class. There is no Lincoln town car waiting for him at the airport. At JetBlue, there are no reserved parking places. The coffee in the kitchen down the hall from his work space is the same as that in the employee lounge at J. F. Kennedy airport. There is only one class on JetBlue planes. The seats that have more legroom are at the back, so people who get off the plane last actually have roomier seats in-flight. The desk and other furniture in his office are the same as that used by everyone else. He tells his pilots: "There are people who make more money at this company than others, but that doesn't mean they should flaunt it."

He can be seen frequently on flights from Florida to New York City. Once the plane settles into its cruising altitude, Neeleman walks to the front of the cabin, grabs the microphone, and introduces himself. He explains that he'll be coming through the cabin serving drinks and snacks along with the crew. He also takes out the garbage when the flight is over. It's his chance to speak directly to JetBlue's customers. JetBlue also has a Crewmember Crisis fund. Everyone donates to it and it's used to help employees in crisis. If someone at JetBlue gets cancer, they have health benefits, but they might tap the fund to pay a babysitter while at chemotherapy.

Employees and customers like the "touchy-feely" aspect of JetBlue. "When you have a leader who's so friendly, it makes everybody feel good about what they're doing," says Jim Small, general manager for San Juan. JetBlue is also generous with travel vouchers when passengers are inconvenienced. Neeleman himself once drove an elderly couple from JFK to Connecticut, where he lives and they were headed, rather then let them spend $200 on a taxi.

For more information on JetBlue, visit this organization's home page at ***http://www.jetblue.com.***

LEARNING OBJECTIVE

2. Identify some personality traits that affect behavior.

PERSONALITY AND BEHAVIOR

The vast number and variety of specific personality traits or dimensions are bewildering. The term **personality trait** *refers to the basic components of personality.* Researchers of personality have identified literally *thousands* of traits over the years. Trait names simply represent the terms that people use to describe each other. However, a list containing hundreds or thousands of terms isn't very useful either in understanding the structure of personality in a scientific sense or in describing individual differences in a practical sense. To be useful, these terms need to be organized into a small set of concepts or descriptions. Recent research has done just that, identifying several general factors that can be used to describe a personality.[8]

Big Five Personality Factors

The **"Big Five" personality factors,** as they often are referred to, describe the individual's emotional stability, agreeableness, extraversion, conscientiousness, and openness.[9] As shown in Figure 11.2, each factor includes a potentially large number and range of specific traits. That is, each factor is both a collection of related traits and a continuum.

FIGURE 11.2 The "Big Five" Personality Factors

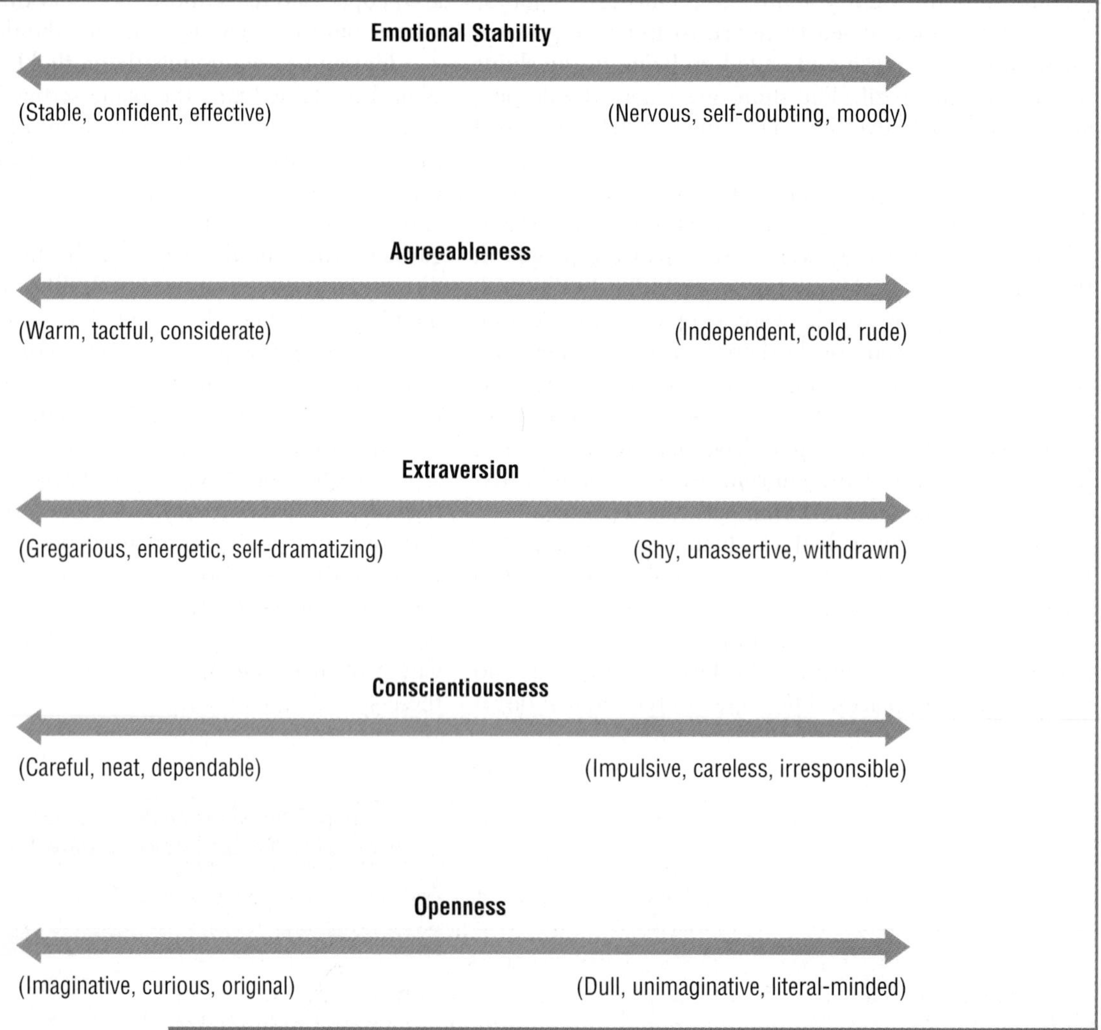

The main reason that we are interested in individual personality in the study of organizational behavior is because of the link between personality and behavior. Researchers have investigated extensively the relationships between the Big Five personality factors and job performance. Their findings indicate that employees who are responsible, dependable, persistent, and achievement oriented perform better than those who lack these traits (the extremes of the *conscientiousness* continuum in Figure 11.2). An individual with a personality at one extreme of the *agreeableness* factor continuum might be described as warm and considerate. But with a personality at this factor's other extreme, the person would be considered cold or rude. The first Experiential Exercise at the end of this chapter contains a questionnaire that you can use to assess yourself in terms of these five personality factors. We invite you to complete it now to help you better understand your own personality and how it impacts others. We will define the terms used in the Big Five now.

Emotional stability *refers to the degree to which a person is relaxed, secure, and unworried.* People who are emotionally stable are poised, calm, resilient, and secure in their interpersonal dealings with others. People with less emotional stability are more excitable, insecure in their dealings with others, reactive, and subject to extreme swings of moods. People with emotional stability handle the stress of managing others better than those who are less emotionally stable. How would you rate David Neeleman's emotional stability?

Agreeableness *refers to a person's ability to get along with others.* Agreeableness causes people to be cooperative, kind, understanding, and good natured in their dealings with others. People who demonstrate low agreeableness are often described as short tempered, uncooperative, and irritable. Highly agreeable people are better at developing and maintaining close relationships with others at work, whereas less agreeable people are not likely to have particularly close working relationships with others, including customers and suppliers. How would you rate Ann Fudge on the agreeableness dimension?

Extraversion *refers to a person's comfort level with relationships.* Sociable people are extraverts. Extraverts are comfortable talking with others and are assertive, talkative, and open to establishing new interpersonal relationships. Less sociable people are usually called *introverts.* They are less likely to establish new relationships with others and are seen by others as less assertive. Research has shown that sociable people tend to be higher performing managers than less sociable people and that they are more likely to be attracted to managerial positions that require good interpersonal skills, such as marketing, sales, and senior management positions. How would you rate David Neeleman on the extraversion dimension?

Conscientiousness *refers to the number of goals on which a person focuses.* People who focus on a few key goals are more likely to be organized, careful, thorough, responsible, and self-disciplined because they concentrate on doing a few things well. Less conscientiousness people tend to focus on a wider array of goals, and as a result, tend to be more disorganized and less thorough. Researchers have found that more conscientious people tend to be higher performers than less conscientious people, especially in sales. How would you rate Ann Fudge on this dimension?

Openness *refers to a person's curiosity and range of interests.* People with high levels of openness are willing to listen to new ideas and to change their own ideas, beliefs, and assumptions in response to new information. Open people tend to have a broad range of interests and be creative. On the other hand, people who demonstrate low openness tend to be less receptive to new ideas and less willing to change their minds. They also tend to have a narrow range of interests and are not curious. Managers who are high on openness tend to be better performers because of their ability to adapt to new situations and their willingness to listen to others who have different points of view. How would you rate Ann Fudge on openness?

Although each personality factor represents a collection of related traits, the link between personality and specific behaviors often is most clear when we focus on a single trait rather than all five factors at once. Here we examine several *specific* personality traits that are particularly important for understanding aspects of organizational behavior. Then, throughout the book, we explain additional personality traits as they relate to topics under discussion—for example, in relation to perception (Chapter 12), work stress and aggression (Chapter 16), and leadership (Chapters 6 and 7).

Self-Esteem

Self-esteem *is the extent to which a person believes that he or she is a worthwhile and deserving individual.*[10] In other words, people develop, hold, and sometimes modify opinions of their own behaviors, abilities, appearance, and worth. These general assessments reflect responses to people and situations, successes and failures, and the opinions of others. Such evaluations are sufficiently accurate and stable to be widely regarded as a basic personality trait or dimension. In terms of the Big Five personality factors, self-esteem most likely would be part of the *emotional stability* factor (see Figure 11.2).

Self-esteem affects behavior in organizations and other social settings in several important ways. It is related to initial vocational choice. For example, individuals with high self-esteem take risks in job selection, are attracted to high-status occupations (e.g., medicine or law), and are more likely to choose unconventional or nontraditional jobs (e.g., forest ranger or jet pilot) than are individuals with low self-esteem. A study of college students looking for jobs reported that those with high self-esteem (1) received more favorable evaluations from recruiters, (2) were more satisfied with the job search, (3) received more job offers, and (4) were more likely to accept jobs before graduation than were students with low self-esteem.

Self-esteem is also related to numerous behaviors. Employees with low self-esteem are more easily influenced by the opinions of other workers than are employees with high self-esteem. Employees with low self-esteem set lower goals for themselves than do employees with high self-esteem. Furthermore, employees with high self-esteem place more value on actually attaining those goals than do employees with low self-esteem. Employees with low self-esteem are more susceptible than employees with high self-esteem to adverse job conditions such as stress, conflict, ambiguity, poor supervision, poor working conditions, and the like. In a general sense, self-esteem is positively related to achievement and a willingness to expend effort to accomplish tasks. Clearly, self-esteem is an important individual difference in terms of work behavior. Both Ann Fudge and David Neeleman appear to be individuals with high self-esteem.[11]

Locus of Control

Locus of control *refers to the extent to which individuals believe that they can control events affecting them.* On the one hand, individuals who have a high **internal locus of control** (internals) *believe that their own behavior and actions primarily, but not necessarily totally, determine many of the events in their lives.* On the other hand, individuals who have a high **external locus of control** (externals) *believe that chance, fate, or other people primarily determine what happens to them.* Locus of control typically is considered to be a part of the *conscientiousness* factor (see Figure 11.2). What is your locus of control? Table 11.1 contains a measure that you can use to assess your own locus of control beliefs.

Many differences between internals and externals are significant in explaining aspects of behavior in organizations and other social settings.[12] Internals control their own behavior better, are more active politically and socially, and seek information about their situations more actively than do externals. Compared to externals, internals are more likely to try to influence or persuade others and are less likely to be influenced by others. Internals often are more achievement oriented than are externals. Compared to internals, externals appear to prefer a more structured, directive style of supervision. As we pointed out in Chapter 1, the ability to manage effectively in the global environment is an important competency. Managers with a

TABLE 11.1 A Locus of Control Measure

For each of these 10 questions, indicate the extent to which you agree or disagree, using the following scale.

1 = strongly disagree
2 = disagree
3 = slightly disagree
4 = neither disagree nor agree
5 = slightly agree
6 = agree
7 = strongly agree

_____ 1. When I get what I want it's usually because I worked hard for it.
_____ 2. When I make plans I am almost certain to make them work.
_____ 3. I prefer games involving some luck over games requiring pure skill.
_____ 4. I can learn almost anything if I set my mind to it.
_____ 5. My major accomplishments are entirely due to my hard work and ability.
_____ 6. I usually don't set goals, because I have a hard time following through on them.
_____ 7. Competition discourages excellence.
_____ 8. Often people get ahead just by being lucky.
_____ 9. On any sort of exam or competition I like to know how well I do relative to everyone else.
_____ 10. It's pointless to keep working on something that's too difficult for me.

To determine your score, reverse the values you selected for questions 3, 6, 7, 8, and 10 (1 = 7, 2 = 6, 3 = 5, 4 = 4, 5 = 3, 6 = 2, 7 = 1). For example, if you strongly disagreed with the statement in question 3, you would have given it a value of "1." Change this value to a "7." Reverse the scores in a similar manner for questions 6, 7, 8, and 10. Now add the 10 point values together.

Your score: _____

A study of college students found a mean of 51.8 for men and 52.2 for women using this questionnaire. The higher your score, the higher your internal locus of control. Low scores are associated with external locus of control.

Source: Adapted from Burger, J. M. *Personality: Theory and Research*. Belmont, Calif.: Wadsworth, 1986, pp. 400–401.

high internal locus of control often adjust more readily to international assignments than do managers with a high external locus of control. What do you think David Neeleman's locus of control score is?

Again, we are particularly interested in the relationship between these personality dimensions and specific behaviors. Figure 11.3 shows some of the important relationships between locus of control and job performance.

Introversion and Extraversion

In everyday usage, the words *introvert* and *extrovert* describe a person's congeniality. **Introversion** *is a tendency to be directed inward and to have a greater affinity for abstract ideas and sensitivity to personal feelings.* Introverts are quiet, introspective, and emotionally unexpressive. Extraversion is an orientation toward other people, events, and objects. Extraverts are sociable, lively, impulsive, and emotionally expressive. Introversion and extraversion are part of the collection of traits that comprise the *sociability* factor (see Figure 11.2). Many experts consider introversion and extraversion to be a personality dimension with a relatively high genetically determined component.

Although some people exhibit the extremes of introversion and extraversion, most are only moderately introverted or extraverted, or are even relatively balanced

FIGURE 11.3 The Effects of Locus of Control on Performance

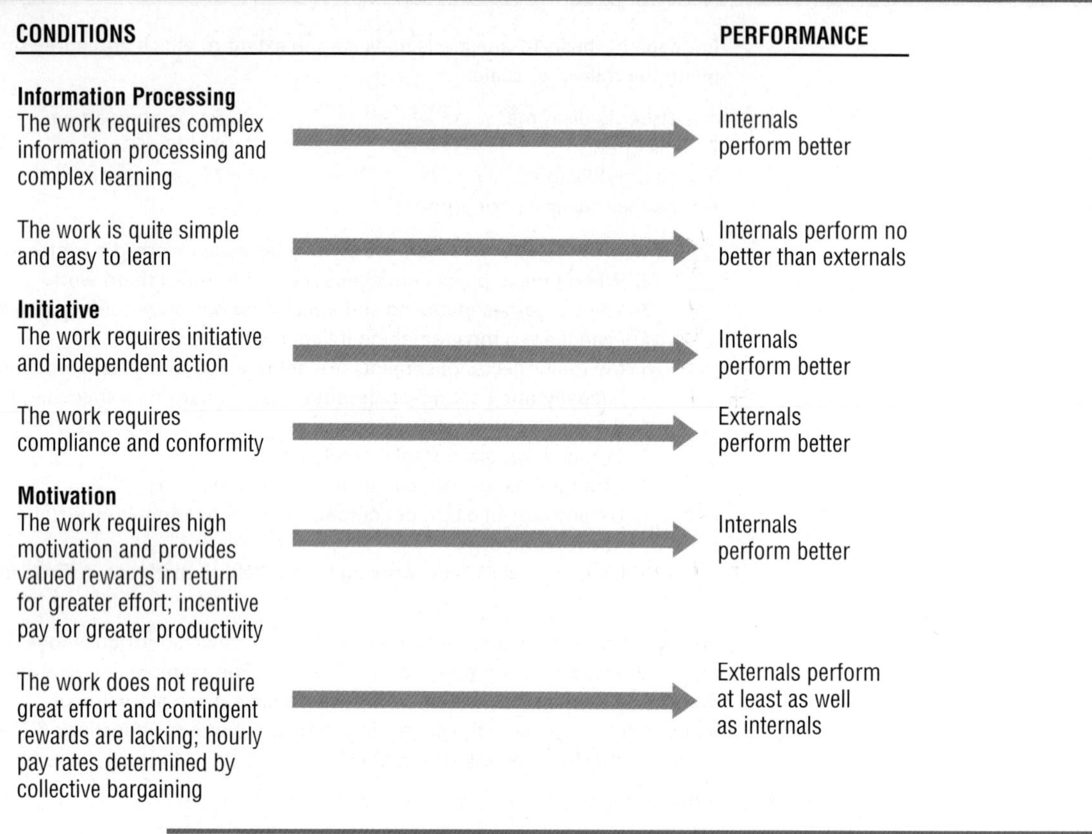

Source: Miner, J. B. *Industrial–Organizational Psychology.* New York: McGraw-Hill, 1992, 151. Reprinted with permission of McGraw-Hill.

between the extremes. Introverts and extroverts appear in all educational, gender, and occupational groups. As might be expected, extraverts are well represented in managerial occupations because the manager's role often involves working with others and influencing them to attain organizational goals. Some people suggest that some extraversion may be essential to managerial success. However, either extreme extraversion or extreme introversion can interfere with an individual's effectiveness in an organization.[13]

One of the most striking implications of the introversion–extraversion personality dimension involves task performance under different working conditions. The evidence suggests that introverts perform better alone and in a quiet environment, whereas extraverts perform better in an environment with greater sensory stimulation, such as a noisy office with many people and a high level of activity.

Emotional Intelligence

Psychologist Daniel Goleman states that emotional intelligence (EQ) is actually more crucial than general intelligence (IQ) in terms of career success.[14] As we indicated in Chapter 1, emotional intelligence refers to how well an individual handles herself and others rather than how smart she is or how capable she is in terms of technical skills. To assess your emotional intelligence, turn to page 336 and complete the questionnaire. Emotional intelligence includes the attributes of self-awareness, social empathy, self-motivation, and social skills.

- **Self-awareness** *refers to recognizing one's emotions, strengths and limitations, and capabilities and how these affect others.* People with high self-awareness know their emotional state, recognize the links between their feelings and what they are thinking, are open to feedback from others on how to continuously improve, and are able to make sound decisions despite uncertainties and pressures. They are able to show a sense of humor. How would you rate David Neeleman on this dimension?

- **Social empathy** *refers to sensing what others need in order for them to develop.* People who are socially aware of themselves show sensitivity, help out based on understanding other people's needs and feelings, challenge bias and intolerance, and act as trusted advisers to others. They are good at acknowledging people's strengths, accomplishments, and development. As a mentor, they give timely coaching advice and offer assignments that challenge a person's competencies.
- **Self-motivation** *refers to being results oriented and pursuing goals beyond what is required.* Highly self-motivated people set challenging goals for themselves and others, seek ways to improve their performance, and readily make personal sacrifices to meet the organization's goals. They operate from hope of success rather than a fear of failure. How would you rate David Neeleman on this dimension?
- **Social skills** *refer to the ability of a person to influence others.* People with effective social skills are good at persuading others to share their vision; stepping forward as a leader, regardless of their position in the organization; leading by example; and dealing with difficult interpersonal situations in a straightforward manner. How would you rate Ann Fudge on this dimension?

Think of EQ as being the social equivalent of IQ. In organizations undergoing rapid change, emotional intelligence may determine who gets promoted and who gets passed over or who gets laid off and who stays. According to Goleman, studies have consistently shown, for example, that the competencies associated with emotional intelligence (e.g., the ability to persuade others, the ability to understand others, and so on) are twice as important for career success as intelligence (IQ) or technical competencies.

Organizational Uses

It should be evident by now that the personality dimensions have important implications for understanding behavior. However, managers or groups should not try to change or otherwise directly control employee personality because being able to do so is generally impossible. Even if such control were possible, it would be highly unethical. Rather, the challenge for managers and employees is to understand the crucial role played by personality in explaining some aspects of human behavior in the workplace. Knowledge of important individual differences provides managers, employees, and students of organizational behavior with valuable insights and a framework that they can use to diagnose events and situations. The following Teams Competency feature describes such a situation at Thrive Networks, an information technology outsourcing company located in Concord, Massachusetts.[15]

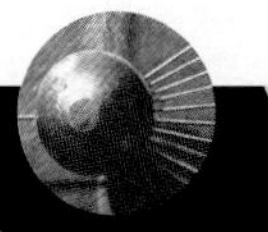

TEAMS COMPETENCY

THRIVE NETWORKS

Thrive Networks is a 35-person firm that used to pay salespeople almost entirely on commission. Of the nine people hired since the company was founded in 2000, only one lasted more than six months. Between the endless networking, cold-calling, meeting with prospects, and closing deals, people simply burned out. The problem was that different people had different personalities. Because the emphasis was on closing deals, people had little incentive to give leads to other salespeople and lose 50 percent of a commission.

Jim Lippie, director of business development, was a proven lead generator and a master networker who brought in dozens of potential customers each week. His personality permitted him to easily meet and greet customers and generate compelling proposals. Nate Wolfson was a closer, the person who could soothe last-minute concerns and make sure that the papers were signed. Both met with John Barrows, Thrive's CEO, and presented a radical new idea. Rather than being paid individually, the two men proposed that Thrive's salespeople pool their commissions and be compensated collectively. At first skeptical, Barrows decided that it was worth a try. Now, each team member receives a base salary and shares commissions based on reaching a monthly team goal. They also can earn more for meeting or exceeding goals.

What have been the results? In the first three months, the number of sales meetings with customers increased by 67 percent and deals took 30 percent less time to complete. For the system to work, all salespeople must understand the others' strengths (personalities). Each salesperson is now part of a team whose members follow up on leads, which demands an outgoing personality; work through the details of a deal, which demands more of an introverted personality; and finally close the deal, which demands a person with high emotional intelligence.

For more information on Thrive Networks, visit the organization's home page at ***http://www.thrivenetworks.com.***

The Person and the Situation

Although understanding differences in personality is important, behavior always involves an interaction of the person and the situation. Sometimes the demands of the situation may be so overwhelming that individual differences are relatively unimportant. For example, if an office building is burning, everyone in it will try to flee. However, the fact that all employees behaved the same way says nothing about the personalities of those individuals. In other situations, individual differences may explain more about behavior.

The relative importance of situational versus personal determinants of behavior continues to be debated, but considerable evidence exists for roles by both. We believe that considering both determinants will help you to understand behavior in organizations. For that reason, our perspective is consistently used throughout this book. You will discover that many of the topics covered, such as leadership, political behavior, power differences, stress, and resistance to change, examine both *personal* and *situational causes* for the organizational behavior discussed. Both *interact* to determine behavior.

LEARNING OBJECTIVE

3. State the role and importance of work attitudes.

WORK ATTITUDES AND BEHAVIOR

Attitudes are another type of *individual difference* that affects an individual's behavior in organizations. **Attitudes** *are relatively lasting feelings, beliefs, and behavioral tendencies aimed at specific people, groups, ideas, issues, or objects.*[16] Attitudes reflect an individual's background and experiences and are formed by a variety of forces, including their personal values, experiences, and their personalities. Attitudes are important because they are the way through which most people express their feelings. An employee's statement that he thinks he is underpaid by his organization reflects his feeling about his pay.

Components of Attitudes

Attitudes are usually viewed as stable individual differences. For a number of reasons, an employee might decide to join an organization. Once she joins that organization, we would expect that person to express a consistently positive attitude toward that organization by telling others about her decision to join, what outstanding products or services the organization offers, and what great challenges the organization will offer her to develop as a professional. People often think of attitudes as a simple concept, but in reality attitudes and their effects on behavior can be extremely complex. An attitude consists of

- an affective component—the feelings, sentiments, moods, and emotions about some person, idea, event, or object;
- a cognitive component—the thoughts, opinions, knowledge, or information held by the individual; and
- a behavioral component—the predisposition to act on a favorable or unfavorable evaluation of something.

These components don't exist or function separately. An attitude represents the *interplay* of a person's affective, cognitive, and behavioral tendencies with regard to something—another person or group, an event, or an issue. For example, suppose that a college student holds a negative attitude about the use of tobacco. During a job interview with the representative of Skippy Peanut Butter, she discovers that Skippy is owned by Kraft Foods, which is a major division of Phillip Morris, a major supplier of cigarettes. She might feel a sudden intense dislike for the company's interviewer (the affective component). She might form a negative opinion of the interviewer based on beliefs and opinions about the type of person who would work for such a company (the cognitive component). She might even be tempted to make an unkind remark to the interviewer or suddenly terminate the interview (the behavioral component). However, the person's *actual* behavior may or may not be easy to predict and will depend on several factors that we discuss shortly.

Key Work-Related Attitudes: Hope, Job Satisfaction, and Organizational Commitment

People form attitudes about many things. Employees have attitudes about their boss, pay, working conditions, promotion possibilities, where they park, food in the company cafeteria, and the like. Some of these attitudes are more important than others because they are more closely linked to performance. Especially important are attitudes of hope, job satisfaction, and organizational commitment.

Hope. **Hope** *involves a person's mental willpower (determination) and waypower (road map) to achieve goals.*[17] Simply wishing for something isn't enough; a person must have the means to make it happen. However, all the knowledge and skills needed to solve a problem won't help if the person doesn't have the willpower to do so. Therefore, a simple definition of hope is

$$\text{Hope} = \text{mental willpower} + \text{waypower to achieve goals.}$$

Answering the questions in Table 11.2 will help you understand this definition of *hope.* The value of this concept is that it applies to a variety of work-related attitudes. The high-hope person enjoys the pursuit of challenging goals and pursues them with a positive attitude. High hope people engage in self-talk, such as "This should be an interesting task" or "I am ready for this challenge." The high-hope person is attentive and focused on the appropriate behaviors for the situation. High-hope people commit themselves to desired positive work outcomes (e.g., good performance) and distance themselves from negative outcomes. Relative to their low-hope counterparts, high-hope individuals establish clear goals, imagine pathways to those goals, and motivate themselves to follow such pathways. The low-hope person is apprehensive about what is to come. This person's attention is quickly diverted from task-relevant behavior to such thoughts as "I'm not doing very well." Quickly the low-hope person may feel a lot of negative emotions. Low-hope people are especially susceptible to feeling great amounts of stress in their jobs and becoming easily derailed by issues in their pursuit of goals. With such derailments, low-hope people perceive that they are not going to reach their desired goal. Their natural tendency is to withdraw from friends and become "loners." For a high-hope person, however, the stressor is seen as a challenge that needs to be worked around. Should the high-hope person be truly blocked in the pursuit of a goal, instead of being full of anger, self-pity, and negative emotions as is the case for low-hope individuals in similar circumstances, high-hope individuals will find another goal that will fulfill similar needs. This is because high-hope individuals have several goals that can bring them happiness. Managers who are hopeful spend more time with employees, establish open lines of communication with employees and others, and help employees set difficult, but achievable, goals. High-hope individuals tend to be more certain of their goals, value progress toward achieving those goals, enjoy interacting with people, readily adapt to new relationships, and are less anxious in stressful situations than are low-hope individuals.

TABLE 11.2 **Hope Scale**

Read each item carefully. For each item, what number best describes you?

1 = definitely false 3 = mostly true
2 = mostly false 4 = definitely true

____ 1. I energetically pursue my work (academic) goals.
____ 2. I can think of many ways to get out of a jam.
____ 3. My past experiences have prepared me well for my future.
____ 4. There are lots of ways around any problem.
____ 5. I've been pretty successful in life.
____ 6. I can think of many ways to get things in life that are most important to me.
____ 7. I meet the goals (work/academic) that I set for myself.
____ 8. Even when others get discouraged, I know I can find a way to solve the problem.

Scoring

Total the eight numbers. If you score higher than 24, you are a hopeful person. If you score less than 24, you probably aren't hopeful. Items 1, 3, 5, and 7 relate to willpower, and items 2, 4, 6, and 8 relate to waypower.

Source: Adapted from Snyder, C. R. Managing for high hope. *R & D Innovator*, 1995, 4(6), 6–7; Snyder, C. R., LaPointe, A. B., Crowson, J. J., and Early, S. Preferences of high- and low-hope people for self-referential input. *Cognition and Emotion*, 1998, 12, 807–823.

Managers can help employees increase their level of hope in at least three ways.[18] First, they can help employees set clear *goals* that have benchmarks so that the employees can track their progress toward the goal; vague goals may actually lessen hope because the result sought is unclear and tracking progress therefore is difficult, if not impossible. Employees who set goals that are slightly higher than previous levels of performance learn to expand their range of hope. They also learn a great deal about which goals are best for them. Second, managers can help employees break overall, long-term goals into *small subgoals* or *steps*. Remember how you learned to ride a bike? Through many falls and wobbles, you learned that each consecutive subgoal (moving the pedals, balancing, going a block without falling) is a stretch. These small steps provided you with positive mental maps about how to reach your goal—riding a bike. Third, managers can help employees figure out how to *motivate* themselves to reach their goals. At Don Herring dealership, the largest Mitsubishi dealership in the United States, the names of all salespersons are posted on a chart in the break room.[19] The typical new-car salesperson sells 8 to 10 cars a month. At Herring, a salesperson sells 20 to 25 a month. How has Herring achieved such results? When a salesperson sells a car, a gold star is placed beside that person's name. The purpose of the chart and gold star is to illustrate positive movement toward achieving a realistic sales goal. The perception of positive movement is crucial for hope.

Job Satisfaction. An attitude of great interest to managers and team leaders is job satisfaction.[20] Do people generally like their jobs? Despite what you may hear in the news about dissatisfied workers going on strike or even acting violently toward their coworkers and/or manager, people are generally quite satisfied with their jobs. These feelings, reflecting attitudes toward a job, are known as job satisfaction. **Job satisfaction** *reflects the extent to which people find fulfillment in their work.* Low job satisfaction can result in costly turnover, absenteeism, tardiness, and even poor mental health. Because job satisfaction is important to organizations, we need to look at the factors that contribute to it.

A popular measure of job satisfaction used by organizations is shown in Table 11.3. It measures five facets of job satisfaction: pay, security, social, supervisory, and growth satisfaction. Take a minute now to complete it. Obviously, you may be satisfied with some aspects of your job and, at the same time, be dissatisfied with others.

The sources of job satisfaction and dissatisfaction vary from person to person. Sources important for many employees include the challenge of the job, interest

TABLE 11.3 Measuring Job Satisfaction

Think of the job you have now, or a job you've had in the past. Indicate how satisfied you are with each aspect of your job below, using the following scale:

1 = Extremely dissatisfied
2 = Dissatisfied
3 = Slightly dissatisfied
4 = Neutral
5 = Slightly satisfied
6 = Satisfied
7 = Extremely satisfied

____ 1. The amount of job security I have.
____ 2. The amount of pay and fringe benefits I receive.
____ 3. The amount of personal growth and development I get in doing my job.
____ 4. The people I talk to and work with on my job.
____ 5. The degree of respect and fair treatment I receive from my boss.
____ 6. The feeling of worthwhile accomplishment I get from doing my job.
____ 7. The chance to get to know other people while on the job.
____ 8. The amount of support and guidance I receive from my supervisor.
____ 9. The degree to which I am fairly paid for what I contribute to this organization.
____ 10. The amount of independent thought and action I can exercise in my job.
____ 11. How secure things look for me in the future in this organization.
____ 12. The chance to help other people while at work.
____ 13. The amount of challenge in my job.
____ 14. The overall quality of the supervision I receive on my work.

Now, compute your scores for the facets of job satisfaction.

Pay Satisfaction:
Q2 + Q9 = __10__ Divided by 2: 5

Security Satisfaction:
Q1 + Q11 = __14__ Divided by 2: 7

Social Satisfaction:
Q4 + Q7 + Q12 = __18__ Divided by 3: 6

Supervisory Satisfaction:
Q5 + Q8 + Q14 = __14__ Divided by 3: 4.67

Growth Satisfaction:
Q3 + Q6 + Q10 + Q13 = __23__ Divided by 4: 5.75

Scores on the facets range from 1 to 7. (Scores lower than 4 suggest there is room for change.) This questionnaire is an abbreviated version of the Job Diagnostic Survey, a widely used tool for assessing individuals' attitudes about their jobs.

Source: J. Richard Hackman & Greg R. Oldham, WORK REDESIGN, © 1980. Reprinted by permission of Pearson Education, Inc., Upper Saddle River, NJ.

that the work holds for the employee, physical activity required, working conditions, rewards available from the organization, nature of coworkers, and the like. Table 11.4 lists work factors that often are related to levels of employee job satisfaction. An important implication suggested is that job satisfaction be considered an outcome of an individual's work experience. Thus high levels of dissatisfaction should indicate to managers that problems exist, say, with working conditions, the reward system, or the employee's role in the organization.

TABLE 11.4 Effects of Various Work Factors on Job Satisfaction

WORK FACTORS	EFFECTS
Work itself	
Challenge	Mentally challenging work that the individual can successfully accomplish is satisfying.
Physical demands	Tiring work is dissatisfying.
Personal interest	Personally interesting work is satisfying.
Reward structure	Rewards that are equitable and that provide accurate feedback for performance are satisfying.
Working conditions	
Physical	Satisfaction depends on the match between working conditions and physical needs.
Goal attainment	Working conditions that promote goal attainment are satisfying.
Self	High self-esteem is conducive to job satisfaction.
Others in the organization	Individuals will be satisfied with supervisors, coworkers, or subordinates who help them attain rewards. Also, individuals will be more satisfied with colleagues who see things the same way they do.
Organization and management	Individuals will be satisfied with organizations that have policies and procedures designed to help them attain rewards. Individuals will be dissatisfied with conflicting roles and/or ambiguous roles imposed by the organization.
Fringe benefits	Benefits do not have a strong influence on job satisfaction for most workers.

Source: Adapted from Landy, F. J. Psychology of Work Behavior, 4th ed. Pacific Grove, Calif.: Brooks/Cole, 1989, 470.

Of special interest to managers and employees are the possible relationships between job satisfaction and various job behaviors and other outcomes in the workplace. A commonsense notion is that job satisfaction leads directly to effective performance. (A happy worker is a good worker.) Yet, numerous studies have shown that a simple, direct linkage between job satisfaction and job performance often doesn't exist.[21] The difficulty of relating attitudes to behavior is important. General attitudes best predict general behaviors, and specific attitudes are related most strongly to specific behaviors. These principles explain, at least in part, why the expected relationships often don't exist. Job satisfaction is a collection of numerous attitudes toward various aspects of the job and represents a general attitude. Performance of a specific task, such as preparing a particular monthly report, can't necessarily be predicted on the basis of a general attitude. However, studies have shown that the level of overall workforce job satisfaction and organizational performance are linked. That is, organizations with satisfied employees tend to be more effective than organizations with unsatisfied employees. Further, management in many organizations recognizes the important link between customer satisfaction and the satisfaction of employees who interact with their customers. Examples of this link are apparent in the following Communication Competency feature.[22]

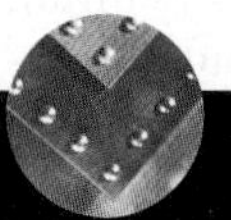

COMMUNICATION COMPETENCY

THE CONTAINER STORE

With employee turnover greater than 100 percent in most retail stores but only at 15 to 25 percent at the Container Store, how do its managers attract and retain employees?

The Container Store recently was named by *Fortune* magazine and the Great Places to Work Institute as one of America's 100 best places to work. Sales exceed $460 million for its 33 stores. What goes into this ranking? Great Places uses five criteria to judge a company: (1) credibility—open communications, integrity; (2) respect—caring for employees as individuals with personal lives; (3) fairness—absence of favoritism in hiring and promotions; (4) pride—the organization's reputation in the community, and (5) camaraderie—sense of family or team.

How does the Container Store rate? First, it practices what it preaches. Every first-year full-time employee gets about 241 hours of training. It is provided both formally and informally by ongoing communication with managers, who not only ask what their people need to do their jobs well, but also regularly assess how to provide necessary assistance. Each store has a back room where new products are housed prior to display. Employees receive formal training on how to display these new products and how to communicate their benefits. According to Garrett Boone and Kip Tindell, the Container Store's CEOs, "Nothing goes out on the sales floor until our people are ready for it." This program is coupled with extensive training programs designed to meet individual skills and job functions and team-based incentive programs. Moreover, a "super sales trainer" serves each store. These trainers are top sales performers who know how to sell the hard stuff and who have an aptitude for leadership and strong communication and presentation skills. These people give on-the-spot help to employees who ask, but employees are encouraged to take responsibility for their own development.

The Container Store pays above-industry salaries to employees. Employees earn 50 to 100 percent more than employees earn at other retailers, such as the Gap, Sample House, and Borders. Employees do not sell on a commission basis. The company is attractive to employees because it offers flexible shifts, allowing college students to earn some cash between classes and mothers to work while their kids are in school (9 A.M. to 2 P.M.).

Guided by what Boone and Tindell call a "do-unto-others" philosophy, the Container Store's more than 2,500 employees, of which 27 percent are minority and 60 percent are women, work in an environment that ensures open communication throughout the company, including regular discussions of store sales, company goals, and expansion plans. Another guiding principle is to offer the best selection, the best service, and the best price. All employees are encouraged to treat customers like they would treat visitors in their homes. Boone and Tindell empathize with those who must cope with multiple demands on their time and energy and need to bring some order to their lives. Balancing both work and motherhood symbolizes their clientele—90 percent of whom are professional women earning more than $42,000.

For more information on the Container Store, visit the organization's home page at ***http://www.containerstore.com.***

THE COMPETENT LEADER

The current challenge is to engage our employees in our business. Managers must personally communicate with their employees.
Cristina Lambert, CEO, Puerto Rico Telephone

Job satisfaction is important for many reasons. Because satisfaction represents an outcome of the work experience, high levels of dissatisfaction help to identify organizational problems that need attention. In addition, job dissatisfaction is strongly linked to absenteeism, turnover, and physical and mental health problems.[23] High levels of absenteeism and turnover are costly for organizations. According to John Semyan, an executive at TNS Partners, Inc., it typically costs firms about 20 percent of a person's salary to recruit a replacement. Thus, when Deloitte & Touche, one of the Big Five accounting firms, loses a $50,000 per year staff accountant, it may have to spend $10,000 to hire a comparable employee. Many management experts suggest that the strong relationship between dissatisfaction and absenteeism and turnover is a compelling reason for paying careful attention to employee job satisfaction.

Organizational Commitment. Another important work attitude that has a bearing on organizational behavior is commitment to the organization. **Organizational commitment** *refers to the strength of an employee's involvement in the organization and identification with it.* Strong organizational commitment is characterized by

- a support of and acceptance of the organization's goals and values,
- a willingness to exert considerable effort on behalf of the organization, and
- a desire to remain with the organization.[24]

Highly committed people will probably see themselves as dedicated members of the organization, referring to the organization in personal terms, such as "we make high-quality products." They will overlook minor sources of job dissatisfaction and have a long tenure with the organization. In contrast, a less committed individual will view his relationship with the organization in less personal terms ("They don't offer quality service"), will express his dissatisfaction more openly about things, and will have a short tenure with the organization.

Organizational commitment goes beyond loyalty to include an active contribution to accomplishing organizational goals. Organizational commitment represents a broader work attitude than job satisfaction because it applies to the entire organization rather than just to the job. Further, commitment typically is more stable than satisfaction because day-to-day events are less likely to change it.

As with job satisfaction, the sources of organizational commitment may vary from person to person. Employees' initial commitment to an organization is determined largely by their individual characteristics (e.g., personality and attitudes) and how well their early job experiences match their expectations. Later, organizational commitment continues to be influenced by job experiences, with many of the same factors that lead to job satisfaction also contributing to organizational commitment or lack of commitment: pay, relationships with supervisors and coworkers, working conditions, opportunities for advancement, and so on. Over time, organizational commitment tends to become stronger because (1) individuals develop deeper ties to the organization and their coworkers as they spend more time with them, (2) seniority often brings advantages that tend to develop more positive work attitudes, and (3) opportunities in the job market may decrease with age, causing workers to become more strongly attached to their current jobs.

Managers are interested in the relationships between organizational commitment and job behavior because the lack of commitment often leads to turnover. The stronger an employee's commitment is to the organization, the less likely the person is to quit. Strong commitment also is often correlated with low absenteeism and relatively high productivity. Attendance at work (being on time and taking little time off) is usually higher for employees with strong organizational commitment. Moreover, committed individuals tend to be more goal directed and waste less time while at work, which has a positive impact on productivity. Effective management can foster increased commitment and loyalty to the organization.

EMOTIONS AND PERFORMANCE

LEARNING OBJECTIVE

4. Describe how emotions affect performance.

Anger, jealousy, guilt, shame, happiness, and relief are all feelings that you have probably experienced in organizations. These feelings are all part of your emotions. **Emotions** *refer to a complex pattern of feelings.* How employees and managers handle their emotions at work has a tremendous impact on their productivity.[25] Positive feelings, such as joy, affection, and happiness, serve many purposes. When people experience these positive emotions, they tend to think more creatively, seek out new information and experiences, behave more flexibly, have greater confidence in their competencies, and be more persistent. Positive emotions can help people bounce back from adversity and live longer and healthier lives. People who experience positive emotions, especially during stressful times, tend to tolerate pain better, cope with and recover from illness faster, and experience less depression. In contrast, negative emotions, such as anger, disgust, and sadness, tend to narrow a person's focus and limit their options to search out alternatives. For example, anger tends to lead to a desire to escape, attack, or take revenge, and guilt/shame can result in a person's desire to withdraw from the situation rather than creatively problem solve.[26]

The distinction between positive and negative emotions is shown in Figure 11.4. Negative emotions are incongruent with the goal you are striving to achieve. For example, which of the six emotions are you likely to experience if you fail the final exam for this course, or if you are dismissed from your job? Failing the exam or losing your job would be incongruent with your goal of graduating or being perceived as an accomplished professional. On the other hand, which of the four positive emotions, shown in Figure 11.4, will you likely experience if you graduate with honors or receive a promotion? The emotions that you would experience in these situations are positive because these are congruent with your goals. Therefore, emotions are goal directed.

Positive emotions have been linked to organizational effectiveness. Leaders who express positive emotions encourage employees to feel positive emotions as well. When people feel positive emotions, they are more likely to set high goals, see and fix mistakes, feel more competent, and have greater problem-solving capabilities. In organizations that recently cut staff, those organizations that had leaders who displayed positive emotions even in such trying times had significantly higher productivity, higher quality, and lower voluntary employee turnover than those leaders who displayed negative emotions. After the Twin Towers toppled on September 11, 2001,

FIGURE 11.4 Positive and Negative Emotions

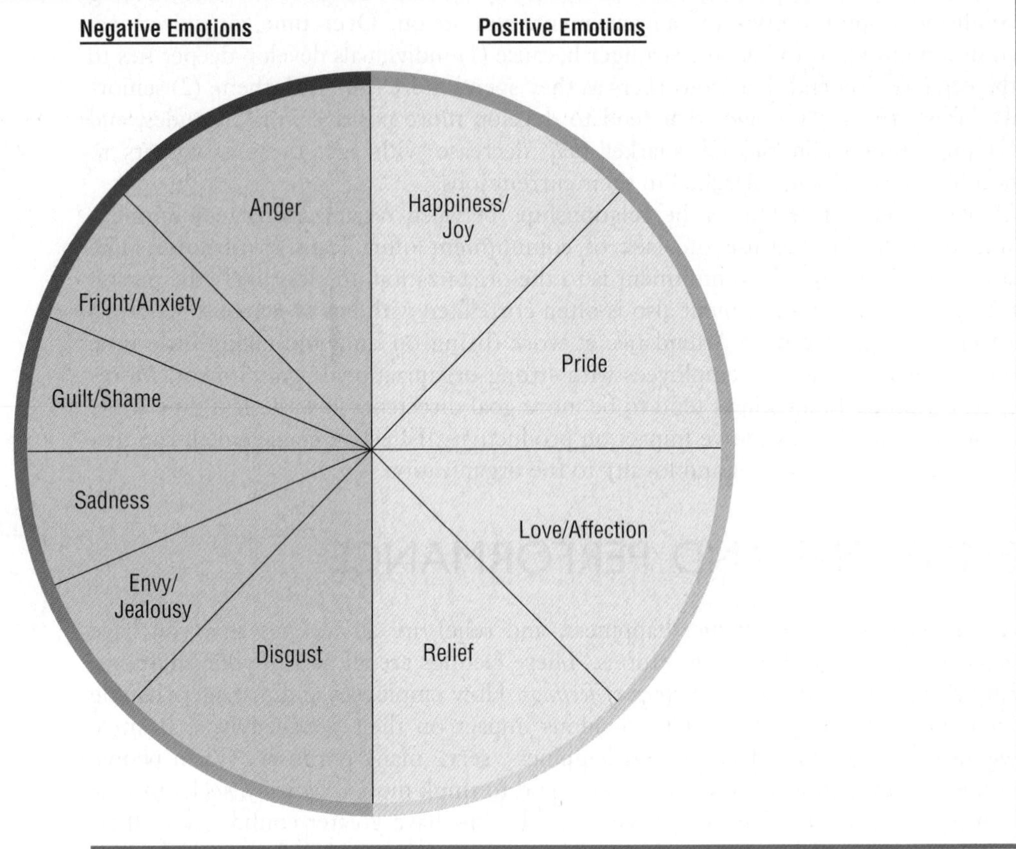

employees at a Starbucks near the Towers were told by their manager that they could leave to protect their safety. Instead, employees and the store managers chose to stay and literally pulled stunned people passing by into the store, giving them food, drink, shelter, and emotional support. As one reporter said: "Embedded in a crisis is an opportunity for employers to build loyalty and wholeheartedly supply positive emotions."

A Model of Emotions

A model of how emotions affect behavior is shown in Figure 11.5.[27] The process starts with a goal. A **goal** *refers to what an individual is trying to accomplish.* That is, a goal is your purpose or intent. A dentist has a goal of seeing 25 patients a week. **Anticipatory emotions** *refer to the emotions that you believe you will feel after achievement or failure of reaching your goal.* For example, at Sewell Automotive in Dallas, Texas, a salesperson's goal is to sell 9 cars a month. If they sell between 9 and 19 cars, they receive special recognition (e.g., flowers, round of golf, choice of cars to drive for the next month) from their boss. If they sell more than 20 cars in any month, they receive a special letter from Carl Sewell, a weekend package at a local hotel with all expenses paid, as well as flowers, golf, etc. If they sell fewer than 9 cars a month, they will receive coaching on their selling tactics. If they sell fewer than 27 cars in three months, they are dismissed. The key motivational device is to have each salesperson imagine the emotions they will feel when they reach their goal. The more desirable the implications are for achieving the goal, the more intense will be the anticipated emotions from achieving that goal. Jenny Craig, Weight Watchers, and other diet organizations ask people to write down their emotions they anticipate when they reach their weight goals. People who had anticipated positive emotions (e.g., I will feel excited, delighted, etc.) lost more weight than those who didn't have such positive anticipatory emotions.

FIGURE 11.5 Role of Emotions in Performance

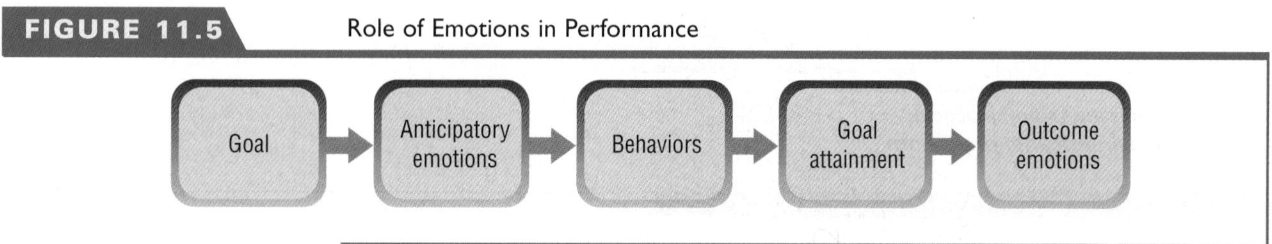

If the anticipatory emotions are of sufficient intensity to motivate the person, the person will engage in those behaviors in order to reach her goal. That is, a person will need to develop a plan, outline the behaviors needed to reach her plan, and exert effort to exhibit those behaviors. Returning to our diet example, if you can imagine strong positive emotions from achieving your weight goal, you need to behave in ways that will enable you to reach that positive emotion. That is, you need to start exercising and dieting. Both of these behaviors are linked to loss of weight. As shown in Figure 11.5, goal attainment is the next step. Did you reach your goal? Yes or no? If yes, then you would experience positive emotions; if no, then you would experience negative emotions. In our dietary plan, researchers found that those people who could anticipate positive emotions from achieving their goal were more likely to diet and exercise and reach their goal than those individuals who didn't engage in these behaviors.

The following Change Competency highlights how Kenneth Chenault, CEO of American Express, ensured that employees and customers felt the care and concern they needed during the September 11, 2001, crisis at the Twin Towers. In good times and in a crisis, positive emotions and behaviors create good feelings in organizations because they create a contagion effect in which people copy each other's emotions. Furthermore, when employees feel gratitude for the goodwill they receive, they want to repay this goodwill with greater loyalty and effort. Therefore, positive emotions in organizations can be a competitive advantage that is not easily copied by competitors.[28]

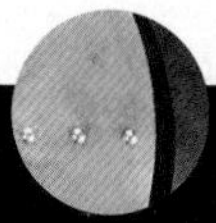

CHANGE COMPETENCY

KENNETH CHENAULT OF AMERICAN EXPRESS

After the events of September 11, 2001, AmEx helped 560,000 stranded cardholders get home, in some cases chartering airplanes and buses to ferry them across the country. It waived millions of dollars in delinquent fees on late-paying cardholders and increased credit limits to cash-starved clients. . . . Most telling, Chenault gathered 5,000 American Express employees at the Paramount Theater in New York on September 20 for a highly emotional "town hall meeting." During the session, Chenault demonstrated the poise, compassion, and decisiveness that vaulted him to the top. He told employees that he had been filled with such despair, sadness, and anger that he had seen a counselor. Twice he rushed to spontaneously embrace grief-stricken employees. Chenault said he would donate $1 million of the company's profits to the families of the AmEx victims. "I represent the best company and the best people in the world," he concluded. "In fact, you are my strength, and I love you." It was a poignant and unscripted moment. Says AmEx board member Charlene

Barshefsky, a partner at Wilmer Cutler & Pickering, who viewed a video of the event, "The manner in which he took command, the comfort and direction he gave to what was obviously an audience in shock was of a caliber one rarely sees."

For more information on American Express, visit the organization's home page at ***http://www.americanexpress.com.***

Organizational Uses. We have listed six ways in which managers can create positive emotions in their organization:

- Express positive emotions—gratitude, generosity, optimism, trust—regularly at work. Start meetings with sincere words of appreciation. Remember that positive emotions are contagious, especially when expressed by direct supervisors and organizational leaders.
- Give unexpected kindness and reach out to others when it is least expected. When you engage in positive emotions and behaviors when it goes against the norm, the element of surprise and courage becomes a powerful example to others, both strengthening people's trust in you and role-modeling behavior for others to follow.
- Help people find positive meaning in their day-to-day work lives. Help employees see how their work contributes to a greater good and whom they are helping through their efforts.
- Provide opportunities for people to help each other and to express appreciation for the help they receive from others.
- Celebrate small wins so that employees experience ongoing success and the associated positive emotions.
- In a crisis, enable employees to experience and express what it feels like to rise to the occasion and find the strength and resources they never knew they had. [29]

CHAPTER SUMMARY

1. Explain the basic sources of personality determinants.

Personality is a person's set of relatively stable characteristics and traits that account for consistent patterns of behavior in various situations. Each individual is like other people in some ways and in some ways is unique. An individual's personality is determined by inherited traits, or tendencies, and life experiences. Experiences occur within the framework of the individual's biological, physical, and social environment—all of which are modified by the culture, family, and other groups to which the person belongs.

2. Identify some personality traits that affect behavior.

An individual's personality may be described by a set of factors known as the Big Five. Specifically, these personality factors describe an individual's degree of adjustment, sociability, conscientiousness, agreeableness, and intellectual openness. Remember that, if you didn't do so earlier, you can assess your own profile in terms of the Big Five by using the Experiential Exercise questionnaire at the end of this chapter. Many specific personality dimensions, including self-esteem, locus of control, introversion/extraversion, and emotional intelligence, have important relationships to work behavior and outcomes. In addition, an understanding of interactions between the person and the situation is important for comprehending organizational behavior.

Attitudes are patterns of feelings, beliefs, and behavioral tendencies directed toward specific people, groups, ideas, issues, or objects. Attitudes have affective (feelings, emotions), cognitive (beliefs, knowledge), and behavioral (a predisposition to act in a particular way) components. The relationship between attitudes and behavior isn't always clear, although important relationships exist. We reviewed how the attitudes of hope, job satisfaction, and organizational commitment affect behavior in many organizations.

3. State the role and importance of work attitudes.

Employees show a variety of emotions during the day. Some of these are positive and can lead to more effective performance, whereas others are negative and can lead to poor performance. We introduced how emotions can influence the productivity of employees.

4. Describe how emotions affect performance.

KEY TERMS AND CONCEPTS

Agreeableness
Anticipatory emotions
Attitudes
"Big Five" personality factors
Conscientiousness
Emotional intelligence
Emotional stability
Emotions
External locus of control
Extraversion
Goal
Hope
Individual differences
Internal locus of control
Introversion
Job satisfaction
Locus of control
Openness
Organizational commitment
Personality
Personality trait
Self-awareness
Self-esteem
Self-motivation
Social empathy
Social skills

DISCUSSION QUESTIONS

1. Identify a specific personality factor that seems particularly interesting to you. Provide an example from your own work or other experience of an instance when this factor seemed strongly related to behavior.
2. Select a strong attitude that you hold and describe it in terms of the three components of an attitude.
3. How can you use the model of emotions to increase your performance?
4. Describe an incident in which you observed an employee with low organizational commitment. What were the effects on his or her performance?
5. What influences on personality development seem most important to you? Why?
6. Identify a personality model. Using this model, describe Ann Fudge's personality and how it impacted the performance of her subordinates at Young & Rubicam.
7. Describe the basic sources of personality differences between yourself and a person you know well.
8. Using the Big Five personality factors, describe the personality of (a) a close family member and (b) a person for whom you have worked. How did these factors affect your behavior toward them?
9. Why is the management of employees' emotions important for a manager?
10. Describe how you can develop your hope attitude to improve your performance.
11. Why do managers give so much attention to job satisfaction?

EXPERIENTIAL EXERCISES

Experiential Exercise: Self Competency

Assessing the Big Five[30]

The Big Five Locator Questionnaire

Instructions: On each numerical scale that follows, indicate which point is generally more descriptive of you. If the two terms are equally descriptive, mark the midpoint.

1. Eager 5 4 3 2 1 Calm
2. Prefer Being with Other People 5 4 3 2 1 Prefer Being Alone
3. A Dreamer 5 4 3 2 1 No-Nonsense
4. Courteous 5 4 3 2 1 Abrupt
5. Neat 5 4 3 2 1 Messy

---

6. Cautious 5 4 3 2 1 Confident
7. Optimistic 5 4 3 2 1 Pessimistic
8. Theoretical 5 4 3 2 1 Practical
9. Generous 5 4 3 2 1 Selfish
10. Decisive 5 4 3 2 1 Open-Ended

---

11. Discouraged 5 4 3 2 1 Upbeat
12. Exhibitionist 5 4 3 2 1 Private
13. Follow Imagination 5 4 3 2 1 Follow Authority
14. Warm 5 4 3 2 1 Cold
15. Stay Focused 5 4 3 2 1 Easily Distracted

---

16. Easily Embarrassed 5 4 3 2 1 Don't Give a Darn
17. Outgoing 5 4 3 2 1 Cool
18. Seek Novelty 5 4 3 2 1 Seek Routine
19. Team Player 5 4 3 2 1 Independent
20. A Preference for Order 5 4 3 2 1 Comfortable with Chaos

---

21. Distractible 5 4 3 2 1 Unflappable
22. Conversational 5 4 3 2 1 Thoughtful
23. Comfortable with Ambiguity 5 4 3 2 1 Prefer Things Clear-Cut
24. Trusting 5 4 3 2 1 Skeptical
25. On Time 5 4 3 2 1 Procrastinate

Big Five Locator Score Conversion Sheet

Norm Score	Emotional Stability	Extraversion	Openness	Agreeableness	Conscientiousness	Norm Score
80						80
79			25			79
78						78
77	22					77
76			24			76
75						75
74						74
73	21		23			73
72		25				72
71				25		71
70	20	24	22			70
69					25	69
68				24		68
67		23	21		24	67
66	19					66
65		22		23	23	65
64			20			64
63					22	63
62	18	21	19	22		62
61					21	61
60		20				60
59	17		18	21	20	59
58						58
57		19				57
56			17			56

Norm Score	Emotional Stability	Extraversion	Openness	Agreeableness	Conscientiousness	Norm Score
55	16	18		20	19	55
54			16	19		54
53						53
52		17			18	52
51	15					51
50		16	15	18	17	50
49						49
48	14	15			16	48
47			14	17		47
46		14			15	46
45			13			45
44	13			16	14	44
43		13				43
42			12			42
41				15	13	41
40	12	12	11			40
39						39
38				14	12	38
37		11	10			37
36	11					36
35		10		13	11	35
34			9			34
33	10	9			10	33
32				12		32
31			8			31
30		8			9	30
29	9			11		29
28		7	7		8	28
27				10		27
26		6			7	26
25	8		6			25
24				9	6	24
23						23
22			5		22	22
21	7	5				21
20				8		20
Enter Norm Scores Here	Es =	Ex =	O =	A =	C =	

Instructions:

1. Find the sum of the circled numbers on the first row of each of the five-line groupings (Row 1 + Row 6 + Row 11 + Row 16 + Row 21 = 13 This is your raw score for "emotional stability." Circle the number in the EMOTIONAL STABILITY column of the Score Conversion Sheet that corresponds to this raw score.
2. Find the sum of the circled numbers on the second row of each of the five-line groupings (Row 2 + Row 7 + Row 12 + Row 17 + Row 22 = 15). This is your raw score for "extraversion." Circle the number in the EXTRAVERSION column of the Score Conversion Sheet that corresponds to this raw score.
3. Find the sum of the circled numbers on the third row of each of the five-line groupings (Row 3 + Row 8 + Row 13 + Row 18 + Row 23 = 17). This is your raw score for "openness." Circle the number in the OPENNESS column of the Score Conversion Sheet that corresponds to this raw score.
4. Find the sum of the circled numbers on the fourth row of each of the five-line groupings (Row 4 + Row 9 + Row 14 + Row 19 + Row 24 = 15). This is your raw score for "agreeableness." Circle the number in the AGREEABLENESS column of the Score Conversion Sheet that corresponds to this raw score.
5. Find the sum of the circled numbers on the fifth row of each of the five-line groupings (Row 5 + Row 10 + Row 15 + Row 20 + Row 25 = 19). This is your raw score for "conscientiousness." Circle the number in the CONSCIENTIOUSNESS column of the Score Conversion Sheet that corresponds to this raw score.

6. Find the number in the far right or far left column that is parallel to your circled raw score. Enter this norm score in the box at the bottom of the appropriate column.
7. Transfer your norm score to the appropriate scale on the Big Five Locator Interpretation Sheet.

Big Five Locator Interpretation Sheet

EMOTIONAL STABILITY: Secure, unflappable, rational, unresponsive, guilt free	Resilient Responsive Reactive 35 45 55 65	WEAK EMOTIONAL STABILITY: Excitable, worrying, reactive, high-strung, alert
INTROVERSION: Private, independent, works alone, reserved, hard to read	Introvert Ambivert Extrovert 35 45 55 65	EXTRAVERSION: Assertive, sociable, warm, optimistic, talkative
LOW OPENNESS: Practical, conservative, depth of knowledge, efficient, expert	Preserver Moderate Explorer 35 45 55 65	HIGH OPENNESS: Broad interests, curious, liberal, impractical, likes novelty
LOW AGREEABLENESS: Skeptical, questioning, tough, aggressive, self-interest	Challenger Negotiator Adapter 35 45 55 65	HIGH AGREEABLENESS: Trusting, humble, altruistic, team player, conflict averse, frank
LOW CONSCIENTIOUSNESS: Spontaneous, fun loving, experimental, unorganized	Flexible Balanced Focused 35 45 55 65	HIGH CONSCIENTIOUSNESS: Dependable, organized, disciplined, cautious, stubborn

Note: The Big Five Locator is intended for use only as a quick assessment for teaching purposes.

Experiential Exercise: Self Competency

Emotional IQ

An individual difference that has recently received a great deal of interest is the notion of *emotional intelligence.* According to psychologist Daniel Goleman, emotional intelligence (EQ) is actually more crucial than general intelligence (IQ) in terms of career success. **Emotional intelligence** refers to how well an individual handles herself and others rather than how smart she is or how capable she is in terms of technical skills. Emotional intelligence includes the attributes of self-awareness, impulse control, persistence, confidence, self-motivation, empathy, and social deftness. We can think of EQ as being the social equivalent of IQ. In organizations undergoing rapid change, emotional intelligence may determine who gets promoted and who gets passed over; or who gets laid off, and who stays, according to Goleman. Studies have consistently shown, for example, that the competencies associated with emotional intelligence (e.g., the ability to persuade others, the ability to understand others, and so on) are twice as important for career success than are raw intelligence (IQ) or technical competencies. You can assess your EQ by using the following scale.

Instructions: Using a scale of 1 through 4, where 1 = strongly disagree, 2 = somewhat disagree, 3 = somewhat agree, and 4 = strongly agree, respond to the ten statements below.

____ 1. I usually stay composed, positive, and unflappable even in trying moments.
____ 2. I am able to admit my own mistakes.
____ 3. I hold myself accountable for meeting my goals.
____ 4. I regularly seek out fresh ideas from a wide variety of sources.
____ 5. I'm good at generating new ideas.
____ 6. I can smoothly handle multiple demands and changing priorities.
____ 7. I pursue goals beyond what's required or expected of me in my current job.

3 8. Obstacles and setbacks may delay me a little, but they don't stop me.

3 9. My impulses or distressing emotions don't often get the best of me at work.

3 10. I operate from an expectation of success rather than a fear of failure.

30 Total points (Add the point values given to items 1 through 10.)

A score below 70 percent (28 of the 40 possible points) may indicate a problem. However, don't despair if your score is lower than you would like. EQ can be learned. In fact, Goleman says, "We are building emotional intelligence throughout life—it's sometimes called maturity."[31]

CHAPTER 12

Perceptions and Attributions

LEARNING OBJECTIVES

When you have finished studying this chapter, you should be able to:

1. Describe the major elements in the perceptual process.
2. Identify the main factors that influence what individuals perceive.
3. Identify the factors that determine how one person perceives another.
4. Describe the primary errors in perception that people make.
5. Explain how attributions influence behavior.

Preview Case: Chet Cadieux, CEO of QuikTrip
THE PERCEPTUAL PROCESS
Across Cultures Competency—Selling Frito-Lay Chips in China
PERCEPTUAL SELECTION
External Factors
Communication Competency—Just My Type
Internal Factors
PERSON PERCEPTION
The Perceived
The Perceiver
The Situation
Impression Management
PERCEPTUAL ERRORS
Accuracy of Judgment
Perceptual Defense
Stereotyping
Diversity Competency—Home Depot
Halo Effect
Projection
The Role of Culture
Self Competency—Doing Business in Arab Countries
ATTRIBUTIONS: WHY PEOPLE BEHAVE AS THEY DO
The Attribution Process
Internal versus External Causes of Behavior
Attributions of Success and Failure
CHAPTER SUMMARY
KEY TERMS AND CONCEPTS
DISCUSSION QUESTIONS
EXPERIENTIAL EXERCISE AND CASE

CHET CADIEUX, CEO OF QUIKTRIP

PREVIEW CASE

Chet Cadieux is the CEO of QuikTrip (QT), a $4 billion privately held firm in Tulsa, Oklahoma, that operates more than 460 convenience stores in nine states and has sales of more than $2.8 billion. It has been listed as one of Fortune's 100 best places to work several times. Turnover rates of its employees are less than 15 percent in an industry where the average turnover is greater than 100 percent. Recently, QT received more than 118,000 job applications for less than 300 jobs. Its stock price has averaged a 17 percent increase in the past years. How has QT achieved these remarkable figures?

First, Cadieux has a clear vision of the competencies his employees need to possess. Some of the key competencies include the ability to work in teams, the ability to learn from others, and an appreciation for diversity. QT puts applicants through a personality assessment designed to reveal how patient and how extroverted they are. If an employee has the right personality, shoppers will sense that when they enter the store. Employees will enjoy working at QuikTrip and will like each other. Second, once the new person is hired, they are assigned a partner who has held the same position previously. These two work the same shifts and perform the same duties. Cadieux believes that this allows the new employee to interact with their peers and get a sense of the pace of work in a busy store. Third, promotions come from within. More than 400 store managers and every top executive started working at a store, stocking shelves, greeting customers, making coffee, etc. Cadieux believes that this fosters teamwork and managers who have empathy for their employees. Front-line managers also have role models to follow. Fourth, Cadieux has created fringe benefits packages that are tailored to employees' needs. For example, depending on a person's tenure, employees' receive 10 to 25 days of vacation, plus 10 days of sick leave, and they can purchase up to an extra two weeks of vacation.

Cadieux has structured a customer service-appraisal system that focuses on the team's performance in satisfying and delighting customers. He employs mystery shoppers who visit stores and report on its service. If the mystery shopper is particularly impressed with an employee, all employees during that shift receive a bonus because he believes that individual rewards would undermine his belief that all employees contribute to the customer's experience. He writes a personal note to the employee thanking him or her for outstanding service. He also tells employees that they will not be fired for well-meant mistakes. He wants to encourage employees to be innovative and take risks. He doesn't want to let the fear of a mistake stifle innovation because employees are often the most important source of new product ideas.[1]

For more information on QuikTrip, visit the organization's home page at ***http://www.quiktrip.com.***

The Preview Case illustrates the importance of how a manager's perceptions of his employees influence their behavior. People base their behaviors on what they *perceive*, not necessarily on what reality *is*. People shop at QuikTrip because of the experience they enjoy while shopping. Cadieux has recognized the difference between the perceptual worlds of their customers and the competitive nature of this industry.

In this chapter, we explore the importance of *perception* and *attribution*. First, we describe the perceptual process. Then, we examine the external and internal factors that influence perception, the ways that people organize perceptions, the process of *person perception*, and various errors in the perceptual process. Finally, we explore the attributions that people make to explain the behaviors of themselves and others.

LEARNING OBJECTIVE

1. Describe the major elements in the perceptual process.

THE PERCEPTUAL PROCESS

Perception *is the process by which people select, organize, interpret, and respond to information from the world around them.* This information is gathered from the five senses—sight, hearing, touch, taste, and smell. It represents the psychological process whereby people take information from the environment and make sense of their worlds.[2]

The key words in the definition of perception are *select* and *organize*. Different people often perceive a situation differently, both in terms of what they selectively perceive and how they organize and interpret the things perceived. Figure 12.1 summarizes the basic elements in the perceptual process from initial observation to final response.

Everyone selectively pays attention to some aspects of the environment and selectively ignores other aspects. For example, when a shopper pulls into the parking lot at QuikTrip, what objects in their environment are they paying attention to and what do they ignore? What do they observe? A well-lighted convenience store, clean areas to pump gas, fully stocked paper towel dispensers with squeegees to wipe and clean windshields, etc., are objects people notice when they pull into this convenience store. A person's selection process involves both external and internal factors. In other words, a complex set of factors, some internal to the person and some in the external environment, combine to determine what the person perceives. We discuss this important process in more detail shortly.

The individual then organizes the stimuli selected into meaningful patterns. How people interpret what they perceive also varies considerably. The Experiential Exercise at the end of this chapter entitled *The Perception Process* permits you to test your current level of perceptual skills. For example, a wave of the hand may be interpreted as a friendly gesture or as a threat, depending on the circumstances and the state of mind of those involved. Certainly, in organizations managers and employees need to recognize that perceptions of events and behaviors may vary among individuals and be inaccurate.

As suggested in Figure 12.1, people's interpretations of their environments affect their responses. Everyone selects and organizes things differently, which is one reason why people behave differently in the same situation. In other words, people often perceive the same things in different ways, and their behaviors depend, in part, on their perceptions.

The way in which individuals select, organize, and interpret their perceptions to make sense of their environments isn't something that managers should ignore. The following Across Cultures Competency feature explores how Frito-Lay is selling its chips in China. The United States is the world's largest snack market with $6 billion in annual sales, but there's little growth. China's snack market is $200 million, but growing by 10 percent. After reading this feature, you should realize that what is being communicated by Frito-Lay may be subtle and based on perceptions.[3]

FIGURE 12.1 The Perceptual Process

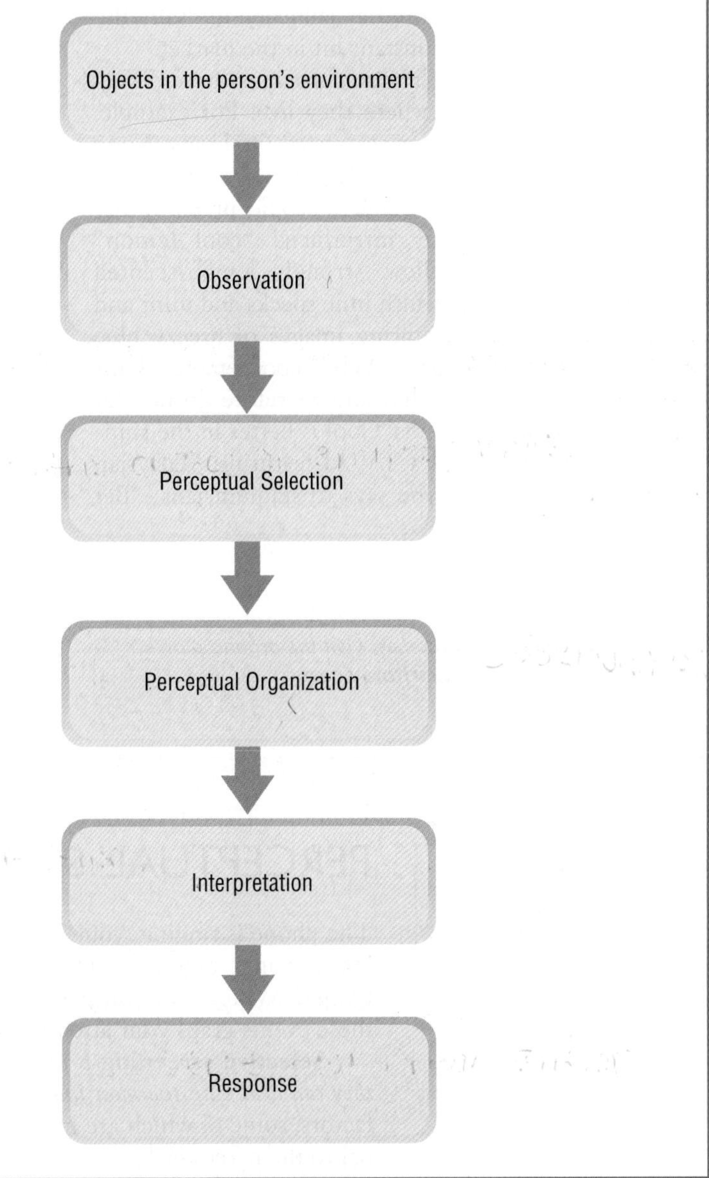

ACROSS CULTURES COMPETENCY

SELLING FRITO-LAY CHIPS IN CHINA

When David Wong was growing up in southern China in the 1970s, he didn't even know what a potato chip was. He snacked on chewy malt candy that he bought from street vendors. Today, he's a senior manager for Frito-Lay in China trying to get people to change their eating habits from chewy malt candy to Frito-Lay's potato chips. In Mandarin, *Lay's* is pronounced "Leshi," which translates into "Happy Things."

Frito-Lay came to China in 1994 with its Cheetos. Unfortunately, Chinese consumers did not like cheese, and Frito-Lay had to change the cheesy flavoring to a corn-based one. Lay's potato chips didn't show up until

1997 because China banned potato imports, forcing Frito-Lay to start raising its own potatoes. Three years after planting its first potato, Lay launched its "salty flavored" chip and it was an instant hit in the market.

Wong realized that Chinese consumers have different tastes depending on where they live. For example, in Shanghai, people like sweet tastes, in Hong Kong people like salty chips, in the western provinces they like spicy flavors, and in Beijing, people prefer meaty ones. Frito-Lay recently introduced "cool lemon" potato chips. These yellow, strongly lemon-scented chips are dotted with greenish lime specks and mint and are sold in a package featuring images of breezy blue skies and rolling green grass. Why "cool lemon?" Chinese consider fried foods hot and therefore do not eat them in the summer months. Cool is better in the summer. Frito also launched a TV ad featuring Malaysian pop star Angelica Lee, who says to stadium fans: "Bet you can't eat just one." Frito also has ads featuring Yao Ming, the Houston Rocket basketball player.

Wong knows that Chinese consumers are much more willing to try a new item outdoors, around a lot of other people, hoping to impress their friends with their sophistication and courage. There is a great demand for foreign products. Thus, an ad for Lay's chips features a mountain climber munching away while perched on a rock face; another climber swings by on a rope and grabs a chip, then return and grabs the whole can. To further capitalize on consumers' curiosity with the new product, Lay's promotes the latest technology. Recently, bags of chips contained a coupon that buyers could use to accumulate electronic money at Lay's website and save toward the purchase of a cell phone or digital camera. In Shanghai, more than 500,000 people have opened play-money accounts.

For more information on Frito-Lay, visit the organization's home page at ***http://www.fritolay.com.***

LEARNING OBJECTIVE

2. Identify the main factors that influence what individuals perceive.

PERCEPTUAL SELECTION

The phone is ringing, your TV is blaring, a dog is barking outside, your PC is making a strange noise, and you smell coffee brewing. Which of these events will you ignore? Which will you pay attention to? Can you predict or explain why one of these events grabs your attention at a particular time?

Selective screening *is the process by which people filter out most information so that they can deal with the most important matters.* Perceptual selection depends on several factors, some of which are in the external environment and some of which are internal to the perceiver.[4]

External Factors

External factors are characteristics that influence whether the event will be noticed. What does Cadieux want its customers to notice when they pull into his convenience store? The following external factors may be stated as *principles* of perception. In each case we present an example to illustrate the principle.

- *Size.* The larger the object, the more likely it is to be perceived. The 90-story Hyatt hotel in Shanghai is more likely to get noticed than a one-story hotel.
- *Intensity.* The more intense an external factor (bright lights, loud noises, and the like), the more likely it is to be perceived. The language in an e-mail message from a manager to an employee can reflect the intensity principle. For example, an e-mail message that reads "Please stop by my office at your convenience" wouldn't fill you with the same sense of urgency as an e-mail message that reads "Report to my office immediately!"
- *Contrast.* External factors that stand out against the background or that aren't what people expect are the most likely to be noticed. In addition, the contrast of

objects with others or with their backgrounds may influence how they are perceived. Figure 12.2 illustrates this aspect of the contrast principle. Which of the solid center circles is larger? The one on the right appears to be larger, but it isn't: The two circles are the same size. The solid circle on the right appears to be larger because its background, or frame of reference, is composed of much smaller circles. The solid circle on the left appears to be smaller because its background consists of larger surrounding circles.

FIGURE 12.2 Contrast Principle of Perception

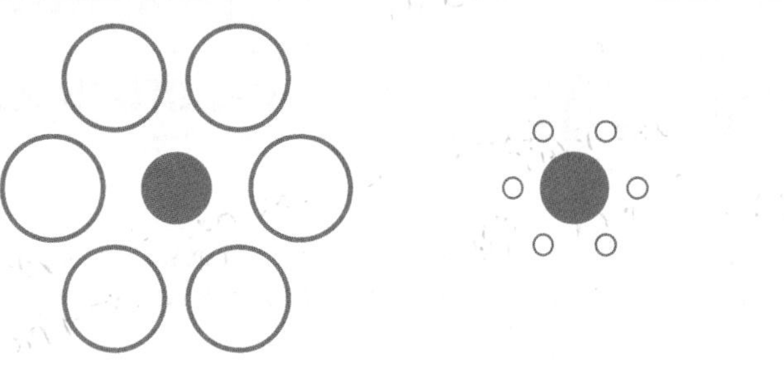

- *Motion.* A moving factor is more likely to be perceived than a stationary factor. PlayStation® games use this to attract people to play them.
- *Repetition.* A repeated factor is more likely to be noticed than a single factor. Marketing managers use this principle in trying to get the attention of prospective customers. An advertisement may repeat key ideas, and the ad itself may be presented many times for greater effectiveness. Marketing managers at Nike have developed the Nike "swoosh" symbol that is consistently used worldwide on all of its products. Similarly, Frito-Lay's ad claiming "Bet you can't eat just one" is repeated around the globe in different languages.
- *Novelty and familiarity.* Either a familiar or a novel factor in the environment can attract attention, depending on the circumstances. People would quickly notice an elephant walking along a city street. (Both novelty and size increase the probability of perception.) Someone is likely to notice the face of a close friend first among a group of approaching people.[5]

A combination of these or similar factors may be operating at any time to affect perception. Along with a person's internal factors, they determine whether any particular stimulus is more or less likely to be noticed.

The visual aspects of a corporation's marketing materials are receiving increasing attention. Typeface designs of advertised brands influence readability and memorability. The following Communication Competency feature illustrates how typefaces (fonts) you use send messages to others about you. Often, these messages are subtle but affect how others perceive you and your message.[6]

COMMUNICATION COMPETENCY

JUST MY TYPE

The "one picture is worth a thousand words" is an old wives' tale that has been used by marketing and advertising companies for decades because people can remember pictures better than words. Similarly, organizations need design styles that are pleasing, engaging, reassuring, and prominent to catch the attention of their customers. Typestyles (fonts) suit the images that they want to send to their customers.

We present you with five different fonts. Circle the letter in front of the font that reflects the image you want to convey to others.

A *Informal Roman*
AncientScript
Enviro
Pepita MT

B Baphomet
EddA
Stonehenge
Paintbrush

C Playbill
Logan
Industria Inline
StencilSet

D NewYorkDeco
Bandstand
SunSpLash
Middle Ages

E AluminumShred
BigDaddy
Ransom
AMAZON

If you chose A, these fonts are considered likable, warm, attractive, interesting, emotional, feminine, and delicate. They do not convey strength, but are reassuring and pleasing.

If you chose B, these fonts convey interest, emotion, excitement, and innovation. They are also unsettling and unfamiliar to most people.

If you chose C, they are generally considered to be cold, unattractive, uninteresting, and unemotional. Companies use these to display characteristics or claims of being countercultural or competing brands.

If you chose D, these fonts represent strength and masculinity. The weighty lines suggest a forcefulness and solidity.

If you chose E, these fonts get high marks for being interesting, elaborate, emotional, exciting, and informal. These fonts could also be considered dishonest, cold, and unattractive.

Internal Factors

Internal factors are aspects of the perceiver that influence their selection. The powerful role that internal factors play in perception shows itself in many ways. Some of the more important internal factors include individual differences (Chapter 11), learning (Chapter 13), and motivation (Chapters 14 and 15).

> **THE COMPETENT LEADER**
>
> A focus on personality characteristics, rather than particular work experiences, allows our company to hire people who will naturally bring the right qualities to the job.
> Chet Cadieux, CEO of QuikTrip

Personality. Personality has an interesting influence on what and how people perceive. Any of the several personality dimensions that we discussed in Chapter 11, along with numerous other traits, may influence the perceptual process. Personality appears to affect strongly how an individual perceives other people. Cadieux at QT believes that understanding an applicant's personality plays a critical part in the hiring process at QT.

In Chapter 11, we introduced you to the Big Five personality factors. To illustrate how personality can influence perception, let's examine one of the Big Five factors, conscientiousness. A conscientious person tends to pay more attention to external environmental cues than does a less conscientious person. On the one hand, less conscientious people are impulsive, careless, and irresponsible. They see their environment as hectic and unstable, which affects the way in which they make perceptual selections. On the other hand, more conscientious people organize their perceptions into neat categories, allowing themselves to retrieve data quickly and in an organized manner. In other words, they are careful, methodical, and disciplined in making perceptual selections.

Learning. Another internal factor affecting perceptual selection is learning. Among other things, learning determines the development of perceptual sets. A **perceptual set** *is an expectation of a particular interpretation based on past experience with the same or a similar object*. What do you see in Figure 12.3? If you see an attractive, elegantly dressed woman, your perception concurs with the majority of first-time viewers. However, you may agree with a sizable minority and see an ugly, old woman. The woman you first see depends, in large part, on your perceptual set.

FIGURE 12.3 Test of Perceptual Set

In organizations, managers' and employees' past experiences and learning strongly influence their perceptions. Managers are influenced by their functional backgrounds (e.g., accounting, engineering, marketing, or production) when making decisions. Thus, under some circumstances, they are likely to interpret problems in terms of their own experiences and values. Shalane Choate, vice president of manufacturing at Sun Roller Corporation, thinks that her firm has a cash flow problem. The firm's accounting manager perceives the problem to be one of extending credit to slow-paying customers, whereas the marketing manager sees the problem as trying to bring in different customers who are used to paying within 60, not 30, days. Successful managers need to "rise above" their own experiences and limitations, accurately recognizing and effectively solving problems in areas other than those with which they are most familiar.[7] Indeed, essential decision-making skills include the ability to recognize the types of knowledge and expertise needed with regard to a particular problem and to avoid framing issues only in terms of the person's own expertise.

Motivation. Motivation also plays an important role in determining what a person perceives. A person's most urgent needs and desires at any particular time can influence perception. For example, imagine that, while taking a shower, you faintly hear what sounds like the telephone ringing. Do you get out of the shower, dripping wet, to answer it? Or do you conclude that it is only your imagination? Your behavior in this situation may depend on factors other than the loudness of the ringing. If you are expecting an important call, you're likely to leap from the shower. If you aren't expecting a call, you're more likely to attribute the ringing sound to shower noises. Your decision, then, has been influenced by your expectations and motivations.

In general, people perceive things that promise to help satisfy their needs and that they have found rewarding in the past. They tend to ignore mildly disturbing events (a barking dog) but will react to dangerous events (the house being on fire). Summarizing an important aspect of the relationship between motivation and perception is the **Pollyanna principle,** *which states that people process pleasant events more efficiently and accurately than they do unpleasant events.* For example, an employee who receives both positive and negative feedback during a performance appraisal session may more easily and clearly remember the positive statements than the negative statements.[8]

LEARNING OBJECTIVE

3. Identify the factors that determine how one person perceives another.

PERSON PERCEPTION

Person perception *is the process by which individuals attribute characteristics or traits to other people.* It is closely related to the attribution process, which we discuss later in this chapter.

The person perception process relies on the same general process of perception shown in Figure 12.1. That is, the process follows the same sequence of observation, selection, organization, interpretation, and response. However, the object being perceived is another person. Perceptions of situations, events, and objects are important, but individual differences in perceptions of other people are crucial at work. For example, suppose that you meet a new employee. To get acquainted and make him feel at ease, you invite him to lunch. During lunch, he begins to tell you his life history and focuses on his accomplishments. Because he talks only about himself (he asks you no questions about yourself), your first impression that he is very self-centered.

In general, the factors influencing person perception are the same as those that influence perceptual selection: Both external and internal factors affect person perception. However, we may usefully categorize factors that influence how a person perceives another as

- characteristics of the perceived,
- characteristics of the perceiver, and
- the situation or context within which the perception takes place.

The Perceived

When perceiving someone else, you need to be aware of various cues given by that person: facial expressions, general appearance, skin color, posture, age, gender, voice quality, personality traits, behaviors, and the like. Such cues usually provide important information about the person. People seem to have implicit theories about the relationships among physical characteristics, personality traits, and specific behaviors.[9] An **implicit personality theory** *is a person's beliefs about the relationships between another's physical characteristics and personality.* Table 12.1 illustrates implicit personality theory in action. People often seem to believe that some voice-quality characteristics indicate that the speaker has certain personality traits. However, the relationships presented in Table 12.1 have no scientific basis. Think about your first contact with someone in a chat room on the Internet. Later, upon meeting, did that person look and act as you expected?

The Perceiver

Listening to an employee describe the personality of a coworker may tell you as much about the employee's personality as it does about that of the person being

TABLE 12.1 Personality Judgments on the Basis of Voice Quality

VOICE QUALITY: HIGH IN	MALE VOICE	FEMALE VOICE
Breathiness	Younger, artistic	Feminine, pretty, petite, shallow
Flatness	Similar results for both sexes:	Masculine, cold, withdrawn
Nasality	Similar results for both sexes:	Having many socially undesirable characteristics
Tenseness	Cantankerous (old, unyielding)	Young, emotional, high-strung, not highly intelligent

Source: Adapted from Hinton, P. R. *The Psychology of Interpersonal Perception*, London: Routledge, 1993, 16.

described. That shouldn't surprise you if you recall that factors internal to the perceiver, including personality, learning, and motivation, influence perception. A person's own personality traits, values, attitudes, current mood, past experiences, and so on, determine, in part, how that person perceives someone else.

Accurately perceiving the personality of an individual raised in another culture often is difficult.[10] For example, Japanese managers in the United States and U.S. managers in Japan may face disorienting experiences as they try to learn how to deal with business associates from the other culture. One reason is that the perceiver interprets the other person's traits and behavior in light of his own cultural experiences, attitudes, and values. Often these factors are inadequate for making accurate judgments about the personality and behavior of people from a different culture. Cross-cultural negotiations are an important part of every global manager's job. The dynamics of negotiating, however, reflects each culture's value and beliefs. In Mexico, personal qualities and social connections influence the selection of a negotiator, whereas in the United States, many companies select negotiators on the basis of position and competence. In U.S.–Japanese negotiations, U.S. companies often prefer to send a small team or only a single person to represent them, whereas the Japanese prefer to send a large group. The large group allows them to have representatives from different areas of the organization present at the negotiations.

The Situation

The situation, or setting, also influences how one person perceives another. The situation may be particularly important in understanding first impressions. For example, if you meet someone for the first time and she is with another person whom you respect and admire, that association may positively influence your assessment of the new acquaintance. But, if she is with someone you dislike intensely, you may form a negative first impression. Of course, these initial perceptions may change over time if you continue to interact with her and get to know her better. Nevertheless, the first impression may continue to color your later perception of the individual.

Impression Management

Impression management *is an attempt by an individual to manipulate or control the impressions that others form about them.* People in organizations use several impression management tactics to affect how others perceive them.[11] They are especially likely to use these tactics when talking with people who have power over them or on whom they are dependent for raises, promotions, and good job assignments. Impression management is used by individuals at all organizational levels as they talk with suppliers, coworkers, managers, and others—and vice versa. Table 12.2

TABLE 12.2 Impression Management Tactics

TACTIC	DESCRIPTION	EXAMPLE
Behavioral matching	Person matches his behavior to that of the perceiver.	Employee tries to imitate her manager's behavior by being aggressive and fast-paced.
Self-promotion	The person tries to present herself in as positive a light as possible.	Employee reminds his boss about his past accomplishments and associates with coworkers who are evaluated highly.
Conforming to norms	Person follows agreed-upon norms for behavior in the organization.	Employee stays late at night even if she has completed all her assignments because staying late is one of the norms of her organization.
Flattering others	Person compliments others. This tactic works best when flattery is not extreme and when it involves a dimension important to the other person.	Employee compliments manager on his excellent handling of a customer who constantly complains about poor service.
Being consistent	Person's beliefs and behaviors are consistent.	Subordinate whose views on diversity are well known flatters her boss for her handling of a conflict between two coworkers of different ethnic backgrounds. When speaking to her boss, the person looks her boss straight in the eye and has a sincere expression on her face.

describes five common impression management tactics: behavioral matching, self-promotion, conforming to norms, flattering others, and being consistent.

Impression management provides another example of an *individual difference.* Some people seem preoccupied with impression management; others are less concerned about how they might be perceived. However, most people care about the impressions they make on others, at least part of the time. Certainly, in organizations the impressions made on others may have significant implications for employees' careers.

LEARNING OBJECTIVE

4. Describe the primary errors in perception that people make.

PERCEPTUAL ERRORS

The perceptual process may result in errors in judgment or understanding. An important part of understanding individual differences in perception is knowing the source of these errors. First, we examine the notion of accuracy of judgment in person perception. Then, we explore five of the most common types of perceptual errors: perceptual defense, stereotyping, the halo effect, projection, and the role of culture.

Accuracy of Judgment

How accurate are people in their perceptions of others? This question is important in organizational behavior. For example, misjudging the characteristics, abilities, or behaviors of an employee during a performance appraisal review could result in an inaccurate assessment of the employee's current and future value to the firm. Another example of the importance of accurate person perception comes from the employment interview. Considerable evidence suggests that interviewers can easily make errors in judgment and perceptions when basing employment decisions on information gathered in face-to-face interviews.[12] The following types of interview errors are the most common:

- *Similarity error*. Interviewers are positively predisposed toward job candidates who are similar to them (in terms of background, interests, hobbies, and the like) and negatively biased against job candidates who are unlike them.
- *Contrast error*. Interviewers have a tendency to compare job candidates to other candidates interviewed at about the same time, rather than to some absolute standard. For example, an average candidate might be rated too highly if preceded by several mediocre candidates; however, an average candidate might be scored too low if preceded by an outstanding applicant.
- *Overweighting of negative information*. Interviewers tend to overreact to negative information as though looking for an excuse to disqualify a job candidate.
- *Race, gender, and age bias*. Interviewers may be more or less positive about a candidate on the basis of the candidate's race, gender, or age.
- *First-impression error*. The primacy effect may play a role in the job interview, because some interviewers are quick to form impressions that are resistant to change.

There are no easy answers to the general problem of ensuring accuracy. Some people accurately judge and assess others, and some people do so poorly. People can learn to make more accurate judgments if they follow some basic guidelines: (1) Avoid generalizing from an observation of a single trait (e.g., tactful) to other traits (e.g., stable, confident, energetic, dependable); (2) avoid assuming that a behavior will be repeated in all situations; and (3) avoid placing too much reliance on physical appearance. Accuracy in person perception can be improved when the perceiver understands these potential biases.

Perceptual Defense

Perceptual defense *is the tendency for people to protect themselves against ideas, objects, or situations that are threatening.* A well-known folk song suggests that people "hear what they want to hear and disregard the rest." Once established, an individual's way of viewing the world may become highly resistant to change. Sometimes perceptual defense may have negative consequences. This perceptual error can result in a manager's inability to perceive the need to be creative in solving problems. As a result, the individual simply proceeds as in the past even in the face of evidence that "business as usual" isn't accomplishing anything.

Stereotyping

Stereotyping *is the belief that all members of specific groups share similar traits and behaviors.* The use of stereotypes can have powerful effects on the decisions that managers make.[13] In a recent study of *Fortune* magazine's top 500 CEOs, it was found that CEOs are mostly white males. The study also found that on the average, male CEOs were almost six feet tall, which reflects a kind of implicit stereotype of the height of CEOs. Given that the average American male is five foot nine, it means that CEOs as a group are about three inches taller. In the United States, about 14.5 percent of all men are six feet or taller and 3.9 percent of white males are six foot two or taller. In this sample, almost a third were six foot two or taller. Furthermore, it was calculated that each inch of height is worth $789 a year in salary. That means that a person who is six feet tall but otherwise identical to someone who is five foot five will make on average $5,525 more per year. Over a career, the difference is in hundreds of thousands of dollars.

An interesting challenge for organizations is to determine whether women managers essentially are like their male counterparts. If they are, gender differences should be only a marginal concern. However, a debate is raging in scientific and management circles around the world with regard to gender differences in thought, emotions, and information processing styles. Some evidence from the research being conducted suggests that women are, on average, superior to men in many organizational roles. Such roles include interacting with customers or clients, facilitating discussions, and smoothing conflicts. With regard to the latter two roles, one study indicated that female project team leaders were more effective, on average, than males in leading cross-functional teams designed to foster high rates of innovation.[14]

One company that has tried hard to eliminate stereotyping people in their hiring practices is Home Depot. As the world's largest home improvement chain, the company operates more than 1,200 stores in the United States, as well as stores in Canada, Argentina, Chile, and Puerto Rico. With more than 227,000 employees, Home Depot is constantly hiring new employees. The following Diversity Competency feature highlights how Home Depot uses a computer system to reduce stereotyping in hiring decisions.[15]

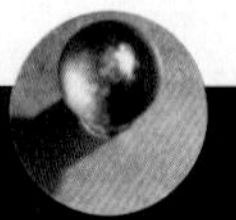

DIVERSITY COMPETENCY

HOME DEPOT

Home Depot settled a class-action lawsuit on behalf of women who claimed they were hired for low-paying cashier positions instead of higher-paying positions for which they were qualified and were not getting promoted because of their gender. Part of the settlement required Home Depot to install a computer system for use in hiring and promoting. The system, called Job Preference Program (JPP), works like this: A Home Depot manager who needs to fill a certain position, in the garden section, for example, enters the position description into JPP. JPP then gives the manager a list of prescreened, qualified individuals for the position, along with advice on how to conduct an interview. Managers like JPP because, rather than having to search for qualified people, JPP does the work for them. Employees seeking promotions register with JPP and are given advice concerning management of their careers. They also are able to update their profiles as they gain more knowledge and experience. Promotions are given only to employees who have registered with JPP.

JPP seems to be helping overcome the effects of stereotyping that lead managers to perceive women inaccurately as not qualified for managerial positions or for certain positions historically considered to be for men only, such as selling building materials. After Home Depot starting using JPP, the number of female managers increased by 30 percent and the number of minority managers increased by 28 percent.

To learn more about Home Depot, visit the organization's home page at ***http://www.homedepot.com.***

Halo Effect

The **halo effect** *refers to evaluating another person solely on the basis of one attribute, either favorable or unfavorable.* In other words, a halo blinds the perceiver to other attributes that also should be evaluated to obtain a complete, accurate impression of the other person. Managers have to guard against the halo effect in rating employee performance. A manager may single out one trait and use it as the basis for judging all other performance measures. Students have been known to evaluate the overall effectiveness of a faculty member in just the first two seconds of the first class. The ratings they gave after these two seconds were almost identical to those rankings after sitting through the instructor's course the entire semester. That's the power of the halo effect.

An important aspect of the halo effect is the self-fulfilling prophecy. The **self-fulfilling prophecy** *is the tendency for someone's expectations about another to cause that individual to behave in a manner consistent with those expectations.*[16] Expecting certain things to happen shapes the behavior of the perceiver in such a way that the expected is more likely to happen. Self-fulfilling prophecies can take both positive and negative forms. In the positive case, *holding high expectations of another tends to improve the individual's performance*, which is known as the **Pygmalion effect.** Subordinates whose managers expect them to perform well do perform well. At Dell Computer, for example, programmers may put in more than 60 hours per week, especially when the team is trying to meet shipment deadlines for new products. Because Dell has an industry reputation for meeting deadlines, positive group-level expectations help create and reinforce an organizational culture of high expectancy for success.[17] The reverse is also true. Subordinates whose managers expect them to perform poorly do in fact perform poorly. Obviously, this effect can be quite devastating.

To increase the likelihood of being positive Pygmalions, managers need to remember three things:

1. *Individuals behave toward others consistent with their expectations of them.* Managers who have high expectations of their employees are supportive and generally give employees more training and challenging jobs. By contrast, managers who have low expectations of their employees aren't supportive and generally won't give employees training and challenging jobs.
2. *A person's behavior affects others.* Not only will those treated positively benefit from special opportunities, but these opportunities will also bolster their self-esteem.
3. *People behave in ways following from how they are treated.* People who have benefited from special treatment and who have confidence in their abilities are likely to be high performers.

Projection

Projection *is the tendency for people to see their own traits in other people.* That is, they project their own feelings, personality characteristics, attitudes, or motives onto others. For example, IBM's decision to lay off employees in New York may cause employees in Texas not only to judge others as more frightened than they are but also to assess various job changes to be more threatening than need be. Projection may be especially strong for undesirable traits that perceivers possess but fail to recognize in themselves. People whose personality traits include stinginess, obstinacy, and disorderliness tend to rate others higher on these traits than do people who don't have these personality traits.

The Role of Culture

Interpretation occurs when an individual gives meaning to observations and their relationships. Interpretation organizes our experience and guides our behavior. Read the following sentence and quickly count the number of Fs:

FINISHED FILES ARE THE RESULT OF YEARS OF SCIENTIFIC

STUDY COMBINED WITH THE EXPERIENCE OF YEARS.

Most people who do not speak English see all six Fs. By contract, many English speakers see only three Fs; they do not see the Fs in the word *of.* Why? Because English-speaking people do not think that the word *of* is important for them to understand the meaning of the sentence. We selectively see those words that are important according to our cultural upbringing.

Because cultural misinterpretations often go on at a subconscious level, we are often unaware of the assumptions we make and their cultural biases. A number of male managers still think that women aren't interested in overseas jobs or won't be effective in them. These managers typically cite dual career issues, a presumed heightened risk of sexual harassment, and gender prejudices in many countries as reasons why their female employees often aren't seriously considered for international assignments. In contrast, a recent survey of female expatriates and their managers revealed that women, on average, are just as interested in foreign assignments and every bit as effective once there. Indeed, some of the traits considered crucial for success overseas—such as knowing when to keep your mouth shut, being a strong team player, and soliciting a variety of opinions and perspectives when solving problems—are more often associated with women's management styles than with men's.[18]

Although we may think that the biggest obstacle to conducting business around the world is understanding other people, the greater issue is to become aware of our own cultural conditioning. We are least aware of our own cultural characteristics and often express surprise when foreigners point these out to us. A way to understand the norms and values of a culture is to pay attention to the behaviors that are rewarded in that society. The following Self Competency feature illustrates a sample of important behaviors that you should be aware of when conducting business in Arab countries.[19]

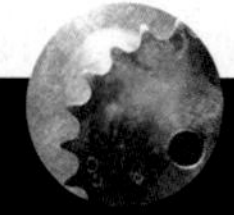

SELF COMPETENCY

DOING BUSINESS IN ARAB COUNTRIES

- *Greeting women.* When you are introduced to a female employee, in all cases you should not greet her with a kiss. If the employee extends her hand to greet you, you may shake it; otherwise greeting with words is appropriate. Do not compliment your host on the beauty of his wife or sister or daughter. This will not be taken as a compliment.
- *Gift giving.* When Arab businesspeople receive a gift, it is not customary to open it in front of the giver. Never give alcohol or products made out of pig.
- *Face concept.* The Arabian culture is a nonconfrontational one. Saving face involves holding one's reactions to give the other party a way to exit the situation with minimal discomfort. It involves compromise, patience, and sometimes looking the other way to allow things time to get back to normal. Pressure sales tactics should be avoided because the Arab managers will associate you with an unpleasant experience.
- *Dress.* The majority of men wear a long-sleeved one-piece dress called a "thoub" that covers the entire body. This garment allows air to circulate in hot summer days. Women dress conservatively in a garment called an "abayah." This is a long black garment that covers a woman's body from the shoulders down to her feet.
- *Social duties.* Managers perform a variety of social duties, including greeting an employee who returns from a trip, visiting an employee who is ill, bringing a gift to a newlywed couple, and visiting the husband and wife after the wife has delivered a new baby.
- *Privacy.* Privacy is important in Arabian societies. Therefore, houses and offices are built with walls that maintain privacy from others. People are not permitted to enter until the manager or host extends his right hand with his palm up saying "Tafaddal," which means come in.

- *Social gatherings.* Men and women meet in separate rooms. Men gather in rooms that are outside the main entrance of a home, away from the rest of the house. Women guests meet in a room inside the house and go through an entrance specifically assigned for female visitors.

ATTRIBUTIONS: WHY PEOPLE BEHAVE AS THEY DO

LEARNING OBJECTIVE

5. Explain how attributions influence behavior.

A question often asked about others is "Why?" "Why did this engineer use these data in his report?" or "Why did Howard Schultz, CEO and founder of Starbucks, start Starbucks?" Such questions are an attempt to get at why a person behaved in a particular way. The **attribution process** *refers to the ways in which people come to understand the causes of their own and others' behaviors.*[20] In essence, the attribution process reflects people's need to explain events through the deliberate actions of others rather than viewing them as random events. To maintain the illusion of control, people need to create causal attributions for events. Attributions also play an important role in perceptions. Attributions made about the reasons for someone's behavior may affect judgments about that individual's basic characteristics (that is, what that person is really like).

THE COMPETENT LEADER

Leaders aren't designated from on high. People become leaders because they attract other talented people who want to work with them. Employees are drawn to them because of their passion for high achievement.
William L. Gore, CEO of Gore-Tex Fabrics

The attributions that employees and managers make concerning the causes of behavior are important for understanding behavior. For example, managers who attribute poor performance directly to their subordinates tend to behave more punitively than do managers who attribute poor performance to circumstances beyond their subordinates' control. A manager who believes that an employee failed to perform a task correctly because he lacked proper training might be understanding and give the employee better instructions or more training. The same manager might be quite angry if he believes that the subordinate made mistakes simply because he didn't try very hard.

Responses to the same outcome can be dramatically different, depending on the attributions made about the reasons for that outcome. Table 12.3 lists some of the possible differences in managerial behavior when employees are perceived positively versus when they are perceived negatively. The relationships between attributions and behavior will become clearer as we examine the attribution process.

TABLE 12.3 Possible Results Stemming from Differences in Perceptions of Performance

BOSS'S BEHAVIOR TOWARD PERCEIVED STRONG PERFORMERS	BOSS'S BEHAVIOR TOWARD PERCEIVED WEAK PERFORMERS
Discusses project objectives. Gives subordinate the freedom to choose own approach to solving problems or reaching goals.	Gives specific directives when discussing tasks and goals.
Treats mistakes or incorrect judgments as learning opportunities.	Pays close attention to mistakes and incorrect judgments. Quick to emphasize what subordinate is doing wrong.

BOSS'S BEHAVIOR TOWARD PERCEIVED STRONG PERFORMERS	BOSS'S BEHAVIOR TOWARD PERCEIVED WEAK PERFORMERS
Is open to subordinate's suggestions. Solicits opinions from subordinate.	Pays little attention to subordinate's suggestions. Rarely asks subordinate for input.
Gives subordinate interesting and challenging assignments.	Gives subordinate routine assignments.
May frequently defer to subordinate's opinions in disagreements.	Usually imposes own views in disagreements.

The Attribution Process

People make attributions in an attempt to understand why people behave as they do and to make better sense of their situations. Individuals don't consciously make attributions all the time (although they may do so unconsciously much of the time).[21] However, under certain circumstances, people are likely to make causal attributions consciously. For example, causal attributions are common in the following situations:

- The perceiver has been asked an explicit question about another's behavior. (Why did she do that?)
- An unexpected event occurs. (I've never seen him behave that way. I wonder what's going on?)
- The perceiver depends on another person for a desired outcome. (I wonder why my boss made that comment about my expense account?)
- The perceiver experiences feelings of failure or loss of control. (I can't believe I failed my midterm exam!)

Figure 12.4 presents a schematic model of the attribution process. People infer "causes" to behaviors that they observe in others, and these interpretations often

FIGURE 12.4 The Attribution Process

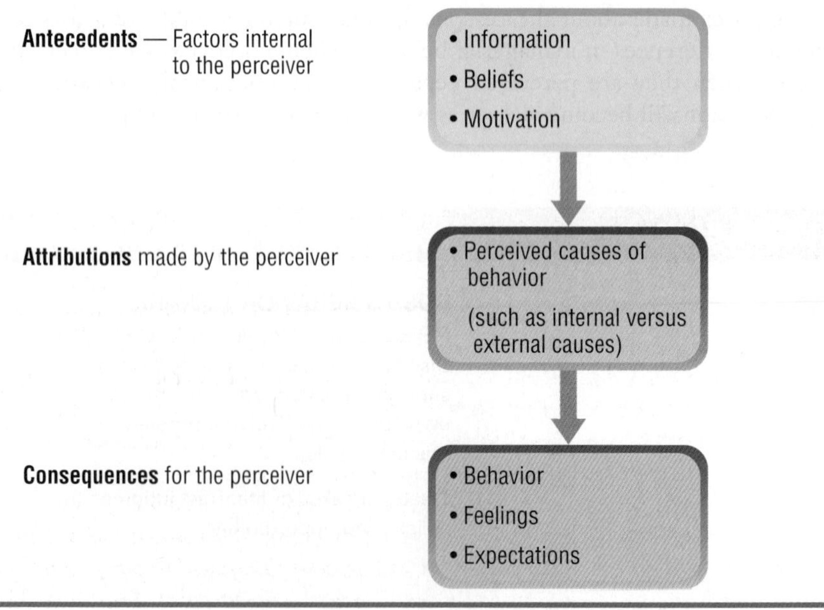

largely determine their reactions to those behaviors. The perceived causes of behavior reflect several antecedents: (1) the amount of information the perceiver has about the people and the situation and how that information is organized by the perceiver; (2) the perceiver's beliefs (implicit personality theories, what other people might do in a similar situation, and so on); and (3) the motivation of the perceiver (e.g., the importance to the perceiver of making an accurate assessment). Recall our discussion of internal factors that influence perception—learning, personality, and motivation. These same internal factors influence the attribution process. The perceiver's information and beliefs depend on previous experience and are influenced by the perceiver's personality.

Internal versus External Causes of Behavior

In applying attribution theory, you should be especially concerned with whether a person's behavior has been internally or externally caused. Internal causes are believed to be under an individual's control—you believe that your website designer's performance is poor because she's often late to work. External causes are believed to be beyond a person's control—you believe that her performance is poor because her Windows operating system is old. According to attribution theory, three factors influence the determination of internal or external cause:

- *Consistency*—the extent to which the person perceived behaves in the same manner on other occasions when faced with the same situation. If your website designer's behavior has been poor for several months, you would tend to attribute it to an internal cause. If her performance is an isolated incident, you would tend to attribute it to an external cause.
- *Distinctiveness*—the extent to which the person perceived acts in the same manner in different situations. If your website designer's performance is poor, regardless of the computer program with which she's working, you would tend to make an internal attribution; if her poor performance is unusual, you would tend to make an external attribution.
- *Consensus*—the extent to which others, faced with the same situation, behave in a manner similar to the person perceived. If all the employees in your website designer's team perform poorly, you would tend to make an external attribution. If other members of her team are performing well, you would tend to make an internal attribution.

As Figure 12.5 suggests, under conditions of high consensus, high consistency, and high distinctiveness, the perceiver will tend to attribute the behavior of the perceived to external causes. When consensus and distinctiveness are low, but consistency is high, the perceiver will tend to attribute the behavior of the perceived to internal causes. For example, when all employees are performing poorly (high consensus), when the poor performance occurs on only one of several tasks (high distinctiveness), and the poor performance occurs only during the last week of the month (high consistency), a supervisor will probably attribute poor performance to an external source, such as peer pressure or an overly difficult task. In contrast, performance will be attributed to an employee (internal attribution) when only the individual in question is performing poorly (low consensus), when the inferior performance is found across several tasks (low distinctiveness), and when the low performance has persisted over time (high consistency). Other combinations of high and low consistency, distinctiveness, and consensus are possible. Some combinations may not provide the perceiver with a clear choice between internal and external causes.

With regard to internal versus external causes of behavior, people often make what is known as the fundamental attribution error. The **fundamental attribution error** *is the tendency to underestimate the influence of situational factors and to overestimate the influence of personal factors in evaluating someone else's behavior.* This error

FIGURE 12.5 You observe a golfer complaining about slow play on a course. To answer "why," you note that:

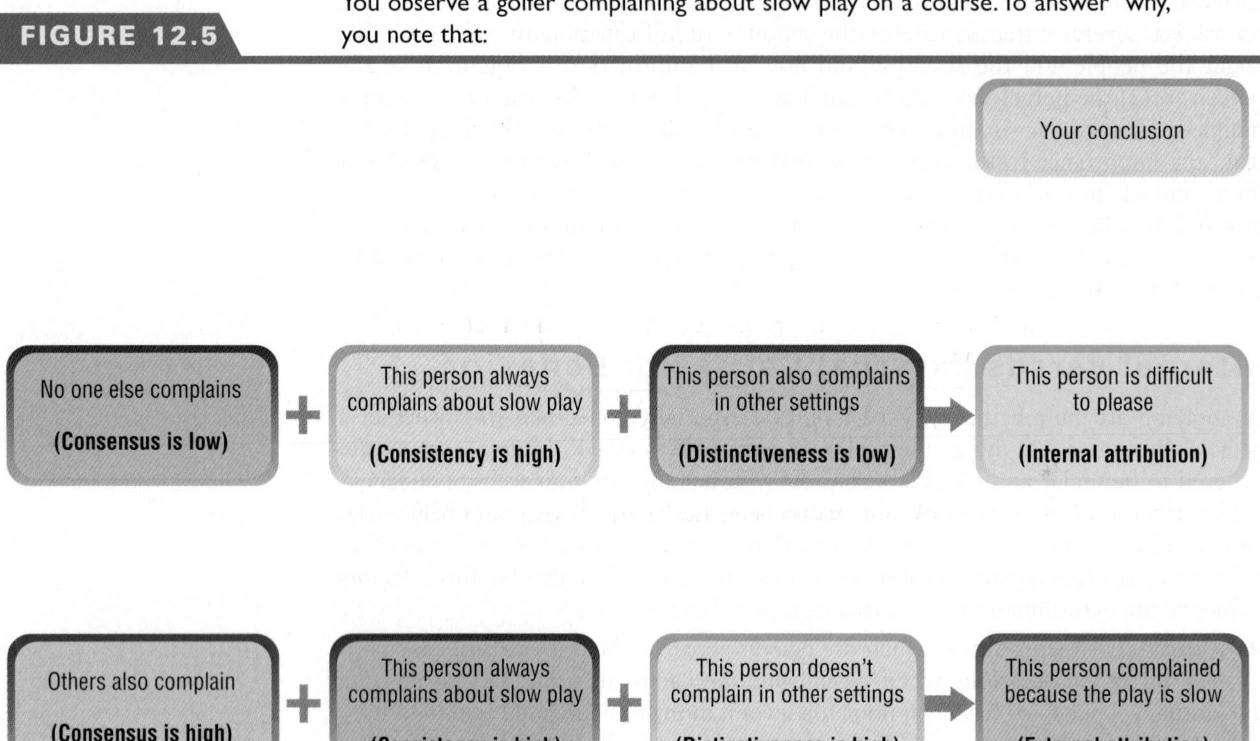

causes perceivers to ignore important environmental factors that often significantly affect a person's behavior. In organizations, employees often tend to assign blame to other departments or individuals and fail to recognize the effect of the situation. For example, a CEO might attribute a high level of political behavior on the part of her vice presidents to aspects of their personalities, not recognizing that competition for scarce resources is causing much of the political behavior.

Some cultural differences exist in the fundamental attribution error. For example, in North America, this type of error would be as just described (underestimating external causes and overestimating internal causes). In India, however, the more common attribution error is for people to overestimate situational or external causes for the observed behavior. This difference in attributions may reflect the way that people view personal responsibility or perhaps differences in "average" locus of control beliefs in the different societies.

The fundamental attribution error isn't the only bias that can influence judgments concerning internal versus external causes of behavior. A study of supervisors showed that they were more likely to attribute effective performance to internal causes for high-status employees and less likely to attribute success to internal causes for low-status employees. Similarly, supervisors were more likely to attribute ineffective performance to internal causes for low-status employees and less likely to attribute failure to internal causes for high-status employees.[22]

Attributions of Success and Failure

The attributions that employees and managers make regarding success or failure are very important. Managers may base decisions about rewards and punishments on their perceptions of why subordinates have succeeded or failed at some task. In general, individuals often attribute their own and others' success or failure to four causal factors: ability, effort, task difficulty, and luck[23]:

- I succeeded (or failed) because I had the competencies to do the task (or because I did not have the competencies to do the task). Such statements are ability attributions.
- I succeeded (or failed) because I worked hard at the task (or because I did not work hard at the task). Such statements are effort attributions.
- I succeeded (or failed) because the task was easy (or because the task was too hard). Such statements are attributions about task difficulty.
- I succeeded (or failed) at the task because I was lucky (or unlucky). Such statements are attributions about luck or the circumstances surrounding the task.

Causal attributions of ability and effort are internal, and causal attributions of task difficulty and luck are external. These attributions about success or failure reflect differences in self-esteem and locus of control—personality dimensions discussed in Chapter 2. Accordingly, the **self-serving bias** *refers to individuals attributing their success to internal factors (ability or effort) and attributing their failure to external factors (task difficulty or luck).* For example, individuals with high self-esteem and high internal locus of control are likely to assess their own performance positively and to attribute their good performance to internal causes.

The tendency of employees to accept responsibility for good performance but to deny responsibility for poor performance often presents a serious challenge for managers during performance appraisals. A self-serving bias may also create other types of problems. For example, it prevents individuals from accurately assessing their own performance and abilities and makes it more difficult to determine why a course of action has failed. The general tendency to blame others for a person's own failures often is associated with poor performance and an inability to establish satisfying interpersonal relationships at work and in other social settings. In general, a version of the self-serving bias seems to operate when people are asked to compare themselves to others in the work setting. That is, managers and employees often view themselves to be more ethical, more effective, better performing, and so on, than the "average" other person.

One of the more traumatic events that can occur to anyone is being fired.[24] Today losing a job doesn't carry the stigma that it once did. But—it still hurts! Inevitably individuals ask themselves: What went wrong? What could I have done differently? And, perhaps most important: What am I going to do now?

For most people, undertaking a job search at any time is always stressful. It has been described as a combination of the worst aspects of a blind date and a fraternity rush party. Undertaking a job search *after* suffering the psychological blow of being fired can be a formidable challenge for anyone. Suppose that you have just been fired. You can take certain constructive actions to increase your chances of success and even end up with a more satisfying job.

1. *Work through the firing psychologically.* Emotionally, you might feel like hiding or taking a sabbatical. But, experts suggest that beginning the search for a new job immediately is crucial. The first contact or two may be hard, but the sooner you get started and the more people you talk to, the more quickly you will find another position. Of course, reestablishing your normal good spirits may be either a long or slow process, depending on your ability to bounce back. Maintaining a sense of humor helps. Hal Lancaster, of the *Wall Street Journal*, suggests that "getting fired is nature's way of telling you that you had the wrong job in the first place."

2. *Figure out what went wrong.* This step is an important part of coming to grips, psychologically, with the situation. Experts suggest that if you don't understand what led to your being fired, you're likely to repeat the same mistakes in the future. Moreover, they suggest that you need to talk to your former employer, coworkers, and friends and seek honest feedback to help you understand your

strengths and weaknesses. Doing so may well be difficult, because many firms' human resource professionals prefer to say as little as possible at the time of dismissal in order to minimize lawsuits. If you can't get insights from your former employer, experts suggest utilizing a career counselor to help you make the same evaluation.

3. *Work with your former employer to develop an exit statement.* Experts almost always recommend that you have something in writing from your former employer that will be an asset in your job search. Specific suggestions include having a paragraph that describes what you accomplished in your former job followed by a paragraph that explains why you are no longer with the firm. There are lots of "socially acceptable" reasons that can be given in such a document: a change in management style, a change in strategy, the desire to pursue interests that no longer fit what the employer wants, and so on. Surprisingly, the fired employee can often get a former boss or other officials to sign such a document. People often want to be helpful, and if such a request is approached in a constructive, problem-solving manner, many times the former employer is willing to help create a letter or other document that condemns neither the company nor yourself. This approach has the advantage of creating a situation where prospective future employers hear the same "story" from both the former employer and the job applicant.

4. *Avoid negative attributions as part of your explanation.* Experts say that you should never say anything bad about your former employer. Don't make excuses; don't trash the people you used to work for; and don't blame everything on other people. Focus on the positive aspects of any written understanding that you have obtained. Accept responsibility for both your failures and successes. Quickly move the discussion to the future, stressing what you've learned from previous jobs and focusing on what you can do for a new employer.

CHAPTER SUMMARY

1. Describe the major elements in the perceptual process.

Perception is the psychological process whereby people select information from the environment and organize it to make sense of their worlds. Environmental stimuli are observed, selected, organized, interpreted, and responded to as a result of the perceptual process. Understanding the two major components of this process—selection and organization—is particularly important.

2. Identify the main factors that influence what individuals perceive.

People use perceptual selection to filter out less important information in order to focus on more important environmental cues. Both external factors in the environment and factors internal to the perceiver influence perceptual selection. External factors can be thought of as characteristics of the event perceived that influence whether it is likely to be noticed. Internal factors include personality, learning, and motivation.

3. Identify the factors that determine how one person perceives another.

How people perceive each other is particularly important for organizational behavior. Person perception is a function of the characteristics of the person perceived, the characteristics of the perceiver, and the situation within which the perception takes place. People may go to great lengths to manage the impressions that others form about them. Understanding the dynamics of impression management is also useful for understanding the behavior of people at work.

4. Describe the primary errors in perception that people make.

The perceptual process may result in errors of judgment or understanding in various ways. The more important and common perceptual errors include perceptual defense, stereotyping, halo effect, projection, and the role of culture. However, through training and experience, individuals can learn to judge or perceive others more accurately.

Attribution deals with the perceived causes of behavior. People infer causes for the behavior of others, and their perceptions of why certain behaviors occur influence their own subsequent behavioral responses and feelings. Whether behavior is internally caused by the nature of the person or is externally caused by circumstances is an important attribution that people make about the behaviors of others. Individuals also make attributions concerning task success and failure, which have important implications for organizational behavior.

5. Explain how attributions influence behavior.

KEY TERMS AND CONCEPTS

Attribution process
Fundamental attribution error
Halo effect
Implicit personality theories
Impression management
Perception
Perceptual defense
Perceptual set
Person perception
Pollyanna principle
Projection
Pygmalion effect
Selective screening
Self-fulfilling prophecy
Self-serving bias
Stereotyping

DISCUSSION QUESTIONS

1. Provide two real examples of the Pygmalion effect.
2. Assume that you take a job in an Arab country. What are some of the factors that you need to be aware of? How will these influence your behavior in that country?
3. Are people who have been laid off from their jobs victims of a fundamental attribution error?
4. Describe a time when the *situation* played a key role in your perception of another person.
   How might that perception have been different if the situation had been different?
5. What style of font are you using on your PC? What hidden message does that send to others about you?
6. Give three examples of the halo effect that you have observed personally.
7. How has Chet Cadieux used impression management tactics to satisfy customers?
8. Provide two examples of where you used impression management to influence others.
9. Describe an important task at which you failed. Describe a second important task at which you succeeded. Identify the attributions that you made to explain your failure and your success.
10. Which type of stereotype do you believe is most persuasive in organizations? Why?

EXPERIENTIAL EXERCISE AND CASE

Experiential Exercise: Diversity Competency

Measuring Perceptions of Women as Managers[25]

Gender role stereotypes limit the opportunity for women to advance to managerial positions in many firms. Although these stereotypes are slowly changing, widely held attitudes about the inadequacies of women as managers represent a barrier to greater career opportunities for many women.

Because specific attitudes and stereotypes can be pervasive and powerful influences on behavior, considering their role in the treatment—by both men and women—of women in managerial positions is important. Attitudes about the managerial abilities of women may affect how a manager or executive judges a woman's performance in a managerial role. In addition, such attitudes may influence the granting or withholding of developmental opportunities. The following questionnaire is designed to help you explore your attitudes toward women as managers.

Instructions: From each set (of three) statements, select the one with which you *most agree* and place an M (for "most agree") in the blank to the right of that statement. For each set, also select the statement with which you *least agree* and place an L (for "least agree") in the blank to the right of that statement. Note that one statement in each set will not be chosen.

1. A. Men are more concerned with the cars they drive than with the clothes their wives wear. ______
   B. Any man worth his salt should not be blamed for putting his career above his family. ______
   C. A person's job is the best single indicator of the sort of person he is. ______
2. A. Parental authority and responsibility for discipline of the children should be divided equally between the husband and the wife. ______
   B. It is less desirable for women than for men to have jobs that require responsibility. ______
   C. Men should not continue to show courtesies to women, such as holding doors open for them and helping them with their coats. ______
3. A. It is acceptable for women to assume leadership roles as often as men. ______
   B. In a demanding situation, a female manager would be no more likely to break down than would a male manager. ______
   C. Some professions and types of businesses are more suitable for men than for women. ______
4. A. Recognition for a job well done is less important to women than it is to men. ______
   B. A woman should demand money for household and personal expenses as a right rather than a gift. ______
   C. Women are temperamentally fit for leadership positions. ______
5. A. Women tend to allow their emotions to influence their managerial behavior more than men do. ______
   B. The husband and the wife should be equal partners in planning the family budget. ______
   C. If both husband and wife agree that sexual fidelity is not important, there is no reason why both should not have extramarital affairs. ______
6. A. A man's first responsibility is to his wife, not to his mother. ______
   B. A man who is able and willing to work hard has a good chance of succeeding in whatever he wants to do. ______
   C. Only after a man has achieved what he wants from life should he concern himself with the injustices in the world. ______
7. A. A wife should make every effort to minimize irritations and inconveniences for the male head of the household. ______
   B. Women can cope with stressful situations as effectively as men can. ______
   C. Women should be encouraged not to become sexually intimate with anyone, even their fiancés, before marriage. ______
8. A. The "obey" clause in the marriage service is insulting to women. ______
   B. Divorced men should help to support their children but should not be required to pay alimony if their former wives are capable of working. ______
   C. Women have the capacity to acquire the necessary skills to be successful managers. ______
9. A. Women can be aggressive in business situations that demand it. ______
   B. Women have an obligation to be faithful to their husbands. ______
   C. It is childish for a woman to assert herself by retaining her maiden name after marriage. ______
10. A. Men should continue to show courtesies to women, such as holding doors open for them or helping them with their coats. ______
    B. In job appointments and promotions, women should be given equal consideration with men. ______
    C. It is all right for a wife to have an occasional casual, extramarital affair. ______
11. A. The satisfaction of her husband's sexual desires is a fundamental obligation of every wife. ______
    B. Most women should not want the kind of support that men traditionally have given them. ______
    C. Women possess the dominance to be successful leaders. ______
12. A. Most women need and want the kind of protection and support that men traditionally have given them. ______

B. Women are capable of separating their emotions from their ideas. ______

C. A husband has no obligation to inform his wife of his financial plans. __L__

Score your responses by using the form and following the instructions given. Your total score indicates your feelings about women managers. The higher your score, the more prone you are to hold negative gender role stereotypes about women in management. Possible total scores range from 10 to 70; a "neutral" score (one that indicates neither positive nor negative attitudes about women as managers) is in the range of 30 to 40.

Instructions:

1. Record your response for the indicated items in the spaces provided.
2. On the basis of the information provided, determine the points for each item and enter these points in the space provided to the right. For example, if in item 3, you chose alternative A as the one with which you *most agree* and alternative B as the one with which you *least agree*, you should receive three points for item 3. Note that items 1 and 6 are "buffer items" and are not scored.
3. When you have scored all 10 scorable items, add the points and record the total at the bottom of this page in the space provided. That is your total score.

POINTS PER ITEM RESPONSE*								
Your Response	Item No.	1	3		5		7	Points
	1	Not Scored						
M __A__ L __C__ 5	2	C(M) B(L)	A(M) B(L)	C(M) A(L)	A(M) C(L)	B(M) A(L)	B(M) C(L)	
M __C__ L __A__ 7	3	A(M) C(L)	A(M) B(L)	B(M) C(L)	C(M) B(L)	B(M) A(L)	C(M) A(L)	
M __A__ L __B__ 3	4	C(M) B(L)	C(M) A(L)	A(M) B(L)	B(M) A(L)	A(M) C(L)	B(M) C(L)	
M __B__ L __C__ 5	5	C(M) A(L)	C(M) B(L)	B(M) A(L)	A(M) B(L)	B(M) C(L)	A(M) C(L)	
M ____ L ____	6	Not Scored						
M __B__ L __A__ 1	7	B(M) A(L)	B(M) C(L)	C(M) A(L)	A(M) C(L)	C(M) B(L)	A(M) B(L)	
M __B__ L __A__ 5	8	C(M) B(L)	C(M) A(L)	A(M) B(L)	B(M) A(L)	A(M) C(L)	B(M) C(L)	
M __A__ L __C__ 3	9	A(M) B(L)	A(M) C(L)	C(M) B(L)	B(M) C(L)	C(M) A(L)	B(M) A(L)	
M __B__ L __C__ 3	10	B(M) A(L)	B(M) C(L)	C(M) A(L)	A(M) C(L)	C(M) B(L)	A(M) B(L)	
M __A__ L __B__ 5	11	C(M) A(L)	C(M) B(L)	B(M) A(L)	A(M) B(L)	B(M) C(L)	A(M) C(L)	
M __A__ L __C__ 5	12	B(M) A(L)	B(M) C(L)	C(M) A(L)	A(M) C(L)	C(M) B(L)	A(M) B(L)	
								Total __48__

*M indicates item chosen as "most"; L indicates item chosen as "least."

Case: Ethics Competency

The Foundation for New Era Philanthropy

In the practice of impression management, creating the desired impression can be greatly aided if others strongly desire to see what you want them to see. The story of the Foundation for New Era Philanthropy provides a classic example of this dynamic.

John G. Bennett Jr. was the founder of what appeared to be a forward-thinking charitable foundation. New Era proposed to pool money from a variety of other charities and wealthy individuals and, through astute investing, fund-raising, and money management, promised to leverage these funds in ways that would allow generous people and charities to dramatically increase their ability to do good works. Specifically, Bennett promised to do the following.

1. Double within 6 months any money contributed to the foundation by selected charities and individuals and return the total to the original charities for distribution. Supposedly New Era had a group of wealthy "anonymous donors" too busy to find their own charities to give to, and it would use this money to double the amount of contributions solicited.
2. Double within 6 months new money that the charities and individuals approached had to promise to raise and return the total to the original charities for distribution.

This sounds too good to be true. Unfortunately, it was.

The beginning of the end came when Prudential Securities was doing a routine audit of $60 million in treasury bills held by New Era. They discovered that the foundation had borrowed $52 million against these bills, but had repaid only $7 million of the loan. Prudential gave New Era 24 hours to come up with the missing money, which it was unable to do. Ensuing events revealed that that there were no "anonymous donors" and that New Era had about $100 million in net liabilities. Basically, New Era was running a classic Ponzi scheme, whereby money from new investors is used to pay off previous investors. Many well-intentioned, supposedly well-informed, sophisticated investors and charities had been taken in by New Era's plan. How could this have happened?

The dynamics of impression management and impression formation coupled with Bennett's personal history seem to offer the best explanation. Bennett was an expansive, likable person who was described as an "incurable optimist." People wanted to believe in him and what he was proposing to do. He had a track record in a business that provided training to nonprofit foundation managers and fund-raisers. As a result he had become well known to the people who managed and contributed to various charities.

Contributing to this positive image was the fact that many of the initial beneficiaries of Bennett's fund-raising were churches and other religious organizations. Bennett himself served on the boards of directors of several Christian groups and was a regular attendant at Philadelphia-area prayer breakfasts. Many of his staunchest supporters were very rich and well connected to the highest levels of government, prestigious universities, investment firms, and the like. Why were so many smart, successful people taken in by this scheme?

One simple explanation, consistent with the notions of impression management, was that "the rich and well connected prefer to believe that they are so because they are smart and enterprising. What worked for Bennett was that these smart and enterprising people are likely to put their faith in other smart and enterprising people. Once Bennett succeeded in developing the *impression* that he was one of them—smart and enterprising—he had it made."[26]

Questions

1. Using the notions of impression management discussed in the chapter, describe Bennett's *impression motivation.*
2. Again, using ideas from the discussion of impression management, speculate about Bennett's *impression construction.*
3. Identify and explain the perceptual errors that may have occurred in this situation.
4. Imagine that you are the managing director of a charity that lost a great deal of money with New Era. Describe the likely attributions that you might make to explain this failure in judgment. Be imaginative and have some fun with this question.

CHAPTER 13

Learning and Reinforcement

LEARNING OBJECTIVES

When you have finished studying this chapter, you should be able to:

1. Explain the role of classical and operant conditioning in fostering learning.
2. Describe the contingencies of reinforcement that influence behavior.
3. List the four schedules of reinforcement and explain when each is effective.
4. Describe how social learning theory explains the development of new behaviors.

Preview Case: Mini Maids

LEARNING THROUGH REWARDS AND PUNISHMENTS
- Classical Conditioning
- Operant Conditioning

CONTINGENCIES OF REINFORCEMENT
- Positive Reinforcement
- *Communication Competency—Gary Logan at Kodak*
- Organizational Rewards
- Negative Reinforcement
- Omission
- Punishment
- *Change Competency—Discipline without Punishment*
- Guidelines for Using Contingencies of Reinforcement

SCHEDULES OF REINFORCEMENT
- Continuous and Intermittent Reinforcement
- Fixed Interval Schedule
- Variable Interval Schedule
- Fixed Ratio Schedule
- *Across Cultures Competency—Northern Shipbuilding of China*
- Variable Ratio Schedule

SOCIAL LEARNING THEORY
- Symbolizing
- Forethought
- Vicarious Learning
- Self-Control
- *Teams Competency—Rowe Furniture's Focused Factory*
- Self-Efficacy
- Organizational Guidelines

CHAPTER SUMMARY

KEY TERMS AND CONCEPTS

DISCUSSION QUESTIONS

EXPERIENTIAL EXERCISE AND CASES

MINI MAIDS

PREVIEW CASE

Mini Maids is a residential cleaning service that Tom Nevant has managed for more than 12 years. His maids are organized into teams of three and travel in company cars to clean homes of customers in the metropolitan Dallas area. Each team has a team leader who is responsible for driving the team to the customer's house. The team leader inspects all cleaning and communicates with the customer.

Tom was faced with the problem of selecting maids who could become assistant team leaders. All of the experienced teams had both assistant and team leaders. Team leaders had to have a Texas driver's license and be able to read a Mapsco map to locate a customer's home. Many maids had never read a Mapsco, rode the bus to and from work, didn't have a Texas driver's license, and used English as their second language. This resulted in cell phone calls to the office for directions and late arrivals at customers' homes. If a customer was promised a cleaning crew between 2:00 and 3:00 P.M. and the assigned team was running behind because of getting lost, then another experienced team "picked up" that customer so as not to break the promised arrival time. This meant that the experienced team had to take work from a less experienced team, which led to frustrations and words between the teams.

A monetary reward was given to those who learned the behaviors needed to become an assistant team leader. An assistant team leader's commission was 14.5 percent of the household cleaning bill (average bill was $104) compared to 13 percent commission for regular maids.

To try to remedy the problem of late arrivals, those who volunteered to become assistant team leaders had to attend a demonstration during working hours. During the demonstration, maids were shown how to read a Mapsco. To qualify as an assistant team leader, the maid would have to find 10 addresses on the map. For each correct address, the maid received $5. To prepare themselves for the test, many of the maids spent up to two hours a day on their own time practicing reading, took Mapsco books home, and helped their fellow maids read. Tom heard one maid jokingly say that "she fell asleep looking at her Mapsco book."

As a result of this training, the number of cell phone minutes decreased from 1,477 in July to 927 minutes in November. Before training, the home office received an average of three calls per day. After training, it received three calls for an entire six weeks. This saved Tom more than $75 per month per person for phone charges. Maids also began arriving on time more often. Maid turnover was reduced by 14.3 percent because they earned more money by arriving on time at the customer's home.

Teams also competed for weekly bonuses that were based on customer compliments and complaints. The experienced teams, whose members could read a Mapsco, were winning bonuses each week and the less experienced teams were regularly losing. Naturally, pride, bragging rights, and good-natured kidding went along with being part of the winning team.[1]

Tom Nevant's motivational tactics are based on specific principles drawn from an area of psychology called *learning*. **Learning** *is a relatively permanent change in knowledge or observable behavior that results from practice or experience.*[2] Desirable work behaviors contribute to achievement of organizational goals; conversely, undesirable work behaviors hinder achievement of these goals. Labeling behavior as *desirable* or *undesirable* may be somewhat subjective and depends on the value systems of the organization (most often represented by an employee's manager) and the employee exhibiting the behavior. For example, a maid at Mini Maids who returns late from lunch exhibits undesirable behavior from the team leader's viewpoint, desirable behavior from the viewpoint of friends with whom the worker chats during the break, and desirable behavior from the worker's viewpoint because of the satisfaction of social needs. Employees quickly learn the difference from the manager's reaction to the behavior and how to change an undesirable to a desirable (from the manager's viewpoint) behavior.

Usually, however, the work setting and organizational norms provide objective bases for determining whether a behavior is desirable or undesirable. The more a behavior deviates from organizational expectations, the more undesirable it is. At Southwest Airlines, undesirable behavior includes anything that results in lost baggage and late departures and arrivals. Expectations vary considerably from one organization to another. For example, at Microsoft's research and development laboratory, engineers and scientists are encouraged to question top management's directives because innovation and professional judgment are crucial to the organization's success.

Effective managers do not try to change employees' personalities or basic beliefs. As we pointed out in Chapters 11 and 12, an individual's personality, emotions, and perceptual processes influence behavior and directly influencing those traits is often difficult, if not impossible. Rather, effective managers focus on identifying observable employee behaviors and the environmental conditions that affect these behaviors. They then attempt to influence external events in order to guide employee behaviors—to help employees learn and exhibit desirable behaviors. In this chapter, we explore three major theories of learning: classical conditioning, operant conditioning, and social learning theory. Each theory proposes a different way by which people learn, but focusing on observable behaviors is common to all three.

LEARNING OBJECTIVE

1. Explain the role of classical and operant conditioning in fostering learning.

LEARNING THROUGH REWARDS AND PUNISHMENTS

In an organization, employees need to learn and practice productive work behaviors.[3] Learning new work often depends on many factors. The manager's task, then, is to provide learning experiences in an environment that will simplify the learning process and promote the employee behaviors desired by the organization. For learning to occur, some types of behavioral change are required. Just as students learn basic educational skills in the classroom, when Mini Maid wanted to change the behavior of its employees, it used the Mapsco training. This training not only prepared employees to effectively use Mapsco to find a customer's home, but it also provided them with incentives to learn and practice these newly learned behaviors.

Classical Conditioning

Classical conditioning *is the process by which individuals learn to link the information from a neutral stimulus to a stimulus that causes a response.* This response may not be under an individual's conscious control.[4] In the classical conditioning process, an unconditioned stimulus (environmental event) brings out a natural response. Then a neutral environmental event, called a *conditioned stimulus*, is paired with the unconditioned stimulus that brings out the behavior. Eventually, the conditioned stimulus alone brings out the behavior, which is called a *conditional response*.

The name most frequently associated with classical conditioning is Ivan Pavlov, the Russian physiologist whose experiments with dogs led to the early formulations of classical conditioning theory. In Pavlov's famous experiment, the sound of a metronome (the conditioned stimulus) was paired with food (the unconditioned stimulus). The dogs eventually exhibited a salivation response (conditioned response) to the sound of the metronome alone. The classical conditioning process is illustrated in Figure 13.1.

FIGURE 13.1 Classical Conditioning

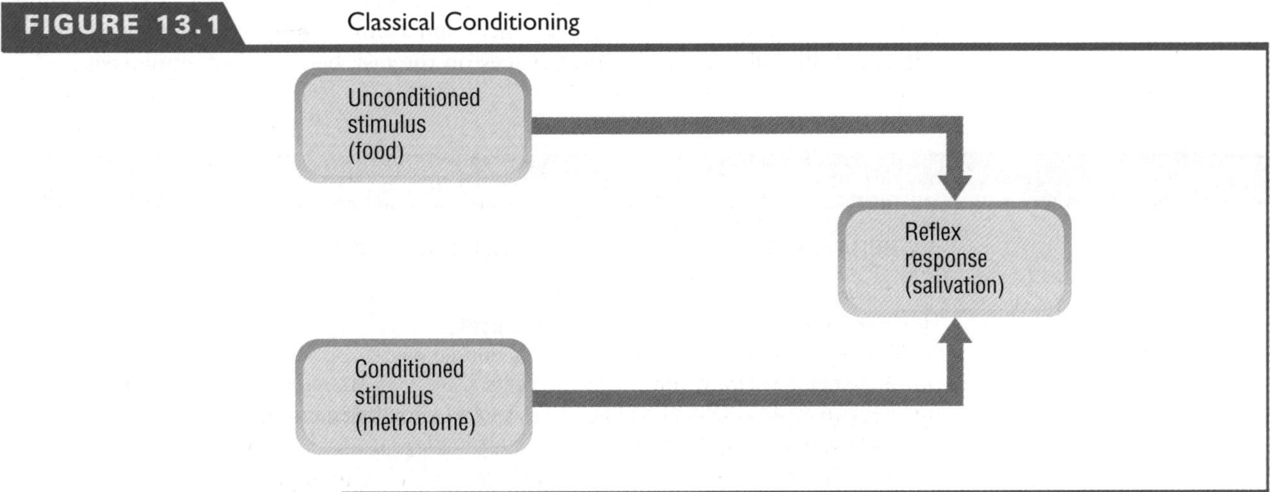

The classical conditioning process helps explain a variety of behaviors that occur in everyday organizational life. At Presbyterian Hospital's emergency room in Plano, Texas, special lights in the hallway indicate that a patient who needs treatment has just arrived. Nurses and other hospital staff report that they feel nervous when the lights go on. In contrast, at a recent luncheon in the dining room at Stonebriar Country Club in Frisco, Texas, Ralph Sorrentino, a partner at Deloitte & Touche, was thanked by his friend Jon Wheeler, vice president of Centex Homes, for introducing a new work system. Now, whenever Sorrentino sees the dining room, he feels good.

Some organizations spend millions of dollars on advertising campaigns designed to link the information value of a stimulus to customer purchase behavior. In a TV ad, AFLAC has successfully created a link between its duck and supplemental insurance. The duck is the unconditioned stimulus, and insurance is the conditioned stimulus. The positive feelings that buyers have toward the duck are associated with insurance, which AFLAC hopes will lead people to buy its products. Similarly, Blue Bell Creameries has linked its cow, Belle, in an award-winning TV ad. When people see Belle (unconditioned stimulus) singing in a pasture of purple flowers, they associate her with Blue Bell ice cream (the conditioned stimulus). By associating the upbeat mood and dairy freshness created by the cow with its product, Blue Bell hopes to lead customers to eat its ice cream. Both organizations have successfully used the concepts of classical conditioning to increase sales of their products.

Classical conditioning isn't widely used in work settings. Employee behaviors usually don't include responses that can be changed with classical conditioning techniques. There is greater interest in the voluntary behaviors of employees and how they can be changed via operant conditioning.

Operant Conditioning

The person most closely linked with this type of learning is B. F. Skinner.[5] He coined the term **operant conditioning** *to refer to a process by which individuals learn voluntary behavior.* Voluntary behaviors are called *operants* because they operate, or have some influence, on the environment. Learning occurs from the consequences of behaviors, and many employee work behaviors are operant behaviors. In fact, most behaviors in everyday life (e.g., talking, walking, reading, or working) are forms of operant behavior. Table 13.1 shows some examples of operant behaviors and their consequences. Managers are interested in operant behaviors because they can influence the results of such behaviors. For example, the frequency of an employee behavior can be increased or decreased by changing the results of that behavior. The crucial aspect of operant conditioning is what happens as a consequence of the behavior. The strength and frequency of operantly conditioned behaviors are determined mainly by consequences. Thus, managers and team members must understand the effects of different types of consequences on the task behaviors of employees.

TABLE 13.1 Examples of Operant Behaviors and Their Consequences

BEHAVIORS	CONSEQUENCES
The Individual	
• works and	is paid.
• is late to work and	is docked pay.
• enters a restaurant and	eats.
• enters a football stadium and	watches a football game.
• enters a grocery store and	buys food.

In operant conditioning, a response is learned because it leads to a particular consequence (reinforcement), and it is strengthened each time it is reinforced. The success of Mini Maids' training program is based on operant conditioning principles. Employees learn to operate in their environment by engaging in specific behaviors (e.g., learning the Mapsco skills to become an assistant team leader) in order to achieve certain consequences (money). At school, you've probably learned that if you study hard, you will receive good grades. If you keep up with your reading throughout the semester, you can cope with the stress of finals week. Thus, you've learned to operate on your environment to achieve your desired goals.

LEARNING OBJECTIVE

2. Describe the contingencies of reinforcement that influence behavior.

CONTINGENCIES OF REINFORCEMENT

A **contingency of reinforcement** *is the relationship between a behavior and the preceding and following environmental events that influence that behavior.* A contingency of reinforcement consists of an antecedent, a behavior, and a consequence.[6]

An **antecedent** *precedes and is a stimulus to a behavior.* Antecedents are instructions, rules, goals, and advice from others that help individuals to know which behaviors are acceptable and which are not and to let them know the consequences of such behaviors. At Mini Maids, antecedents were the Mapsco instructions that Tom Nevant sent to all maids about reaching a customer's home on time. Antecedents play an essential educational role by letting employees know in advance the consequences (extra money) of different behaviors (learning to read the Mapsco map).

A **consequence** *is the result of a behavior, which can be either positive or negative in terms of goal or task accomplishment.* A manager's response to an employee is contingent on the consequence of the behavior (and sometimes on the behavior itself, regardless of consequence). The consequence for the employees at Mini Maids is meeting their goals and those of the organization and earning a bonus.

Figure 13.2 shows an example of contingent reinforcement. First, the employee and manager jointly set a goal (e.g., selling $100,000 worth of equipment next

FIGURE 13.2 Example of Contingent Reinforcement

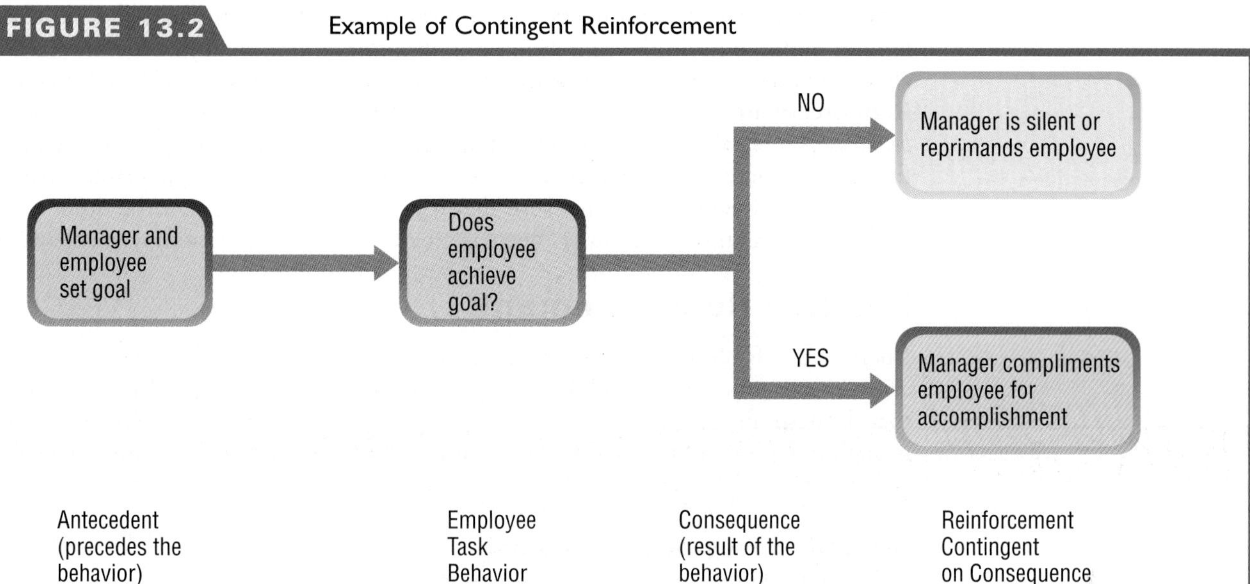

month). Next, the employee performs tasks to achieve this goal (e.g., calling on four new customers a week, having regular lunches with current buyers, and attending a two-day training program on new methods of selling). If the employee reaches the sales goal, the manager praises the employee—an action contingent on achievement of the goal. If the employee fails to reach the goal, the manager doesn't say anything or reprimands the employee.

The contingency of reinforcement concept involves three main types of contingencies. First, an event can be presented (applied) or withdrawn (removed), contingent on employee behavior. The event also may be positive or aversive. **Positive events** *are desirable, or pleasing, to the employee.* **Aversive events** *are undesirable, or displeasing, to the employee.* Figure 13.3 shows how these events can be combined to

FIGURE 13.3 Types of Contingencies of Reinforcement

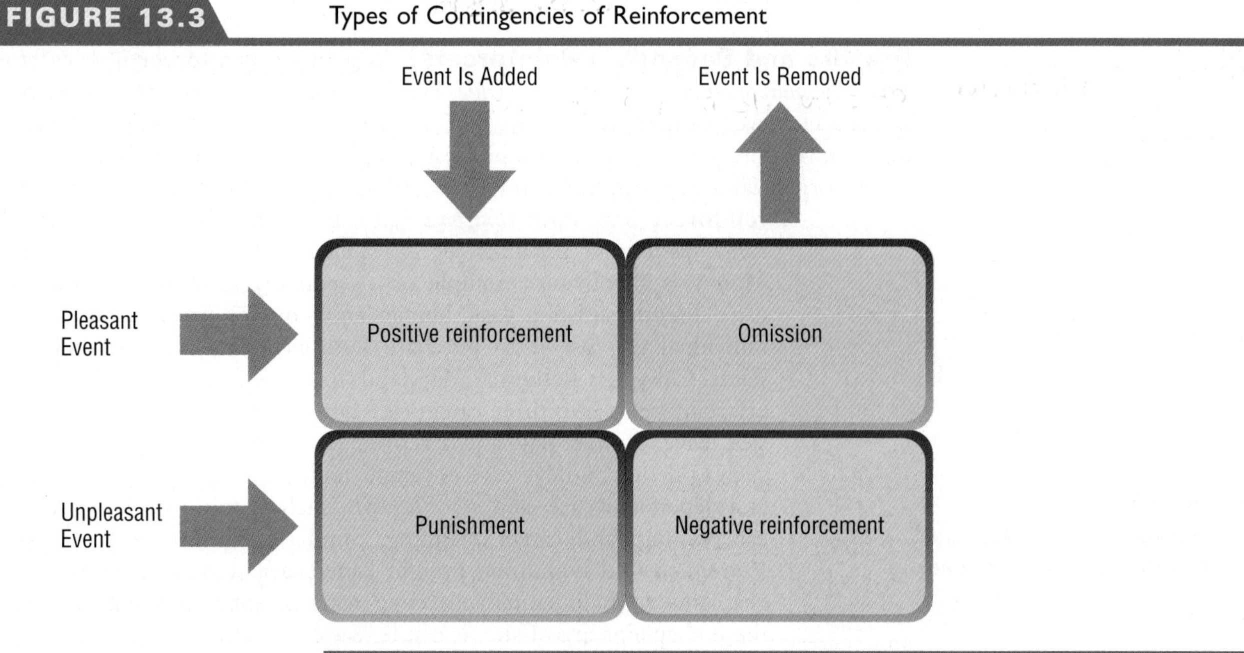

produce four types of contingencies of reinforcement. It shows whether a particular type of contingency is likely to increase or decrease the frequency of the behavior. It also is the basis for the following discussion of contingencies of reinforcement. **Reinforcement** *is a behavioral contingency that increases the frequency of a particular behavior that it follows.* On the one hand, reinforcement, whether positive or negative, always increases the frequency of the employee behavior. If you want a behavior to continue, you must make sure that it is being reinforced. On the other hand, omission and punishment always decrease the frequency of the employee behavior.

Positive Reinforcement

Positive reinforcement *entails presenting a pleasant consequence after the occurrence of a desired behavior* (see Figure 13.3). That is, a manager rewards an employee's behavior that is desirable in terms of achieving the organization's goals. Robert Gooch brought a cup of coffee to John McElhanney while discussing the improved quality of his work, and his work continued to improve (positive reinforcement).

Reward versus Reinforcement. The terms *reinforcement* and *reward* are often confused in everyday usage. A **reward** *is an event that a person finds desirable or pleasing.* Whether a reward acts as a reinforcer is influenced by the culture.[7] For example, praise and appreciation of employees in family-dominated cultures such as Greece, Italy, Singapore, and South Korea may mean just as much to the recipient as money. Certain material rewards can also carry unexpected consequences. In China, for example, organizations often distribute food to employees as holiday gifts. Employees in higher positions get more and better food items than lower-level workers. The same reactions may occur with nonmaterial rewards. A manager who singled out and praised a Japanese employee in front of coworkers for finding an error in the team's report believed that she was reinforcing the desired behavior. Later, however, she learned that the employee was given the silent treatment by other team members and had stopped looking for errors.[8]

To qualify as a reinforcer, a reward must increase the frequency of the behavior it follows. Recall that at Mini Maids, maids can only earn higher commissions if they qualify to become assistant team leaders. Money can be regarded as a positive reinforcer for a particular individual only if the frequency of the desired behavior (in this case, high performance) increases. A reward doesn't act as a reinforcer if the frequency of the behavior decreases or remains unchanged.

Primary and Secondary Reinforcers. A **primary reinforcer** *is an event for which the individual already knows the value.* Food, shelter, and water are primary reinforcers. However, primary reinforcers don't always reinforce. For example, food may not be a reinforcer to someone who has just completed a five-course meal.

In organizations, secondary reinforcers influence most behaviors. A **secondary reinforcer** *is an event that once had neutral value but has taken on some value (positive or negative) for an individual because of past experience.* Money is an obvious example of a secondary reinforcer. Although it can't directly satisfy a basic human need, money has value because an individual can use it to purchase both necessities and discretionary items. Calvert, a Bethesda, Maryland, financial firm, groups its secondary reinforcers into three categories: *core benefits,* such as life insurance, sick leave, holiday pay, and a retirement savings plan; *optional benefits,* such as dental and eye care coverage, and spending accounts for health and dependent care; and *other benefits,* such as tuition reimbursement, car pooling, and career planning. Similarly, Tyson Foods, Pilgrim's Pride, and Old Dominion Freight Lines have started hiring part-time chaplains to help employees cope with personal problems. Because these chaplains are offsite, it can be easier for employees to build rela-

> **THE COMPETENT LEADER**
>
> I want our customers to become a better spouse, a better parent, and more personally self-fulfilled. We're in the people business, not the suit business.
>
> George Zimmer, founder of the Men's Wearhouse

tionships with them and seek help in the time of need. Chaplains charge the company $250 to $100,000 per month, depending on the number of employees who use their services.[9]

Managers at State Farm Insurance Company have discovered that when people are given a choice of things to do, whatever they consistently choose can be used as a reinforcer for the behaviors not chosen. At work, this means that if a manager can watch how people spend their time when they have a choice, they can identify the reinforcers for them. If an assistant spends most of his or her time reading murder novels instead of doing something else, we can assume that reading murder novels is a reinforcer to that person. In fact, we invite you to make a list of all the things that you need to do. Rank these from things you most want to do or enjoy doing to the things you least like to do. Then start working at the bottom of the list. You will quickly notice that when you start at the bottom, every time you finish a task, the next one on the list is more desirable. If you start at the top of your list, the consequence of completing that task is that the next one is more undesirable, difficult, or boring. Using this approach, you quit. Starting from the bottom and working to the top, you don't want to quit until all tasks are done.

Gary Logan, department manager of Kodak's Image Loops and Sundries Department put this to the test. The following Communication Competency feature illustrates how reinforcers can be used to increase productivity.[10]

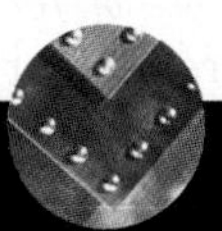

COMMUNICATION COMPETENCY

GARY LOGAN AT KODAK

Logan observed that operators in his department enjoyed certain special work-related projects. These were usually team activities aimed at improving production quality and efficiency. Improvement in both areas is beneficial to Kodak. Logan and his production supervisor, Karyn Johnson, decided to use team activities to reinforce the operators for meeting weekly production efficiency and quality goals.

When the operators reached their weekly goal for each type of image loop, Logan let Johnson shut down the production line and the workers could then work on other projects. On their own initiative, the team developed ideas for improving the operation and formed two ad hoc teams to implement these ideas.

Johnson noted that 10 to 15 improvements have been made by these teams. According to Logan, Kodak's production goals are not easy to meet, but there have been times when the goal was met late Thursday and then the team worked on other projects all day Friday. He also noticed that for other weeks, the team had a difficult time meeting its production goal, making it just before the end of the shift. There was no guarantee that the team would make its production goal, but when it did, Logan and Johnson let the team members work on their special interest projects.

Johnson found that the operators thrived on the challenge. They monitored their own progress on a large 6- by 10-foot bar graph. Their graph reflected the cumulative efforts of all teams. Each team had its own color to show its contribution to production, which made each team's results visible. In this way, the teams get feedback on how they are doing and how they are contributing toward the weekly goal. Highly visible daily feedback toward a common goal has inspired the operators to find ways to eliminate unneeded paperwork.

Johnson found that people were so motivated to move on to their special projects that on several occasions, some operators finished early and volunteered to continue working to make up a previous week's shortfall of another team. Then they were able to get to their team activities and enjoyed the challenge of catching up. Of course, quality doesn't take a back seat to quantity. The operators perform random daily quality audits, graphing those results as well.

Principles of Positive Reinforcement. Several factors influence the effectiveness of positive reinforcement. These factors can be thought of loosely as principles because they help explain optimum reinforcement conditions.[11]

The **principle of contingent reinforcement** *states that the reinforcer must be administered only if the desired behavior is performed.* A reinforcer administered when the desired behavior has not been performed is ineffective. At Mini Maids, just as soon as the maid passes the Mapsco test and becomes an assistant team leader, her salary increases.

The **principle of immediate reinforcement** *states that the reinforcer will be most effective if administered immediately after the desired behavior has occurred.* This is what Gary Logan used at Kodak. The more time that elapses after the behavior occurs, the less effective will be the reinforcer.

The **principle of reinforcement size** *states that the larger the amount of reinforcer delivered after the desired behavior, the more effect the reinforcer will have on the frequency of the desired behavior.* The amount, or size, of the reinforcer is relative. A reinforcer that may be significant to one person may be insignificant to another person. Thus, the size of the reinforcer must be determined in relation both to the behavior and the individual. ARAMARK, a supplier of food services to college campuses, gives T-shirts to workers with perfect attendance for a month and a $50 gift certificate to those with perfect attendance for a semester.

The **principle of reinforcement deprivation** *states that the more a person is deprived of the reinforcer, the greater effect it will have on the future occurrence of the desired behavior.* However, if an individual recently has had enough of a reinforcer and is satisfied, the reinforcer will have less effect.

Organizational Rewards

The material rewards—salary, bonuses, fringe benefits, and the like—that organizations commonly use are obvious. Most organizations also offer a wide range of other rewards, many of which aren't immediately apparent. They include verbal approval, assignment to desired tasks, improved working conditions, and extra time off. At Toyota's Camry assembly plant in Georgetown, Kentucky, management rewards employees for *kaizens.* A **kaizen** *is a suggestion that results in safety, cost, or quality improvements.*[12] The awards are distributed equally among all members of a team. The awards aren't cash payments; rather, they are gift certificates redeemable at local retail stores. Toyota learned that an award that could be shared by the employees' families was valued more than extra money in the paycheck. These awards instill pride and encourage other employees to scramble for new ideas and products in the hope that they, too, will receive them. In addition, self-administered rewards are important. For example, self-congratulation for accomplishing a particularly difficult assignment can be an important personal reinforcer. Table 13.2 contains an extensive list of organizational rewards. Remember, however, that such rewards will act as reinforcers only if the individuals receiving them find them desirable or pleasing.

Negative Reinforcement

Negative reinforcement (see Figure 13.3) *means an unpleasant event that precedes the employee behavior is removed when the desired behavior occurs.* This procedure increases the likelihood that the desired behavior will occur. Negative reinforcement is sometimes confused with punishment because both use unpleasant events to influence behavior. Negative reinforcement is used to increase the frequency of a desired behavior. In contrast, punishment is used to decrease the frequency of an undesired behavior. You stay late on Monday night to revise a presentation on Tuesday morning because you know if it isn't perfect, your manager will criticize you (negative reinforcement).

Managers and team members frequently use negative reinforcement when an employee hasn't done something that is necessary or desired. For example, air-traffic controllers want the capability to activate a blinking light and a loud buzzer in the

TABLE 13.2 Rewards Used by Organizations

MATERIAL REWARDS	SUPPLEMENTAL BENEFITS	STATUS SYMBOLS
Pay	Company automobiles	Corner offices
Pay raises	Health insurance plans	Offices with windows
Stock options	Pension contributions	Carpeting
Profit sharing	Vacation and sick leave	Drapes
Deferred compensation	Recreation facilities	Paintings
Bonuses/bonus plans	Child-care support	Watches
Incentive plans	Club privileges	Rings
Expense accounts	Parental leave	Private restrooms
SOCIAL/ INTERPERSONAL REWARDS	**REWARDS FROM THE TASK**	**SELF-ADMINISTERED REWARDS**
Praise	Sense of achievement	Self-congratulation
Developmental feedback	Jobs with more responsibility	Self-recognition
Smiles, pats on the back, and other nonverbal signals	Job autonomy/self-direction	Self-praise
Requests for suggestions	Performing important tasks	Self-development through expanded knowledge/skills
Invitations to coffee or lunch		Greater sense of self-worth
Wall plaques		

cockpits of planes that come too close to each other. The air-traffic controllers wouldn't shut these devices off until the planes moved farther apart. This type of procedure is called *escape learning* because the pilots quickly learn to move their planes away from each other to escape the light and buzzer. **Escape learning** *means an unpleasant event occurs until an employee performs a behavior, or terminates it.* In most instances, use of negative reinforcements generates enough behavior to escape or avoid punishment. Doing "just enough to get by" is typical.

Omission

Omission *is the removal of all reinforcing events.* Whereas reinforcement increases the frequency of a desirable behavior, omission decreases the frequency and eventually extinguishes an undesirable behavior (see Figure 13.3). Managers use omission to reduce undesirable employee behaviors that prevent achievement of organizational goals. The omission procedure consists of three steps:

1. identifying the behavior to be reduced or eliminated,
2. identifying the reinforcer that maintains the behavior, and
3. stopping the reinforcer.

Omission is a useful technique for reducing and eventually eliminating behaviors that disrupt normal workflow. For example, a team reinforces the disruptive behavior of a member by laughing at the behavior. When the team stops laughing (the reinforcer), the disruptive behavior will diminish and ultimately stop.

Omission can also be regarded as a failure to reinforce a behavior positively. In this regard, the omission of behaviors may be accidental. If managers fail to reinforce desirable behaviors, they may be using omission without recognizing it. As a result, the frequency of desirable behaviors may inadvertently decrease.

Most managers feel that doing nothing has no effect on performance. The fact is that when managers do nothing following a behavior, they change that performance.

If people are taking the initiative to go beyond what is required, those behaviors will stop if they are not reinforced. If people are taking shortcuts in areas of safety and quality and nothing is said, then omission will cause the undesirable behaviors to continue.

Punishment

Punishment (see Figure 13.3) *means an unpleasant event follows a behavior and decreases its frequency.* Remember when you tried to use a PC for the first time? You probably inadvertently deleted a document you had been working on for hours (punishment). Now, you probably hit the "Save" option regularly. As in positive reinforcement, a punishment may include a specific antecedent that cues the employee that a consequence (punisher) will follow a specific behavior. A positive contingency of reinforcement encourages the frequency of a desired behavior. In contrast, punishment decreases the frequency of an undesired behavior.

To qualify as a punisher, an event must decrease the undesirable behavior. Just because an event is thought of as unpleasant, it isn't necessarily a punisher. The event must actually reduce or stop the undesired behavior before it can be defined as a punisher.

Organizations typically use several types of unpleasant events to punish individuals.[13] Material consequences for failure to perform adequately include a cut in pay, a disciplinary suspension without pay, a demotion, or a transfer to a dead-end job. The final punishment is the firing of an employee for failure to perform. In general, organizations reserve the use of unpleasant material events for cases of serious behavior problems.

Interpersonal punishers are used extensively. They include a manager's oral reprimand of an employee for unacceptable behavior and nonverbal punishers such as frowns, grunts, and aggressive body language. Certain tasks themselves can be unpleasant. The fatigue that follows hard physical labor can be considered a punisher, as can harsh or dirty working conditions. However, care must be exercised in labeling a punisher. In some fields and to some employees, harsh or dirty working conditions may be considered as just something that goes with the job.

Three of the principles of positive reinforcement discussed earlier have equivalents in punishment. For maximum effectiveness, a punisher should be directly linked to the undesirable behavior (principle of contingent punishment); the punishment should be administered immediately (principle of immediate punishment); and, in general, the greater the size of the punisher, the stronger will be the effect on the undesirable behavior (principle of punishment size).

Negative Effects of Punishment. A criticism for using punishment is the chance that it will have negative effects, especially over long or sustained periods of time. Punishment may stop an undesirable employee behavior. However, the potential negative consequences may be greater than the original undesirable behavior. Figure 13.4 illustrates some potential negative effects of punishment.

Punishment may cause undesirable emotional reactions. An employee who has been reprimanded for staying on break too long may react with anger toward the manager and the organization. Such reactions may lead to behavior detrimental to the organization. Sabotage, for example, typically is a result of a punishment-oriented management system. Chapter 16 will discuss aggressive behavior in the workforce more completely.

Punishment frequently leads only to short-term suppression of the undesirable behavior, rather than to its elimination. Thus, suppression of an undesirable behavior over a long period of time usually requires continued and, perhaps, increasingly severe punishment. Another problem is that control of the undesirable behavior

FIGURE 13.4 Potential Negative Effects of Punishment

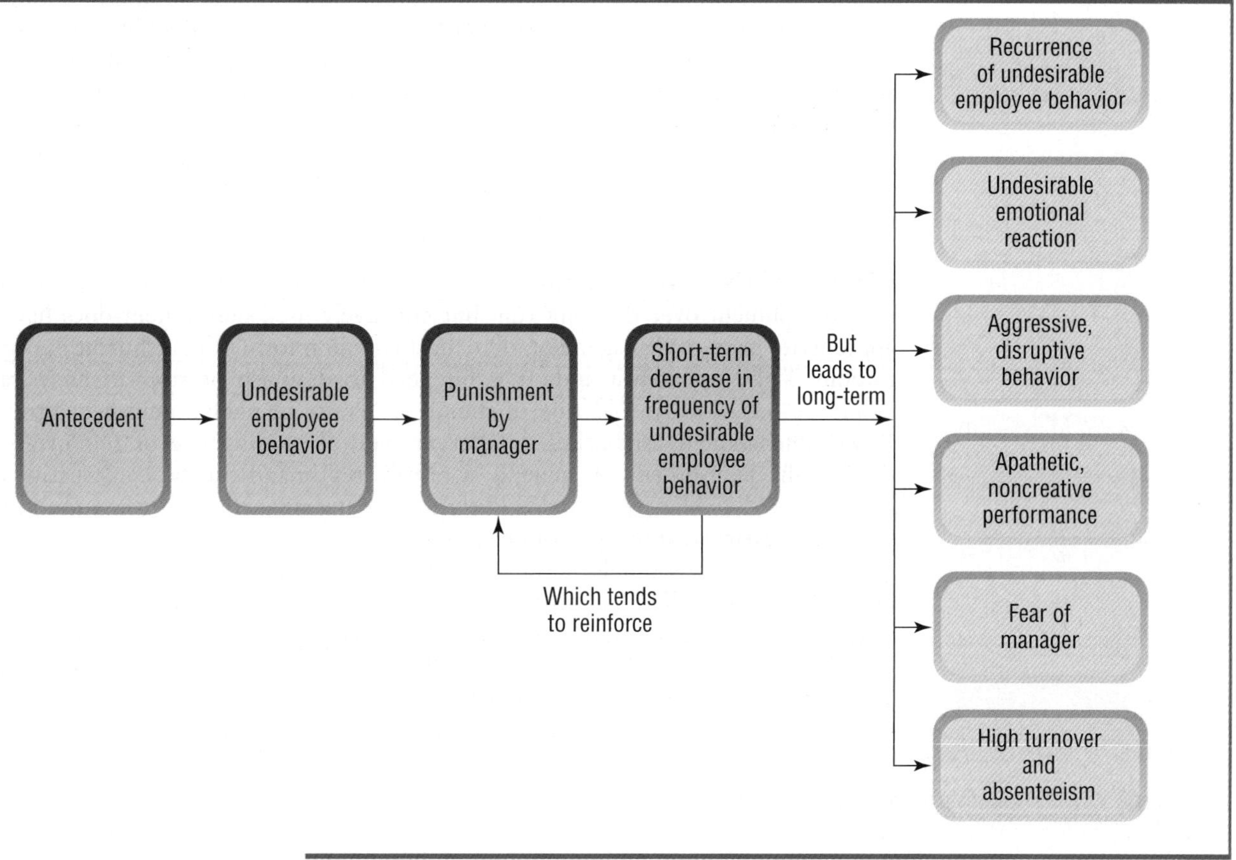

becomes contingent on the manager's presence. When the manager isn't around, the undesirable employee behavior is likely to recur.

In addition, the punished individual may try to avoid or escape the situation. From an organizational viewpoint, this reaction may be unacceptable if an employee avoids a particular, essential task. High absenteeism is a form of avoidance that is likely to occur when punishment is used frequently. Quitting is the employee's final form of escape, and organizations that depend on punishment are likely to have high rates of employee turnover. Some turnover is desirable, but excessive turnover is damaging to an organization. For instance, recruitment and training average more than $600 per employee at fast-food restaurants.

Punishment suppresses employee initiative and flexibility. Reacting to punishment, many an employee has said: "I'm going to do just what I'm told and nothing more." Such an attitude is undesirable because organizations depend on the personal initiative and creativity that individual employees bring to their jobs. Overusing punishment produces apathetic employees who are not an asset to an organization. Sustained punishment can also lead to low self-esteem. Low self-esteem, in turn, undermines the employee's self-confidence, which is necessary for performing most jobs (see Chapter 11).

Punishment produces a conditioned fear of management. That is, employees develop a general fear of punishment-oriented managers. Such managers become an environmental cue, indicating to employees the probability that an aversive event will occur. So if operations require frequent, normal, and positive interaction between employee and manager, such a situation can quickly become intolerable. Responses to fear, such as "hiding" or reluctance to communicate with a manager, may well hinder employee performance.

A manager may rely on punishment because it often produces fast results in the short run. In essence, the manager is reinforced for using punishment because the approach produces an immediate change in an employee's behavior. That may cause the manager to ignore punishment's long-term detrimental effects, which can be cumulative. Although a few incidents of punishment may not produce negative effects, its long-term, sustained use most often results in negative outcomes for the organization.

Effective Use of Punishment. Positive reinforcement is more effective than punishment over the long run, but effectively used punishment does have an appropriate place in management. The most common form of punishment in organizations is the oral reprimand. It is intended to diminish or stop an undesirable employee behavior. An old rule of thumb is "Praise in public; punish in private." Private punishment establishes a different type of contingency of reinforcement than public punishment. In general, a private reprimand can be constructive and informative. A public reprimand is likely to have negative effects because the person has been embarrassed in front of her peers.

Oral reprimands should never be given about behavior in general and especially never about a so-called bad attitude. An effective reprimand pinpoints and specifically describes the undesirable behavior to be avoided in the future. It focuses on the target behavior and avoids threatening the employee's self-image. The effective reprimand punishes specific undesirable behavior, not the person. Behavior is easier to change than the person.

> **THE COMPETENT LEADER**
>
> Tell me why I shouldn't fire the whole lot of you. We needed to make changes or we would be out of business.
>
> Carol Bartz, CEO of Autodesk

Punishment (by definition) trains a person in what not to do, not in what to do. Therefore, a manager must specify an alternative behavior to the employee. When the employee performs the desired alternative behavior, the manager must then reinforce that behavior positively.

Finally, managers should strike an appropriate balance between the use of pleasant and unpleasant events. The absolute number of unpleasant events isn't important, but the ratio of pleasant to unpleasant events is. When a manager uses positive reinforcement frequently, an occasional deserved punishment can be quite effective. However, if a manager never uses positive reinforcement and relies entirely on punishment, the long-run negative effects are likely to counteract any short-term benefits. Positive management procedures should dominate in any well-run organization.

John Huberman, a Canadian psychologist, began promoting the idea of positive discipline in the mid-1960s, but it wasn't until the 1970s when Richard Grote introduced positive discipline at Frito-Lay that the idea took hold. Grote began searching for a better management technique after a customer discovered a vulgar message written by a disgruntled employee on a corn chip. Grote gave the employee a day off with pay and called it "positive discipline." **Positive discipline** *emphasizes changing employee behaviors by reasoning rather than by imposing increasingly severe punishments.*[14] Management's primary duty is to help employees understand that the needs of the organization require certain standards of behavior and performance. A manager's task is to coach employees, issuing oral and then written reminders only when they fail to maintain behavioral and performance standards. It is the employee's responsibility to exercise self-discipline in achieving those standards. Many have used positive discipline to deal with problem employees and change undesirable employee behaviors. On the face of it, this approach sounds like a contradiction in terms. However, as illustrated in the following Change Competency feature about General Electric's approach, positive discipline places the responsibility for behavioral change with the one person who can best change that behavior—the employee.

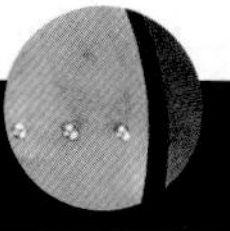

CHANGE COMPETENCY

DISCIPLINE WITHOUT PUNISHMENT

General Electric's program at its Vermont plant works as follows. An employee who comes to work late, does a sloppy job, or mistreats another employee gets an oral reminder about the behavior rather than a written reprimand. If the undesirable behavior continues, the employee is issued a written reminder. If the behavior still persists, the employee is suspended with pay for a day, called a "decision-making day." The purpose of the day is for the employee to decide whether to conform to the standards. The company pays the employee for this day to demonstrate its sincere effort to help him change. Paying the employee accomplishes two important things. First, it gives GE the opportunity to tell the employee that it is serious about the problem and wants the employee to use time this to think through whether GE is the right place for him. One boss said: "But if you decide to remain with us, another disciplinary problem will result in your termination." Second, paying the employee often eliminates the anger that commonly results from a person's ultimately being fired. The purpose of the day off with pay is to send a wake-up call.

Discipline without punishment does two things. First, it communicates to the employee that the organization is serious about the matter. The specific gap between the employee's performance and the performance GE expects is highlighted. It reminds the employee of his responsibility to meet GE's standards and gains the employee's agreement to solve this problem. Second, it sends a clear message to other employees who have been thinking about challenging the standards that the organization doesn't put up with unacceptable behavior—that GE's values and standards will not be compromised. Finally, the suspension provides tangible evidence that the employee's job is at risk.

General Electric's approach has been very successful. More than 85 percent of the employees going through the positive discipline program have changed their behaviors and stayed with the organization. Since the program started, reported written warnings and reminders dropped from 39 to 23 to 12 during a recent two-year period. Employees that don't change their behaviors are fired.

For more information on General Electric, visit the organization's home page at ***http://www.ge.com.***

Guidelines for Using Contingencies of Reinforcement

For a positive reinforcer to cause an employee to repeat a desired behavior, it must have value to that employee. If the employee is consistently on time, the manager or team leader positively reinforces this behavior by complimenting the employee. But, if the employee has been reprimanded in the past for coming to work late and then reports to work on time, the manager or team leader uses negative reinforcement and refrains from saying anything, because the employee is expected to come to work on time.

If the employee continues to come to work late, the manager or team leader can use either omission or punishment to try to stop this undesirable behavior. The team leader who chooses omission doesn't praise the tardy employee but simply ignores the employee. The use of punishment may include reprimanding, fining, or suspending—and ultimately firing—the employee if the behavior persists.

The following guidelines are recommended for using contingencies of reinforcement in the work setting.

- Do not reward all employees in the same way.
- Carefully examine the consequences of nonactions as well as actions.
- Let employees know which behaviors will be reinforced.
- Let employees know what they are doing wrong.
- Don't punish employees in front of others.
- Make the response equal to the behavior by not cheating workers out of their just rewards.[15]

LEARNING OBJECTIVE

3. List the four schedules of reinforcement and explain when each is effective.

SCHEDULES OF REINFORCEMENT

Managers using reinforcement to encourage the learning and performance of desired behaviors must choose a schedule for applying reinforcers. Although the schedule of reinforcement often depends on practical considerations (e.g., the nature of the person's job and the type of reinforcer being used, deliberately or not), reinforcement is always delivered according to some schedule.

Continuous and Intermittent Reinforcement

Continuous reinforcement *means that the behavior is reinforced each time it occurs and is the simplest schedule of reinforcement.* An example of continuous reinforcement is dropping coins in a soft-drink vending machine. The behavior of inserting coins is reinforced (on a continuous schedule) by the machine delivering a can of soda (most of the time!). Verbal recognition and material rewards generally are not delivered on a continuous schedule in organizations. In organizations such as Mary Kay Cosmetics, Tupperware, and Amway, salespeople are paid a commission for each sale, usually earning commissions of 25 to 50 percent of sales. Although the reinforcer (money) isn't paid immediately, as it is at Mini Maids, people track their sales immediately and quickly convert sales into amounts owed them by the organization. However, most managers who supervise employees other than salespeople seldom have the opportunity to deliver a reinforcer every time their employees demonstrate a desired behavior. Therefore, behavior typically is reinforced intermittently.

Intermittent reinforcement *refers to a reinforcer being delivered after some, but not every, occurrence of the desired behavior.* Intermittent reinforcement can be subdivided into (1) interval and ratio schedules and (2) fixed and variable schedules. In an **interval schedule,** *reinforcers are delivered after a certain amount of time has passed.* In a **ratio schedule,** *reinforcers are delivered after a certain number of behaviors have been performed.* These two schedules can be further subdivided into fixed (not changing) or variable (constantly changing) schedules. Figure 13.5 shows these four primary types of intermittent schedules: fixed interval, variable interval, fixed ratio, and variable ratio.[16]

Fixed Interval Schedule

A **fixed interval schedule** *means a constant amount of time must pass before a reinforcer is provided.* The first desired behavior to occur after the interval has elapsed is reinforced. For example, in a fixed interval, one-hour schedule, the first desired behavior that occurs after an hour has elapsed is reinforced.

Administering rewards according to this type of schedule tends to produce an uneven pattern of behavior. Prior to the reinforcement, the behavior is frequent and energetic. Immediately following the reinforcement, the behavior becomes less frequent and energetic. Why? Because the individual rather quickly figures out that

FIGURE 13.5 Four Types of Reinforcement Schedules

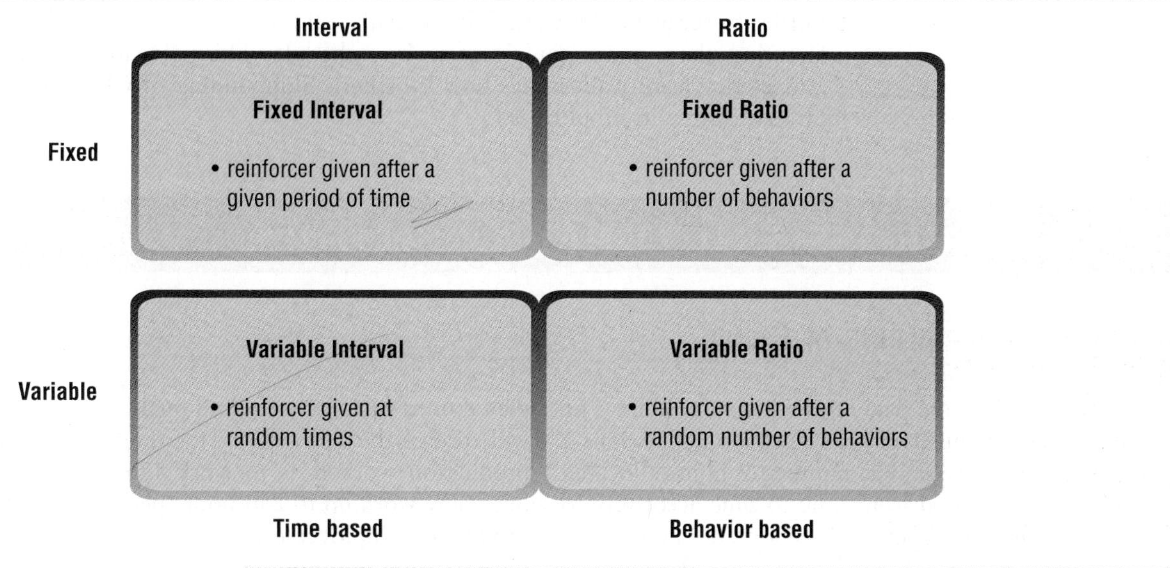

another reward won't immediately follow the last one—a certain amount of time must pass before it is given again. A common example of administering rewards on a fixed interval schedule is the payment of employees weekly, biweekly, or monthly. That is, monetary reinforcement comes regularly at the end of a specific period of time. Such time intervals, unfortunately, are generally too long to be an effective form of reinforcement for newly acquired work-related behavior. For example, Carl Sewell, owner of Sewell Lexus, tells all salespeople that they must sell at least 27 cars in three months. Therefore, during the third month, if a salesperson hasn't sold his or her quota, they try hard to sell cars by calling former clients, asking for referrals from existing clients, etc.

Variable Interval Schedule

A **variable interval schedule** *represents changes in the amount of time between reinforcers.* Jack Gustin, COO for University Hospitals in Cleveland, Ohio, uses a variable interval schedule to observe and reinforce the behaviors of housekeeping personnel. A person receives $100 for perfect attendance and a score above 92 percent on 23 performance indicators (e.g., floor swept, trash baskets emptied, room dusted, etc.). To observe their behavior, Gustin announced to all housekeeping employees that, during the month, he would make seven inspections at random times. During the first week, he observed and recorded the performance of employees on Tuesday between 3:00 and 4:00 P.M. and Wednesday from 6:00 to 7:30 A.M. The following week, he made no observations. During the third week, he observed employees on Monday between 10:00 and 11:00 A.M. and Friday from 12:00 to 1:45 P.M. During the fourth week, he observed employees on Monday between 8:00 and 9:00 P.M. and from 11:00 P.M. to 12:00 A.M. and on Thursday from 2:00 to 3:30 P.M. If he didn't change his schedule, the employees would anticipate his tours and adjust their behaviors to get a reward.

Fixed Ratio Schedule

In a **fixed ratio schedule,** *the desired behavior must occur a specified number of times before it is reinforced.* Administering rewards under a fixed ratio schedule tends to produce a high response rate when the time for reinforcement is close, followed by periods of steady behavior. The employee soon determines that reinforcement is based on the number of responses and performs the responses as quickly as possible in order to receive the reward. The individual piece-rate system used in many manufacturing plants is an example of such a schedule. The following Across Cultures Competency feature illustrates how Northern Shipbuilding of China uses this system to motivate its employees.[17]

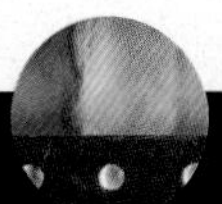

ACROSS CULTURES COMPETENCY

NORTHERN SHIPBUILDING OF CHINA

Production workers are paid on the basis of pieces. The firm allocates a number of hours per job and assigns a unit price to each piece. The number of hours allocated to each job is reviewed from time to time according to whether production targets are being met. The workers are paid 9.6 RMB (or US $1.17) per piece. Workers can complete several pieces per hour. If the job is completed on time to the required quality standard, workers will receive the full amount for the job. The norm for production workers is to work 176 hours per month, but many work up to 250 hours per month. An average production employee can earn 2,500 to 3,000 RMB per month.

Variable Ratio Schedule

In a **variable ratio schedule,** *a certain number of desired behaviors must occur before the reinforcer is delivered, but the number of behaviors varies around some average.* Managers frequently use a variable ratio schedule with praise and recognition. For example, team leaders at Alcatel vary the frequency of reinforcement when they give employees verbal approval for desired behaviors. Gambling casinos, such as Bally's and Harrah's, among others, and state lotteries use this schedule of reinforcement to lure patrons to shoot craps, play poker, feed slot machines, and buy lottery tickets. Patrons win, but not on any regular basis. The reason why variable ratio schedules are effective is that they create uncertainty about when the consequence will occur. Using this schedule makes sense for giving praise or auditing the behavior of people. People know that a consequence will be delivered, but not when. To avoid consequences of either punishment or omission, the person keeps demonstrating the desired behaviors.

Table 13.3 summarizes the four types of intermittent reinforcement schedules. The ratio schedules—fixed or variable—usually lead to better performance than do interval schedules. The reason is that ratio schedules are more closely related to the occurrence of desired behaviors than are interval schedules, which are based on the passage of time. The particular schedule of reinforcement is not as critical as the fact that reinforcement is based on the performance of desired behaviors.[18]

LEARNING OBJECTIVE

4. Describe how social learning theory explains the development of new behaviors.

SOCIAL LEARNING THEORY

Although operant conditioning accurately describes some of the major factors that influence learning, certain aspects are not covered by this theory. For example, a person's feelings and thoughts aren't considered. Albert Bandura and others have

TABLE 13.3 Comparison of Reinforcement Schedules

SCHEDULE	INFLUENCE ON PERFORMANCE	EXAMPLE
Fixed interval	Leads to average performance	Monthly paycheck
Fixed ratio	Leads quickly to high and stable performance	Piece-rate pay
Variable interval	Leads to moderately high and stable performance	Occasional praise by team members
Variable ratio	Leads to very high performance	Random quality checks with praise for zero defects

extended and expanded Skinner's work by demonstrating that people can learn new behavior by watching others in a social situation and then imitating their behavior.[19] **Social learning theory** *refers to knowledge acquisition through the mental processing of information.* In other words, the social part acknowledges that individuals learn by being part of a society and the learning part recognizes that individuals use thought processes to make decisions. People actively process information when they learn. By watching others perform a task, people develop mental pictures of how to perform the task. Bandura suggested that observers often learn faster than those who do not observe the behaviors of others because they don't need to unlearn behaviors and can avoid needless and costly errors.

Social learning theory has five dimensions—symbolizing, forethought, vicarious learning, self-control, and self-efficacy—as shown in Figure 13.6. These five dimensions can help you understand why different employees may behave differently when facing the same situation.

FIGURE 13.6 Five Dimensions of Social Cognitive Theory

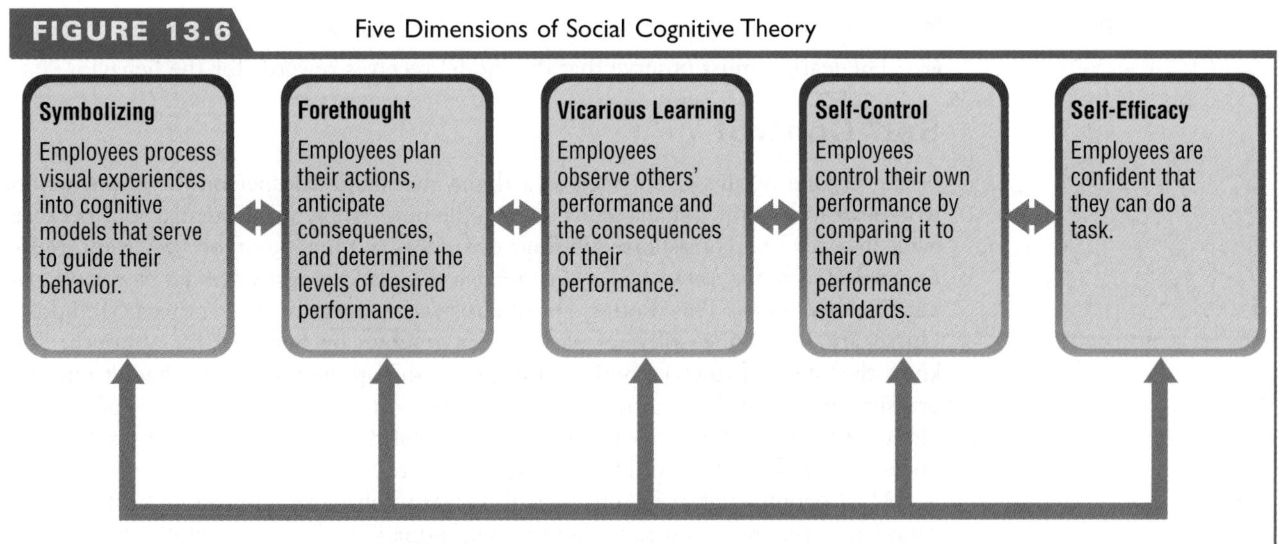

Source: Adapted from Stajkovic, A.D., and Luthans, F. Social cognitive theory and self-efficacy. *Organizational Dynamics*, Spring 1998, 65. Reprinted with permission.

Symbolizing

Individuals have an ability to use *symbols* that enable them to react to their environment. By using symbols, people process visual experiences and use the memories of them to guide their behavior. People imitate parents, friends, teachers, heroes, and others because they can identify with them. The symbolic process yields guidelines for behavior. If a golfer observes the swings of Tiger Woods or Anika Sorenstam on their web pages, this observation creates an image (symbol) in that person's mind of what a good golf swing looks like. Such images or symbols help the person swing a golf club the next time she plays golf. In a social situation, when those at the head of the table at a formal dinner begin to eat, their actions let the other diners know that starting to eat now is appropriate.

Forethought

People use *forethought* to anticipate, plan, and guide their behaviors and actions. For example, as the golfer who has watched the video of Woods or Sorenstam approaches a shot from a sand trap, she recalls the clips in the video where the pro was getting out of a trap. As a result, she adjusts her hands, feet, and body posture to the correct playing position to hit the shot. She anticipates where the ball will land and mentally plans her next shot.

Vicarious Learning

Vicarious learning *occurs when a person observes the behavior of others and the consequences of that behavior.* Employees' capacity to learn by observation enables them to obtain accurate information without having to perform these behaviors through trial and error. All self-help videos rely on vicarious learning. For vicarious learning to occur, several conditions must be met:

- The learner must observe the other person—the model—when the behavior is being performed.
- The learner must accurately perceive the model's behavior.
- The learner must remember the behavior.
- The learner must have the skills and abilities necessary to perform the behavior.
- The learner must observe that the model receives rewards for the behavior.[20]

Self-Control

Not everyone is cut out to work as a flight attendant, salesperson, or construction worker or to become a manager. Many people never apply for particular jobs because what they see isn't consistent with their own ideas of the type of job they want. **Self-control** *leads to the learning of a new behavior because a person selects his own goals and ways to reach them.* Tina Potter, an administrative assistant at Southern Methodist University, had a new software package for graphics on her desk for a month. She knew that she had to learn how to use it even though her supervisor hadn't put any pressure on her to do so. She worked Saturdays on her own to learn this new technique. Potter's goal was to learn to use the software to produce figures for this book—which she achieved. Her approach exhibited self-control.

Most people engage in self-control to learn behaviors both on and off the job. Mundane tasks (e.g., learning how to use e-mail) and more complex tasks (e.g., preparing a subordinate's performance appraisal) can be learned. When an employee learns through self-control, managers don't need to be controlling because the employee takes responsibility for learning and performing the desired behaviors. In fact, if a manager exercises control, it may well be redundant and counterproductive.

In recent years, the concept of teams, especially self-directed teams, has taken the business world by storm. Unfortunately, in many cases, management continues to exert too much control over teams, whose members then have few opportunities to apply self-control to their tasks. For teams to be effective, managers must empower their members to make decisions. **Empowerment** *means giving employees* *the authority, skills, and self-control to perform their tasks.*[21] The following Teams Competency feature highlights how Rowe Furniture empowers teams to improve productivity. Located in Virginia, Rowe supplies midpriced furniture to more than 1,500 retailers. Rowe makes upholstered furniture—sofas, ottomans, and such. One of the ways that Bruce Birnbach, Rowe's CEO, believes that his company can stay ahead of its competition is to offer more styles, better quality, and manufacture sofas in 10 days instead of six weeks like Rowe Furniture's competitors do.

TEAMS COMPETENCY

ROWE FURNITURE'S FOCUSED FACTORY

Rowe's specialized teams for cutting, sewing, framing, and upholstering were scattered throughout the plant with little interaction among them. The goal was to have the maximum amount of work in progress, with batches of inventory for other departments on the floor. There were problems with this system, including overdue orders being held back to create a batch and materials being easily lost. It was taking 27.5 hours for a cushion that required just 10 minutes to stitch to make it to stuffing, the next spot on the production line.

Rowe managers called town hall meetings with all 1,400 workers. In small groups, Birnbach said that changes were needed to keep Rowe competitive. One of the ideas that came from these sessions was the focus factory. Each focus factory was to be self-contained within the larger plant. This eliminates wasted floor space, and greatly reduces unnecessary walking and material handling. Cutters, sewers, framers, and upholsters sit together in a U-shape, roughly in production sequence, close enough to hand some pieces to one another. These workers are cross-trained so they can help each other out when needed. A sewer can reach for supplies and perform different operations in one place rather than walking to separate machines.

Once the line was up and running, workers were expected to improve its efficiency. Each week, a different worker is given a legal pad of paper. They are expected to use it to tell management five things they are doing right and five things that need improvement. Each morning, the members of the team assign a set number of pieces for that day. If the team finishes early, everyone goes home early, but they still get paid for a full day.

What are the results? Rowe produces 5 percent more furniture with 10 percent fewer workers. Since each focus factory operates like its own business, personnel savings get shared among team members. Work gets inspected and repaired immediately within each focus factory. The error rate is 0.1 percent compared to an industry average of 3 percent. One of the reasons for the jump in quality is because workers who sew arm pieces can now see the upholsters attach them to the frames. They now realize the need for a precise seam to make a snug fit. Absenteeism is nearly half of what it was previously at Rowe.

Self-Efficacy

Self-efficacy *refers to the individual's estimate of his or her own ability to perform a specific task in a particular situation.*[22] The greater the employee's perceived ability to perform the task, the higher will be the employee's self-efficacy. Employees with high self-efficacy believe that (1) they have the ability needed, (2) they are capable of the effort required, and (3) no outside events will keep them from performing at a high level. If employees have low self-efficacy, they believe that no matter how hard they try, something will happen to prevent them from reaching the desired level of performance. Self-efficacy influences people's choices of tasks and how long they will spend trying to reach their goals.[23] For example, a novice golfer who has taken only a few lessons might shoot a good round. Under such circumstances, the golfer might attribute the score to "beginner's luck" and not to ability. But, after many lessons and hours of practice, a person with low self-efficacy who still can't break 100 may decide that the demands of the game are too great to justify spending any more time on it. However, a high self-efficacy individual will try even harder to improve her game. This effort might include taking more lessons, watching videotapes of the individual's own swing, and practicing even harder and longer.

Self-efficacy has an impact on learning in three ways:

- *It influences the activities and goals that individuals choose for themselves.* In a sales contest at Pioneer Telephone Cooperative in Kingfisher, Oklahoma, employees with low self-efficacy didn't set challenging, or "stretch" goals. These people weren't lazy; they simply thought that they would fail to achieve a lofty goal. The high self-efficacy employees thought that they were capable of achieving high-performance goals—and did so.
- *It influences the effort that individuals exert on the job.* Individuals with high self-efficacy work hard to learn new tasks and are confident that their efforts will be rewarded. Low self-efficacy individuals lack confidence in their ability to succeed and see their extra effort as futile because they are likely to fail anyway.
- *It affects the persistence with which a person stays with a complex task.* Because high self-efficacy people are confident that they will perform well, they are likely to persist in spite of obstacles or in the face of temporary setbacks. At IBM, low-performing employees were more likely than high-performing employees to dwell on obstacles hindering their ability to do assigned tasks. When people believe that they aren't capable of doing the required work, their motivation to do a task will be low.

Organizational Guidelines

Managers (and fellow team members) can use social learning theory to help employees learn to believe in themselves. Past experience is the most powerful influence on behavior. At work, the challenge is to create situations in which the employee may respond successfully to the task(s) required. A manager's expectations for a subordinate's performance—as well as the expectations of peers—also can affect a person's self-efficacy. If a manager holds high expectations for an employee and provides proper training and suggestions, the person's self-efficacy is likely to increase. Small successes boost self-efficacy and lead to more substantial accomplishments later. If a manager holds low expectations for an employee and gives little constructive advice, the employee is likely to form an impression that he can't achieve the goal and, as a result, perform poorly.

Guidelines for using social learning theory to improve behavior in organizations include the following:[24]

- Identify the behaviors that will lead to improved performance.
- Select the appropriate model for employees to observe.
- Be sure that employees are capable of meeting the technical skills required by the new behaviors.
- Structure a positive learning situation to increase the likelihood that employees will learn the new behaviors and act accordingly.
- Provide positive consequences (praise, raises, or bonuses) to employees who perform as desired.
- Develop organizational practices that maintain the newly learned behaviors.

The effective use of self-control in learning requires that several conditions be met.[25] First, the person must engage in behaviors that he wouldn't normally want to perform. This distinguishes performing activities that the person enjoys from those involving self-control. At Mini Maids, not all employees wanted to be assistant team leaders. They had to take the initiative to learn how to read the Mapsco and other additional tasks. Second, the person must be able to use self-reinforcers, which are rewards that individuals give themselves. Some self-reinforcers include buying oneself a present, going out to a "great" restaurant, playing a round of golf at a nice course, and the like. Self-reinforcers come simply from a feeling of accomplishment or achievement. Third, the person must set goals that determine when self-reinforcers are to be applied. A person high in self-control doesn't randomly reward himself, but sets goals that determine when to self-reinforce. In doing so, the person relies on his own past performance, the performance of others on similar kinds of tasks, or some standard set by others. For example, one of the authors of this book is an accomplished golfer with a single-digit handicap. After playing a round in the 70s, he frequently buys himself a golf shirt as a self-reinforcer for a good round. Finally, the person must administer the self-reinforcer when the goal is achieved. The author buys himself a golf shirt only when he shoots a round in the 70s.

CHAPTER SUMMARY

1. Explain the role of classical and operant conditioning in fostering learning.

Classical conditioning began with Pavlov's work. He started a metronome (conditioned stimulus) at the same time food was placed in the dog's mouth (unconditioned stimulus). Quickly the sound of the metronome alone evoked salivation. Operant conditioning focuses on the effects of reinforcement on desirable and undesirable behaviors. Changes in behavior result from the consequences of previous behavior. People tend to repeat a behavior that leads to a pleasant result and not to repeat a behavior that leads to an unpleasant result. In short, when a behavior is reinforced, it is repeated; when it is punished or not reinforced, it is not repeated.

2. Describe the contingencies of reinforcement that influence behavior.

The two types of reinforcement are (1) positive reinforcement, which increases a desirable behavior because the person is provided with a pleasurable outcome after the behavior has occurred; and (2) negative reinforcement, which also maintains the desirable behavior by presenting an unpleasant event before the behavior occurs and stopping the event when the behavior occurs. Both positive and negative reinforcement increase the frequency of a desirable behavior. Conversely, omission and punishment reduce the frequency of an undesirable behavior. Omission involves stopping everything that reinforces the behavior. A punisher is an unpleasant event that follows the behavior and reduces the probability that the behavior will be repeated.

3. List the four schedules of reinforcement and explain when each is effective.

There are four schedules of reinforcement. In the fixed interval schedule, the reward is given on a fixed time basis (e.g., a weekly or monthly paycheck). It is effective for maintaining a level of behavior. In the variable interval schedule, the reward is given around some average time during a specific period of time (e.g., the plant manager walking through the plant an average of five times every week). This schedule of reinforcement can maintain a high level of performance because employees don't know when the reinforcer will be delivered. The fixed ratio schedule ties rewards to certain outputs (e.g., a piece-rate system). This schedule maintains a steady level of behavior once the person has earned the reinforcer. In the variable ratio schedule, the reward is given around some mean, but the number of behaviors varies (e.g., a payoff from a slot machine). This schedule is the most powerful because both the number of desired behaviors and their frequency change.

4. Describe how social learning theory explains the development of new behaviors.

Social learning theory focuses on people learning new behaviors by observing others and then modeling their own behaviors on those observed. The five factors emphasized in social learning theory are symbolizing, forethought, vicarious learning, self-control, and self-efficacy.

KEY TERMS AND CONCEPTS

Antecedent
Aversive events
Classical conditioning
Consequence
Contingency of reinforcement
Continuous reinforcement
Empowerment
Escape learning
Fixed interval schedule
Fixed ratio schedule
Intermittent reinforcement
Interval schedule
Kaizen
Learning
Negative reinforcement
Omission
Operant conditioning
Positive discipline
Positive events
Positive reinforcement
Primary reinforcer
Principle of contingent reinforcement
Principle of immediate reinforcement
Principle of reinforcement deprivation
Principle of reinforcement size
Punishment
Ratio schedule
Reinforcement
Reward
Secondary reinforcer
Self-control
Self-efficacy
Social learning theory
Variable interval schedule
Variable ratio schedule
Vicarious learning

DISCUSSION QUESTIONS

1. What are the basic differences between classical conditioning and operant conditioning? Which type is most important for managers? Why?
2. What principles of reinforcement did Mini Maids use?
3. What schedule(s) of reinforcement can a manager use to improve productivity? What schedules of reinforcement did Logan use at Kodak?
4. How can a team leader use punishment effectively?
5. How did Rowe Furniture use social learning theory to improve employee performance?
6. When are employees likely to engage in self-control?
7. Steven Kerr wrote an article entitled "On the Folly of Rewarding A While Hoping for B." The essence of the article is that organizations often unintentionally reward behaviors that they don't want to occur. Find some examples of this behavior.
8. Visit either a local health club or diet center and schedule an interview with the manager. What types of rewards does it give its members who achieve targeted goals? Does it use punishment?
9. How do producers of self-help videos use social learning theory to change a person's behavior?
10. How can a manager or a team raise an employee's level of self-efficacy?

EXPERIENTIAL EXERCISE AND CASES

Experiential Exercise: Self Competency

What Is Your Self-Efficacy?[26]

The following questionnaire gives you a chance to gain insights into your self-efficacy in terms of achieving academic excellence. Please answer the following seven questions in the spaces provided, using the following five-point scale. An interpretation of your score follows the questions.

5 = Strongly agree
4 = Agree
3 = Moderate
2 = Disagree
1 = Strongly disagree

1. I am a good student. 5 4 3 2 1
2. It is difficult to maintain a study schedule. 5 4 3 2 1
3. I know the right things to do to improve my academic performance. 5 4 3 2 1
4. I find it difficult to convince my friends who have different viewpoints on studying than mine. 5 4 3 2 1
5. My temperament is not well suited to studying. 5 4 3 2 1
6. I am good at finding out what teachers want. 5 4 3 2 1
7. It is easy for me to get others to see my point of view. 5 4 3 2 1

Add your scores to questions 1, 3, 6, and 7. Enter that score here _____. For questions, 2, 4, and 5, reverse the scoring key. That is, if you answered question 2 as strongly agree, give yourself 1 point, agree is worth 2 points, and so on. Enter your score here for questions 2, 4, and 5 ______. Enter your combined score here _________. This is your *self-efficacy* score for academic achievement. If you scored between 28 and 35, you believe that you can achieve academic excellence. Scores lower than 18 indicate that you believe, no matter how hard you try to achieve academic excellence, something may prevent you from reaching your desired level of performance. Scores between 19 and 27 indicate a moderate degree of self-efficacy. Your self-efficacy may vary with the course you are taking. In courses in your major, you may have greater self-efficacy than in those outside of your major.

Case: Ethics Competency

Medical Incentives

Members of Harris Methodist Health Plan, a 310,000 member health maintenance organization (HMO) in Dallas, Texas, sued the HMO because it fined primary care doctors (general practitioners, pediatricians, and internists) who wrote more prescriptions than their contracts allowed. Texas regulators found that most of Harris's compensation arrangement with physicians violated the law. Under Harris's contracts, the insurer pays its physicians a set percentage (ranging from 10 to 12.8 percent) of each member's monthly premium to cover all services that a person might need. Doctors who can keep their patients healthy and out of the office can make a profit. Like most HMOs, Harris offers bonuses to doctors who meet a predetermined budget for hospitalizations and referrals to specialists. Harris had a policy of firing physicians who wrote more prescriptions than their contracts allowed. In 1997, doctors spent $4.5 million over the limit, resulting in a loss to the HMO of $1.5 million. As a result, physicians stopped referring patients to a specialist and dropped writing prescriptions that had to be filled at the Harris pharmacy in order not to be fined and/or fired.

Richard Hubner, a primary care physician, sued the HMO because it withheld more than $8,000 from him because of deficits in his pharmacy budget. He contended that his patients needed drugs to return to their health and that he shouldn't be fined for helping patients. Kent Clay, an attorney for patients, is also suing the HMO for not referring patients to specialists because it is affecting the primary care physician's pocketbook. The HMO is accused of not providing quality care because this level of care affects the HMO's profitability and its profits are shared with all primary care physicians.[27]

Questions

1. What contingencies of reinforcement did Harris HMO adopt to pay its primary care physicians? How have these methods affected patient care?
2. What are some of the ethical dilemmas facing Harris HMO?
3. If you were the chief administrator of Harris HMO, what would you do to correct the problem?
4. What elements of the Ethics Competency are represented in this case (see Chapter 1)?

Case: Change Competency

Westinghouse

At the Westinghouse plant in College Station, Texas, management was committed to develop a high-commitment culture that would motivate employees to feel a sense of responsibility for the electronic parts they were making. Employees worked in 8- to 12-person teams and tracked and monitored their own performance. All employees were on salary, and raises were based on performance. Thus workers who showed proficiency in various jobs could boost their pay significantly.

When the plant first opened, management's attendance goal was 98 percent. After approximately 18 months of operation, this attendance goal was not being achieved, although management didn't have a system in place to track attendance specifically. Managers believed that attendance was somewhere around 93 percent, with the industry average between 93 and 97 percent. Westinghouse management estimated that each 1 percentage-point drop in attendance cost the company an additional $80,000. Management believed that this figure, based solely on hiring temporary workers for the day, was conservative and didn't account for lower team productivity, increased scrap costs, lost customer orders, and the like.

A task force of managers and employees was formed to design and implement a process to monitor attendance and make suggestions for improvement. The group designed a program that its members hoped would motivate employees to meet or exceed a 97 percent attendance rate. Attendance performance was categorized as follows.

Level 1: Perfect (100%), with no make-up time.
Level 2: Good to excellent (97–100%), including make-up time.
Level 3: Needing improvement (95–96.9%), including make-up time.
Level 4: Unacceptable (below 95%).

Positive reinforcement was used at Levels 1 and 2. Perfect attendance for 1 month was rewarded by listing employee names in the Westinghouse newsletter; perfect attendance for the entire team led to its being mentioned in the local newspaper. Perfect attendance for 6 months brought a letter of commendation from the plant manager, a paid luncheon, and reserved parking privileges. Perfect attendance for a year brought a $100 gift certificate, letters of commendation from headquarters, listing the employee's name on plaques displayed in the plant, and reserved parking. For Level 2 attendance, longer amounts of time were needed to earn rewards. It took 3 months for an individual to have his or her name mentioned in the Westinghouse newspaper, 6 months for an employee to get a paid luncheon, and 1 year for an employee to receive a commendation from the department manager and receive a gift certificate for $50.

At Level 3, employees were verbally warned by their manager to improve their attendance. Steps to increase their attendance were discussed with the team leader and department manager. Employees in Level 3 had to develop an action plan to improve their attendance. A follow-up meeting at the end of 2 months was scheduled to evaluate their performance and/or revise their action plans.

At Level 4, additional verbal warnings were given; a formal document was prepared by the team leader and department manager and forwarded to the plant manager; and a person's pay was docked. Termination was discussed unless attendance improved to 97 percent within the next month.[28]

Questions

1. What contingencies of reinforcement did the task force recommend to improve attendance? What schedule(s) of reinforcement did it recommend?
2. Given these rewards, would you improve your attendance? If so, why? If not, why?
3. What do you think happened at the plant? Did attendance improve?
4. Using the concepts outlined in this chapter, support your answer.

CHAPTER 14

Fundamentals of Motivation

LEARNING OBJECTIVES

When you have finished studying this chapter, you should be able to:

1. Explain the motivational process.
2. Describe two basic human needs approaches to motivation.
3. Explain how the design of jobs affects motivation.
4. Describe the expectancy model of motivation.
5. State how feelings of equity and inequity affect motivation.

Preview Case: Starbucks

THE BASIC MOTIVATIONAL PROCESS

Core Phases

Motivational Challenges

MOTIVATING EMPLOYEES THROUGH SATISFYING HUMAN NEEDS

Needs Hierarchy Model

Achievement Motivation Model

Self Competency—John Schnatter of Papa John's Pizza

MOTIVATING EMPLOYEES THROUGH JOB DESIGN

Motivator–Hygiene Model

Job Characteristics Model

Teams Competency—SEI Investments

Cultural Influences

MOTIVATING EMPLOYEES THROUGH PERFORMANCE EXPECTATIONS

Expectancy Model

Across Cultures Competency—McProgrammers

MOTIVATING EMPLOYEES THROUGH EQUITY

Equity Model: Balancing Inputs and Outcomes

Ethics Competency—Employee Theft

Procedural Justice: Making Decisions Fairly

CHAPTER SUMMARY

KEY TERMS AND CONCEPTS

DISCUSSION QUESTIONS

EXPERIENTIAL EXERCISE AND CASE

STARBUCKS

PREVIEW CASE

The Starbucks Support Center is located at Starbucks Coffee Company's headquarters in Seattle. As one of *Fortune* magazine's "100 Best Companies to Work for in America," not to mention one of the world's fastest-growing chains of coffee houses, Starbucks has been treating its employees well since it started in 1971. Woven into the company's mission statement is the objective to "provide a great work environment and treat each other with respect and dignity." It takes more than company declarations to motivate and inspire people. So how does this company on an aggressive growth track motivate more than 74,000 people and inspire balance and a team spirit?

The answer is what Starbucks refers to as "a special blend of employee benefits" and a work/life program that focuses on the physical, mental, emotional, and creative aspects of each person. Starbucks developed an innovative work/life program to create a committed coffee culture—and a long-term partnership. In fact, employees at Starbucks are called *partners.*

Joan Moffat, the Starbucks manager of partner relations and work/life, is responsible for the company's work/life program. It includes on-site fitness services, referral and educational support to help employees meet child-care and eldercare needs, an info-line for convenient information, and the Partner Connection—a program that links employees with shared interests and hobbies. Starbucks has comparatively low health-care costs, low absenteeism, and one of the strongest retention rates in the industry. "Our turnover rate is 60 percent, which is excellent as compared to the restaurant and retail industry," says Moffat. Moreover, employees reap the benefits of the company's ongoing success.

Starbucks is committed to providing an atmosphere that fosters respect and values the contributions that people make each day, regardless of who or where they are within the company. All partners who work a minimum 20 hours a week receive full medical and dental coverage, vacation days, and stock options as part of the Starbucks Bean Stock program. Eligible partners can choose health coverage from two managed care plans or a catastrophic plan. They also can select one of two dental plans or a vision plan. Because its workforce is young and healthy, Starbucks has low health-benefit costs. According to Annette King, the human resources (HR) benefits manager, the company's health-care costs are approximately 20 percent lower than the national average.

The company also provides disability and life insurance, a discounted stock purchase plan, and a retirement savings plan with company matching contributions. These benefits provide a powerful incentive for partners, particularly those working part time, to stay with the company, thus reducing Starbucks' recruiting and training costs. "We have historically had low turnover, most of which can be attributed to the culture and a sense of community," says Moffat.

Several years ago, the HR staff began examining how the company could become more attuned to employees' wants and needs. For instance, some employees who started with the company when they were in college are now buying homes and dealing with the realities of child care and elder care. Starbucks responded by providing flexible work schedules as part of its work/life program. "Our environment lends itself to meet multiple life demands. By virtue of our strong sales and accelerated growth, flex schedules have not hurt productivity in the least," says Moffat. "Flexibility is particularly inherent in our stores because of our extended hours of operation and the diversity of our workforce—from students to parents—who need to work alternative hours."

For more information on Starbucks, visit the organization's home page at ***http://www.starbucks.com.***

Recent studies have shown that 60 percent of U.S. workers have child-care or elder-care responsibilities. Starbucks recognized—as many other companies have—that partners less encumbered by personal stress and obligations are more innovative and productive. Starbucks implemented several programs that specifically address the life stages and personal needs of its workforce. To help deal with the fast-paced and demanding environment at Starbucks, it also provides referral services for partners and eligible dependents enrolled in the medical plan. It connects them with information that helps make extraordinary life demands more manageable. Moffat recently put the program to use when she needed elder-care advice for her grandmother. In another case, a partner needed emergency child care for his ill son. Starbucks' Working Solutions program made prompt arrangements for a certified in-home caretaker, no work was missed, and Starbucks covered half the cost.[1]

Howard Schultz, chairman and CEO of Starbucks, says that his greatest challenge is to attract, develop, and manage a worldwide workforce. He believes that Starbucks must provide motivational systems that will cut costs while maintaining high quality. Permitting employees to participate in the incentive programs described in the Preview Case, among others, has led to greater productivity. Starbucks can be found in restaurants, hotels, offices, on airline flights, and in more than 8,800 stores in 30 countries, including Australia, Germany, Japan, China, the United States, and the United Kingdom. There is even a Starbucks in China's Forbidden City.[2]

LEARNING OBJECTIVE

1. Explain the motivational process.

THE BASIC MOTIVATIONAL PROCESS

The question of exactly what it takes to motivate people to work has received a great deal of attention. In addressing this question, we focus on four different approaches: (1) meeting basic human needs, (2) designing jobs that motivate people, (3) enhancing the belief that desired rewards can be achieved, and (4) treating people equitably. The interrelated nature of these approaches is illustrated in Figure 14.1. Before turning our attention to these approaches, we need to define motivation.

FIGURE 14.1 Basics of Workplace Motivation

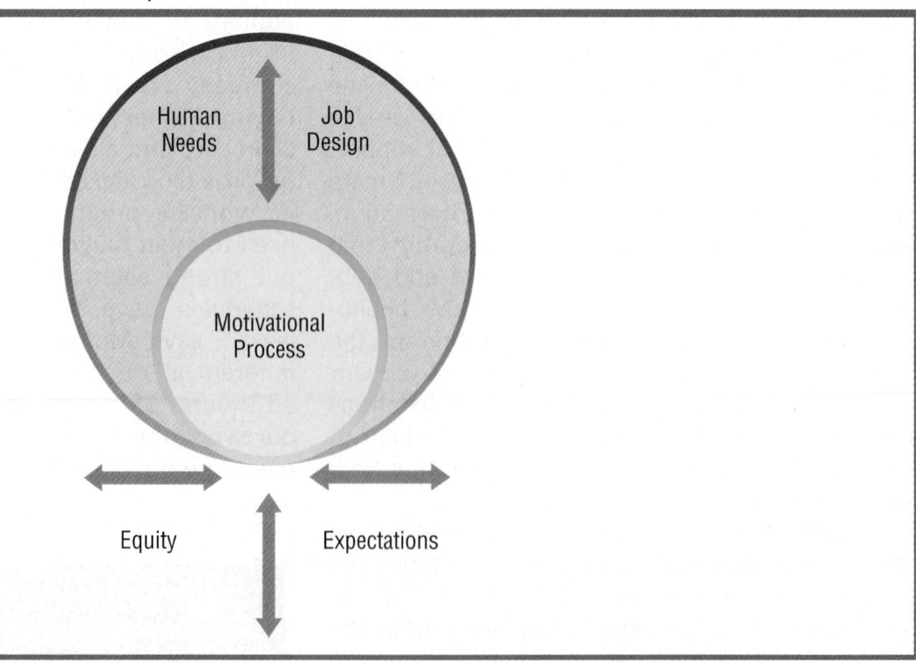

Motivation *represents the forces acting on or within a person that cause the person to behave in a specific, goal-directed manner.*[3] Because motives of employees affect their productivity, one of management's jobs is to channel employee motivation effectively toward achieving organizational goals. However, motivation isn't the same as performance. Even the most highly motivated employees may not be successful in their jobs, especially if they don't have the competencies needed to perform the jobs or work under unfavorable job conditions. Although job performance involves more than motivation, motivation is an important factor in achieving high performance.[4]

Experts might not agree about everything that motivates employees—and the effects of working conditions on their careers—but they do agree that an organization must

- attract people to the organization and encourage them to remain with it,
- allow people to perform the tasks for which they were hired, and
- stimulate people to go beyond routine performance and become creative and innovative in their work.

Thus, for an organization to be effective, it must tackle the motivational challenges involved in arousing people's desires to be productive members of the organization.

Core Phases

A key motivational principle states that performance is a function of a person's level of ability and motivation. This principle is often expressed by the following formula:

$$\text{Performance} = f\,(\text{ability} \times \text{motivation}).$$

According to this principle, no task can be performed successfully unless the person who is to carry it out has the ability to do so. **Ability** *is the person's natural talent, as well as learned competencies, for performing goal-related tasks.* Regardless of a person's competence, however, ability alone isn't enough to ensure performance at a high level. The person must also *want* to achieve a high level of performance. Thus, discussions of motivation generally are concerned with (1) what drives behavior, (2) what direction behavior takes, and (3) how to maintain that behavior.

The motivational process begins with identifying a person's needs, shown as phase 1 in Figure 14.2. **Needs** *are deficiencies that a person experiences at a particular time* (phase 1). These deficiencies may be psychological (e.g., the need for recognition), physiological (e.g., the need for water, air, or food), or social (e.g., the need for friendship). Needs often act as energizers. That is, needs create tensions within the individual, who finds them uncomfortable and therefore is likely to make an effort (phase 2) to reduce or eliminate them.

Motivation is goal directed (phase 3). A **goal** *is a specific result that an individual wants to achieve.* An employee's goals often are driving forces, and accomplishing those goals can significantly reduce needs. For example, some employees have strong drives for advancement and expectations that working long hours on highly visible projects will lead to promotions, raises, and greater influence. Such needs and expectations often create uncomfortable tension within such individuals. Believing that certain specific behaviors can overcome this tension, these employees act to reduce it. Employees striving to advance may seek to work on major problems facing the organization in order to gain visibility and influence with senior managers (phase 4). Promotions and raises are two of the ways in which organizations attempt to maintain desirable behaviors. They are signals (feedback) to employees that their needs for advancement and recognition and their behaviors are appropriate or inappropriate (phase 5). Once the employees have received either rewards or punishments, they reassess their needs (phase 6).

FIGURE 14.2 Core Phases of the Motivational Process

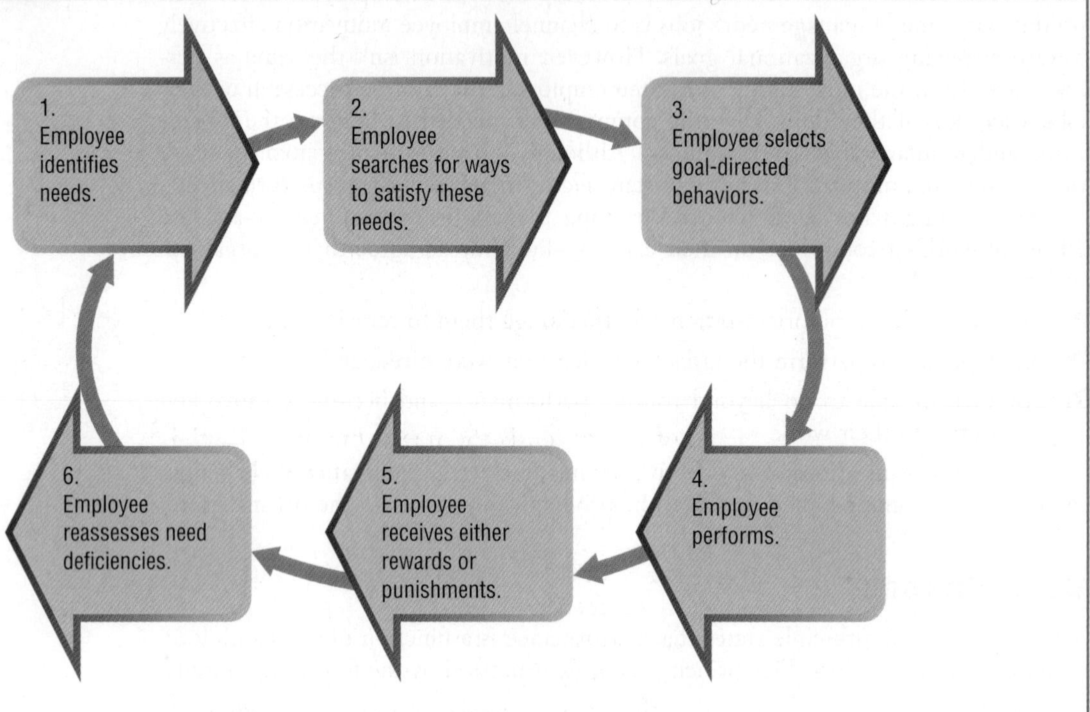

Motivational Challenges

In concept, the basic motivational process just described is simple and straightforward. In the real world, of course, the process isn't as clear-cut. The first challenge is that motives can only be inferred; they cannot be seen. Leslie Lenser, head of project and systems management at American Computer Systems, observed two employees in her department who were debugging software programs that estimate service requirements for the company. She knows that both employees are responsible for the same type of work, have received similar training, have similar competencies, and have been with the organization for about five years. One employee is able to spot problems more easily and quickly than the other, so the difference in their output strongly suggests that they have different levels of motivation. Lenser recognized that she would have to investigate further to determine what motivates each person.

A second challenge centers on the dynamic nature of needs. As we pointed out in the Preview Case, Starbucks has developed numerous programs in its attempt to meet employee needs. Doing so is always difficult because, at any one time, everyone has various needs, desires, and expectations. Moreover, these factors change over time and may also conflict with each other. Employees who put in many extra hours at work to fulfill their needs for accomplishment may find that these extra work hours conflict directly with needs for affiliation and their desires to be with their families.

A third challenge involves the considerable differences in people's motivations and in the energy with which people respond to them. Just as different organizations produce a variety of products and offer a variety of services, different people have a variety of motivations. Chris Koski, a marketing manager for Celanese Chemical Corporation in the United States, took a three-year assignment with her company in Sweden. She quickly joined a group of American managers so she could satisfy her need to belong to such a group and to learn quickly about Swedish management practices. She discovered that Swedes frequently bypass formal lines of communication and go directly to the person most likely to have the information and expertise, not necessarily their boss. If a Swedish employee would work in the Italian branch of her organization, this behavior would be a sign of disrespect. Why? Italian managers believe that frequently bypassing a boss indicates a poorly designed organization.[5]

All of these challenges are things that managers can do something about. They can determine what motivates employees and use this knowledge to channel employees' energies toward the achievement of the organization's goals. With this opportunity in mind, we devote the rest of the chapter to various approaches to motivation that managers can apply.

MOTIVATING EMPLOYEES THROUGH SATISFYING HUMAN NEEDS

LEARNING OBJECTIVE

2. Describe two basic human needs approaches to motivation.

Needs Hierarchy Model

The most widely recognized model of motivation is the **needs hierarchy model.** Abraham H. Maslow suggested *that people have a complex set of exceptionally strong needs, that can be arranged in a hierarchy.*[6] Underlying this hierarchy are the following basic assumptions:

- Once a need has been satisfied, its motivational role declines in importance. However, as one need is satisfied, another need gradually emerges to take its place, so people are always striving to satisfy some need.
- The needs network for most people is very complex, with several needs affecting behavior at any one time. Clearly, when someone faces an emergency, such as desperate thirst, that need dominates until it is gratified.
- Lower level needs must be satisfied, in general, before higher level needs are activated sufficiently to drive behavior.
- There are more ways of satisfying higher level than lower level needs.

This model states that a person has five types of needs: physiological, security, affiliation, esteem, and self-actualization. Figure 14.3 shows these five needs categories, arranged in Maslow's hierarchy.

FIGURE 14.3 Maslow's Needs Hierarchy

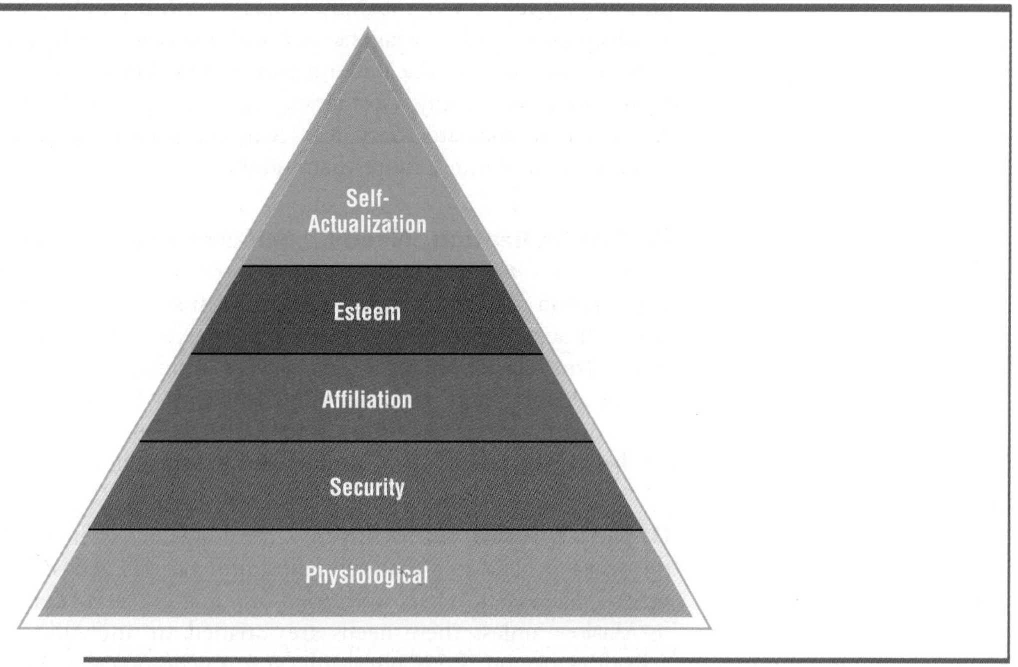

Physiological Needs. **Physiological needs** *are the desire for food, water, air, and shelter.* They are the lowest level in Maslow's hierarchy. People concentrate on satisfying these needs before turning to higher order needs. Managers should understand that, to the extent employees are motivated by physiological needs, their concerns do not center on the work they are doing. They will accept any job that meets those needs. Managers who focus on physiological needs in trying to motivate subordinates assume that people work primarily for money. Hershey Foods, for example, offers insurance rebates to employees who live healthy lifestyles (e.g., physically fit nonsmokers) and raise premiums for those at greater risk. In this way, they offer incentives to encourage wellness activities.

Security Needs. **Security needs** *are the desire for safety, stability, and absence of pain, threat, or illness.* Like physiological needs, unsatisfied security needs cause people to be preoccupied with satisfying them. People who are motivated primarily by security needs value their jobs mainly as defenses against the loss of basic needs satisfaction. Managers who feel that security needs are important focus on protecting workers from hazards in their environment by providing them with hard hats, goggles, and ergonomic keyboards (which prevent carpal tunnel syndrome). Psychological safety is also important. By offering health, life, and disability insurance, organizations promote their employees' sense of security and well-being.

Affiliation Needs. **Affiliation needs** *are the desire for friendship, love, and a feeling of belonging.* When physiological and security needs have been satisfied, affiliation needs emerge. Managers should realize that, when affiliation needs are the primary source of motivation, people value their work as an opportunity for finding and establishing warm and friendly interpersonal relationships. Managers and team leaders who believe that employees are striving primarily to satisfy these needs are likely to act supportively. They emphasize employee acceptance by coworkers, extracurricular activities (e.g., organized sports programs, cultural events, and company celebrations), and team-based norms.

Esteem Needs. *The desire for feelings of achievement, self-worth and recognition or respect are all* **esteem needs.** People with esteem needs want others to accept them for what they are and to perceive them as competent and able. Managers who focus on esteem needs try to motivate employees with public rewards and recognition for achievements. Such managers may use lapel pins, articles in the company paper, achievement lists on the bulletin board, and the like to foster employees' pride in their work. Mary Kay Cosmetics rewards top performers with a pink Cadillac. According to the late Mary Kay Ash, the founder of her company, people want recognition and praise more than money.

Self-Actualization Needs. **Self-actualization needs** *involve people realizing their full potential and becoming all that they can become.* People who strive for self-actualization seek to increase their problem-solving abilities. Managers who emphasize self-actualization may involve employees in designing jobs, make special assignments that capitalize on employees' unique skills, or give employee teams leeway in planning and implementing their work. The self-employed often have strong self-actualization needs. When Mary Kay Ash founded her firm in 1963, she acted on her belief that, when a woman puts her priorities in order, she can indeed have it all.

Organizational Guidelines. Maslow's needs hierarchy model also suggests the types of behaviors that will help fulfill various needs. *The three lowest categories of needs—physiological, safety, and social—are also known as* **deficiency needs.** According to Maslow, unless these needs are satisfied, an individual will fail to develop into a healthy person, both physically and psychologically. In contrast, *esteem and self-*

actualization needs are known as **growth needs.** Satisfaction of these needs helps a person grow and develop as a human being.

This model provides incomplete information about the origin of needs. However, it implies that higher level needs are present in most people, even if they don't recognize or act to meet those needs. These higher level needs will motivate most people if nothing occurs to block their emergence.

The needs hierarchy is based on U.S. cultural values. In cultures that value uncertainty avoidance, such as Japan and Greece, job security and lifelong employment are stronger motivators than self-actualization. Moreover, in Denmark, Sweden, and Norway, the value and rewards of a high quality of life are more important than productivity. Thus, social needs are stronger than self-actualization and self-esteem needs. In countries such as China, Japan, and Korea that value collectivist and community practices over individual achievements, belonging and security are considerably more important than meeting growth needs. Therefore, although the needs that Maslow identified may be universal, the logic or sequence of the hierarchy differs from culture to culture.[7]

Maslow's work has received much attention from managers, as well as psychologists.[8] Research has found that top managers are better able to satisfy their esteem and self-actualization needs than are lower level managers; part of the reason is that top managers have more challenging jobs and opportunities for self-actualization. Employees who work on a team have been able to satisfy their higher level needs by making decisions that affect their team and organization. At the Miller Brewing Company's plant in Trenton, Ohio, groups of employees are trained to perform multiple tasks, including hiring and training team members—and even firing those who fail to perform adequately. As team members learn new tasks, they start satisfying their higher level needs. Employees who have little or no control over their work (e.g., assembly-line workers) may not even experience higher level needs in relation to their jobs. Studies have also shown that the fulfillment of needs differs according to the job a person performs, a person's age and background, and the size of the company. "Not everyone is motivated in the same way. You shouldn't assume that it's a one-size-fits-all solution. You have to understand people's needs," says Susan Dallas, a manager for business development at Gartner, an information technology consulting firm in San Diego.

Achievement Motivation Model

David McClelland proposed a learned needs model of motivation that he believed to be rooted in culture.[9] He argued that everyone has three particularly important needs: for achievement, affiliation, and power. Individuals who possess a *strong power motive* take action that affects the behaviors of others and has a strong emotional appeal. These individuals are concerned with providing status rewards to their followers. Individuals who have a *strong affiliation motive* tend to establish, maintain, and restore close personal relationships with others. Individuals who have a *strong achievement motive* compete against some standard of excellence or unique contribution against which they judge their behaviors and achievements.

McClelland has studied achievement motivation extensively, especially with regard to entrepreneurship. His **achievement motivation model** *states that people are motivated according to the strength of their desire either to perform in terms of a standard of excellence or to succeed in competitive situations.* According to McClelland, almost all people believe that they have an "achievement motive," but probably only about 10 percent of the U.S. population is strongly motivated to achieve. The amount of achievement motivation that people have depends on their childhood, their personal and occupational experiences, and the type of organization for which they work. Table 14.1 shows an application of McClelland's model to presidents of the United States. Presidents' motives can be documented by the legislation they have proposed and the policies they have pursued during their tenures. Look at the table and see if you would rank the presidents' motives in the same way we did.

TABLE 14.1 Presidents' Needs for Power, Achievement, and Affiliation

PRESIDENT	NEEDS Power	Achievement	Affiliation
Bush, G. W.	Moderate	High	Low
Clinton, B.	Moderate	High	High
Reagan, R.	High	Moderate	Low
Kennedy, J. F.	High	Low	High
Roosevelt, F. D.	High	Moderate	Low
Lincoln, A.	Moderate	Low	Moderate
Washington, G.	Low	Low	Moderate

According to McClelland's model, motives are "stored" in the preconscious mind just below the level of full awareness. They lie between the conscious and the unconscious, in the area of daydreams, where people talk to themselves without quite being aware of it. A basic premise of the model is that the pattern of these daydreams can be tested and that people can be taught to change their motivation by changing these daydreams.

Measuring Achievement Motivation. McClelland measured the strength of a person's achievement motivation with the **Thematic Apperception Test (TAT).** *The TAT uses unstructured pictures that may arouse many kinds of reactions in the person being tested.* Examples include an inkblot that a person can perceive as many different objects or a picture that can generate a variety of stories. There are no right or wrong answers, and the person isn't given a limited set of alternatives from which to choose. A major goal of the TAT is to obtain the individual's own perception of the world. The TAT is called a *projective method* because it emphasizes individual perceptions of stimuli, the meaning each individual gives to them, and how each individual organizes them (recall the discussion of perception in Chapter 12).

One projective test involves looking at the picture shown in Figure 14.4 for 10 to 15 seconds and then writing a short story about it that answers the following questions.

- What is going on in this picture?
- What is the woman thinking?
- What has led up to this situation?

Write your own story about the picture. Then compare it with the following story written by a manager exhibiting strong achievement motivation, which McClelland would describe as a high achiever.

> The individual is an officer in a small entrepreneurial organization that wants to get a contract for her company. She knows that the competition will be tough, because all the big firms are bidding on this contract. She is taking a moment to think how happy she will be if her company is awarded the large contract. It will mean stability for the company and probably a large raise for her. She is satisfied because she has just thought of a way to manufacture a critical part that will enable her company to bring in a low bid and complete the job with time to spare.

What motivational profile did you identify? Does it match the executive's?

Characteristics of High Achievers. Self-motivated high achievers have three main characteristics.[10] First, they like to set their own *goals*. Seldom content to drift aimlessly and let life happen to them, they nearly always are trying to accomplish something. High achievers seek the challenge of making tough decisions. They

FIGURE 14.4 Sample Picture Used in a Projective Test

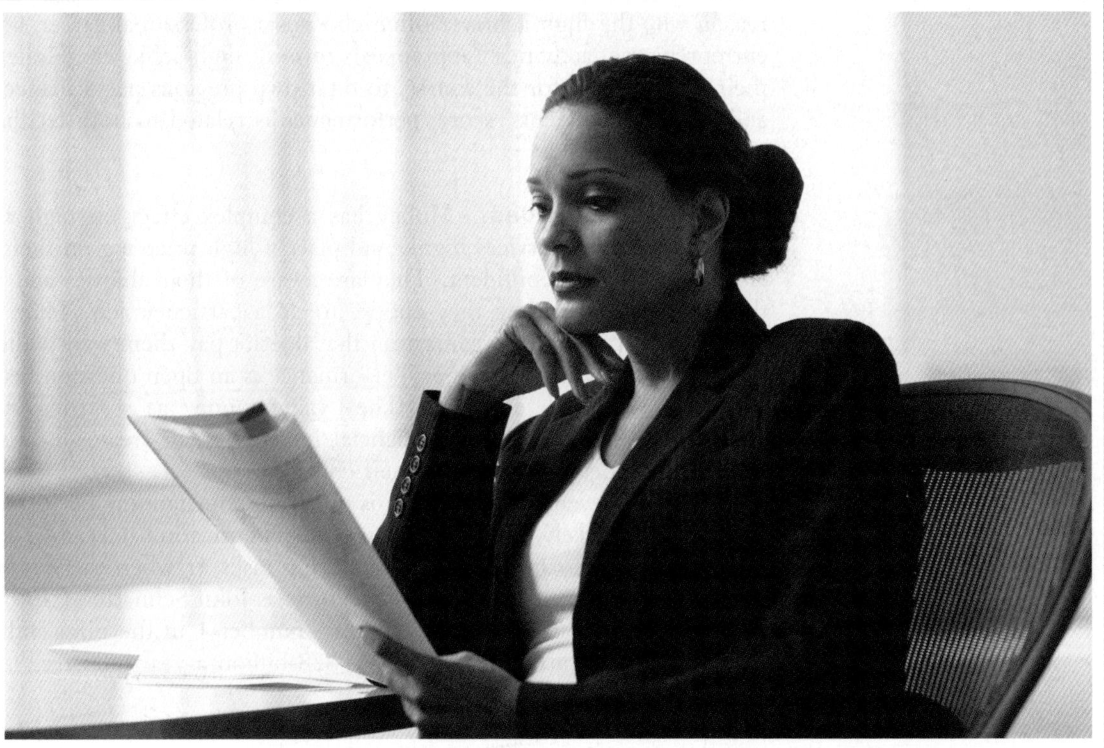

are selective about the goals to which they commit themselves. Hence, they are unlikely to automatically accept goals that other people, including their superiors, attempt to select for them. They exercise self-control over their behaviors, especially the ways in which they pursue the goals they select. They tend to seek advice or help only from experts who can provide needed knowledge or skills. High achievers prefer to be fully responsible for attaining their goals. If they win, they want the credit; if they lose, they accept the blame. For example, assume that you are given a choice between rolling dice with one chance in three of winning or working on a problem with one chance in three of solving the problem in the time allotted. Which would you choose? A high achiever would choose to work on the problem, even though rolling the dice is obviously less work and the odds of winning are the same. High achievers prefer to work at a problem rather than leave the outcome to chance or to other people.

Second, high achievers avoid selecting extremely difficult goals. They prefer *moderate goals* that are neither so easy that attaining them provides no satisfaction nor so difficult that attaining them is more a matter of luck than ability. They gauge what is possible and then select as difficult a goal as they think they can attain. The game of ring toss illustrates this point. Most carnivals have ring toss games that require participants to throw rings over a peg from some minimum distance but specify no maximum distance. Imagine the same game but with people allowed to stand at any distance they want from the peg. Some will throw more or less randomly, standing close and then far away. Those with high-achievement motivation will seem to calculate carefully where they should stand to have the greatest chance of winning a prize and still feel challenged. These individuals seem to stand at a distance that isn't so close as to make the task ridiculously easy and isn't so far away as to make it impossible. They set a distance moderately far away from which they can potentially ring a peg. Thus, they set personal challenges and enjoy tasks that will stretch their abilities.

Third, high achievers prefer tasks that provide *immediate feedback*. Because of the goal's importance to them, they like to know how well they're doing. That's one reason why the high achiever often chooses a professional career, a sales career, or entrepreneurial activities. Golf appeals to most high achievers: Golfers can compare their scores to par for the course, to their own previous performance on the course, and to their opponents' score; performance is related to both feedback (score) and goal (par).

Financial Incentives. Money has a complex effect on high achievers. They usually value their services highly and place a high price tag on them. High achievers are usually self-confident. They are aware of their abilities and limitations and thus are confident when they choose to do a particular job. They are unlikely to remain very long in an organization that doesn't pay them well. Whether an incentive plan actually increases their performance is an open question because they normally work at peak efficiency. They value money as a strong symbol of their achievement and adequacy. A financial incentive may create dissatisfaction if they feel that it inadequately reflects their contributions.

When achievement motivation is operating, outstanding performance on a challenging task is likely. However, achievement motivation doesn't operate when high achievers are performing routine or boring tasks or when there is no competition against goals. An example of a high achiever is John Schnatter, CEO and founder of Papa John's. Schnatter's drive to become number 1 in the pizza industry has made Papa John's a major competitor in this $28-billion-a-year industry.[11]

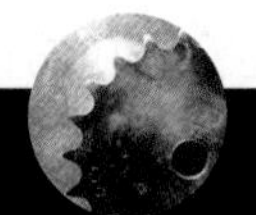

SELF COMPETENCY

JOHN SCHNATTER OF PAPA JOHN'S PIZZA

As a high school student working at a local pizza shop in Jeffersonville, Indiana, Schnatter in the early 1980s realized that there were no national pizza chains. So in 1984, he knocked out a broom closet located in the back of his father's tavern, sold his prized Z28 Camaro, purchased $1,600 worth of used restaurant equipment, and began selling pizzas to the tavern's customers. The business grew so fast that he decided to move next door. He eventually opened his first Papa John's restaurant in 1985.

Today, Papa John's is number three behind Pizza Hut and Domino's in the takeout pizza market with more than 3,000 pizzerias worldwide. With 27 percent of the market share, Schnatter's goal is to take market share away from Pizza Hut (which has about 38 percent) and Domino's (which has about 30 percent) by having better ingredients and making a better pizza. He has achieved remarkable results by being singularly obsessive about high quality and performance. He preaches to his employees about pizza in very passionate terms. He requires all employees to memorize the company's Six Core Values, including stay focused, customer satisfaction must be superior, and people are priority No. 1 *always*—and calls on employees during meetings to stand up and shout them out. He created a Ten Point Perfect Pizza Scale that measures the quality of pizzas. For example, pieces of the toppings should not touch, there should be no "peaks or valleys" along the pizza's border, all mushrooms should be sliced to 0.25 inches, and no splotchy coloring should appear on the crust. The employee newsletter carries articles such as "The Papa John's Black Olive Story" or "The Papa John's Tomato Story." Such articles inform employees about how special ingredients are used to make Papa John's pizza.

At headquarters in Louisville, Kentucky, most employees (including Schnatter) wear Papa John's teal-blue polo shirts, with Pizza Wars embroidered across them. Employees even have their own clothing embroidered with Papa John's logo. By 2007, Schnatter wants Papa John's to be the number one pizza brand in the world in terms of name recognition and by 2008, the leader in sales.

*For more information on Papa John's, visit the organization's home page at **http://www.papajohns.com.***

Organizational Guidelines. McClelland and his associates at McBer and Company have conducted most of the research supporting the achievement motivation model. Based on this research, they recommend the following approach:

- Arrange tasks so that employees receive periodic feedback on their performance. Feedback enables employees to modify their behaviors as necessary.
- Provide good role models of achievement. Employees should be encouraged to have heroes to emulate.
- Help employees modify their self-images. High-achievement individuals accept themselves and seek job challenges and responsibilities.
- Guide employee aspirations. Employees should think about setting realistic goals and the ways in which they can attain them.
- Make it known that managers who have been successful are those that are higher in power motivation than in affiliation motivation.

One of the main problems with the achievement motivation model is also its greatest strengths. The TAT method is valuable because it allows the researcher to tap the preconscious motives of people. This method has some advantages over questionnaires, but the interpretation of a story is more of an art than a science. As a result, the method's reliability is open to question. The permanency of the model's three needs has also been questioned. Further research is needed to explore the model's validity.[12]

MOTIVATING EMPLOYEES THROUGH JOB DESIGN

LEARNING OBJECTIVE

3. Explain how the design of jobs affects motivation.

Motivator–Hygiene Model

Frederick Herzberg and his associates took a different approach to examining what motivates people. He and his staff simply asked people to tell them when they felt exceptionally good about their jobs and when they felt exceptionally bad about their jobs. As shown in Table 14.2, people identified somewhat different things when they felt good or bad about their jobs. From this study they developed the *two-factor theory*, better known as the **motivator–hygiene model,** *which proposes that two sets of factors—motivators and hygienes—are the primary causes of job satisfaction and job dissatisfaction.*[13]

TABLE 14.2 Sources of Job Satisfaction and Job Dissatisfaction

MOTIVATOR FACTORS THAT AFFECT JOB SATISFACTION	HYGIENE FACTORS THAT AFFECT JOB DISSATISFACTION
• Achievement	• Organizational rules and policies
• Advancement	• Relationships with coworkers
• Autonomy	• Relationships with supervisors
• Challenge	• Salary
• Feedback	• Security
• Responsibility	• Working conditions

Motivator Factors. **Motivator factors** *include the work itself, recognition, advancement, and responsibility.* These factors are related to an individual's positive feelings about the job and to the content of the job itself. These positive feelings, in turn, are associated with the individual's experiences of achievement, recognition, and responsibility. They reflect lasting rather than temporary achievement in the work setting. In other words, motivators are **intrinsic factors,** *which are directly related to the job and are largely internal to the individual.* The organization's policies may have only an indirect impact on them. But, by defining exceptional performance, for example, an organization may enable individuals to feel that they have performed their tasks exceptionally well. Can you identify some motivators that Starbucks uses to motivate its employees? (See the Preview Case.)

Hygiene Factors. **Hygiene factors** *include company policy and administration, technical supervision, salary, fringe benefits, working conditions, and interpersonal relations.* These factors are associated with an individual's negative feelings about the job and are related to the environment in which the job is performed. Hygienes are **extrinsic factors,** *or factors external to the job.* They serve as rewards for high performance only if the organization recognizes high performance. Can you identify the hygiene factors used by Starbucks to attract new employees?

Job Characteristics Model

The job characteristics model is one of the best-known approaches to job design.[14] The job characteristics model uses Herzberg's recommendations of adding motivators to a person's job and minimizing the use of hygiene factors.

Framework. The **job characteristics model** *involves increasing the amounts of skill variety, task identity, task significance, autonomy, and feedback in a job.* The model proposes that the levels of these job characteristics affect three critical psychological states: (1) experienced meaningfulness of the tasks performed, (2) experienced personal responsibility for task outcomes, and (3) knowledge of the results of task performance. If all three psychological states are positive, a reinforcing cycle of strong work motivation based on self-generated rewards is activated. A job without meaningfulness, responsibility, and feedback is incomplete and doesn't strongly motivate an employee. Figure 14.5 illustrates the elements of the job characteristic model and their relationships.

Job characteristics. Five job characteristics hold the key to this model. They are defined as follows:

1. **Skill variety**—*the extent to which a job requires a variety of employee competencies to carry out the work.*

FIGURE 14.5 Job Characteristics Enrichment Model

Core Job Characteristics		Critical Psychological States		Personal and Work Outcomes
Skill variety Task identity Task significance	→	Experienced meaningfulness of the work		High internal work motivation High quality work performance High satisfaction with the work Low absenteeism and turnover
Autonomy	→	Experienced responsibility for outcomes of the work	→	
Job feedback	→	Knowledge of the actual results of the work		

Individual Differences

- Knowledge and skill
- Growth-need strength
- Satisfaction with contextual factors

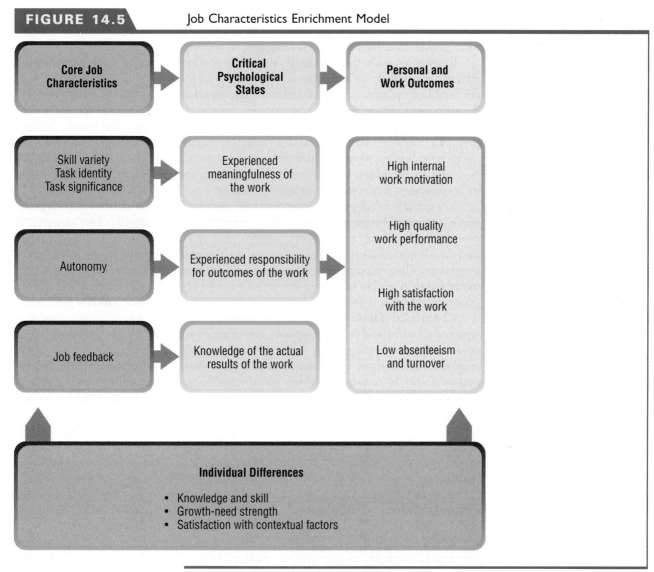

Source: J. Richard Hackman & Greg R. Oldham, WORK REDESIGN, ©1980. Reprinted by permission of Pearson Education, Inc., Upper Saddle River, NJ.

2. **Task identity**—*the extent to which a job requires an employee to complete a whole and identifiable piece of work, that is, doing a task from beginning to end with a visible outcome.*
3. **Task significance**—*the extent to which an employee perceives the job as having a substantial impact on the lives of other people, whether those people are within or outside the organization.*
4. **Autonomy**—*the extent to which the job provides empowerment and discretion to an employee in scheduling tasks and in determining procedures to be used in carrying out those tasks.*
5. **Job feedback**—*the extent to which carrying out job-related tasks provides direct and clear information about the effectiveness of an employee's performance.*

Individual Differences. The individual differences (see Figure 14.5) identified in this model influence how employees respond to enriched jobs. They include knowledge and skills, strength of growth needs, and satisfaction with contextual factors.

These individual differences have an impact on the relationship between job characteristics and personal or work outcomes in several important ways. Managers, therefore, should consider them when designing or redesigning jobs.

Employees with the *knowledge* and *skills* needed to perform an enriched job effectively are likely to have positive feelings about the tasks they perform. Employees unable to perform an enriched job may experience frustration, stress, and job dissatisfaction. These feelings and attitudes may be especially intense for employees who desire to do a good job but realize that they are performing poorly because they lack the necessary skills and knowledge. Accordingly, assessing carefully the competencies of employees whose jobs are to be enriched is essential. A training and development program may be needed along with an enrichment program to help such employees attain the needed competencies.

The extent to which an individual desires the opportunity for self-direction, learning, and personal accomplishment at work is called **growth-need strength.** This concept is essentially the same as Maslow's esteem and self-actualization needs concepts. Individuals with high growth needs tend to respond favorably to job enrichment programs. They experience greater satisfaction from work and are more highly motivated than people who have low growth needs. High growth-need individuals are generally absent less and produce better quality work when their jobs are enriched.

Contextual factors *include organizational policies and administration, technical supervision, salary and benefit programs, interpersonal relations, travel requirements, and work conditions (lighting, heat, safety hazards, and the like).* The extent to which employees are satisfied with contextual factors at work often influences their willingness or ability to respond positively to enriched jobs. Contextual factors are similar to hygiene factors. Employees who are extremely dissatisfied with their superiors, salary levels, and safety measures are less likely to respond favorably to enriched jobs than are employees who are satisfied with these conditions. Other contextual factors (e.g., employee satisfaction with the organizational culture, power and the political process, travel requirements, and team norms) also can affect employee responses to their jobs.

Organizational Guidelines. The two most used approaches for designing enriched jobs are vertical loading and the formation of natural work teams.

Vertical loading *is the delegation to employees of responsibilities and tasks that were formerly reserved for management or staff specialists.* Vertical loading includes the empowerment of employees to

- set schedules, determine work methods, and decide when and how to check on the quality of the work produced;
- make their own decisions about when to start and stop work, when to take breaks, and how to assign priorities; and
- seek solutions to problems on their own, consulting with others only as necessary, rather than calling immediately for the manager when problems arise.

The formation of *natural teams* combines individual jobs into a formally recognized unit (e.g., a section, team, or department). The criteria for the groupings are logical and meaningful to the employee and include the following:

- *Geographic*: Salespeople or information technology consultants might be given a particular region of the state or country as their territory.
- *Types of business*: Insurance claims adjusters might be assigned to teams that serve specific types of businesses, such as utilities, manufacturers, or retailers.
- *Organizational*: Word-processing operators might be given work that originates in a particular department.
- *Alphabetic or numeric*: File clerks could be made responsible for materials in specified alphabetical groups (A to D, E to H, and so on); library-shelf readers might check books in a certain range of the library's cataloging system.

- *Customer groups*: Employees of a public utility or consulting firm might be assigned to particular industrial or commercial accounts.

To illustrate the benefits of enriched jobs, the following Teams Competency illustrates how SEI Investments uses the concepts shown in Figure 14.5.[15] After reading this feature, you should be able to identify the five major job characteristics and methods by which SEI enriched workers' jobs.

TEAMS COMPETENCY

SEI INVESTMENTS

The first sign that there's something unusual about SEI Investments, a $169 million financial company, is the design of its headquarters building in Oaks, Pennsylvania. On the outside, it looks like a Playskool version of a farm. On the inside, it looks like a beehive. All the furniture is on wheels so that employees can create their own work areas. Colorful cables spiral down from the ceiling, carrying electricity, Internet access, and telephone cords. Many employees often move their desks. As a result, SEI created software to map everyone's location. There are no secretaries, walls, or organizational charts. Tasks are distributed among 140 self-managed teams. Some are permanent, designed to serve big customers, but many are temporary teams. Employees come together to solve a problem and disband when the work is finished. Different employees work on different parts of a problem until it is completed.

All employees know the goals that matter most: earnings per share and assets under management. SEI establishes corporate-level goals and translates these into goals for the teams. According to Henry Greer, SEI's president, "Our goals are passed out to the teams and they figure out what they have to do to hit them. Once the team understands its goal(s), everyone on that team drives toward that goal." Greer and his assistants do not care how many vacation days people take, so long as they hit their goals.

To motivate employees to work together in teams, Greer and his staff follow a basic principle: Self-managed teams need leaders. Employees must demonstrate competencies to be chosen by their fellow employees to be team leaders. Team leaders need communication and change management competencies that enable them to use a "soft" hand to guide the team. It's up to the team leader to describe the project in an enthusiastic manner so that others will want to join the team. Once the team leader has assembled the team, all its members are expected to work together to reach the goal.

Team work is a major part of an employee's pay. SEI uses incentive team-based compensation whereby employees can earn anywhere from 10 to 100 percent of their base pay. "Each team gets a pot of money," says Greer, "and decides how to distribute it." Some teams have members vote on each other's bonuses, while other teams defer to the team leader.

For more information about SEI Investments, visit the organization's home page at ***http://www.SEI.com.***

Cultural Influences

One of the important themes of this book is recognizing and addressing cultural diversity in the workforce. As U.S. organizations continue to expand overseas and foreign organizations establish manufacturing operations in Canada, Mexico, and the United States, managers must be aware of cultural differences and how these differences can affect the motivation of employees.[16] With the passage of the North American Free Trade Agreement (NAFTA), managers and employees in North America began working more closely with others who don't necessarily share similar work motivations. It didn't take U.S. managers very long to realize that employees in Mexico have different attitudes toward work. In the United States workers generally favor taking the initiative, having individual responsibility, and taking failure personally. They are competitive, have high goals, and live for the future. Workers are comfortable operating in a group, with the group sharing both success and failure. They tend to be cooperative, flexible, and enjoy life as it is now.

THE COMPETENT LEADER

Dependence on and loyalty to family are incredibly strong in Mexico. If forced to choose between family and work, family will be the choice.
Humberto Gutierrez-Olvera, Director of E-Commerce, Comp USA

In Mexico, employees' priorities are family, religion, and work—in that order. During the year, plant managers host family dinners to celebrate anniversaries of employees who have worked there 5, 10, 15, and 20 years. Employees may use the company clubhouse for weddings, baptisms, anniversary parties, and other family celebrations. Organizations also host a family day during which employees' families can tour the plant, enjoy entertainment and food, and participate in sports.

The typical workday in Mexico is 8 A.M. to 5:30 P.M. Employees are picked up by a company bus at various locations throughout the city. Employees like to eat their main meal in the middle of the day, the cost of which is heavily subsidized (as much as 70 percent) by the company. Interestingly, managers serve the employees this meal.

LEARNING OBJECTIVE

4. Describe the expectancy model of motivation.

MOTIVATING EMPLOYEES THROUGH PERFORMANCE EXPECTATIONS

Besides creating jobs that people find challenging and rewarding, people are also motivated by the belief that they can expect to achieve certain rewards by working hard to attain them. Believing that you can get an "A" in this class by expending enough effort can be a very effective motivator. If you can clearly see a link between your study behaviors (effort) and your grade, you will be motivated to study. If you see no link, why study at all? To better understand this approach to motivation, let's take a look at the expectancy model.

Expectancy Model

The **expectancy model** *states that people are motivated to work when they believe that they can achieve things they want from their jobs*. These things might include satisfaction of safety needs, the excitement of doing a challenging task, or the ability to set and achieve difficult goals. A basic premise of the expectancy model is that employees are rational people. They think about what they have to do to be rewarded and how much the rewards mean to them before they perform their jobs. Four assumptions about the causes of behavior in organizations provide the basis for this model.

First, a combination of forces in the individual and the environment determines behavior. Neither the individual nor the environment alone determines behavior. People go to work for organizations with expectations about their jobs that are based on their needs, motivations, and past experiences. These factors influence how people respond to an organization, but they can and do change over time.

Second, individuals decide their own behaviors in organizations, even though many constraints are placed on individual behavior (e.g., through rules, technology, and work-group norms). Most individuals make two kinds of conscious decisions: (1) decisions about coming to work, staying with the same organization, and joining other organizations (membership decisions); and (2) decisions about how much to produce, how hard to work, and the quality of workmanship (job-performance decisions).

Third, different individuals have different needs and goals. Employees want different rewards from their work, depending on their gender, race, age, and other characteristics. Of the many rewards that Starbucks offers to its employees, which do you find attractive? Why? In five years, are these same rewards likely to be attractive to you?

Fourth, individuals decide among alternatives based on their perceptions of whether a specific behavior will lead to a desired outcome. Individuals do what they perceive will lead to desired outcomes and avoid doing what they perceive will lead to undesirable outcomes.[17]

In general, the expectancy model holds that individuals have their own needs and ideas about what they desire from their work (rewards). They act on these needs and ideas when making decisions about what organization to join and how hard to work. This model also holds that individuals are not inherently motivated or unmotivated but rather that motivation depends on the situations that individuals face and how their responses to these situations fit their needs.

To help you understand the expectancy model, we must define its most important variables and explain how they operate. They are first-level and second-level outcomes, expectancy, instrumentality, and valence.

First-Level and Second-Level Outcomes. *The results of behaviors associated with doing the job itself are called* **first-level outcomes.** They include level of performance, amount of absenteeism, and quality of work. **Second-level outcomes** *are the rewards (either positive or negative) that first-level outcomes are likely to produce.* They include a pay increase, promotion, and acceptance by coworkers, job security, reprimands, and dismissal.

Expectancy. **Expectancy** *is the belief that a particular level of effort will be followed by a particular level of performance.* It can vary from the belief that there is absolutely no relationship between effort and performance to the certainty that a given level of effort will result in a corresponding level of performance. Expectancy has a value ranging from 0, indicating no chance that a first-level outcome will occur after the behavior, to +1, indicating certainty that a particular first-level outcome will follow a behavior. For example, if you believe that you have no chance of getting a good grade on the next exam by studying this chapter, your expectancy value would be 0. Having this expectancy, you shouldn't study this chapter. Good teachers will do things that help their students believe that hard work will lead students to achieve better grades.

Instrumentality. **Instrumentality** *is the relationship between first-level outcomes and second-level outcomes.* It can have values ranging from –1 to +1. A –1 indicates that attainment of a second-level outcome is inversely related to the achievement of a first-level outcome. For example, Sharron Coon, a staff manager at AT&T, wants to be accepted as a member of her work group, but it has a norm for an acceptable level of performance. If she violates this norm, her work group won't accept her. Therefore, Coon limits her performance so as not to violate the group's norm. A +1 indicates that the first-level outcome is positively related to the second-level outcome. For example, if you received an A on all your exams, the probability that you would achieve your desired second-level outcome (passing this course) approaches +1. If there were no relationship between your performance on a test and either passing or failing this course, your instrumentality would be 0.

Valence. **Valence** *is an individual's preference for a particular second-level outcome.* Outcomes having a positive valence include being respected by friends and coworkers, performing meaningful work, having job security, and earning enough money to support a family. Valence is just not the amount of the reward received, but what it means to the person receiving it. Outcomes having a negative valence are things that you want to avoid, such as being laid off, being passed over for a promotion, or being discharged for sexual harassment. An outcome is positive when it is preferred and negative when it is not preferred or is to be avoided. An outcome has a valence of 0 when the individual is indifferent about receiving it.

Putting It All Together. In brief, the expectancy model holds that work motivation is determined by individual beliefs regarding effort–performance relationships and the desirability of various work outcomes associated with different performance levels. Simply put, you can remember the model's important features by the saying:

> People exert work effort to achieve performance that leads to valued work-related outcomes.

The Expectancy Model in Action. The five key variables just defined and discussed lead to a general expectancy model of motivation, as shown in Figure 14.6. Motivation is the force that causes individuals to expend effort, but effort alone isn't enough. Unless an individual believes that effort will lead to some desired performance level (first-level outcome), he won't make much of an effort. The effort–performance relationship is based on a perception of the difficulty of achieving a particular behavior (say, working for an A in this course) and the probability of achieving that behavior. On the one hand, you may have a high expectancy that, if you attend class, study the book, take good notes, and prepare for exams, you can achieve an A in this class. That expectancy is likely to translate into making the effort required on those activities to get an A. On the other hand, you may believe that, even if you attend class, study the book, take good notes, and prepare for exams, your chances of getting an A are only 20 percent. That expectancy is likely to keep you from expending the effort required on these activities to achieve an A.

FIGURE 14.6 Expectancy Model in Action

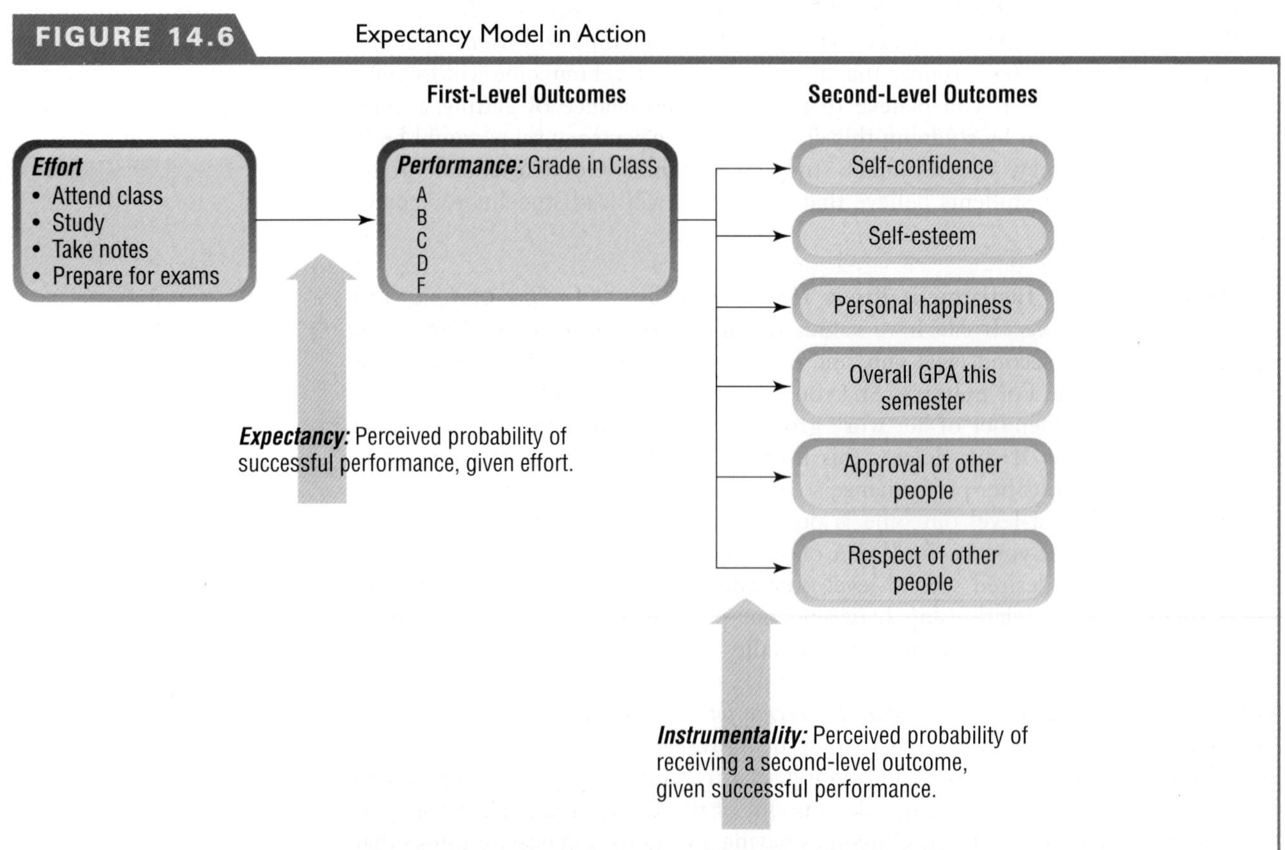

Source: VandeWalle, D., Cron, W.L., and Slocum, J.W. The role of goal orientation following performance feedback. *Journal of Applied Psychology,* 2001, 86, 629-640.

Performance level is important in obtaining desired second-level outcomes. Figure 14.6 shows six desirable second-level outcomes: self-confidence, self-esteem, personal happiness, overall GPA this semester, approval of other people, and respect of other people. In general, if you believe that a particular level of performance (A, B, C, D, or F) will lead to these desired outcomes, you are more likely to try to perform at that level. If you really desire these six second-level outcomes and you can achieve them only if you get an A in this course, the instrumentality between receiving an A and these six outcomes will be positive. But, if you believe that getting an A in this course means that you won't gain personal happiness and the approval and respect of other people, the instrumentality between an A and these outcomes will be negative. That is, if the higher the grade, the less likely you are to experience personal happiness, you might choose not to get an A in this course. Once you have made this choice, you will lessen your effort and start cutting class, not studying for exams, and so on.

Researchers are still working on ways to test this model, which has presented some problems:[18]

- The model tries to predict choice or the amount of effort an individual will expend on one or more tasks. However, there is little agreement about what constitutes choice or effort for different individuals. Therefore, this important variable is difficult to measure accurately.
- The model doesn't specify which second-level outcomes are important to a particular individual in a given situation. Although researchers are addressing this issue, comparison of the limited results to date is often difficult because each study is unique. Take another look at the second-level outcomes in Figure 14.6. Would you choose them? What others might you choose?
- The model contains an implicit assumption that motivation is a conscious choice process. That is, the individual consciously calculates the pain or pleasure that she expects to attain or avoid when making a choice. The expectancy model says nothing about unconscious motivation or personality characteristics. In fact, people often do not make conscious choices about which outcomes to seek. Can you recall going through this process concerning your grade while taking this course?
- The model works best in cultures that emphasize internal attribution. The expectancy model works best when people in a culture believe that they can control their work environment and their own behavior, such as in the United States, Canada, and the United Kingdom.[19] In cultures where people believe the work environment and their own behavior aren't completely under their control, such as in Brazil, Saudi Arabia, Iran, Japan, and China, the assumptions of the model might not be valid. For example, a Canadian manager in Japan decided to promote one of her young female Japanese sales representatives to manager (a status and monetary reward). To her surprise, the promotion diminished the new Japanese manager's performance. Why? Japanese have a high need for harmony—to fit in with their colleagues. The promotion, an individualistic reward, separated the new manager from her colleagues, embarrassed her, and therefore diminished her work motivation.

Organizational Uses. The expectancy model has some important implications for motivating employees. These implications can be grouped into seven suggestions for action:[20]

1. Managers should try to determine the outcomes that each employee values. Two ways of doing so are observing employee reactions to different rewards and asking employees about the types of rewards they want from their jobs. However, managers must recognize that employees can and do change their minds about desired outcomes over time.

2. Managers should define good, adequate, and poor performance in terms that are observable and measurable. Employees need to understand what is expected of them and how these expectations affect performance. When the Baxter Pharmaceutical Company announced a new examination table for doctors, its salespeople wanted to know what behaviors, such as cold-calling on new accounts or trying to sell the new tables to their existing accounts, would lead to more sales. To the extent that Baxter was able to train its salespeople in selling its new product, it was able to link salespeople's efforts with performance.[21]

3. Managers should be sure that desired levels of performance set for employees can be attained. If employees feel that the level of performance necessary to get a reward is higher than they can reasonably achieve, their motivation to perform will be low. For example, Nordstrom tells its employees: "Respond to Unreasonable Customer Requests." Employees are urged to keep scrapbooks with "heroic" acts, such as hand-delivering items purchased by phone to the airport for a customer leaving on a last-minute business trip, changing a customer's flat tire, or paying a customer's parking ticket when in-store gift wrapping has taken longer than expected. It is hardly surprising that Nordstrom pays its employees much more than they could earn at a rival's store. For those who love to sell and can meet its demanding standards, Nordstrom is nirvana.

4. Managers should directly link the specific performance they desire to the outcomes desired by employees. Recall the discussion in Chapter 4 of how operant conditioning principles can be applied to improve performance. If an employee has achieved the desired level of performance for a promotion, the employee should be promoted as soon as possible. If a high level of motivation is to be created and maintained, it is extremely important for employees to see clearly and quickly the reward process at work. Concrete acts must accompany statements of intent in linking performance to rewards.

5. Managers should never forget that perceptions, not reality, determine motivation. Too often, managers misunderstand the behavior of employees because they tend to rely on their own perceptions of the situation and forget that employees' perceptions may be different.

6. Managers should analyze situations for conflicts. Having set up positive expectancies for employees, managers must look at an entire situation to determine whether other factors conflict with the desired behaviors (e.g., the informal work group or the organization's formal reward system). Motivation will be high only when employees perceive many rewards and few negative outcomes associated with good performance.

7. Managers should be sure that changes in outcomes or rewards are large enough to motivate significant efforts. Trivial rewards may result in minimal efforts, if any, to improve performance. Rewards must be large enough to motivate individuals to make the effort required to substantially change performance.

THE COMPETENT LEADER

High performance is not a matter of chance, it is a matter of choice; it is not a thing to be waited for, it is a thing to be achieved.
Nancy Smith, Vice President, Field Merchandising, 7-11

Rajendra Pawar has created a global chain of computer schools that graduate low-cost technicians for call centers and software firms. Pawar is the cofounder and chairman of the National Institute for Information Technology (NIIT), a company that started in 1981. The company operates in 42 countries and has an enrollment of more than 500,000 students. More than 3 million people have graduated from NIIT. He has used many of the expectancy model's recommendations, as the following Across Cultures competency feature illustrates.[22]

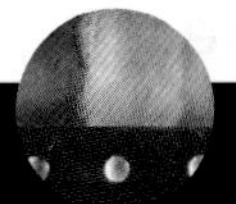

ACROSS CULTURES COMPETENCY

McPROGRAMMERS

Crammed into a small classroom near a New Delhi shopping center, 20 of Pawar's students practice on their keyboards, pausing slightly to look up at a whiteboard full of equations and text. The students are in their teens and most come from families whose average income is less than $2,000. These students expect to earn considerably more someday, which explains why they are so engrossed with learning the intricacies of creating applications for Microsoft's.Net and Oracle's high-end databases.

Who attends NIIT? Naveen Panthary is a typical NIIT student who comes from a small town called Sagar. He is one of four children of a policeman whose salary topped out at about $2,000 a year. After graduating from high school, Panthary couldn't find a job. He made his way to New Delhi and enrolled in an NIIT program. Four years later, he is a trainee at an electronic company making $120 a month and expects to make more than $800 a month after he graduates and starts working full time.

The growth of NIIT has been tremendous. After watching McDonald's expand into a global fast-food chain, Pawar came up with a unique twist. The NIIT course syllabus reads like a McDonald's menu: Dollar Menu, Combo Meals, and Sides. For each menu item, there is a list of courses that the student can choose from, the number of hours required to complete the course, and the total cost for the course. The syllabus for each course is very specific with objectives assigned to each lesson. Students get feedback on their own progress by accessing the intranet. NIIT's course offerings are also offered over the Internet for as little as US $17. It also sells training manuals to Microsoft and Sun Microsystems.

Copying McDonald's notion of franchising, Pawar came up with a uniquely Indian twist. He got the most respected families in small communities to sign up as his franchisees. Indians put great emphasis on pride and respect, known as *izzat.* To lose *izzat* is to lose everything. Pawar figured if he could get respected families to be his franchisees, they'd have a powerful incentive to manage the school well—protecting their *izzat*—along with the NIIT brand name. The franchisees pay for marketing, space, desks, and computers. NIIT provides all the course materials and selects and trains all faculty members. In return, NIIT gets royalties of 20 percent on student tuitions and is paid for all supplies. For franchisees, if well run, the profits can exceed 30 percent on their investment.

MOTIVATING EMPLOYEES THROUGH EQUITY

LEARNING OBJECTIVE

5. State how feelings of equity and inequity affect motivation.

Feelings of unfairness were among the most frequent sources of job dissatisfaction reported to Herzberg and his associates. Some researchers have made this desire for fairness, justice, or equity a central focus of their models. Assume that you just received a 5 percent raise. Will this raise lead to higher performance, lower performance, or no change in performance? Are you satisfied with this increase? Would your satisfaction with this pay increase vary with the consumer price index, with what you expected to get, or with what others in the organization performing the same job and at the same performance level received?

Equity Model: Balancing Inputs and Outcomes

The **equity model** *focuses on an individual's feelings of how fairly she is treated in comparison with others.*[23] It is based on the belief that people are motivated to maintain a fair, or equitable, relationship between themselves and others and to avoid relationships that are unfair or inequitable. It contains two major assumptions. The first is that individuals evaluate their interpersonal relationships just as they would evaluate the buying or selling of a home, shares of stock, or a car. The model views relationships as exchange processes in which individuals make contributions and expect certain results. The second assumption is that individuals don't operate in a vacuum. They compare their situations to those of the others in the organization to determine fairness. In other words, what happens to individuals is important when they compare themselves to similar others (e.g., coworkers, relatives, and neighbors).

General Equity Model. The equity model is based on the comparison of two variables: inputs and outcomes. **Inputs** *represent what an individual contributes to an exchange;* **outcomes** *are what an individual receives from the exchange.* Some typical inputs and outcomes are shown in Table 14.3. A word of caution: The items in the two lists aren't paired and don't represent specific exchanges.

TABLE 14.3 Examples of Inputs and Outcomes in Organizations

INPUTS	OUTCOMES
Age	Challenging job assignments
Attendance	Fringe benefits
Interpersonal skills, communication skills	Job perquisites (parking space or office location)
Job effort (long hours)	Job security
Level of education	Monotony
Past experience	Promotion
Performance	Recognition
Personal appearance	Responsibility
Seniority	Salary
Social status	Seniority benefits
Technical skills	Status symbols
Training	Working conditions

According to the equity model, individuals assign weights to various inputs and outcomes according to their perceptions of the situation. Because most situations involve multiple inputs and outcomes, the weighting process isn't precise. However, people generally can distinguish between important and less important inputs and outcomes. After they arrive at a ratio of inputs and outcomes for themselves, they compare it with their perceived ratios of inputs and outcomes of others who are in the same or a similar situation. These relevant others become the objects of comparison for individuals in determining whether they feel equitably treated.[24]

Equity exists whenever the perceived ratio of a person's outcomes to inputs equals that for relevant others. For example, an individual may feel properly paid in terms of what he puts into a job compared to what other workers are getting for their inputs. Inequity exists when the perceived ratios of outcomes to inputs are unequal. Jay Loar, a director of program engineering at Lockheed Martin, works

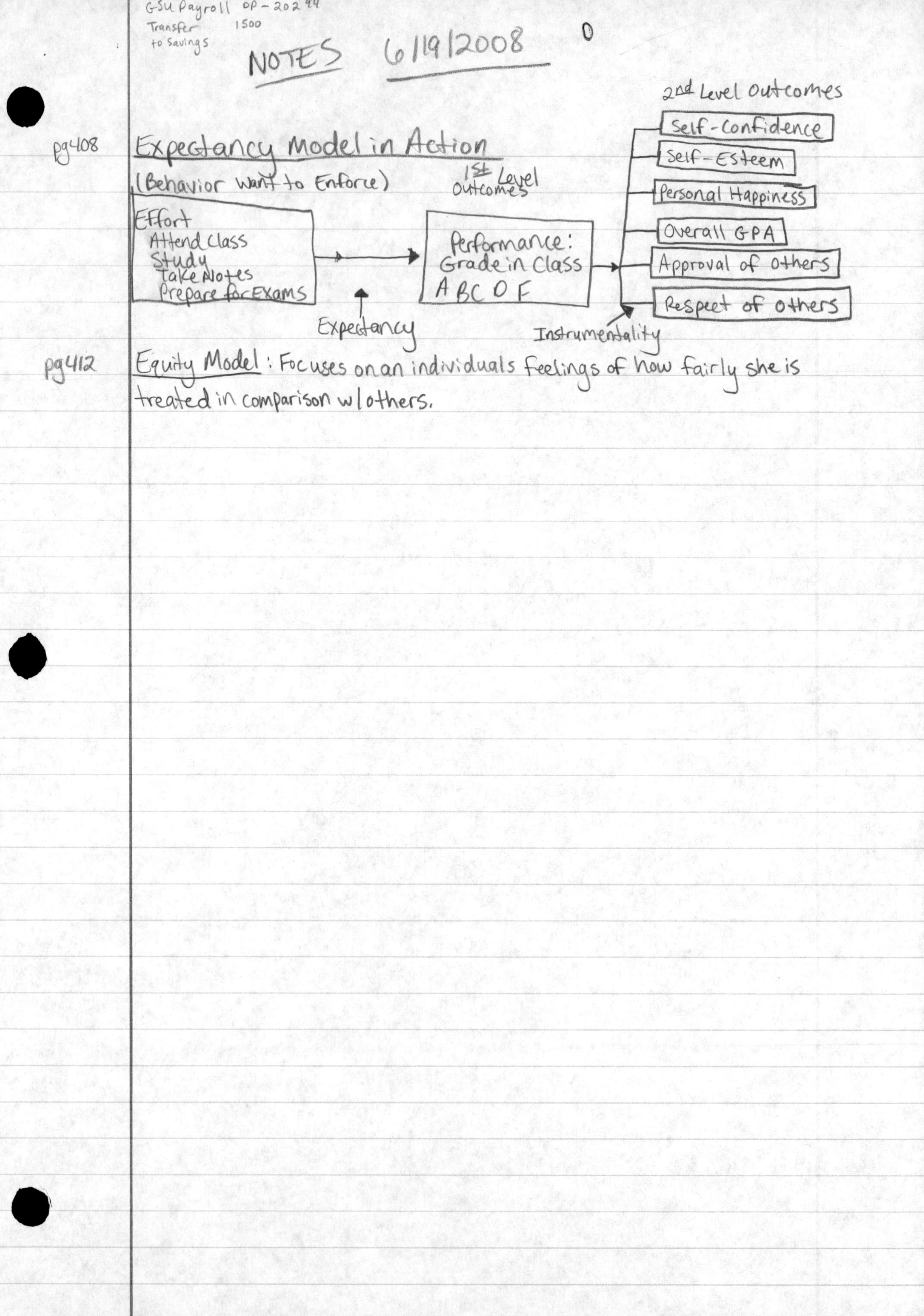

GSU Payroll OP - 202 94
Transfer 1500
to Savings
NOTES 6/19/2008
pg408
Expectancy Model in Action
(Behavior want to Enforce)
Effort
Attend Class
Study
Take Notes
Prepare for Exams
Expectancy
1st Level Outcomes
Performance: Grade in Class
A B C D F
Instrumentality
2nd Level Outcomes
Self-Confidence
Self-Esteem
Personal Happiness
Overall GPA
Approval of others
Respect of others
pg412
Equity Model: Focuses on an individuals feelings of how fairly she is treated in comparison w/others.

harder than his coworkers, completes all his tasks on time even though others don't, and puts in longer hours than others, but receives the same pay raise as the others. What happens? Loar believes that his inputs are greater than those of his coworkers and therefore should merit a greater pay raise. Inequity can also occur when people are overpaid. In this case, the overpaid employees might be motivated by guilt or social pressure to work harder to reduce the imbalance between their inputs and outcomes and those of their coworkers.

Consequences of Inequity. Inequity *causes tension within and among individuals.* Tension isn't pleasurable, so people are motivated to reduce it to a tolerable level, as illustrated in Figure 14.7. To reduce a perceived inequity and the corresponding level of tension, people may choose to act in one or more of the following ways:

FIGURE 14.7 Inequity as a Motivational Process

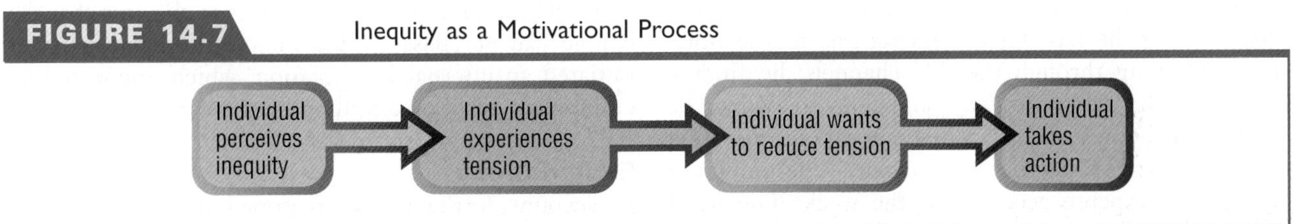

- People may either increase or decrease their inputs to what they feel to be an equitable level. For example, underpaid people may reduce the quantity of their production, work shorter hours, be absent more frequently, and so on.
- People may change their outcomes to restore equity. Many union organizers try to attract nonmembers by pledging to improve working conditions, hours, and pay without an increase in employee effort (input).
- People may distort their own inputs and outcomes. As opposed to actually changing inputs or outcomes, people may mentally distort them to achieve a more favorable balance. For example, people who feel inequitably treated may distort how hard they work ("This job is a piece of cake") or attempt to increase the importance of the job to the organization ("This really is an important job!").
- People may leave the organization or request a transfer to another department. In doing so, they hope to find an equitable balance.
- People may shift to a new reference group to reduce the source of the inequity. The star high school athlete who doesn't get a scholarship to a major university might decide that a smaller school has more advantages, thereby justifying a need to look at smaller schools when making a selection.
- People may distort the inputs or outcomes of others. They may come to believe that others in a comparison group actually work harder than they do and therefore deserve greater rewards.

Keeping these six actions in mind, let's take a look at employee theft as a reaction to inequity. Employee theft is one of the most serious problems facing organizations. Each day they lose an average of $9 per employee. Employee theft and shoplifting are consistently the two largest sources of inventory lost. Employee theft is the greatest in furniture shops (85 percent) and lowest in camera (5 percent) shops. Shoplifting occurs most frequently in apparel (38 percent) and is least likely in furniture (< 1 percent). The National Retail Security Association estimates that employee theft costs U.S. organizations more than $33.6 billion a year. Billions are also stolen from retail department stores and over the Internet. Theft is up almost 25 percent a year for the past five years.[25] After reading both accounts in the following Ethics Competency feature, how would you explain such behaviors?[26]

ETHICS COMPETENCY

EMPLOYEE THEFT

Account 1

An employee is working out of town for several days. One evening, he has dinner and returns to the hotel room. Flipping through the TV channels, he finds a movie that he wants to watch and does so. When he checks out the next day, a $5 item appears on the hotel bill. For what? A pay-per-view movie. The employee submits his expense account for the week. The hotel bill is $500. The accounts payable clerk crosses off the $5 movie charge and reimburses the employee $495 for the hotel bill. Why? Because movies are a personal expense and their reimbursement is against company policy.

Account 2

A young couple purchased a home in an exclusive area of Dallas and applied to join Stonebriar Country Club, which has a membership entrance fee of $38,500. On the application the wife indicated that she worked as a clerk for a local bank. The country club manager called her manager to verify employment. The husband was a local high school math teacher. The club manager called the local school district to verify his employment. The bank manager was aware of the high entrance fee at Stonebriar and the costs of homes in the area that the couple had purchased. On a hunch, the bank manager initiated an internal investigation, which uncovered an embezzlement of $1.8 million by the wife.

Explanations

In account 1, the person reasoned that he had been away from home, working 10 to 12 hours a day. He's earning his company three times his salary of $65,000. He's missing his kids' soccer games and parent–teacher meetings. He feels justified in charging this small amount to the company for relaxation.

In account 2, the wife was motivated to steal from her bank because she and her husband needed money to support a lifestyle like that enjoyed by their friends. She believed that the bank owed her more money because she was more highly qualified (she had a college degree, was older, and had worked at the bank for more than 15 years before accepting this position) for her job than any of the other clerks (all of whom were only high school graduates, 19 years old, and were working at their first jobs).

Procedural Justice: Making Decisions Fairly

Equity theory focuses on the outcomes people receive after they have expended effort, time, or other inputs. It doesn't deal with how decisions leading to outcomes were made in the first place. Procedural justice examines the impact of the process used to make a decision. *The perceived fairness of rules and how decisions are made is referred to as* **procedural justice.**[27] Procedural justice holds that employees are going to be more motivated to perform at a high level when they perceive as fair the procedures used to make decisions about the distribution of outcomes. In organizations procedural justice is very important to most employees, who are motivated to attain fairness in how decisions are made, as well as in the decisions themselves.

Reactions to pay raises, for example, are greatly affected by employees' perceptions about the fairness of how the raises were determined. If in the minds of the employees the pay raises were administered fairly, the employees are usually more satisfied with their increases than if the employees judged the procedures used to make these increases to be unfair. The perceived fairness of the procedures used to allocate pay raises is a better predictor of satisfaction than the absolute amount of pay received. Similarly, students base their faculty member evaluations on perceptions of fair grading decisions.

In both the pay and evaluation situations, the individual can't directly control the decision but can react to the procedures used to make it. Even when a particular decision has negative outcomes for the individual, fair procedures help ensure that the individual feels that her interests are being protected.

Employees' assessments of procedural justice have also been related to their trust in management, intention to leave the organization, evaluation of their supervisor, employee theft, and job satisfaction. Consider some of the relatively trivial day-to-day issues in an organization that are affected by procedural justice: decisions about who will cover the phones during lunch while others are away from their desks, the choice of the site of the company picnic, or who gets the latest software for a personal computer.

Procedural justice has also been found to affect the attitudes of workers who survive a layoff. When workers are laid off, survivors (those who remain on the job) are often in a good position to judge the fairness of the layoff in terms of how it was handled. When a layoff is handled fairly, survivors feel more committed to the organization than when they believe that the laid-off workers were treated unfairly.[28]

Going Beyond the Call of Duty. In many organizations, employees perform tasks that are not formally required.[29] **Organizational citizenship behavior** *exceeds formal job duties but is often necessary for the organization's survival, including its image and acceptance.* Examples of organizational citizenship behavior include helping coworkers solve problems, making constructive suggestions, volunteering to perform community service work (e.g., blood drives, United Way campaigns, and charity work). Although not formally required by employers, these behaviors are important in all organizations. Helping coworkers is an especially important form of organizational citizenship behavior when it comes to computers. Every organization has some computer gurus, but often it's the secretary who doesn't go to lunch who can fix a problem easier and without putting down the struggling user. Managers often underestimate the amount of this informal helping that takes place in organizations.

Employees have considerable discretion over whether to engage in organizational citizenship behaviors. Employees who have been treated fairly and are satisfied are more likely to do so than employees who feel unfairly treated. Fairly treated employees engage in citizenship behaviors because they want to give something back to the organization. Most people desire to have fair exchanges with coworkers and others in their organization.

Howard Johnson, vice president of internal auditing for Lowe's, a national hardware store chain, developed a simple yet innovative method to acknowledge organizational citizenship behaviors at his North Carolina office. At the beginning of the year, Johnson gives each of his 10 employees a jar containing 12 marbles. Throughout the year, employees may give marbles to others who have helped them in some way or who have provided an extraordinary service. Employees are recognized throughout the year and are proud of the number of marbles they accumulate, even though they receive no monetary reward from Johnson.

Organizational Uses. Managers often use the equity model in making a variety of decisions, such as taking disciplinary actions, giving pay raises, allocating office and parking space, and dispensing other perquisites (perks). The equity model leads to two primary conclusions. First, employees should be treated fairly. When individuals believe that they are not being treated fairly, they will try to correct the situation and reduce tension by means of one or more of the types of actions identified previously in this section. A sizable inequity increases the probability that individuals will choose more than one type of action to reduce it. For example, individuals may partially withdraw from the organization by being absent more often, arriving at work late, not completing assignments on time, or stealing. The organization may try to reduce the inputs of such employees by assigning them to monotonous jobs, taking away some perks, and giving them only small pay increases.

Second, people make decisions concerning equity only after they compare their inputs and outcomes with those of comparable employees.[30] These relevant others may be employees of the same organization or of other organizations. The latter present a major problem for managers, who cannot control what other organizations pay their employees. For example, Ralph Sorrentino, a partner at Deloitte Consulting, hired a recent business school undergraduate for $47,500, the maximum the company could pay for the job. The new employee thought that this salary was very good until she compared it to the $55,250 that fellow graduates were getting at Boston Consulting, McKinsey, and Bain. She felt that she was being underpaid in comparison with her former classmates, causing an inequity problem for her (and the company).

The idea that fairness in organizations is determined by more than just money has received a great deal of attention from managers. Organizational fairness is influenced by how rules and procedures are used and how much employees are consulted in decisions that affect them.

CHAPTER SUMMARY

1. Explain the motivational process.

A six-stage motivational model indicates that individuals behave in certain ways to satisfy their needs. Managers have three motivational challenges—motives can only be inferred, needs are dynamic, and there are considerable differences in people's motivations.

2. Describe two basic human needs approaches to motivation.

Two human needs models of motivation are widely recognized. Maslow proposed that people have five types of needs: physiological, security, affiliation, esteem, and self-actualization and that when a need is satisfied it no longer motivates a person. McClelland believed that people have three learned needs (achievement, affiliation, and power) that are rooted in the culture of a society. We focused on the role of the achievement need and indicated the characteristics associated with high achievers, including that they like to set their own moderate goals and perform tasks that give them immediate feedback.

3. Explain how the design of jobs affects motivation.

Herzberg claimed that two types of factors affect a person's motivation: motivator and hygiene factors. Motivators, such as job challenge, lead to job satisfaction but not to job dissatisfaction. Hygiene factors, such as working conditions, prevent job dissatisfaction but can't lead to job satisfaction. Managers need to structure jobs that focus on motivators because they lead to high job satisfaction and performance. The job characteristics model focuses on adding five motivators to the job (skill variety, task identity, task significance, autonomy, and feedback). Whether an employee responds favorably to an enriched job is dependent on her knowledge and skill, growth-need strength, and contextual factors.

4. Describe the expectancy model of motivation.

The expectancy model holds that individuals know what they desire from work. They choose activities only after they decide that the activities will satisfy their needs. The primary components of this model are first- and second-level outcomes, expectancy, instrumentality, and valence. An individual must believe that effort expended will lead (expectancy) to some desired level of performance (first-level outcome) and that this level of performance will lead (instrumentality) to desired rewards (second-level outcomes and valences). Otherwise, the individual won't be motivated to expend the effort necessary to perform at the desired level.

5. State how feelings of equity and inequity affect motivation.

The equity model focuses on the individual's perception of how fairly he is treated in comparison to others in similar situations. To make this judgment, an individual compares his inputs (experience, age) and outcomes (salary) to those of relevant others. If equity exists, the person isn't motivated to act. If inequity exists, the person may engage in any one of six behaviors to reduce this inequity. Both procedural justice and organizational citizenship behavior are based on the equity model and have significant implications for employees' perceptions of equity. Procedural justice examines the impact of the process (rules and procedures) used to make a decision. Organizational citizenship behaviors are employee behaviors that go above and beyond their job requirements.

KEY TERMS AND CONCEPTS

Ability
Achievement motivation model
Affiliation needs
Autonomy
Contextual factors
Deficiency needs
Equity model
Esteem needs
Expectancy
Expectancy model
Extrinsic factors
First-level outcomes
Goal
Growth-need strength
Growth needs
Hygiene factors
Inequity
Inputs
Instrumentality
Intrinsic factors
Job characteristics model
Job feedback
Motivating potential score (MPS)
Motivation
Motivator factors
Motivator–hygiene model
Needs
Needs hierarchy model
Organizational citizenship behavior
Outcomes
Physiological needs
Procedural justice
Second-level outcomes
Security needs
Self-actualization needs
Skill variety
Task identity
Task significance
Thematic Apperception Test (TAT)
Valence
Vertical loading

DISCUSSION QUESTIONS

1. Why do employees steal and/or shoplift from their employers?
2. What steps can an organization take to encourage procedural justice by its managers?
3. Why was Pawar successful in motivating employees at McProgrammers?
4. Imagine that you have just been selected to become a new sales manager for Dell Computers in Mexico. What would you do to motivate employees to become high producers?
5. "I'm bored," says Amna Kirmani, a clerk at Lowe's. What would you recommend to make her job more interesting?
6. Identify the hygiene factors in the Starbucks Preview Case. According to Herzberg, what role do they play? Do hygiene factors attract people to jobs? Explain.
7. Think about the worst job you've had. What motivational approach was used in that organization? Now think about the best job you've had. What motivational approach was used in that organization?

8. What are your own assumptions about motivation? How do they reflect the culture in which you were raised?
9. Why is job satisfaction not strongly related to job performance?
10. What are the motivational assumptions at SEI Investments?
11. How could someone like John Schnatter, CEO of Papa John's, apply McClelland's model of motivation to motivate his employees?

EXPERIENTIAL EXERCISE AND CASE

Experiential Exercise: Self Competency

What Do You Want from Your Job?

We have listed the 16 most often mentioned characteristics that employees want from their jobs in random order.[31] Please rank them in order of both their importance to you and then in terms of satisfaction for you. Rank these characteristics 1 (most important), 2 (next most important), 3 (next most important), and so on, through 16 (least important). Use the same procedure to rank satisfaction. Then compare your answers to those of managers working in a wide variety of jobs and industries provided at the end of this exercise.

Job Characteristics	Importance Rank	Satisfaction Rank
1. Working independently	_____	_____
2. Chances for promotion	_____	_____
3. Contact with people	_____	_____
4. Flexible hours	_____	_____
5. Health insurance and other benefits	_____	_____
6. Interesting work	_____	_____
7. Work important to society	_____	_____
8. Job security	_____	_____
9. Opportunity to learn new skills	_____	_____
10. High income	_____	_____
11. Recognition from team members	_____	_____
12. Vacation time	_____	_____
13. Regular hours	_____	_____
14. Working close to home	_____	_____
15. Little job stress	_____	_____
16. A job in which I can help others	_____	_____

Answers

For job importance, the rank order of characteristics is 1–6; 2–14; 3–15; 4–16; 5–1; 6–2; 7–13; 8–3; 9–4; 10–11; 12–5; 13–8; 14–12; 15–10; 16–9.

For job satisfaction, the rank order of characteristics is 1–3; 2–14; 3–2; 4–6; 5–13; 6–4; 7–9; 8–7; 9–11; 10–12; 11–15; 12–8; 13–5; 14–1; 15–16; 16–10.

Questions

1. Choose any model of motivation and think about your answers. What situational factors (such as being in school, looking for a new job, desiring more responsibility, desiring to work for a foreign organization, and the like) influenced your ranking of importance?
2. What characteristics gave most of the respondents their greatest job satisfaction? What model of motivation helps you understand these rankings?

Case: Teams Competency

SAS Institute[32]

Jim Goodnight funded the SAS Institute in Cary, North Carolina, in 1976. It is probably the least-well-known major software company in the world. In simplest terms, SAS writes software that makes it possible to gather and understand data, to sift through mountains of information in order to find patterns and meaning. SAS—which stands for "statistical analysis software"—started out as a tool for statisticians. Goodnight originally developed it to analyze agricultural-research data in North Carolina. These days Marriott Hotels uses the software to manage a frequent-visitor program; Merck & Co. and Pfizer Inc. use it to develop new drugs; the U.S. government uses SAS to calculate the Consumer Price Index. The software is not cheap. A charge of $50,000 a year for 50 users is typical. All but 2 of the 100 largest U.S. public companies use it. Its sales exceed $1.3 billion. The company employs 9,300 people worldwide, up from 5,400 people five years ago.

What is truly unusual about SAS is not the software it creates but the unusual way in which it does business. The freedom and exuberance associated with the new economy has a dark side: Work is so demanding, so all-consuming, that is can become unsatisfying. In that context, SAS may be the world's sanest company. Why?

First, there's the mood of the place. SAS operates in a competitive arena full of buzzwords—"data mining," "knowledge management"—and builds cutting-edge products that set the industry standard. Yet the one word that employees universally use to describe the company's work environment is "relaxed."

Second, there's also the stability of the company. It is an article of faith in the software business that the only way to attract and keep talented employees is to offer them stock options, along with extraordinary salaries. SAS, a private company, offers no stock, and its salaries are no better than its competition. SAS treats its employees so well—there is no limit on how many sick days they can take; they can even stay home to care of sick family members—that employees remain fanatically devoted to the company. Last year, its turnover rate was 3.7 percent; never in the history of the company has the rate been higher than 5 percent.

Third, there's the sense of balance between work and family life found at SAS. At a time when companies are trying to mix work and family, SAS has the largest on-site daycare operation in North Carolina. To encourage families to eat lunch together, the SAS cafeteria supplies baby seats and high chairs. To encourage families to eat dinner together, the company has adopted a seven-hour workday. Indeed, most people at SAS keep work hours that are far from typical of the new economy. They leave the office by 5 P.M.

It's just past 6 A.M., and Larnell Lennon is loosening up with some buddies in the SAS fitness center. Despite the hour, the place is moderately busy. SAS has 36,000 square feet of gym space, which includes a large, hardwood aerobics floor; two full-length basketball courts; a private, skylit yoga room; and workout areas segregated by gender. People are too shy to ride an exercise bike in front of coworkers of the opposite sex. Outside, there are soccer and softball fields. Massages are available several times a week, and classes are offered in golf, African dance, tennis, and tai chi.

Lennon, a software tester in the display-products group, remembers the first time he saw the gym, 13 years ago, when it was part of a workout complex that was only two-thirds as large as the current one. "I had heard the company's name, but nothing more," Lennon says. "I had a friend here at SAS, and he invited me over to the gym during lunch. That gym caught my attention. I saw how people related to each other." At the time, Lennon was just a year out of school, working as a programmer at Nortel. "The professional standards there were great," he says. "But you went to your cubicle in the morning, and then you left at the end of the day. The atmosphere was tight." His first visit to the SAS gym was in February 1991. Two months later, Lennon interviewed for the position of development tester. That June, he was hired. "I came back, and I met managers. The atmosphere went beyond the gym. I liked what I heard." How much did he like it? He took a 10 percent pay cut to join SAS: "It's better to be happy than to have a little more money."

Lennon had more surprises coming. In what may qualify as the most over-the-top health benefit around, SAS launders his (and other employees') sweat-soaked workout clothes and then returns them, fresh and fluffy, the next day—a service that many people's spouses wouldn't even consider providing. "This is a no-excuses facility," says Kelli Dutrow, a wellness coordinator. At SAS, you can't use grungy workout clothes as a reason not to exercise. The point of the human resources strategy is to make it impossible for people not to do their work. If you're worried about finding an assisted-living center for your aging mom up in New York, call the company's elder-care coordinator, who will make calls for you. If you need allergy shots, why shouldn't you be able to get them on campus, at the SAS health clinic? Says David Russo: "Jim's idea is that if you hire adults and treat them like adults, then they'll behave like adults."

The history of the company's benefits is revealing. The story begins when SAS was still a startup in 1976—a startup with a number of women working for it. "Our women employees were two or three years into their careers—at the top of their talent curve—and they started deciding to stay home and have kids," says Russo. "We knew and they knew that they'd have to start from scratch if they stepped out. Jim said, 'We can't lose those people. We're too small a company.' So we started providing day care in the basement. We began with 4 or 5 kids; now we have 528 (including some who attend a nearby private facility)." SAS was by no means obligated to offer day care. It couldn't, however, afford to lose its female employees. Today 51 percent of SAS managers are women. A group at the company meets monthly to discuss proposed new benefits, evaluating them in the context of a three-part test: Would the benefit accord with SAS's culture? Would it serve a significant number of employees? And would it be cost accountable—that is, would its perceived value be at least as high as it cost? Every benefit has to pass all three tests.

SAS is owned by just two people—Jim Goodnight, who owns two-thirds of it, and John Sall, senior vice president, who owns the rest. Since both of them are billionaires, they can do what they want. If Goodnight wants a sculpture, he opens up his wallet and buys it. In fact, SAS has a full-time, four-person art group, headed by an artist who was originally hired to create paintings for the company.

The benefits build a foundation of loyalty that supports the bottom line. The payoff starts with turnover. A typical software company of SAS's size loses 1,000 employees per year. At SAS, the number lost is about 130—which translates into almost 900 employees per year whom SAS doesn't have to replace. The result is a huge reduction in expenses for recruiting candidates, for flying them in for interviews, and for moving new hires across the country, as well as a reduction in the amount of work time lost while jobs remain unfilled. Two consulting companies—Hewitt Associates and the Saratoga Institute—have estimated that the cost of replacing a worker runs between 1 and 2.5 times the salary of the open job. The more sophisticated the job, the higher the cost. Given a factor of 1.5 and an average SAS salary of $50,000, the company arguably saves $67.5 million a year, compared with what its competitors spend to attract new employees. That comes to an extra $12,500 per year per employee that SAS can spend on fringe benefits. Russo's department pays for many of those work-life benefits. "Is that my budget, $67 million? No way," says Russo. "That's the beauty of it. The cost of the buildings, of running the gym—that's pretty inexpensive. There's no way I could spend all of the money we save."

A subtle critique of the SAS corporate culture is that it might spawn unintended management problems. It might create a work atmosphere so relaxed, so playful, that urgency and quality could end up taking a back seat to finishing a workout. Russo seems unconcerned: "If you're out sick for six months, you'll get cards and flowers, and people will come to cook dinner for you. If you're out sick for six Mondays in a row, you'll get fired. We expect adult behavior."

John Sall, in addition to being a co-owner of SAS, runs his own small group within the company that develops statistical-analysis software for desktop machines. Except for a summer job in the melting room of a foundry, he has never worked anywhere else. So how does SAS prevent people from taking advantage of its policies? What if people desired to spend all day playing billiards or Ping-Pong? The question has clearly never occurred to Sall. "I can't imagine that playing Ping-Pong would be more interesting than work."

On a midsummer afternoon, Kathy Passarella is sitting in the main cafeteria at SAS. The room is airy and busy; live piano music plinks in the background. The crowd is so young and informally dressed that the place seems more like a college campus than a corporate one. Passarella has been at SAS for a year and a half, training new R&D employees in computer skills. In one of her previous jobs, she worked as a programmer at Bell Labs. She connects SAS's approach to benefits to the performance of the people who receive them. "You're given the freedom, the flexibility, and the resources to do your job. Because you're treated well, you treat the company well." When she joined SAS she noted that when you walked down the halls here, it's rare to hear people talking about anything but work.

The informal environment at SAS can be misleading. This is a company built on accountability. SAS is a decentralized company, but tracks key performance data closely. From his computer, Goodnight can look up detailed sales and performance information; he can track data on technical support calls, which are sorted by product and by time-to-resolution; he can monitor bug reports in new software, noting how quickly testers and developers are eliminating flaws in products headed for release. The sense of accountability also extends to documentation. Every SAS product manual includes the names of the developers and testers who created or updated the software. The sense of accountability is so ingrained, and the lines of reporting are so simple that the company needs no formal organization chart. As it grows, SAS tends to get wider—spawning new divisions—rather than adding more layers of management. Indeed, the company is so brutally flat that on the Cary campus, many of the several thousand frontline employees who work there—from housekeepers to coders with Ph.D.s—are just two or three levels in the corporate hierarchy from Jim Goodnight.

Larnell Lennon says that what surprised him most when he arrived at SAS—besides getting his own office—was how his manager spent his time. "My manager is doing what I'm doing," says Lennon. "She is in the trenches, writing code. Dr. Goodnight was once in the same group that I'm in. At my last job, my manager was just making sure that everything got done. Here, we all do that." Xan Gregg works in John Sall's group. Sall has plenty to say "about the details of how code is written," says Gregg. "That's unusual for an executive vice president. Usually managers are not very technical." Sall, an almost impossibly shy and unassuming billionaire, says that he sees himself primarily as "a statistician and a software developer—not a businessperson or a manager." Managers who understand the work that they oversee can make sure that details don't slide. At SAS, groups agree on deadlines, and managers understand what their group does. Unrealistically optimistic promises about timetables and completion dates are relatively rare.

Bob Snyder, an applications developer who was recently hired away from Texas Instruments, where he had worked on the guidance systems for Paveway bombs, says, "Here, I know everything I do has an impact on the final product. That gives you a sense of responsibility to get things done right and on time."

SAS is also a typical organization. It's a place where product releases run late, where sales quotas don't get met, where groups are understaffed, where people clash over both substance and style. One recent hire griped that SAS is too family friendly: "It's hard to eat lunch without stepping on a rug-rat."

Some might even suggest that the mood at SAS—the cheeriness, the contentment—could become grating. The place can come across as being a bit too perfect, as if working there might mean surrendering some of your personality. Outsiders have occasionally referred to SAS as "Stepford Corporation"—a place with a sophisticated plantation mentality, where the boss lives (as Goodnight does) in a mansion adjacent to the corporate campus, and where your lunch tab is automatically deducted from your paycheck. You may not owe your salary to the company store, but what about your soul?

Questions

1. How has Jim Goodnight used the characteristics found in the needs model to motivate his employees?
2. What's motivating Jim Goodnight?
3. Would you like to work for SAS?

CHAPTER 15

Motivation through Goal Setting and Reward Systems

LEARNING OBJECTIVES

When you have finished studying this chapter, you should be able to:

1. Explain how goal setting affects performance.
2. State the effects of goal setting on job satisfaction and performance.
3. Describe reward systems for fostering high performance.

Preview Case: UPS
MODEL OF GOAL SETTING AND PERFORMANCE
Importance of Goal Setting
Challenge
Teams Competency—NASCAR Racing
Moderators
Mediators
Performance
Ethics Competency—The Gap
Rewards
Satisfaction
EFFECTS OF GOAL SETTING
Impact on Performance
Communications Competency—The Ritz-Carlton Hotel
Limitations to Goal Setting
Organizational Guidelines
REWARD SYSTEMS FOR HIGH PERFORMANCE
Gain-Sharing Programs
Profit-Sharing Programs
Skill-Based Pay
Flexible Benefit Plans
Organizational Guidelines
Across Cultures Competency—Reward Practices in Different Cultures
CHAPTER SUMMARY
KEY TERMS AND CONCEPTS
DISCUSSION QUESTIONS
EXPERIENTIAL EXERCISE AND CASE

UPS

PREVIEW CASE

Steve Menkhaus, a UPS delivery driver in Sharonville, Ohio, didn't see himself as a salesperson. However, since UPS began a sales lead incentive program in 1993, more than 100,000 delivery drivers have generated more than a half a million sales leads. After a driver initiates a lead, a UPS representative follows up, usually in a day, with additional information and a contract offer. Forty-three percent of these new sales leads have turned into new customers, generating millions in new company revenue. Menkhaus's efforts in the sales lead incentive program not only added new business for UPS, but they also enabled him to accrue points that he could exchange for merchandise and trips. What Menkhaus did sounds simple, but it represents a dramatic and fundamental change in the way UPS motivated its drivers.

The need to change was fueled by competitors, such as the U.S. Postal Service, Emery, and DHL, all of which expanded their services to attract UPS customers. Offering customized and convenient services, each competitor chipped away at UPS's business as they carved out their own niches. To respond to the competition, UPS cut costs by offering an early retirement program to managers, which many took. This program left UPS with fewer managers and put more demands on front-line employees, such as Menkhaus.

UPS's motivation plan was to involve each employee in soliciting new business. In essence, UPS was entrusting nonmanagement people with determining the best ways to attract and serve customers. Most of the drivers embraced their new autonomy and saw tremendous opportunities to get valued rewards. Before UPS turned its drivers into salespeople, it gave each driver tips on selling.

UPS drivers were allowed to spend up to thirty minutes per week of unstructured time on the job. [Remember, this is a company that scheduled its drivers to the tenth of an hour and told them how to carry the clipboard (under the right arm) and the package (under the left)]. As a result, drivers can now spend more time with customers—to listen and to come up with solutions to meet their needs. Thirty minutes a week may not sound like much, but it is a huge financial commitment. At $29 per hour, UPS drivers are the highest paid in the nation. For UPS, thirty minutes per week per driver means a commitment of approximately $36 million a year.

What have been the results? Revenues have exceeded $35 billion and profits were up substantially. UPS handled more than 13.7 million packages a day, the best in the history of the company. Recently, UPS has set a goal to become the number one supply chain company in the world.

To accomplish this goal, UPS has aggressively acquired other logistics companies and has started to manage the in-house supply chain operations for customer companies. For example, Nike uses UPS to handle its entire supply chain. Every few hours, Nike sends a batch of orders from Nike.com to a UPS facility in Louisville, Kentucky. Within a few minutes, a UPS employee, using a radio-frequency barcode reader, grabs the item—usually made in Asia and delivered directly to a UPS warehouse located by a major airport—off the shelf. The product is then checked by another UPS employee for accuracy, packed, and shipped within 24 hours to the store.[1]

For more information on UPS, visit the organization's home page at ***http://www.UPS.com.***

To survive in today's global competitive market, setting challenging goals that take into account the crucial factors of time and quality and providing feedback to employees is no longer an option. It must happen!

The motivational practices that produce the achievements in UPS are based on setting goals, developing feedback systems, and providing reward systems that get individuals to strive to reach those goals. Goals play an important part in motivating individuals to strive for high performance. The basic concepts in goal setting remain an important source for motivating employees.[2]

In this chapter, we begin by presenting a model of goal setting and performance based on the individual. Then we focus on four commonly used reward systems that reinforce desired behaviors of employees.

LEARNING OBJECTIVE

1. Explain how goal setting affects performance.

MODEL OF GOAL SETTING AND PERFORMANCE

Goals *are future outcomes (results) that individuals and groups desire and strive to achieve.*[3] An example of an individual goal is "I intend to graduate with a 3.2 grade point average by the end of the spring semester, 2009." **Goal setting** *is the process of specifying desired outcomes toward which individuals, teams, departments, and organizations will strive and is intended to increase organizational efficiency and effectiveness.*

Importance of Goal Setting

The goal-setting process is no easy task, but the effort is not only worthwhile, it is also becoming essential in the current highly competitive global business and institutional environments. The most important reasons for having goals include the following:

- Goals guide and direct behavior. They increase role clarity by focusing effort and attention in specific directions, thereby reducing uncertainty in day-to-day decision making.
- Goals provide challenges and indicators against which individual, team, departmental, or organizational performance can be assessed.
- Goals justify the performance of various tasks and the use of resources to pursue them.
- Goals define the basis for the organization's design. They determine, in part, communication patterns, authority relationships, power relationships, and division of labor.
- Goals serve an organizing function for the person's work.
- Goals reflect what employees and managers alike consider important and thus provide a framework for planning and controlling activities.[4]

Just as organizations strive to achieve certain goals, individuals also are motivated to strive for and attain goals. In fact, the goal-setting process is one of the most important motivational tools for affecting the performance of employees in organizations. In this section we consider one of the most widely accepted models of goal setting and indicate how goal-setting techniques can be applied to motivate individuals and teams.

Ed Locke and Gary Latham developed a sophisticated model of individual goal setting and performance. Figure 15.1 presents a simplified version of their model. It shows the key variables and the general relationships that can lead to high individual performance, some of which we have discussed in previous chapters. The basic idea behind this model is that a goal serves as a motivator because it allows people to compare their present performance with that required to achieve the goal. To the extent that people believe they will fall short of a goal, they will feel dissatisfied and work harder to attain it as long as they believe that it can be achieved.

Having a goal also may improve performance because the goal makes clear the type and level of performance expected. At PPG, a Pittsburgh-based paint and glass manufacturer, employee objectives are called SMART goals, an acronym for "Specific, Measurable, Agreed-upon by the employee and manager, Realistic, Time-bound," says George Kock, director of human resource planning. Before the SMART goal system was implemented, a sales manager would be told by her boss to increase sales for the next year. Now she might be asked to develop, by September 30, three new customers in three Southeast regions with annual sales volume of $250,000 each. Thanks to SMART, sales performance has increased by more than 25 percent.[5]

FIGURE 15.1 Model of Goal Setting

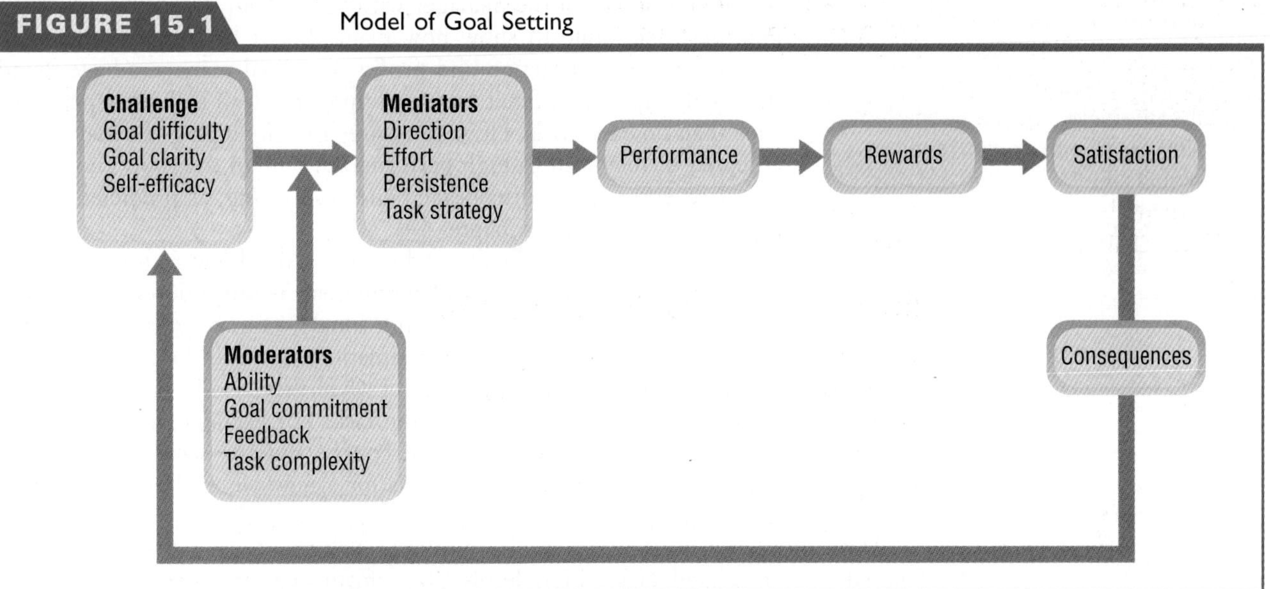

Source: Adapted from Locke, E. A., and Latham, G.P. *A Theory of Goal Setting and Task Performance.* Englewood Cliffs, N.J.: Prentice Hall, 1990, 253.

Challenge

Stated another way, goal setting is the process of developing, negotiating, and establishing targets that challenge the individual. Employees with unclear goals or no goals are prone to work slowly, perform poorly, exhibit a lack of interest, and accomplish less than employees whose goals are clear and challenging. In addition, employees with clearly defined goals appear to be more energetic and productive. They get things done on time and then move on to other activities (and goals).

Goals may be implicit or explicit, vague or clearly defined, and self-imposed or externally imposed. Whatever their form, goals serve to structure the individual's time and effort. Two key attributes of challenging goals are particularly important: goal difficulty and goal clarity.

- **Goal difficulty.** *A goal should be challenging but not impossible to achieve.* If it is too easy, the individual may delay or approach the goal lackadaisically. If it is too difficult, the individual may not really accept the goal and thus not try to meet it.
- **Goal clarity.** *A goal must be clear and specific if it is to be useful in directing effort.* The individual thus will know what is expected and not have to guess. For instance, FedEx's customer service agents are expected to answer customers' questions within 140 seconds.

Clear and challenging goals lead to higher performance than do vague or general goals. **Management by objectives** (MBO) *is a management system that uses goal difficulty and goal clarity as its foundation for motivating employees.* In essence, this management system involves managers and employees jointly setting goals for performance and personal development, periodically evaluating the employee's progress toward achieving these goals, and then rewarding the employee. One company that has made extensive use of management by objectives is Cardinal Health. At the beginning of each year, all 55,000 employees are asked to identify at least one performance objective that supports one of the four corporate goals of growth, operational excellence, leadership development, and customer focus. In addition, at the end of the year, managers are asked to rate employees on a set of core leadership competencies, such as self-management, teamwork, sound judgment, relationship building, and the like. By combining the ratings from the manager with those from the employees, Cardinal has been able to show how management by objectives leads to both employee satisfaction and profits. Cardinal managers have found that goals that are difficult but not impossible lead to higher performance than do easy goals. However, unrealistically high goals may not be accepted or may lead to high performance only in the short run.[6] Individuals eventually get discouraged and stop trying, as predicted by the expectancy model (see Chapter 14).

THE COMPETENT LEADER

Our people are motivated financially to reach their goals. We believe that the goal-setting process is not something that has been pulled out of a textbook, but is the guideline for running our company.
David Disiere, CEO, Deep South

Along with goal difficulty and clarity, a third key factor that influences the establishment of challenging goals is self-efficacy. In Chapter 13, we defined *self-efficacy* as the individual's estimate of his or her own ability to perform a specific task in a particular situation. As might be expected, individuals who set high goals perform at a high level when they also have high self-efficacy. A person's self-efficacy is dependent on the task. For example, a golfer with a low handicap has high self-efficacy on the golf course. But the same person might have low self-efficacy when meeting sales quotas for a new piece of equipment that her company has just introduced.[7]

With clear and challenging goals, employee behaviors are more likely to be focused on job-related tasks, high levels of performance, and goal achievement. Table 15.1 provides a summary of the key links between goal setting and individual performance.

TABLE 15.1 Impact of Goals on Performance

WHEN GOALS ARE	PERFORMANCE WILL TEND TO BE
Specific and clear	Higher
Vague	Lower
Difficult and challenging	Higher
Easy and boring	Lower
Set participatively	Higher
Set by management (top down)	Lower
Accepted by employees	Higher
Rejected by employees	Lower
Accompanied by rewards	Higher
Unrelated to rewards	Lower

The following Teams Competency feature illustrates how people in teams use the basic concepts of goal challenge, goal clarity, and self-efficacy to instill teamwork. In NASCAR racing, it is often how well the pit crew performs that determines whether the driver wins the race.[8]

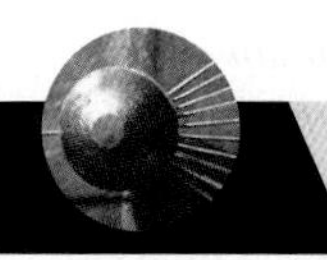

Teams Competency

NASCAR Racing

Ray Evernham is considered by many NASCAR people to be a premier crew chief. Over a recent span of five years, he and Jeff Gordon have won more races than any other NASCAR team. Evernham and Gordon give much of the credit to their pit crew, known as the Rainbow Warriors, because crew members wear rainbow-striped jumpsuits.

When the Rainbow Warriors crew was assembled, its members decided to do things differently. In the past, mechanics who had worked on a race car all week also suited up on Sunday to work as the pit crew. The car was the number one priority. The crew relied on horsepower and the driver to win the race. Pit crews didn't practice and set goals. Evernham and Gordon knew that all drivers have essentially the same equipment. They thought the ingredient that would separate winning from losing drivers was their ability to create a team. They decided to have two crews: The first crew was responsible for the mechanics of the car (e.g., engine and suspension components); the second—the pit crew—was responsible for the car during the race.

Under Evernham and Gordon's leadership, the Rainbow Warriors hired a coach to develop specifically the teamwork competency of the pit crew. Training included rope climbing, scaling walls, wind sprints, guys carrying each other on their backs, and the like. All members of the pit crew were trained to perform all necessary tasks so that they could rotate tasks among themselves, depending on race conditions. By analyzing other NASCAR drivers, Evernham determined that, if Gordon's car could leave the pit 1 second faster than the competition, Gordon would gain 300 feet on the competition (a car going 200 mph travels nearly 300 feet a second). The pit crew set a goal of having the car exit the pit in 17 seconds or less. During a race, all crew members listen to each other on their scanners. They use special code words to signal whether they are changing two or four tires when Gordon pulls into the pit. The crew also determines whether to gas the car fully or just to put in enough gas to finish the race. Evernham and his crew also determine when Gordon should come in for a pit stop. Before the race, all the Rainbow Warriors sit in a circle to discuss race strategy. The circle symbolizes that the team is stronger than any individual. When Gordon wins a race, signs a personal services contact, or is paid to sign autographs, all the members of both crews receive a percentage of that money.

For more information on NASCAR, visit the organization's home page at ***http://www.nascar.com****.*

Moderators

Figure 15.1 also shows four of the factors that moderate the strength of the relationship between goals and performance: ability, goal commitment, feedback, and task complexity. We begin with ability because it limits an individual's capacity to respond to a challenge.

Ability. The relation of goal difficulty to performance is curvilinear, not linear. That is, performance levels off as the limits of a person's ability are approached. In Chapter 14, we learned that motivation is an important part of a person's ability to perform. Some individuals believe that they have the ability to acquire new competencies and master new situations. They seek challenging new assignments that open their eyes to new ways of doing tasks. Others believe that their ability to complete a task is relatively stable and avoid placing themselves in a situation in which they might receive a negative evaluation.[9]

Goal Commitment. The second factor, **goal commitment,** *refers to an individual's determination to reach a goal, regardless of whether the goal was set by that person or someone else.* What is your goal commitment in this class? Take a minute and complete the questionnaire in Table 15.2. Your commitment to achieve a goal is likely to be stronger if you make it publicly, if you have a strong need for achievement, and if you believe that you can control the activities that will help you reach that goal.

TABLE 15.2 Goal Commitment Questionnaire

	RESPONSE CATEGORY				
ITEM	STRONGLY AGREE	AGREE	UNDECIDED	DISAGREE	STRONGLY DISAGREE
1. I am strongly committed to achieving a grade of ______.	_____	_____	_____	_____	_____
2. I am willing to expend the effort needed to achieve this goal.	_____	_____	_____	_____	_____
3. I really care about achieving this grade.	_____	_____	_____	_____	_____
4. Much personal satisfaction can be gained if I achieve this grade.	_____	_____	_____	_____	_____
5. Revising my goal, depending on how other classes go, isn't likely.	_____	_____	_____	_____	_____
6. A lot would have to happen to abandon my grade goal.	_____	_____	_____	_____	_____
7. Expecting to reach my grade goal in this class is realistic for me.	_____	_____	_____	_____	_____

Scoring: Give yourself 5 points for each Strongly Agree response; 4 points for each Agree response; 3 points for each Undecided response; 2 points for each Disagree response; and 1 point for each Strongly Disagree response. The higher your total score, the greater is your commitment to achieve your grade goal in this class.

Source: Adapted from Cron, Wm. L., Slocum, J.W., Jr VandeWalle, D. and Fu, F. The role of goal orientation on negative emotions and goal setting when initial performance falls short of one's performance goal. *Human Performance*, 2005, 18(1), 55–80; Hollenbeck, J.R. Williams, C.R., and Klein, H.J. An empirical examination of the antecedents of commitment to goals. *Journal of Applied Psychology*, 1989, 74, 18–23.

The effect of participation on goal commitment is complex. Positive goal commitment is more likely if employees participate in setting their goals, which often leads to a sense of ownership. In a study by the Corporate Leadership Council of 50,000 employees, the council found that increased commitment can lead to a 57 percent improvement in discretionary effort—employees' willingness to exceed the normal job duties. That effort produces, on the average, a 20 percent individual performance improvement and an 87 percent reduction in a desire to leave the organization. Not expecting or wanting to be involved in goal setting reduces the importance of employee participation in terms of goal commitment. Even when a manager has to assign goals without employee participation, doing so leads to more focused efforts and better performance than if no goals are set or if a person is told simply to "do their best."[10]

The expected rewards for achieving goals play an important role in the degree of goal commitment. The greater the extent to which employees believe that positive rewards (merit pay raises, bonuses, promotions, opportunities to perform interesting tasks, and the like) are contingent on achieving goals, the greater is their commitment to the goals. These notions are similar to the ideas contained in the expectancy model of motivation. Similarly, if employees expect to be punished for not achieving goals, the probability of goal commitment also is higher. However, recall that punishment and the fear of punishment as the primary means of guiding behavior may create long-term problems (see Chapter 13).

Employees compare expected rewards against rewards actually received. If received rewards are consistent with expected rewards, the reward system is likely to continue to support goal commitment. If employees think that the rewards they receive are much less than the rewards they expected, they may perceive inequity. If perceived or actual inequity exists, employees eventually reduce their goal commitment.

Teamwork and peer pressures are other factors that affect a person's commitment to a goal. Health First, a nonprofit chain of hospitals in Rockledge, Florida, has successfully matched corporate goals with those of its employees. Health First management set five goals, including patient care and managing costs. Why five? Because Health First wants to keep managers focused on a handful of high-priority items that are measurable. At the beginning of the year, department heads sit down with their employees and communicate these five goals. They discuss how the employee plans to reach that goal. If the manager of the OB-GYN department needs to reduce his operating costs by 5 percent, he can log into the hospital intranet to see how costs are tracking for his department during the year. Half of a person's pay increase is based on individual and team performance. If a manager is not reaching his goal, then human resource managers give him input on how to achieve the goal. According to Bob Suttles, vice president for human resources, "The monitoring system holds managers accountable to motivate their staffs to their highest performance."[11]

Feedback. Feedback makes goal setting and individual responses to goal achievement (performance) a dynamic process. **Feedback** *provides information to the employee about how well he or she is doing.* It enables the individual to relate received rewards to those expected in terms of actual performance. This comparison, in turn, can influence changes in the degree of goal commitment.

Task Complexity. **Task complexity** *is the last moderator of the strength of the relationship between goals and performance that we consider.* For simple tasks (e.g., answering telephones at Marriott's reservation center), the effort encouraged by challenging goals leads directly to high task performance. For more complex tasks (e.g., studying to achieve a high grade), effort doesn't lead directly to effective performance. The individual must also decide where and how to allocate effort.

Mediators

Let's assume that an individual has challenging goals and that the moderating factors support achievement of these goals. How do the four mediators—direction, effort, persistence, and task strategy—affect performance? *Direction of attention* focuses behaviors on activities expected to result in goal achievement and steers the individual away from activities irrelevant to achieving the goals. The *effort* a person exerts usually depends on the difficulty of the goal. That is, the greater the challenge, the greater will be the effort expended, assuming that the person is committed to reaching the goal. *Persistence* involves a person's willingness to work at the task over an extended period of time until the results are achieved. Most sports require participants to practice long and hard to hone their competencies and maintain them at a high level. Finally, *task strategy* is the way in which an individual—often through experience and instruction—decides to tackle a task. That is, what to do first.

Performance

Performance is likely to be high when (1) challenging goals have been set, (2) the moderators (ability, goal commitment, feedback, and task complexity) are present, and (3) the mediators (direction, effort, persistence, and task strategy) are operating. Destiny Health, an Oak Brook, Illinois, company that offers health plans for small businesses, offers employees a program called the Vitality Program. The program was created to encourage employees to seek preventive medical care. This program awards points to employees who take care of themselves. For example, enrollment in a stop smoking program is worth 3,000 points, which can be redeemed for consumer electronics, movie tickets, magazine subscriptions, and vacation packages. Points can also be converted into frequent-flier miles on selected airlines. Companies whose employees each earn more than 45,000 points a year qualify for discounted health insurance.[12]

Three basic types of quantitative indicators can be used to assess performance: units of production or quality (amount produced or number of errors); dollars (profits, costs, income, or sales); and time (attendance and promptness in meeting deadlines). When such measures are unavailable or inappropriate, qualitative goals (customer satisfaction, teamwork) and indicators may be used. In addition, many organizations have developed a code of ethics to support employees in setting ethical goals and making ethical decisions. Creating ethics guidelines has several advantages that the Gap, GE, and Johnson & Johnson, among others, consider important. Some of the advantages for setting ethical goals are

- to help employees identify what their organization recognizes as acceptable behaviors;
- to legitimize the consideration of ethics as part of decision making;
- to avoid uncertainties among employees about what is right and wrong; and
- to avoid inconsistencies in decision making caused by an organizational reward system that appears to reward unethical behavior.[13]

The Gap, Inc., has recently issued a 42-page social responsibility report that spells out the problems facing this $6.5 billion clothing retailer found in its more than 3,000 factories contracted to produce clothing for the Gap, Old Navy, and Banana Republic brands. The company discovered persistent wage, health, and safety violations in many regions where it does business, including China, Africa, India, and Central and South America. The infractions ranged from a failure to provide proper protective equipment to physical abuse and coercion. The Gap pulled its business from 136 factories and turned down bids from more than 100 others when they failed to meet the Gap's labor standards. The following Ethics Competency feature highlights what the Gap has done to improve working conditions.[14]

ETHICS COMPETENCY

THE GAP

What has the Gap done to improve the working conditions at the factories around the world that manufacture its apparel? First, it appointed Anne Gust, Gap's chief administrative and compliance officer, who authorized the publication of a report. This 42-page report divulges information on the Gap's social responsibility practice to its shareholders and financial institutions. This report honestly told of the labor violations and admits that the Gap does not have all of the answers to fix them. Many of the labor problems are widespread in this industry.

Second, it has built an elaborate monitoring system that has 93 members who perform more than 8,500 factory inspections each year. Of those, 75 percent of these passed inspection and were accepted into the Gap's approved supplier list. During a follow-up visit, 136 factories were found to violate the Gap's policies and were kicked off the Gap's approved supplier list. All production facilities are now monitored and violations are reported to Gust.

Third, it has outlined goals to achieve in each of its supplier factories. The Gap has agreed to rethink accepted garment industry practices. Some of these include the use of child or forced labor (prisoners), unrealistic production cycles, requiring employees to work more than 60 hours a week, and expecting employees to work unpaid overtime.

Fourth, Gust and her assistant have met with several labor-advocacy groups in an effort to make the-Gap's labor policies very clear. The Gap has shown a willingness to go public and reveal its responses to these groups.

Fifth, it supported the efforts by El Salvadoran garment workers to unionize its apparel factory.

Sixth, many factories in India have added benefits like on-site child care and health care, as well as free meals. These have reduced employee turnover and improved productivity.

For more information on the Gap, visit the organization's home page at ***http://www.Gap.com.***

Rewards

When an employee attains a high level of performance, rewards can become important inducements for the employee to continue to perform at that level. Rewards can be external (bonuses, paid vacations, and the like) or internal (a sense of achievement, pride in accomplishment, and feelings of success). UPS, PPG, and Jeff Gordon's NASCAR organization all reward people for high performance. However, what is viewed as a reward in one culture may not be viewed as a reward in another. For example, doing business in Vietnam requires the exchange of gifts during the first day of a business meeting. Although they may be small and relatively inexpensive, gifts with a company logo are highly valued. The gifts should be wrapped, but white or black paper should not be used because these colors are associated with death. In contrast, exchanging gifts at a business meeting in the United States generally is not expected. Praising an individual in public for achievement in Vietnam will embarrass the individual. Rewards are not to be given in public. Conversely, public acclaim for achievement in the United States is valued.[15]

Satisfaction

Many factors—including challenging work, interesting coworkers, salary, the opportunity to learn, and good working conditions—influence a person's satisfaction with the job (see Chapter 11). However, in the Locke–Latham model, the primary focus is on the employee's degree of satisfaction with performance. Employees who set extremely high, difficult goals may experience less job satisfaction than employees who set lower, more easily achievable goals. Difficult goals are less frequently achieved, and satisfaction with performance is associated with success. Thus some compromise on goal difficulty may be necessary in order to maximize both satisfaction and performance. However, some level of satisfaction is associated with simply striving for difficult goals, such as responding to a challenge, making some progress toward reaching the goals, and the belief that benefits may still be derived from the experience regardless of the outcome.

LEARNING OBJECTIVE

2. State the effects of goal setting on job satisfaction and performance.

EFFECTS OF GOAL SETTING

What conditions increase or decrease the benefits of goal setting? Five essential pieces must come together for managers to gain the benefits of a goal-setting program:[16]

1. The person must have the knowledge and ability to attain the goal. If the goal is to increase sales by 15 percent within the next 12 months and the employee lacks the sales competencies needed to attain it, urging them to set "stretch goals" usually isn't effective. It can make employees so anxious to reach the goal that they scramble to discover ways (ethical and unethical) to reach the goal, but do not learn the behaviors that are needed to be effective.
2. The person must be committed to the goal, especially if the goal is difficult. Achieving a difficult goal requires a great deal of effort.
3. People need feedback on their progress toward the goal. Feedback enables employees to adjust their effort and behavior necessary for goal attainment. When employees discover that they are not reaching their goals, they typically increase their efforts because of the pride they have in their performance.
4. Tasks that are complex need to be broken down so that the employee can set subgoals that can be attained. These subgoals yield information for employees as to whether their progress is consistent with what is required for them to attain their goal.
5. Situational constraints can make goal attainment difficult. One of the primary roles of a leader is to ensure that employees have the resources necessary to attain their goals and to remove obstacles in the way of accomplishing those goals.

Impact on Performance

One of the consequences of goal setting is that it motivates individuals to achieve high performance. There are several reasons for this. First, difficult but achievable goals prompt people to concentrate on achievement of the goals. At Enterprise Rent-A-Car, agents focus on customer satisfaction goals because they know that results are measured monthly and ranked and that these rankings affect their chances for advancement. Second, difficult goals motivate people to spend lots of time and effort on developing methods for achieving them. At Enterprise, agents communicate with customers, sometimes at length, so that the agents understand their needs and can provide the most suitable vehicle to them, whether it is a sedan, convertible, pickup, or SUV. Customer satisfaction and loyalty are vital to the success of the business. Third, difficult goals increase people's persistence in trying to achieve them. If people perceive that goals can be reached by luck or with little effort, they tend to dismiss the goals as irrelevant and not follow through with the actions needed to reach them.

To sum up, specific, difficult goals affect motivation and performance by

- encouraging people to develop action plans to reach these goals,
- focusing people's attention on these goal-relevant actions,
- causing people to exert the effort necessary to achieve the goals, and
- spurring people to persist in the face of obstacles.

One of the many firms that have put these steps into practice is the Ritz-Carlton Hotel. As described in the following Communications Competency, communications during an employee's orientation is critical. It is during this orientation that the hotel's values and goals are communicated.[17]

COMMUNICATION COMPETENCY

THE RITZ-CARLTON HOTEL

Employees who work for The Ritz-Carlton Hotel are proud of the fact that the company is a two-time winner of the Baldrige National Quality Award. The awards for excellent customer service they represent don't just happen by accident. It begins with the hiring process—the company knows what types of people perform well in each job, and it is careful to employ only the people who have demonstrated empathy and teamwork and present a low-key demeanor.

Orientation comes next. This is the first step in creating a team of employees who all share the same goals. During orientation, the company communicates its "soul" according to Horst Schultz, former president. During orientation, Schultz would explain that every employee was essential to the company's reaching its performance goals. If they didn't making checking in a pleasure and respond to the guests' every need, the company would not reach its quality service goals. Quality service includes 24-hour room service, twice-a-day maid service, complimentary shoeshines, and club rooms with a private lounge and concierge.

After a general orientation program, Ritz-Carlton provides more specific training for employees, reflecting their specific jobs. The training is designed and delivered by the five best employees who perform each job. These employees, called *5 Star Awardees*, are superior performers who have been nominated by their peers, guests, and managers. Working as a team, those who are best at doing each job develop a set of principles that everyone doing that job needs to know and practice. And the communication of these principles never stops. For the first 15 minutes of each day, all employees participate in the "line-up," which is used to remind all employees that they should strive to live the company's values throughout their workday. At these line-ups, department heads inform employees of special events that day and bring up potential problems, such as food, language, monetary exchange rates, and transportation needs. By constantly communicating with employees what the company hopes to achieve, it teaches them habits that will serve their guests well. To reward employees for practicing these behaviors, managers give out *Gold Standard Coupons* to those employees who are "caught" meeting the hotel's standards for quality. The coupons can be exchanged for weekend accommodations at the hotel or merchandise in the hotel's gift shop.

For more information on The Ritz-Carlton, visit this organization's home page at ***http://www.RitzCarlton.com.***

Limitations to Goal Setting

Goal setting has been shown to increase performance in a variety of settings. However, you should be aware of three limitations.[18] First, when employees lack the skills and abilities needed to perform at a high level, goal setting doesn't work. Giving an employee a goal of writing a computer program will not lead to high performance if the worker doesn't know how to write such a program. To overcome this limitation, new hires at The Ritz-Carlton are required to attend training sessions at which they are taught how to process requests and complaints, build customer loyalty, and establish relationships with restaurants, taxi services, golf courses, and others services frequently requested by guests.

Second, successful goal setting takes longer when employees are given complicated tasks that require a considerable amount of learning. Good performance on complicated tasks also requires that employees be able to direct all their attention to the tasks and not be interrupted by side issues. Ray Evernham's Rainbow Warriors pit crew is able to perform complicated tasks quickly because they are the only tasks that the crew is focusing on while the car is in the pit.

Third, goal setting can lead to major problems when it rewards the wrong behaviors. Rod Rodin is the CEO of Marshall Industries, a billion-dollar electronics distributor in Los Angeles that serves more than 30,000 customers who order more than 700,000 parts a month. He quickly recognized that the company's reward system was encouraging behaviors that led to poor service, dissatisfied customers, and, ultimately, lower profits. Rodin found that more than 20 percent of each month's sales were shipped to clients during the last 3 days of the month. Managers were hiding customer returns or opening bad credit accounts just to make their monthly sales goals. Divisions were hiding products from each other or saying that products had been shipped when they really had none on hand. Salespeople fought over how to split commissions on revenue from a customer who did design work in Chicago but made purchases in Cleveland. Employee and team performance was reviewed and ranked on the basis of numerical criteria, such as receivables outstanding and gross sales dollars. Rodin's solution was to scrap the incentive compensation system. He declared that there would be no more contests, prizes, or bonuses for individual achievements. Everyone at Marshall was put on a salary and shared in a companywide bonus pool if the organization as a whole met its goals.[19]

THE COMPETENT LEADER

Running a business is like going to a track meet. You have to make a decision on how high to put the bar on a high jump. My job is to encourage people to put the bar up as high as realistically possible and encourage them to figure out how they can get over it.
Kurt Wiedenhaupt, CEO, American Precision Industries

Organizational Guidelines

Individuals who are both satisfied with and committed to an organization are more likely to stay with it and to accept the challenges that it presents than are individuals who are less satisfied and committed. Turnover and absenteeism rates for satisfied individuals are low. This link brings us full circle to the beginning of the Locke–Latham goal-setting model. What might happen if things go badly and an individual who had been satisfied becomes dissatisfied? Individual responses fall into at least six categories: (1) job avoidance (quitting); (2) work avoidance (absenteeism, arriving late, and leaving early); (3) psychological defenses (alcohol and/or drug abuse); (4) constructive protest (complaining); (5) defiance (refusing to do what is asked); and (6) aggression (theft or assault). Quitting is the most common outcome of severe dissatisfaction.[20]

The goal-setting model has important implications for employees, managers, and teams alike. First, it provides an excellent framework to assist the manager or team in diagnosing the potential problems with low- or average-performing employees. Diagnostic questions might include these: (1) How were the goals set? (2) Are the goals challenging? (3) What is affecting goal commitment? and (4) Does the employee know when he has done a good job? Second, it provides concrete advice to the manager on how to create a high-performance work environment. Third, it portrays the system of relationships and interplay among key factors, such as goal difficulty, goal commitment, feedback, and rewards, to achieve high performance.

LEARNING OBJECTIVE

3. Describe reward systems for fostering high performance.

REWARD SYSTEMS FOR HIGH PERFORMANCE

In Chapters 13 and 14 we discussed types of rewards that organizations make available to employees. From the concepts discussed in those chapters, along with the concepts presented so far in this chapter, you should by now recognize that one of the basic goals of managers should be to motivate employees to perform at their highest levels. The term **high-performance work system** *is often used to describe the* *integration of well-established methods of motivation with new technologies that link pay and performance.* Managers agree that tying pay to job performance is essential. However, the actual implementation of programs designed to bring about such a relationship is often quite difficult. Questions that arise include "Should pay increases be tied to the performance of an individual or team?" Recall that Rod Rodin, CEO of Marshall Industries, found that rewarding individuals created unhealthy competition among employees and destroyed morale. Deciding to reward all employees in the organization raises another question: Should the reward be based on cost savings or profits and be distributed annually or when people retire or otherwise leave the organization? The accounting procedures required by cost savings plans are enormous and complex, but if efficient they allow rewards to be distributed relatively quickly. Moreover, many employees view fringe benefits, salaries, opportunities to engage in challenging assignments, and the achievement of difficult goals as rewards.

Considerable research has been done on how rewards affect individual and team performance. From this research, the ability of rewards to motivate individuals or team to high performance was found to depends on six factors:

1. *Availability.* For rewards to reinforce desired performance, they must be available. Too little of a desired reward is no reward at all. For example, pay increases are often highly desired but unavailable. Moreover, pay increases that are below minimally accepted standards may actually produce negative consequences, including theft, falsifying records, and the like.
2. *Timeliness.* Like performance feedback, rewards should be given in a timely manner. A reward's motivating potential is reduced to the extent that it is separated in time from the performance it is intended to reinforce.
3. *Performance contingency.* Rewards should be closely linked with particular performances. If a goal is met, the reward is given. The clearer the link between performance and rewards, the better able rewards are to motivate desired behavior. Forty percent of employees nationwide believe that there is no link between their performance and pay.
4. *Durability.* Some rewards last longer than others. Intrinsic rewards, such as increased autonomy, challenge, and accountability, tend to last longer than extrinsic rewards, such as pay increases.
5. *Equity.* Employees' motivation to perform is improved when they believe that the pay policies of their organization are fair and equitable.
6. *Visibility.* To promote a reward system, management must ensure that rewards are visible throughout an organization. Visible rewards, such as assignments to important committees or promotion to a new job, send signals to employees that rewards are available, timely, and based on performance.

To the extent that reward systems are used to motivate employees to achieve high performance, we discuss four popular reward systems: gain sharing, profit sharing, skill-based pay, and flexible benefit plans. The strengths and limitations of each are summarized in Table 15.3.

Gain-Sharing Programs

Gain-sharing programs *are designed to share with employees the savings from productivity improvements.* The underlying assumption of gain sharing is that employees and the employer have similar goals and thus should share in economic gains. Regular cash bonuses are provided to employees for increasing productivity, reducing costs, or improving quality. According to Michael Murphy, a compensation consultant for Hewitt Associates, more than 25 percent of all U.S. companies had some type of gain-sharing pay plan for their employees. The average payout for employees was 7.6 percent, up from 5.9 percent just a few years ago. Many organizations, such as Georgia-Pacific, Huffy Bicycle Company, TRW, Inland Container Corporation, and General Electric, are discovering that, when designed correctly, gain-sharing plans

TABLE 15.3 Reward Systems in High-Performance Work Settings

REWARD SYSTEM	STRENGTHS	LIMITATONS
Gain-sharing programs	Rewards employees who reach specified production levels and control costs.	Formula can be complex; employees must trust management.
Profit-sharing programs	Rewards organizational performance.	Individuals and teams are not likely to have an impact on overall organizational performance.
Skill-based pay	Rewards employee with higher pay for acquiring new skills.	Labor costs increase as employees master more skills. Employee can "top out" at the highest wage rate.
Flexible benefits	Tailored to fit individual needs.	Administrative costs are high and the program is difficult to use with teams.

can contribute to employee motivation and involvement. Specific formulas tailor-made for each organization are used to calculate both performance contributions and gain-sharing awards. Many gain-sharing plans encourage employees to become involved in making decisions that will affect their rewards. Gain-sharing plans are tied to a plant, division, or department's improvement.[21]

A popular version of gain sharing is the Scanlon plan, named after Joe Scanlon, a union leader in the 1930s.[22] The **Scanlon plan** *is a system of rewards for improvements in productivity.* This plan is designed to save labor costs, and incentives are calculated as a function of labor costs relative to the sales value of production. Working together, employees and managers develop a formula that bases the distribution of rewards on a ratio of total labor costs to total sales volume. If actual labor costs are less than expected, the surplus goes into a bonus pool. For example, Baltimore County workers calculated that they needed $100,000 worth of labor to generate $500,000 worth of services to residents of that county. In the following year, the same services were provided for $80,000 worth of labor. Forty percent of the $20,000 saved was then distributed to the employees, with the county keeping the balance. Employee bonuses were based on a percentage of salary.[23] In many cases, the bonus pool is equally split between organization and employees.

Gain-sharing programs are better suited to certain situations than to others. Table 15.4 illustrates a list of conditions favoring this plan. In general, gain-sharing programs seem suited to small organizations with a good market, simple measures of performance, and production costs controllable by employees. Top management should support the plan and the employees should be interested in and knowledgeable about gain sharing.

Although gain-sharing plans sound good, there have been notable failures. The Fleet Financial Group recently abandoned its gain-sharing program. As a part of a two-year cost-cutting effort, management had created a gain-sharing program tied to the company's ratio of expenses to revenue and its stock prices. The more costs were cut and the higher the stock rose, the more employees were supposed to be rewarded. But when Fleet's stock price remained depressed even after cost cutting, workers got the minimum payout—averaging $615 per employee. Many employees stated that, considering the blood, sweat, and tears that went into getting the bonus, it turned out to be meaningless. What further enraged employees was that top management received big bonuses that weren't tied to the same measures. Another fail-

TABLE 15.4 Conditions Favoring Gain-Sharing Plans

ORGANIZATIONAL CHARACTERISTIC	FAVORABLE CONDITION
Size of organization	Usually fewer than 500 employees
Product costs	Controllable by employees
Organizational climate	Open, high level of trust
Style of management	Participative
Union status	No union, or one that is favorable to a cooperative effort
Communication policy	Open, willing to share financial results
Plant manager	Trusted, committed to plan, able to articulate goals and ideals of plan
Management	Technically competent, supportive of participative management style, good communication skills, able to deal with suggestions and new ideas
Workforce	Technically knowledgeable, interested in participation and higher pay, financially knowledgeable and interested

Source: Adapted from Cummings, T. G., and Worley, C. G. *Organization Development and Change*, 7th ed. Cincinnati: South-Western, 2001, 403.

ure occurred at Ameristeel Corporation. After seven years of the gain-sharing plan and with the worldwide overcapacity in steel production and declining prices, top management had to cancel the plan. Ameristeel's gain-sharing plan, which paid out largely based on productivity gains, has been replaced by a plan based on employees' ability to operate efficiently by cutting costs and waste and by reducing imperfections that require steel to be rerolled.[24]

Profit-Sharing Programs

Profit-sharing programs *give employees a portion of the company's earnings.* As the name suggests, profit-sharing plans distribute profits to all employees. Average profit-sharing figures are difficult to calculate, but according to some experts they typically range between 4 and 6 percent of a person's salary. According to Steve Watson, managing director at Stanton Chase, an executive-recruiting firm, profit sharing may have a limited impact because employees may feel that they can do little to influence the organization's overall profitability. That is, company profits are influenced by many factors (e.g., competitor's products, state of the economy, and inflation rate) that are well beyond the employees' control. However, profit-sharing plans are very popular in Japan. For example, at Seiko Instruments many managers and workers receive bonuses twice a year that equal four or five months' salary. These bonuses are based on the company's overall performance.[25]

What are the characteristics of successful profit-sharing programs? According to Hewitt Associates, more than one-third of the companies that use profit sharing do not track the results of such programs, while 28 percent indicate that profit-sharing plans do not meet the objectives. To avoid failure, Hewitt Associates recommends the following:

- Involve line managers and employees in the plan's creation to ensure they'll support it.
- Set clear goals for the plan.
- Ensure that the employees understand the metrics that the plan is measuring.
- Tie the plan to the company's strategy.

- Give the plan time to succeed. It takes two or three years for a plan to change overall company performance.
- Provide up-to-date information that allows employees to see how well they are performing against their goals.[26]

Skill-Based Pay

Paying people according to their value in the labor market makes a great deal of sense. After all, employees having highly developed skills, and those who develop multiple skills are particularly valuable assets to the organization. As we have emphasized earlier, competencies such as managing communication, team building, and change are often based on mastering a number of individual skills, such as verbal, written, and media presentations. **Skill-based pay** *depends on the number and level of job-related skills that an employee has learned.*[27] Skill-based pay compensates employees for the skills they can use in the organization, rather than for specific jobs they are performing. Pay changes do not necessarily go along with job changes. There is also little emphasis on seniority. The underlying assumption is that by focusing on the individual rather than the job, skill-based reward systems recognize learning and growth. Employees are paid according to the number of different skills they can perform.

More than 16 percent of the Fortune 1000 companies use skill-based pay systems to motivate employees. In the United Kingdom, the Norwich and Peterborough Building Society, a mortgage and banking business, had a reward system that had 12 levels, proved to be ineffective in curbing turnover, covered only some of the employees, and basically confused employees. The new plan centers on five-level job skills, such as customer service and relationship management, that are linked to pay rate changes in the market. Sixty-seven percent of employees now know that their pay progression is linked to the attainment of these five-level job skills. As a result, employee turnover has dropped to 17 percent from 25 percent, productivity has increased, customer satisfaction has improved, and employees report that the new pay system is simple and transparent, and they understand what skills they need to learn to increase their pay. For managers, they do not have to answer the question "Why is that person earning more than I am?"[28]

Of course, skill-based pay programs have some limitations. There is a major drawback of skill-based pay: the tendency to "top out." Topping-out occurs when employees learn all the skills there are to learn and then run up against the top end of the pay scale, with no higher levels to attain. Some organizations, such as GE and United Technologies, have resolved the topping-out effect by installing a gainsharing program after most employees have learned all the skills required. Other organizations have resolved this problem by making skills obsolete, eliminating them, and adding new ones, thus raising the standards of employee competence. Other drawbacks include inadequate management commitment to the plan, conflicts between the employees included in and those excluded from the skill-based pay plan, inadequate training of managers, and poor plan designs that increase labor costs without providing offsetting organizational benefits. Skill-based pay systems also require a heavy investment in training, as well as a measurement system capable of telling when employees have learned the new skills.

Flexible Benefit Plans

Flexible benefit plans *allow employees to choose the benefits they want, rather than having management choose for them. Flexible benefit plans often are called* **cafeteria-style benefits plans.** According to John Semyan, partner with TNS Consulting, a typical corporation's benefits plan currently is about 36 percent of its total employee compensation package.[29] That represents a huge cost, considering that only 3 percent or less is set aside for merit pay increases in most organizations. Under flexible benefit plans, employees decide—beyond a base program—which additional benefits they want, tailoring the benefits package to their needs. The idea is that employees can make important and intelligent decisions about their benefits. Some employees take all their discretionary benefits in cash; others choose additional life insurance, child or elder care, dental insurance, or retirement plans. Extensive benefit options may be highly attractive to an employee with a family. However, many benefits might be only minimally attractive to a young, single employee. Older employees value retirement plans more than younger employees and are willing to put more money into them. Employees with elderly parents may desire financial assistance in providing care for them. At Traveler's Insurance Company employees can choose benefits of up to $5,000 a year for the care of dependent elderly parents.

Thousands of organizations now offer flexible benefits plans. They have become very popular because they offer three distinct advantages. First, they allow employees to make important decisions about their personal finances and to match employees' needs with their benefits plans. Second, such plans help organizations control their costs, especially for health care. Employers can set the maximum amount of benefit dollars they will spend on employees' benefits and avoid automatically absorbing cost increases. Third, such plans highlight the economic value of many benefits to employees. Most employees have little idea of the cost of benefits because the organization is willing to pay for them even though employees might not want some of them or might prefer alternatives.

Moreover, the changing workforce is causing employers to consider flexible benefits as a tool to recruit and retain employees. Starbucks Coffee Company believes that its use of flexible benefits plans has cut employee turnover from 150 to 60 percent (see Chapter 14). Starbucks calculates that hiring an employee costs $550. If so, a competitor with 300 percent turnover would have to hire three people at a cost of 3 x $550 = $1,650 per job per year, whereas Starbucks would need to spend only 0.6 x $550 = $330 per job per year.

Some limitations are associated with flexible benefit plans. First, because different employees choose different benefits packages, record keeping becomes more complicated. Sophisticated computer systems are essential for keeping straight the details of employees' records. Second, accurately predicting the number of employees that might choose each benefit is difficult. Such uncertainty may affect the firm's group rates for life and medical insurance, because the costs of such plans are based on the number of employees covered.

Organizational Guidelines

Management must make certain trade-offs when choosing among these four reward systems. Figure 15.2 provides some guidance for choosing a suitable reward system. It shows under what circumstances an individual or team plan is appropriate and under what situations specific individual or team plans are most effective. If you answer the first five diagnostic questions *yes*, reward systems that permit individuals to calculate their own rewards might be of value. If you answer the first five diagnostic questions *no*, team, department, or organizationwide reward systems might be more appropriate. If you want to reward individuals' performance, you should then ask three additional questions. If the answers to all of these questions are *yes*, a skill-based or gainsharing system is appropriate. Similarly, if a group or team reward system seems appropriate, you should ask three additional questions. If the answers to all of these questions are *yes*, profit-sharing and flexible benefit programs are appropriate.

Organizations in various countries utilize different reward systems. Cultural values learned in childhood are passed down from one generation to the next and serve to differentiate one country from another. The information shown in Table 15.5 was taken from several large international studies. The researchers examined reward system differences in more than 50 cultures. In Chapter 1, we presented a framework to examine differences in thinking, feelings, ideas, and values that differentiate

FIGURE 15.2 Deciding among Alternative Reward Systems

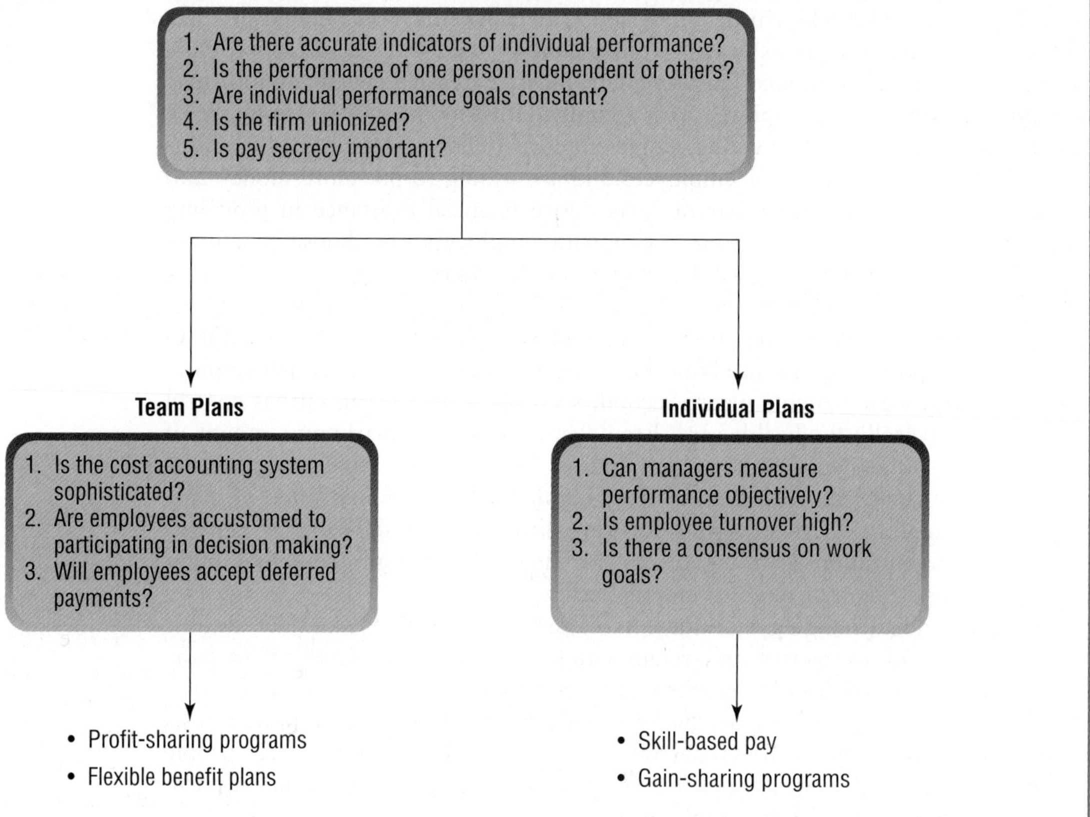

Source: Adapted from Wagner, J. A., and Hollenbeck, J. R. *Organizational Behavior,* 3rd ed. Englewood Cliffs, N.J.: Simon and Schuster, 1998, 100.

TABLE 15.5 Cultures and Reward Systems

CULTURE	REWARD SYSTEM
Power distance	Pay based on individual performance
	Status symbols are important
	Pay tied to level in the organization's hierarchy
	Stock options to MBO
Individualism-collectivism	Pay based on team performance
	Profit sharing
	Little emphasis on extrinsic rewards
Gender role orientation	Extensive use of fringe benefits
	Gain sharing
	Goals set by participation linked to team achievements
	Pay equality
Uncertainty avoidance	Pay focuses on long-term orientation
	Seniority is important

Source: Adapted from Tosi, J. L., and Greckhamer, T. Culture & CEO compensation. *Organization Science*, 2004, 15, 657–670; and Hofstede, G. *Cultures Consequences*, 2nd ed. Thousand Oaks, CA: Sage, 2001.

people of one culture from another.[30] We discussed the four dimensions that cultures can vary on, including uncertainty avoidance, power distance, individualism-collectivism, and gender role orientation.

Please reread pages 19-22 to refresh yourself with these dimensions. Using these dimensions, the following Across Cultures competency feature highlights how cultural differences impact differences in reward systems.[31]

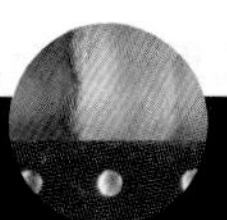

ACROSS CULTURES COMPETENCY

REWARD PRACTICES IN DIFFERENT CULTURES

In high *uncertainty avoidance* cultures, reward systems emphasize seniority. There is strong loyalty to the company that leads to long-term employment. Rewards based on seniority are easy to administer and understand. These systems expose the employee to little risk because they are based on the performance of the company and not on individual and/or team efforts. In Japan and other Asian cultures, employees receive their annual pay raise on their anniversary date (the day they joined the company). Instead of dismissing an employee for poor performance, managers move people from one department to another or into a "window seat," a job with little authority and responsibility. These practices allow the employee to save face.

In high *power distance* cultures, rewards are based on one's level within the managerial hierarchy. There are wide salary ranges between the top and lower level employees. Perquisites and status symbols are popular and expected. Profit sharing and other forms of variable compensation systems are relied on to motivate employees. Subordinates are motivated by the threat of sanctions.

In *individualistic cultures*, organizations expect individuals to look out for their own personal interests. The employee–employer relationship is a business deal based on what the "labor market" will pay. Incentives are given to individuals. Therefore, skill-based pay and MBO systems are popular because they reward an individual's achievements. In collective cultures, team gain sharing is used to reinforce the team or group's achievements. At NSK, a ball-bearing manufacturer, and Toto, a toilet producer, when business slows down, these companies permit all workers to work shorter shifts and receive smaller paychecks. In cultures that do not have a strong gender role orientation, equality among members is stressed. There are few differences between gender and pay. Flexible benefits plans that allow the individual a wide choice of non–work-related benefits (e.g., child care, sabbatical leaves) are used to motivate employees to perform. For example, in Sweden, women in management take having families for granted and expect managers to find creative ways to help them work through this childbearing time.

CHAPTER SUMMARY

1. Explain how goal setting affects performance.

Goal setting is a process intended to increase efficiency and effectiveness by specifying the desired outcomes toward which individuals, departments, teams, and organizations should work.

The goal-setting model developed by Locke and Latham emphasizes the challenges provided for the individual: goal difficulty, goal clarity, and self-efficacy. Setting difficult but clear and achievable goals for individuals who believe that they have the ability to complete their tasks leads to high performance. Four moderators

—ability, goal commitment, feedback, and task complexity—influence the strength of the relationship between challenging goals and performance. If the individual has the ability, is committed to the goal, and is given feedback on progress toward achievement of the goal—and if the task is complex—high performance will result. All four moderators must be present to motivate a person to achieve goals. Four mediators—direction, effort, persistence, and task strategy—facilitate goal attainment. That is, these four characteristics channel or focus the person's motivational efforts. Performance, rewards, satisfaction, and consequences complete the model.

2. State the effects of goal setting on job satisfaction and performance.

Goal setting is one of the key mechanisms for increasing job satisfaction and performance because it permits employees to be self-motivated. Five requirements must be in place for goal setting to have positive benefits for the employee and organization: the employee's knowledge and ability, the employee's commitment to a goal, feedback on the task, establishment of subgoals on complex tasks, and a leader who removes obstacles that prevent employees from reaching their goals.

3. Describe reward systems for fostering high performance.

Reward systems represent a powerful means for motivating high levels of individual and team performance. Four reward systems, in particular, are designed to enhance performance: gain sharing, profit sharing, skilled-based pay, and flexible benefits. Gain-sharing programs are regular cash bonuses for employees who increase their productivity, reduce costs, or improve quality. A similar program is profit sharing, which gives employees a portion of the organization's profits. Skilled-based pay systems pay a person according to the number and level of job-related skills that the employee masters. The value of these skills is determined by the organization. Flexible benefit plans allow employees to choose the benefits that are important to them.

KEY TERMS AND CONCEPTS

Cafeteria-style benefit plans
Feedback
Flexible benefit plans
Gain-sharing programs
Goal clarity
Goal commitment
Goal difficulty
Goal setting
Goals
High-performance work system
Management by objectives (MBO)
Profit-sharing programs
Scanlon plan
Skill-based pay

DISCUSSION QUESTIONS

1. Cindy Baker, a financial manager for the Marriott, said that many times, managers commit the error of measuring the wrong behaviors with excruciating accuracy. What implications does this pose for managers using management by objectives?
2. What are the similarities and differences between gain-sharing and profit-sharing plans? Which system would motivate you to achieve greater performance? Why?
3. If a manager for CompUSA based in Dallas were transferred to Japan, what cultural issues that might she encounter when rewarding employees?
4. Explain UPS's program according to the concepts presented in the goal-setting model. Why is it so successful?
5. What factors influenced your level of goal commitment to this course? Did your level of commitment change after receiving feedback on an assignment or test? Explain.
6. Can a flexible benefits plan be tied to employee performance? If so, what are the advantages of doing so? The disadvantages?
7. What are some problems that employees might face in an organization that has adopted a skill-based pay program?

8. Marc Occhuiti, a manager for American Airlines' food and beverage service, said: "If you cannot define it and measure it, you are not going to get it." What implications does this statement have for setting goals? For measuring them?

9. Use the goal-setting model to analyze Ray Evernham's NASCAR team, the Rainbow Warriors. Why is it so effective?

10. List your five most important personal goals. Evaluate the difficulty and clarity of each goal. Can these be measured? What are the implications, if any, of this assessment for your future?

EXPERIENTIAL EXERCISE AND CASE

Experiential Exercise: Self-Competency

Goal Setting[32]

Instructions

The following statements refer to a job you currently hold or have held. Read each statement and then select a response from the following scale that best describes your view. You may want to use a separate sheet of paper to record your responses and compare them with the responses of others.

Scale

Almost Never 1 2 3 4 5 Almost Always

_____ 1. I understand exactly what I am supposed to do on my job.
_____ 2. I have specific, clear goals to aim for on my job.
_____ 3. The goals I have on this job are challenging.
_____ 4. I understand how my performance is measured on this job.
_____ 5. I have deadlines for accomplishing my goals on this job.
_____ 6. If I have more than one goal to accomplish, I know which are most important and which are least important.
_____ 7. My goals require my full effort.
_____ 8. My manager tells me the reasons for giving me the goals I have.
_____ 9. My manager is supportive with respect to encouraging me to reach my goals.
_____ 10. My manager lets me participate in the setting of my goals.
_____ 11. My manager lets me have some say in deciding how I will go about implementing my goals.
_____ 12. If I reach my goals, I know that my manager will be pleased.
_____ 13. I get credit and recognition when I attain my goals.
_____ 14. Trying for goals makes my job more fun than it would be without goals.
_____ 15. I feel proud when I get feedback indicating that I have reached my goals.
_____ 16. The other people I work with encourage me to attain my goals.
_____ 17. I sometimes compete with my coworkers to see who can do the best job in reaching our goals.
_____ 18. If I reach my goals, my job security will be improved.
_____ 19. If I reach my goals, my chances for a pay raise are increased.
_____ 20. If I reach my goals, my chances for a promotion are increased.
_____ 21. I usually feel that I have a suitable action plan(s) for reaching my goals.
_____ 22. I get regular feedback indicating how I am performing in relation to my goals.
_____ 23. I feel that my training was good enough so that I am capable of reaching my goals.
_____ 24. Organization policies help rather than hurt goal attainment.
_____ 25. Teams work together in this company to attain goals.
_____ 26. This organization provides sufficient resources (e.g., time, money, and equipment) to make goal setting effective.
_____ 27. In performance appraisal sessions, my supervisor stresses problem solving rather than criticism.
_____ 28. Goals in this organization are used more to help you do your job well rather than punish you.
_____ 29. The pressure to achieve goals here fosters honesty as opposed to cheating and dishonesty.
_____ 30. If my manager makes a mistake that affects my ability to attain my goals, he or she admits it.

Scoring and Interpretation

Add the points shown for items 1 through 30. Scores of 120 to 150 may indicate a high-performing, highly satisfying work situation. Your goals are challenging and you are committed to reaching them. When you achieve your goals, you are rewarded for your accomplishments. Scores of 80 to 119 may suggest a highly varied work situation with some motivating and satisfying features and some frustrating and dissatisfying features. Scores of 30 to 79 may suggest a low-performing, dissatisfying work situation.

Questions

1. Using the concepts found in the Locke and Latham model, how might you increase work performance?
2. What type of high-performance reward system would support the changes suggested in your answer to Question 1?

Case: Change Competency

Improving Safety

Safety issues continue to be of great concern to employees and managers. Since the passage of the Occupational Safety and Health Act (OSHA) in 1970, managers have been particularly alert to the need for reducing injury-related accidents at work and ways of doing so. In a certain farm machinery company, three departments had particularly troublesome safety records: final assembly, parts, and raw material preparation. Although management had posted safety warnings, safety violations were still occurring too frequently.

The company hired four consultants who developed a checklist based on the company's safety manual. The consultants then randomly observed workers in the three departments to determine whether they followed the company's safety rules (e.g., did employees wear safety glasses with shields on both sides when working underneath equipment and did they wear leather gloves?). These observations were made two to four times a week in full view of the employees. A total of 167 observations were made during the study. After each observation session, the safety performance of each of the three departments was computed by dividing the number of employees working safely by the total number of departmental employees observed and multiplying by 100. Weekly departmental safety performance was determined by averaging the results of the observations during that week. The results were posted so that all employees knew their department's safety performance score. The average safety record for the raw material department was 72 percent, for the final assembly department it was 53 percent, and for the parts department it was 48 percent.

The consultants designed a training program to improve safety in these departments. All employees attended a 30-minute meeting during which management told them that the safety goal would be related to their department's weekly safety performance. Management also said that 100 percent weekly safety performance was unrealistically high and therefore not expected. The employees were told further that, if 90 percent of the employees performed their jobs safely, not only would the goal be attained, but the frequency of injuries also would decline.[33]

Questions

1. Design a goal-setting program for achieving a 90 percent accident-free environment in the three departments. You may choose to work through the goal-setting model presented in the text as a start.
2. What type of reward system would you design to achieve a high-performance work system? State your reasons.

CHAPTER 16

Managing Stress and Aggressive Behavior

LEARNING OBJECTIVES

When you have finished studying this chapter, you should be able to:

1. Explain the concept of stress and an employee's response to stress.
2. Describe the role of personality in reactions to stress.
3. Identify the primary sources of stress in organizations.
4. Outline the possible impacts of stress on health, performance, and job burnout.
5. Identify individual and organizational practices for managing workplace stress.
6. Discuss four major types of workplace aggression: bullying, sexual harassment, violence, and aggression toward the organization itself.

Preview Case: Erica Benson
CONCEPT OF STRESS
Fight-or-Flight Response
The Stress Experience
ROLE OF PERSONALITY IN STRESS
The Type A Personality
The Hardy Personality
PRIMARY SOURCES OF STRESS
Organizational Sources
Teams Competency—Bruce Goode of Works Corporation
Life Stressors
IMPACTS OF STRESS
Impacts on Health
Impacts on Performance
Impacts on Job Burnout
Self Competency—John Houghom's Burnout Experience
MANAGING STRESS
Individual Practices
Organizational Practices
Change Competency—Dofasco's Wellness Program
WORKPLACE AGGRESSION
Workplace Bullying
Sexual Harassment
Diversity Competency—OfficeWorks' Sexual Harassment Policy
Workplace Violence
Aggression toward the Organization
CHAPTER SUMMARY
KEY TERMS AND CONCEPTS
DISCUSSION QUESTIONS
EXPERIENTIAL EXERCISE AND CASE

ERICA BENSON

PREVIEW CASE

"It was as if the very life was being sucked out of me. The expectation was for me to give, give, give, produce, produce, produce, and I had nothing left to give. It was just entirely too much," says Erica Benson. Today, she works from home as the sole proprietor of A-Solution. Located in Bear, Delaware, it offers job coaching and other professional services. Before that, she was a compliance manager for First USA. According to Benson, this position actually required three employees. Aside from pressures at work, Benson had obligations at home to her husband and two daughters. Balancing the two had become mentally and physically burdensome.

"I was always too fatigued or busy with work when I was at home to really enjoy my family in the evening. I would rush my kids through their bath, or to bed, so that I could finish a project. I would make promises to do things with my kids, but then ended up being too tired to hold true to my promise. I also noticed that I was short-tempered with my family over little things."

Benson thought the façade of a happy face would pull her through. Although her husband suggested she seek help, Benson was hesitant to ask for professional assistance. She states: "Of course, I was in denial. There was no way that a strong black woman such as me could be in depression. And even if there was a remote chance that this was true, I kept telling myself that I could handle it on my own. I thought I could do everything." Trying to manage everything, however, took its toll. Benson felt angry about being overworked and undercompensated. She also felt guilty about neglecting her daughters. She became extremely irritable and tired. The stress of it all had even caused chest pains that were growing more intense.

"My body was throwing out all kinds of signs [both physical and mental] that it was about to break down. I even had an episode one morning where the whole left side of my body froze, and I couldn't move any part of it for about three minutes. I was beating myself up mentally because I had the twisted perception that because I had not yet made V.P., I was a failure." After being diagnosed with anxiety and depression, she chose to leave her demanding job.

"Once I knew that I had made the decision to leave, I started feeling better. There was a wonderful peace with my decision. Every day that I was away from that company, I felt myself getting stronger, healthier, and happier." Benson used her expertise to start a home-based business, which has also allowed her to spend more time with her family.[1]

Erica Benson's story is not that unusual. Job stress has become a common and costly problem in the workplace, leaving few workers untouched. For example, studies of workplace stress report the following:

- One-fourth of employees say they are "almost always" mentally and physically drained at the end of the workday.
- Forty percent of workers report that their job is very or extremely stressful.
- Thirty-five percent of employees say their jobs are harming their physical or emotional health.
- Nearly 50 percent of employees say they need help in learning how to manage stress and 42 percent think their coworkers need such help.
- The estimated financial costs of stress vary widely. One estimate by the U.S. Bureau of Labor Statistics indicates that stress costs employers $10,000 per worker per year because of stress-related sickness, absenteeism, turnover, shoddy work, and workplace aggression.[2]

Organizations that ignore stress management, or assign it a low priority, are likely to suffer declines in productivity and morale and perhaps increased legal costs. The negative consequences of stress are so dramatic that managers need to (1) work hard to reduce excessive stress in the workplace and (2) assist employees in developing stress-coping skills. Erica Benson experienced both physical and emotional consequences of high levels of stress.

In this chapter, we (1) explain the nature of stress, (2) discuss the role of personality differences in handling stress, (3) identify key sources of stress, (4) review the effects of stress, (5) outline actions that can be taken to help manage stress, and (6) discuss four types of workplace aggression.

LEARNING OBJECTIVE

1. Explain the concept of stress and an employee's response to stress.

CONCEPT OF STRESS

Stress *is the excitement, feeling of anxiety, and/or physical tension that occurs when the demands placed on an individual are thought to exceed the person's ability to cope.*[3] This most common view of stress is often called *distress* or negative stress. **Stressors** *are the physical or psychological demands in the environment that cause this condition.* They can take various forms, but all stressors have one thing in common: They create stress or the potential for stress when an individual perceives them as representing a demand that exceeds that person's ability to respond.

Fight-or-Flight Response

Numerous changes occur in a person's body during a stress reaction. Breathing and heart rates increase so that the body can operate with maximum capacity for physical action. Brain wave activity goes up to allow the brain to function maximally. Hearing and sight become momentarily more acute, and muscles ready themselves for action. An animal attacked by a predator in the wild basically has two choices: to fight or to flee. The animal's bodily responses to the stressor (the predator) increase its chances of survival. The **fight-or-flight response** *refers to the biochemical and bodily changes that represent a natural reaction to an environmental stressor.*[4] Similarly, our cave-dwelling ancestors benefited from this biological response mechanism. People gathering food away from their caves would have experienced a great deal of stress upon meeting a saber-toothed tiger. In dealing with the tiger, they could have run away or stayed and fought. The biochemical changes in their bodies prepared them for either alternative and contributed to their ability to survive.

The human nervous system still responds the same way to environmental stressors. This response continues to have survival value in a true emergency. However, for most people most of the time, the "tigers" are imaginary rather than real. In work situations, for example, a fight-or-flight response usually isn't appropriate. If an employee receives an unpleasant work assignment from a manager, physically assaulting the manager or storming angrily out of the office obviously is inappropriate. Instead, the employee is expected to accept the assignment calmly and do the best job possible. Remaining calm and performing effectively may be especially difficult when the employee perceives an assignment as threatening and the body is prepared to act accordingly.

Medical researcher Hans Selye first used the word *stress* to describe the body's biological response mechanisms. Selye considered *stress* to be the nonspecific response of the human body to any demand made on it.[5] However, the body has only a limited capacity to respond to stressors. The workplace makes a variety of demands on people, and too much stress over too long a period of time will exhaust their ability to cope with those stressors.

The Stress Experience

A variety of factors influence how an individual experiences stress. Figure 16.1 identifies four of the primary factors: (1) the person's perception of the situation, (2) the person's past experiences, (3) the presence or absence of social support, and (4) individual differences in reacting to stress.

FIGURE 16.1 Common Influences on the Stress Experienced

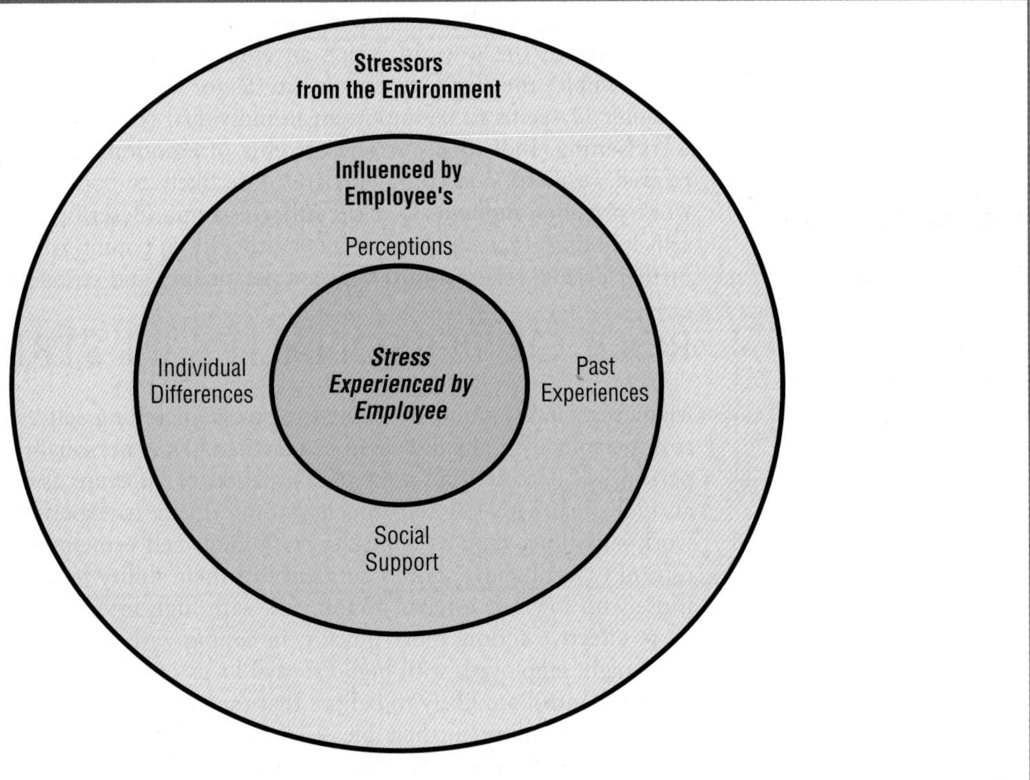

Perception. In Chapter 12 we defined *perception* as a process whereby a person selects and organizes environmental information into a concept of reality. Employee perceptions of a situation can influence how (or whether) they experience stress. For example, two employees, Gail and John, have their jobs duties substantially changed—a situation likely to be stressful for many people. Gail views the new assignment as an opportunity to learn new competencies and thinks that the change is a vote of confidence from management in her ability to be flexible and take on new challenges. In contrast, John perceives the same situation to be extremely threatening and concludes that management is unhappy with his performance.

Past Experiences. John may perceive a situation as more or less stressful, depending on how familiar he is with the situation and his prior experiences with the particular stressors involved. Past practice or training may allow Gail to deal calmly and competently with stressors that would greatly intimidate less experienced or inadequately trained employees. The relationship between experiences and stress is based on reinforcement (see Chapter 13). Positive reinforcement or previous success in a similar situation can reduce the level of stress that a person experiences under certain circumstances; punishment or past failure under similar conditions can increase stress under the same circumstances.

Social Support. The presence or absence of other people influences how individuals in the workplace experience stress and respond to stressors.[6] The presence of coworkers may increase John's confidence, allowing him to cope more effectively with stress. For example, working alongside someone who performs confidently and competently in a stressful situation may help John behave similarly. Conversely, the presence of fellow workers may irritate Gail or make her anxious, reducing her ability to cope with stress.

Individual Differences. The individual's motivation, attitudes, personality, and abilities also influence whether the person experiences work stress and, if so, how he responds to it.[7] Simply stated, each person is different, as we pointed out in Chapters 11 and 12. What one person considers a major source of stress, another may hardly notice. Personality characteristics, in particular, may explain some of the differences in the ways in which an employee experiences and responds to stress. For example, the Big Five personality factor that we labeled emotional stability in Chapter 11 seems to be important in individual responses to various stressors in the work setting. Individuals at one extreme of emotional stability (described as stable, relaxed, resilient, and confident) are more likely to cope well with a wide variety of work stressors; individuals at the other extreme (described as reactive, nervous, and self-doubting) typically have greater difficulty in coping with the same stressors. We further discuss relationships between personality and stress in the following section.

LEARNING OBJECTIVE

2. Describe the role of personality in reactions to stress.

ROLE OF PERSONALITY IN STRESS

Many personality traits are related to stress, including self-esteem and locus of control (personality traits discussed in Chapter 11). A personality trait may affect how a person will perceive and react to a situation or an event as a stressor.[8] For example, an individual with low self-esteem is more likely to experience stress in demanding work situations than is a person with high self-esteem. Individuals high in self-esteem typically have more confidence in their ability to meet job demands than do those with low self-esteem. Employees with high internal locus of control may take more effective action, more quickly, in coping with a sudden emergency (a stressor) than might employees with high external locus of control. Individuals high in internal locus of control are likely to believe that they can moderate the stressful situation.

Before reading further, please respond to the statements in Table 16.1. This self-assessment exercise is related to the discussion that follows.

The Type A Personality

The **Type A personality** *refers to a person involved in a never-ending struggle to achieve more and more in less and less time.* Characteristics of this personality type include

- a chronic sense of urgency about time;
- an extremely competitive, almost hostile orientation;
- thinking about other things while talking to someone;
- an impatience with barriers to task accomplishment; and
- sense of guilt when relaxing or taking a vacation.[9]

TABLE 16.1 A Self-Assessment of Type A Personality

Choose from the following responses to answer the questions below:

A. Almost always true C. Seldom true
B. Usually true D. Never true

_____ 1. I do not like to wait for other people to complete their work before I can proceed with my own.
_____ 2. I hate to wait in most lines.
_____ 3. People tell me that I tend to get irritated too easily.
_____ 4. Whenever possible, I try to make activities competitive.
_____ 5. I have a tendency to rush into work that needs to be done before knowing the procedure I will use to complete the job.
_____ 6. Even when I go on vacation, I usually take some work along.
_____ 7. Even when I make a mistake, it is usually due to the fact that I have rushed into the job before completely planning it through.
_____ 8. I feel guilty for taking time off from work.
_____ 9. People tell me I have a bad temper when it comes to competitive situations.
_____ 10. I tend to lose my temper when I am under a lot of pressure at work.
_____ 11. Whenever possible, I will attempt to complete two or more tasks at once.
_____ 12. I tend to race against the clock.
_____ 13. I have no patience for lateness.
_____ 14. I catch myself rushing when there is no need.

Score your responses according to the following key:

- *An intense sense of time urgency* is a tendency to race against the clock, even when there is little reason to. The person feels a need to hurry for hurry's sake alone, and this tendency has appropriately been called "hurry sickness." Time urgency is measured by items 1, 2, 8, 12, 13, and 14. Every A or B answer to these six questions scores one point.

Your score = _____

- *Inappropriate aggression and hostility* reveal themselves in a person who is excessively competitive and who cannot do anything for fun. This inappropriately aggressive behavior easily evolves into frequent displays of hostility, usually at the slightest provocation or frustration. Competitiveness and hostility is measured by items 3, 4, 9, and 10. Every A or B answer scores one point.

Your score = _____

- *Polyphasic behavior* refers to the tendency to undertake two or more tasks simultaneously at inappropriate times. It usually results in wasted time due to an inability to complete the tasks. This behavior is measured by items 6 and 11. Every A or B answer scores one point.

Your score = _____

- *Goal directedness without proper planning* refers to the tendency of an individual to rush into work without really knowing how to accomplish the desired result. This usually results in incomplete work or work with many errors, which in turn leads to wasted time, energy, and money. Lack of planning is measured by items 5 and 7. Every A or B response scores one point.

Your score = _____
TOTAL SCORE = _____

If your score is 5 or greater, you may possess some basic components of the Type A personality.

Source: Reproduced with permission of the Robert J. Brady Co., Bowie, Maryland, 20715, from its copyrighted work *The Stress Mess Solution: The Causes and Cures of Stress on the Job*, by G. S. Everly and D. A. Girdano, 1980, 55.

Two medical researchers first identified the Type A personality when they noticed a recurrent personality pattern in their patients who suffered from premature heart disease.[10] In addition to the characteristics just listed, *extreme* Type A individuals often speak rapidly, are preoccupied with themselves, and are dissatisfied with life. They tend to give quick replies to questions with no pause to deliberate before answering the questions. Type A personalities may give sarcastic, rude, and hostile responses. They may try to appear to be humorous, but with the underlying intent to be hurtful.

The questionnaire in Table 16.1 measures four sets of behaviors and tendencies associated with the Type A personality: (1) time urgency, (2) competitiveness and hostility, (3) polyphasic behavior (trying to do several things at once), and (4) a lack of planning. Medical researchers have discovered that these behaviors and tendencies often relate to life and work stress. They tend to cause stress or make stressful situations worse than they otherwise might be.

Current research suggests that the Type A personality description is too broad to predict adverse health impacts accurately. Rather, research now indicates that only those individuals with certain aspects of the Type A personality—particularly anger, hostility, and aggression—may be related to severe stress and health reactions.[11] Type A individuals with these specific attributes appear to be two to three times more likely to develop adverse health impacts than are Type B individuals. The **Type B personality** *refers to a person who tends to be easygoing and relaxed, patient, a good listener, and takes a long-range view of things.*

The Hardy Personality

What aspects of personality might protect individuals from the negative health impacts of stress? Individual traits that seem to counter the effects of stress are known collectively as the **hardy personality**—*a person with a cluster of characteristics that includes feeling a sense of commitment, responding to each difficulty as representing a challenge and an opportunity, and perceiving that one has control over one's own life.*[12] The hardy personality is characterized by

- a sense of personal control over events in one's life;
- a tendency to attribute one's own behavior to internal causes (recall the discussion of attribution in Chapter 12);
- a strong commitment to work and personal relationships; and
- an ability to view stress and change as challenges and opportunities for growth, instead of threats.[13]

A high degree of **hardiness** reduces the negative effects of stressful events. Hardiness seems to reduce stress by altering the way in which people perceive stressors. The concept of the hardy personality provides a useful insight into the role of individual differences in reactions to stressors. An individual having a low level of hardiness perceives many events as stressful; an individual having a high level of hardiness perceives fewer events as stressful. A person with a high level of hardiness isn't overwhelmed by challenging or difficult situations. Rather, faced with a stressor, the hardy personality copes or responds constructively by trying to find a solution—to control or influence events. This behavioral response typically reduces stress reactions, moderates blood pressure increase, and reduces the probability of adverse health impacts.

Through development of the *self competency*, we contend that a person may come to reflect the attributes of the hardy personality. Recall from Chapter 1 that the self competency involves the ability to assess your own strengths and weaknesses, set and pursue professional and personal goals, balance work and personal life, and engage in new learning—including new or changed skills, behaviors, and attitudes.

PRIMARY SOURCES OF STRESS

Employees often experience stress in both their personal and work lives. Understanding these sources of stress and their possible interaction is important. To consider either source in isolation may give an incomplete picture of the stress that an employee is experiencing.

LEARNING OBJECTIVE

3. Identify the primary sources of stress in organizations.

Organizational Sources

In the Preview Case on Erica Benson, stress in the workplace is a problem of considerable significance to her and the organization. Organizational sources of stress take a variety of forms. Thus, managers and employees need a framework for thinking about and diagnosing organizational sources of work stress. Figure 16.2 presents such a framework, identifying seven principal work stressors and showing that internal factors influence the ways in which employees experience these stressors.

Workload. For many employees, having too much work to do and not enough time or resources to do it can be stressful. **Role overload** *exists when demands of the job exceed the capacity of a manager or employee to meet all of them adequately.* Many stressful jobs may be in a continuous condition of role overload. Surveys commonly identify work overload or "having to work too hard" as a major source of stress.[14]

FIGURE 16.2 Work Stressors and Stress Experienced

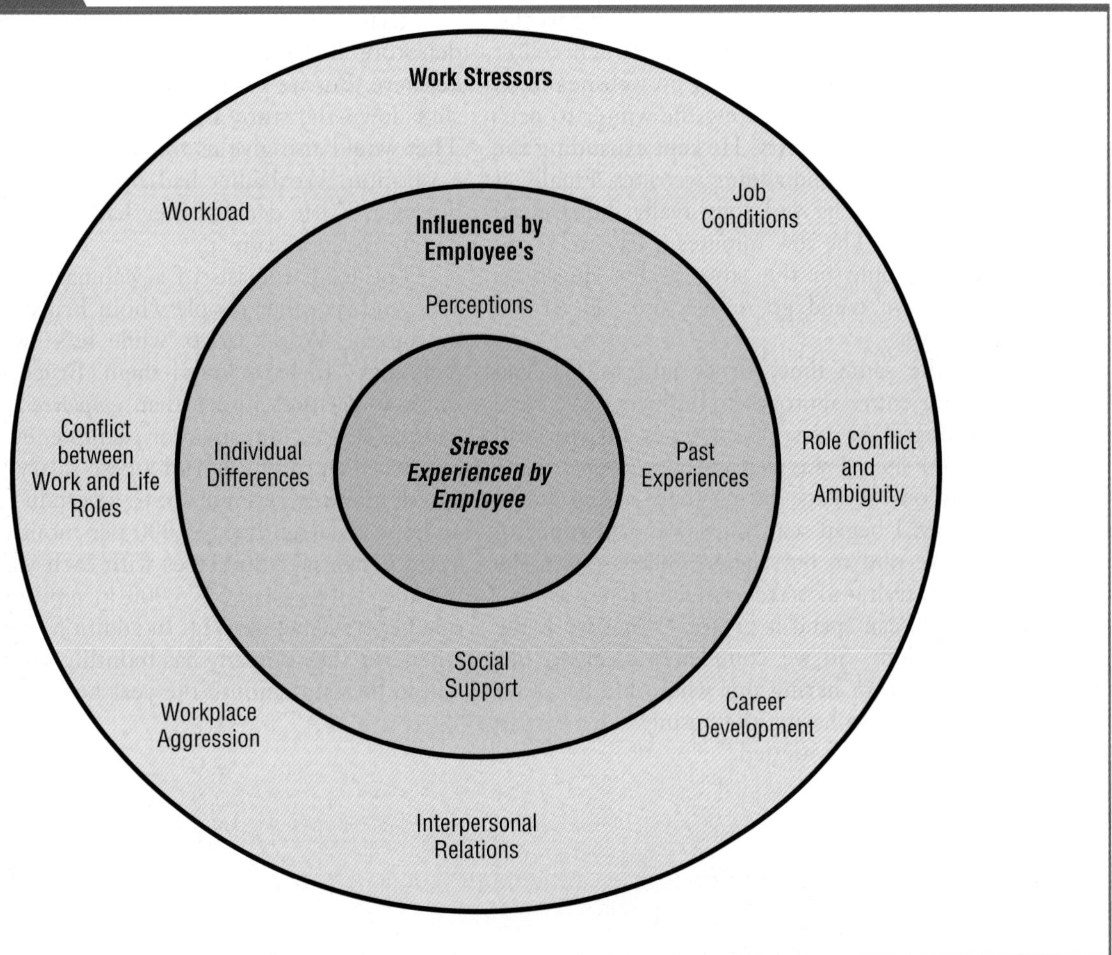

Recall the Preview Case. Erica Benson felt she was working to the point of exhaustion. The demands she experienced allowed little room for rest, flexibility, and family.

Having too little work to do also may create stress. Have you ever had a job with so little to do that the workday seemed never to end? If so, you can understand why many people find too little work stressful. Managers sometimes are guilty of trying to do their subordinates' work, or *micromanage*, when their jobs aren't challenging enough. Micromanaging might reduce the manager's stress caused by boredom, but it is likely to increase subordinates' stress because the superior constantly watches them or second-guesses their decisions.

Bruce Goode is the founder and CEO of Works Corporation. This is an Internet retailer of outdoor garden and home products based in Boise, Idaho. The following Teams Competency feature reports on the work overload he and his spouse, Jody, experienced at one time and how they learned to use a team-based approach in their new business.[15]

Teams Competency

Bruce Goode of Works Corporation

Bruce Goode used to work long days and long weeks. He and Jody, his spouse, owned a small garden center in Boise, Idaho. Goode began putting up websites in an effort to sell garden products during the winter to people in other parts of the country. He kept expanding the online product offerings and adding websites. Finally, it dawned on Bruce that he and Jody really didn't need the store anymore. "The few minutes a day we could get away from people in the store asking questions about $9 items, we could go online and sell $1,000 items," Bruce says.

At about the same time, Bruce and Jody began questioning their entire approach to business. "We were working like dogs," he says. "Sometimes I'd work all night putting up sites. I was getting burned out, and I was completely out of shape sitting there eating at the computer all day. I began realizing I was a prisoner of the business. We said to ourselves, 'There's got to be more to life than trying to make as much money as possible whether you can spend it or not.' What we really wanted was freedom. So we completely changed our way of thinking—from having our whole life be about building the business to having the business be a way to sustain the kind of life we wanted."

That meant, among other things, closing the garden store. Bruce says: "We had a really good niche market here. But we realized we could do even better if we shut down the store and concentrated on the Internet. That would also give us freedom to go camping or take a vacation. We hadn't had one in seven years." First, however, Bruce decided they had to hire some employees and build a team.

The team consists of a webmaster, an office manager, and six other people whom Bruce trusts implicitly to run the Works Corp. while he's away. He says he feels lucky to have found them. Bruce strives to treat them as partners rather than *employees*, a word he has banned at the company. For example, everyone, including Bruce and Jody, is paid a base salary plus a percentage of monthly revenue above a certain threshold. That amount is currently $175,000 per month. The percentage a person gets increases with each year of service. If revenue is less than $175,000 in any given month, no one gets revenue sharing. In addition, there are bonuses whenever the company has monthly sales higher than it had in the same month the year before.

For more information on the Works Corp., visit the organization's home page at ***http://www.workscorp.com.***

Job Conditions. Poor working conditions represent another important set of job stressors. Temperature extremes, loud noise, too much or too little lighting, radiation, and air pollution are but a few examples of working conditions that can cause stress in employees. Heavy travel demands or long-distance commuting are other aspects of jobs that employees may find stressful. Poor working conditions, excessive travel, and long hours all add up to increased stress and decreased performance. Recall Erica Benson's distress related to her long hours: "I was always too fatigued or busy with work when I was at home to really enjoy my family in the evening." In addition, cutting-edge technology, while clearly of great benefit to society in general and many individuals in particular, nevertheless has created job conditions that may be quite stressful. Many employees are receiving massive volumes of e-mail and voice mail messages. A number of technology-assisted jobs have both maximum flexibility and maximum stress. Computers have lowered the entry barriers to many high-stress jobs, from accounting to programming, by making it possible to perform them anytime, anywhere.[16] For some employees, this makes it difficult to draw mental boundaries between work and home. They can end up being the same place, as experienced by Erica Benson in the Preview Case.

Role Conflict and Ambiguity. **Role conflict** *refers to differing expectations of or demands on a person at work that become excessive.* (We discuss role conflict in detail in Chapter 9.) **Role ambiguity** *occurs when an employee is uncertain about assigned job duties and responsibilities.* Role conflict and role ambiguity are particularly significant sources of job-related stress. Many employees suffer from role conflict and ambiguity, but conflicting expectations and uncertainty particularly affect managers. Having responsibility for the behavior of others and a lack of opportunity to participate in important decisions affecting their job are other aspects of employees' roles that may be stressful. Recall in the Preview Case that Erica Benson often felt that she was caught in the difficult situation of trying to resolve the conflicting pressures between family and her view of the company's expectations to "give, give, give, produce, produce, produce. . . . I would make promises to do things with my kids, but then ended up being too tired to hold true to my promise."

Career Development. Major stressors related to career planning and development involve job security, promotions, transfers, and developmental opportunities. An employee can feel stress from underpromotion (failure to advance as rapidly as desired) or overpromotion (promotion to a job that exceeds the individual's competencies). The current wave of reorganizations and downsizings may seriously threaten careers and cause stress. The acquisition of Gillette by Procter & Gamble resulted in more than 3,000 managers and other professionals being dismissed in an effort to save money and be more efficient. When jobs, teams, departments, or entire organizations are restructured, employees often have numerous career-related concerns: Can I perform competently in the new situation? Can I advance? Is my new job secure? Typically, employees find these concerns very stressful.

Interpersonal Relations. Teams and groups have a great impact on the behavior of employees. (We explore these dynamics in Chapter 8.) Good working relationships and interactions with peers, subordinates, and superiors are crucial aspects of organizational life, helping employees achieve personal and organizational goals. When relationships are poor, they can become sources of stress. In a recent national poll, 90 percent of respondents believed that incivility at work and elsewhere has become a major problem. **Incivility** *implies rudeness and disregard of others.* It includes the violation of workplace norms for mutual respect. Consider two anonymous employee reports of workplace incivility and their feelings of distress:

> *Female employee:* "During a presentation that I was making to all of the company's international country managers and vice presidents, the division president stood up and shouted, 'No one is interested in this stuff.' His comment made

me so nervous and upset that I could barely go on. I had been with this company for many years; you'd think he could have offered me a little respect for that alone."

Male employee: "I was pulling off a payroll cycle for a month during December, and I entered '12' (the calendar month) when I should have entered '6' (the fiscal month). The cycle was garbage accordingly. The accountant called me insulting names with my new boss sitting right there next to me. It was humiliating and unfair. It was my first payroll with the company. I was new—it was an honest mistake."[17]

A high level of political behavior, or "office politics," also may create stress for managers and employees. The nature of relationships with others may influence how employees react to other stressors. In other words, interpersonal relationships can be either a source of stress or the social support that helps employees cope with stressors.

Workplace Aggression. A disturbing source of stressors is workplace aggression. We discuss four types of workplace aggression in the last major part of this chapter, including bullying, sexual harassment, workplace violence, and aggression toward the organization.

Conflict between Work and Life Roles. A person has many roles in life (e.g., breadwinner, family member, little league coach, and/or church volunteer, to name a few), only one of which is typically associated with work (although some individuals may hold more than one job at a time). These roles may present conflicting demands that may become sources of stress. Furthermore, work typically meets only some of a person's goals and needs. Recall the Preview Case in which Erica Benson expressed conflicting pressures and stress among her roles as manager, mother, and spouse.

Other goals and needs may conflict with career goals, presenting an additional source of stress. For example, employees' personal desires to spend time with their families or have more leisure time may conflict with the extra hours they must work to advance their careers. This source of stress was evident in our previous Teams Competency feature on Bruce and Jody Goode. He comments further: "We've hit a number where we can make enough money to live very comfortably and travel, and everybody's happy. Too much growth in the business could mess it up."[18] Also, current demographic trends, such as the increasingly large number of dual-career couples, have brought work and family role conflicts into sharp focus.

Life Stressors

The distinction between work and nonwork stressors isn't always clear, although a primary source of stress for many employees clearly is pressures between work and family demands.[19] As Figure 16.3 illustrates, both work and family pressures may contribute to work–family stress because pressures in one area can reduce a person's ability to cope with pressures in the other. These incompatible pressures trigger stress, which, in turn, lead to work–family conflicts. These conflicts trigger possible outcomes such as dissatisfaction, frustration, and depression.

Life stressors *refer to tensions, anxieties, and conflicts that stem from pressures and demands in people's personal lives.* People must cope with a variety of life stressors; they deal with these stressors differently because of personality, age, gender, experience, and other characteristics. Events that cause stress for one person may not do so for another person. However, life stressors that affect almost everyone are those caused by significant changes: divorce, marriage, death of a family member, and the like. People have a limited capacity to respond to stressors. Too much change too quickly can exhaust the body's ability to respond, with negative consequences for a person's physical and mental health.

FIGURE 16.3 The Path of Work–Family Pressures, Stress, and Conflict

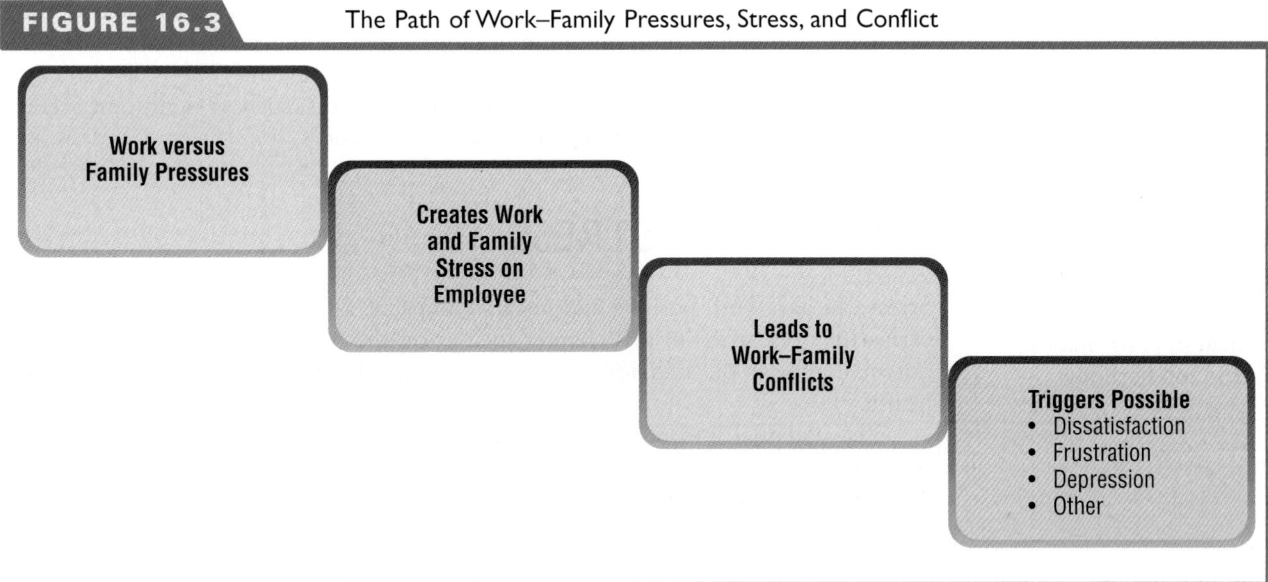

Table 16.2 contains some stressful events that college students typically face. These events are rated on a 100-point scale, with 1 indicating the least stressful event and 100 the most stressful. Events labeled "high levels of stress" might be assigned 71 to 100 points, depending on the specific circumstances of the student being evaluated. "Moderate levels of stress" might be scored from 31 to 70 points, and "low levels of stress" assigned scores from 1 to 30 points. During the course of a year, if a student faces events that total 150 points or more, the student has a 50–50 chance of getting sick as a result of excessive stress.[20]

TABLE 16.2 Stressful Events for College Students

EVENTS HAVING HIGH LEVELS OF STRESS
- Death of parent
- Death of spouse
- Divorce
- Flunking out
- Unwed pregnancy

EVENTS HAVING RELATIVELY LOW LEVELS OF STRESS
- Change in eating habits
- Change in sleeping habits
- Change in social activities
- Conflict with instructor
- Lower grades than expected

EVENTS HAVING MODERATE LEVELS OF STRESS
- Academic probation
- Change of major
- Death of close friend
- Failing important course
- Finding a new love interest
- Loss of financial aid
- Major injury or illness
- Parents' divorce
- Serious arguments with romantic partner
- Outstanding achievement

Source: Adapted from Baron, R. A., and Byrne, D. *Social Psychology: Understanding Human Interaction*, 6th ed. Boston: Allyn & Bacon, 1991, 573.

Recall that stress is the body's general response to any demand made on it. Note that the list of stressful events in Table 16.2 contains both unpleasant events, such as failing a course, and pleasant events, such as finding a new love interest. This dual nature of life stressors demonstrates that they involve both negative and positive experiences. For example, vacations and holidays actually may be quite stressful for some people but very relaxing and refreshing for others. In addition, viewing unpleasant life events as having only negative effects is incorrect. People often can both cope with and grow from experiencing unpleasant events. They can also enjoy the positive effects and stimulation of pleasurable events, such as significant accomplishments, vacations, or gaining a new family member.

LEARNING OBJECTIVE

4. Outline the possible impacts of stress on health, performance, and job burnout.

IMPACTS OF STRESS

Stress can have both positive and negative impacts, as we have suggested. Our concern with work stress in this chapter focuses on the negative impacts because of its potential effects on individual and organizational effectiveness as well as one's health.

The potential impacts of high levels of work stress occur in three main areas: physiological, emotional, and behavioral.[21] Examples of the impacts of severe distress in these areas are as follows:

- Physiological impacts of stress include increased blood pressure, increased heart rate, sweating, hot and cold spells, breathing difficulties, muscular tension, gastrointestinal disorders, and panic attacks.
- Emotional impacts of stress include anger, anxiety, depression, low self-esteem, poor intellectual functioning (including an inability to concentrate and make decisions), nervousness, irritability, resentment of supervision, and job dissatisfaction.
- Behavioral impacts of stress include poor performance, absenteeism, high accident rates, high turnover rates, high alcohol and substance abuse, impulsive behavior, and difficulties in communication.

These impacts of work stress have important implications for organizational behavior and organizational effectiveness. We examine some of these impacts in terms of health, performance, and job burnout.

Impacts on Health

Health problems commonly associated with stress include back pain, headaches, stomach and intestinal problems, upper respiratory infections, and various mental problems. Although determining the precise role that stress plays in individual cases is difficult, some illnesses appear to be stress related.[22]

Stress-related illnesses place a considerable burden on people and organizations. The costs to individuals seem more obvious than the costs to organizations. However, at least some of the organizational costs associated with stress-related disease can be identified. First, costs to employers include increased premiums for health insurance, as well as lost workdays from serious illnesses (e.g., ulcers) and less serious illnesses (e.g., headaches). Estimates are that each employee who suffers from a stress-related illness loses an average of 16 days of work a year. Second, more than three-fourths of all industrial accidents are caused by a worker's inability to cope with emotional problems worsened by stress. Third, legal problems for employers are growing. The number of stress-related worker compensation claims is increasing. The link between the levels of stress in the workplace and worker compensation claims is clear. When employees experience higher amounts of stress, more worker compensation claims are filed. Studies have shown similar patterns in many different industries.[23]

Post-traumatic stress disorder *is a psychological disorder brought on, for example, by horrible experiences in combat during wartime, acts of violence and terrorism, and the like.* Courts are now recognizing post-traumatic stress disorder as a condition that may justify a damage claim against an employer. Employees have successfully claimed suffering from this disorder as a result of sexual harassment, violence, and other traumatic circumstances in the workplace. Awards of damages in the millions of dollars have resulted from court cases involving workplace post-traumatic stress disorder claims.

Impacts on Performance

The positive and negative effects of stress are most apparent in the relationship between stress and performance. Figure 16.4 depicts the general stress–performance relationship in the shape of an arch. At low levels of stress, employees may not be sufficiently alert, challenged, or involved to perform at their best. As the curve indicates, increasing the amount of stress may improve performance—but only up to a point. An optimal level of stress probably exists for most tasks. Beyond that point, performance begins to deteriorate.[24] At excessive levels of stress, employees are too agitated, aroused, or threatened to perform well.

FIGURE 16.4 Typical Relationship between Performance and Stress

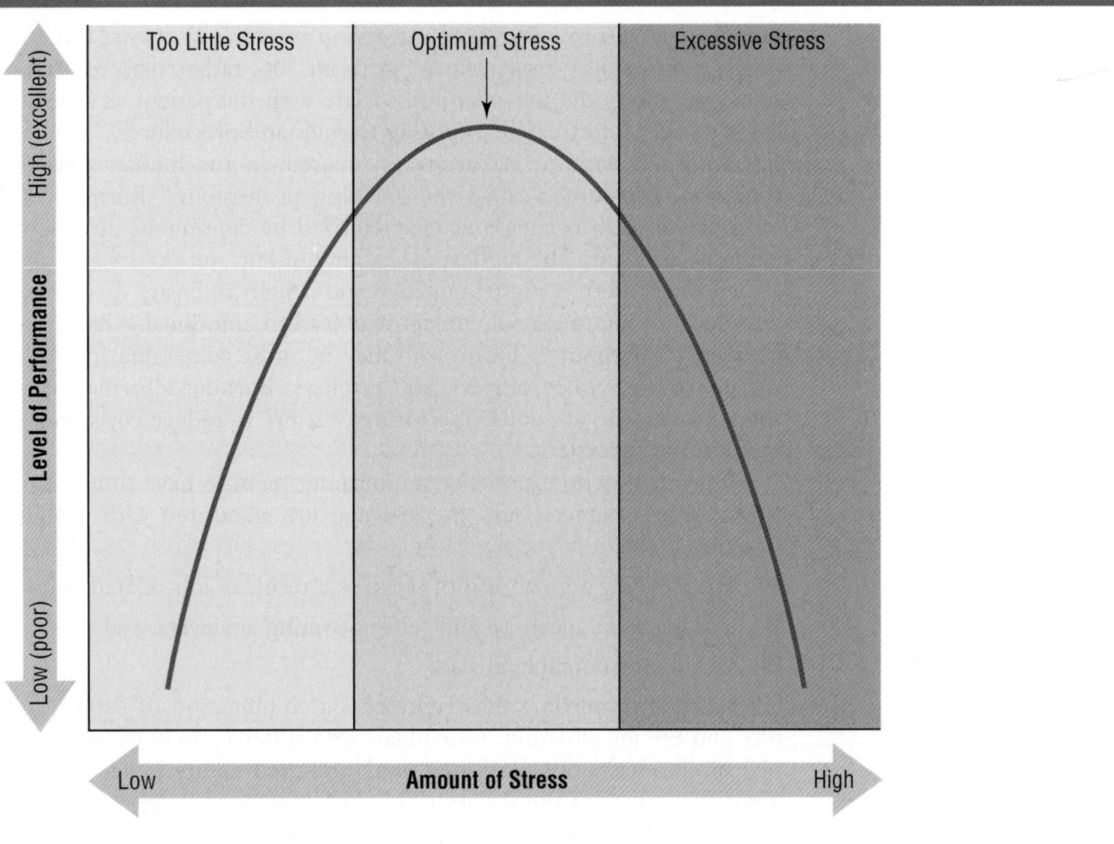

Managers often want to know the optimum stress points for both themselves and their subordinates. This information, however, is difficult to pin down. For example, an employee may be absent from work frequently because of boredom (too little stress) or because of overwork (excessive stress). The curve shown in Figure 16.4 changes with the situation; that is, it varies for different people and different tasks. Too little stress for one employee may be just right for another on a particular task. Similarly, the optimal amount of stress for a specific individual for one task may be too much or too little for that person's effective performance of other tasks.

As a practical matter, managers should be more concerned about excessive stress than with how to add to stress. Motivating individuals to perform better is always important, but attempting to do so by increasing the level of stress is shortsighted.

Studies of the stress–performance relationship in organizations often show a strong negative association between the amount of stress in a team or department and its overall performance. That is, the greater the stress that employees are experiencing, the lower will be their productivity. This negative relationship indicates that these work settings are operating on the right-hand side (excessive stress) of the curve shown in Figure 16.4. Managers and employees in these situations need to find ways to reduce the number and magnitude of stressors.

Impacts on Job Burnout

Job burnout *refers to the adverse effects of working conditions under which stressors seem unavoidable and sources of job satisfaction and relief from stress seem unavailable.* The burnout phenomenon typically contains three components:

- a state of emotional exhaustion,
- depersonalization of individuals, and
- feelings of low personal accomplishment.[25]

Depersonalization *refers to the treatment of people as objects.* For example, a nurse might refer to the "broken knee" in room 306, rather than use the patient's name. Doing so allows the nurse to disassociate with the patient as a person. The patient becomes seen and treated according to rules and procedures.

Most job burnout research has focused on the human services sector of the economy—sometimes called the "helping professions." Burnout is thought to be most prevalent in occupations characterized by continuous direct contact with people in need of aid. The highest probability of burnout occurs among those individuals who have both a high frequency and a high intensity of interpersonal contact. This level of interpersonal contact may lead to emotional exhaustion, a key component of job burnout.[26] Those who may be most vulnerable to job burnout include social workers, police officers, and teachers. Burnout also may affect managers or shop owners who are under increasing pressure to reduce costs, increase profits, and better serve customers.

Individuals who experience job burnout seem to have some common characteristics. Three characteristics in particular are associated with a high probability of burnout:

- experiencing a great deal of stress as a result of job-related stressors,
- tending to be idealistic and self-motivating achievers, and
- seeking unattainable goals.[27]

The burnout syndrome thus represents a combination of certain individual attributes and the job situation. Individuals who suffer from burnout often have unrealistic expectations concerning their work and their ability to accomplish desired goals, given the nature of the situation in which they find themselves. Job burnout is not something that happens overnight: The entire process typically takes a great deal of time. The path to job burnout is illustrated by Figure 16.5. One or more of the working conditions listed, coupled with the unrealistic expectations or ambitions of the individual, can lead eventually to a state of complete physical, mental, and emotional exhaustion. Under conditions of burnout, the individual can no longer cope with the demands of the job and willingness to try drops dramatically.

John Houghom is the senior vice president of health-care improvement and chief information officer of PeaceHealth, headquartered in Bellevue (near Seattle), Washington. PeaceHealth operates six acute care hospitals, a variety of health clinics, and other outpatient care facilities in Washington, Oregon, and Alaska. In the following Self Competency feature, we share excerpts from his journey into a state of burnout and recovery.[28]

FIGURE 16.5 The Path to Job Burnout

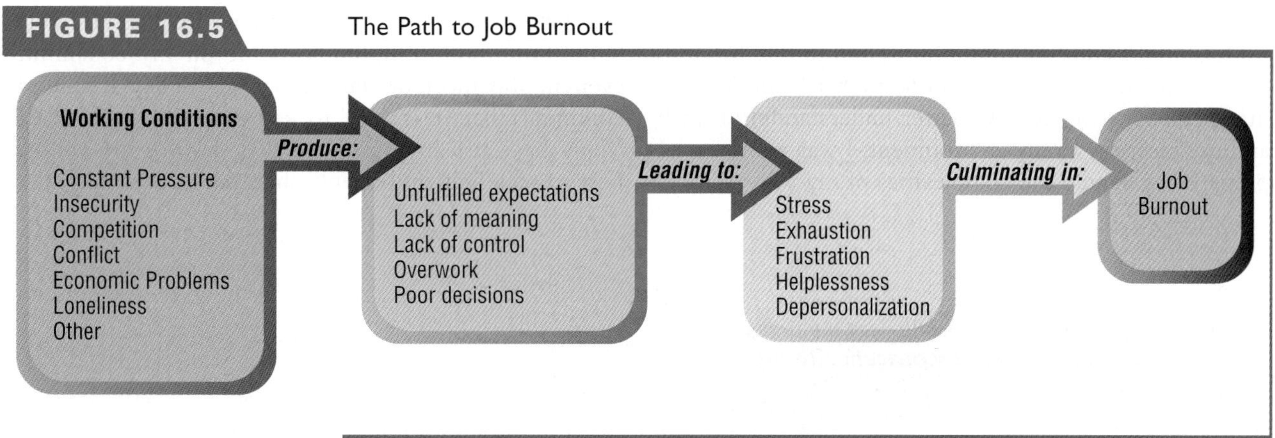

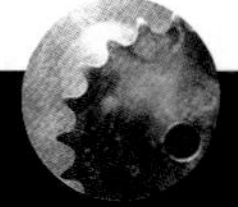

SELF COMPETENCY

JOHN HOUGHOM'S BURNOUT EXPERIENCE

For more than 25 years, I believed I could accomplish just about anything professionally. And I often did. Following medical school, I enjoyed 15 years of practice before accepting a senior leadership role in PeaceHealth, a nonprofit health-care organization in the Pacific Northwest. My job quickly grew until I had responsibility for corporate-wide clinical quality and all information technology initiatives. PeaceHealth launched an aggressive campaign to implement an advanced IT infrastructure supporting both operations and clinical care. The centerpiece of the effort was our Community Health Record project, a network of community-wide medical records designed to support patient care in each of the communities we serve.

Little did I know how difficult this role would prove to be. Resistance was monumental and seemed to come from everywhere in the organization—from skeptical board members and executives to hostile physicians. My workday typically began by 6 A.M., when I would send e-mails and return voice messages from home. Arriving at the office before 7:30 A.M., my days were characterized by a blur of conference calls, tense meetings and voluminous e-mail exchanges. Around 7 P.M., I would stagger out of the office to catch a quick meal with my wife, before heading to my home office where I would continue working until 10 or 11 P.M. My four sons grew accustomed to not seeing their dad even on the weekends.

Despite the resistance, with the staunch support of my CEO, we literally moved mountains. In roughly four years, PeaceHealth went from virtually no automation to a highly advanced infrastructure including a full-blown electronic medical records system supporting care in all of our hospitals and clinics with nearly everything online.

However, managing the project was the most stressful job I had ever undertaken. My engine reached its breaking point. Each night I would lie in bed and replay my day at work, sleeping only a few hours. At the office, I uncharacteristically began snapping at people. My colleagues began wondering what happened to the affable, mild-mannered, resilient "old John." Finally, one morning, I realized that I could not go on. I literally had no reserve, finding it difficult to even get out of bed, much less manage my professional responsibilities. Admitting this to myself was one of the hardest things I have ever done, but it was also one of the most important.

My boss, the corporate CEO, graciously granted me a three-month sabbatical. A couple of days into it, I sought professional help from the Professional Renewal Center, an outpatient center dedicated to helping executives deal with stress. It turned out to be exactly the right thing to do. With rest, counseling, and introspection, I rediscovered myself and my zest for life. Equally important, I learned vital coping and stress management skills that have allowed me to return to work and be as productive as before, yet with a healthier balance of my professional and personal life. I feel as though I have been given a great gift. I returned to work armed with new insights on leadership. The key to effective leadership depends on how you respond to the demands and challenges of your position, internal conflicts or interpersonal struggles. By better understanding myself and my response to my environment, I was vastly better prepared to handle the complexities of my role.

Those around me have seen a noticeable difference. Colleagues have complimented me on my equanimity even in the most difficult situations. They frequently comment that it is nice to see the "old John" back. Many have privately told me they admire my willingness to seek help and openly share my experience.

For more information on PeaceHealth, visit the organization's home page at ***http://www.peacehealth.org.***

LEARNING OBJECTIVE

5. Identify individual and organizational practices for managing workplace stress.

MANAGING STRESS

Individual and organizational practices to help managers and employees cope with stress have become increasingly popular as stress has become more widely recognized as a problem. A variety of initiatives are available to individuals and organizations for managing stress and reducing its harmful effects. **Stress management** *refers to any initiative that reduces stress by helping people understand the stress response, recognize stressors, and use coping techniques to minimize the negative impact of stress.*[29]

Individual Practices

Managing stress by individuals includes activities and behaviors designed to (1) eliminate or control the sources of stress and (2) make the individual more resistant to or better able to cope with stress. The first step in individual stress management involves recognizing the stressors that are affecting the person's life. Next, the individual needs to decide what to do about them. Personal goals and values, coupled with practical stress management skills, can help individuals cope with stressors and reduce negative stress reactions.

Basic practices for managing stress by individuals include the following.

- Plan ahead and practice good time management.
- Get plenty of exercise, eat a balanced diet, get adequate rest, and generally take care of yourself.
- Develop a sound philosophy of life and maintain a positive attitude as well as a sense of humor.
- Concentrate on balancing your work and personal life. Always take time to have fun.
- Learn relaxation techniques.[30]

Individuals can use relaxation techniques during the workday to cope with job demands. For example, a common "relaxation response" to stress is to (1) choose a comfortable position, (2) close your eyes, (3) relax your muscles, (4) become aware of your breathing, (5) maintain a passive attitude when thoughts surface, and (6) continue for a set period of time (e.g., 20 minutes).[31]

An in-depth study of successful top executives revealed that they used similar methods of coping with stress.[32] These executives came from a variety of industries and included the president of an oil field service company, the founder of a residential real estate firm, the CEO of a large commercial bank, and a U.S. Navy admiral. First, they worked hard at balancing work and family concerns. Work was central to their lives, but it wasn't their sole focus. These executives also made effective use of leisure time to reduce stress. In addition, they were skilled time managers and goal setters. Important components of their effective use of time were identifying crucial goals and constructively planning how to reach them. Finally, these executives cited the essential role of social support in coping with stress. They didn't operate as loners; rather they received emotional support and important information from a diverse network of family, friends, coworkers, and industry colleagues. Additionally, these executives worked hard at maintaining fair exchanges in these relationships. That is, they both received support from and gave support to others in their networks.

Organizational Practices

As suggested in Figure 16.6, organizational stress management programs are often designed to reduce the harmful effects of stress (distress) in one or more of the following ways: (1) Identify and reduce or eliminate the work stressors, (2) assist employees in changing their perceptions of the stressors and experienced stress, and (3) assist employees cope more effectively with the outcomes from stress.

FIGURE 16.6 Targets of Organizational Stress Management Programs

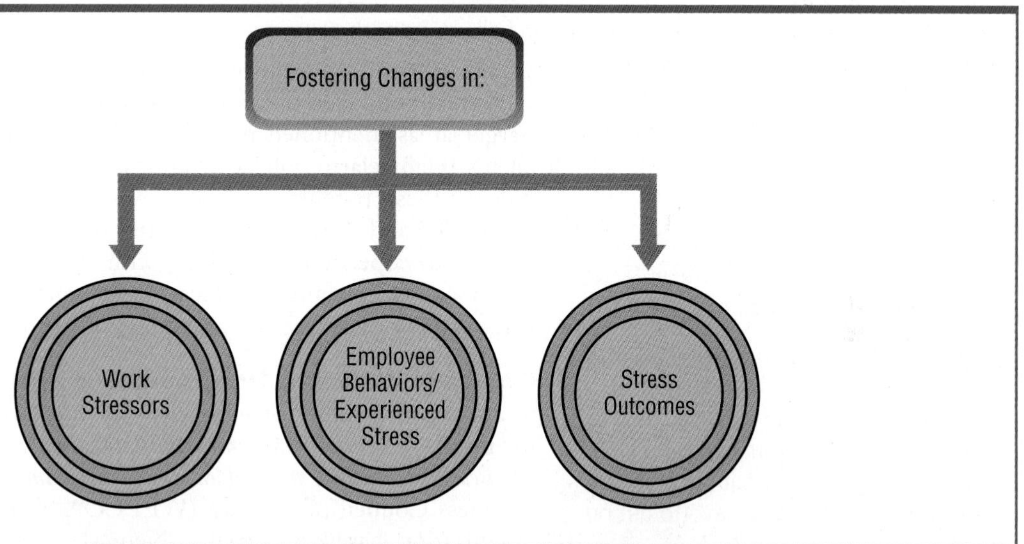

Reducing Work Stressors. Practices aimed at eliminating or modifying work stressors include

- improvements in the physical work environment;
- job redesign;
- changes in workloads and deadlines;
- changes in work schedules, more flexible hours, and sabbaticals; and
- greater levels of employee participation, particularly in planning changes that affect them.

Actions that promote role clarity and role analysis can be particularly useful in removing or reducing role ambiguity and role conflict—two main sources of stress. When diagnosing stressors in the workplace, managers should be particularly aware that uncertainty and perceived lack of control heighten stress. The greatest stress occurs when jobs are high in stressors and low in controllability. Thus, involvement of employees in organizational changes that will affect them, work redesign that reduces uncertainty and increases control over the pace of work, and improved clarity and understanding of roles all should help reduce work stress. An important way to provide employees with more control and less stress is to give individuals more control over their time.

Sam Noble, a heath-care analyst who works for Value Management Group in Dallas, perhaps typifies the type of employee who attaches great importance to time. Noble says, "There's a point where money doesn't matter anymore after I have a certain amount of disposable income. It's more important to have reduced stress, a relaxed work style, and the time I need to be with my children and family." He was attracted to Value Management by its avowed corporate philosophy: "Make sure you get the job done and done well. Then, take what time you need as long as you don't abuse it."[33]

Modifying Behaviors. Programs targeted at behaviors and experiences of stress and outcomes of stress include

- team building,
- career counseling and other employee assistance programs,
- workshops on time management,
- workshops on job burnout to help employees understand its nature and symptoms, and
- training in relaxation techniques.

Dividing stress management programs into these categories doesn't mean that they are not related. In addition, such programs might overlap in terms of their impact on the three target areas mentioned previously. For example, a workshop dealing with role problems might clarify job descriptions and duties, reducing the magnitude of these potential stressors. At the same time, through greater knowledge and insight into roles and role problems, employees might be able to cope more effectively with this source of stress. Similarly, career counseling might reduce career concerns as a source of stress while improving the ability of employees to cope with career problems.

> **THE COMPETENT LEADER**
>
> There is no question that workplace wellness is worth it. The only question is whether you're going to do it today or tomorrow. If you keep saying you're going to do it tomorrow, you'll never do it. You have to get on it today.
>
> Warren Buffett, Chairman, Berkshire Hathaway

Creating Wellness Programs. One comprehensive method of improving the ability of individuals to cope with stress is a **wellness program**—*a health management initiative that incorporates the components of disease prevention, medical care, self-care, and health promotion.*[34] The Wellness Council of America (WELCOA) is a nonprofit membership organization based in Omaha, Nebraska, that is dedicated to promoting healthier lifestyles. Its primary focus is on building *Well Workplaces*—organizations dedicated to the health of their employees. The council provides a blueprint to help organizations create programs to help employees make better lifestyle choices and that can have a positive impact on the organization's profits. To date, more than 600 organizations have received the Well Workplace Award. WELCOA and other wellness programs are driven by, among other factors, the continuous increases in health-care costs and research that suggest that leading causes of illness are often preventable. Tobacco use, alcohol and substance abuse, sedentary lifestyles, poor nutritional habits, excessive and unnecessary stressors in the workplace, and inadequate employee abilities to cope with stress are examples of targets of wellness programs.[35] The scope and features of wellness programs among organizations vary widely.

The following Change Competency feature provides an overview of Dofasco's wellness program that has evolved over time.[36] Dofasco Inc. is headquartered in Hamilton, Ontario, in Canada and has more than 7,000 employees. The company makes hot-rolled, cold-rolled, galvanized, and tin-plate steels, as well as tubular steel products. Most of its customers are in the packaging, distribution, construction, and automotive industries.

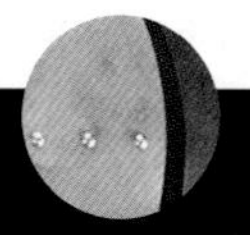

CHANGE COMPETENCY

DOFASCO'S WELLNESS PROGRAM

Dofasco has increased its emphasis on health and wellness initiatives. At the same time, it has experienced reduced absenteeism, short-term disability claims, workplace compensation injuries, and workers' compensation costs, according to Brian Mullen, director of Human Resources. Mullen comments: "It's the whole approach to wellness, lifestyles, safety and the work environment. We have seen what we consider positive impacts."

Evidence of Dofasco's longstanding commitment to employee health and well-being can be seen in the F. H. Sherman Recreation and Learning Centre. It includes a twin-pad arena, double gymnasium, and playing fields. These facilities are located a 15-minute drive from the plant. Recently, the company added its third fitness center located on the plant site itself. The three gyms combined see a total of 4,000 visits a month. Mullen states: "It's a case of healthy bodies, healthy minds. It's an investment in our employees that reflects the company's values."

Dofasco's medical services department works closely with the lifestyle resources group, an active grassroots volunteer committee with about 35 members. The volunteers organize an annual two-day health and safety fair with a broad choice of speakers and exhibits. Organizations like St. John's Ambulance, the Canadian Mental Health Association, and the Diabetes Association have booths. About 4,000 people attend the fair. The medical services group provides free screening for cholesterol, blood pressure, and other health threats such as unhealthy blood sugar levels. It gives people a heads-up on their overall health status, flagging issues that can be discussed with a company doctor or family physician. Individual departments also hold their own health and safety days.

Tai chi classes, yoga, aerobics, and smoking cessation programs are just some of the offerings. Some plant areas where there has been a high incidence of muscle strains have implemented stretching programs at the beginning of a shift.

Mullen comments: "Issues like stress, depression and mental health may be news to some companies, but they're across the community, they're across the country, they're things that need to be addressed. Stress is a little like water for sponges. Not all stress is work related, but people can only absorb so much, so if the stress they're encountering externally is high, then perhaps what they can tolerate work-wise is low. And if external stress is low, maybe the stress level that they can absorb at work is higher."

Dofasco recently completed a company-wide survey based on one-on-one interviews of employees by medical professionals working with the Institute for Work and Health in Toronto, Ontario. The data were analyzed for factors that might impact stress levels, allowing the company to compare its staff to the institute's Canadian normative data. The findings "allowed us to look at our organization on almost any sort of breakdown that we want—age, gender, responsibility," or plant area, looking at factors individually or in combination. This has helped Dofasco target things like stress reduction programs to where they're needed most.

For more information on Dofasco Inc., visit the organization's home page at ***http://www.dofasco.ca.***

WORKPLACE AGGRESSION

LEARNING OBJECTIVE

6. Discuss four major types of workplace aggression: bullying, sexual harassment, violence, and aggression toward the organization itself.

Workplace aggression *includes a variety of behaviors, ranging from psychological acts such as shouting to physical assault.*[37] Aggressive workplace behavior can be grouped into three broad categories: (1) expressions of hostility—hostile, verbal or symbolic behaviors such as "the silent treatment"; (2) obstructionism—behaviors that are designed to hamper the individual's performance such as refusing to provide needed resources; and (3) overt aggression—many types of assault and destruction of property.[38] A variety of defense mechanisms have been identified for the rationalization of workplace aggression. Some of the underlying defense mechanisms used by individuals to justify aggressive behaviors include the following:

- **Hostile attribution bias**—*implicit assumption that people tend to be motivated by desires to harm others.* This bias is used at times to explain why others behave as they do. Individuals with a strong motive to aggress may even see friendly acts by others as being driven by hidden/hostile agendas that are designed to inflict harm. This type of attribution enables aggressive persons to rationalize their own hostile behaviors as acts of self defense intended to head off physical or verbal attack by others.
- **Potency bias**—*the implicit assumption by the aggressive individual that interactions with others are contests to establish dominance versus submissiveness.* This bias rationalizes the use of aggression to dominate others as demonstrating strength, bravery, control, and fearlessness. The failure to act aggressively is seen as weakness, fear, and cowardice. Thus, aggressive individuals see their behaviors as a means of gaining respect from others and that to show weakness is to encourage powerful others to take advantage of them.
- **Retribution bias**—*aggressive individuals think that taking revenge (retribution) is more important than preserving relationships.* There is a tendency to see retaliation as a more rational behavior than reconciliation. For example, aggression is seen as justifiable if it is thought to restore respect or exact retributions for a perceived wrong. Retaliation is seen by aggressive individuals as more reasonable than forgiveness, vindication is seen as more reasonable than reconciliation, and obtaining revenge is seen as more reasonable than maintaining a relationship. This bias often underlies justification for aggressions stimulated by wounded prided, reduced self-esteem, and perceived disrespect.
- **Derogation of target bias**—*aggressive individuals see those they wish to make (or have made) targets of aggressions as evil, immoral, or untrustworthy.* This type of influence enables them to see the targets of aggression as deserving of it.
- **Social discounting bias**—*aggressive individuals believe that social customs reflect free will and the opportunity to satisfy their own needs.* They have a disdain for traditional ideals and conventional beliefs and are often cynical and critical of social events. They show a lack of sensitivity, empathy, and concern for social customs. Thus, socially deviant behaviors intended to harm others are justified by claiming that they allow the aggressive individuals to obtain freedom of expression, relief from the cycles of social customs, and liberation from social relationships. These and other underlying mechanisms for rationalizing aggression may be seen in incidents of bullying, sexual harassment, and workplace violence.[39]

In the remainder of this section, we present the core features of four major types of workplace aggression—bullying, sexual harassment, violence, and aggression toward the organization. As suggested in Figure 16.7, there are potential overlaps and relationships among these types of workplace aggression. For example, an employee may encounter a variety of bullying behaviors, some of which may escalate into the category of workplace violence and destruction or theft of organizational property.

Workplace Bullying

Workplace bullying *is the repeated and unreasonable behavior directed toward an employee or group of employees that creates a risk to health and safety.* Unreasonable behavior refers to acts that a reasonable person, when considering all of the circumstances, would see as victimizing, humiliating, undermining, or threatening an employee or group of employees. Bullying often involves a misuse or abuse of power. For the employees subject to it, they can experience difficulties in defending themselves.[40] Bullying cuts across race, religion, and gender. It involves offensive behaviors that a reasonable person would see as creating an intimidating, hostile, or

FIGURE 16.7 Potential Overlaps Among Four Types of Workplace Aggression

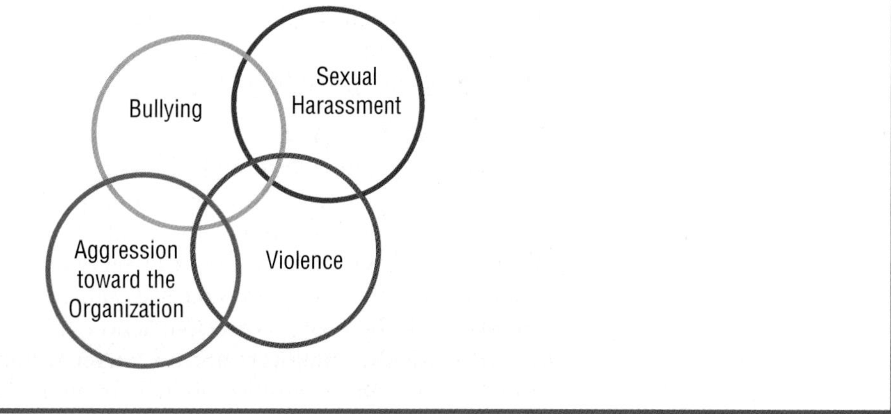

abusive work environment. Normally, bullying must involve repeated incidents and a pattern of behavior.

Bullies at work engage in a variety of behaviors ranging from condescension to rage. The top 10 acts of workplace bullying have been identified as follows:

1. Talking about others behind their back.
2. Continuously interrupting others when they are speaking or working.
3. Flaunting status or authority, acting in a condescending manner.
4. Belittling someone's opinion to others.
5. Repeated failure to return phone calls or respond to memos.
6. Giving others the silent treatment.
7. Insults, yelling, and shouting.
8. Verbal forms of sexual harassment.
9. Staring, dirty looks, or other negative eye contact.
10. Intentionally damning with faint praise.

Women as well as men bully others at work. Women bullies target other women an overwhelming 84 percent of the time. Men bullies target women in 69 percent of the cases. Women are most often the targets of bullying.

A critical characteristic of workplace bullying is that it harms the health of the individual subject to it. Health concerns from bullying need to be distinguished from routine office politics, teasing, incivilities, and boorishness.[41] All of the effects of stress identified previously may be experienced as a result of bullying. In addition, individuals who report severe forms of bullying identify experiencing the following major symptoms:

- **General anxiety disorder**—*evidenced by anxiety, excessive worry, disruptive sleep, stress headaches, and racing heart rate.*
- **Clinical depression**—*evidenced by loss of concentration, disruptive sleep, obsession over details at work, exhaustion (leading to an inability to function), and diagnosed depression.*
- **Post-traumatic stress disorder**—*evidenced by feeling edgy or irritable and constantly on guard; having recurrent nightmares and flashbacks, and needing to avoid the feelings or thoughts that remind the bullied person of the trauma.*[42]

In addition to the potential terrible effects of bullying on the individual, the organization has much at stake in preventing or dealing with bullying in a direct way. A variety of organizational effects have been associated with bullying. A few of these include (1) high absenteeism resulting from time taken off by the bullied employees, (2) reduced productivity among bullied workers, (3) stress-related illnesses that increase health-care costs to the organization, (4) reduced customer service due to bullied employees feeling less loyalty to the organization because it is not protecting them from bullying, and (5) increased employee turnover—82 percent of people targeted by a bully quit.[43]

Addressing Bullying. Many remedies are suggested to address bullying in the workplace. We note just several of them here. As a start, organizations should have an anti-bullying or workplace aggression policy that defines expectations for interpersonal relationships. Employees should understand what is and is not acceptable behavior in the workplace. This will serve as one step in creating a culture where people treat each other with courtesy and respect. Organizations encourage a culture of respect by taking corrective action against those engaged in bullying behaviors. Increasingly, employers are no longer dismissing bullying as simply a socially acceptable side effect of office politics. In addition to strong sexual harassment policies, a number of firms are developing policies that address bullying. A few examples include American Express, Burger King, and J.C. Penney. The failure of organizations to address bullying has resulted in successful legal action against those firms.[44]

A variety of suggestions have been offered to address bullying. Several of these are noted as follows:

1. Speak directly to the bully. Tell the individual that you find his or her behaviors unacceptable and to stop them. Often this is all that is needed.
2. In some cases, the bullying behaviors are not seen by others. Thus, tell a friend or work colleague. You may soon learn that you are not the only one who has been subject to the person's bullying.
3. Keep a diary of the specific behaviors and incidents of bullying and when each occurred. Many of the incidents in isolation may seem minor, but when put together, they can establish a serious pattern over time.
4. Discuss the experience of bullying with your manager. If your manager is one who is doing the bullying, you may need to discuss the matter with a person in the human resources department or the appropriate person designated by organizational policy, if one exists.
5. If these initial steps are not effective, it may be necessary to file a formal complaint, consistent with the organization's policies. There is no assurance that these steps will be effective.

Unfortunately, too often individuals have found it necessary to resign from their positions or seek a transfer to a different department to remove themselves from the bullying activity.[45]

A special type of bullying in the workforce is **mobbing**—*the ganging up by coworkers, subordinates, or superiors to force someone out of the workplace through humor, intimidation, humiliation, discrediting, and/or isolation.* As with the traditional form of bullying, mobbing may result in high turnover, low morale, decreased productivity, increased absenteeism, and a loss of key individuals. More broadly, it may eventually lead to diminished teamwork, trust, and a toxic workplace culture.

Research suggests that the prime targets of mobbers are high achievers, enthusiastic employees, those of high integrity and ethical standards, those who don't belong to the "in-group," women with family responsibilities, and even those with different religious or cultural orientations.[46] Mobbing is much more difficult for the individual to deal with than bullying. The person is not simply dealing with the actions of another, but rather that of many of his or her coworkers and/or superiors. While training employee work teams, George Gates reports on his witnessing mobbing: "I noticed a young man, relatively new to the company, who sat alone. Whenever he spoke, someone hurled a wisecrack his way. If he entered or left the room, jibes from his 'teammates' followed. At a break, I asked if this harassment was typical. 'Oh,' he answered, 'it's been like that since I got here. It's not everybody, just four or five guys. I guess I have to put up with it because I'm new.' I offered to address the obnoxious behavior or get help from his manager, but he refused. 'Don't,' he pleaded. 'That'll only make it worse. I just try to put up with it.'"[47]

The person subject to mobbing may find that colleagues no longer meet with her. Management may not provide the possibility to communicate, the person may be isolated in a work area, perhaps the individual is given meaningless work assignments, or the individual may be repeatedly left out of the information loop critical to his or her work. Taken together and repeated over times, these kinds of actions may be devastating for the individual. In too many cases, the only recourse for the individual is to seek a transfer within the organization or resign the position.

Sexual Harassment

Sexual harassment is one of the many categories of harassment that may occur in the workplace. **Harassment** *refers to verbal or physical conduct that denigrates or shows hostility or aversion toward an individual because of that person's race, skin color, religion, gender, national origin, age, or disability.* Harassment can also occur if conduct is directed toward a person's relatives, friends, or associates. Harassment does one or more of the following:

- Has the purpose or effect of creating an intimidating, hostile, or offensive work environment.
- Has the purpose or effect of unreasonably interfering with an individual's work performance.
- Otherwise aversely affects an individual's employment opportunities.

Sexual harassment *generally refers to unwelcome sexual advances, requests for sexual favors, and other verbal or physical conduct of a sexual nature.*[48] Any harassment policy, including one on sexual harassment, should contain (1) a definition of the harassment, (2) a harassment prohibition statement, (3) a description of the organization's complaint procedure, (4) a description of disciplinary measures for such harassment, and (5) a statement of protection against retaliation.[49]

The following Diversity Competency feature provides an excellent example of a sexual harassment policy.[50] It includes the state of California's and the U.S. federal government's core regulatory requirements and prohibitions related to sexual harassment. More excerpts of this policy are from OfficeWorks, a specialized health-care staffing organization with headquarters in Tarzana, California. The firm specializes in placing medical support and medical administrative personnel. OfficeWorks has 300 employees with 13 offices in five states. In addition to staffing, the firm will also provide full services by actually running a private doctor's or medical group's office, from human resources to billing. OfficeWorks functions under the corporate name of Healthcare Consulting, Inc.

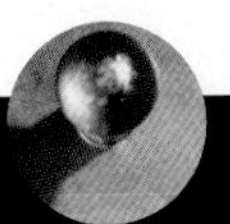

DIVERSITY COMPETENCY

OfficeWorks' Sexual Harassment Policy

OfficeWorks is committed to providing a work environment that is free of discrimination. In keeping with this commitment, we maintain a strict policy prohibiting unlawful harassment, including sexual harassment. Sexual harassment is prohibited by this Company and is against the law. Every employee should be aware of: (1) what sexual harassment is; (2) steps to take if harassment occurs; (3) the personal liability of harassers; and (4) prohibited retaliation for reporting sexual harassment.

What Is Sexual Harassment.
It's against the law for females to sexually harass males or other females, and for males to harass other males or females.

California Law. California law defines harassment due to sex as sexual harassment; gender harassment; and harassment due to pregnancy, childbirth; or related medical conditions. This includes:

- Verbal harassment—epithets, derogatory coments, or slurs. *Examples:* Name-calling, belittling, sexually explicit or degrading words to describe an individual, sexually explicit jokes, comments about an employee's anatomy and/or dress, sexually oriented noises or remarks, questions about a person's sexual practices, use of patronizing terms or remarks, verbal abuse, graphic verbal commentaries about the body.
- Physical harassment—assault, impeding or blocking movement, or any physical interference with normal work or movement, when directed at an individual. *Examples:* Touching, pinching, patting, grabbing, brushing against or poking another employee's body, requiring an employee to wear sexually suggestive clothing.
- Visual harassment—derogatory posters, cartoons, or drawings. *Examples:* Displaying sexual pictures on a PC or wall, writings, or objects, obscene letters or invitations, staring at an employee's anatomy, leering, sexually oriented gestures, mooning, unwanted love letters or notes.
- Sexual favors—unwanted sexual advances which condition an employment benefit upon an exchange of sexual favors. *Examples:* Continued requests for dates, any threats of demotion, termination, etc., if requested sexual favors are not given, making or threatening reprisals after a negative response to sexual advances, propositioning an individual.

Federal Law. Under federal law, unwelcome sexual advances, requests for sexual favors, and other verbal or physical conduct of a sexual nature constitute sexual harassment when:

- Submission to such conduct is made either explicitly or implicitly a term or condition of an individual's employment;
- Submission to or rejection of such conduct by an individual is used as the basis for employment decisions affecting such individual; or
- Such conduct has the purpose or effect of unreasonably interfering with an individual's work performance creating an intimidating, hostile, or offensive working environment.

Stopping Sexual Harassment.

1. When possible, simply tell the harasser to stop. The harasser may not realize the advances or behavior is offensive. When it is appropriate and sensible, simply tell the harasser the behavior or advances are unwelcome and must stop.
2. You are strongly encouraged to report sexual harassment. Contact your supervisor, another manager, or your staffing coordinator. Sexual harassment or retaliation should be reported in writing or verbally. You may report such activities even though you were not the subject of harassment.
3. An investigation will be conducted. OfficeWorks will investigate, in a discreet manner, all reported incidents of sexual harassment and retaliation.
4. Appropriate action will be taken. Where evidence of sexual harassment or retaliation is found, disciplinary action, up to and including termination, may result.

Protection against Retaliation.
Company policy and California state law forbid retaliation against any employee who opposes sexual harassment, files a complaint, testifies, assists, or participates in any manner in an investigation, proceeding, or hearing conducted by OfficeWorks, the Department of Fair Employment and Housing, or the Fair Employment and Housing Commission. Prohibited retaliation includes but is not limited to: (1) demotion, (2) suspension, (3) failure to hire or consider for hire, (4) failure to give equal consideration in making employment decisions, and (5) adversely affecting working conditions or otherwise denying any employment benefit to an individual.

For more information on OfficeWorks, visit the organization's home page at ***http://www.pharmacystaffing.com.***

From a legal perspective, there are two different sets of grounds for claiming sexual harassment. Under the quid pro quo form of harassment, a person in authority (usually a supervisor or manager) demands sexual favors of a subordinate as a condition of getting or keeping a job benefit. Frequently, a quid pro quo situation does not exist. Many sexual harassment victims are never threatened with termination or lack of advancement. Rather, they suffer the abuse of a hostile work environment, which is an alternate ground for bringing sexual harassment legal action. A **hostile work environment** *refers to a situation in which a coworker or supervisor, engaging in unwelcome and inappropriate sexually based behavior, renders the workplace atmosphere intimidating, hostile, or offensive.*[51] Today, courts are more likely to find a hostile work environment as being present when the workplace includes sexual propositions, pornography, extremely vulgar language, sexual touching, degrading comments, or embarrassing questions or jokes.

The previous Diversity Competency feature on OfficeWorks clearly sets forth the prohibition against quid pro quo sexual harassment and hostile work environment harassment. The behaviors associated with each are clearly developed. The course of action to stop such sexual harassment is stated in the policy by OfficeWorks. The potential consequences to harassers are identified. A statement of protection against retaliation is expressed. Organizations with policies such as OfficeWorks' and, perhaps more importantly, the implementation of such policies are likely to have a reduced number of sexual harassment incidents.

Sexual harassment continues to be a serious problem in the United States. In a review of a number of studies of the incidents of sexual harassment in the United States, it was found that 58 percent of the women respondents report having experienced potentially harassing behaviors and 24 percent report having experienced sexual harassment at work.[52] Sexual harassment continues to be a serious form of workplace aggression because it may lead to one or more of the discussed reactions outlined for bullying and in previous parts of this chapter.[53] As with bullying, management has a strong responsibility to do everything in its power to prevent sexual harassment from occurring. When it does occur, it needs to be dealt with quickly and firmly. An excellent policy statement, along with its implementation, was presented in the Diversity Competency related to the sexual harassment policy at OfficeWorks.

Workplace Violence

Workplace violence *refers to aggressive behavior that can range from threats and extreme verbal abuse to physical assault and homicide.*[54] Within the United States, it is estimated that some 2 million acts of workplace violence are committed annually. As might be expected, the vast majority (75 percent) of these incidents were viewed as simple assaults, while an additional 19 percent were aggravated assaults. There are approximately 800 workplace homicides each year within the United States. The instances of verbal violence (simple assaults) are three times that of physical violence. Moreover, most of the forms of physical and severe verbal attacks come from strangers (such as doing a robbery) or customers. Further, it is estimated that workplace violence costs organizations and communications more than $36 billion per year in lost productivity, comps and services, legal fees, and court awards—in addition to injuries, loss of life, and loss of managers' time spent dealing with crises. Also included in the total cost is 1.7 million days of lost work.[55]

A wide variety of behaviors are considered as forms of workplace violence. Some of these include homicide, rape, robbery, wounding, battering, physical assaults, kicking, biting, punching, spitting, scratching, squeezing or pinching, stalking, intimidation, threats, leaving offensive messages, rude gestures, swearing, harassment (including sexual, racial, and other), bullying, and mobbing. Numerous types of behaviors have been considered by some to follow under the general category of workplace violence.

Harm Model. As noted previously and in Figure 16.7, there are potential overlaps in the types of workplace aggressive behaviors that are considered to constitute bullying, sexual harassment, and workplace violence. These relationships and overlaps are suggested in the **harm model of aggression**—*a continuum that ranges from harassment to aggression to rage to mayhem.*[56] The types of conduct related to each level of aggressive or threatening behavior occur on an ascending scale, as follows:

- *Harassment.* The first level of behavior on the violence continuum is harassment. This behavior may or may not cause harm or discomfort to the individual. But it is generally considered inappropriate conduct for the workplace. Examples of harassment include acting in a condescending way to a customer, slamming an office door, glaring at a colleague, playing frequent, practical, and cruel jokes (particularly on a single employee), or telling a lie about a coworker.
- *Aggression.* Aggressive behaviors that cause harm to or discomfort for another person or for the organization might include shouting at a customer, slamming a door in someone's face, spreading damaging rumors about a coworker, or damaging someone's personal belongings. Clearly, all of these behaviors are inappropriate for the workplace.
- *Rage.* The third level on the continuum is rage. Rage is seen through intense behaviors that often cause fear in other persons and that may result in physical or emotional harm to people or damage to property. Rage typically makes the inappropriate behaviors physical and visible. Examples of rage can range from pushing a customer to sabotaging a coworker's presentation or leaving hate statements on someone's desk.
- *Mayhem.* The final stage is mayhem. This stage represents physical violence against people or the violent destruction of property. Activity in this category can range from punching a customer or ransacking to physically punching a coworker or superior to destroying a facility to shooting a coworker or superior to death.

THE COMPETENT LEADER

When a confrontational situation develops, that's the time to back away and say "Let's just cool off a little bit." If the person is venting, you need to know what to do in that situation.

Robert Cartwright, Loss Prevention Manager, Bridgestone/Firestone

Warning Signs. Individuals who engage in workplace violence at the rage and mayhem levels frequently exhibit clear observable warning signs, which are often newly acquired behaviors. These warning signs include:

1. Violent and threatening behavior—including hostility and approval of the use of violence.
2. "Strange" behavior—becoming reclusive, deteriorating personal appearance/hygiene, and erratic behavior.
3. Performance problems—including problems with attendance or tardiness.
4. Interpersonal problems—including numerous conflicts, types of sensitivity, and expressions of resentment.
5. "At the end of his (or her) rope"—indicators of impending suicide, the expression of an unspecified plan to "solve all problems" and the like, and statements of access to and familiarity with weapons.[57]

Triggering Events. There are identifiable sets of triggering events. The triggering event is seen to the violence prone individual as the last straw that creates a mind-set of "no way out" or no more options. The most common sets of triggering events that lead to rage or mayhem are

1. being fired, laid off or suspended, or passed over for promotion;
2. disciplinary action, poor performance review, severe criticism from one's superior or coworkers;
3. bank or court action such as foreclosure, restraining orders, or custody hearings;

4. benchmark date—the anniversary of the employee at the organization, chronological age, a date of some horrendous event (such as September 11, 2001), and the like; or
5. failed or spurned romance or a personal crisis such as separation, divorce, or death in family.[58]

These types of triggering events are indicators that allow employers to anticipate or predict the potential of an individual who exhibits these warning signs for engaging in rage or mayhem.

Prevention. There are a variety of ways for organizations to help prevent workplace violence. During the hiring process, careful interviewing and background checks are essential. For the existing workforce, management's application of the foundation competencies developed throughout this book will minimize the conditions that trigger incidents of workplace violence. Employee training related to workplace violence is increasingly seen as essential. When the early warning signs of the potential for an individual to engage in workplace violence occur, the appropriate use of counseling, employee assistance program referral, sound security measures, and preventive disciplinary actions will be helpful. A zero-tolerance violence policy that is consistently communicated and enforced is a foundation element in minimizing and taking corrective action with respect to workplace violence.[59]

Aviza Technology, headquartered in Scotts Valley, California (near San Jose), employs approximately 400 people worldwide. The company provides processing equipment to help firms such as Intel manufacture their chips. Aviza Technology's workplace violence prevention policy outlines the essential elements that all organizations should consider for inclusion in their policies. The following paragraphs report on Aviza Technology's violence prevention policy.[60]

> Aviza is committed to preventing workplace violence and to maintaining a safe work environment. Given the increasing violence in society in general, Aviza has adopted the following guidelines to deal with intimidation, harassment, or other threats of (or actual) violence that may occur during business hours or on its premises.
>
> All employees, including supervisors and temporary employees, should be treated with courtesy and respect at all times. Employees are expected to refrain from fighting, "horseplay," or other conduct that may be dangerous to others. Firearms, weapons, and other dangerous or hazardous devices or substances are prohibited from the premises of Aviza without proper authorization.
>
> Conduct that threatens, intimidates, or coerces another employee, a customer, or a member of the public at any time, including off-duty periods, is banned. This ban includes all acts of harassment, including harassment that is based on an individual's sex, race, age, or any characteristic protected by federal, state, or local law. All threats of (or actual) violence, both direct and indirect, should be reported as soon as possible to your immediate supervisor or any other member of management. This includes threats by employees, as well as threats by customers, vendors, solicitors, or other members of the public. When reporting a threat of violence, you should be as specific and detailed as possible. All suspicious individuals or activities should also be reported as soon as possible to a supervisor. Do not place yourself in peril. If you see or hear a commotion or disturbance near your workstation, do not try to intercede or see what is happening.
>
> Aviza will promptly and thoroughly investigate all reports of threats of (or actual) violence and of suspicious individuals or activities. The identity of the individual making a report will be protected as much as is practical. In order to maintain workplace safety and the integrity of its investigation, Aviza may suspend employees, either with or without pay, pending investigation. Anyone determined to be responsible for threats of (or actual) violence or other conduct

that is in violation of these guidelines will be subject to prompt disciplinary action up to and including termination of employment.

Aviza encourages employees to bring their disputes or differences with other employees to the attention of their managers or the Human Resources Department before the situation escalates into potential violence. Aviza is eager to assist in the resolution of employee disputes, and will not discipline employees for raising such concerns.

Aggression toward the Organization

Our discussion has focused on three of the types of workplace aggression as they impact the employee or groups of employees. An employee who feels unjustly treated, whether for a good cause or self-serving rationalization, may also engage in aggressive behaviors against the organization. At times, the aggression toward the organization is seen as a way of retaliating against the person's manager or higher levels of management. Direct aggression toward management may be seen as resulting in reprisals, such as disciplinary actions or dismissal. The employee might ignore customers and their requests or be rude to them, but not to the point that the customers are likely to complain to higher management. Or, the person might say negative things as a way of blaming the customers' problems on higher management.

Other forms of aggression against the organization may include (1) theft of equipment, supplies, or money, (2) damaging or destroying equipment and facilities, and (3) slacking off whenever possible and withholding ideas for improvements.[61]

CHAPTER SUMMARY

1. Explain the concept of stress and an employee's response to stress.

Stress is the excitement, feeling of anxiety, and/or physical tension that occur when the demands placed on individuals exceed their ability to cope. This view of stress is often negative stress. Individual's general biological responses to stressors prepare them to fight or flee—behaviors generally inappropriate in the workplace. Many factors determine how employees experience work stress, including their perception of the situation, past experiences, the presence or absence of social support, and a variety of individual differences.

2. Describe the role of personality in reactions to stress.

Several personality characteristics are related to differences in how individuals cope with stress. Individuals with a Type A personality are more prone to stress and have an increased chance of physical ailments due to it. Some dimensions of the Type A personality, such as hostility, are particularly important in terms of stress-related illness. In contrast, the collection of personality traits known as hardiness seems to reduce the effects of stress.

3. Identify the primary sources of stress in organizations.

Organizational sources of stress at work often include (1) workload, (2) job conditions, (3) role conflict and ambiguity, (4) career development, (5) interpersonal relations, (6) workplace aggression, especially bullying, sexual harassment, and violence, and (7) conflict between work and other roles. In addition, significant changes or other events in an individual's personal life may also be sources of stress.

4. Outline the possible impacts of stress on health, performance, and job burnout.

Stress impacts individuals physiologically, emotionally, and behaviorally. Severe stress is linked to various health problems. An arch-shaped relationship exists between stress and performance. In other words, an optimal level of stress probably exists for any particular task. Less or more stress than that level may lead to reduced performance. Job burnout is a major result of unrelieved and intense job-related stress.

Stress is a real issue for both individuals and organizations. Fortunately, various initiatives, both organizational and individual, can help managers and employees manage stress in the workplace. These initiatives often focus on identifying and removing workplace stressors as well as helping employees cope with stress. Wellness programs are particularly promising in helping employees cope with stress. Workplace aggression as discussed in the last part of the chapter requires additional organizational practices.

5. Identify individual and organizational practices for managing workplace stress.

Workplace aggression includes a variety of behaviors: psychological acts such as shouting or intimidating remarks, physical assault, and destruction or theft of property. Four of the more common types of workplace aggression include bullying, sexual harassment, workplace violence, and aggression toward the organization itself. There may be overlaps in the behaviors associated with each type, as suggested by the *harm model.* This model represents a continuum of levels of violence from harassment to aggression to rage to mayhem. Mayhem may include murder or destruction of organizational property. A variety of suggestions for minimizing and taking corrective action with respect to bullying, sexual harassment, and workplace violence were reviewed.

6. Discuss four major types of workplace aggression: bullying, sexual harassment, violence, and aggression toward the organization itself.

KEY TERMS AND CONCEPTS

Clinical depression
Depersonalization
Derogation of target bias
Fight-or-flight response
General anxiety disorder
Harassment
Hardiness
Hardy personality
Harm model of aggression
Hostile attribution bias
Hostile work environment
Incivility
Job burnout
Life stressors
Mobbing
Post-traumatic stress disorder
Potency bias
Retribution bias
Role ambiguity
Role conflict
Role overload
Sexual harassment
Social discounting bias
Stress
Stress management
Stressors
Type A personality
Type B personality
Wellness program
Workplace aggression
Workplace bullying
Workplace violence

DISCUSSION QUESTIONS

1. Give an example of your use of the fight-or-flight response. In that situation, all things considered, was your response effective or ineffective?
2. Identify and list some of the stressors in a job that you have held. Which were the most difficult to deal with? Why?
3. Either from your own experience or from something you have read or seen in the business media, describe a real-world example of job burnout. What was its likely cause?
4. Describe a situation in which you coped well with stress. Describe another situation in which you didn't cope well with stress. How did your perception of the two situations differ?
5. Have you experienced or witnessed workplace bullying? If yes, did the management deal with it effectively? Explain.
6. Have you experienced or witnessed workplace violence? If yes, did the management deal with it effectively? Explain.
7. If you have not experienced or witnessed workplace bullying, what factors in the organization do you think accounted for the absence of it?

8. What techniques, approaches, and competencies do you use to cope with stress? Which seem to work best for you?
9. How would you describe yourself in comparison to (a) the Type A personality, (b) the Type B personality, and (c) the hardy personality?
10. Provide an example from your own experience that illustrates the arch-shaped relationship between stress and performance.
11. How do your individual differences (e.g., age, gender, past experience, and personality) contribute to your stress? Explain.
12. Describe a personal work situation that you found stressful. Use Figures 16.1 and 16.2 to identify the factors causing the stress and explain their impact on you.

EXPERIENTIAL EXERCISE AND CASE

Experiential Exercise: Self Competency

Determining Your Stress Level[62]

The following questionnaire has been widely used to measure stress levels. As you answer the questions, think only of the past month. After selecting an answer for each question, add your points to obtain a total.

_____ 1. How often have you been upset because of something that happened unexpectedly?

0 = never
1 = almost never
2 = sometimes
3 = fairly often
4 = very often

_____ 2. How often have you felt that you were unable to control the important things in your life?

0 = never
1 = almost never
2 = sometimes
3 = fairly often
4 = very often

_____ 3. How often have you felt nervous and "stressed"?

0 = never
1 = almost never
2 = sometimes
3 = fairly often
4 = very often

_____ 4. How often have you felt confident about your ability to handle your personal problems?

4 = never
3 = almost never
2 = sometimes
1 = fairly often
0 = very often

_____ 5. How often have you felt that things were going your way?

4 = never
3 = almost never
2 = sometimes
1 = fairly often
0 = very often

_____ 6. How often have you been able to control irritations in your life?

4 = never
3 = almost never
2 = sometimes
1 = fairly often
0 = very often

_____ 7. How often have you found that you could not cope with all the things that you had to do?

0 = never
1 = almost never
2 = sometimes
3 = fairly often
4 = very often

_____ 8. How often have you felt that you were on top of things?

4 = never
3 = almost never
2 = sometimes
1 = fairly often
0 = very often

_____ 9. How often have you been angered because of things that were outside your control?

0 = never
1 = almost never
2 = sometimes
3 = fairly often
4 = very often

_____ 10. How often have you felt difficulties were piling up so high that you could not overcome them?

0 = never
1 = almost never
2 = sometimes
3 = fairly often
4 = very often

_____ TOTAL POINTS

Stress levels vary among individuals. Compare your total score to the following averages.

Age Average Score	Average Score
18–29 . . . . 14.2	Men. 12.1
30–44 . . . . 13.0	Women 13.7
45–54 . . . . 12.6	
55–64 . . . . 11.9	
65 and over . . 12.0	

Questions

1. If your score is above the average for your age or gender, does your score suggest that you need to take action to lower your stress level? If "yes," what actions do you think would be most effective?
2. What three competencies are likely to be most effective and important to you in managing your stress level?

Case: Change Competency

Stress Management at Metropolitan Hospital

This stress management program was carried out over a 2-year period at Metropolitan Hospital. The initial impetus for the project was widespread complaints from middle managers about feeling stress, overworked, and subject to unexpected changes in policies and procedures. Top administrators sought help in dealing with these problems from external organization development (OD) consultants with skills and experience in stress management.

The initial stage of the project consisted of diagnosing the causes and consequences of experienced stress at the hospital. Understanding the sources of stress was seen as a necessary prelude to developing an appropriate plan for managing stress. The consultants developed a questionnaire to collect data from the 45 middle managers responsible for almost every phase of operation of the hospital. The design of the questionnaire was guided by a conceptual model of stress similar to that shown in Figure 16.2. The questionnaire included items about various organizational stressors, including ongoing, recurrent stressors as well as those associated with recent changes. It also included questions about the managers' use of stress management techniques, such as exercise, nutritional awareness, and the creation of support systems. The questionnaire ended with items about possible immediate stress effects (e.g., irritability, sleep difficulty, and changes in eating and drinking patterns) and longer term impacts (e.g., reduced general health, job dissatisfaction, and poor work performance).

Analysis of the data showed that many of the organizational change events and ongoing working conditions were significantly related to the managers' levels of perceived stress. Among the most stressful organizational change events were major and frequent changes in instructions, policies, and procedures; numerous unexpected crises and deadlines; and sudden increases in the activity level or pace of work. The ongoing working conditions contributing most to stress included work overload, feedback only when performance was unsatisfactory, lack of confidence in management, and role conflict and ambiguity. The managers reported little use of stress management techniques to help them cope with these stressors. Only 20 percent engaged in regular physical exercise, and, surprisingly, 60 percent had marginally or poorly balanced diets. Among the most commonly reported health problems were tension headaches, diarrhea or constipation, common colds, and backaches.

Based on the data, senior management with the help of the consultants implemented several organizational improvements. To reduce work overload and role ambiguity, each managerial position was analyzed in terms of work distribution, job requirements, and performance standards. Actions based on this analysis resulted in more balanced workloads across the jobs and in clearer job descriptions. Hospital administrators also began working with department managers to define job descriptions and expectations and to provide ongoing performance feedback. The managers were given training in time management, how to organize their workloads better, and in general how to delegate work to subordinates more effectively.

The "fire-fighting" climate at the hospital had caused many managers to focus on their own departments while neglecting important lateral relations with other units. Monthly cross-departmental meetings were implemented to improve lateral relations among department heads and supervisors. Efforts were also made to provide an organizational culture that encouraged the building of peer-support groups.

To reduce uncertainty about organizational changes, senior managers spent more time informing and educating middle managers about forthcoming changes. Top management also held quarterly information meetings with first-line supervisors in order to clear up misunderstandings, misinterpretations, and rumors.

In addition to the changes aimed at reducing organizational stressors, measures were taken to help managers identify and cope with stress more effectively. The hospital instituted yearly physical examinations to detect stress-related problems. It also trained managers to identify stress symptoms and problems both in themselves and subordinates. The hospital developed an exercise club and various sports activities and offered weekly yoga classes. It also created a training program combining nutritional awareness with techniques for coping with tension headaches and backaches. Fresh fruit was made available as an alternative to doughnuts in all meetings and training sessions.

Initial reactions to the stress management program were positive, and the hospital's management is assessing the longer term effects. Measures of stressors and experienced stress will be taken every 12 to 18 months to monitor the program so that further changes can be made as necessary.[63]

Questions

1. Identify the primary ideas and concepts from the chapter that appear in this case in one form or another.
2. Using Figure 16.2, diagnose the work stressors at Metropolitan Hospital.
3. Using Figure 16.6, analyze Metropolitan Hospital's stress management program.

References

CHAPTER 1

1. Adapted from Boland, M.A., and Katz, J.P. Jack Gherty, president and CEO of Land O'Lakes, on leading a branded food and farm supply cooperative. *Academy of Management Executive*, 2003, 17(3), 24–30.
2. Boland and Katz, Jack Gherty . . . , 30.
3. Conger, J.A., and Ready, D.A. Rethinking leadership competencies. *Leader to Leader*, 2004, 32, 41–48; Jossey-Bass Publishers (Ed.). *Management Skills: A Jossey-Bass Reader.* San Francisco: Jossey-Bass/Pfeiffer, 2005.
4. Adapted from Organizational Behavior Division of the Academy of Management. Available at http://www.aomonline.org/ (accessed January 18, 2005).
5. Zeidner, M., Matthews, G., and Roberts, R.D. Emotional intelligence in the workplace: A critical review. *Applied Psychology*, 2004, 53, 371–399; Law, K.S., Wong, C.S., and Song, L.J. The construct and criterion validity of emotional intelligence and its potential utility for management studies. *Journal of Applied Psychology*, 2004, 83, 483–490.
6. Boland and Katz, Jack Gherty . . . , 29.
7. Hall, D.T. *Careers In and Out of Organizations.* Thousand Oaks, CA: Sage, 2002; King, Z. Career self-management: Its nature, causes and consequences. *Journal of Vocational Behavior*, 2004, 65, 112–133.
8. Adapted from Wademan, D. The best advice I ever got. *Harvard Business Review*, 2005, 83(1), 35–44.
9. This section draws from Ellinor, L., and Gerard, G. *Dialogue: Rediscover the Transforming Power of Conversations.* New York: John Wiley & Sons, 1998; Conrad, C., and Poole, M.S. *Strategic Organizational Communication: In a Global Economy*, 6th ed. Belmont: CA: Wadsworth, 2005.
10. Wademan, The best advice, 37.
11. Adapted from Clinebell, S., and Rowley, D.J. Former CEO of the Security Traders Association on managing through chaos. *Academy of Management Executive*, 2003, 17(2), 30–36.
12. This section draws from Thomas, K.M. *Diversity Dynamics in the Workplace.* Belmont, CA: Wadsworth, 2004; Powell, G.N. *Managing a Diverse Workforce: Learning Activities.* Thousand Oaks, CA: Sage, 2004.
13. Salett, E.P. Defining multiculturalism. *Washington Post*, May 24, 2001, 16A.
14. Bucher, R.D. *Diversity Consciousness: Opening Our Minds to People, Cultures, and Opportunities*, 2nd ed. Old Tappan, NJ: Prentice-Hall, 2004; Stockdale, M., and Crosby, F.J. *The Psychology and Management of Workplace Diversity.* Malden, MA: Blackwell, 2003; Carr-Ruffino, N. *Making Diversity Work.* Old Tappan, NJ: Prentice-Hall, 2005.
15. Catalyst. *Facts about Working Women.* Available at http://www.catalystwomen.org (accessed January 20, 2005).
16. Diversity—Part I: Building a competitive workforce. *Forbes*, May 13, 1999. Special insert, 1–31; Aetna's company demographics. http://www.aetna.com/diversity/ (accessed January 21, 2005).
17. Catalyst. *The Bottomline: Connecting Corporate Performance and Gender Diversity.* Available at http://www.catalyst.com (accessed January 21, 2005).
18. Tossi, M. Labor force projections to 2012: The graying of the U.S. workforce. *Monthly Labor Review*, 2004, 127(2), 37–58.
19. Tossi, Labor force projections, 38.
20. IBM. Hoovers Online. Available at http://www.hoovers.com (accessed January 22, 2005).
21. Letter from IBM's Vice President of Global Work Force Diversity. Available at http://www.ibm.com (accessed January 21, 2005); also see Thomas, D.A. Diversity as strategy. *Harvard Business Review*, September 2004, 98–108.
22. This section draws from Donaldson, T., and W[illegible]ane, P. (eds.). *Ethical Issues in Business: A Philosoph[illegible]roach.* Upper Saddle River, NJ: Prentice-Hall, [illegible]errell, O.C., Fraedrich, J., and Ferrell, L. *Business [illegible]thical Decision Making and Cases*, 6th ed. Bosto[illegible]ghton Mifflin, 2005.
23. Greenberg, J., and Colquitt, J.A. (eds.). *H[illegible]ook of Organizational Justice.* Mahwah, NJ: Lawrenc[illegible]lbaum Associates, 2005.
24. Cohen, M. *101 Ethical Dilemmas.* New Yor[illegible]tledge, 2003.
25. McNamara, C. *Complete Guide to Ethics Management: An Ethics Toolkit for Managers.* Available at http://www.managementhelp.org/ethics/ethxgde.htm (accessed November 2005).
26. Swanson, W.H. Ethics: Setting your moral compass. Available at http://www.raytheon.com/ethics (accessed January 25, 2005).
27. Adapted from *Raytheon: Code of Business Ethics and Conduct.* Available at http://www.raytheon.com (accessed January 25, 2005).
28. Jury awards $500,000 in Raytheon harassment case. Available at http://www.boston.com (accessed January 11, 2005).
29. Harris, P.R., Moran, R.T., and Moran, S. *Managing Cultural Differences: Global Strategies for the 21st Century*, 6th ed. Burlington, MA: Butterworth-Heineman, 2005; M. Gannon and K. Newman (eds.). *The Blackwell Handbook of Cross-Cultural Management.* Malden, MA: Blackwell, 2001.
30. Adler, N.J. *International Dimensions of Organizational Behavior*, 4th ed. Cincinnati, OH: South-Western, 2002.
31. Hofstede, G., and Hofstede, G.J. *Cultures and Organizations: Software of the Mind.* New York: McGraw-Hill, 2005.
32. Kirkman, B.L., Gibson, C.B., and Shapiro, D.L. "Exporting" teams: Enhancing the implementation and effectiveness of work teams in global affiliates.

Organizational Dynamics, 2001, 30, 12–29.

33. Javidan, M., and House, R.J. Cultural acumen for the global manager: Lessons from project GLOBE. *Organizational Dynamics*, 2001, 29, 289–305.
34. Fang, T. A critique of Hofstede's fifth national culture dimension. *International Journal of Cross Cultural Management*, 2003, 3, 347–368; Triandis, H.C. The many dimensions of culture. *Academy of Management Executive*, 2004, 18(1), 88–93.
35. Adapted from Osland, J.S., and Bird, A. Beyond sophisticated stereotyping: Cultural sensemaking in context. *Academy of Management Executive*, 2000, 14(1), 65–76.
36. Adapted from Zhang, C. How the Internet has changed the world's most populous nation. *Academy of Management Executive*, 2004, 18(4), 143–150.
37. Beatty, C.A., and Barker Scott, B. *Building Smart Teams: A Roadmap to High Performance.* Thousand Oaks, CA: Sage, 2005; LaFasto, F.M.J., and Larson, C.E. *When Teams Work Best: 6000 Team Members and Leaders Tell What It Takes to Succeed.* Thousand Oaks, CA: Sage, 2001.
38. Adapted from Kreuzer, J.E., and Ormsby, J.L. Teams work to contain costs in $16.2 million hospital turnaround. *Managed Health Care Executive*, 2004, 14(2), 31–34; West Suburban Health Care. Available at http://www.westsub.com (accessed January 24, 2005).
39. Boland and Katz, Jack Gherty . . . , 28.
40. Muczyk, J.P., and Steel, R.P. Leadership style and the turnaround executive. *Business Horizons*, March/April 1998, 39–46.
41. Adapted from Fitzgerald, M. The next best thing to being there. *INC Magazine*, July 2004, 44–45; Case studies: Alaska Indoor Sports Distributing, Ltd. Available at http://www.groove.net (accessed January 24, 2005).
42. Adapted from Hill-Stocks, H. Diversity Self-Assessment Questionnaire, 1994. Used with permission.
43. Adapted from Puffer, S.M. CompUSA's CEO James Halpin on technology rewards and commitment. *Academy of Management Executive*, May 1999, 29–36.

CHAPTER 2

1. Adapted from Davis, G.L. Business ethics: It's all inside—JC Penney grounded in golden rules of business conduct. *Mid-American Journal of Business*, 2004, 19(1), 7–10; JC Penney about us. Available at http://www.jcpenney.net (accessed May 2005).
2. Ferrell, O.C., Fraedrich, J., and Ferrell, L. *Business Ethics: Ethical Decision Making and Cases*, 6th ed. Boston: Houghton Mifflin, 2004; Carroll, A.B., and Buchholtz, A.K. *Business and Society: Ethics and Stakeholder Management*, 6th ed. Mason, OH: South-Western, 2006.
3. Adapted from Ethics Resource Center. National business ethics survey. Available at http://www.ethics.org (accessed May 2005). Also see Brown, M.T. *Corporate Integrity: Rethinking Organizational Ethics and Leadership.* New York: Cambridge University Press, 2005.
4. The framework for this section is based primarily on James, T.M. Ethical decision making by individuals in organizations: An issue-contingent model. *Academy of Management Review*, 1991, 16, 366–395; May, D.R., and Paul, K.P. The role of moral intensity in ethical decision making. *Business and Society*, 2002, 41, 84–118; Carlson, D.S. The impact of moral intensity dimensions on ethical decision making: Assessing the relevance of orientation. *Journal of Managerial Issues*, 2002, 14, 15–31; Watley, L.D., and May, D.R. Enhancing moral intensity: The roles of personal and consequential information in ethical decision-making. *Journal of Business Ethics*, 2004, 49, 105–126.
5. DeGeorge, R. *Business Ethics*, 6th ed. Upper Saddle River, NJ: Prentice Hall, 2005; Johnson, C.E. *Meeting the Ethical Challenges of Leadership: Casting Light or Shadow.* Thousand Oaks, CA: Sage, 2005.
6. Bauer, C. An ethics self-exam. *Internal Auditor*, June 2004, 27–31.
7. Weiss, J.W. *Business Ethics: A Stakeholder and Issues Management Approach*, 4th. ed. Mason, OH: South-Western, 2006; Bowie, N.E., and Werhane, P.H. *Management Ethics.* Malden, MA: Blackwell, 2005.
8. O'Harrow, R. *No Place to Hide: Behind the Scenes of Our Emerging Surveillance Society*. New York: Free Press, 2005; Solove, D.J. *The Digital Person: Technology and Privacy in the Information Age.* New York: New York University Press, 2005.
9. Turkington, R.C., and Allen-Castellitto, A.L. *Privacy Law: Cases and Materials*, 2nd ed. Eagan, MN: West Group Publishing, 2002.
10. Etzioni, A. *The Limits of Privacy*. New York: Basic Books, 2000; Cohn, M. *101 Ethical Dilemmas.* New York: Routledge, 2003.
11. Greenwold, J. Privacy issues creating dilemma for employers. *Business Insurance*, February 16, 2004, 1–3; Privacy Rights Clearinghouse. Workplace privacy. Available at http://www.privacyrights.org (accessed May 2005).
12. U.S. Equal Employment Opportunity Commission. The Equal Pay Act of 1963. Available at http://www.eeoc.gov/policy/ (accessed November 2005).
13. Roussouw, D. *Business Ethics*, 2nd ed. New York: Oxford University Press, 2002.
14. BambooWeb Dictionary. At-will employment. Available at http://www.bambooweb.com (accessed May 2005).
15. Janove, J. Keep 'em at will, treat 'em for cause. *HRMagazine*, 2005, 50(5), 111–116; Grossenbacher, K. What happened to at will? *National Law Journal*, April 4, 2005, 26–27; Roehling, M.V., and Wright, P. Organizationally sensible vs. legal-centric responses to the eroding employment at-will doctrine. *Employee Responsibilities and Rights Journal*, 2004, 16, 89–103.
16. Institute for Global Ethics. *Global Values, Moral Boundaries: A Pilot Survey.* Camden, MA: Institute for Global Ethics, 1997; Baker, W.E. *America's Crisis of Values: Reality and Perception.* Princeton, NJ: Princeton University Press, 2004.
17. Greenpeace: About us. Available at http://www.greenpeace.org (accessed June 2005).

18. Jackson, P.M. Ethical decision making: Some economic foundations. *International Journal of Management & Decision Making*, 2005, 6, 203–212.
19. Rowan, J.R. The foundation of moral rights. *Journal of Business Ethics*, 2000, 24, 355–361; Johnson, C. *Meeting the Ethical Challenges of Leadership*, 2nd ed. Thousand Oaks, CA: Sage, 2005.
20. Adapted from Brodsky, N. Just say yes: A policy that sounds tough can turn into a lifeline for some. *Inc.*, November 2004, 67–68.
21. Anderson, D.R., Sweeney, D.J., and Williams, T.A. *An Introduction to Management Science: Quantitative Approaches to Decision Making*, 11th ed. Mason, OH: South-Western, 2005.
22. Adapted from Xerox Consensus Matrix. Available at http://www.xbrg.com (accessed June 2005).
23. Hammond, J.S., Keeney, R.L., and Raiffa, H. *Smart Choices: A Practical Guide to Making Better Decisions.* Boston: Harvard Business School Press, 1999; Koller, G. *Risk Assessment and Decision Making in Business and Industry*, 2nd ed. Boca Raton, FL: CRC Press, 2005.
24. QAD Company. Available at http://www.qad.com (accessed June 2005).
25. Adapted from Muoio, A. Decision, decisions. *Fast Company*, October 1998, 93–97; Bylinsky, G. The queen of elegant software. *Fortune*, March 19, 2001, 4–8.
26. Chakravarti, B. Whether to bet, reserve options or insure: Making certain choices in an uncertain world. *Ivey Business Journal Online*, January/February 2004, 1–3.
27. Montgomery, H., Lipshitz, R., and Brehmer, B. (eds.). *How Professionals Make Decisions.* Mahwah, NJ: Lawrence Erlbaum Associates, 2005; Betsch, T., and Haberstroh (eds.). *The Routines of Decision Making.* Mahwah, NJ: Lawrence Erlbaum Associates, 2005.
28. Adapted from Herper, M. Doctors, untethered. Forbes.com. June 21, 2004, 20–21; Gruman, G. Caging wireless. *CIO Magazine*, July 15, 2004, 1–4; Williams, C.T. Inside a closed loop medication strategy. *Nursing Management*, October 2004, 8–9, 24.
29. About St. Vincent Hospital. Available at http://www.stv.org (accessed June 2005).
30. Simon, H.A. *Administrative Behavior: A Study of Decision-Making Processes in Administrative Organizations*, 4th ed. New York: Free Press, 1997. Also see Kohler, D.J. and Harvey, N. *Blackwell Handbook of Judgment and Decision Making.* Malden, MA: Blackwell Publishing, 2005.
31. Roach, J.M. Simon says: Decision making is "satisficing" experience. *Management Review*, January 1979, 8–9; Dequech, D. Bounded rationality, institutions, and uncertainty. *Journal of Economic Issues*, 2001, 35, 911–930.
32. Armstrong, R.W., Williams, R.J., and Barrett, J.D. The impact of banality, risky shift, and escalating commitment on ethical decision making. *Journal of Business Ethics*, 2004, 53, 365–370.
33. Montealegre, R., and Keil, M. Deescalating information technology projects: Lessons from the Denver International Airport. *MIS Quarterly*, 2000, 24, 417–447.
34. Petrakis, P.E. Risk perception, risk propensity, and entrepreneurial behavior: The Greek case. *Journal of Academy of Business*, 2005, 7, 233–242.
35. Bernstein, P.L. *Against the Gods: The Remarkable Story of Risk.* Somerset, NJ: John Wiley & Sons, 1997; Gladwell, M. *Blink: The Power of Thinking without Thinking.* New York: Little, Brown, 2005.
36. Kahneman, D., and Tversky, A. *Choices, Values and Frames.* New York: Cambridge University Press, 2000.
37. Schoemaker, P.J.H., and Russo, J.E. A pyramid of decision approaches. *California Management Review*, Fall 1993, 9–31.
38. Adapted from Nutt, P.C. Surprising but true: Half the decisions in organizations fail. *Academy of Management Executive*, 1999, 13(4), 75–90; Nutt, P.C. Expanding the search for alternatives during strategic decision-making. *Academy of Management Executive*, 2004, 18(4), 13–28.
39. Patriotta, G. *Organizational Knowledge in the Making: How Firms Create, Use, and Institutionalize Knowledge.* New York: Oxford University Press, 2005.
40. Adapted from Conley, L. Julie Rodriguez. *Fast Company*, May 2005, 72; Rodriguez, J. A message from the president. *Working Under Pressure* (EPIC newsletter), Third Quarter Issue, 2003, 1–2; Rodriguez, J. Letter from the CEO. *Working Under Pressure* (EPIC newsletter) First Quarter Issue, 2003, 1–2.
41. About Epic Companies. Available at http://www.epicompanies.com (accessed June 2005).
42. Pfeffer, J. *Managing with Power: Politics and Influence in Organizations.* Boston: Harvard Business School Press, 1992; Kramer, R.M., and Neale, M.A. (eds.). *Power and Influence in Organizations.* Thousand Oaks, CA: Sage, 1998.
43. Funk, S. Risky business. *Across the Board*, July/August 1999, 10–12.
44. Dulebohn, J.H., and Ferris, G.R. The role of influence tactics in perceptions of performance evaluations' fairness. *Academy of Management Journal*, 1999, 42, 288–303; Bacharach, S.B. *Get Them on Your Side.* Woodbury, NY: Platinum Press, 2005.
45. Hamel, G., Gould, S.J., and Weick, K.E. *On Creativity, Innovation and Renewal.* San Francisco: Jossey-Bass, 2002.
46. Thompson, L.L., and Choi, H. (eds.). *Creativity and Innovation in Organizational Teams.* Mahwah, NJ: Lawrence Erlbaum Associates, 2005; McLean, L.D. Organizational culture's influence on creativity and innovation: A review of the literature and implications for human resource development. *Advances in Developing Human Resources*, 2005, 7, 226–246; Egan, T.B. Factors influencing individual creativity in the workplace: An examination of quantitative empirical research. *Advances in Developing Human Resources*, 2005, 7, 160–181; Leonard, D., and Swap, W. *When Sparks Fly: Harnessing the Power of Group Creativity.* Boston: Harvard Business School Press, 2005.
47. deBono, E. *Serious Creativity: Using the Power of Lateral Thinking to Create New Ideas.* New York: HarperCollins, 1993; Fisher, J.R., Jr. The need for lateral thinking in the new century. *National Productivity Review*, Spring

2000, 1–12; Edward De bono personal website. Available at http://www.edwarddebono.com (accessed June 2005).
48. Amabile, T.M. How to kill creativity. *Harvard Business Review*, September/October 1998, 77–87; Gogatz, A., and Mondejar, R. *Business Creativity: Breaking the Invisible Barriers.* New York: Palgrave Macmillan, 2005.
49. Gryskiewicz, S.S., and Epstein, R. Cashing in on creativity at work. *Psychology Today*, September/October 2000, 62–67; Maurzy, J., and Harriman, R.A. Three climates for creativity. *Research Technology Management*, 2003, 46, 27–31.
50. Adapted from Underwood, R. Donna Kacmar on questioning assumptions. *Fast Company*, December 2004, 44; Profile: Dona Kacmar. *Architecture and Community Involvement.* Available at http://www.aia.org (accessed June 2005).
51. About Architect Works, Inc. Available at http://www.architectworks.com (accessed November 2005).
52. Cosier, R.A., and Schwenk, C.R. Agreement and thinking alike: Ingredients for poor decisions. *Academy of Management Executive*, 1990, 4(1), 69–74.
53. Adapted from Duran, G.J., Gomar, E.E., Stiles, M., Vele, C.A., and Vogt, J.F. Living ethics: Meeting challenges in decision making. In *The 1997b Annual: Volume 1, Training*. Copyright © 1997 by Pfeiffer, An Imprint of Jossey-Bass, Inc., Publishers, San Francisco, Calif., 127–135. Used with permission.
54. Adapted from Is Opportunity Knocking? Copyright © 1995 by Cis Hawk, The Citizenship Foundation, Houston, Texas. Written as a basis for classroom discussion. Distributed by the International Case Clearinghouse. Used with permission.

CHAPTER 3

1. Adapted from Pitts, R.A., and Lei, D. *Strategic Management: Building and Sustaining a Competitive Advantage*, 4th ed. Cincinnati, OH: South-Western, 2006, 230–233.
2. Colbert, B.A. The complex resource-based view: Implications for theory and practice of strategic human resource management. *Academy of Management Review*, 2004, 29, 341–358.
3. Henderson A.D., and Stern, I. Selection-based learning: The coevolution of internal and external selection in high-velocity environments. *Administrative Science Quarterly*, 2004, 49, 39–75; Ketchen, D.J., Jr., Snow, C.C., and Hoover, V.L. Research on competitive dynamics: Recent accomplishments and future challenges. *Journal of Management*, 2004, 30, 779–804.
4. Hall, R.H. *Organizations: Structures, Processes and Outcomes*, 8th ed. Upper Saddle River, NJ: Prentice Hall, 2002, 201–235; Gerwin, D.J., and Ferris, S.J. Organizing new product development projects in strategic alliances. *Organization Science*, 2004, 15, 22–37.
5. Porter, M. *Competitive Strategy.* New York: Free Press, 1980; Hambrick, D.C., and Fredrickson, J.W. Are you sure you have a strategy? *Academy of Management Executive*, 2001, 15(4), 48–59; Joyce, W.F. What really works: Building the 4 + 2 organization. *Organizational Dynamics*, 2005, 34, 118–129.
6. Personal communication with Kevin Elliott, vice president, Merchandising, 7-Eleven, Dallas, TX, January 2005.
7. Thompson, J.D. *Organizations in Action.* New York: McGraw-Hill, 1967; Van der Vegt, G.S., and Janssen, O. Joint impact of interdependence and group diversity on innovation. *Journal of Management*, 2003, 29, 729–752.
8. Burns, T., and Stalker, G. *The Management of Innovation.* London: Social Science Paperbacks, 1961, 96–125.
9. Adapted from Weber, M. *The Theory of Social and Economic Organization* (trans. Parsons, T.). New York: Oxford University Press, 1947, 329–334.
10. Hellriegel, D., Jackson, S.J., and Slocum, J.W., Jr. *Management: A Competency-Based Approach*, 10th ed. Cincinnati, OH: South-Western, 2005, 302–303.
11. Becker, T.H. *Doing Business in New Latin America.* Westport, CT: Praeger, 2004, 112–147.
12. http://www.hoovers.com (accessed January 2005); Kirkpatrick, J. Cinemark chief hopes to land another big deal. *Dallas Morning News*, May 13, 2004, D1, D9.
13. http://www.hoovers.com (accessed January 2005).
14. Personal conversation with M. Bohn, director of business systems, Celanese Chemical Corporation, Dallas, TX, January 2005.
15. See http://www.utc.com (accessed January 2005).
16. Lei, D., and Slocum, J.W., Jr. Strategic and organizational requirements for competitive advantage. *Academy of Management Executive*, 2005, 19, 31–45.
17. Roth, K., and Kostova, T. The multinational corporation as a research context. *Journal of Management*, 2003, 29, 883–902.
18. Christmann, P. Multinational companies and the natural environment: Determinants of global environmental policy standardization. *Academy of Management Review*, 2004, 47, 747–759.
19. Gupta, A., and Govindarajan, V. Converting global presence into global competitive advantage. *Academy of Management Executive*, 2001, 15(2), 45–58.
20. Biediger, J., DeCicco, T., Green, T., Hoffman, G., Lei, D., Mahadevan, K., Ojeda, J., Slocum, J.W., Jr., and Ward, K. Strategic action at Lenovo. *Organizational Dynamics*, 2005, 34, 89–102.
21. http://www.hoovers.com (accessed January 2005).
22. Martins, L.L., Gilson, L.L., and Maynard, M.T. Virtual teams: What do we know and where do we go from here? *Journal of Management*, 2004, 30, 805–836.
23. Lichenstein, B.B. Self-organized transitions: A pattern amidst the chaos of transformative change. *Academy of Management Executive*, 2000, 14, 128–141; Alvarez, S.A., and Barney, J.B. How entrepreneurial firms can benefit from alliances with large partners. *Academy of Management Executive*, 2001, 15, 139–148.
24. Saunders, C., Van Slyke, C., and Vogel, D. My time or yours? Managing time in global virtual teams. *Academy of Management Executive*, 2004, 18, 19–31; Markus, M.L., Manville, B., and Agres, C.E. What makes a virtual organization work? *Sloan Management Review*, 2000, 42(1), 13–27.

25. Adapted from http://www.hoovers.com (accessed January 2005) and http://www.dreamworks.com (accessed January 2005).
26. Adapted from Pasmore, W.A. *Designing Effective Organizations: The Sociotechnical Systems Perspective.* New York: John Wiley & Sons, 1988, 157–186.
27. Moingeon, B., Ramanantsoa, B., Metais, E., and Orton, J.D. Another look at the strategy–structure relationships: The resource-based view. *European Management Journal*, 1998, 16, 297–305.

CHAPTER 4

1. Adapted from Warner, M. What can your company learn from Google? *Business 2.0*, June 2004, 100–106; Piper, P.S. Google spawn: The culture surrounding Google. *Searcher*, 2004, 12(6), 26–33; Delany, K.J., and Lublin, J.S. Google goes public. *Wall Street Journal*, August 20, 2004, C3 (Eastern ed.); http://www.google.com (accessed February 2005).
2. Mike, B., and Slocum, J.W., Jr. Changing culture at Pizza Hut and YUM! Brands, Inc. *Organizational Dynamics*, 2003, 32, 319–330.
3. Mason, R. Lessons in organizational ethics from the *Columbia* disaster: Can a culture be lethal? *Organizational Dynamics*, 2004, 33, 128–142.
4. Lee, S.K.J., and Yu, K. Corporate culture and organization performance. *Journal of Managerial Psychology*, 2004, 19, 340–359.
5. Gibson, C.B., and Zellmer-Bruhn, M.E. Metaphors and meaning: An intercultural analysis of the concept of teamwork. *Administrative Science Quarterly*, 2001, 46, 274–298.
6. Schein, E.H. *Organizational Culture and Leadership.* San Francisco: Jossey-Bass, 1985.
7. Ibid., 49–84.
8. Schein, E.H. Organizational culture. *American Psychologist*, 1990, 45, 109–119.
9. Adapted from Gutierrez-Olvera, H. Cultural impact of the acquisition of CompUSA by Mexico based Grupo Carso S.A. de C.V. Unpublished paper, Cox School of Business, Southern Methodist University, February 2005.
10. Chatman, J.A., Polzer, J.T., Barsade, S.G., and Neale, M.A. Being different yet feeling similar: The influence of demographic composition and organizational culture on work process and outcomes. *Administrative Science Quarterly*, 1998, 43, 749–779.
11. Eisenberg, D. Where people are never let go. *Time*, June 18, 2001, 40–41; Goff, L. The top five. *Computerworld*, June 28, 1999, 4ff.
12. Mason, Lessons in organizational ethics.
13. Mike and Slocum, Changing culture at Pizza Hut.
14. Personal conversations with Fred Flores, director, Mary Kay Cosmetics, February 2005; Karen Mortazavi, salesperson, Mary Kay Cosmetics, February 2005.
15. Mardenfeld, S. Mary Kay Ash. *Incentive*, January 1996, 54–55; Farnharn, A. Lessons in leadership. *Fortune*, September 1993, 68–75.
16. Schein, Organization culture, 109–119.
17. Sorensen, J.B. The strength of corporate culture and the reliability of firm performance. *Administrative Science Quarterly*, 2002, 47, 70–91.
18. Adapted from Kuglin, H., Kuglin, F., and Slocum, J. W., Jr. A route to building a competitive advantage: Harley-Davidson. *Nanyang Business Review*, 2005, 4(1), 23–43. Bacon, T. You are how you behave: Customers can't be fooled. *Journal of Business Strategy*, 2004, 35(4), 35–41.
19. Hellriegel, D., Jackson, S.J., and Slocum, J.W., Jr. *Management: A Competency-Based Approach*, 10th ed. Cincinnati, OH: South-Western, 2005, 517–521.
20. Kerr, J., and Slocum, J.W., Jr. Managing corporate cultures through reward systems. *Academy of Management Executive*, 1987, 1(2), 99–108.
21. Mike and Slocum, Changing culture at Pizza Hut, 322.
22. Schein, *Organizational Culture and Leadership.*
23. Maher, K. Global companies face reality of instituting ethics programs. *Wall Street Journal*, November 9, 2004, B8; Personal communication with Ralph Sorrentino, partner, Deloitte Touche Tohmatsu, February 2005.
24. Van der Merwe, R., Pitt, L., and Berthon, P. Are excellent companies ethical? *Corporate Reputation Review*, 2003, 5, 343–356; Totterdell, P., Wall, T., Holman, D., Diamond, H., and Epitropaki, O. Affect networks: A structural analysis of the relationship between work ties and job related affect. *Journal of Applied Psychology*, 2004, 89, 854–869.
25. Adapted from Near, J.P., Rehg, M. T., VanScotter, J.R., and Miceli, M.P. Does type of wrongdoing affect the whistle-blowing process? *Business Ethics Quarterly*, 2004, 14, 219–242.
26. Adapted from Smith, D.M. *Women at Work.* Upper Saddle River, NJ: Prentice Hall, 2000, 139–143.
27. Filstad, C. How newcomers use role models in organizational socialization. *Journal of Workplace Learning*, 2004, 16, 396–410.
28. Van Vianen, A.E., DePrater, I.E., Kristof-Brown, A.L., and Johnson, E.C. Fitting-in: Surface-and-deep-level cultural differences and expatriates' adjustment. *Academy of Management Journal*, 2004, 47, 697–710.
29. See the Walt Disney Company website, http://www.disney.com (accessed February 2005); Brannen, M.Y. When Mickey loses face: Recontextualization, semantic fit and semiotics of foreignness. *Academy of Management Review*, 2004, 29, 593–616.
30. Bowen, D.E., and Ostroff, C. Understanding HRM-firm performance linkages: The role of the "strength" of the HRM system. *Academy of Management Review*, 2004, 29, 203–221.
31. Adapted from Reiss, M.C., and Mitra, K. The effects of individual difference factors on the acceptability of ethical or unethical workplace behaviors. *Journal of Business Ethics*, 1998, 17, 1581–1593.
32. Adapted from Zellner, W. Dressed to kill competitors. *Business Week*, February 21, 2005, 60–61; Smith, G. An evolution of the corporate culture of Southwest Airlines. *Measuring Business Excellence*, 2004, 8(4), 26–34; Trottman, M. New atmosphere: Inside Southwest Airlines storied culture feels strains. *Wall Street Journal*, July 11, 2003, A1ff.

CHAPTER 5

1. Adapted from Loomis, C.J. Why Carly's big bet is failing. *Fortune*, February 7, 2005, 50–64; Elgin, B. Carly's challenge. *Business Week*, December 13, 2004, 98ff; Tam, P.W. Hewlett-Packard board considers a reorganization. *Wall Street Journal*, January 24, 2005, A1, A6; Rosenberg, W. Making a profit ... and a difference: HP invents an organization to drive sustainability. *Journal of Organizational Excellence*, Summer 2004, 3–13; Elgin, B. Can anyone save HP? *Business Week*, February 21, 2005, 28–35.
2. Weick, K., and Sutcliffe, K.M. *Managing the Unexpected.* San Francisco: Jossey-Bass, 2001.
3. Kersetter, J., and Burrows, P. A CEO's last stand. *Business Week*, July 26, 2004, 64ff.
4. Juggernaut in the works. *Dallas Morning News*, January 29, 2005, 2D; Akhter, S.H. Is globalization what it's cracked up to be? Economic freedom, corruption, and human development. *Journal of World Business*, 2004, 29, 283–295.
5. Leonidas, L., and Theodosiou, M. The export marketing information system: An integration of extant knowledge. *Journal of World Business*, 2004, 39, 12–26.
6. Siehman, P. How a tighter supply chain extends the enterprise. *Fortune*, November 8, 1999, 272A–272B.
7. Personal communication with Will Sowell, vice president of strategic initiatives, GE Capital-Card Services, January 28, 2005.
8. Schweiger, D.M., Atamer, T., and Calori, R. Transnational project teams and networks: Making the multiorganization more effective. *Journal of World Business*, 2003, 38, 127–140.
9. Ambos, B., and Schlegelmilch, B.B. The use of international R&D teams: An empirical investigation of selected contingency factors. *Journal of World Business*, 2004, 39, 37–48.
10. Brewster, M. The freelance conundrum. *INC.*, December 1, 2004, 38.
11. Gavin, J.H., and Mason, R.O. The virtuous organization. *Organizational Dynamics*, 2004, 33, 379–392. This entire issue is dedicated to healthy, happy, and productive work and is edited by Quick, J.C., and Quick, J.A. *Organizational Dynamics*, 2004, 33, 329–439.
12. Adapted from Zachary, G.P. Give me your tired, your hungry, your cash. *Business 2.0*, 2004, October, 66–69; Lubove, S. On the backs of the poor. *Forbes*, November 15, 2004, 156–160.
13. Goodman, P.S., and Rousseau, D.M. Organizational change that produces results: The linkages approach. *Academy of Management Executive*, 2004, 18, 7–22.
14. Beer, M., and Nohria, N. Resolving the tension between theories E and O of change. In M. Beer and N. Nohria (eds.), *Breaking the Code of Change.* Boston: Harvard Business School Press, 2000, 1–34.
15. Ibid.
16. Boyle, M. The Wegman's way. *Fortune*, January 24, 2005, 61–68.
17. Buderi, R. GE finds its inner Edison. *Technology Review*, 2003, 106(8), 46ff; Useem, J. Another boss, another revolution. *Fortune*, April 5, 2004, 112–118; Sonnenfeld, J.A. A return to the power of ideas. *Sloan Management Review*, 2004, 45(2), 30–33.
18. Balogun, J., and Johnson, G. Organizational restructuring and middle manager sensemaking. *Academy of Management Journal*, 2004, 46, 523–549; Dent, E.B., and Goldberg, S.G. Challenging "resistance to change." *Journal of Applied Behavioral Science*, 1999, 35, 25–41.
19. EDS website. http://www.eds.com; EDS executive says job isn't over. *Dallas Morning News*, January 21, 2005, 1D.
20. Tully, S. Mr. Cleanup. *Fortune*, November 15, 2004, 151ff; Faust, D. Breathing life into HealthSouth, *Business Week*, February 7, 2005, 72–73.
21. Tomlinson, R. Troubled waters at Perrier. *Fortune*, November 29, 2004, 173–195.
22. Adapted from Nutt, P.C. *Making Tough Decisions.* Jossey Bass, © 1989.
23. Grow, B. Thinking outside the big box. *Business Week*, October 214, 2004, 70ff.
24. Weld, L., Bergevin, P.M., and Magrath, L. Anatomy of a financial fraud. *The CPA Journal*, 2004, 74(10), 44–50.
25. Kelleher, K. Giving dealers a raw deal. *Business 2.0*, December 2004, 82–84.
26. http://www.dallascowboys.com; Cartwright, G. Arlington team. *Texas Monthly*, 2004, 32(10), 78–81.
27. Lewin, K. *Field Theory in Social Science.* New York: Harper & Row, 1951; Lewin, K. Frontiers in group dynamics. *Human Relations*, 1947, 1, 5–41; Zand, D.E. Force field analysis. In N. Nicholson (ed.), *Blackwell Encyclopedic Dictionary of Organizational Behavior.* Oxford, England: Blackwell, 1995, 160–161.
28. Adapted from Maxwell, R. How do we break out of the box we're stuck in? *Fast Company*, November 2000, 260ff.
29. Cummings, T.S., and Worley, C.G. *Organization Development and Change*, 8th ed. Mason, OH: Thomson South-Western, 2005, 134–140; Born, D., and Mathieu, J.E. Differential effects of survey-guided feedback: The rich get richer and the poor get poorer. *Group & Organization Development*, 1996, 21, 388–404.
30. Whetten, David A.; Cameron, Kim S., *Developing Management Skills*, 6th edition, © 2005. Adapted by permission of Pearson Education, Inc., Upper Saddle River, NJ.
31. Polzer, J. T. *Identity Issues in Teams.* Boston, MA: Harvard Business School, Case #9-403-095, 2003; Lencioni, P. *The Five Dysfunctions of a Team.* San Francisco: Jossey-Bass, 2002.
32. Grow, B. Don't discount this discounter. *Business Week*, May 24, 2004, 84–86.
33. O'Reilly, C.A., and Tushman, M.L. The ambidextrous organization. *Harvard Business Review*, 2004, 82(4), 74–81; Cummings and Worley, *Organization Development and Change*, 130–139.
34. Adapted from Just in time. *Forbes*, July 5, 2004, 66–68.
35. Lowman, R.L. (ed.). *The Ethical Practice of Psychology in Organizations.* Washington, DC: American Psychological Association, 1998.
36. Adapted from Maurer, R. Working with resistance to

change: The support for change questionnaire. In J.W. Pfeiffer (ed.), *The 1996 Annual—Volume 2 Consulting*. San Diego: Pfeiffer & Company, 1996, 161–174.

37. Adapted from *Organization Development and Change*, 6th ed., by T.G. Cummings and C.G. Worley. Copyright © 1997. By permission of South-Western College Publishing, a division of International Thomson Publishing, Inc., Cincinnati, Ohio 45227.

CHAPTER 6

1. Adapted from Brinkley, A. Critical qualities of leadership. *Executive Speeches*, 2003, 17(6), 29–33; Brinkley, A. Ethics and ethos: The timeless importance of character. Speech at the Wharton Women Annual Dinner, November 4, 2004. Available at http://www.bankofamerica.com/newsroom/speeches/ (accessed February 23, 2005).
2. Tichy, N.M. The teachable point of view. *Journal of Business Strategy*, January/February 1998, 29–33; Tichy, N.M. *The Cycle of Leadership: How Great Leaders Teach Their Companies to Win*. New York: Harperbusiness, 2004.
3. March, J.G., and Weil, T. *On Leadership*. Malden, MA: Blackwell Publishing, 2005.
4. French, J.R.P., and Raven, B. The bases of social power. In D. Cartwright (ed.), *Studies in Social Power.* Ann Arbor: University of Michigan Institute for Social Research, 1959, 150–167.
5. See, for example, the classic work by Barnard, C.I. *The Functions of the Executive*. Cambridge, MA: Harvard University Press, 1938, 110.
6. Fryer, B. Bosses from heaven—and hell! *Computerworld*, August 9, 1999, 46–47.
7. Ibid.
8. Ibid.
9. Ibid.; see also VanDerWall, S. *The Courageous Follower: Standing Up To and For Our Leaders*. San Francisco: Berret-Koehler, 1998.
10. Fryer, Bosses from heaven–and hell!
11. Scarnati, J.T. The godfather theory of management: An exercise in power and control. *Management Decision*, 2002, 40, 834–841.
12. Cross, R., and Parker, A. *The Hidden Power of Social Networks: Understanding How Work Really Gets Done in Organizations*. Boston: Harvard Business School Press, 2004; Harvard Business Essentials, *Power, Influence, and Persuasion*. Boston: Harvard Business School Press, 2005.
13. Christie, N. Managing office politics. *Office Solutions*, 2003, 20(5), 5–8; Treadway, D.C., Hochwarter, W.A., Ferris, G.R., Kacmar, C.J., Douglas, C., Ammeter, A.P., and Buckley, M.R. Leader political skill and employee reactions. *Leadership Quarterly*, 2004, 15, 493–513.
14. Madison, D.L., Allen, R.W., Porter, L.W., Renwick, P.A., and Mayes, B.T. Organizational politics: An exploration of managers' perceptions. *Human Relations*, 1980, 33, 79–100; Finkelstein, S. *Why Smart Executives Fail: What You Can Learn from Them*. Bergenfield, NJ: Penguin, 2003; Ahearn, K.K., Ferris, G.R. Hochwarter, C.D., and Ammeter, A.P. Leader political skill and team performance. *Journal of Management*, 2004, 3, 309–327.
15. Broom, M.F. *The Infinite Organization: Celebrating the Positive Use of Power in Organizations*. Palo Alto, CA: Davies-Black, 2002.
16. Higgins, C., Judge, T.A., and Ferris, G.R. Influence tactics and work outcomes. A meta-analysis. *Journal of Organizational Behavior*, 2003, 24, 89–106.
17. Gioia, D.A., and Longenecker, C.O. Delving into the dark side: The politics of executive appraisal. *Organizational Dynamics*, Winter 1994, 54; Akella, A. *Unlearning the Fifth Discipline: Power, Politics, and Control in Organizations*. Thousand Oaks, CA: Sage, 2004.
18. Gioia and Longenecker, Delving into the dark side, 56. Also see Delpo, A. *The Performance Appraisal Handbook: Legal and Practical Rules for Managers*. Berkeley, CA: NOLO, 2005.
19. Adapted from Jenkins, M. Getting the corner office. *Black Enterprise*, August 2004, 78–84.
20. About State Farm: Did You Know? Available at http://www.statefarm.com (accessed February 26, 2005).
21. Northouse, P.G. *Leadership: Theory and Practice*, 3rd ed. Thousand Oaks, CA: Sage, 2003; Barlow, C.B., Jordon, M., and Hendrix, W.H. Character assessment: An examination of leadership levels. *Journal of Business and Psychology*, 2003, 17, 563–584.
22. Adapted from Augustine, N.R. Ethics and business: An oxymoron? Available at http://www.ethics.org (accessed November 2005).
23. For information on the Ethics Resource Center, go to http://www.ethics.org.
24. Lockheed Martin Corporation. Hoover's Online. Available at http://www.hoovers.com (accessed February 28, 2005).
25. Bass, B.M. *Bass and Stogdill's Handbook of Leadership*, 3rd ed. New York: Free Press, 1990.
26. Fleishman, E.A., and Harris, E.E. Patterns of leadership behavior related to employee grievances and turnover: Some post hoc reflections. *Personnel Psychology*, 1998, 51, 825–834; Fleishman, E.A. Consideration and structure: Another look at their role in leadership research. In F. Danserau and F.J. Yammarino (eds.), *Leadership: The Multi-Level Approaches*. Greenwich, CT: JAI Press, 1998, 285–302; Littrell, R.F. Desirable leadership behaviours of multi-cultural managers in China. *Journal of Management Development*, 2002, 21, 5–74.
27. Hersey, P., et al. *The Management of Organizational Behavior: Leading Human Resources*, 8th ed. Escondido, CA: Center for Leadership Studies, 2001.
28. *Source:* Hersey, P. Blanchard, K.H., and Johnson, D.E. *The Management of Organizational Behavior: Leading Human Resources.* © 2001 Center for Leadership Studies. Used with permission.
29. Adapted from Buckingham, M. What great managers do. *Harvard Business Review*, 2005, 83(3), 70–79; Buckingham, M. *The One Thing You Need to Know*. New York: Free Press, 2005.
30. About Walgreens. Available at http://www.walgreens.com/about/ (accessed February 28, 2005).
31. Vecchio, R.P., and Boatwright, K.J. Preferences for idealized styles of supervision. *Leadership Quarterly*, 2002,

13, 327–337; Magnificent leadership. *T+D Magazine*, 2005, 59(1), 62–64; Avery, G.C., and Ryan, J. Applying situational leadership in Australia. *Journal of Management Development*, 2002, 21(4), 242–262; Zigarmi, D., Blanchard, K.H., Cooper, M., and Edeburn, C. *The Leader Within: Knowing Enough About Yourself to Lead Others*. Escondido, CA: Ken Blanchard Companies, 2004.

32. Vroom, V.H., and Jago, A.G. *The New Leadership*. Englewood Cliffs, N.J.: Prentice-Hall, 1988; Also see Sternberg, R.J., and Vroom, V. The person versus the situation in leadership. *Leadership Quarterly*, 2002, 13, 321–323.
33. The discussion of the revised model is based on Vroom, V.H. New developments in leadership and decision making. *OB News*. Briarcliff Manor, NY: Organizational Behavior Division of the Academy of Management, headquartered at Pace University, Spring 1999, 4–5; Vroom, V.H. Leadership and the decision-making process. *Organizational Dynamics*, Spring 2000, 82–93; Vroom, V.H. Educating managers for decision making and leadership. *Management Decision*, 2003, 41(10), 968–978.
34. Adapted from Vroom, V.H. Leadership and the decision-making process, 90–91. Also see Duncan, W.J., LaFrance, K.G., and Ginter, P.M. Leadership and decision making: A retrospective application and assessment. *Journal of Leadership & Organizational Studies*, 2003, 9, 1–20.
35. Adapted from Reddy, W.B., and Williams, G. The visibility/credibility inventory: Measuring power and influence. In J.W. Pfeiffer (ed.), *The 1988 Annual: Developing Human Resources*. San Diego: University Associates, 1988, 115–124; Also see Ferris, G.R., Treadway, D.C., Kolodinsky, R.W., Hochwarter, W.A., Kacmar, C.J., Douglas, C., and Frink, D.D. Development and validation of the political skill inventory. *Journal of Management*, 2005, 31, 126–152.
36. *Source:* This case was prepared by Claire McCarty Kilian, Edwin C. Leonard, Jr., and Roy A. Cook, *Ashley Automotive—Changing Times*. Case appeared in Cheryl L. Noll (ed.), *Society for Case Research 2004 Proceedings*, 113–116. It is intended to be used as a basis for class discussion rather than to illustrate either effective or ineffective handling of the situation. Copyright © 2004 by Claire McCarty Kilian, Edward C. Leonard, Jr., and Roy A. Cook. The views presented here are those of the case authors and do not necessarily reflect the views of the Society for Case Research. The names of the organization, individuals, location, and financial information have been disguised to preserve anonymity. Edited for *Organizational Behavior*, 11th edition, and used with permission.
37. Kouzes, J.M., and Posner, B.Z. *The Leadership Challenge: How to Get Extraordinary Things Done in Organizations*. San Francisco: Jossey-Bass, 1987, 3.

CHAPTER 7

1. Adapted from Kirsner, S. One tough assignment. *Fast Company*, September 2004, 76–77; McClenahen, J.S. Restoring credibility. *Industry Week*, February 2005, 12–13; Tully, S. Mr. cleanup. *Fortune*, November 15, 2004, 151–157; Pillmore, E.M. How we're fixing up Tyco. *Harvard Business Review*, 2003, 81(12), 96–103; Letter from Ed Breen. Available at http://www.tyco.com (accessed November 2005).
2. Antonakis, J., Cianciolo, A.T., and Sternberg, R.J. (eds.). *The Nature of Leadership*. Thousand Oaks, CA: Sage, 2004.
3. Bass, B.M. Does the transactional-transformational leadership paradigm transcend organizational and national boundaries? *American Psychologist*, 1997, 52, 130–139.
4. Avolio, B.J. *Leadership Development in Balance: Made/Born*. Mahwah, NJ: Lawrence Erlbaum Associates, 2005, 15.
5. Adapted from Tsui, A.S., Wang, H., Xin, K., Zhang, L., and Fu, P.P. Let a thousand flowers bloom: Variations of leadership styles among Chinese CEOs. *Organizational Dynamics*, 2004, 33(1), 5–20.
6. Drucker, P.F. What makes an effective executive. *Harvard Business Review*, 2004, 82(6), 58–63.
7. Bryant, S.E. The role of transformational and transactional leadership in creating, sharing and exploiting organizational knowledge. *Journal of Leadership & Organizational Studies*, 2003, 9(4), 32–44; Judge, T.A., and Piccolo, R.F. Transformational and transactional leadership: A meta-analytic test of their relative validity. *Journal of Applied Psychology*, 2004, 89, 755–768.
8. Conger, J.A., and Kanungo, R.N. *Charismatic Leadership in Organizations*. Thousand Oaks, CA: Sage, 1998; Avolio, B.J., and Yammarino, F.J. (eds.). *Transformational and Charismatic Leadership: The Road Ahead*. Oxford, UK: Elsevier Science, 2002.
9. de Hoogh, A.H., den Hartog, D.N., Koopman, P.L., and Thierry, H. Charismatic leadership, environmental dynamism, and performance. *European Journal of Work and Organizational Psychology*, 2004, 13, 447–471; de Hoogh, A.H., den Hartog, D.N., Koopman, P.L., Thierry, H., Van den Berg, P.T., Van der Weide, J.G., and Wilderom, C.P. Leader motives, charismatic leadership, and subordinates' work attitude in profit and voluntary sector. *Leadership Quarterly*, 2005, 16, 17–38.
10. Adapted from Deutschman, A. The gonzo way of branding. *Fast Company*, October 2004, 87–96; Kets de Vries, M.F.R. *The New Global Leaders: Richard Branson, Percy Barnevik, and David Simon*. San Francisco: Jossey-Bass, 1999; Wells, M. Red baron. *Forbes*, July 3, 2000, 151–160.
11. About Virgin. Available at http://www.virgin.com/aboutus/ (accessed March 10, 2005).
12. Beyer, J.M., and Browning, L.D. Transforming an industry in crisis: Charisma, routinization, and supportive cultural leadership. Working paper, University of Texas at Austin, 2000, 8.
13. Washington, J.M., and King, M.L., Jr. (eds.). *A Testament of Hope: The Essential Speeches and Writings of Martin Luther King, Jr.* San Francisco: Harper, 1990.
14. Howell, J.M., and Shamir, B. The role of followers in the charismatic leadership process: Relationships and their consequences. *Academy of Management Review*, 2005, 30, 96–112.

15. Raelin, J.A. The myth of charismatic leaders. *T+D Magazine*, 2003, 573(3), 47–54.
16. Avolio, B. Luthans, F., and Walumbwa, F.O. Authentic leadership: Theory-building for veritable sustained performance. Working paper, Gallup Leadership Institute, University of Nebraska, Lincoln, 2005.
17. This discussion is based on Avolio, B.J., Gardner, W.L., Walumbwa, F.O., Luthans, F., and May, D.R. Unlocking the mask: A look at the process by which authentic leaders impact follower attitudes and behaviors. *Leadership Quarterly*, 2004, 15, 801–823; Gardner, W.L., and Schermerhorn, J.R. Unleashing individual potential: Performance gains through positive organizational behavior and authentic leadership. *Organizational Dynamics*, 2004, 33, 270–281; George, B. *Authentic Leadership: Rediscovering the Secrets to Creating Lasting Value*. San Francisco: Jossey Bass, 2003; Ward, B. The authentic leader: Losing the mask. Available at http://www.affinitymc.com (accessed March 27, 2005). For an excellent critique of this research, see Cooper, C.D., Scandura, T.A., and Schriesheim, C.A. Looking forward but learning from our past: Potential challenges to developing authentic leadership theory and authentic leaders. *Leadership Quarterly*, 2005, 16, 475–493.
18. Adapted from Lapchick, R. Interview of Robert L. Johnson on leading talented people. *Academy of Management Executive*, 2004, 18(1), 114–119.
19. Anderson, T.D. *Transforming Leadership: Equipping Yourself and Challenging Others to Build the Leadership Organization*, 2nd ed. Boca Raton, FL: CRC Press, 1998.
20. This section draws from Avolio, B.E. *Full Leadership Development: Building the Vital Forces in Organizations*. Thousand Oaks, CA: Sage Publications, 1999, 43–49; Bass, B.M. *Transformational Leadership: Industry, Military, and Educational Impact*. Mahwah, NJ: Lawrence Erlbaum Associates, 1998; Rafferty, A.E., and Griffin, M.A. Dimensions of transformational leadership: Conceptual and empirical extensions. *Leadership Quarterly*, 2004, 15, 329–354; Smith, B.N., Montagno, R.V., and Kuzmenko, T.N. Transformational and servant leadership: Content and contextual comparisons. *Journal of Leadership and Organizational Studies*, 2004, 10, 80–91; Gillespie, N.A., and Mann, L. Transformational leadership and shared values: The building blocks of trust. *Journal of Managerial Psychology*, 2004, 19, 588–607; Zhu, W. Chew, I.K., and Spangler, W.D. CEO transformational leadership and organizational outcomes: The mediating role of human-capital-enhancing human resource management. *Leadership Quarterly*, 2005, 16, 39–52.
21. Egan, G. *Change Agent Skills*. Monterey, CA: Brooks/Cole, 1985, 204.
22. Adapted from Frayne, C.A., and Callahan, R.E. Safeco CEO Mike McGavick on leading a turnaround. *Academy of Management Executive*, 2004, 18, 143–150.
23. Adapted from Reagon, G. The managers of the 21st century inventory. In *The 1997 Annual: Volume 1—Training*. Copyright © 1997 by Pfeiffer, An Imprint of Jossey-Bass, Inc. Publishers, San Francisco, pp. 187–189. Used with permission.
24. Adapted from Sellers, P. eBay's secret. *Fortune*, October 18, 2004, 160–168; Schonfeld, E. The world according to eBay. *Business 2.0*, January/February 2005, 76–80; Schonfeld, E. How to manage growth. *Business 2.0*, December 2004, 98–99; Malone, M.S. Meet Meg Whitman. *Wall Street Journal*, March 16, 2005, A24, A26. Business: Queen of the online flea market. *Economist*, January 3, 2004, 48–49; Brown, E. How can a dot-com be this hot? *Fortune*, January 21, 2002, 78–84; Bannan, K. Sole survivor. *Sales and Marketing Management*, July 2001, 36–41; Fishman, C. Facetime: Meg Whitman. *Fast Company*, May 2001, 79–82; Rogers, A. CRN interview, Meg Whitman. *CRN*, November 12, 2001, 20–22; Schonfeld, E. eBay's secret ingredient. *Business 2.0*, March 2002, 52–58.

CHAPTER 8

1. Adapted from Berry, L.L. Leadership lessons from Mayo Clinic. *Organizational Dynamics*, 2004, 33, 228–242; Berry, L.L., and Bendapui, N. Clueing in customers. *Harvard Business Review*, 2003, 81(1), 100–1[illegible].
2. Homans, G.C. *The Human Group*. New Y[illegible]k: Harcourt, Brace and World, 1959, 2.
3. Levi, D. *Group Dynamics for Teams*. Thousand Oaks, CA: Sage, 2001; Edmondson, A.C. *Teams That Learn: What Leaders Must Do to Foster Organizational Learning*. New York: Wiley, 2006.
4. Wheelan, S.A. *Creating Effective Teams: A Guide for Members and Leaders*, 2nd ed. Thousand Oaks, CA: Sage, 2005.
5. Morton, S.C., Brookes, N.J., Smart, P.K., Backhouse, C.J., and Burns, N.D. Managing the informal organization: Conceptual model. *International Journal of Productivity and Performance Management*, 2004, 53, 214–227.
6. Herrenkohl, R.C. *Becoming a Team: Achieving a Goal*. Mason, OH: South-Western/Thomson, 2004.
7. Adapted from Gehrki, B. Designing new ORs for efficiency. *OR Manager Newsletter*, January 2002, 1–3.
8. LaFasto, F., and Larson, C. *When Teams Work Best*. Thousand Oaks, CA: Sage, 2001.
9. Adapted from Johnson, K. Stoner: Built on a strong foundation. *Quality Progress*, August 2004, 40–47.
10. Adapted from Cross, L. Combating rework. *Graphic Arts Monthly*, August 2004, 34–37.
11. Michalski, W.J., and King, D.G. (eds.). *40 Tools for Cross-Functional Teams: Building Synergy for Breakthrough Creativity*. Portland, OR: Productivity Press, 1998; Mohamed, M., Stankosky, M., and Murray, A. Applying knowledge management principles to enhance cross-functional team performance. *Journal of Knowledge Management*, 2004, 8, 127–140.
12. Adapted from Smith, S. Walking the talk at Bell Helicopter. *Occupational Hazards*, December 2004, 20–22.
13. Tata, J., and Prasad, S. Team self-management, organizational structure, and judgments of team effectiveness. *Journal of Managerial Issues*, 2004, 16, 248–266.
14. Kirkman, B.I., and Rosen, B. Beyond self-management: Antecedents and consequences of team empowerment. *Academy of Management Journal*, 1999, 42, 58–74; Seibert, S.E., Silver, S.R., and Randolph, W.A. Taking

empowerment to the next level: A multiple-level model of empowerment, performance, and satisfaction. *Academy of Management Journal*, 2004, 47, 332–349.

15. Cooney, R. Empowered self-management and the design of work teams. *Personnel Review*, 2004, 33, 677–690.
16. Van Mierlo, H., Rutte, C.G., Kompier, M.A., and Doorewaard, H.A. Self-managing teamwork and psychological well being: Review of a multicultural research domain. *Group & Organization Management*, 2005, 30, 211–235.
17. Kirkman, B.L., and Rosen, B. Powering up teams. *Organizational Dynamics*, 2000, 28(3), 48–66; Batt, R. Who benefits from teams? Comparing workers, supervisors, and managers. *Industrial Relations*, 2004, 43, 183–212; Langfred, C.W. Too much of a good thing? Negative effects of high trust and individual autonomy in self-managing teams. *Academy of Management Journal*, 2004, 47, 385–399; Urch Druskat, V., and Wheeler, J.V. How to lead a self-managing team, *Sloan Management Review*, 2004, 45(4), 65–71.
18. Adapted from Grazier, P. Living with a self-directed work team and why self-direction works. Available at http://www.teambuilding.com (accessed January 24, 2005); Bayer's Myerstown plant. Available at http://www.bayerus.com/communities/myerstown/ (accessed April 28, 2005).
19. Powell, A., Piccoli, G., and Ives, B. Virtual teams: A review of current literature and directions for future research. *Database for Advances in Information Systems*, 2004, 35, 6–37.
20. Edwards, A., and Wilson, J.R. *Implementing Virtual Teams*. Abingdon, Oxon, UK: Gower Publishing, 2004; Jones, R. Oyung, R., and Pace, L. *Working Virtually: Challenges of Virtual Teams*. Hershey, PA: IRM Press, 2005.
21. Gould, D. Virtual teams. Available at http://www.seanet.com/~daveg/ (accessed April 28, 2005); Gibson, C.B., and Cohen, S.G. (eds.). *Virtual Teams That Work: Creating Conditions for Virtual Team Effectiveness*. San Francisco: Jossey-Bass, 2003.
22. Jarvenpaa, S.L., and Leider, D.E. Communication and trust in global virtual teams. Available at http://jcmc.indiana.edu (accessed November 2005).
23. This presentation is based primarily on Townsend, D.M., DeMarie, S.M., and Hendrickson, A.R. Virtual teams: Technology and the workplace of the future. *Academy of Management Executive*, 1998, 12(3), 17–29; Malhotra, A., and Majchrzak, A. Virtual workspace technologies. *Sloan Management Review*, 2005, 46(2), 11–14.
24. Beise, C.M., Niederman, F., and Mattord, H. IT project managers' perceptions and use of virtual team technologies. *Information Resources Management Journal*, 2004, 17(4), 73–89; Maruping, L.M., and Agarwal, R. Managing team interpersonal processes through technology: A task-technology fit perspective. *Journal of Applied Psychology*, 2004, 89, 975–990.
25. Marquardt, M. *Global Teams: How Multinationals Span Boundaries and Cultures with Teamwork*. Mountain View, CA: Davis-Black Publishing, 2001; Golden, T.D., and Veiga, J.F. Spanning boundaries and borders: Toward understanding the cultural dimensions of team boundary spanning. *Journal of Managerial Issues*, 2005, 17, 178–198.
26. Barczak, G., and McDonough III, E.F. Leading global product teams. *Research Technology Management*, 2003, 46(6), 14–19.
27. Saunders, C., Van Slyke, C., and Vogel, D.R. My time or yours? Managing time visions in global virtual teams. *Academy of Management Executive*, 2004, 18(1), 19–31.
28. Adapted from Majchrzak, A., Malhotra, A., Stamps, J., and Lipnack, J. Can absence make a team grow stronger? *Harvard Business Review*, 2004, 82(5), 131–137.
29. Davis, D.D. The Tao of leadership in virtual teams. *Organizational Dynamics*, 2004, 33, 47–62; Zakaria, N., Amelinckx, A., and Wilemon, D. Working together apart? Building a knowledge-sharing culture for global virtual teams. *Creativity and Innovation Management*, 2004, 13, 15–29.
30. Tuckman, B.W. Development sequence in small groups. *Psychological Bulletin*, 1965, 62, 384–399; Tuckman, B.W., and Jensen, M.A.C. Stages of small group development revisited. *Group & Organization Studies*, 1977, 2, 419–427; Obert, S.L. Developmental patterns of organizational task groups: A preliminary study. *Human Relations*, 1983, 36, 37–52.
31. Richards, T., and Moger, S. Creative leadership processes in project team development: An alternative to Tuckman's stage model. *British Journal of Management*, 2000, 4, 273–283.
32. Caouette, M., and O'Connor, B. The impact of group support systems on corporate teams' stages of development. *Journal of Organizational Computing and Electronic Commerce*, 1998, 8, 57–81; Also see Lee-Kelley, L., Grossman, A., and Cannings, A. A social interaction approach to managing the "invisibles" of virtual teams. *Industrial Management & Data Systems*, 2004, 104, 650–657.
33. Adapted from Furst, S.A., Reeves, M., Rosen, M., and Blackburn, R.S. Managing the life cycle of virtual teams. *Academy of Management Executive*, 2004, 18(2), 6–20.
34. Ibid.
35. Ibid.
36. Lencioni, D. *The Five Dysfunctions of Teams*. San Francisco: Jossey-Bass, 2002.
37. Janis, I.L. *Groupthink*, 2nd ed. Boston: Houghton Mifflin, 1982; Whyte, G. Groupthink reconsidered. *Academy of Management Review*, 1989, 14, 40–56; Brownstein, A.L. Biased decision processing. *Psychological Bulletin*, 2003, 129, 545–591.
38. Albanese, R., and Van Fleet, D.D. Rational behavior in groups: The free-riding tendency. *Academy of Management Review*, 1985, 10, 244–255; Chen, X., and Bachrack, D.G. Tolerance of free-riding: The effects of defection size, defection pattern, and social orientation in a repeated public good dilemma. *Organizational Behavior and Human Decision Processes*, 2003, 90, 139–147.
39. Schnake, M.E. Equity in effort: The "sucker effect" in co-acting groups. *Journal of Management*, 1991, 17, 41–55; Murphy, S.M., Wayne, S.J., Liden, R.C., and

Erdogan, B. Understanding social loafing: The role of justice perceptions and exchange relationships. *Human Relations*, 2003, 56, 61–84.

40. Harris, T.E., and Sherblom, J.C. *Small Group and Team Communication*, 3rd ed.. Upper Saddle River, NJ: Allyn & Bacon, 2004.
41. Lencioni, *The Five Dysfunctions of Teams.*
42. Berry, Leadership lessons from Mayo Clinic, 231.
43. Denton, D.K. How a team can grow. *Quality Progress*, June 1999, 53–58.
44. Berry, Leadership lessons from Mayo Clinic, 229.
45. Hackman, J.R. *Leading Teams: Setting the Stage for Great Performances.* Boston: Harvard Business School Press, 2002; Bradner, E., Mark, G., and Hertel, I.D. Team size and technology fit: Participation, awareness, and rapport in distributed teams. *IEEE Transactions on Professional Communication*, 2005, 48, 68–77.
46. Kuipers, B.S., and de Witte, M.C. Teamwork: A case study on development and performance. *International Journal of Human Resource Management*, 2005, 16, 185–201.
47. Bales, R.F. *Interaction Process Analysis.* Cambridge, MA: Addison Wesley, 1950; Klein, K.J., Lim, B., Saltz, J.L., and Mayer, D.M. How do they get there? An examination of the antecedents of centrality in team networks. *Academy of Management Journal*, 2004, 47, 952–963.
48. Lustig, M.W. Bales' interpersonal rating forms: Reliability and dimensionality: *Small Group Behavior*, 1987, 18, 99–107; Gorse, C.A., and Emmitt, S. Investigating interpersonal communication during construction progress meetings: Challenges and opportunities. *Engineering, Construction, and Architectural Management*, 2003, 10, 234–245.
49. Hobman, E.V., Bordia, P., and Gallois, C. Perceived dissimilarity and work group involvement: The moderating effects of group openness to diversity. *Group & Organization Management*, 2004, 29, 560–587.
50. Jackson, S.J., and Joshi, A. Diversity in social context: A multi-attribute, multilevel analysis of team diversity and sales performance. *Journal of Organizational Behavior*, 2004, 25, 675–702; van Knippenberg, D., De Dreu, C.K., and Homan, A.C. Work group diversity and group performance: An integrative model and research agenda. *Journal of Applied Psychology*, 2004, 89, 1008–1022.
51. Chatman, J.A., and Flynn, F.J. The influence of demographic heterogeneity on the emergence and consequences of cooperative norms in work groups. *Academy of Management Journal*, 2001, 44, 956–974; Hoobler, J.M. Lip service to multiculturalism: Docile bodies of the modern organization. *Journal of Management Inquiry*, 2005, 14, 49–57.
52. Ehrhart, M.G., and Naumann, S.E. Organizational citizenship behavior in work groups: A group norms approach. *Journal of Applied Psychology*, 2004, 89, 960–974.
53. Feldman, D.C. The development and enforcement of group norms. *Academy of Management Review*, 1984, 9, 47–53.
54. Besser, T.L. *Team Toyota.* Ithaca: State University of New York Press, 1996; Ehrhart, M.G., and Naumann, S.E. Organizational citizenship behavior in work groups: A group norms approach. *Journal of Applied Psychology*, 2004, 89, 960–974.
55. Spoor, J.R., and Kelly, J.R. The evolutionary significance of affect in groups: Communication and group bonding. *Group Processes and Interpersonal Relations*, 2004, 7, 398–412; Man, D.C., and Lam, S. The effects of job complexity and autonomy on cohesiveness in collectivistic and individualistic work groups: A cross-cultural analysis. *Journal of Organizational Behavior*, 2003, 24, 979–1001.
56. Lipman-Blumen, J., and Leavitt, H.J. *Hot Groups: Seeding Them, Feeding Them, and Using Them to Ignite Your Organization.* New York: Oxford University Press, 1999.
57. Adapted from Sullivan, L. Team of the year. *InformationWeek*, December 13, 2004, 38–42; Tahmincioglu, E. Linda Dillman. *New York Times*, April 25, 2004, 3.
58. La Barre, P. Weird ideas that work. *Fast Company*, January 2002, 68–73; see also Sutton, R. *Weird Ideas That Work: 11 1/2 Practices for Promoting, Managing, and Sustaining Innovation.* New York: Free Press, 2001; Thompson, L.I. Improving the creativity of organizational work groups. *Academy of Management Executive*, 2003, 17(1), 96–111.
59. Major portions of this discussion for the nominal group technique are based on Woodman, R.W. Use of the nominal group technique for idea generation and decision making. *Texas Business Executive*, Spring 1981, 50–53; Leonard, D.A., and Swap, W.C. *When Sparks Fly: Harnessing the Power of Group Creativity.* Boston: Harvard Business School Press, 2005.
60. Duggan, E.W., and Thachenkary, C.S. Integrating nominal group technique and joint application development for improved systems requirements determination. *Information & Management*, 2004, 41, 399–411.
61. McGlynn, R.P., McGurk, D., Sprague Effland, V., Johll, N.L., and Harding, D.J. Brainstorming and task performance in groups constrained by evidence. *Organizational Behavior and Human Decision Processes*, 2004, 93, 75–87; Osborn, A.F. *Applied Imagination*, rev. ed. New York: Scribner, 1957.
62. Santanen, E.L., Briggs, R.O., and de Vreede, G. Causal relationships in creative problem solving: Comparing facilitation interventions for ideation. *Journal of Management Information Systems*, 2004, 20, 167–197; Gilson, L.L., and Shalley, C.E. A little creativity goes a long way: An examination of teams' engagement in creative processes. *Journal of Management*, 2004, 30, 453–470.
63. Play about us. Available at http://www.lookatmorestuff.com (accessed April 18, 2005); Dahle, C. Mind games. *Fast Company*, January/February 2000, 169–180.
64. For a description of the wide array of collaborative software products and services offered by GroupSystems, visit this organization's home page at http://www.groupsystems.com (accessed April 18, 2005).
65. Dennis, A.R., and Reinicke, B.A. Beta versus VHS and the acceptance of electronic brainstorming technology. *MISQuarterly*, 2004, 28, 1–20.

66. Eastman Chemical—Creativity and team center case study. Available at http://www.groupsystems.com (accessed April 19, 2005).
67. Adapted from *The Student Audit Instrument.* Developed by Jon M. Werner, a faculty member in the Department of Management at the University of Wisconsin–Whitewater; Edmondson, A. Psychological safety and learning behavior in work teams. *Administrative Science Quarterly*, 1999, 44, 350–383.
68. Prepared by and adapted with permission from Barnes, F.C., University of North Carolina at Charlotte.

CHAPTER 9

1. Adapted from Weiss, J., and Hughes, J. Want collaboration? Accept—and actively manage—conflict. *Harvard Business Review*, 2005, 83(3), 92–101; Roberts, B. How KLA-Tencor yields innovation. *Electronic Business*, January 2005, 44–48.
2. Rahim, M.A. *Managing Conflict in Organizations*, 3rd ed. Westport, CT: Quorum Books, 2001.
3. Mayer, B. *Beyond Neutrality: Confronting the Crisis in Conflict Resolution.* San Francisco: Jossey-Bass, 2004.
4. Nicholson, N., Pillutla, M., and Audia, P. *Blackwell Encyclopedia of Management: Organizational Behavior.* Malden, MA: Blackwell, 2005.
5. Fogler, J.P., Poole, M.S., and Stutman, R.K. *Working through Conflict: Strategies for Relationships, Groups, and Organizations*, 5th ed. Boston: Allyn & Bacon, 2005; Huxham, C., and Vangen, S. *Managing to Collaborate: The Theory and Practice of Collaborative Advantage.* New York: Routledge, 2005.
6. Spector, B. (ed.). *Family Business Conflict Resolution Handbook.* Philadelphia: Family Business, 2005.
7. Pervin, A. Preserving your sibling connection: Set up the rules to resolve sibling conflicts. Available at http://www.pervinfamilybusiness.com (accessed May 2005).
8. Eagly, A.H., Baron, R.M., and Hamilton, L.V. (eds.). *The Social Psychology of Group Identity and Social Conflict.* Washington, DC: American Psychological Association, 2004.
9. Daft, R.L. *Organization Theory and Design*, 8th ed. Mason, OH: South-Western, 2004, 488–492.
10. Fortune's 100 best companies to work for. Available at http://www.fortune.com/fortune/bestcompanies/ (accessed April 2005); Fortune's best companies for minorities. Available at http://www.fortune.com/diversity/ (accessed April 2005).
11. Society for Human Resource Management. What are employee networks? Available at http://www.shrm.org/diversity/ (accessed April 2005).
12. Hankin, H. *The New Workforce.* New York: AMACOM, 2005.
13. Adapted from Diversity at Georgia Power. Available at http://www.georgiapower.com (accessed November 2005).
14. Thomas, K.W. Conflict and negotiation processes in organizations. In Dunnette, M.D., and Hough, L.M. (eds.), *Handbook of Industrial and Organizational Psychology*, 2nd ed., vol. 3, Palo Alto, CA: Consulting Psychologists Press, 1992, 651–717; Conerly, K., and Tripathi, A. What is your conflict style? *Journal for Quality and Participation*, 2004, 27(2), 16–20.
15. Adapted from Tam, P., and Wingfield, N. As tech matures, workers file a spate of salary complaints. *Wall Street Journal*, February 24, 2005, A1, A11.
16. Gross, M.A., and Guerrero, L.K. Managing conflict appropriately and effectively: An application of the competence model to Rahim's organizational conflict styles. *International Journal of Conflict Management*, 2000, 11, 200–226; Brew, F.P., and Cairns, D.R. Styles of managing interpersonal workplace conflict in relation to status and face concern: A study with Anglos and Chinese. *International Journal of Conflict Management*, 2004, 15, 25–56; Horn, A. *Face It: Recognizing and Conquering the Hidden Fear That Drives All Conflict.* New York: AMACOM, 2004.
17. Adapted from Kessendides, D. Getting started: Happy together. *INC*, November 2004, 54–55; Fitzgerald, J. Billings partners use their friendship to build ATM Express. *Knight Ridder Tribune Business News*, January 30, 2005, 1–2.
18. Lewicki, R.J., Barry, B., and Saunders, D.M. *Negotiation*, 5th ed. Boston: McGraw-Hill/Irwin, 2006, 1.
19. Adapted from Cormick, G.W. *Negotiation Skills for Board Professionals.* Mill Creek, WA: CSE Group, 2005.
20. Walton, R.E., and McKersie, R.B. *A Behavioral Theory of Labor Negotiations*, 2nd ed. Ithaca, NY: ILR Press, 1991; Kolb, D.M., and Williams, J. Breakthrough bargaining. *Harvard Business Review*, February 2001, 89–97.
21. Fisher, R., and Ury, W. *Getting to Yes: Negotiating Agreement without Giving In*, 2nd ed. New York: Penguin Books, 1991; Camp, J. *Start with NO. . .The Negotiating Tools that the Pros Don't Want You to Know.* New York. Crown Business, 2002; Spector, B. Introduction: An interview with Roger Fisher and William Ury. *Academy of Management Executive*, 2004, 18(3), 101–108.
22. Hensel, Jr., B. Continental, unions agree on cuts. *Houston Chronicle*, March 1, 2005, D1, D5; Schofield, A. Continental unions ratify most cuts, attendants hold out. *Aviation Daily*, April 1, 2005, 1–2.
23. Fisher and Ury, *Getting to Yes;* Bazerman, M.H. (ed.). *Negotiation, Decision Making and Conflict Management.* Northampton, MA: Edward Elgar Publishing, 2005; Raiffa, H., Richardson, J., and Metcalfe, D. *Negotiation Analysis: The Science and Art of Collaborative Decision Making.* Cambridge, MA: Harvard University Press, 2003.
24. Adapted from Powers of persuasion. *Fortune*, October 12, 1998, 160–164; Shapiro, R. Spotlight on credit congress. *Business Credit*, April 2000, 52–54; Shapiro, R., and Jankowski, M. *The Power of Nice: How to Negotiate So Everyone Wins—Especially You*, rev. ed. New York: John Wiley & Sons, 2002.
25. Adapted from Keeping collections in-house. *American Gas*, March 2005, 20–22; Johnson, T. The CIS transfer. *Electric Perspectives*, March/April 2005, 14–20.
26. Cinergy corporate overview. Available at http://www.cinergy.com (accessed November 2005).

27. Excerpts from Tyler, K. The art of give-and-take. *HR Magazine*, November 2004, 107–116.
28. Friedman, R.A. *Front Stage Backstage: The Dynamic Structure of Labor Negotiations.* Cambridge, MA: The MIT Press, 1994; O'Connor, K.M. Negotiators' bargaining histories and their effect on future negotiation performance. *Journal of Applied Psychology*, 2005, 90, 350–362.
29. Moore, C.W. *The Mediation Process: Practical Strategies for Resolving Conflict*, 3rd ed. San Francisco: Jossey-Bass, 2004.
30. Abramson, H.I. *Mediation Representation: Advocating in a Problem Solving Process.* South Bend, IN: National Institute of Trial Advocacy, 2004; Baruch Bush, R.A., and Folger, J.P. *The Promise of Mediation: The Transformative Approach to Conflict*, rev. ed. San Francisco: Jossey-Bass, 2004.
31. Culture and negotiation. Available at http://www.negotiations.org (accessed April 2005).
32. Ghauri, P.N., and Usunier, J.C. *International Business Negotiations.* New York: Elsevier Science, 1996; Salacuse, J.W. Ten ways that culture affects negotiating style: Some survey results. *Negotiation Journal*, 1998, 14, 221–[illegible] Sheer, V.C., and Chen, L. Successful Sino-Western business negotiation: Participants' accounts of national and professional cultures. *Journal of Business Communication*, 2003, 40, 50–85.
33. Paik, Y., and Tung, R.L. Negotiating with East Asians: How to attain "win–win" outcomes. *Management International Review*, 1999, 37, 103–122; Brett, J.M., and Ukumura, T. Inter- and intracultural negotiation: U.S. and Japanese negotiators. *Academy of Management Journal*, 1998, 41, 495–510.
34. Adapted from Jassawalla, A., Truglia, C., and Garvey, J. Cross-cultural conflict and expatriate manager adjustment: An exploratory study. *Management Decision*, 2004, 42, 837–849.
35. Griffin, T.J., and Daggatt, W.R. *The Global Negotiator: Building Strong Business Relationships Anywhere in the World.* New York: HarperBusiness, 1990, 29–30.
36. Adapted from Ghauri, P., and Usunier, J. (eds.). *International Business Negotiations.* New York: Pergamon, 2006; Boyer, M.A. *Negotiating in a Complex World: An Introduction to International Negotiation*, 2nd ed. London: Littlefield Brown Publishers, 2005; Gelfand, M.J., and Brett, J.M. (eds.). *The Handbook of Negotiation and Culture.* Palo Alto, CA: Stanford University Press, 2004.
37. Adapted from Graham, J.L., and Lam, N.M. The Chinese negotiation. *Harvard Business Review*, 2003, 81(10), 82–91. Also see Miles, M. Negotiating with the Chinese. *Journal of Applied Behavioral Science*, 2003, 39, 453–472; Faing, T. *Chinese Business Negotiating Style.* Thousand Oaks, CA: Sage, 1999; Palich, L.E., Carini, G.R., and Livingstone, L.P. Comparing American and Chinese negotiating styles: Influence of logic paradigms. *Thunderbird International Business Review*, 2002, 44, 777–798.
38. Adapted from Baskerville, D.M. How do you manage conflict? *Black Enterprise*, May 1993, 63–66; Thomas, K.W., and Kilmann, R.H. *The Thomas-Kilmann Conflict Mode Instrument.* Tuxedo, NY: Xicom, 1974; Rahim, M.A. A measure of styles of handling interpersonal conflict. *Academy of Management Journal*, 1983, 26, 368–376.
39. Adapted from Elangovan, A.R. Deciding how to intervene in employee disputes. In R.J. Lewicki, D.M. Saunders, and J.W. Minton (eds.), *Negotiation*, 3rd ed. Boston: Irwin/McGraw-Hill, 1999, 458–469.

CHAPTER 10

1. Adapted from Cambie, S. David Radcliffe's NECK. *Communication World*, March/April 2005, 28–31; Hogg Robinson. Available at http://www.hoggrobinson.co.uk (accessed May 2005).
2. DeVito, J.A. *The Interpersonal Communication Book*, 10th ed. Boston: Allyn & Bacon, 2004.
3. Personal interview with D. Bitterman, director–investments, CIBC Oppenheimer, Dallas, T[illegible]002.
4. Russ, G.S., Daft, R.L., and Lengel, R.H. Media selection and managerial characteristics in organizational communications. *Management Communication Quarterly*, 1990, 4, 151–175; Robert, L.P., and Dennis, A.R. Paradoxes of richness: A cognitive model of media choice. *IEE Transactions on Professional Communication*, 2005, 48, 10–21; Sheer, V.C., and Chen, L. Improving media richness theory. *Management Communication Quarterly*, 2004, 18, 76–93.
5. Mortensen, C.D., and Ayres, C.M. *Miscommunication.* Thousand Oaks, CA: Sage, 1997.
6. Cambie, David Radcliffe's NECK, 31.
7. Scott, J.C. Differences in American and British vocabulary: Implications for international business. *Business Communication Quarterly*, December 2000, 27–39.
8. Brinson, S.L., and Benoit, W.L. The tarnishing Star. *Management Communication Quarterly*, 1999, 12, 483–510; Labich, K. No more crude at Texaco. *Fortune*, September 6, 1999, 205–212.
9. Zivuska, S., Kacmar, K.M., Carlson, D.S., and Bratton, V.K. Interactive effects of impression management and organizational politics on job performance. *Journal of Organizational Behavior*, 2004, 25, 627–641; Bolino, M.C., and Turnley, W.H. More than one way to make an impression: Exploring profiles of impression management. *Journal of Management*, 2003, 29, 141–160.
10. Varner, I., and Beamer, L. *Intercultural Communication in the Global Workplace*, 3rd ed. Burr Ridge, IL: McGraw-Hill/Irwin, 2005.
11. Hofstede, G. The universal and the specific in 21st century management. *Organizational Dynamics*, Summer 1999, 34–44; Gudykunst, W.B. (ed.). *Theorizing about Intercultural Communication.* Thousand Oaks, CA: Sage, 2005.
12. Berger, K. Ethnocentrism: What is it? Available at http://www.iupui.edu/~anthkb/ (accessed May 2005).
13. Adapted from Kinsey Gorman, C. Unleashing the power of creative collaboration. *Communication World*, November/December 2004, 14–17.
14. Caterpillar Inc. Available at http://www.hoovers.com (accessed May 2005).
15. Cambie, David Radcliffe's NECK, 31.

16. Ellinor, L., and Gerard, G. *Dialogue: Rediscovering the Transforming Power of Conversation.* New York: Wiley, 1998; Hardy, C., Lawrence, T.B., and Grant, D. Discourse and collaboration: The role of conversations and collective identity. *Academy of Management Review*, 2005, 30, 58–77.
17. Van Wert, G. Honesty not the easiest, but the best policy. *American Printer*, September 2003, 6–7.
18. Sheridan's company purpose and values. Available at http://www.sheridanpress.com (accessed May 2005).
19. Heracleous, L., and Marshak, R.J. Conceptualizing organizational discourse as situated symbolic action. *Human Relations*, 2004, 1285–1313; Hoogervorst, J., van der Flier, H., and Koopman, P. Implicit communication in organizations: The impact of culture, structure and management practices on employee behavior. *Journal of Managerial Psychology*, 2004, 19, 288–311.
20. Pillutla, M.M., and Chen, X. Social norms and cooperation in social dilemmas: The effects of context and feedback. *Organizational Behavior & Human Decision Processes*, 1999, 78(2), 81–93; London, M. *Job Feedback: Giving, Seeking, and Using Feedback for Performance Improvement*, 2nd ed. Mahwah, NJ: Lawrence Erlbaum Associates, 2003.
21. DeNisi, A.S., and Kluger, A.N. Feedback effectiveness: Can 360-degree appraisals be improved? *Academy of Management Executive*, 2000, 14(1), 129–139; Atwater, L.E., and Brett, J.F. Antecedents and consequences of reactions to developmental 360° feedback. *Journal of Vocational Behavior*, 2005, 66, 532–548.
22. Petrino, S. (ed.). *Balancing the Secrets of Private Disclosures.* Mahwah, NJ: Lawrence Erlbaum Associates, 2000.
23. McCall, C. *Listen! There's a World Waiting to Be Heard, The Empowerment of Listening.* Scottsdale, AZ: Institute for Global Listening and Communication, 2005; Brownell, J. *Listening: Attitudes, Principles, and Skills*, 3rd ed., Boston: Allyn & Bacon, 2006.
24. Adapted from McCallen, J. Conversation culture. *Journal of Financial Planning*, September/October 2004, 20–21; About FPA. Available at http://www.fpanet.org (accessed May 2005).
25. Center for Nonverbal Studies. Nonverbal communication. Available at http://members.aol.com/nonverbal2/index.htm (accessed May 2005).
26. Riggio, R.E., and Feldman, R.S. (eds.). *Applications of Nonverbal Communication.* Mahwah, NJ: Lawrence Erlbaum Associates, 2005.
27. Adapted from Beall, A.E. Body language speaks. *Communication World*, March/April 2004, 18–20; Knapp, M.L., and Hall, J.A. *Nonverbal Communication in Human Interaction*, 6th ed. Belmont, CA: Wadsworth, 2006.
28. Wong, E. *A Master Course in Feng-Shui.* Boston: Shambhala Publications, 2001.
29. Zeer, D. *Office Feng Shui: Creating Harmony in Your Work Space.* San Francisco: Chronicle Books, 2004.
30. Tsang, E.W. Toward a scientific inquiry into superstitious business decision-making. *Organization Studies*, 2004, 25, 923–946.
31. Hickson, M.L., Stacks, D.W., and Moore, N. *Nonverbal Communication: Studies and Applications.* Los Angeles: Roxbury, 2002; Jandt, F.E. *An Introduction to Intercultural Communication*, 4th ed. Thousand Oaks, CA: Sage, 2004.
32. Bluedorn, A.C., Kaufman, C.F., and Lane, P.M. How many things do you like to do at once? An introduction to monochronic and polychronic time. *Academy of Management Executive*, 1992, 6(4), 17–26; Kaufman-Scarborough, C., and Lindquist, J.D. Time management and polychronicity comparisons, contrasts, and insights for the workplace. *Journal of Managerial Psychology*, 1999, 14, 288–312; Crossan, M., Cunha, M.P., Vera, D., and Cunha, J. Time and organizational improvisation. *Academy of Management Review*, 2005, 30, 129–145.
33. Ting-Toomey, S. *Communicating across Cultures.* New York: Guilford Press, 1999; Von Glinow, M.A., Shapiro, D.L., and Brett, J.M. Can we talk, and should we? Managing emotional conflict in multicultural teams. *Academy of Management Review*, 2004, 29, 578–592.
34. Latane, B., Liu, J.H., Nowak, A., Bonevento, M., and Zheng, L. Distance matters: Physical space and social impact. *Personality and Social Psychology Bulletin*, 1995, 21, 795–805.
35. Aquino, K., Brover, S.L., Bradfield, M., and Allen, D.G. The effects of negative affectivity, hierarchical status, and self-determination on workplace victimization. *Academy of Management Journal*, 1999, 42, 260–272.
36. Adapted from Zielinski, D. *Presentations*, April 2001, 36–42.
37. Adapted from Baber, D., and Wayman, L. Internal networking: The key to influence. *Canadian HR Reporter*, June 17, 2002, 12–13.
38. Ahearn, K.K., Ferris, G.R., Hochwarter, W.A., Douglas, C., and Ammeter, A.P. Leader political skill and team performance. *Journal of Management*, 2004, 30, 309–327.
39. Ferris, G.R., Treadway, D.C., Kolodinsky, R.W., Hochwarter, W.A., Kacmar, C.J., Douglas, C., and Frink, D.D. Development and validation of the political skill inventory. *Journal of Management*, 2005, 31, 128. Also see Treadway, D.C., Hochwarter, W.A., Kacmar, C.J., and Ferris, G.R. Political will, political skill, and political behavior. *Journal of Organizational Behavior*, 2005, 26, 229–246.
40. Keyton, J. *Communication and Organizational Culture: A Key to Understanding Work Experiences.* Thousand Oaks, CA: Sage, 2005.
41. Adapted from Burke, L.A., and Morris Wise, J. The effective care, handling, and pruning of the office grapevine. *Business Horizon*, 2003, 46(3), 71–76.
42. Kemmel, A.J. *Rumors and Rumor Control: A Manager's Guide to Understanding and Combatting Rumors.* Mahwah, NJ: Lawrence Erlbaum Associates, 2004.
43. Michelson, G., and Mouly, V.S. Do loose lips sink ships? The meaning, antecedents and consequences of rumor and gossip in organizations. *Corporate Communications: An International Journal*, 2004, 9, 189–201.
44. Adapted from Taylor, M., and Elsey, G. Building commitment to a new business strategy at Sensis. *Strategic Communication Quarterly*, April/May 2005, 3–17.

45. Sensis today. Available at http://www.sensis.com (accessed May 2005).
46. Adapted from Douglas Roberts, formerly manager of training, LTV Missiles and Electronics Group, Grand Prairie, TX. Used with permission.
47. Catlin, L., and White, T. *Cultural Sourcebook and Case Studies*. Cincinnati: South-Western, 1994, 40–41. Used with permission.

CHAPTER 11

1. Adapted from Brady, D. Act II. *Business Week*, March 29, 2004, 73ff; Howard, T. Y&R leader seeks views from client, employees. *USA Today*, May 20, 2003.
2. Pervin, L.A., and John, O.P. *Handbook of Personality*, 2nd ed. New York: Guilford, 1999.
3. Janada, L. *The Psychologist's Book of Personality Tests*. New York: John Wiley & Sons, 2001; Judge, T.A., Bono, J.A., and Locke, E.A. Personality and job satisfaction: The mediating role of job characteristics. *Journal of Applied Psychology*, 2000, 85, 237–249.
4. Turkheimer, E. Heritability and biological explanation. *Psychological Review*, 1998, 105, 782–791; Plomin, R., and Caspi, A. Behavioral genetics and personality. In L.A. Pervin and O.P. John (eds.), *Handbook of Personality*, 2nd ed. New York: Guilford, 1999, 251–276.
5. Furnham, A., Petrides, K.V., Tsaousis, I., Pappas, K., and Garrod, D. A cross-cultural investigation into the relationship between personality and work values. *Journal of Psychology*, 2005, 139, 5–33.
6. Brunk, B.P., Aukje, N., and Molleman, E. In search of the group animal. *European Journal of Personality*, 2005, 91(1), 69–81.
7. Adapted from Newman, R. Preaching JetBlue. *Chief Executive*, October 2004, 26–30; Brodsky, N. Street Smarts: Learning from JetBlue. *Inc.*, March 2004, 59ff.
8. Raja, U., Johns, G., and Ntalianis. The impact of personality on psychological contracts. *Academy of Management Journal*, 2004, 47, 350–367; Robins, R.W., Noftle, E.E., and Tzesniewski, K.H. Do people know how their personality has changed? *Journal of Personality*, 2005, 73(2), 489–521.
9. Barrick, M.R., and Mount, M.K. The big five personality dimensions and job performance: A meta-analysis. *Personnel Psychology*, 1991, 44, 1–26; Thorese, C.J., Bradley, J.C., Bliese, P.D., and Thoresen, J.D. The Big Five personality traits and individual job performance growth trajectories in maintenance and transitional job stages. *Journal of Applied Psychology*, 2004, 89, 835–854; Bozionelos, N. The big five of personality and work involvement. *Journal of Managerial Psychology*, 2004, 19, 88–110.
10. Pierce, J.L., and Rodgers, L. The psychology of ownership and worker-owner productivity. *Group & Organization Management*, 2004, 29 (5), 588–613.
11. Chen, G., Gully, S.M., and Eden, D. General self-efficacy and self-esteem: Toward theoretical and empirical distinction between correlated self-evaluations. *Journal of Organizational Behavior*, 2004, 25 (4), 439–459.
12. Bono, J.E., and Judge, T.A. Core-self evaluations: A review of trait and its role in job satisfaction and job performance. *European Journal of Personality*, 2003, 17 (suppl. 1), 5–18; Judge, T.A., Erez, A., and Bono, J.E. The core self-evaluations scale: Development of a measure. *Personnel Psychology*, 2003, 56(2), 303–331.
13. Huifang, Y., and Shuming, Z. Research on the personality types of business managers. *Psychological Science*, 2004, 27(4), 983–985.
14. Goleman, D. *Working with Emotional Intelligence*. New York: Bantum Press, 1998; Goleman, D. What makes a leader? In Taylor, R.L., and Rosenbach, W.E. (eds.), *Military Leadership: In Pursuit of Excellence*, 5th ed. Boulder, CO: Westview Press, 2005, 53–68; Law, K.S., Wong, C., and Lynda, J.S. The construct and criterion validity of emotional intelligence and its potential utility for management studies. *Journal of Applied Psychology*, 2004, 89, 483–497.
15. Adapted from Cannella, C. Kill the sales commission. *Inc.*, August 2004, 38.
16. Kraimer, M.L., Wayne, S.J., and Liden, R.C. The role of job security in understanding the relationship between employees' perceptions of temporary workers and employees' performance. *Journal of Applied Psychology*, 2005, 90, 350–362.
17. Snyder, C.R., Berg, C., and Woodward, J.T. Hope against the cold. *Journal of Personality*, 2005, 73, 287–312; Snyder, C.R. Hope and other strengths: Lessons for animal farm. *Journal of Social and Clinical Psychology*, 2004, 23, 624–727.
18. Luthans, F. Positive organizational behavior. *Academy of Management Executive*, 2003, 16, 57–75.
19. Box, T. The little dealership that could. *Dallas Morning News*, August 23, 2001, D-1ff.
20. Staw, B.A., and Choen-Charash, Y. The dispositional approach to job satisfaction: More than a mirage, but not an oasis. *Journal of Organizational Behavior*, 2005, 26, 59–79; Schleicher, D.J., Watt, J.D., and Greguras, G.J. Reexamining the job satisfaction-performance relationship. *Journal of Applied Psychology*, 2004, 89, 176–178.
21. Siebert, S.E., Silver, S.R., and Randolph, W.A. Taking empowerment to the next level: A multiple-level model of empowerment, performance and satisfaction. *Academy of Management Journal*, 2004, 47, 332–349; Janssen, O., and Yperen, W.V. Employees' goal orientations, the quality of leader-member exchange, and the outcomes of job performance and job satisfaction. *Academy of Management Journal*, 2004, 47, 368–384.
22. Adapted from Gavin, J.H., and Mason, R.O. The value of happiness in the workplace. *Organizational Dynamics*, 2004, 33, 379–392; Powers, V. Finding workers who fit the Container Store built a booming business for neatniks who turned out to be their best employees. *Business 2.0*, November 2004, 74ff.; http://www.greatplacetowork.com; http://www.containerstore.com (accessed July, 2005).
23. Johnson, S., Cooper, G., Cartwright, S., Ian, D., Taylor, P., and Clare, M. The experience of work-related stress across occupations. *Journal of Managerial Psychology*, 2005, 20, 178–188; Cable, D.M., and Edwards, J.R. Complementary and supplementary fit: A theoretical

and empirical integration. *Journal of Applied Psychology*, 2004, 89, 822–835.

24. Mowday, R.T., Porter, L.W., and Steers, R.M. *Employee–Organization Linkages: The Psychology of Commitment, Absenteeism, and Turnover.* New York: Academic Press, 1982; Siegel, P.A., Post, C., Brockner, J., Fishman, A.Y., and Garden, C. The moderating influence of procedural fairness on the relationship between work-life conflict and organizational commitment. *Journal of Applied Psychology*, 2005, 90, 13–25.
25. The seminal work in the field was done by Lazarus, R. *Emotion and Adaption.* New York: Oxford University Press, 1991. Also see Cron, W.L., Slocum, J.W., Jr., VandeWalle, D., and Fu, F. The role of goal orientation on negative emotions and goal setting when initial performance falls short of one's goal. *Human Performance*, 2005, 18, 55–80; Dalvir, S. Managerial elites making rhetorical and linguistic "moves" for emotional display. *Human Relations*, 2004, 57(9), 1103–1143.
26. Bagozzi, R.P., Wong, N., and Yi, Y. The role of culture and gender in the relationship between positive and negative emotions. *Cognition and Emotion*, 1999, 16, 641–672.
27. Huy, Q.N. Emotional balancing of organizational continuity and radical change: The contribution of middle managers. *Administrative Science Quarterly*, 2002, 47, 31–69; Bagozzi, R.P., Baumgartner, H., and Pieters, R. Goal-directed emotions. *Cognition and Emotion*, 1998, 12, 1–26; Brown, S.P., Cron, W.L., and Slocum J.W., Jr. Effects of goal-directed emotions on sales person's volitions, behavior and performance. *Journal of Marketing*, 1997, 61, 39–50.
28. Adapted from Caproni, P. J. *Management Skills for Everyday Life.* Upper Saddle River, NJ: Pearson/Prentice Hall, 2005, 103.
29. Cameron, K.S., Dutton, J.E., and Quinn, R. (eds.). *Positive Organizational Scholarship.* San Francisco: Berrett-Koehler Publishing, 2003, 3–14; Peterson, C.M., and Seligman, M.E.P. Positive organizational studies: Lessons from positive psychology. In *Positive Organizational Scholarship*, 14–29.
30. Reprinted with permission from Howard, P.J., Medina, P.L., and Howard, J.M. The big five locator: A quick assessment tool for consultants and trainers. In J.W. Pfeiffer (ed.), *The 1996 Annual: Volume 1, Training.* San Diego: Pfeiffer & Company, 1996, 119–122. Copyright © 1996 Pfeiffer, an imprint of Jossey-Bass, Inc., Publishers. All rights reserved.
31. Adapted from Fisher, A. Success Secret: A high emotional IQ. *Fortune*, October 26, 1998, 293–298.

CHAPTER 12

1. Adapted from Bendaudi, N., and Bendapudi, V. Creating a living brand. *Harvard Business Review*, May 2005, 124–132; http://www.quiktrip.com (accessed July 2005).
2. Rolf, V.D., and Jost, S. Should I Stay or Should I go? Turnover intentions with organizational identification and job satisfaction. *British Journal of Management*, 2004, 15(4), 351–360.
3. Adapted from Flannery, R. China is a big prize. *Forbes*, May 10, 2004, 163–165.
4. Henderson, J.M., and Hollingworth, A. High-level scene perception. *Annual Review of Psychology*, 1999, 50, 243–271.
5. Farah, M.J., Wilson, K.D., Drain, M., and Tanaka, J.N. What is "special" about face perception? *Psychological Review*, 1998, 105, 482–498.
6. Adapted from Henderson, P.W., Giese, J.L., and Cote, J.A. Impression management using typeface designs. *Journal of Marketing*, 2004, 68(4), 60–72.
7. Armstrong, S.J. The impact of supervisors' cognitive styles on the quality of research supervision in management education. *British Journal of Educational Psychology*, 2004, 74(4), 599–616.
8. Diener, E. What is positive about positive psychology: The curmudgeon and Pollyanna. *Psychology Inquiry*, 2003, 14(2), 115–120.
9. Heslin, P.A., Latham, G.P., and VandeWalle, D. The effect of implicit person theory on performance appraisals. *Journal of Applied Psychology*, JAP, 2005, 90, 842–856.
10. McCrae, R.R., and Terracciano, A. Universal features of personality traits from the observer's perspective: Data from 50 cultures. *Journal of Personality and Social Psychology*, 2005, 88, 547–561.
11. Wei-Chi, T., Chen, C., and Chiu, S. Exploring boundaries of the effects of application impressions management tactics in job interviews. *Journal of Management*, 2005, 31, 108–125.
12. Hayes, T.L. The first 90 days. *Personnel Psychology*, 2004, 57, 1073–1076.
13. Cable, D.M., and Judge, T.A. The effect of physical height on workplace success and income: Preliminary test of a theoretical model. *Journal of Applied Psychology*, 2004, 89, 428–441; Siegel, P.A., and Brockner, J. Individual and organizational consequences of CEO claimed handicapping: What's good for the CEO may not be good for the firm. *Organizational Behavior and Human Decision Processes*, 2005, 96, 1–22.
14. Clair, J.A., Beatty, J.E., and MacLean, T.L. Out of sight, but not out of mind: Invisible social identities in the workplace. *Academy of Management Review*, 2005, 30, 78–95; Atwater, L.E., Brett, J.F., and Waldman, D. Men's and women's perceptions of the gender typing of management subroles. *Sex Roles*, 2004, 50, 191–199.
15. Home Depot launches national hiring initiative. *The Officer*, November 2004, 5–7; http://www.homedepot.com (accessed June 2005).
16. Kierein, N.M. Pygmalion in work organizations: A meta-analysis. *Journal of Organizational Behavior*, 2000, 21(8), 913–914; McNatt, D.B. Ancient Pygmalion joins contemporary management: A meta-analysis result. *Journal of Applied Psychology*, 2000, 75, 314 –322.
17. Personal communication with Mel Parakh, director of sales, Dell Computer, North Texas, May 2005.
18. Jun, S., and Gentry, J.W. An exploratory investigation of the relative importance of cultural similarity and per-

sonal fit in the selection and performance of expatriates. *Journal of World Business*, 2005, 40, 1–8; Selmer, J., and Chin, R. Required human resources competencies in the future: A framework for developing HR executives in Hong Kong. *Journal of World Business*, 2004, 39, 324–336; Bossard, A.B., and Peterson, R.B. The repatriate experience as seen by American expatriates. *Journal of World Business*, 2005, 40, 9–28.

19. Adapted from http://www.traderscity.com/abcg/culture8.htm (accessed May 2005).
20. Ployhart, R.E., Ehrhart, K., Holcombe, H., and Hayes, S.C. Using attributions to understand the effects of applicant reactions. *Journal of Applied Social Psychology*, 2005, 35, 259–296.
21. Elkins, T.J., and Phillips, J.S. Evaluating sex discrimination claims: The mediating role of attributions. *Journal of Applied Psychology*, 1999, 84, 186–199.
22. Nurcan, E., and Murphy, S.E. Cross-cultural variations in leadership perceptions and attribution of charisma to the leader. *Organizational Behavior and Human Decision Processes*, 2003, 92(1–2), 52–66; Bartel, C.A. Social comparison in boundary-spanning work: Effects of community outreach on members' organizational identity and identification. *Administrative Science Quarterly*, 2001, 379–413.
23. Westman, M., Etzion, D., and Danon, E. Job insecurity and crossover of burnout in married couples. *Journal of Organizational Behavior*, 2001, 22, 467–484; Wiesenfeld, B.M., Brockner, J., and Thibault, V. Procedural fairness, manager's self-esteem, and managerial behaviors after a layoff. *Organizational Behavior and Human Decision Processes*, 2000, 83, 1–32.
24. Landry, J.L.B., Sathi, M., and Hartman, S. The changing nature of work in the age of e-business. *Journal of Organizational Change Management*, 2005, 18, 132–145.
25. Adapted from Yost, E.B., and Herbert, T.T. Attitudes toward women as managers. In L.D. Goodstein and J.W. Pfeiffer (eds.), *The 1985 Annual: Developing Human Resources*. San Diego: University Associates, 1985, 117–127. Reprinted with permission.
26. Adapted from Ritti, R.R. *The Ropes to Skip and the Ropes to Know: Studies in Organizational Behavior*, 5th ed. New York: John Wiley & Sons, 1998, 30–31.

CHAPTER 13

1. Adapted from Nevant, T. "Mini Maids." Unpublished Executive MBA case, Cox School of Business, Southern Methodist University, Dallas, TX, 2005. Used with permission.
2. Weiss, H.M. Learning theory and industrial and organizational psychology. In M.D. Dunnette and L.M. Hough (eds.), *Handbook of Industrial & Organizational Psychology*, 2nd ed. Palo Alto, CA: Consulting Psychologist Press, 1990, 170–221.
3. Kanfer, R. Motivation theory and industrial and organizational psychology. In Dunnette and Hough, *Handbook of Industrial & Organizational Psychology*, 75–169.
4. Daniels, A.C. *Bringing Out the Best in People*, 2nd ed. New York: McGraw-Hill, 2000, 25–78.
5. Skinner, B.F. *About Behaviorism*. New York: Knopf, 1974; Dragoi, V., and Staddon, J.E.R. The dynamics of operant conditioning. *Psychological Review*, 1999, 106, 20–24.
6. Thompson, H., Iwata, B.A., Hanley, G.P., Dozier, C.L., and Samaha, A. The effects of extinction, noncontingent reinforcement, and different reinforcement of other behavior as control procedures. *Journal of Applied Behavior Analysis*, 2003, 36, 221–239.
7. Adler, N.J. *International Dimensions of Organizational Behavior*, 4th ed. Cincinnati, OH: South-Western, 2002; Fey, C.E., Pavlovskaya, A., and Tang, N. Does one shoe fit everyone? *Organizational Dynamics*, 2004, 33, 79–97.
8. Paik, Y., and Sohn, J.D. Expatriate managers and MNC's ability to control international subsidiaries: The case of Japanese MNCs. *Journal of World Business*, 2004, 39, 61–70.
9. Eidan, M. Got worries? Tell them to the chaplain. *Business Week*, February 9, 2004, 16.
10. Adapted from Daniels, *Bringing Out the Best in People*, 59–60.
11. Simons, R. Designing high-performance jobs. *Harvard Business Review*, July/August 2005, 55–62.
12. Besser, T.L. Rewards and organizational goal achievement: A case study of Toyota Motor manufacturing in Kentucky. *Journal of Management Studies*, 1995, 32, 383–401; Lustgarten, A. Elite factories. *Fortune*, September 6, 2004, 240ff.
13. Sunstein, C.R. On the psychology of punishment. *Supreme Court Economic Review*, 2003, 11, 171–189.
14. Grote, D.F. Discipline without punishment. *Across the Board*, September/October 2001, 52–57.
15. Stajkovic, A.D., and Luthans, F. A meta-analysis of the effects of organizational behavior modification on task performance. *Academy of Management Journal*, 1997, 40, 1122–1149.
16. Reed, P. Human response rates and causality judgments on schedules of reinforcement. *Learning and Motivation*, 2001, 32, 332–348.
17. Adapted from Smyth, R., Wang, J. and Deng, X. Equity-for-debt swaps in Chinese big business: A case study of restructuring in one large state-owned enterprise. *Asia Business Review*, 2004, 10(3/4), 382–401.
18. Latham, G.P., and Huber, V.L. Schedules of reinforcement: Lessons from the past and issues for the future. *Journal of Organizational Behavior Management*, 1992, 12, 125–150.
19. Bandura, A. *Social Learning Theory*. Upper Saddle River, NJ: Prentice Hall, 1977; Bandura, A. *Self-Efficacy: The Exercise of Self-Control*. New York: W. H. Freeman, 1997.
20. Caligiuri, P.M., and Phillips, J.M. An application of self-assessment realistic job previews to expatriate assignments. *International Journal of Human Resource Management*, 2003, 14, 1102–1117.
21. Adapted from Salter, C. When couches fly. *Fast Company*, July 2004, 80–81.
22. Judge, T.A., and Bono, J.E. Relationship of core self–self-evaluations traits—self-esteem, generalized self-

efficacy, locus of control, and emotional stability—with job satisfaction and job performance: A meta-analysis. *Journal of Applied Psychology*, 2001, 86, 80–93; Stajkovic, A.D., and Luthans, F. Social cognitive theory and work-related performance: A meta-analysis. *Psychological Bulletin*, 1998, 124, 240–261.

23. Kehr, H.M. Integrating implicit motives, explicit motives, and perceived abilities: The compensatory model of work motivation and volition. *Academy of Management Review*, 2004, 29, 479–499.
24. Locke, E.A., and Latham, G.P. What should we do about motivation theory? Six recommendations for the twenty-first century. *Academy of Management Review*, 2004, 29, 388–403.
25. Kanfer, R., and Ackerman, P.L. Aging adult development and work motivation. *Academy of Management Review*, 2004, 29, 440–458.
26. Adapted from Lee, C., and Bobko, P. Self-efficacy beliefs: Comparison of five measures. *Journal of Applied Psychology*, 1994, 79, 364–370; Maurer, T.J., and Pierce, H.R. A comparison of Likert scale and traditional measures of self-efficacy. *Journal of Applied Psychology*, 1998, 83, 324–330.
27. Adapted from Fuquay, J. Texas health plan doctors settle lawsuit. *Fort Worth Star-Telegram*, September 27, 1997, 1ff; Ornstein, C. Members sue Harris Methodist Plan, Dallas area's largest HMO. *Knight-Ridder/Tribune News*, May 14, 1998, 1ff; Ornstein, C. Arlington, Texas-based HMO to pay $1.1 million to settle doctors' lawsuit. *Dallas Morning News*, September 3, 1998, 1ff. For additional information, visit the Dallas Morning News Web site at http://www.dallasnews.com.
28. Adapted from Beard, J.W., Woodman, R.W., and Moesel, D. Using behavioral modification to change attendance patterns in the high-performance, high-commitment environment. In R.W. Woodman and W.A. Pasmore (eds.), *Research in Organizational Change and Development*, vol. 11. Stamford, Conn.: JAI Press, 1998, 183–224. For additional information, visit the Westinghouse Web site at http://www.westinghouse.com.

CHAPTER 14

1. Adapted from Stopper, W.G. Establishing and maintaining the trust of your employees. *Human Resource Planning*, 2004, 27(2), 21–22; Hammers, M. Please employees, pouring profits. *Workforce Management*, 2003, 82 (10), 58–60; http://www.starbucks.com (accessed December 2004).
2. For additional information, visit the company's home page at http://www.starbucks.com.
3. LePine, J.A., LePine, M.A., and Jackson, C.L. Challenge and hindrance stress: Relationships with exhaustion, motivation to learn and learning performance. *Journal of Applied Psychology*, 2004, 98, 883–891.
4. Maurer, T.J., Weiss, E.M., and Barbeite, F.G. A model of motivation in work-related learning and development activity: The effects of individual, situational, motivational, and age variables. *Journal of Applied Psychology*, 2003, 88, 707–724.
5. Adler, N.J. *International Dimensions of Organizational Behavior*, 4th ed. Cincinnati, OH: South-Western, 2002, 174–181.
6. Maslow, A.H. *Motivation and Personality*. New York: Harper & Row, 1970. For an excellent overview of motivation models, see Ambrose, M.L., and Kulik, C.T. Old friends, new faces: Motivation research in the 1990s. *Journal of Management*, 1999, 25, 231–237.
7. Lovett, S., and Coyle, T. Job satisfaction and technology in Mexico. *Journal of World Business*, 2004, 39, 217–232.
8. Maslow, A.H., and Kaplan, A.R. *Maslow on Management*. New York: John Wiley & Sons, 1998; Landy, F.L., and Becker, W.S. Motivation model reconsidered. In Cummings, L.L., and Staw, B.M. (eds.), *Research in Organizational Behavior*, Vol. 9. Greenwich, CT: JAI Press, 1987, 1–38.
9. McClelland, D.C., and Burnham, D. Power is the great motivator. *Harvard Business Review*, March/April 1976, 100–111; Payne, D.K. *Training Resources Group*. Boston: McBer & Company, 1998.
10. Baum, J.R., and Locke, E.A. The relationship of entrepreneurial traits, skill and motivation to subsequent venture growth. *Journal of Applied Psychology*, 2004, 89, 587–598; McClelland, D.C. *Motivational Trends in Society*. Morristown, NJ: General Learning Press, 1971.
11. Adapted from http://www.papajohns.com (accessed December 2004).
12. Collins, C.J., Hanges, P.J., and Locke, E.A. The relationship of achievement motivation to entrepreneurial behavior: A meta-analysis. *Human Performance*, 2004, 17, 95–117.
13. Herzberg, F.I., Mausner, B., and Snyderman, B.B. *The Motivation to Work*. New York: John Wiley & Sons, 1959.
14. Hackman, J.R., and Oldham, G.R. *Work Redesign*. Reading, MA: Addison-Wesley, 1980; Parker, S.K., and Wall, T.D. Work design: Learning from the past and mapping a new terrain. In Anderson, N., and Deniz, S. (eds.), *Handbook of Industrial, Work, and Organizational Psychology*. London: Sage Publications, 2002, 90–109.
15. Adapted from http://www.seiinvestments.com (accessed December 2004).
16. Gomez, C. The influence of environmental, organizational and HRM factors on employee behaviors in subsidiaries: A Mexican case study of organizational learning. *Journal of World Business*, 2004, 39, 1–11; Schuler, R.S., and Jackson, S.E. A quarter-century review of human resource management in the U.S.: The growth in importance of the international perspective. *Management Review*, 2005, 16 (1), 1–25.
17. Vroom, V.H. *Work and Motivation*. New York: John Wiley & Sons, 1964.
18. Erez, A., and Isen, A.M. The influence of positive affect on the components of expectancy motivation. *Journal of Applied Psychology*, 2002, 87, 1055–1067.
19. Adler, N. International Dimensions of Organizational Behavior, 179–182.
20. Stewart-Williams, S., and Podd, J. The placebo effect: Dissolving the expectancy versus conditioning debate. *Psychological Bulletin*, 2004, 130, 324–340.

21. Personal interview with J. Cones, senior vice president, NATRECOR, December 2004.
22. Adapted from Malik, O. McProgrammers. *Business 2.0*, August 2004, 97–102.
23. Adams, J.S. Toward an understanding of inequity. *Journal of Abnormal and Social Psychology*, 1963, 67, 422–436.
24. Scheer, L.K., Kuman, N., and Steenkamp, J.B. Reactions to perceived inequity in U.S. and Dutch interorganizational relationships. *Academy of Management Journal*, 2003, 46, 303–316.
25. Hollinger, R.C., and Langton, L. *2003 National Retail Security Survey*. Gainesville: Center for Studies in Criminology and Law, University of Florida, 2004.
26. Folger, R., and Husted, B.W. Fairness and transaction costs: The contribution of organizational justice theory to an integrative model of economic organization. *Organization Science*, 2004, 15, 719–929; Colella, A. Coworkers' distributive fairness judgments on the workplace accommodation of employees with disabilities. *Academy of Management Review*, 2001, 26, 100–116.
27. Ramamoorthy, N., and Flood, P.C. Gender and employee attitudes: The role of organizational justice. *British Journal of Management*, 2004, 15, 247–253; Tepper, B.J., Duffy, M.K., and Hoobler, J. Moderators of the relationships between coworkers' organizational citizenship behavior and fellow employees' attitudes. *Journal of Applied Psychology*, 2004, 89, 455–465.
28. DeConinck, J.B., and Stilwell, C.D. Incorporating organizational justice, role states, pay satisfaction and supervisor satisfaction in a model of turnover intentions. *Journal of Business Research*, 2004, 57, 225–231; Onne, J. How fairness perceptions makes innovative behavior more or less stressful. *Journal of Organizational Behavior*, 2004, 25, 201–215.
29. Lee, T.W., Mitchell, T.R., and Sablynski, C.J. The effects of job embeddedness on organizational citizenship: Job performance, volitional absences, and voluntary turnover. *Academy of Management Journal*, 2004, 47, 711–722.
30. Liden, R.C., Wayne, S.J., and Jaworski, R.A. Social loafing: A field investigation. *Journal of Management*, 2004, 30, 285–304; Ehrhart, M.G. Leadership and procedural justice climate as antecedents of unit-level organizational citizenship behavior. *Personnel Psychology*, 2004, 57, 61–94.
31. Adapted from a survey of employees conducted by Seglin, J.L. The happiest worker in the world, *Inc.*, May 1996, 62–76.
32. Fishman, C. Sanity Inc. *Fast Company*, January 21, 1999, 84ff; Florida, R., and Goodnight, J. Managing for creativity. *Harvard Business Review*, July/August 2005, 124–13; http://www.sas.com (accessed July 2005).

CHAPTER 15

1. Adapted from Donnelley, S.B. Out of the box: UPS still delivers packages, of course, but it's also helping firms like Nike and Toshiba assemble, store, and repair products. Who knew? *Time*, November 8, 2004, 2Aff; http://www.UPS.com.
2. Latham, G.P. The motivational benefits of goal-setting. *Academy of Management Executive*, 2004, 18, 126–129; Shaw, K.N. Changing the goal-setting process at Microsoft. *Academy of Management Executive*, 2004, 18, 139–143.
3. Locke, E.A., and Latham, G.P.A *Theory of Goal Setting & Task Performance*. Englewood Cliffs, NJ: Prentice-Hall, 1990, 7; Steers, R.M., Mowday, R.T., and Shapiro, D.L. Introduction to special topic form: The future of work motivation theory. *Academy of Management Review*, 2004, 29, 379–387.
4. Locke, E.A., and Latham, G.P. Building a practically useful theory of goal setting and task motivation: A 35-year odyssey. *American Psychologist*, 2002, 57, 705–717.
5. Locke and Latham, *A Theory of Goal Setting*, 252–257; Latham, G.P. A five step approach to behavior change. *Organizational Dynamics*, 2003, 32, 309–318; Locke, E.A. and Latham, G.P. Goal setting theory: Theory building by induction. In M. Hitt and K.G. Smith (eds.). *Oxford Handbook of Management Theory: The Process of Theory Development*. London: Oxford University Press, 2005, 128–150.
6. Moos, B. These workers heed their health, then reap rewards. *Dallas Morning News*, December 19, 2004, D7ff; Mullich, J. Get in line. *Workforce Management*, 2003, 82(13), 43–47; Erez, A., and Judge, T.A. Relationship to core self-evaluations to goal setting, motivation and performance. *Journal of Applied Psychology*, 2001, 86, 1270–1279.
7. Bandura, A., and Locke, E.A. Negative self-efficacy and goal effects revisited. *Journal of Applied Psychology*, 2003, 88, 87–99; Stajkovic, A.D., and Luthans, F. Social cognitive theory and self-efficacy. *Organizational Dynamics*, Spring 1998, 62–75.
8. Adapted from Vasilash, G.S. Teamwork and technology: How Evernham Motorsports goes fast. *Automotive Design and Production*, 2003, 115(10), 30–33.
9. Cron, W. L., Slocum, J.W., Jr. VandeWalle, D., and Fu, F. The role of goal orientation, negative emotions and goal setting when initial performance falls short of one's performance goal. *Human Performance*, 2005, 18, 55–50; Seijts, G.H., Latham, G.P., Tasa, K., and Latham, B.W. Goal setting and goal orientation: An integration of two different yet related literatures. *Academy of Management Journal*, 2004, 47, 227–240.
10. Adapted from Wright, P.M., O'Leary-Kelly, A.M., Cortina, J.M., Klein, H.J., and Hollenbeck, J.R. On the meaning and measurement of goal commitment. *Journal of Applied Psychology*, 1994, 79, 795–808. Also see Buchanan, L. The things they do for love. *Harvard Business Review*, December 2004, 19–20.
11. Mullich, Get in line.
12. Gossage, B. Lose weight, get a toaster. *Inc.*, January 2005, 24.
13. Schweitzer, M.E., Ordonez, L., and Douma, B. Goal setting as a motivator of unethical behavior. *Academy of Management Journal*, 2004, 47, 422–432; Cullen, J.B., Parboteeah, K.P., and Hoegl, M. Cross-national differences in managers' willingness to justify ethically suspect

behaviors: A test of institutional anomie theory. *Academy of Management Journal*, 2004, 47, 411–421.

14. Adapted from Dahle, C. Gap's new look: The see-through. *Fast Company*, September 2004, 69–71; Malone, S. Gap report cites action against violating factories. *WWD*, May 12, 2004, 23.
15. Borton, L. Working in a Vietnamese voice. *Academy of Management Executive*, 2000, 14(4), 20–31; Smith, E.D., Jr., and Pham, C. Doing business in Vietnam: A cultural guide. *Business Horizons*, May/June 1996, 47–51.
16. Latham, G.P. The motivational benefits of goal-setting. *Academy of Management Executive*, 2004, 18, 125–126; Goldman, B.M., Masterson, S.S., and Locke, E.A. Goal-directedness and personal identity as correlates of life outcomes. *Psychological Reports*, 2002, 91, 152–166.
17. Adapted from http://www.ritz-carlton.com (accessed December 2004); Himelstein, B.J. Sales meets human resources. *Sales & Marketing Management*, 2003, 155(7), 64–65.
18. Guthrie, J.P., and Hollensbe, E.C. Group incentives and performance: A study of spontaneous goal setting, goal choice and commitment. *Journal of Management*, 2004, 30, 263–284; Locke, E.A. Linking goals to monetary incentives. *Academy of Management Executive*, 2004, 18, 130–134; Miner, J.B. The rated importance, scientific validity, and practical usefulness of organizational behavior theories: A quantitative review. *AOM Learning and Education*, 2003, 2, 250–268.
19. Adapted from Dess, G.P., and Picken, J.C. *Beyond Productivity*. New York: American Management Association, 1999, 164–167.
20. Locke, E.A. Setting goals for life and happiness. In Snyder, C.R., and Lopez, S.J. (eds.), *Handbook of Positive Psychology*. London: Oxford University Press, 2002, 299–312; Kerr, S., and Landauer, S. Using stretch goals to promote organizational effectiveness and personal growth: General Electric and Goldman Sachs. *Academy of Management Executive*, 2004, 18, 134–138.
21. Personal communication with Michael Murphy, Hewitt Associates, Frisco, TX, December 2004.
22. Schuler, R.S., and Jackson, S.J. *Human Resource Management*, 6th ed. Cincinnati, OH: South-Western, 2000; Tyler, L.S., and Fisher, B. The Scanlon concept: A philosophy as much as a system. *Personnel Administrator*, July 1983, 33–37.
23. Fox, J., and Lawson, B. Gainsharing program lifts Baltimore employees' morale. *American City and County*, September 1997, 112(10), 93–94.
24. Scott, K.D. Scanlon & skill: Two compensation plans for difficult times. *Pay for Performance*, December 2002, 1ff; Lee, C., Law, K.S., and Bobko, P. The importance of justice perceptions on pay effectiveness: A two-year study of a skilled-base pay plan. *Journal of Management*, 1999, 25, 851–873.
25. Personal conversation with Steve Watson, managing director, Stanton Chase, Dallas, TX, December 2004; see also Long, R. Employee profit-sharing: Consequences and moderators. *Industrial Relations* (Canadian), 2000, 55, 477–505.
26. Sammer, J. Making incentives pay: Regular reviews of reward programs insure their worth. *Industry Week*, August 2002, 66–68; Ready, D.A. How to grow great leaders. *Harvard Business Review*, December 2004, 93–100.
27. Guthrie, J.P. Alternative pay practices and employee turnover: An organization economics perspective. *Group & Organization Management*, 2000, 25, 419–439.
28. Mullich, Get in line.
29. Personal conversation with John Semyan, partner, TNS Consulting, Dallas, TX, December, 2004. Also see Sturman, M.C., Hannon, J.M., and Milkovich, G.T. Computerized decision aids for flexible benefits decisions: The effects of an expert and decision support system on employee intentions and satisfaction with benefits. *Personnel Psychology*, 1996, 49, 883–908.
30. Hofstede, G. *Cultures Consequences*, 2nd ed. Thousand Oaks, CA: Sage, 2001. Also see Yamazaki, Y., and Kayes, D.C. An experiential approach to cross-cultural learning: A review and integration of competencies for expatriate adaptation. *Academy of Management Learning & Education*, 2004, 3, 362–379.
31. Tosi, H.L., and Greckhamer, T. Culture & CEO compensation. *Organization Science*, 2004, 15, 657–670; Schuler, R.S., and Jackson, S.J. A quarter-century review of human resource management in the U.S.: The growth in importance of the international perspective. *Management Review*, 2005, 16(1) 1–25; Carlo, G., Roesch, S.C., and Knight, G.P. Between or within culture variation? Cultural group as a moderator of the relations between individual differences and resource allocation preferences. *Journal of Applied Developmental Psychology*, 2001, 22, 559–579.
32. Adapted from Locke and Latham, *A Theory of Goal Setting*, 355–358.
33. Adapted from Reber, R.A., Wallim, J.A., and Chhokar, J.S. Improving safety performance with goal setting and feedback. *Human Performance*, 1990, 3(1), 51–61.

CHAPTER 16

1. Adapted from Jackson, L.A. When your job really makes you sick. *Black Enterprise*, December 2003, 63–65.
2. American Institute of Stress. Job stress. Available at http://www.stress.org (accessed February 1, 2005); McGinn, T. Quitting time. *Newsweek*, May 24, 2004, 12.
3. J. Barling, Kelloway, E.K., and Frone, M.R. (eds.). *Handbook of Work Stress*. Thousand Oaks, CA: Sage, 2005.
4. Sikora, P.B., Beaty, E.D., and Forward, J. Updating theory on organizational stress: The asynchronous multiple overlapping change (AMOC) model of workplace stress. *Human Resource Development Review*, 2004, 3, 3–35.
5. Selye, H. History of the stress concept. In L. Goldberger and S. Breznitz (eds.), *Handbook of Stress*, 2nd ed. New York: Free Press, 1993, 7–20; Selye, H. *The Stress of Life*, 2nd ed. New York: McGraw-Hill, 1978, 1.
6. G. Fink (ed.), *Encyclopedia of Stress*. Burlington, MA: Academic Press, 2001.
7. Zeidner, M., Matthews, G., and Roberts, R.D. Emotional intelligence in the workplace. *Applied Psychology: An International Review*, 2004, 53, 371–399.

8. Terluin, B., Van Rhenen, W., Schaufeli, W.B., and De Haan, M. The four-dimensional symptom questionnaire (4DSQ): Measuring distress and other mental health problems in a working population. *Work & Stress*, 2004, 18, 187–207.
9. Krell, E. *Personality Counts.* H. R. M. Magazine, November, 2005, 46–53.
10. Friedman, M., and Rosenman, R. *Type A Behavior and Your Heart.* New York: Knopf, 1974.
11. Stress and the heart: Treatment helps. *Harvard Men's Health Watch*, February 2005, 7–8.
12. Benishek, L.A., Feldman, J.M., Wolf, S.R., Mecham, S.D., and Lopez, F.G. Development and evaluation of the revised academic hardiness scale. *Journal of Career Assessment*, 2005, 13, 59–76.
13. Turnipseed, D.L. Hardy personality: A potential link with organizational citizenship behavior. *Psychological Reports*, 93, 2003, 529–543; Jacobs, G.D. Developing a stress-hardy personality. Available at http://www.truestarhealth.com (accessed February 3, 2005).
14. Gryna, F.M. *Work Overload: Redesigning Jobs to Minimize Stress and Burnout.* Milwaukee, WI: ASQ Quality Press, 2004.
15. Adapted from Burlingham, B. How big is big enough? *Inc.*, Fall 2004, 40–43.
16. Raghuram, S., and Wiesenfeld, B. Work–nonwork conflict and job stress among virtual workers. *Human Resource Management*, 2004, 43, 259–277.
17. Pearson, C.M., Andersson, L.M., and Porath, C.L. Assessing and attacking workplace incivility. *Organizational Dynamics*, 2000, 29(2), 123–137.
18. Burlingham, How big is big enough?, 42.
19. Kossek, E.E., and Lambert, S.J. (eds.). *Work and Life Integration: Organizational, Cultural, and Individual Perspective.* Mahwah, NJ: Lawrence Erlbaum Associates, 2005.
20. Holmes, T.H., and Rahe, R.H. The social readjustment rating scale. *Journal of Psychosomatic Medicine*, 1967, 11, 213–218.
21. Clarke, S., and Cooper, C. (eds.). *Managing the Risk of Workplace Stress.* New York: Routledge, 2003.
22. Atkinson, W. Stress: Risk management's most serious challenge. *Risk Management*, 2004, 51(6), 20–26.
23. McDermott, H., Lopez, K., and Weiss, B. Computer ergonomics programs: Risk-based approaches maximize their impact. *Professional Safety*, 2004, 49(6), 34–40.
24. Jex, S.M. *Stress and Job Performance.* Thousand Oaks, CA: Sage, 1998.
25. Fernet, C., Gray, F., and Senécal, C. Adjusting to job demands: The role of work, self-determination and job control in predicting burnout. *Journal of Vocational Behavior*, 2004, 65, 39–56.
26. Moore, J.E. Why is this happening? A causal attribution approach to work exhaustion consequences. *Academy of Management Review*, 2000, 25, 335–349; Angerer, J.M. Job burnout. *Journal of Employment Counseling*, 2003, 40, 98–107.
27. Toppinen-Tanner, S., Kalimo, R., and Mutanen, P. The process of burnout in white-collar and blue-collar jobs: Eight-year prospective study of exhaustion. *Journal of Organizational Behavior*, 2002, 23, 555–567.
28. Adapted from Houghom, J.L. How to pass the stress test: An IT executive tells the story of his stress-related breakdown and recovery, and reveals what you can do about the abyss. *CIO*, 2003, 16(14), 1–4; Daniels, C. The last taboo, *Fortune*, October 28, 2002, 137–140.
29. Seaward, B.L. *Managing Stress: Principles and Strategies for Health and Well-Being*, 4th ed. Sudbury, MA: Jones & Bartlett Publishers, 2004.
30. Joshi, V. *Stress: From Burnout to Balance.* Thousand Oaks, CA: Sage, 2005.
31. Linden, W. Stress Management: From Basic Science to Better Practice. Thousand Oaks, CA: Sage, 2004.
32. Delbecq, A.L., and Friedlander, F. Strategies for personal and family renewal: How a high-survivor group of executives cope with stress and avoid burnout. *Journal of Management Inquiry*, 1995, 4, 262–269.
33. Adapted from Shellenbarger, S. Employees who value time as much as money now get their reward. *Wall Street Journal*, September 22, 1999, B1.
34. Hattie, J.A., Myers, J.E., and Sweeney, T.J. A factor structure of wellness: Theory, assessment, analysis, and practice. *Journal of Counseling and Development*, 2004, 82, 354–365.
35. For extensive information on wellness programs, go to the Website for the Wellness Council of America at http://www.welcoa.org (accessed November 2005).
36. Adapted from Mullen, B. Employee wellness. *Canadian HR Reporter*, February 23, 2004, 9–13; Di Giacomo, G. Dofasco's healthy lifestyles program. Available at http://www.dofasco.com (accessed February 8, 2005).
37. LeBlanc, M.M., and Barling, J. Workplace aggression. *Current Directions in Psychological Science*, 2004, 13, 9–12.
38. Dupre, K.E., and Barling, J. Workplace aggression. In A. Sagie, Stashevsky, S., and Kolowsky, M. (eds.). *Misbehavior and Dysfunctional Attitudes in Organizations.* New York: Palgrave/Macmillan, 2003, 13–32.
39. James, L.R., and Associates. A conditional reasoning measure for aggression. *Organizational Research Methods*, 2005, 8, 69–99.
40. European Agency for Safety and Health at Work. Bullying at work. Available at http://www.agency.osha.eu.int (accessed February 9, 2005).
41. Gardner, S., and Johnson, P.R. The leaner, meaner workplace: Strategies for handling bullies at work. *Employment Relations Today*, 2001, 28(2), 23–36.
42. Naime, G. *U.S. Hostile Workplace Survey.* Available at http://bullyinginstitute.org (accessed February 14, 2005).
43. Naime, G. *WBTI 2003 Report on Abusive Workplaces.* Available at http://bullyinginstitute.org (accessed February 14, 2005); Naime, G., and Naime, R. *The Bully at Work.* Naperville, IL: Sourcebooks, 2003; Agervold, M., and Gemozoe-Mikkelsen, E. Relationship between bullying, psychosocial work environment, and individual stress reactions. *Work & Stress*, 2004, 18, 336–351.
44. Einarse, S., Hoel, H., Zapf, D., and Cooper, C. (eds.). *Bullying and Emotional Abuse in the Workplace: International Perspectives.* New York: Taylor & Francis, 2002.

45. Yamada, D. The phenomenon of "workplace bullying" and the need for status behind hostile work environment protection. *Georgetown Law Journal*, 2000, 88, 475–550.
46. Prince, S. *Bully-Free at Work.* Sun Valley, NV: Good Heart Products and Services, 2003.
47. Gates, G. Bullying and mobbing. *Pulp & Paper*, 2004, 78(10), 31–33; Davenport, N., Schwartz, R.D., and Elliott, G.P. *Mobbing: Emotional Abuse in the American Workplace*, 2nd ed. Ames, IA: Civil Society Publishing, 2002.
48. CCH Incorporated. *Creating a Harassment Policy.* Available at http://www.toolkit.cch.com (accessed February 13, 2005).
49. Zapf, D., and Einarsen, S.E. Mobbing at work: Escalated conflicts in organizations. In Fox, S., and Spector, P.E. (eds.), *Counterproductive Workplace Behavior: Investigations of Actors and Targets.* Washington, DC: American Psychological Association, 2005, 237–270.
50. Equal Opportunity Commission. *Sexual Harassment.* Available at http://www.eeoc.gov (accessed February 15, 2005); Gregory, R.F. *Unwelcome and Unlawful: Sexual Harassment in the American Workplace.* Ithaca, NY: Cornell University Press, 2004.
51. Adapted from OfficeWorks sexual harassment policy. Available at http://pharmacystaffing.com (accessed February 15, 2005).
52. Daniel, T.D. Developing a "culture of compliance" to prevent sexual harassment. *Employment Relations Today*, 2003, 30(3), 33–42.
53. Ilies, R., Hauserman, N., Schwochau, S., and Stibal, J. Reported incidence rates of work-related sexual harassment in the United States. *Personnel Psychology*, 2003, 56, 607–632.
54. O'Leary-Kelly, A.M., Paetzold, R.L., and Griffin, R.W. Sexual harassment as aggressive behavior. *Academy of Management Review*, 2000, 25, 372–389.
55. Rudewicz, F.E. The road to rage. *Security Management*, 2004, 48(2), 40–47.
56. National Institute of Occupational Safety and Health. *Violence in the Workplace.* Available at http://www.cdc.gov/niosh/ (accessed February 15, 2005).
57. Viollis, P.M. Helping clients head off workplace violence. *American Agent & Broker*, 2003, 75(11), 30–38.
58. Perline, I.H., and Goldschmidt, J. *The Psychology and Law of Workplace Violence.* Springfield, IL: Charles C. Thomas Publisher, 2004.
59. Blythe, B.T., and Butler-Stivarius, T. Defusing threats of workplace violence. *Employment Relations Today*, 2004, 30(4), 63–70; Kirk, D.J., and McClure-Franklin, G. Violence in the workplace: Guidance and training advice for business owners and managers. *Business and Society Review*, 2003, 108, 523–537.
60. Adapted from Aviza Technology. *Workplace Violence Prevention Policy.* Available at http://www.avizatechnology.com (accessed February 16, 2005).
61. Jawahar, I.M. A model of organizational justice and workplace aggression. *Journal of Management*, 2002, 28, 811–834; Dietz, J., Robinson, S.L., Folger, R., Baron, R.A., and Schultz, M. The impact of community violence and organization's procedural justice climate on workplace aggression. *Academy of Management Journal*, 2003, 46, 317–326.
62. Adapted from a questionnaire developed by Sheldon Cohen contained in Adler, J. Stress. *Newsweek*, June 14, 1999, 63.
63. Adapted from Cummings, T.G., and Worley, C.G. *Organization Development and Change*, 6th ed. Copyright 1997. By permission of South-Western College Publishing, a division of International Thomson Publishing Inc., Cincinnati, OH 45227.

Index

A

Abaco Grupo Financiero, 298–99
ability
  defined, 393
  performance and, 427
absence of trust, 225–26
accommodating style, 256
accuracy of judgment, 348–49
achievement motivation model, 397–400
across cultures competency, 18–23. *See also* culture; organizational culture
  abilities, 19
  Caterpillar, 285–86
  Chinese negotiating style, 270–71
  communication, 295–97
  defined, 18–23
  emotional intelligence, 268
  ethnocentrism, 284
  Frito-Lay, 341–42
  Grupo Carso, 102
  high context culture, 284
  intercultural communication, 284
  low context culture, 284
  negotiating, 266–70
  NIIT, 411
  Northern Shipbuilding, 380
  reward practices, 441
  Unilever Latin America, 220–21
  Western Union, 131–32
  Zhang on China, 22–23
active listening, 8, 292–93
Activision, 90
adapters, 293–94
adjourning stage, 222, 224
Aetna, 13
affiliation needs, 395–97
affinity, 253–54
age, 10, 14, 349
aggression. *See* workplace aggression
agreeableness, 316, 317
airline industry, 52, 72, 141, 150, 261–62
AirTran, 150
Alaska Indoor Sports Distributing Ltd., 26–27
Allen, Sharon, 225
Amazon.com, 111
Ambuehl, Marty, 258–59
American Computer Systems, 394
American Express, 331–32
American Printing Company, 214
Ameristeel Corporation, 437
analogy technique, 58
Anderson, T., 265
antecedents, 368
anticipatory emotions, 330
approach-approach conflict, 249
approach-avoidance conflict, 250
Arab countries, perception and, 352–53
ARAMARK, 138–39
Architect Works, Inc., 58–59
Arnold, Bill, 99
Arthur Andersen, 113–14
Artist's Way at Work, The (Fudge), 311
Ash, Mary Kay, 396
A-Solution, 448
assertive communication, 286–87
ATM Express, 258–59
attitude, 12–13, 322–29
  attitudinal structuring, 264
  hope, 323–25
  job satisfaction, 325–28
  organizational commitment, 328–29
  personality, 322–29
attitudinal structuring, 264
attribution process, 353–58. *See also* perception
  fundamental attribution error, 355–56
  internal/external causes, 355–56
  job loss, 357–58
  self-serving bias, 357
authentic leadership, 194–97, 202
autonomy, 403
Avedisian, J., 137
aversive events, 369–70
Aviza Technology, 473–74
avoidance-avoidance conflict, 250
avoiding style of conflict, 255

B

Badham, R., 56, 166
Bank of America, 161–62
Barbaro, Ronald, 58
Baron, R.A., 457
Barrett, Colleen, 118
Barrows, John, 322
Barshefsky, Charlene, 331–32
Bartz, Carol, 376
BATNA (Best Alternative To a Negotiated Agreement), 259–60
Baxter Pharmaceutical Company, 410
BayerUS, 217, 224, 229
Becker, T.H., 80
behavior. *See also* attribution process; leadership; teams
  Behavioral Leadership Style (questionnaire), 172
  behavioral model of leadership, 170–73
  Ethical Intensity of Selected Behaviors (questionnaire), 41
  personality, 316–22
  stress management, 462–65
Bell Helicopter Textron, 214–15
Benjamin, Maria, 133
Benson, Erica, 447
Beyer, J.M., 106
Bezos, Jeff, 111
Big Five personality factors, 316–18
  perception, 345
  stress, 450
Birnbach, Bruce, 383
Black Entertainment Television (BET), 196
Bleustein, Jeff, 108
Blue Bell Creameries, 367
body language, 297. *See also* nonverbal communication
Boeing, 83, 85
Bontagnali, Gottardo, 285–86
Boone, Garrett, 327–28
bounded rationality decision-making model, 51–54
Bradford, S., 11
brainstorming, 237–39
Branson, Richard, 192, 193
Breen, E., 140
Breen, Ed, 140, 187–88
Brin, Sergey, 97
Brinker International, 74
Buchanan, D., 56, 166
Buckingham, Marcus, 312
Buffett, Warren, 464
bullying, 466–69
bureaucracy, 75
bureaucratic culture, 109–10
Burger, J.M., 319
burnout, 460, 461–62. *See also* stress
Bush, George W., 398
Business Travel International (BTI), 286
Byrne, D., 457

C

Cadieux, Chet, 339–40, 344
cafeteria-style benefits plans, 438–39
Calloway Golf, 72–73
Calvert, 370
Cardinal Health, 426
careers, 6–7, 455
Carmike Cinemas, 81
Carrier, 83–84
Cartwright, Robert, 472
Caterpillar, 285–86
Celanese Corporation, 82, 394–95
Centennial Medical Center, 99
centralization, 76
CEOs, perception, 349–50
chain of command, 78
Challenges of change, 128–38
  economic approach, 133
  globalization, 129–30
  information technology, 130
  organizational development, 133–34
  success indicators, 134–36
  workforce changes, 131–32
change. *See* organizational change
change competency, 25–27
  abilities, 25
  Alaska Indoor Sports Distributing Ltd., 26–27

change competency, continued
American Express, 331–32
Dofasco, 465
7-Eleven, 71
General Electric, 377
Harley-Davidson, 107–8
leadership, 180
Play, 238
Safeco, 200
St. Vincent's Hospital, 50
Your Leadership as Director of Research (exercise), 180
channels, 279–80
charismatic leadership, 190–93, 202
Chase Manhattan Bank, 105
Chatman, J.A., 100
Chenault, Kenneth, 331–32
Chevron Texaco, 283
Childs, Ted, Jr., 14–15
Chili's, 74
China, 21–23, 70
conflict resolution, 270–71
interpersonal communication, 286, 295
learning and reinforcement, 380
organizational design, 72
perception, 340–42
China Post Savings Bureau, 270–71
Choate, Shalane, 345
chromatics, 295–96
chronemics, 296
Chubb, 83–84
Cinergy, 263–64
clan culture, 109, 110
Clark, Neil, 258–59
classical conditioning, 366–67
clinical depression, 467
Clinton, Bill, 398
cluster chain, 300
coaching, 104–5
Coca-Cola Enterprise, Inc., 82
codes of ethics, 37, 430. *See also* ethics
coercive power, 164
cognitive theory. *See* social learning theory
cohesiveness, 233–34
collaborating style of conflict, 256–57
collaborative software, 219
collectivism, 19–20, 22, 79
college students, stressful events for, 457
communication competency, 7–9. *See also* interpersonal communication
abilities, 6
ATM Express, 258–59
Container Store, 327–28
DreamWorks SKG, 89–90
Electrolux, 86–87
Epic Divers and Marine, 54
Financial Planning Association (FPA), 292–93
Kodak, 371
Korens on communicating, 9
Mayo Clinic, 211–12
Ritz-Carlton Hotel, 432–33
Sensis, 301–2
Toyota, 151–52
typestyles, 343–44
Virgin Group, 192, 193
Walgreens, 176
What Would You Do? (questionnaire), 114
communication openness, 288–89
compensation. *See also* financial issues; rewards
income, 11
skill-based pay, 438
U.S. Equal Pay Act of 1963, 43
competencies, 3–24. *See also* competency features throughout
across cultures competency, 18–23
change competency, 25–27
communication competency, 7–9
diversity competency, 9–15
ethics competency, 15–18
self competency, 5–7
teams competency, 23–25
competency, 4
competitors, 69
compliance conformity, 233
compromising style, 257–58
CompUSA, 102
concentration of effect, 40
conditioned response, 366–67
conditioned stimulus, 366–67
conditioning
classical, 366–67
operant, 367–68, 380
conflict. *See also* stress; workplace aggression
accommodating style, 256
across cultures competency, 270
affinity groups, 253
approach-approach conflict, 249
approach-avoidance conflict, 250
ATM Express, 258
attitudinal structuring, 264
avoidance-avoidance conflict, 250
avoiding style, 255
BATNA, 259
Cinergy, 263
collaborating style, 256
communication competency, 258
compromising style, 257
concern for others, 254
concern for self, 254
conflict management, 248
cross-cultural negotiation, 266–71
defined, 248
dimensions, 248
distributive negotiations, 261
diversity, 252–53
emotional intelligence, 268
forcing style, 255
integrative negotiations, 262
intergroup conflict, 252
interpersonal conflict, 250
interpersonal conflict-handling styles, 254–59
interrole conflict, 251
intersender role conflict, 251
intragroup conflict, 251
intraorganizational negotiations, 264
intrapersonal conflict, 249
intrasender role conflict, 251
KLA-Tencor, 247
levels, 249–54
mediation, 266
motivation, 410
negotiating across cultures, 266
negotiation, 259–66
negotiation stages, 259
negotiator's dilemma, 265
person-role conflict, 251
role, 250
role ambiguity, 251
role conflict, 250
role episode model, 250
role set, 250
task interdependency, 252
teams competency, 263
work-family pressures, 456–57
Conoco, 58
conscientiousness, 316, 317, 345
consensus, 355
consequences, 368
consideration, 171, 199–200
consistency, 355
consult individually style, 177
consult team style, 177
contact, in nonverbal communication, 293–94
Container Store, 327–28
contextual factors, 404
Continental Airlines, 262
contingencies of reinforcement, 368–70. *See also* learning; reinforcement; rewards
guidelines, 377–78
negative reinforcement, 372–73
omission, 373–74
organizational rewards, 372
positive reinforcement, 370–72
principle of contingent reinforcement, 372
reinforcement, 370
contingent workforce, 131
continuous reinforcement, 378
contrast principle of perception, 342–43
Cook, Scott, 51
Coon, Sharon, 407
Cooper, Cynthia, 113–14
Corporate Leadership Council, 428
Cosier, R.A., 60
Cotsakos, Christos, 111
creativity
analogy technique, 58
Architect Works, Inc., 59
cross-fertilization techniques, 58
cultural blocks, 56
devil's advocate method, 59
electronic brainstorming, 238–39
emotional blocks, 56
lateral thinking method, 57
nominal group technique, 235–37
organizational creativity, 56
perceptual blocks, 56
reversal technique, 58
team, 235–39
traditional brainstorming, 237–38
crises, 104
Cron, W.L., 408, 428
cross-fertilization technique, 58
cross-functional teams, 214–15
Crowson, J.J., 324
cues, 280, 293–95

cultural blocks, to creativity, 56–57
cultural context, 284–85
cultural racism, 13–14
cultural symbols, 99
cultural values, 99, 100
culture
abilities, 19
across cultures competency, 18–23
attribution error, 356
careers, 6
China, 22
chromatics, 295
chronemics, 296
collectivism, 19
conflict, 256
cultural values, 18
ethics, 113–15
gender role orientation, 21
global mind-set, 19
global team, 219
goals, 431
individualism, 19
interpersonal communication, 284–86, 295–97
long-term orientation, 21
motivation, 394–95, 397, 405–6, 409
negotiation, 266–71
perception, 347, 351–53
personality, 313–14
polychronic time schedule, 296
power distance, 20
reinforcement, 370
reward systems, 437, 439–41
stereotypes, 22
uncertainty avoidance, 21
culture-performance relationships, 111–12
Cummings, J.G., 135
Cummings, T.G., 437
customers, 69

D

Dallas, Susan, 397
Dallas Cowboys, 144
data, 280
Davis, Gary, 37–38, 45
De Bono, E., 58
decide style, 177
decision making. *See also* teams
analogy technique, 58
balancing interests principles, 42
bounded rationality model, 51
change competency, 50
communication competency, 54
concentration of effect, 40
concern for others principles, 43
creativity, 235–39
cross-fertilization technique, 58
cultural blocks, 56
devil's advocate method, 59
dictionary rule, 53
emotional blocks, 56
Epic Divers and Marine, 54
escalating commitment, 52
ethical decisions, 38–48
ethical intensity, 39–41
ethics, 38
explicit knowledge, 54
influence methods, 55
information, 52
JC Penney, 37
knowledge management, 53
lateral thinking method, 57
limited search, 52
magnitude of consequences, 39
managerial models, 48–56
organizational creativity, 56
perceptual blocks, 56
political model, 55
power, 55
probability of effect, 40
problem framing, 53
proximity, 40
rational model, 48
reversal technique, 58
risk propensity, 52
satisficing, 51
self competency, 59
self-serving principles, 42
social consensus, 40
St. Vincent Hospital, 50
tacit knowledge, 53
temporal immediacy, 40
vertical thinking method, 57
Xerox six-stage process, 48
decision significance, 178, 180
decision-time penalty, 178–80
decoding, 281
deficiency needs, 396–97
delegating style, 174, 175, 177
Dell Computer, 351
Deloitte Consulting, 75, 78
Deloitte Touche Tohmatsu, 112–13
Denver International Airport, 52
departments, of organizations, 66
depersonalization, 460
DePeters, Jack, 133
depression, 467
derogation of target bias, 466
describing skills, 8
design. *See* organizational design
Destiny Health, 430–31
devil's advocate method, 59–60
dialogue, 286, 287
dictionary rule, 53
differentiation strategy, 71
Dillman, Leonard Wayne, 235
Dillman, Linda, 234–35
Di Matteo, Piero, 163
direction of attention, 429
disclosure principle, 43
Disiere, David, 426
Disney World, 119
distinctiveness, 355
distortion, 283
distributive justice principle, 43
distributive negotiations, 261–62
distributors, 68–69
diversity
abilities, 9
affinity groups, 253
age, 14
attitudes, 12
categories, 10–12
challenges, 115
conflict, 252
cultural, 115
dilemmas, 119
diversity competency, 9–15
ethnic groupings, 12
ethnicity, 14
gender, 13
glass ceiling, 13
IBM, 14
language differences, 12
Levi Strauss, 116
organizational culture, 115–17
organizational socialization, 117
primary categories, 11
programs, 116
questionnaire, 117
race, 13
racism, 13
secondary categories, 11
socialization, 117
socialization process, 118
team, 231
workplace, 12
diversity competency, 9–15
Georgia Power, 253–54
Home Depot, 350
IBM, 14–15
OfficeWorks, 469–70
division of labor, 76–77
divisions, of organizations, 66
Dofasco Inc., 464–65
Dollar General, 70
Don Herring Mitsubishi, 325
DreamWorks SKG, 89–90, 110, 127
drug testing, 47–48
Dunlap, Al, 133
DuPont, 115
Duran, G.J., 44

E

Early, S., 324
Eastman Chemical, 239
eBay, 70, 164
economic approach to organizational change, 133, 140–41
EDS, 140, 210
education, 11
effective groups, 211
effort, 429
Electrolux, 86–87
Electronic Arts, 75
electronic brainstorming, 238–39
El Salvador, 431
Emerson, Ralph Waldo, 6
emotional blocks, to creativity, 56–57
emotional intelligence (EQ), 5–6, 320–21
cross-cultural negotiations, 268–69
emotional stability, 316–18, 450
emotions
leadership, 195
model of, 330
performance, 329–32
empathizing skills, 8

employees
  financial costs of stress, 448
  hiring practices and organizational culture, 104, 105
  readiness for change, 137
  socialization, 117–20
  theft, 413–14
  turnover, 77, 439
  workforce changes, 12–13
employment at will, 45
empowerment, 215–16, 382–83
encoding, 281
Enron, 111, 112, 113–14
Enterprise Rent-A-Car, 432
entrepreneurial culture, 109, 110–11
environment, personality, 313–15
environmental factors, in organizational design, 68–69, 80
Epic Divers and Marine, 54
equity model, 411–12, 412–14
  procedural justice, 414–16
errors
  fundamental attribution error, 355–56
  perception, 348–53
escalating commitment, 52
escape learning, 373
esteem needs, 395–97, 404
ethics
  abilities, 15
  authentic leadership, 194
  Brodsky, Norm, 47
  concentration of effect, 40
  decision making, 38–48
  disclosure principle, 43
  distributive justice principle, 43
  employment at will, 45
  Ethical Assessment of an Incident, 44
  ethical dilemmas, 16
  ethical intensity, 39–41
  Ethical Intensity (questionnaire), 41
  Ethical Practices Questionnaire, 16–17
  ethics competency, 15–18, 47
  golden rule principle, 43
  hedonist principle, 42
  interpersonal communications, 286–92
  magnitude of consequences, 39
  means-end principle, 280
  might-equals-right principle, 42
  organizational change, 152
  organizational culture, 112–15
  organization interests principle, 42
  privacy, 280
  probability of effect, 40
  professional standards principle, 42
  proximity, 40
  rights, 46
  social consensus, 40
  temporal immediacy, 40
  Tyco International, 188
  utilitarian principle, 42
  whistle-blowing, 113
ethics competency, 15–18
  abilities, 15
  Black Entertainment Television, 196
  drug testing case, 46–48
  employee theft, 414
  Gap, Inc., 430–31
  Lockheed Martin, 169–70
  Raytheon Company, 17–18
Ethics Resource Center, 38
ethnicity, 11, 12, 13–14
ethnocentrism, 284–85
E*Trade, 111
Everly, G.S., 451
Evernham, Ray, 427
existence of adapters, nonverbal communication, 293–94
expectancy, 407
expectancy model, 406–10
expert power, 164
explicit knowledge, 54
expressions, nonverbal communication, 293–94
external adaptation and survival, 101
external factors
  of behavior, attribution, 355–56
  perception, 340, 342–44
external locus of control, 318–19, 450
external networks, 299
extraversion, 316, 317, 319–20
extrinsic factors, 402
eyes, nonverbal communication, 293–94

F

facilitate style, 177
failure, attribution, 356–57
family, personality determinant, 314
family-friendly attitude, 10
family-run businesses, 251
family-unfriendly attitude, 10
Farmers Insurance, 74
FBI, 113–14
feedback, 393
  360-degree, 290
  diagnosis of practices, 290–91
  goal setting, 429
  interpersonal communication, 280–82, 289–91
  motivation, 400, 403
  survey, 147
feng shui, 295
F.H. Sherman Recreation and Learning Centre, 465
fight-or-flight response, 448–49
film industry, 88–90
financial issues. *See also* compensation; rewards
  motivation, 400
  organizational change, 143
Financial Planning Association (FPA), 292–93
Fiorina, Carly, 127–28
firing, from employment, 357–58
first-level outcomes, 407
fixed interval schedule, 378–79
fixed ratio schedule, 379–80
Fleet Financial Group, 436–37
flexible benefit plans, 438–39
Flight Systems, 83–84
focused strategy, 72–73
follower identification, 195
fonts, perception, 343–44
FOODCO, 223–24, 225–26
force field analysis, 144–46
forcing style, 255–56
forethought, 382
forming stage of team development, 221–22
Fote, Charles, 131–32
foundation competencies
  abilities, 8
  Effectiveness, 4
free riders, 225
friendship groups, 210
Frito-Lay, 340–42, 376
Fu, F., 428
Fudge, Ann, 311–12
functional design, 81–82
functional teams, 212–13
fundamental attribution error, 355–56

G

gain-sharing programs, 435–37
Gamble, G. Arlivia Babbage, 167–68
Gap, Inc., 430–31
Gardenswartz, L., 117
Gates, George, 468
Geffen, David, 89–90
gender, 11, 13
  perception, 349
  role orientation, 21
  workplace bullying, 467
general anxiety disorder, 467
General Electric, 130, 377
General Mills, 69
General Motors, 85–86
geographic location
  diversity, 12
  place design, 82–83
George, B., 197
Georgia Power, 253–54
Gerstner, Lou, 145
Gherty, Jack, 3–4, 6, 25
Gillette, 455
Girdano, D.A., 451
glass ceiling, 13
Glick, Linda, 115–16
globalization, 102, 129–30
global mind-set, 19
Global Negotiation Project, 264
global teams, 219–21
goals. *See also* attitude; motivation
  defined, 393, 424
  emotions, 330
  goal commitment, 428
  goal setting, 424–34
  high achievers, 398–400
  network design, 87
  performance, 424–34
  setting, 324–25
  team effectiveness, 227–28
  teams, 232
  Type A personality, 451
  virtual teams, 218
Goal setting, 424–41
  impact on performance, 426–27; 160
  limitations of, 433–34
  Locke and Latham, 424–32
  management by objectives, 425
  model, 425
  organizational guidelines, 434

Go-e-biz.com, 104
golden rule principle, 43
Gomar, E.E., 44
Gonzales, Claudia, 298
Gonzales, Henry, 239
Goode, Bruce, 454, 456
Goode, Jody, 454
Goodyear Tire and Rubber Company, 143
Google, 97
Gordon, Jeff, 427
Gore, William L., 353
gossip chain, 300
grapevine, 300
Greenhalgh, L., 248
Greenpeace, 46
Greer, Henry, 405
Grinney, Jay, 143
Groove Networks, Inc., 26–27
Grote, Richard, 376
groups
  defined, 210
  effective, 211
  informal, 210–11
  membership, 314
GroupSystems, 238
groupthink, 225
growth needs, 397
growth-need strength, 404
Grupo Carso, 102–3
guanxi, 270
Guinan, P.J., 56
Guo, Guangchang, 189–90
Gust, Anne, 430–31
Gustin, Jack, 379
Gutierrez-Olivera, H., 406

H

habits, organizational change, 139–40
Hackman, J.R., 326, 403
Hackworth, Michael L., 38
Hall, E., 285
Hall, Reggie, 288
Hallmark Cards, 58
halo effect, 350–51
harassment, 469, 472. *See also* workplace aggression
hardiness, 452
hardy personality, 452
Harley-Davidson, 107–8
harm model of aggression, 472
health, stress, 458–59. *See also* workplace aggression
Health First, 429
HealthSouth Corporation, 143
hedonist principle, 42
Heinecke, Bill, 68–69
heredity, personality, 313
Hermle, Lynne, 256
Herzberg, F.I., 411
Hewitt Associates, 437–38
Hewlett-Packard (HP), 89, 127–28
hierarchy of authority, 76
high achievers, 398–400
high-context culture, 284
high-performance work system, 434–35
Hinton, P.R., 347
Hogg Robinson Limited, 277
Hollenbeck, J.R., 428
Home Depot, 142–43, 350
Honda, 107
Honeywell-Bull, 270–71
Hoojberg, R., 109
hope, 195, 323–25
Hope Scale, 324
hostile attribution bias, 466
hot groups, 233
Huberman, John, 376
Hughes, Keith, 296
Huse, Steve, 59
Huse Food Group, 59
Hutton, Shirly, 106
hygiene factors, 402. *See also* motivator-hygiene model

I

IBM, 14–15, 85
"I Have a Dream" (King), 198, 201
immediate reinforcement, principle of, 372
Immelt, Jeff, 134
impersonality, 77–78
implicit personality theory, 346
importance of commitment, 178, 180
impression management, 283–84, 347–48. *See also* perception
incivility, 455–56
income, 11. *See also* compensation; rewards
India, 356, 431
individual behavior, 27–28. *See also* goals; motivation; performance
  effectiveness of, 28
  expectancy model, 406–10
  organizational change, 138–42, 147–50
  stress management, 462–63
individual differences, 312. *See also* personality
  job characteristics model, 403–4
  stress, 450
individual gestures, 293–94
individualism, 19–20, 24–25, 79, 441
individual racism, 13–14
industrial accidents, 458
inequity, 413
influence, idealized, 199
influence methods, 55–56
informal groups, 210–11
informal leaders, 234
information technology (IT), 130
initiating structure, 171
inputs, equity model, 412–14
institutional racism, 13–14
instrumentality, 407
integrative negotiations, 262–63
intellectual openness, 10
intellectual stimulation, 199
intercultural communication, 284–86
intergroup conflict, 252–53
intermittent reinforcement, 378
internal factors
  attribution, 355–56
  perception, 340, 344–46
internal integration, 101
internal locus of control, 318–19, 450
Internet, 8, 26
interorganizational agreements, 143–44
interpersonal communication. *See also* communication competency
  across cultures competency, 285
  assertive communication, 286
  barriers, 282–84
  body language, 297
  Caterpillar's piazza, 285
  channels, 280
  chromatics, 295
  chronemics, 296
  communication competency, 292, 301
  communication openness, 288
  cultural barriers, 284
  cultural context, 284
  cultural differences, 295
  decoding, 281
  defined, 278
  360-degree feedback, 290
  Diagnosis of Feedback Practices (questionnaire), 290
  dialogue, 286
  distortion, 283
  elements, 278–86
  encoding, 281
  ethics, 286–92
  ethnocentrism, 284
  expressions, 294
  eyes, 294
  feedback, 282, 289
  feng shui, 295
  formal employee network, 301
  gestures, 294
  grapevine, 300
  high-context culture, 284
  impression management, 283
  individual network, 298
  informal group network, 300
  interpersonal communication network, 298
  Interpersonal Communication Practices (questionnaire), 36
  language routines, 283
  listening, 292
  low-context culture, 284
  lying, 283
  meaning, 280
  media richness, 280
  messages, 279
  meta-communication, 288
  noise, 282
  nonverbal communication, 287, 293
  organizational change, 145
  PERCEIVE, 293
  political skill, 299
  polychromic time schedule, 296
  proximity, 294
  Radcliffe, David, 277
  receiver, 278
  receptors, 279
  relative orientation, 294
  self-disclosure, 291
  semantics, 282
  sender, 278
  Sensis, 301

interpersonal communication, continued
status differences, 297
stress, 455–56
transmitters, 279
interpersonal conflict, 250–51, 254. *See also* conflict; interpersonal communication
accommodating style, 256
avoiding style, 255
collaborating style, 256–57
compromising style, 257–58
effectiveness, 258
forcing style, 255–56
interval schedule, 378
interviews, 349
intragroup conflict, 251
intraorganizational negotiations, 264–65
intrapersonal conflict, 249–50
intrinsic factors, 402
introversion, 317
Italy, 395
izzat, 411

J

Janis, I.L., 225
Japan, 21, 22, 409
conflict resolution, 267, 268
perception, 347
reward systems, 437, 441
JC Penney, 12, 37–38, 45
Jehn, K.A., 100
Jensen, M.A.C., 222
JetBlue, 315
job burnout, 460
job characteristics model, 402–5
job conditions, stress, 455
job design
motivation, 401–5
job feedback, 403. *See also* feedback
job satisfaction, 325–28. *See also* motivation
equity, 411–16
goals, 431–32
measuring, 325–26
work factors, 326
Johnson, Howard, 415
Johnson, Karyn, 371
Johnson, Robert, 195–96
Jordan, Michael, 140
J.R. Simplot, 68

K

Kacmar, Donna, 58–59
Kadoka Holdings, 90
Kahn, R.L., 250
kaizens, 372
Karsten Manufacturing, 72–73
Katzenbach, J.R., 149
Katzenberg, Jeffrey, 89–90, 127
Kay, Mary, 106
Keebler Foods, 65–66
Keegan, Robert, 143
Kellogg Company, 65–66, 68, 76, 78, 83
Kendall-Futuro Inc., 227
Kennedy, John F., 398
KFC, 118. *See also* YUM Brands
King, Annette, 391
King, M.L., Jr., 193, 198, 201
Kirkman, B.L., 216
KLA-Tencor, 247
knowledge management, 53
Knowling, Robert, 127
Kock, George, 425
Kodak, 371
Kohlberg, Andrew, 82
Kordestani, Omid, 97
Korens, Lee, 8, 9
Kormanski, C., 222
Koski, Chris, 394–95
Kozlowski, Dennis, 140, 187, 193
Kraft Foods, 311
Krispy Kreme, 73
Krol, Jack, 187
Kusin, Gary, 133

L

Lambert, Cristina, 328
Lancaster, Hal, 357
Land O'Lakes, 3–4
language, 12
cues, 281
language routines, 283
LaPointe, A.B., 324
lateral networks, 299
lateral thinking method, 57–58
Latham, G.P., 431, 434
Latin America, 78–80
Lay, Ken, 111, 113
Lay, Sharon, 111
Lazarus, Shelly, 6–8
leader expertise, 178
leaders, 162
leadership. *See also* behavior; personality; teams
authentic leadership, 194
Behavioral Leadership Style Questionnaire, 172
behavioral model of leadership, 170
Branson, Richard, 192
Breen, Ed, 188
change competency, 180, 200
charismatic leadership, 190
coercive power, 164
communication competency, 176, 192
leadership, 192
competencies, 202
consideration, 171
consult individually style, 177
consult team style, 177
contemporary models, 202
contingent rewards, 188
decide style, 177
decision significance, 178
decision-time penalty, 178
defined, 162
delegate style, 177
delegating style, 175
effectiveness, 28
ethics, 169
ethics competency, 169, 196
facilitate style, 177
follower identification, 195
hope, 195
idealized influence, 199
individualized consideration, 199
initiating structure, 171
inspirational motivation, 198
integrity, 169
intellectual stimulation, 199
Johnson, Richard, 196
leader, 162
leader expertise, 178
legitimate power, 163
management by exception, 189
McGavick, Mike, 200
optimism, 195
participating style, 175
performance appraisal, 167
political behavior, 165
political tactics, 166
power, 163–68
readiness, 175
referent power, 164
relationship behavior, 174
reward power, 163
self competency, 167, 189
selling style, 175
situational leadership model, 173
synergy, 201
task behavior, 173
team behaviors, 28–29, 234–35
team competence, 178
team expertise, 178
teams, 234
team support, 178
telling style, 175
traits model of leadership, 168
transactional leadership, 188
transformational leadership, 197
trust, 195
vision, 191
Vroom-Jago time-driven leadership style, 177
zone of indifference, 163
learning
classical conditioning, 366–67
contingencies of reinforcement, 368–78
defined, 366
framework for, 27–29
negative reinforcement, 372–73
omission, 373–74
operant conditioning, 367–78
organizational rewards, 372–73
perceptual set, 345
positive discipline, 376–77
positive reinforcement, 370–72
principles of positive reinforcement, 372
punishment, 374–77
rewards and punishments, 366–68
schedules of reinforcement, 378–81
social learning theory, 380–85
Lee, Angelica, 342
legal issues. *See* workplace aggression
legitimate power, 163
Lenser, Leslie, 394
Leonard, Joseph, 150
Levi Strauss and Company, 115–16

Lewicki, R.J., 248
life experiences, 314
life stressors, 456–58
Lincoln, Abraham, 398
Lincoln Electric, 104
Lippie, Jim, 322
listening, 292–93
Locke, E.A., 431
Lockheed Martin, 169–70
locus of control, 318–19
  performance, 320
  stress, 450
Logan, Gary, 371
long-term orientation, 21
Lopker, Pam, 48–49
low-context culture, 284
low-cost strategy, 70
Lowe's, 415
Luthans, F., 381
lying, 283

M

magnitude of consequences, 39
Maldia, Mark, 50
management. *See also* decision making; ethics
  fear, 375–76
  organizational change, 151
  organizational culture, 103–4
management by objectives (MBO), 426
Mangean, Craig, 255
manufacturing firms, design, 81–82
marital status, 11
market culture, 109, 111
Marriott, 12
Marshall Industries, 434
Mary Kay Cosmetics, 98, 105–6, 129, 396
Maslow, A.H., 404
Mayo, William, 209
Mayo Clinic, 209–12, 224, 227
McBer and Company, 401
McBride, Douglas, 26–27
McCullen, Janet, 292–93
McDonald's, 68, 99–100, 129, 411
McGavick, Mike, 200–201
McNealey, Scott, 129
meaning, 280–82
means-end principle, 42
mechanistic organizations, 74–80
media richness, 280, 281
mediation, 266
mediators, goals, 429
Medical City of Dallas, 88
Menkhaus, Steve, 423–24
messages, 279–80
meta-communication, 288
Mexico, 102–3, 406
micromanaging, 454
might-equals-right principle, 42
Miller, Michelle, 175–76
Miller, Steve, 146
Miller Brewing Company, 397
Miner, J.B., 320
Ming, Yao, 342
Mini Maids, 365–66
Minton, J.W., 248
mobbing, 468–69
moderators, goals, 427–29
Moffat, Joan, 391
money, motivation and, 400
monochronic time schedule, 296
Morimoto, Hidetomo, 256
Moroone, Michael E., 164
Morris, Edna, 6
motivation. *See also* goals; organizational change
  Achievement Motivation Model, 397–401
  achievement motivation model, 397–400
  basic model of, 392–95
  core phases of, 393–94
  defined, 393
  equity, 411–16
  expectancy model, 406–11
  goals, 325, 424–34
  high achiever characteristics, 398–401
  job characteristics model, 402–6
  job design, 401–6
  Maslow, 395–97
  McClelland, 397–401
  needs, 395–401
  needs hierarchy model, 395–97
  organizational citizenship behavior, 415–16
  perception, 345–46
  performance expectations, 406–11
  process, 392–95
  reward systems and performance, 434–41
  transformational leadership, 198
motivator-hygiene model, 401–2
Mulcahy, A.M., 37
Mullen, B., 465
multidivisional design (M-form), 84–85
multinational design, 85–86
Munson, Eddie, 16
Munter, M., 285
Murphy, M., 435

N

Nardella, Bob, 142–43
NASA, 105
NASCAR, 426–27
National Institute for Information Technology (NIIT), 410–11
National Retail Security Association, 413
NBC, 89
needs, 393. *See also* motivation
  achievement motivation model, 397–400
  needs hierarchy model, 395–97, 404
Neeleman, David, 315
negative reinforcement, 372–73
negotiation. *See also* conflict
  across cultures, 266–71
  across cultures competency, 270
  assessing stage, 260
  attitudinal structuring, 264
  BATNA, 259
  Chinese negotiating style, 270
  Cinergy, 263
  collaborating style, 256
  communication, 269
  compromising style, 257
  distributive negotiations, 261
  emotional intelligence, 268
  forcing style, 255
  implementation stage, 260
  influences, 264–66
  integrative negotiations, 262
  intraorganizational negotiations, 264
  matrix of outcomes, 265
  mediation, 266
  negotiating stage, 260
  negotiators, 267
  negotiator's dilemma, 265
  process, 269
  process stage, 260
  Shapiro, Ron, 263
  stages, 259–61
  teams competency, 263
  time, 269
negotiator's dilemma, 265
Nestlé, 141
network design, 87–89, 301
Nevant, Tom, 365–66
Nike, 143–44, 343, 423
Noble, Sam, 464
noise, 282
nominal group technique (NGT), 235–36
nonverbal communication, 8, 293
Nordstrom (stores), 71
norming stage of team development, 222, 223
norms, 231–33
North American Free Trade Agreement (NAFTA), 405–6
Northern Shipbuilding, 380
Norwich and Peterborough Building Society, 438
Novak, David, 107, 118–19
NSK, 441

O

office politics, 456. *See also* organizational politics
OfficeWorks, 469–70
Ogilvy, David, 7
Ogilvy & Mather Worldwide, 6–7
Ohio Department of Claims, 53
Ohio State University, 171
Oldham, G.R., 326, 403
omission, 373–74
openness, 316, 317–18
operant conditioning, 367–68, 380
optimism, 195–96
organic organizations, 74–80
organization, aggression toward, 474. *See also* workplace aggression
organizational behavior, 5
organizational change
  Are You Ready to Change?, 141–42
  ethics, 152–53
  individual resistance, 138–42
  interpersonal methods, 147
  leading positive change, 148

organizational change, continued
- organizational diagnosis, 136–38
- organizational methods, 150–53
- organizational resistance, 142–44
- organizational use, 134–36
- overcoming resistance, 144–47
- pressure, 129–32
- promoting, 147–52
- resistance, 138–46
- team building, 148–50
- team methods, 147–50
- types of approaches, 132–34

organizational citizenship behavior, 415
organizational commitment, 328–29
organizational creativity, 56–60, 150
organizational culture. *See also* across cultures competency; culture
- bureaucratic culture, 109–10
- changing a culture, 106–8
- clan culture, 110
- culture-performance relationships, 111–12
- diversity, 115–17
- dynamics, 98–108
- emergence, 101
- entrepreneurial culture, 110–11
- ethical behavior, 112–15
- forming a culture, 101–3
- layers, 99
- maintaining, 104
- market culture, 111
- organizational change, 142–43, 149–50
- socialization of new employees, 117–20
- socialization process, 118–20
- sustaining a culture, 103–6
- types, 108–12
- whistle-blowing, 113–15

organizational design, 29, 64–67
- chain of command, 78
- contemporary, 85–90
- defined, 66
- differentiation strategy, 71–72
- division of labor, 76–77
- environmental factors, 68–69, 80
- focused strategy, 72–73
- functional design, 81–82
- hierarchy authority, 76
- impersonality, 77–78
- key factors, 67–74
- Latin America *versus* U.S., 79–80
- low cost strategy, 70
- mechanistic and organic organizations, 74–80
- M-form, 84–85
- multinational design, 85–87
- network design, 87–90
- organizational change, 142
- place design, 82–83
- product design, 83–84
- rules & procedures, 77
- selected dimensions, 76–80
- span of control, 78–80
- strategic factors, 68–73
- technological factors, 68, 73–74, 80
- traditional, 80–85

organizational development approach, 133–34
organizational diagnosis, 136–38
organizational politics, 165–66. *See also* office politics
organizational rewards, 372
organizational rites and ceremonies, 105–6
organizational socialization, 117–20
organizational stress management programs, 463–64
organization charts, 66, 67, 81, 83, 90
organization interests principle, 42
Otis, Elisha Graves, 83
Otis Elevator, 83–84
outcomes, in equity model, 412–14

P

PacificCare, 136
Pacific Software Publishing, 256
Page, Larry, 97
Panarello, Jay, 262
Panthary, Naveen, 411
Papa John's Pizza, 400–401
parental status, 12
participating style of leadership, 174, 175
Pavlov, I., 367
Pawar, Rajendra, 410–11
PeaceHealth, 460–62
PepsiCo, 111
perception, 338–53. *See also* attribution process
- defined, 340
- errors, 348–53
- external factors, 342–44
- impression management, 283–84, 347–48
- internal factors, 344–46
- motivation, 410
- perceived/perceiver roles, 346–47
- perceptual blocks, to creativity, 56–57
- perceptual defense, 349
- perceptual process, 340–42
- perceptual selection, 342–46
- perceptual set, 345
- person perception, 340, 346–48
- stress, 449–50

perceptual errors, 348–53
- defense, 349
- halo effect, 350–51
- judgment, 348–49
- projection, 351
- Pygmalion effect, 351
- role of culture, 351–53
- self-fulfilling prophecy, 351
- stereotyping, 349–50

performance
- attribution, 353–54, 357
- emotions, 329–32
- goals, 424–34
- job satisfaction, 327
- locus of control, 320
- motivation, 406–11
- reward systems, 434–41
- stress, 459–60

performance appraisal, 167
performing stage of team development, 222, 223–24
Perrier, 140–41
persistence, goals, 429
personal acceptance conformity, 233
personality, 310–22
- behavior, 316–22
- behavior and work attitude, 322–29
- Big Five, 316–18 (334–36)
- defined, 312–13
- determinants, 312–15
- emotional intelligence, 320–22; 336–37
- emotions and performance, 329–32
- hardy, 452
- Hope Scale, 324
- introversion/extraversion, 319–20
- job satisfaction, 325–28
- locus of control, 318–19
- organizational change, 139
- perception, 344–46
- self-esteem, 318
- sources of differences in, 313
- stress, 450–53
- traits model of leadership, 170
- Type A, 450–52
- Type B, 452

personalized charismatic leaders, 193
personal style, 12
person perception, 340, 346–48
Petrock, F., 109
Pfeiffer, J.W., 11, 222
physical abilities, 11
physical environment, nonverbal communication, 295
physiological needs, 395–97
Pittenger, Linda, 292
Pizza Hut, 68–69
place design, 82–83
planned organizational change, 132
Play, 237–38
political behavior, stress, 456
political decision-making model, 55–56
political skill, 299–300
Pollyanna principle, 346
polychronic attitude index, 296
polychronic time schedule, 296
polyphasic behavior, 451
pooled interdependence, 74, 80
Porter, M., 70
positive discipline, 376–77
positive events, 369–70
positive reinforcement, 370–72
post-traumatic stress disorder, 458–59, 467
potency bias, 466
Potter, Tina, 382
power. *See also* motivation
- inequality, 79
- leadership, 163–68
- organizational change and, 140
- political decision-making model and, 55–56
- presidents' need for, 398

power distance, 20–21, 441
Power of Nice, The (Shapiro), 263
PPG, 425
Pratt & Whitney, 83–84
Presbyterian Hospital, 367
primary categories, of diversity, 10–11
primary reinforcers, 370–71
principles of positive reinforcement, 372
privacy issues, 42–43
probability chain, 300
probability of effect, 40

problem framing, 53
problem-solving teams, 212–14
procedural justice, 414–16
procedures, in organizational design, 77
Procter & Gamble, 129–30, 455
product design, 83
productivity, 233–34. *See also* motivation; rewards
professional standards principle, 42
profit-sharing programs, 437–38
projection, 351
projective method, 398
proximity
 ethical decisions, 40
 nonverbal communication, 293–94
Prudential Insurance, 58
punishment. *See also* reinforcement
 effective use, 376–77
 learning through, 366–68
 motivation, 393
 negative effects, 374–76
Pygmalian effect, 351

Q

QAD, Inc., 48–49
quality of work life (QWL), 131
questioning skills, 8
QuikTrip, 339–40, 344
Quinn, R.E., 109
Quorum Hotel (Marriott), 12

R

race, 10, 13–14, 349
racism, 13–14
Radcliffe, David, 282, 286
Radio Shack, 75, 102
rage, 472. *See also* workplace aggression
Rainbow Warriors, 427
Ralcorp Holdings, 69
rational decision-making model, 48–50
ratio schedule, 378
Raytheon Company, 17–18
readiness, 175
Reagan, Ronald, 398
receivers, 278–79
receptors, 279
reciprocal interdependence, 74, 80
recruitment, 105
Reddy, W.B., 231
referent power, 164
Reid, Grady, 263–64, 265
reinforcement. *See also* contingencies of reinforcement; learning; rewards
 defined, 370
 schedules, 378–81
reinforcement deprivation, principle of, 372
reinforcement size, principle of, 372
relationship behavior, 174
relations-oriented roles, 229–30
relative orientation, in nonverbal communication, 293–94
relaxation techniques, 462–63. *See also* stress
religious beliefs, 11
retaliatory discharge, 45
retribution bias, 466
reversal technique, 58
reward power, 163–64
rewards. *See also* reinforcement
 culture impact, 439–41
 examples, 373
 goals, 429, 431
 learning through, 366–68
 motivation, 393, 410
 organizational, 372
 organizational change, 136
 organizational culture, 105, 118–19
 political behavior, 166–67
 reinforcement *vs.*, 370
 systems for high performance, 434–41
 team creativity, 235
 team goals, 228
 transactional leadership, 188–89
Ridge, Garry C., 173
rights, determination, 46–48
risk propensity, 52
risk taking, 26
Ritz-Carlton Hotel, 99, 104–5, 432–33
Robert J. Brady Co., 451
Rodin, Rod, 434
Rodriguez, Julie, 54
role, 250
role ambiguity, 251, 455
role conflict, 250–51, 455
role modeling, 104–5
role-oriented behavior, 230–31
role overload, 453–54
role senders, 250
role sets, 250
Roosevelt, Franklin D., 398
Rosen, B., 216
Rowe, A., 117
Rowe Furniture, 383
Rowley, Coleen, 113–14
Royal Dutch/Shell, 146
rules, 77

S

Safeco, 200–201
Salonek, Tom, 104
Sarbanes-Oxley Act of 2002, 112–13
SAS Institute, 75
satisficing, 51–52
Saunders, D.M., 248
Scanlon, Joe, 436
Scanlon plan, 436
schedules of reinforcement, 378–81
 continuous, 378
 fixed interval, 378–79
 fixed ratio, 379–80
 variable interval, 379
 variable ratio, 380
Schnatter, John, 400–401
Schriesheim, C.A., 172
Schrivenk, C. R., 60
Schultz, Horst, 433
Schultz, Howard, 392
Scott Paper, 133
secondary categories, diversity, 10–12
secondary reinforcers, 370–71
second-level outcomes, 407
security needs, 395–97
SEI Investments, 405
Seiko Instruments, 437
selective screening
 external factors, 342–44
 internal factors, 344–46
self-actualization needs, 395–97, 404
self-awareness, 320–21
self competency, 5–7. *See also* self-efficacy
 abilities, 25
 Arab business practices, 352–53
 Architect Works, Inc., 59
 Are You Ready to Change? (questionnaire), 141–42
 burnout, 461–62
 career development, 6
 emotional intelligence, 5
 JetBlue, 315
 Levi Strauss and Company, 116
 Papa John's Pizza, 400–401
 Shanghai Fortune High Technology Group, 189–90
 State Farm Insurance Company, 167–68
 stress, 452
 Wal-Mart, 234–35
self-control, 382–85
self-disclosure, 291
self-efficacy, 383–84
 goal setting, 426
self-esteem, 318, 450
self-fulfilling prophecy, 351
self-managed teams, 215–17
self-motivation, 321
self-oriented roles, 230–31
"Self-Reliance" (Emerson), 6
self-serving bias, 357
selling style of leadership, 174, 175
semantics, 282–83
senders, 278–79
Sensis, 301–2
sequential interdependence, 74
7-Eleven, 71
Sewell, Carl, 330
Sewell Automotive, 330
sexual harassment, 469–71
sexual orientation, 11
Shanghai Fortune High Technology Group, 189–90
Shapiro Negotiation Institute, 263
shared behaviors, 99
Shell, 146
Sheridan Press, 287
Shoeneck, Kelly, 133
Siegel, M., 100
Simon, H.A., 53
single-strand chain, 300
situational determinants
 behavior, 322
 perception, 347
situational leaders, 3
Situational Leadership® Model, 173–77
skill-based pay, 438
skill variety, 402
Skinner, B.F., 381

Slim Helú, Carlos, 102
Slocum, J.W., Jr., 408, 428
Smith, D.K., 149
Smith, Nancy, 410
Snyder, C.R., 324
sociability factor, 319. *See also* extraversion
social consensus, 40
social discounting bias, 466
social empathy, 321
socialization, 117–20, 150
socialized charismatic leaders, 193
social learning theory, 380–85
  forethought, 382
  organizational guidelines, 384–85
  self-control, 382–83
  self-efficacy, 383–84
  symbolizing, 381–82
  vicarious learning, 382
social skills, 321
SOHU.com, 22–23
Sorell, Martin, 311
Sorrentino, Ralph, 367, 416
Sottolano, D., 56
Southwest Airlines, 72
span of control, 78
Spielberg, Steven, 89–90
St. Vincent's Hospital, 50
Stajkovic, A.D., 381
Starbucks, 330, 391–92, 439
State Farm Insurance Company, 82, 167–68, 371
status, 230
  interpersonal communication, 297–98
  organizational culture, 105
stereotypes, 268–69
  avoiding, 22
  perception, 349–50
Stettheimer, Timothy, 50
Stiles, M., 44
Stoner, Inc., 213
storming stage of team development, 222–23
strategic factors, organizational design, 68–73
stress. *See also* conflict; workplace aggression
  behavioral impacts, 458
  career development, 455
  clinical depression, 467
  college students, 457
  competitiveness, 452
  cost, 448
  defined, 448
  depersonalization, 460
  emotional impacts, 458
  fight-or-flight response, 448
  frequency, 448
  general anxiety disorder, 467
  hardy personality, 452
  harm model of aggression, 472
  health, 458
  hostile work environment, 471
  impact, 458–62
  incivility, 455
  individual differences, 450
  interpersonal relations, 455
  job burnout, 460
  job conditions, 455
  life role, 456
  life stressors, 456
  management, 462–65
  micromanage, 454
  mobbing, 468
  modifying behaviors, 464
  perception, 449–50
  performance, 459
  personality, 450–53
  physiological impacts, 458
  polyphasic behavior, 452
  post-traumatic disorder, 458, 467
  prevention, 462–65
  reduction, 462–65
  role ambiguity, 455
  role conflict, 455
  role overload, 453
  Selye, Hans, 449
  sexual harassment, 469–71
  social support, 450
  sources, 453–58
  stressors, 448, 453–58, 462–65
  time urgency, 452
  Type A personality, 450
  Type B personality, 452
  wellness programs, 464
  work-family pressures, 457
  workplace aggression, 456, 465–74
  workplace bullying, 466
  workplace violence, 471
subcultures, 107
success, attribution of, 356–57
sucker effect, 225
Sun Microsystems, 129
Sun Roller Corporation, 345
superordinate goals, 228
suppliers, 68
survey feedback, 147
Suttles, Bob, 429
Swartz, Mark, 140
Sweden, 394–95, 441
symbolizing, 381–82
symbols, cultural, 99
synergy, 201

T

tacit knowledge, 53
Target, 69, 75
task behavior, 173–74
task complexity, 429
task groups, 210
task identity, 403
task interdependency, 73–74, 252
task-oriented roles, 229
task significance, 403
task strategy, 429
TDIndustries, 105
teaching, organizational culture and, 104–5
teams. *See also* behavior; leadership; teams competency
  across cultures competency, 220
  adjourning stage, 224
  autonomy, 216
  change, 147–50
  change competency, 238
  cohesiveness, 233–34
  communication competency, 211
  compliance conformity, 233
  context, 226
  creativity, 235–39
  cross-functional team, 214
  defined, 212
  development, 221–26
  Dillman, Linda, 234
  diversity, 231
  dysfunctions, 224
  effectiveness, 28, 211, 226–35
  electronic brainstorming, 238
  FOODCO, 223
  forming stage, 221
  free rider, 225
  friendship group, 210
  functional team, 212
  global team, 219
  goals, 232
  groupthink, 225
  hot group, 233
  impact, 216
  individual abilities, 23
  influences, 226–35
  informal group, 210
  job characteristics model, 404
  Kendall-Futuro, 227
  leadership, 28–29, 234
  Leading Positive Change (questionnaire), 148
  Mayo Clinic, 210
  meaningfulness, 215
  nominal group technique, 235–37
  norming stage, 223
  norms, 231–32
  organizational change, 147–50
  organizational culture, 103–4
  performing stage, 223
  personal acceptance conformity, 233
  potency, 215
  problem-solving team, 213
  productivity, 233
  relations-oriented role, 229
  roles, 229
  rules, 232
  self competency, 234
  self-managed team, 215
  self-oriented role, 230
  Situational Leadership® Model, 178
  size, 228
  stages, 221–24
  storming stage, 222
  sucker effect, 225
  superordinate goals, 228
  task group, 210
  task interdependency, 252
  task-oriented role, 229
  team building, 148–49
  team empowerment questionnaire, 215
  team goals, 227
  teams competency, 23–25, 217
  technology, 218
  traditional brainstorming, 237
  trust, 225
  types, 212–21
  virtual team, 218
teams competency, 23–25, 210
  abilities, 23
  BayerUS, 217

teams competency, continued
- Cinergy, 263–64
- NASCAR, 426–27
- Rowe Furniture, 383
- SEI Investments, 405
- Shell, 146
- Thrive Networks, 321–22
- West Suburban Hospital, 24–25
- Works Corporation, 454

technology, 26
- defined, 73
- informal groups, 210
- information technology (IT), 130
- jobs, 455
- organizational design, 68, 73–74, 80
- virtual teams, 218–19

Teerlink, Richard, 107–8
telling style, 174, 175
temporal immediacy, 40
temporary employment agencies, 131
Teng, C.T., 270–71
Texaco, 283
Textron, Inc., 214–15
Thailand, 68–69
Thematic Apperception Test (TAT), 398
360-degree feedback, 290
Thrive Networks, 321–22
time, nonverbal communication, 295
Tindell, Kip, 327–28
topping-out effect, 438
Toto, 441
Toyota, 85–86, 151–52
traditional brainstorming, 237
Tragge-Lakra, Cynthia, 201
traits model of leadership, 168–70
transactional leadership, 188–90, 202
transmitters, 279
Traveler's Insurance Company, 439
Trice, H.M., 106
trust, 195, 200
trust, absence of, 225–26
Tuckman, B.W., 222
two-factor theory, 401. *See also* motivator-hygiene model
Tyco International, 140, 187–88
Type A personality
- defined, 450–52
- Self-Assessment (questionnaire), 451

Type B personality, 452
typefaces, perception, 343–44

U

uncertainty avoidance, 21, 79, 397
Unilever Latin America, 220–21
United Parcel Service (UPS), 77
United Technologies, 83–84
unity of command, 78
University Hospitals (Cleveland, Ohio), 379
UPS, 423–24
Ury, W., 264
U.S. Bureau of Labor Statistics, 131, 448
U.S. Department of Labor, 115
U.S. Equal Pay Act of 1963, 43
U.S. Naval Academy, 118
utilitarian principle, 42

V

valence, 407–8
VandeWalle, D., 408, 428
variable interval schedule, 379
variable ratio schedule, 379, 380
Vele, C.A., 44
verbal communication, 8
vertical loading, 404
vertical networks, 298–99
vertical thinking method, 57–58
vicarious learning, 382
violence in the workplace, 471–74. *See also* workplace aggression
Virgin Group, 192, 193
virtual organizations, 87
virtual teams, 130, 218–19
vision, 135, 198–99
Vogt, J.F., 44
voice
- nonverbal communication, 293–94
- perception, 347

Volvo, 229
Vroom-Jago time-driven leadership model, 177–81

W

Walgreens, 176
Wal-Mart, 69, 70, 129, 234–35
Ward, Steve, 269
Washington, George, 398
Watkins, Sherron, 113–14
Wegman's, 133
Weingart, Bill, 163
Weisman, Joan, 287
Welch, Jack, 25, 134
Welch, Shawn, 214
Wellness Council of America (WELCOA), 464
wellness programs, 464
Western Union, 131–32
West Suburban Hospital, 24–25
whistle-blowing, 113–15
Whitman, Meg, 70, 164
Wiedenhaupt, Kurt, 434
Williams, C.R., 428
"window seat" jobs, 441
Wingo, Renée, 231
Wolfson, Nate, 322
Wong, David, 341–42
Woolmark Company, 238
work attitudes, 322–29. *See also* attitude
work ethic, 314
work experience, 11
workplace aggression. *See also* conflict; stress
- clinical depression, 467
- cost, 471
- defined, 465
- derogation of target bias, 466
- diversity, 469
- effects, 467
- general anxiety disorder, 467
- harassment, 469
- harm model of aggression, 472
- hostile attribution bias, 466
- hostile work environment, 471
- laws, 470
- mayhem, 472
- mobbing, 468
- post-traumatic stress disorder, 467
- potency bias, 466
- prevention, 473
- rage, 472
- remedies, 468
- retribution bias, 466
- sexual harassment, 469
- social discounting bias, 466
- targeted individuals, 468
- toward the organization, 474
- triggering events, 472
- workplace bullying, 466
- workplace violence, 471

workplace stress. *See* stress
work-related cultural values, 19–22
Works Corporation, 454
WorldCom, 113–14
Worley, C.G., 135, 437
Worthington Foods, 65
WPP Group, 311
written communication, 8

Xerox Corporation, 48–49

Yarmouth, M.E., 285
Young & Rubicam, Inc., 311–12
Yukl, G., 56
YUM Brands, 75, 98, 110, 129

Z

Zanussi, 86
Zeira, Y., 137
Zhang, Charles Chao Yang, 22–23
Zimmer, George, 370
zone of indifference, 163